Auditing Organizational Communication

Auditing Organizational Communication is a thoroughly revised and updated new edition of the successful *Handbook of Communication Audits for Organisations*, which has established itself as a core text in the field of organizational communication. Research studies consistently show the importance of effective communication for business success. They also underscore the necessity for organizations to put in place validated techniques to enable them to systematically measure and monitor their communications. This handbook equips readers with the vital analytic tools required to conduct such assessments. Owen Hargie, Dennis Tourish and distinguished contributors drawn from both industry and academia:

- Provide a comprehensive analysis of research, theory and practice pertaining to the communication audit approach
- Review the main options confronting organizations embarking on audit
- Discuss the merits and demerits of the approaches available
- Provide case studies of the communication audit process in action
- Illustrate how findings can be interpreted so that suitable recommendations can be framed
- Outline how reports emanating from such audits should be constructed.

This second edition arrives at a time of considerable growing interest in the area. A large volume of research has been published since the last edition of the book, and the text has been comprehensively updated by reviewing this wealth of data. In addition, new chapters on social network analysis and auditing electronic communication have been added, together with new case study chapters illustrating audits in action.

Owen Hargie is Professor of Communication at the University of Ulster, and **Dennis Tourish** is a Professor at Aberdeen Business School, Robert Gordon University. They have previously co-authored *Key Issues in Organizational Communication*, *Communication in Management*, and *Communication Skills for Effective Management*.

Auditing Organizational Communication

A handbook of research, theory and practice, second edition

Edited by Owen Hargie and Dennis Tourish

Routledge
Taylor & Francis Group

LONDON AND NEW YORK

First published 2009
by Routledge
27 Church Road, Hove, East Sussex BN3 2FA

Simultaneously published in the USA and Canada
by Routledge
270 Madison Ave, New York, NY 10016

*Routledge is an imprint of the Taylor & Francis Group,
an Informa business*

Typeset in Times by
RefineCatch Limited, Bungay, Suffolk
Printed and bound in Great Britain by
TJ International Ltd, Padstow, Cornwall
Paperback cover design by Hybert Design

This publication has been produced with paper manufactured to
strict environmental standards and with pulp derived from
sustainable forests.

British Library Cataloguing in Publication Data
A catalogue record for this book is available from the British Library

Library of Congress Cataloging-in-Publication Data
Auditing organizational communication : a handbook of research,
theory and practice / edited by Owen Hargie and Dennis Tourish. –
2nd ed.
    p. cm.
    Rev. ed. of: Handbook of communication audits for organisations /
edited by Owen Hargie and Dennis Tourish. 2000.
    Includes bibliographical references and index.
    1. Communication in organizations – Auditing.   2. Management
audit.   I. Hargie, Owen.   II. Tourish, Dennis.   III. Handbook of
communication audits for organisations.
    HD30.3.H3537 2009
    658.4'013 – dc22   2008029009

ISBN: 978–0–415–41445–6 (hbk)
ISBN: 978–0–415–41446–3 (pbk)

We dedicate this book to our late colleague and very dear friend, Dr David Dickson. He was a consummate academic and a wonderful human being, who enriched our lives both personally and professionally. It was indeed a privilege and a pleasure to have worked closely with him for so many years.

Contents

Illustrations

CHARTS

BOXES

Contributors

Allyson D. Adrian is Adjunct Assistant Professor of Business, Georgetown University.

Laurey Berk is a senior consultant with MetaComm, a communications consulting firm.

Phillip G. Clampitt is the Hendrickson Professor of Business at the University of Wisconsin, Green Bay.

Menno D.T. de Jong is Associate Professor of Communication Studies at the University of Twente, The Netherlands.

David Dickson was Senior Lecturer in the School of Communication at the University of Ulster, Northern Ireland.

Cal W. Downs is Professor Emeritus of Communication at the University of Kansas and President of Communication Management, Inc.

Judy H. Gray is Associate Professor in Organizational Leadership in the Education Faculty at Monash University, Melbourne, Australia.

Owen Hargie is Professor of Communication at the University of Ulster, Northern Ireland.

Albert Hydeman is President of Albert Hydeman Associates, Los Angeles, California.

Heather M. Laidlaw is Head of Human Resources at Holy Trinity Brompton and Alpha International, London.

Rita Marcella is Dean of the Aberdeen Business School at The Robert Gordon University, Scotland.

Donna McAleese is Project Leader for Knowledge Management with the Patton Group, Northern Ireland.

Rob Millar is Lecturer in Guidance and Counselling in the School of Psychology at the University of Ulster, Northern Ireland.

Colleen E. Mills is Associate Professor of Organization Studies at the University of Canterbury, New Zealand.

Paula O'Kane is Lecturer in Organizational Behaviour in the School of Business Organization and Management at the University of Ulster, Northern Ireland.

Dennis Quinn is a communications consultant and trainer in Northern Ireland, having previously been in a management position within a major police organization.

Myra Skipper is a communications consultant and trainer in Northern Ireland, having previously been a senior speech and language therapist.

Dennis Tourish is Professor of Leadership and Management at Aberdeen Business School, The Robert Gordon University, Scotland.

Naheed Tourish is Lecturer in Communication within Aberdeen Business School at The Robert Gordon University, Scotland.

Anne Tracey is Lecturer in Counselling Psychology in the School of Psychology at the University of Ulster, Northern Ireland.

Karen H. Zwijze-Koning is Assistant Professor of Communication Studies at the University of Twente, The Netherlands.

Introduction

There has been an enormous growth of interest in the field of organizational communication since the first edition of this book was published. In part, this is because the volume and variety of communications have expanded exponentially. Across the world, literally billions of e-mails fly round cyberspace and people send billions of text messages every day. Employees never really 'switch off' as they take their virtual office with them wherever they go. The company internet site has become increasingly important for attracting and maintaining the customer base, and the intranet is now central to internal communications. Furthermore, a highly educated, articulate and assertive workforce no longer just wishes to be consulted and listened to – Generation Y demand and expect that this will be the case. One result of this is that employees want workplace communication to be like modern food – instant and always available when they need it. Organizations therefore ignore communications at their peril. The problem for businesses, of course, is how to manage all of this effectively. This book helps to provide important solutions.

The central purpose of the book is to explore how organizations can evaluate their internal and external communications, in order to improve their effectiveness. A core tenet that underpins the text is that high quality communication inside organizations, and between them and their external publics, produces many tangible benefits. These include a sane internal atmosphere where teamwork is the norm, more satisfied employees and customers, greater levels of productivity and innovation, and sustained competitive advantage. It is our belief that the tools of communication are an organization's most vital resource in the daily battle for survival. This book is dedicated to establishing how these tools can best be employed.

George Bernard Shaw once said 'The biggest single problem in communication is the illusion that it has taken place.' This is an error made all too often by managers, who fail to remember that message sent does not equal message received. We need to check for feedback to ensure that messages are indeed being received and understood. It is also worth noting that many organizations make the error of acknowledging the need for improvements while continuing to repeat the well-learned mistakes of yesterday. Good intentions are not enough. Merely declaring the need for improvement does not bring it any nearer. We need to know exactly what the current baseline position is and what these improvements will look like. We also need to be able to measure the degree of the improvement so that we can compare this against the baseline. We do not believe that there is bad faith on the part of those organizations and managers who express a desire to improve communications without actually doing anything about it. Most genuinely wish to move forward. But they have encountered many apparently insurmountable problems in the attempt to turn aspiration into accomplishment. The difficulties faced include:

- Accurately diagnosing current communication practices. How do you measure the complexities of communication?
- Tracking the impact of particular measures designed to improve communication. How do we know what works, and what doesn't?
- Evaluating the overall contribution that communication makes to business success. How do we know that any of it matters?
- Learning how to inculcate different behaviours at all levels of the organization. It isn't that people necessarily face the new challenges with indifference. It is just that, like a drunk trying to appear sober, they often do the wrong things very, very, carefully.

These difficulties can be overcome. We have produced this book in the belief that communication audits build bridges between managers' aspirations and reality. What gets measured gets done. Auditing communication involves the assessment of current practice (*diagnosis*) in order to determine what steps are required to secure improvements (*prescription*). This book offers a series of methodologies that are commonly employed to evaluate communication effectiveness. It includes invited contributions from academic leaders in this field in the UK, Europe, the United States, Australia and New Zealand. The purpose is to equip readers with vital analytic tools, enabling them to benchmark performance and effect significant improvements.

In what follows, we and our fellow contributors generally do not distinguish between audits of internal or external communication. Having said that, this book focuses particularly on auditing internal communication. We recognize that there is a growing body of research in the field of public relations and marketing communications into assessing external communications. This research is usually referred to as 'monitoring', 'scanning' or 'evaluation', rather than auditing. It is beyond the remit or scope of this book to review this material in depth. A number of the most standard instruments reflect the internal communications bias of the present book, such as the Audit Questionnaire presented in the Appendix to this text. At the same time, other approaches, such as mystery shopping, are more widely used in audits of external communications. Furthermore, in principle, most of the methods discussed in the book can be adapted to meet both situations. We refer to this issue at various points throughout the book. Likewise, some of the case study chapters examine external communications (see for example Chapter 15). Overall, we would encourage readers to be creative in their approach. There is no need to feel imprisoned by precedent. The deciding factor in what techniques to use must be the needs and resources of the organizations and researchers concerned. However, it is always useful to remember that when a conflict flares up between the ideal and the possible, it is generally wise to side with the latter. Like a battle plan, most research designs have to be changed when they engage with the real world.

The book is structured in four parts: review, methods, case studies and overview. In Part I, a range of issues involved in auditing communication is reviewed. Chapter 1 provides an overall theoretical underpinning for the approaches explored. In particular, we discuss the contribution that communication makes to securing business success. It is increasingly clear that positive human resources policies are a prime determinant of organizational effectiveness. However, within this category, it is our conviction that how information is produced, exchanged and processed is a pivotal binding ingredient, joining together all the working parts of the organization. We also look at the benefits of good communication with customers, and the costs incurred when it goes wrong. Managers are busy people and the change agenda for most of them is already stretched to breaking point. We can only justify devoting time and other resources to improving communication if it is clear that tangible, substantial and measurable benefits will accrue. In Chapter 2, the specific contribution that audits can make to the assessment of communication practices is discussed. The origins of the audit process in the academic and business literature are also charted.

Part II provides a detailed analysis of a range of audit methodologies, and discusses the advantages and disadvantages of each. The approaches discussed include questionnaires, focus groups, interviews, diary and log analysis, mystery shopping, and techniques that may be less well known, such as social network analysis, constitutive ethnography and the Delphi technique. No one method works for every organization. The intention here is to equip managers and researchers with a fuller understanding of the available alternatives, and so help them to decide on the most appropriate approach for whatever communication challenges they are facing. This section also contains a chapter on auditing e-communications. There have been huge developments in this field, and these present new challenges that auditors must be ready to explore. In addition, Part II contains a chapter on writing an audit report. This chapter raises issues other than the nuts and bolts of report writing, such as breaking bad news to senior managers, devising recommendations in response to particular findings, and how to persuade key change agents within the organization to respond positively to audit findings.

Throughout the book, it is our intention to intimately connect theory with practice. Part III therefore illuminates the approaches discussed through a range of carefully chosen case studies. Those selected include both the retention of some classic audit studies from the first edition, together with a selection of new audit chapters. They embrace a variety of methods discussed in this book, and encompass internal and external communications, in both the public and private sectors. The aim is to explore audits in action, through illustrating how they have been employed to solve genuine problems in the real world. Each case study outlines the general context in which the audit occurred, the precise problems of the organization concerned, the audit methodology employed (and why it was selected), and the recommendations and changes to which the intervention gave rise. These chapters provide further examples of tools and techniques that should be of enormous help to those readers undertaking audits of their own. They will also prove fruitful for those seeking audit case studies to stimulate class-based discussion.

Finally, we conclude the book in Part IV by outlining a framework for the development of communication strategies, which integrates the implementation of audits into the strategic planning process. In this context, we discuss the criteria that should be employed in choosing between the multifarious audit tools available. This chapter also looks at the potential role of audits as a research tool, and in the teaching of management communication.

Overall, this text offers a unique blend of theory, research and practice in the field of communication auditing. The communication side of organizational life looks set to attract ever growing attention. The present book will therefore be essential for managers, communications practitioners, researchers and students concerned with organizational communication. In the period since the first edition of this book was published we have received considerable feedback from managers, consultants, lecturers and students who have experienced audits at first hand. We are grateful for this feedback, which has helped to develop and shape the new edition.

Communication breakdowns are always a barometer of greater storms and mishaps ahead. Equipped with the tools discussed here, organizations will be in a better position to identify icebergs in advance of collisions (one *Titanic* was enough), and so chart a safe passage through the turbulent oceans of the 21st-century marketplace.

Owen Hargie and Dennis Tourish
January 2009

Acknowledgements

We would like to acknowledge the assistance of a number of people in producing this text. We are grateful to the International Communication Association for giving us permission to develop and adapt their Audit Questionnaire, and for allowing us to publish the revised version in the Appendix to this text. Appreciation is also given to Noel Wilson who greatly assisted us with statistical analysis in relation to this questionnaire. Thanks to Philip Burch and David Barr, graphic design technicians at the University of Ulster, who assisted us with the figures and diagrams that feature at various points in the book. We acknowledge with gratitude the editorial staff at Routledge, especially Becci Waldron and Tara Stebnicky, for their unfailingly helpful and empathetic approach as we wrestled with the task of welding many themes into a coherent whole.

Finally, we pay tribute to our late friend and colleague Dr David Dickson with whom we worked for over three decades. He was a constant source of insight, humour, wisdom and inspiration, but always in his own inimitable, understated, style. His advice at many points in the conception and execution of this book, and his own contribution in Chapter 5, were a reflection both of his academic prowess and of his unfailing friendship. Thanks for everything, David.

Part I

Audits in context

Chapter 1

Communication and organizational success

Dennis Tourish and Owen Hargie

INTRODUCTION

The central purpose of this book is to explore how audits provide a clear picture of the communication climate that organizations face, internally and externally. However, this approach has to be anchored within a wider context, which establishes why anyone should bother to investigate the effectiveness of their communications programmes in the first place. Managers already face a surfeit of challenges. This chapter explores the benefits derived from treating organizational communication with the same diligence normally reserved for such functions as finance. A manager's intuitive feel for whether the company's books show a profit, or are splashed in red ink, is not normally regarded as sufficient. Hard evidence is required, to establish whether further success or imminent insolvency is in prospect. But, bizarrely, organizations often seek to determine whether they are communicating well without recourse to any kind of objective data. A moment's reflection shows that this is not a credible approach. As this book will demonstrate, it can be incredibly difficult to diagnose an organization's communication climate with any degree of accuracy. We therefore offer a systematic approach to the construction of a seaworthy communications strategy, and the rigorous evaluation of all steps taken along the way.

It is our contention that many business problems are the product of poor communications policies. Early action could avert shipwreck later in the day. For example, customers often take their business elsewhere because they receive inadequate information about company products; staff seek new jobs where they will have a better opportunity to contribute their ideas; levels of innovation are low because key players in rival departments are barely on speaking terms. Communication audits can be used to identify and reward good practice, prepare against possible storms sooner rather than later, and improve business performance.

In this chapter, we review:

- How organizational communication can be best defined and theorized.

- The central importance of communication in the day-to-day work of managers.
- The growing evidence to show that internal communication helps determine an organization's prospects of success. In the process, we highlight examples of good practice from leading companies. These suggest steps that other organizations should consider taking, in the drive to reach world class levels of performance.
- The role of communication in maintaining customer loyalty, and the importance of such loyalty in ensuring business success.
- The implications of these issues for our general conception of the communication function.

A recurrent theme in what follows is the importance of accurately appraising what we do today, in order to establish what we must do tomorrow. Traditionally, a ship's captain was the last person to find out that his crew intended to mutiny. Communication audits identify the symptoms of discontent, before either customers or employees storm the bridge. They are an organization's early warning system. What follows shows why they are necessary, and how they can help.

THE NATURE OF COMMUNICATION

Traditionally, communication tended to be viewed as a relatively simple linear process, in which a message was transmitted by a sender to a source, who then understood, internalized and acted on the message (Goldhaber *et al.*, 1978). Research in the organizational field concentrated on how this process could be managed, in order to improve productivity, performance and profitability. Communication audits have their origin within this framework, and were initially conceived in straightforward terms as a means of assisting managers to get their message across to employees more effectively. It is not surprising that, in the immediate post-war period, the study of communication itself was often a somewhat peripheral topic in universities, with its agenda imitating those set by more established social science disciplines that included industrial psychology, management and economics (Redding, 1985).

However, a paradigm shift has occurred since the early 1980s. Scholars still recognize that communication involves information transmission – the so-called conduit metaphor (Axley, 1984). But it is also clear that this conception does not do full justice to the phenomenon. Increasingly, organizational communication scholars study the dynamic relationships between communication processes and wider systems of human organizing (Mumby, 2007). In particular, what has become known as 'the linguistic turn' has focused attention on the central importance of language use in a huge variety of contexts, where its role had previously been under-emphasized (Grant *et al.*, 2004).

As such, the study of communication increasingly explores the co-construction of meaning between organizational actors, who influence each other in the context of asymmetrical power relationships, during which they compete for power, resources, voice and legitimacy (Tourish, 2007a). Individuals, and small and large groups, create multiple, contested realities to which they must then respond (Craig, 1999; Deetz, 1992; Fairhurst, 2005; Putnam, 1983; Smircich and Morgan, 1982; Weick, 1979). Language is no longer viewed as representative of reality, in some kind of neutral sense, but as also constitutive of it (Cooren *et al.*, 2006). This means that narratives, storytelling and sensemaking are fundamental units of organization, without which organizations could scarcely be said to exist. The assumption is that organizations are best viewed 'as complex discursive formations where discursive practices are both "in" organizations and productive of them' (Deetz, 2001, pp. 5–6). In short, communication *reflects* the relationships between all organizational actors; it also *creates* those relationships, and defines, shapes and explains them to ourselves and others, with varied degrees of success. Communication audits increasingly, but not always, seek to illuminate these processes. Inevitably, the issues raised are by no means simple.

Traditionally, managerial accounts of organization have had a privileged epistemological status, and in many accounts still emerge as articulating a reality that simply 'is', and is therefore beyond interrogation. Within this framework, the role of communication was straightforward. It was to deliver management messages to employees and other constituencies, so that everyone signed up for the vision and direction set by the top management team. In varied forms, this notion can still be found. But, although couched in timeless and universalist terms, such discourse is often more consistent with particular sectional interests than it acknowledges (Willmott, 1993). Thus: do managers and employees invariably share a common interest? Does a given organizational direction serve everyone's interests – or only those of a few? Is there only one generally agreed truth about where the organization is at and how it has got there, or are there multiple versions of reality? If the latter, whose version of reality will prevail? How are these competing stories communicated? Advocates of 'the linguistic turn' have therefore challenged the view of organizations as having a taken for granted existence as material entities, separate and apart from their discursive constructions (Westwood and Linstead, 2001; Gergen, 2000). Our notion of what constitutes communication, and therefore what denotes material for examination in communication audits, has undergone a radical transformation.

Communication clearly is about much more than 'making and sending messages and moving information as a copyable, distributable resource' (Varey, 2006, p. 184); rather, it can be viewed as dealing with how 'socially constructed institutions are reproduced and transformed by the accounting activities of people in interdependent (joint) action as they make sense of what they do together' (Varey, 2006, p. 191). Organization, ultimately, emerges as a phenomenon that is produced and reproduced (within certain limits) by the discursive interactions between organizational actors. It also, as Varey suggests, involves co-action and cooperation, as well as conflict, competition, uncertainty and anxiety. Increasingly, communication auditors seek to explore these more complex realities, and the often highly charged meanings that organizational actors attach to particular phenomena. Thus, organizations are studied as communicative sites of power and politics (Mumby, 2007). As part of this, issues of organizational diversity and 'voice' have come to the fore. In the past, organizations were often considered as neat and tidy formations, easily explained, with communication a peripheral lens through which scholars could study how people coordinated message exchange in conveniently bite-sized interactions. It might be more appropriate today to view the organizational landscape as a mess, littered with debris, and in which competing groups attempt to scavenge some sense of meaning from the chaos – not always successfully.

It follows from this that our view of communication audits has shifted in recent years. Audits increasingly study language, meaning, power relationships, voice, and gender, sometimes critically. Mumby's (2007) very useful overview also suggests that research on organizational communication must turn its efforts to exploring the in situ, moment-to-moment, everyday communication practices of organization members. This means extending communication research beyond pen and pencil self-report techniques that, while providing careful measurement, rarely capture the full complexities, ambiguities and frustrations of really occurring organizational behaviour. It is in this context that we offer the resources and ideas contained in this book.

Thus, some chapters offer methods and case studies that are concerned with careful measurement, often involving the information transmission aspects of communication in organizations. But we also provide examples of more interpretively oriented studies and techniques that, depending on the purpose of whatever audit readers may be contemplating, can furnish a richer and more qualitative account of how people communicate in organizations. Many auditors may seek to employ a combination of the various methods and theoretical perspectives that are available. Consistent with this discussion, we would not claim that any approach will ever produce a full account of communication. All methods and theoretical orientations have their strengths – and weaknesses. It is our hope that this book will help readers to develop a more sophisticated understanding of what can be achieved, and therefore make more informed choices about what suits their purpose.

COMMUNICATION IN MANAGEMENT

These issues come into sharp relief when we consider the role of communication in the context of how managers perform their jobs. Management is generally held to involve crafting a strategic vision to enhance organizational effectiveness. Turning this lofty aspiration into reality means creating and sustaining a unifying sense of purpose, on the part of many people. Organizations can be defined as 'social entities in which the behaviour of individuals is shaped and directed to achieve common goals' (Hargie, 2007, p. 25). Arguably, they are therefore best viewed as partnership arrangements, in which the principles of coalition building are the key to success (Tourish, 1998). Intuitively, many managers understand this, and the importance that it places on the effective management of people. Delbridge *et al.* (2006) cited a survey of UK managers that explored their perceptions of what most impacts on competitive advantage. More than half of the respondents cited the central role of 'effective people management', as against 14% who emphasized Research and Development and a meagre 7% who highlighted new capital investment. Most managers know that they need the active enthusiasm and commitment of their people if they are to succeed. However, managerial practice is riddled with paradoxes, and many organizations fail to implement the policies that will generate precisely this kind of commitment. For example, employees cannot buy into ideas that they neither know nor understand. There is a growing body of evidence to the effect that if people are excluded from the decision making process it becomes more difficult to secure their commitment to whatever decisions have been reached by the top management team (Clampitt and Williams, 2007). In turn, if they are not committed, they are less likely to deal with customers in the manner necessary to secure repeat business.

Unfortunately, it appears that most organizations are performing below par on these vital issues. An engagement index devised by the polling organization, Gallup, found that only 16% of UK employees were positively engaged with their work – that is, loyal and committed to the organization (Caulkin, 2007). The rest were unengaged or actively disengaged – that is, physically present but psychologically absent. These data are consistent with international trends. A Towers-Perrin (2006) study of 86,000 people in 16 countries across four continents found that only 14% of employees worldwide were fully engaged on the job – that is, able and willing to give sustained discretionary effort to help their organizations succeed. Nearly a quarter were actively disengaged, with 62% moderately engaged. Interestingly, China fared particularly poorly, with no more than 8% of Chinese workers highly engaged. In Europe, only 11% of employees were highly engaged, with 22% disengaged. In the US, comparable figures show that 21% of people were highly engaged, 63% moderately engaged and 16% disengaged. The costs to management credibility of this situation are enormous. For example, a study of over 3000 people across 18 countries found that while 42% of people said they would view 'a person like myself' as a 'credible' spokesperson for an organization, only 16% were willing to regard CEOs in the same light (Smythe, 2007) – a blow for many communication strategies that push the CEO to the fore of corporate publicity campaigns!

It is clear that huge opportunities to build cooperative, engaged and more productive workplaces are being missed, often as a result of management practices that alienate employees. In particular, we believe that insufficient attention to constructing positive communication programmes systematically undermines organizational performance. Consistent with this interpretation, Towers-Perrin (2006) concluded from their study that one of the key obstacles to employee engagement was a failure to build appropriate connections between senior managers and the workforce. Likewise, a survey of 2000 UK employees by the Chartered Institute of Personnel Development (CIPD, 2006), designed to explore employee engagement, found that around a third of employees had managers who 'rarely' or 'never' discussed their training and development needs with them. Only two in five reported getting feedback on how they were performing; 30% said that their manager rarely or never gave them performance feedback, and 25% said that their manager rarely or never made them feel that their work counts.

Communication emerged as an explicit theme in responses. Thus, while 46% of employees felt 'fairly well informed' about important organizational issues, 29% said they received only 'a limited amount of information' and 13% reported that they received 'not much at all'. The direct and indirect effects are enormous, with 47% of employees reportedly looking for another job or already in the process of leaving. Interestingly, the CIPD reported that, in terms of employment engagement, people most appreciated having opportunities to feed their views upward, being well informed about what is happening in the organization, and thinking that their manager was committed to the organization. At least two of these criteria are fundamentally concerned with organizational communication. They are also consistent with other empirical work which has found that feedback from managers to employees, and a belief that managers listen to their people, are critical factors in shaping communication climate and employee commitment (Van Vuuren et al., 2007). Despite this, and the need to unleash people's sense of involvement by inverting traditional organizational hierarchies, many communications programmes, regrettably, remain locked in a now dysfunctional tradition of command and control (Smythe, 2007). It is a tradition that wiser managers, and more successful organizations, are seeking to break.

In essence, communication is the most fundamental and pervasive of all management activities. Management involves an overwhelming focus on sharing information with others; seeking feedback on either the manager's ideas or those of other staff, customers, outside suppliers or franchise holders; making decisions (often in groups); commenting on proposals; and attending meetings. Information exchange, in all its multi-faceted forms, is central to the effective performance of the management function. Yet, paradoxically, the absence of adequate communication is among the most common findings of employee attitude surveys (Sirota et al., 2008). In seeking to remedy this dismal reality, Welch and Jackson (2007) describe one of the key goals of internal communication as the promotion of a positive sense of belonging by employees, and the consequent creation of relationships characterized by commitment.

Such an orientation reflects the pivotal role of communication in what managers actually do, as opposed to what old textbooks taught they ought to be doing. For example, Luthans and Larsen (1986) found that managers typically spend between 60% and 80% of their time communicating. One study of 60 front line supervisors at a Midwest US steel manufacturing plant found that 70% spent between eight and 14 hours per week in writing-related activities alone (Mabrito, 1997). These involved producing disciplinary action reports, clarifying job procedures, dealing with formal grievances, writing memos, producing instructional documents to subordinates, drafting incident reports and writing external letters or reports to customers. It appears that the burden of these activities is increasing. Thus Gurchiek (2006) reported a Canadian study, which found that 58% of respondents spent between 2 and 4 hours per day reading e-mails, reports, memos, the Internet and intranet. A US study by the American Management Association found 10% of respondents spending more than half the workday on e-mail (Pfeffer, 2007).

It has been suggested that effective managers are particularly inclined to spend a great deal of their time in communication-based activities. Kotter's landmark study into the role of general managers (1982) challenged the notion that effective executives spend their time holed up in offices where they plan, organize and motivate by manipulating pieces of paper. Kotter followed 15 chief executives through the day-to-day routines of their companies. He concluded that the most successful executives used a variety of influencing techniques in predominantly face-to-face interaction, as their primary method of motivating people and effecting successful change.

This is consistent with a variety of research findings, which generally suggests that supervisors spend between one-third and two-thirds of their time interacting with what are sometimes still termed 'subordinates' (Zorn, 1995). Most such communication is face to face, and most of it is task related rather than personal in content. Managers spend their day communicating with many people, in brief interactions that are nevertheless of enormous significance in determining the communication and cultural climate of their organizations. Effective management depends on open communication, and requires an interpersonal style characterized by warmth, candour, supportiveness and a commitment to dialogue rather than monologue. No wonder that Mintzberg (1989, p. 18), having surveyed a wide range of evidence, drew the following conclusion: 'The manager does not leave meetings or hang up the telephone in order to get back to work. In large part, communication *is* his or her work.' Studies of leadership in management have reaffirmed the point – effective leadership in the workplace requires a constant use of the tools of communication to create meaning, share visions and build a common focus on the agenda for change (Sims and Lorenzi, 1992). It is scarcely surprising, therefore, that studies have found that the more skilled and competent a leader is at communicating, the more likely employees are to be satisfied with their jobs (Madlock, 2008).

It is, therefore, scarcely surprising that many surveys have shown that most people in organizations, from top to bottom, are keen to secure improved communications (e.g. Hargie and Tourish, 1996a; Tourish and Tourish, 1997; Kalla, 2005), and that such improvements are correlated with job satisfaction and commitment. These could be considered worthwhile gains in their own right. There is also now a considerable research literature to indicate that increased commitment is positively associated with improved organizational functioning and that even small changes in employee performance often have a significant impact on the bottom line (Cushman and King, 2001; Delbridge *et al.*, 2006). These issues are of fundamental importance. As Argyris (1998) has argued, questions such as morale, satisfaction and commitment need to be viewed as a vital concern in human relations policies – but they are not decisive. That pole position is reserved for business performance. The evidence on this issue strongly suggests that positive communications programmes improve overall performance – a further justification for utilizing communication audit methodologies as the first stage towards benchmarking and then securing further improvements. It is to a detailed consideration of this evidence that we now turn.

COMMUNICATION AND ORGANIZATIONAL EFFECTIVENESS

Organizations that treat their people well, and that communicate with them fully and forthrightly, do better in the marketplace. For example, the UK *Sunday Times* lists the 100 best companies to work for each year, based on widespread surveys of employees. This has found that those scoring high as good workplaces consistently outperformed the average in terms of shareholder returns on the FTSE 1200 index over a 5-year period (*Sunday Times*, 2006). Within the top ten best companies, an astonishing 91% of employees felt proud to work for their company, and said they would 'strongly recommend' it to others. These companies had 63% of their employees strongly engaged, compared with just 28% for the non-listed companies. Unsurprisingly, communication emerges as a recurrent theme. Barchester Healthcare was ranked number 2 in the list of top 20 'big companies' to work for. Its senior managers explicitly embrace proactive communication as a key to their success. They visit all locations throughout the year, hold regular meetings with employees, make intense use of a company intranet, issue regular newsletters and prioritize one-to-one communication with their people.

Other examples abound. The CEO of Continental Airlines holds an 'open house' each month in his office at which employees are invited to show up and speak with him about anything. At JetBlue airline, each employee spends his or her first day at an orientation that includes spending an hour with the company President, CEO and other top managers (Argenti, 2007). Such activities are a vital part of CEO communication programmes that seek to demonstrate visible and vocal support for, and championship of, the company vision and strategy (Sanchez and McCann, 2005). While effective communication practices will not be enough to deliver employee engagement and commitment by themselves, it seems likely that they will improve morale, promote a sense of engagement, heighten employee retention and productivity, and thereby help organizations to compete more effectively in the marketplace.

Similarly, Kanter (1988) argued that communication within and between organizations and sections of organizations stimulates higher levels of innovation. For this reason, research has shown that team based organizations generally outperform their rivals, and are more effective at unleashing the cooperative energies of employees (Ancona and Bresman, 2007). When groups work in isolation, with people sharing minimal information across inflexible boundaries, the locomotive of change slows to a crawl. Communication audits conducted by us suggest one contributing factor to this. We have found that poor inter-departmental communication generates considerable feelings of isolation and dissatisfaction, and is in turn correlated with low levels of involvement in the decision making process. Thus, poor information exchange exacerbates uncertainty, increases alienation and produces a segmented attitude to work that is inimical to the spirit of innovation. Kanter's conclusion is that contact at as many levels as possible is vital to wholehearted, widespread involvement in the achievement of organizational goals and the creation of a supportive climate for innovation.

Similar views have since been propounded in a series of anecdotal management books written by successful managers. One of the most interesting of such autobiographical accounts is provided by Semler (1989, 1993). He described how he turned around Brazil's largest marine and food processing machinery manufacturer. Facing ruin in 1980, by 1989 productivity and profits were rising at an annual rate of 40%. Semler identified a strong focus on communications as a crucial part of the package that ensured his company's survival. The efforts made and results obtained included the following:

- Factory workers set their own production quotas.
- Employees set their own salaries, with no strings attached.
- Before people are hired or promoted into management positions they are interviewed and approved by those they will be managing.
- Managers are reviewed on their performance every 6 months, by those who work under them.
- Information about all aspects of organizational performance are openly shared. For example, there is full disclosure of salary levels and personal earnings.

- Semco has grown sixfold, despite buffeting recessions.
- Productivity has increased sevenfold.
- Profits have risen fivefold.

While Semco is unusual in the extent to which it implements these practices, it is far from unique. For example, Whole Foods is both very profitable and ranked 15 in the top 100 of the US's best places to work for. All of its employees are free to look up any one else's salary, from the top to the bottom of the company (Levering and Moskowitz, 2006).

Participation is also emerging as a major issue in the research literature (Harley *et al.*, 2005). Participative forms of management inevitably assume that many people within the organization, outside the ranks of management, need to be kept informed of key corporate issues and that they in turn feel keen to contribute to building the organization's success. A much more open flow of information is indispensable to the effective management of such programmes. As the requirement of participation is further extended, the communication challenges can only grow.

How does improved participation impact on organizational outcomes? Miller *et al.* (1990) surveyed over 700 people in one large organization. They found that participation in decision making and the existence of social support reduced workplace stress and burnout, while raising levels of satisfaction and commitment. This is connected to productivity. One meta-analysis of 43 studies concluded that profit-sharing, worker ownership and worker participation in decision making were all positively associated with increased productivity (Doucouliagos, 1995).

There appears to be a correlation between high performance and the existence of internal communications programmes. A survey of 293 communications professionals in UK companies classified their organizations into well performing and poorly performing categories (Stewart, 1999). The former were defined as companies that had excellent or good financial performance for all of the 3 preceding years, whereas those whose financial performance had been poor or very poor for all 3 years were classified as poorly performing organizations. Over half those in the former category had formal communications programmes. This compared to only 25% of their poorly performing counterparts.

The evidence on these issues is by now extensive. One of the most detailed, and therefore most interesting, accounts available concerns General Motors (GM). Few organizations have tracked exactly what they have done and its effects so precisely. It is therefore worth recounting the nature of GM's communications programme, and the results in some detail. These have been recounted in depth by McKeans (1990), Smith (1991) and O'Reilly and Pfeffer (2000).

The communications programme began in 1982 in one division, led by a senior manager who wished to transform the division's communication and performance. His first move was to motivate senior colleagues by getting them to read widely into the basics of effective internal communications. He then upgraded the division's newsletter, increased the frequency of its publication and included much more key business information. A variety of other publications were also produced, including one jointly written and funded with trade union organizations.

A communications review group was set up, which met monthly, and evaluated the range of publications being issued. This group involved top management and institutionalized their personal involvement in the programme. Other steps were as follows:

- A quarterly video news magazine was produced, allowing management to present detailed business information if not in person, then at least on camera. This was shown during working hours in scheduled meetings, and served as a launch pad for face-to-face discussions between supervisors and staff.
- Face-to-face meetings were held. Managers met with randomly selected small groups of staff, with the express purpose of facilitating open discussion on highly sensitive issues.
- Regular audits, video surveys and quality culture surveys were conducted to track the impact of the programme. Thus, follow up audits were conducted every 2 years.

It is noteworthy that none of these steps is enormously radical. Internal communications programmes that effect significant improvements are often characterized by their simplicity. However, in their totality they can be summed up as the adoption of a creative approach to ensuring the maximum amount of interaction between as many groups of people as possible, and a new openness in the sharing of information. The results, for GM at any rate, can be evaluated in terms of both the quality of communication, and bottom line business performance.

- Less than 50% of GM employees said they believed the information supplied by management in 1982. By 1986 this had risen to over 80%.
- Budget savings amounted to 2.8% for the first year, 4.9% in the second, then 3.2%, 3.7% and 2.2%.
- Sales doubled over a 7-year period.
- By 1988 delays in delivering service parts were eliminated.
- Suggestion scheme savings per employee were $864 in 1981, $1220 in 1982, $1306 the following year, followed by $1741, $1547 and $5748 in 1987.

This focus has been maintained. Team meetings are held twice a month, when the assembly line is stopped for 30 minutes so that people can review their performance. The impact on employee engagement is significant. In 1998, workers made an average of 3.2 suggestions each, of which 81% were implemented. Furthermore, during that year, over 86% of employees made suggestions. By contrast, in too many workplaces the average number of employee suggestions unfortunately comes in at approximately zero.

A number of factors stand out in this case study. First, top management commitment is reaffirmed as necessary. This is partly because communications take time and effort – simply holding regular meetings is a big commitment, and there is a temptation on the part of managers to regard it as 'dead time'. Second, the measures involved in effective communications are in themselves simple, and involve taking imaginative steps to increase the general flow of information through more face-to-face and informal communications. Third, it is impossible from these data to definitively establish a causal link between the programme discussed and the resulting outcomes. However, it appears that a correlation of some kind exists. It is unlikely that the benefits the GM executives observed were unconnected with the communications efforts they initiated. Wider longitudinal studies into the effect of similar programmes, particularly in split site workforces, is necessary to resolve the full extent of this issue.

Some studies of the kind discussed with regard to GM have also been conducted in healthcare settings. Arnold (1993) reported on the quality improvement programme that he initiated as President of the largest for-profit medical centre in the United States. His paper argued that communication was central to the programme adopted. Arnold literally implemented an 'open door policy', by having his office door taken from its hinges; he moved the nearest coffee machine into his office, so that people had little option but to interact with him; department leaders received an organization-wide monthly financial report once a month; open forums were held once a month, and the questions and answers raised at them were distributed in written form throughout the organization. Bottom line results from the management effort, reported by Arnold, included:

- A staff turnover rate of 30% in 1989 down to 12% by 1991.
- Accounts receivable running at 71 days in 1989, down to 44 days.
- Bad debt percentage down from 3.2% to an average of 0.4% per month.

It is notable that this account of quality focuses on the benefits of communication, rather than the formal apparatus of quality improvement (e.g. certification) on which many organizations choose to concentrate. Such measures clearly help to reduce status differentials among organizational members – differentials that the evidence generally suggests have negative effects on people's level of involvement and engagement in their jobs (Messe *et al.*, 1992; Ravlin, 2005).

From all of this, a general agreement exists in the literature concerning the nature of the activities that characterize proactive and effective communications policies. We summarize some examples of good practice in Box 1.1, drawing in particular on accounts of communication within Microsoft (Love, 2006), Sun Microsystems (McKenzie, 2007), the Mayo Clinic (Davis, 2006a), Southwest Airlines (Hardage, 2006), British Petroleum (Croston, 2005), and Royal Mail in the UK (Kennedy and McCarthy, 2008). In addition, Chapter 11 of this book contains a case study, documenting how particular communication interventions in the aftermath of a communication

---

Box 1.1 Best communications practices by leading companies

1   Communications training is an ongoing activity for all personnel, *especially* senior leaders.
2   Communicators treat employees as adults, honestly acknowledging problems rather than spinning failure as 'success temporarily postponed'. Managers at Sun Microsystems are encouraged to talk about problems (P), then talk about solutions (S), and then report regularly on progress from P to S.
3   Microsoft has created a 'network' of those responsible for communication, who are brought together to share their planning and best practice. This is a significant investment of time, energy and human resources.
4   The Mayo Clinic has also created an informal network to obtain regular employee feedback. Each communication team member selects ten employees whom they know informally. These receive one or two e-mails per month, soliciting feedback on a range of issues, such as 'What question would you like to ask the CEO?' This serves as an inexpensive but regular communication audit.
5   Southwest Airlines sends out a daily newsletter through the intranet, e-mail and bulletin boards, and issues a weekly newsline broadcast from the CEO. It also ensures that the CEO and president visit every major employee location at least once a year and delivers what they term a 'Message to the field'.
6   Each quarter, BP produces a *Performance in Perspective* programme, which takes the organization's quarterly results, and interviews the CEO about their significance. It also includes media reaction, comment from external analysts and reports from some of BP's main businesses. The first programme was watched by 5000 employees; this has now grown to over 54,000 in 75 countries.
7   Royal Mail has a 'work time listening and learning' (WTLL) session each week, lasting for 30 minutes, in which teams discuss issues of local importance and how they might improve their workplace.

audit also resulted in measurable improvements in the organization's communication climate. Regular evaluation, clear objectives, and an intense desire to secure two-way involvement are among the recurrent themes.

COMMUNICATION AND THE MOTIVATION OF STAFF

We have, above, identified significant gains from a management focus on improving communication. The question arises: why should an emphasis on relationships have such a profound impact on people's ability to perform the tasks for which they are hired, and on organizational outcomes?

The explanation is that people do not set aside their normal human needs during working hours. We therefore need to stop viewing organizations through the distorting lens of positivist inspired machine metaphors. Such metaphors tend as a matter of course to assume a watertight division between thinking and feeling, and conceptualize organizations as impersonal systems, to be manipulated into new forms exclusively at management's will. This is far from the case. Organizations are chiefly systems of human interaction (Edwards and Wajcman, 2005). People carry their emotions and wider social needs into work with them. They also then discuss and share these in groups. Such needs must be addressed, or they will become a source of dysfunctional dissatisfaction.

The implications of this become clear when we consider the issue of change management. Increasingly, communications programmes are dominated by the management of change (Carnall, 2007). Change is also rampant, as a study by Worrall and Cooper (2006) demonstrated. They surveyed 1541 UK managers and found 89% had experienced some form of organizational change in the previous year. In fact, over half had gone through more than three major changes in that timeframe. Given the data on the importance of employee commitment, and the degree to which managers themselves admit its importance, one might expect that these changes were geared at promoting better workplace relationships and enhancing employee participation, engagement and commitment. Instead, 63% of managers reported that cost reduction programmes were the most common form of change they had experienced. Predictably, almost two-thirds reported that job security and morale had decreased as a result. Half thought that motivation levels, loyalty and employee well being had been negatively affected. As a considerable amount of research has demonstrated (including Chapter 14 in this book), change programmes (such as downsizing) that attack people's job security and sense of self-worth tend to have such adverse effects, irrespective of the communication strategies employed to implement them (Tourish et al., 2004).

The problem is compounded by the manner in which change is normally managed. When managers are introducing change and a new culture they frequently regard resistance primarily as something to be overcome rather than as useful feedback. *Star Trek* has regularly featured a marauding group of intergalactic aliens called the Borg, who solemnly inform everyone they meet that 'resistance is futile'. Their goal is to 'assimilate' all new species, so that they lose their individuality and become part of 'the Borg collective'. Likewise, management inspired changes that treat resistance (or even questions) as a futile gesture risk producing the sort of monolithic cultures, stifling norms and organizational frameworks that are incompatible with innovation, and which therefore undermine competitive advantage (Tourish and Robson, 2006). Rather, feedback must be institutionalized into organizational decision making, in order to avoid the emergence of a 'collective' consciousness characterized by drab uniformity – and profits that sink in tandem with staff morale. 'Uniform thinking', in any event, is an oxymoron. Some researchers have found that, in many cases, it is the manner in which change is introduced rather than change per se that alienates people (Turnbull and Wass, 1998). A lack of consultation and communication is particularly prone to spark resistance. The problem of managing change is therefore, to a very large extent, a problem of managing communication. Communication about change should therefore explain why the change is needed, what will be different as a result, what success will ultimately look like, how people will be supported during the change, and how the results will be measured (McKenzie, 2007).

This perspective is reinforced if we consider the issue of motivation. It is clear that the quality of relationships with co-workers is a crucial factor in determining levels of job satisfaction. Yet this is far removed from the primary task-focused rationale that is generally the original spur for the creation of most organizations. Summarizing a number of research investigations, Argyle (1987) concluded that job satisfaction correlated highly with popularity or acceptance by group members in many studies. In a later text, Argyle (1994) cited a study which found that while 34% of respondents regarded their job primarily as a means of earning a living, 66% thought that it was more than that, and placed a particular value on sociability with colleagues and their use of skills. In line with this research, one study involving 302 employees at two manufacturing firms found a strong relationship between positive communication (such as accurate information, high levels of trust and a desire for interaction) and levels of job satisfaction (Petit *et al.*, 1997). However, the same study found only a weak to moderate relationship between satisfaction with communication and job performance, indicating the need for further research into this issue.

Plainly, co-workers provide material and social rewards. If, as appears to be the case, the exchange of rewards is essential to the smooth functioning of most relationships (Dickson *et al.*, 1993), the expectation of rewards must operate within peer groups at work and become translated into generalized feelings about the entire job. Hence, Argyle (1994) reported that job satisfaction is higher for those who are accepted by co-workers and who belong to what are described as cohesive groups. If this is true, it suggests that job satisfaction cannot be achieved by an exclusive emphasis on tasks. In short, we would argue that effective organizations must be aware of their members' personal needs, and take care to nurture relationships at all levels. Communication is a vital means of furthering this objective. Through opening the channels of communication people can articulate their needs, reduce uncertainty by gaining access to information, develop opportunities to influence the decision making process and satisfy the fundamental human need to make a difference. The alternative is a policy of exclusion, which threatens well being on all fundamental levels and produces a workforce so preoccupied with its own unmet needs that it is incapable of responding to the needs of clients or customers.

There is a clear suggestion here that effective communication promotes organizational cohesion and effectiveness because it answers to people's basic motivational impulses. Employees tend to be preoccupied by six basic questions. These can be divided into two parts. Thus:

Part One	*Part Two*
What's my job?	How are we doing?
How am I doing?	How do we fit in to the whole?
Does anybody give a damn?	How can I help?

These form two categories – the WIIFME questions (*What's In It For Me?*), and the WIIFU questions (*What's In It For Us?*) Many programmes address only the issues in Part Two. However, it appears that unless the first set is accorded equal significance people will simply be unable to hear what comes next. It is also clear that real involvement only occurs when employees ask the final question (How can I help?), and that corporate communications programmes are ultimately designed to get the maximum number of employees thinking at this level.

Business success rests on serving a need at a profit. However, people are not intrinsically motivated by the knowledge that a sound business plan underwrites their activities, that shareholders have received an adequate return on their investment, or that the CEO has met all his or her performance targets for the year (and perhaps received handsome stock options in return). It appears that the commitment of employees to the enterprise is primarily engaged, in the first instance, by the amount of attention that is paid to their perceived needs.

Thus, people are not fundamentally rational creatures. In the long term, business success is vital for individual as well as societal well being. However, the evidence reviewed here suggests that, in order to grasp this wider picture, the fundamental human needs that people bring into the workplace with them must be addressed. This is certainly a messy picture, and makes the management task even more difficult than it already is. There is an inherent ambiguity to the job of management, which sometimes makes the task feel akin to one of juggling with cannon balls. It also suggests that communication should be regarded as a competence of core management, underpinning the many people management skills that organizations are now battling to develop. Unless such realities are faced head-on it is unlikely that organizations will be able to achieve anything like their full competitive potential. The costs will be incalculable.

CUSTOMERS, EMPLOYEES AND COMMUNICATION

Communication with clients and customers is also a vital ingredient of overall success. As Cornelissen *et al.* (2006, p. 114) summarize prevalent research: 'in today's society the future of any one company depends critically on how it is viewed by key stakeholders and investors, customers and consumers, employees, and members of the community in which the company resides'. In particular, an organization's perceived trustworthiness, competence and attractiveness have a particular potency to influence whether people want to work there, or customers wish to buy its products and services. Empirical studies show that potential investors also tend to assume that companies with a high reputational ranking will offer better investment opportunities (Helm, 2007). For this reason, corporate reputation is increasingly regarded as a vital barometer of health and financial well being (Dowling, 2006). This can be defined as 'a set of collectively held beliefs about a company's ability to satisfy the interests of its various stakeholders' (Gabbionta *et al.*, 2007, p. 99).

It has also been found that customers welcome communication from the businesses they deal with. The Henley Centre for Forecasting found that 68% of customers actively wanted information from such companies and 60% were more likely to buy from suppliers who kept in touch (Jones, 1997). A recognition of such factors has led to the growth of what has been defined as 'relationship marketing', in which primary importance is attached to the quality of relationships between customers and the companies they deal with (Day *et al.*, 1998).

There appears to be a direct correlation between the willingness of organizations to address their external customer relations on the one hand, and their management of internal communication issues on the other. For example, Hartline and Ferrell (1996) found that managers who were committed to the quality of customer services were more inclined to empower employees and use behaviour-based evaluations.

In turn, a recognition of such links is one means of achieving competitive advantage, by differentiating the organization from its rivals. Hutton (1996) discusses what is called a 'culture-to-customer' philosophy, which recognizes the importance of what employees believe and do, and how this is perceived by customers. The assumption is that the organization should first define its own culture, then communicate its basic tenets internally, and finally ensure that these values are made visible to customers, via the behaviour and attitude of employees. As Hutton (1996, p. 40) expressed it: 'Customers are then able to identify and "connect" or "associate" with the organization, with a particular product class, that best matches their own values or aspirations.' A number of key companies and the guiding values that help them stand out in the marketplace are identified. These include:

- IBM (service)
- Ben and Jerry's/Body Shop (social conscience)
- Apple/Saturn/Benetton (non-conformity/new attitude)
- Pepsi (youth)
- 3M/General Electric (innovative products that make life more enjoyable).

Market pressures are likely to strengthen these links in the future. Many companies already highlight those aspects of their culture that they believe will most impress customers. Johnson and Johnson view their 'Credo' as being at the core of their vision and strategy (Forman and Argenti, 2005). This is a short statement that is widely distributed and contains such typical statements as 'We are responsible to our employees, the men and women who work with us throughout the world.' The Body Shop publishes what it calls a 'Values Report', an independently audited account of its record on the environment, animal protection and human relationships (Kent, 1996). There is, indeed, growing evidence to suggest that customers are influenced in their purchase decisions by these and other criteria. Scott (1996) reported one survey which found that 84% of consumers were prepared to pay more for goods when manufacturers paid employees a reasonable wage. While one can debate the degree to which this is merely aspirational, rather than a reflection of actual consumer behaviour, the fact remains that all of us are increasingly bombarded with information that enables us to base our purchase decisions on such criteria, if we so choose.

The role of the media adds an extra dimension of importance to the issue of corporate reputation. The media pay enormous attention to 'organizational secrets' – the bigger, the better. Believing that news is what someone doesn't want known, and anything else is advertising, it has a tendency to focus on stories critical of business practice. The impact of such exposure can be devastating. Thus, one study into the impact of bad news found that perceived levels of trustworthiness were the first and biggest casualty of negative publicity (Renkema and Hoeken, 1998). Like money, trust is hard to acquire but is easily squandered. Thus, customers who defect because of poor service or communication, and staff who blow the whistle on management malpractice or publicize a mood of imminent insurrection, can follow a well-trodden pathway to the airwaves. The conclusion is that best practice companies should see internal and external communications as part of a seamless whole, and devote considerable resources to monitoring their effectiveness.

Customers can fall into three main categories: promoters (enthusiastic advocates on behalf a company), passives (who are indifferent) and detractors (who consciously run it down). Having a superior ratio of customers in the first category as opposed to the other two turns out to be one of the simplest and most powerful metrics behind business success or failure. For example, a study of the airline industry in the US found that no airline had superior growth over a 3-year period without 'a superior ratio of promoters to detractors' (Reichheld, 2006, p. 42). Evidently, customer attitudes hit the bottom line, and do so at warp speed. Despite this, the evidence suggests that most businesses underestimate the importance of evaluating their communications with customers. Thus, Reichheld (2003) found that US companies lose 50% of their customers every 5 years. Bizarrely, most of them make little effort to find out why.

The costs of these problems are enormous. Research has shown that it costs about six times more to get a new customer than to keep an existing one (Hargie *et al.*, 2004). A significant body of evidence, covering organizations such as MBNA, BancOne, Southwest Airlines and Taco Bell, also shows that even small increases in customer retention lead to large increases in profitability (Bowen *et al.*, 1999). In some cases, 5% increases in the former have led to 75–100% gains in the latter. This is because retention is associated with higher levels of satisfaction, and a series of related commercial benefits. For example, customers in the retail sector who report that they are 'very satisfied' as opposed to merely 'satisfied' are four times more likely to come back, are more likely to make recommendations to others, and spend more money when they do visit the retail outlet (Buckingham and Cowe, 1999). With this in mind, Reichheld (2003) argued that tools should be employed to learn from customer defections, and turn the data into a strategy for reducing their loss. In our view, communication audits constitute an important part of the toolkit of businesses anxious to focus on this area.

When attention is paid to these issues the returns are substantial. For example, Sears, Roebuck and Company (a leading US retailer) spent much of the 1990s redesigning itself around what it characterized as an employee–customer–profit chain. As Rucci *et al.* (1998, p. 84) comment in analysing this company, anyone:

> with even a limited experience in retailing understands intuitively that there is a chain of cause and effect running from employee behaviour to customer behaviour to profits, and it's not hard to see that behaviour depends primarily on attitudes.

They go on to point out that the biggest problem with these variables is measurement, with the result that 'many companies do not have a realistic grasp of what their customers and employees actually think and do' (p. 84). Sears, Roebuck has tackled the problem by developing a process of data collection, analysis, modelling and experimentation around a series of Total Performance Indicators. A crucial stage in their development was intense communication within the ranks of senior management, with employees and with customers. For example, a senior representative from the corporate communications team served in the change process group, managers were trained in the communication aspects of the changes being implemented (including how to handle employees' emotions), and formal communication plans became part of the implementation process (Forman and Argenti, 2005). The basis for long-term executive compensation was changed, so that it relied one-third on employee measures, one-third on customer measures and one-third on traditional investor returns. The result is that a company that recorded a mind-boggling $3.9 billion loss in 1992 ended the decade by, once again, turning in a healthy profit.

Overall, good relationships and communication with customers are essential to business success. Customer loyalty hinges on innumerable communicative episodes that have been termed 'Moments of Truth' (Ryder, 1998). One indifferent, unmotivated or surly employee is often enough to poison a relationship, and lose valuable customers. Studies repeatedly find that customers identify the quality of communication with the organizations where they do business as a key factor in determining the overall quality of their relationship with that organization (Madden and Perry, 2003). In turn, this affects how they communicate with others. Thus, Davis (2006a) reported that 95% of the Mayo Clinic's patients stated that they said 'good things' about the clinics after their visits, and that they told these on average to 46 other people. Management's job, therefore, is to create numerous positive Moments of Truth, which make the customer experience unforgettable for all the right rather than all the wrong reasons. Accordingly, Caywood (1998) has suggested that customer communications should be guided by questions along the following lines:

1   How many different methods (e.g. readership surveys, e-mail response/ tracking mechanisms, focus groups) are employed for gathering feedback from stakeholders?
2   To what degree does the organization solicit input from different audiences when it is determining corporate and/or communications goals?
3   Does the organization segment its audiences, enabling it to deliver more appropriate communications messages?
4   Is every contact point between the company and its audiences treated like a communications opportunity?

An example of how this might work in practice can be drawn from the experience of the SAS Institute, a statistical analysis software company

(Reichheld, 2006). It organizes its 275 phone technical representatives into small teams. Each team appoints a member to serve on a customer ballot committee. This group reports regularly on customer problems, attitudes and issues in general. They then discuss responses and solutions to such problems. But the process goes further. Each year, the group compiles its feedback and solutions into a list of actions that the company could take to ensure that the problems disappear and the solutions become permanent. These are published on the company's website. Customers then vote on what improvements they most want to see in the company's software. Internal SAS meetings are held, at which key directors report on which items have received the most customer votes and what actions could be taken to begin the improvements. Previous years' commitments and results are also reviewed. The essence of the process is simple: it is grounded in a philosophy of *listening* to customers, and creating systems that institutionalize this into the heart of the company's operations. The only surprise is that this approach is more the exception than the norm.

Previously, organizations have underestimated the importance of these issues, but are now coming under pressure to be more proactive. In particular, audit tools have been used infrequently, despite their utility. They represent a valuable means of providing managers with the data that can then inform action plans. As this discussion shows, insight into what is happening now prepares the ground for a wider understanding of what must happen tomorrow. The pressure of the marketplace is now such that communication with customers cannot be treated in the cack-handed way that may have sufficed in the past.

THE CHANGING ROLE OF COMMUNICATIONS

Given this context, communications practitioners have been attempting to delineate the impact of new thinking and recent practice on their approach. In the past, the job of internal communicators was viewed, rather simplistically, as one of providing information to employees (McKenzie, 2007). Such a role is primarily concerned with one-way communications, the regulation of the behaviour of employees and ensuring compliance with centrally decreed instructions. Much of it is also still necessary. When decisions have been made centrally it is imperative that they are disseminated widely within the organization, as quickly as possible, and that people understand the response that is required from them. However, as this chapter has made clear, organizations are increasingly attempting to unleash the creative involvement and participation of people as well. This suggests that the success of leadership should increasingly be measured by the extent to which it promotes open communication, involvement, participation and power-sharing, rather than in the number of visionary strategies emanating from the Chief Executive's office (TQM, re-engineering, downsizing, delayering, Investors in People, 'just in time . . .') (Tourish, 2005). Most such strategies fail. Many do so because CEOs frequently rush into dramatic change programmes before they have anything like enough evidence to judge whether they will help or hinder their organizations (Pfeffer and Sutton, 2006). Overall, we would counsel a lower volume of change management and an increased emphasis on communication about core values, strategic priorities and organizational vision.

This renders it impossible to sustain the argument that people only need to know whatever the organization decides they need to know in order to do their jobs. It is worth pointing out that if managers treat staff on a 'need to know' basis, what is known as 'the norm of reciprocity' suggests that this attitude will be returned from the shop floor, with important information then being withheld from managers. When someone is hit, the natural human instinct is to retaliate. This will further inflame the already difficult problem of securing accurate upward feedback. As we have seen, improving communication with customers may be one of the most important steps that companies can take to increase their profits. In addition, coherent internal communication enables the organization to present a consistent and clear image to its external publics: absolutely vital to any prospect of sustaining internal cohesion and marketplace advantage.

The underlying perspective on organizations advocated in this chapter is integrative – that is, the organization is viewed as an interconnected whole, which needs to be focused on agreed objectives in order to go through organizational transformation without collapsing into internal strife. As Grunig and Grunig (2006, p. 6) noted: 'Effective organizations are able to achieve their goals because they choose goals that are valued by their strategic constituencies both inside and outside the organization . . . Ineffective organizations cannot achieve their goals, at least in part, because their publics do not support and typically oppose management efforts to achieve what publics consider illegitimate goals.' Within this framework, a spirit of collaboration has been seen as a primary integrative force. The objective is to increase employees' level of involvement in the organization, so that they are prepared to exceed the effort required to perform narrowly defined job tasks – in short, the promotion of what has been termed organizational citizenship behaviour (Tang and Ibrahim, 1998). In this model, employees have rights in terms of information exchange, but they also have corresponding responsibilities to contribute to the achievement of important business goals. Issues of involvement, participation, democracy and power-sharing are also inevitably raised. Nevertheless, it has been noted that 'seldom has the vast literature on forms and practices of leadership been brought into direct dialogue with research on employee participation and workplace democracy' (Cheney *et al.*, 1998, p. 40). This is a serious weakness.

Management clearly has the biggest responsibilities to rectify this situation. We view auditing communication as part of an overall package designed to evaluate effectiveness, identify best practice within and without the organization, and create a climate within which such practices can become more widely applied.

CONCLUSION

This chapter has identified what can be gained from a proactive focus on communications, both internally and externally. To do so is to put a greater premium on relationships with staff, business suppliers and customers. However, the question arises: how can this perspective be reconciled with the self-evident fact that staff are often treated as a dispensable liability, customers as little more than a damned nuisance, and suppliers as potential industrial spies? For example, increasing employee commitment has become one of the central thrusts of business life (Riketta and Van Dick, 2005). Yet the desire for such commitment is at odds with the downsizing and delayering processes characteristic of much management practice. Delayering has been described as 'the process by which people who barely know what's going on get rid of those who do' (Mintzberg, 1996, p. 62). It is not without significance that practitioners of the noble art of firing people generally seek refuge behind a dense and ever expanding smoke-screen of euphemisms. No one is ever fired – they are 'let go', a process that sounds almost pleasant. We know of one top executive who announced a wave of redundancies by telling those affected that he was giving them 'the opportunity to fulfil your potential elsewhere'. People are not overworked – they are 'empowered', and so choose to do more. Employees in some organizations have even taken to joking that management jargon has acquired the status of a new language, known as 'Desperanto'. The results are predictable, if depressing. Cynicism has grown, while loyalty has declined, as our discussion of employee engagement earlier in this chapter has demonstrated.

In the present competitive economic climate it is vital that these issues are managed more effectively. As Argenti (2007, p. 137) noted: 'Most of today's employees are well educated, have higher expectations of what they will get out of their careers than their parents did, and want to understand more about the companies they work for.' The evidence reviewed here suggests that organizations employing positive communication policies would be better positioned to reap significant competitive benefits. The corollary is also true: poor communications programmes will contribute to lost competitive edge.

Thus hierarchical and autocratic models of management run counter to what the available evidence suggests is most effective. Nor do the data suggest that practices such as 'downsizing' yield returns on bottom line financial indicators. A major study of 3628 US companies over a 15-year period concluded that companies that downsized saw their return on assets (ROA) *decline* in the year of downsizing and in the year after. It recovered slightly in the following year, but not to the levels that existed before the lay-offs occurred (Morris *et al.*, 1999). Nevertheless, support for such practices remains strong on the part of top managers. One survey of 562 chairmen, CEOs and managing directors in the UK found that three-quarters of the respondents would be willing to conduct an annual cull of staff with the aim of raising productivity (Hudson, 2007). One in six, in defiance of all the evidence to the contrary, imagined that they could get rid of 20% of employees without damaging performance or morale. Half even reckoned that firing up to 5% a year would be a good idea. The fact that such fads are widely practised, or that such destructive ideas are endorsed by senior managers, is no recommendation.

Popular support for an opinion (e.g. 'women are inferior to men', and, more recently, 'men are inferior to women') does not constitute evidence that it is correct. Alternative courses of action are both possible and necessary. In the final analysis, competitive advantage is gained from doing something different to everyone else, rather than from enthusiastically emulating their mistakes. Communicating with employees is now a core requirement to build successful businesses. Failures on this score damage the bottom line. But better informed and involved employees can help to build better organizations. As Sudhakar and Patil (2006, p. 33) argued: 'Employees need to understand that the organization cares for them, that their opinion matters, that their involvement is respected, and that the company takes action on the input they give.'

Having identified internal and external communication as vital ingredients of organizational success the issue arises: what should be done about it? This book argues that by auditing what currently happens, the ground is prepared for substantial improvements. It therefore explores the tools and techniques that will assist organizations to achieve this objective.

Chapter 2

Auditing communication to maximize performance

Dennis Tourish and Owen Hargie

INTRODUCTION

Organizations that communicate badly can be likened to a theatrical production in which no one knows which part they are playing and constantly speaks the wrong lines, often interrupting other performers to do so. Meanwhile, the audience is either ignored or insulted. A focused communication strategy helps to avert such chaos. It provides the opportunity for organizations to enjoy a long running performance in the marketplace. Such a strategy must be based on accurate information about current practices. Few managers would dispute the notion that businesses must have an accurate impression of how they are viewed externally, and what staff think of how they receive and transmit information. To achieve this, key questions must be answered:

- Is the right message getting through?
- Do people feel informed, or merely patronized?
- Has the communications programme really addressed the issues that most concern people, or has it missed the moving target of public opinion?

To answer these questions, accurate information about how both internal and external customers perceive the communication climate is vital. Illusions, hopes and pretence have to give way to an appraisal of reality. This constitutes the fundamental rationale for auditing communication. The need to do so is widely recognized. For example, Argenti (2007, p. 139) pointed out that the most appropriate way to ascertain how effective a company's internal communication efforts is 'by determining what employees' attitudes are about the firm. This can be done through a communication audit. Based on audit results, communications professionals can design the right program for the organization.' However, in common with most textbooks on corporate communication that make similar statements, Argenti does not explain in any depth what a communication audit consists of or how to implement one. It is this gap that this book seeks to remedy.

In this chapter, we define the term communication audit, outline its origins in the academic and management literature, and propose an implementation framework that can be applied to the auditing of both internal and external communication. A word of caution is in order at the outset. As many other scholars have recognized, there is no one 'right' method for auditing communication. This book does not seek to become a 'cookbook' of audits, in which recipes for every contingency can be found. Each method has its strengths and limitations, and each organization has its own unique needs, culture and problems in the marketplace. There is no perfect recipe, guaranteeing a meal to satisfy all tastes. However, we believe that it is possible to specify some ingredients which, in our experience, consistently characterize good practice. Within this framework, subsequent chapters explore a variety of auditing tools in more depth, from which readers are encouraged to select those most appropriate to their needs.

THE NATURE OF AUDIT

The term 'audit' has by now been applied to an enormous range of activities. Its very ubiquity often generates confusion (Baker, 1999). Indeed, the *Concise Oxford Dictionary* notes the existence of an audit ale, a special beer once brewed in English colleges for consumption on the day an audit was undertaken. (It is questionable whether the critical acumen of auditors was sharpened by the imbibing of such liquids.) Historically, the practice of auditing is most commonly associated with scrutiny of an organization's financial health, and the principle is clearly derived from this area.

At its most basic, an audit is simply an evaluation of a designated process (Hogard and Ellis, 2006). As Henderson (2005, p. 312) expressed it:

> The communications audit process is designed to examine and evaluate an organization's communication program; to reveal hurdles to effective communication, to reveal gaps in the communication process, and to provide suggestions for improvement.

It assists managers by

> providing an objective picture of what is happening compared with what senior executives think (or have been told) is happening.
>
> (Hurst, 1991, p. 24)

The term first emerged in the general academic literature in the early 1950s (Odiorne, 1954), and its use has since been frequently urged on business, human resources and public relations practitioners (e.g. Campbell, 1982; Kopec, 1982; Stanton, 1981; Strenski, 1984). Researchers have drawn attention to its role in not-for-profit organizations (Lauer, 1996), in evaluating how well marketing communication messages resonate with various targeted audiences (Schimmel *et al.*, 2007), as an important ingredient of strategic marketing in the healthcare sector (Stone, 1995) and of communication involving health professionals more generally (Hogard *et al.*, 2005). Its utility as a pedagogic instrument in the teaching of management communication has been asserted (Conaway, 1994; Shelby and Reinsch, 1996; Zorn, 2002), while communication audits have been recognized as a valuable ingredient of employee relations audits in general (Jennings *et al.*, 1990). Audits can also be readily employed to assess communication with customers, suppliers and other businesses outside the organization.

Communication audits share a number of characteristics with more established audit practices in such spheres as finance, medicine and accounting (Hargie and Tourish, 1993). These include:

1 *The accumulation of information.* In the case of finance, the goal is to check the efficacy of financial accounting procedures by sampling a representative cross-section of transactions within the organization. In communication terms, a similar goal is to assess a sample of communication episodes, in order to determine key trends. This might be termed the *diagnostic* phase of the auditing process.
2 *The creation of management systems.* Systems are developed to control the flow of information and resources over a given period. This is the *prescriptive* phase of the audit process.
3 *The comparison of communication practices with publicly declared standards.* Leaving aside Enron and similar business scandals, a finance audit normally ensures that funds are appropriately managed and that efficient methods of financial management are being applied (Singleton and Singleton, 2007). Clinical audits monitor the effectiveness and efficiency of medical activity, and contrast both with national and international benchmarks (Shapiro, 1999). Communication audits provide similar performance benchmarks, generating a much enhanced ability to measure both performance and the impact of specific measures designed to improve it. This is the *accountability* phase of the audit process.

Organizations require all three of these strands to be applied to their internal and external communication systems. Given the propensity of communications to break down, at untold cost, a strong case can be made for ascertaining their general level of effectiveness. Managers need to know who they are communicating with, through what channels and with what effect. Proper procedures must be developed to achieve these goals. There should also be some accountability for the flow of information within the organization. At a practical level, this means that if vital information is not getting through to its key target audiences the blockages in the channels of communication must be identified and dealt with.

Considerable attention was devoted to the issue of communication audits by the International Communication Association (ICA) during the 1970s (Goldhaber and Krivonos, 1977), while the issue also attracted the attention of a number of prominent communication scholars (e.g. Greenbaum and White, 1976). A seminal text was published from the work of the ICA towards the end of the decade (Goldhaber and Rogers, 1979). This identified a number of key issues to be evaluated by a communication audit, including:

- The amount of information underload or overload for major topics, sources and channels of communication.
- The quality of information communicated between various sources.
- Communication relationships, including interpersonal trust, supportiveness, sociability and job satisfaction.
- Operational communication networks (including for rumours, social and job related messages), and how they compare with formal networks.
- Bottlenecks and gatekeepers of information.
- Positive and negative communication experiences.
- Individual, group and organizational patterns of actual communication behaviours related to sources, channels, topics, length and quality of interactions.

Other suggestions have been made as to what should constitute reasonable audit objectives in most organizations. Cheney *et al.* (2004) identified various ingredients of organizational communication, which many communication audits therefore seek to explore. These include:

- *Symbols* (including logos, architecture, uniforms, etc.).
- *Structures* (e.g. rules, reporting mechanisms, operating procedures).
- *Patterns* of practices (such as the informal means by which news is habitually spread).
- *Discrete messages* (particular announcements, CEO statements, or press releases).
- *Interactions* (such as those that might occur during performance appraisal interviews or disciplinary hearings).
- *Relationships* (such as those between different departments).
- *Narratives* (such as stories about how the organization was born, evolved or survived a crisis).
- *Meetings.*
- *Networks* (both formal and informal).
- *Rituals* (such as coffee mornings or celebrations).
- *Myths* or stories (such as 'Jane got early promotion, and you can too').
- *Broad discourses*, (such as a company's firm belief in its ethical values).

It would be difficult, if not impossible, for one audit or audit process to look comprehensively at all of these. Much depends on immediate priorities and needs. Different tools, discussed in the chapters that follow, will be more or less appropriate for the study of the above issues, and the resources of the audit team concerned.

However, Hargie and Tourish (1996b) argued that audits generally aim to tell managers and organizations:

- Who they are talking to.
- Who they should be talking to.
- What issues people are talking about.
- From which sources most people get their information.
- Whether information reaches people through the media, face-to-face discussions with managers, internal publications or other communication channels.
- The impact of all this on working relationships.

In short, a communication audit strips away myths, fears and illusions about the communication climate within organizations, and about the wider culture within which the organization works. In their place, it provides an accurate diagnosis of the organization's communicative health.

Gildea and Rosenberg (1979, p. 7) compared communication audits to 'an annual physical', viewing it as 'a sound diagnostic procedure that can pinpoint functions and dysfunctions in organizational communication'. As Bedien (1980) noted, this approach means that audits allow organizations to determine whether communication problems are interrelated, and facilitates the implementation of solutions on a company wide basis. Thus, audit measures typically focus on issues such as:

- Who is communicating with whom.
- Which issues receive the most attention and arouse the most anxiety.
- How much information people are receiving and sending on crucial issues.
- How much interpersonal trust exists.
- How the overall quality of working relationships can be characterized.

Such issues are among the core concerns of efforts to establish what has been termed 'organizational climate'. This 'reflects beliefs about the organization's environment that are shared among members and to which members attach psychological meaning to help them make sense of their environment' (Dickson *et al.*, 2006, p. 351). It is the result of interaction between an organization's structure, systems, leader behaviours and employees' psychological needs (Srivastav, 2006), and is strongly determined by people's emotional responses to a wide range of issues, including communication (Patterson *et al.*, 2004). Communication climate is therefore a crucial component of overall organizational climate.

Various attempts have been made to establish the ingredients of an ideal communication climate. In an early study, Redding (1972) identified the following five dimensions of communication climate as being of particular importance:

- supportiveness
- participative decision making
- trust, confidence and credibility
- openness and candour
- high performance goals.

Creating such a climate involves five key information sharing practices, including communication about job, personal, operational and strategic issues, alongside robust systems for upward communication (Robertson, 2005). It has a direct impact on building a workforce that is satisfied with both the organization and the work that it does (Robertson, 2003). In one sense audits amount to an investigation of organizational climate, which helps managers recognize whether storms, earthquakes or sunshine lie ahead. In this way, major improvements in communication can be effected.

When such evaluations are turned into quantitative and qualitative data, managers acquire a clear, comprehensive picture of how things actually are. This subverts both their own natural tendency towards self-aggrandizement, and the traditional reluctance of staff and customers to provide honest feedback to those perceived as having a higher status than they do (Milliken *et al.*, 2003; Kassing, 2007) – in this case, top executives. In turn, this provides managers with the opportunity to develop a compelling sense of direction, indispensable for success in a crowded marketplace. Communication audits therefore perform a useful diagnostic and prescriptive role in strategic management.

Having said this, Jones (2002, p. 469), in advocating a more 'interpretivist' perspective, challenges what she sees as an overemphasis on the notion of auditors as expert diagnosticians, bringing a special wisdom to management deliberations. Instead, she urges auditors to 'listen with a trained interpretive ear to a range of organisational choices, provide powerful feedback offered in an open and tentative spirit, and collaborate with members of an organisation to frame inquiries, carry out investigations, and generate knowledge about communication'. Others have expressed similar views (e.g. Meyer, 2002; Salem, 2002).

Such an orientation is consistent with the growing emphasis on language analysis in organizational studies (Gabriel, 2004; Cornelissen, 2006; Amernic *et al.*, 2007). This conceives of organizations as narrative spaces in which stories and accounts are employed by all participants to facilitate the process of sensemaking (this is discussed in depth in Chapter 19). In this context, leaders engage 'in a process of rhetorical negotiation with their audience, trying out words, phrases, and literary constructions to better and more convincingly communicate their vision of their organization' (Cuno, 2005, p. 205). It follows that communication auditors should pay considerable attention to language in use – for example, in reports, memos, conversation and formal letters. The interpretive challenge that this poses is to tease out the implicit, probable or possible meanings likely to be attached to the language concerned by different audiences. Thus, interest in interpretive approaches to communication auditing is growing, and we provide a case study of one in action in Chapter 14.

Our own position is that communication audits should always be conducted in a spirit of open-ended inquiry, thus avoiding predetermined outcomes and allowing all organizational voices to be heard. They should proceed in partnership with key organizational stakeholders, and they should engage the energies of varied constituencies in the search for solutions to communication problems. It would be fatal for any prospect of implementation and progress to conduct an audit in conditions of semi-secrecy, doing it *to* staff rather than *with* them, and springing surprises on top managers at the end, when they should be apprised of progress and emergent findings throughout. Nevertheless, communication auditors will normally have special expertise in the area, and frequently also have considerable experience of conducting audits in a variety of organizational contexts. In our experience, they are expected to bring additional insight to the table, and be better positioned to help organizations move forward. A completely open-ended approach, and a reluctance to adopt a definite position, would be likely to alienate those most crucial to building communication improvements. As with many things, balance is the key to success. The various tools that can be used to achieve this are discussed in separate chapters in this book.

IMPLEMENTING COMMUNICATION AUDITS: A STRATEGIC FRAMEWORK

Overall, this chapter is intended to provide a rationale for the use of communication audits as a management tool. It is also necessary to suggest a sequence of practical steps that auditors should follow to operationalize the process. It has been argued that audits of various kinds go through at least five stages (Baker, 1999). These are:

- The selection of a topic.
- The specification of desired performance in terms of criteria and standards.

- The collection of objective data to determine whether the standards are met.
- The implementation of appropriate changes to improve performance.
- The collection of data for a second time, to check whether any changes introduced have affected performance.

In reality, the audit process does not proceed in the straightforward linear sequence that might easily be assumed. For example, the specification of desired performance *should* occur at the beginning of the whole exercise. However, it will also occur *afterwards*, when the audit team uses its data to help establish what standards of performance are most appropriate to the organization concerned. It may be that the audit itself reveals previously exalted standards as impractical, or discloses that people's sights have been set too low.

The topic under investigation in this book is obviously communication. Our experience as practising auditors suggests that management teams frequently give the whole issue little thought, and have only the haziest idea of what questions should be explored during an audit. For example, many assume that communication is concerned exclusively with the transmission of messages from managers to staff. In reality, it also encompasses the *exchange* of information vertically, horizontally and diagonally. To be effective, communication therefore needs to be two-way, and hence dialogic, in nature (Deetz, 1995; Fairhurst, 2007). Our own discussion in Chapter 1 of this text of how organizational communication can be defined and theorized reinforces this point. It provides a key theoretical rationale for how communication auditors can conceptualize the communication process, and which therefore needs to inform all decisions about how audits are planned, implemented, reported and evaluated.

The case study chapters in this book discuss different approaches to implementing an audit. Given that the each organization has unique needs, there is no absolutely cut and dried process that will apply everywhere, irrespective of local circumstances. As we warned at the outset, it is not our intention to prescribe one allegedly best method for auditing communication. Nevertheless, we can extract the most pertinent themes from the research, in order to identify a number of stages that are normally followed, irrespective of the underlying method of data collection. We would suggest that the following sequence is a summary of the best general practice available. It takes account of the need to integrate auditing into the process of strategy development – a theme to which we return in the final chapter, Chapter 20. Auditors who depart from it should have compelling reasons for doing so. Thus, the process of audit implementation should generally encompass the following stages.

Engage senior management commitment

A variety of studies have suggested that unless senior managers are actively involved in any change process, and passionately committed to its success, it will fail (Karp, 2006). New tools designed to assist organizational development inevitably appear threatening to some. Most people greet change from a firmly established 'No Zone', and only reluctantly enter a 'Go Zone', in which it is embraced and implemented (Craine, 2007). To secure such an outcome, an intense level of senior management involvement is needed throughout. At the outset of the audit process a problem focused workshop between senior management and the auditors should be held. Such an event serves to:

(1) *Clarify in depth the value of audits, their role in this particular organization and the commitment required from management if maximum advantage is to be obtained.* For example, the following issues should be addressed:

- What timescale best ties in with the business planning cycle?
- Will other organizational development issues need to be rescheduled?
- How can evaluating communication channels with customers support the marketing strategy?
- How can we involve staff in framing audit questions, interpreting the results and making suggestions for improvements?
- What plans can be made to circulate the audit results as widely as possible?

(2) *Identify the top half dozen issues on which people should be receiving and sending information.* An audit cannot examine every conceivable issue, in depth. Our own research has generally found that information flow on a few key issues tends to be typical of the overall communication climate (Tourish and Hargie, 1998). Restricting the number of issues to be explored in this way is sufficient to provide valid data, while ensuring that the audit remains practicable. For example, if the audit is concerned with external communication, what are the most important issues that the company wants its customers to be aware of? Conversely, what does it want to hear from its customers about? These data can then be incorporated into the materials being used during the audit exercise. If questionnaires are being employed, a section should explore information flow on the key issues identified.

This also offers a good opportunity to delineate the extent of the audit exercise, and therefore clarify managers' conception of the communication process. It is essential, at this stage, to establish both what audits can and cannot do. Managers must have realistic expectations about what can be achieved. When too much (or too little) is envisioned the audit will be less likely to achieve its full potential as a tool for facilitating organizational development. For example, it is difficult to use data obtained from focus groups to set statistical benchmarks (see Chapter 5). If the focus group is the only tool that the organization can use, and there are many circumstances in which this is the case, it is unrealistic to think that future audits will be able to measure precisely the extent of any progress that has been made. Novice auditors may be inclined to promise more than they can deliver, thereby generating retribution and recrimination from disappointed managers further along in the process.

Nevertheless, we would generally urge that auditors utilize more than one method of data collection. In particular, survey results can be difficult to interpret on a stand-alone basis, as Zwijze-Koning and de Jong (2007) demonstrated in a study conducted in The Netherlands. They utilized survey methods in conjunction with the Critical Incident Technique (see Chapter 8 for a fuller discussion of what this technique involves). Their findings demonstrated how survey items exploring issues such as employee dissatisfaction and the openness and honesty of top management communication could be conflated, misinterpreted or simply produce data too indeterminate for practical purposes. They therefore recommended that such approaches be complemented by more qualitative investigations, such as focus groups and interviews, to tease out the full complexity of the communication dynamics under examination.

(3) *Discuss the communication standards the management team believes they should adopt and live up to.* For example, in the UK, the National Health Service Management Executive published standards for communication in 1995, and circulated them throughout the main management tiers of the organization. Similar approaches have been used in many organizations, where senior managers commit to particular behaviours designed to foreground the importance of communication, and to demonstrate their commitment to improvement (Robertson, 2005). In the case of the NHS, a summary of best general practice was produced, recommending that commitments be made to:

- board level discussions
- regular audits
- upward appraisal
- training for effective communications
- the consideration of communication during the business planning cycle, and
- the identification and reward of good practice.

Having established standards, answers must then be formulated to a number of key questions:

- What do they mean in practice?
- How will every organizational unit be transformed if they are implemented?
- What has stopped such implementation in the past?
- How much can be agreed and how much will remain in dispute for the foreseeable future?
- How quickly can change begin?
- What training needs have to be met?

The audit can then reveal the extent to which the standards are being implemented, stimulate further discussion on the gap between current practice and the characteristics of a world class communication system, and encourage overt commitments to the key publics concerned, internally and/or externally.

(4) *The identification of a senior person or persons prepared to act as link between the organization and the external audit team.* If the audit is being conducted in-house, a link between those handling the project and top management is still vital. This is not to suggest that auditors should surrender their independence. However, ongoing contact with key people is vital to keep doors open; prevent sabotage or obstruction; ensure that the audit timescale remains on track; and provide essential information on the organization's structure, history, internal politics, business challenges, main priorities and climate.

Prepare the organization for the audit

Usually, a simple letter is sufficient to inform staff of the nature of the audit process, and the timescale that is envisaged. We would generally recommend that it be issued by the Chief Executive Officer, thus putting the authority of this office behind the audit. This helps to ensure that managers facilitate access to audit participants, and generally engage with what is going on. It also binds the top management team into the audit exercise, by publicly identifying them with it. This makes it more likely that the results of the audit will be taken seriously and used to effect improvements in performance. In the case of external audits, a sample of customers or supply businesses can be addressed in a similar manner. Alternatively, internal or external newsletters, videos or team briefing mechanisms can be employed.

Those involved in conducting audits should also follow rigorous ethical standards. There is now a considerable body of research to show that an unethical style of operating will almost certainly cause long-term damage to the organization (Clampitt, 2005; Hargie *et al.*, 2004). A code for communication professionals was put forward by Montgomery *et al.* (2001), and the following elements of this should be borne in mind by auditors.

- *Do not harm others*. The principle of *non-maleficence* should be followed. For example, no individual should suffer in any way during the collection of data or in the presentation of the report. Where guarantees are given to respondents of anonymity or confidentiality these must be adhered to.
- *Act professionally at all times*. Auditors themselves have to be appropriate ethical role models, practising what they preach. This means that all commitments given should be honoured. The auditor must be knowledgeable about all aspects of the audit process, and behave in such a way as to inspire confidence.
- *Treat others justly*. The integrity of individuals needs to be recognized. All respondents should be treated equally, regardless of their position or power in the corporate hierarchy. Individually must know what is expected of them and how their responses will be processed. Their contribution to the audit must be recognized, and the audit findings should be made available to all respondents.
- *Be open and honest*. The purpose and objectives of the audit should be made clear to all those involved. It is also important that the audit results are told as they are, that figures are not massaged, and that no attempt is made to camouflage negative findings.

Recurring staff worries that tend to arise here include confidentiality, how widely available the results will be, and the time commitment required of audit respondents (Tourish and Tourish, 1996). The most difficult of these issues is confidentiality. Respondents are often wary of honestly expressing their views, in case what they say will be used against them at a later stage. It may be necessary to address these issues during initial communications with audit participants. The following general rules help:

- *Participants should be assured, orally and in writing, that their responses will be treated confidentially*. Research shows that the more often a message is repeated the more likely people are to accept that it is true (Cialdini, 2001). Accordingly, these assurances should be reiterated on a number of occasions – the more publicly, the better. The steps proposed to ensure confidentiality should be explained in detail. Most importantly, these promises should be kept.
- *Wherever possible, participants should be selected randomly*. This reinforces the message that the aim of the exercise is not to single people out with a view to imposing sanctions. There are hazards to this. When administering questionnaires to a group during one of our audits, one of the people present approached us to remark that it was the third time in 6 months he had been 'randomly selected' to complete questionnaires, dealing with a variety of organizational development issues. Intense persuasion was required to convince him that we were not part of a management plot against him!

- *Only the audit team should have access to questionnaires, tape recordings or anything else that might identify individual respondents.* All such materials should be destroyed at the conclusion of the audit. This policy should be communicated clearly to all audit participants.
- *Care should be taken, in writing the report, to ensure that it does not inadvertently enable readers to identify particular respondents.* For example, if only one person works in the payroll department the report should not cite comments, good or bad, from 'a payroll respondent'.
- *Audit instruments should be administered well away from the gaze of managers.* Again, during one of our audits, we had just spent some time explaining the confidential nature of the exercise to a group of questionnaire respondents, when a member of the senior management team dropped by simply to see how many people had turned up. Unfortunately, the effect was to discredit our assurances of confidentiality with the people concerned.

Normally, these procedures are sufficient to ensure that this problem is eased. However, it remains one of the strongest arguments in favour of using external rather than internal auditors. If a top manager turns up to administer questionnaires or conduct interviews, or if the person concerned is viewed as being close to managers, confidentiality assurances have low credibility.

Data gathering

This normally proceeds in two phases. A small number of preliminary first round interviews familiarizes the audit team with staff or customer views, as well as management concerns. Typically, respondents will be randomly selected. Feedback obtained by this approach helps in the design of final questionnaires, if this is the main method to be used. A number of typical issues have been suggested that should be explored in preliminary interviews (Tourish and Tourish, 1996). The bulk of these are applicable to both internal and external audits:

- how decisions are made
- communication channels
- communication relationships
- communication obstacles
- organizational structure
- responsiveness (e.g. the quality of information flow during a crisis).

Finally, the main audit exercise is embarked on. A pilot test is vital. This makes it possible to detect shortcomings in the design and implementation of questionnaires, or other approaches being employed (Brown, 2006). However, as Remenyi *et al.* (1998, p. 174) pointed out, 'in business and management research there is usually time and considerable financial pressure to get the project started'. Pilots are therefore often selected opportunistically, on grounds of convenience, availability, proximity or cost. We do not view this as a major problem. A pilot is a test case, undertaken to double check the viability of the approach chosen. It should not, even in ideal circumstances, become so elaborate that it develops into a main study in its own right. For example, Tourish's (2007b) study of upward communication in organizations, which eventually led to 105 interviews in four organizations, had a pilot study consisting of three interviews. This was sufficient to fine tune the proposed interview schedule, and determine how long interviews were likely to last. Once the pilot is complete, the main study can proceed.

It has been argued that information technology (particularly email, the intranet and the internet) has drastically simplified the process of data gathering. Goldhaber (2002) counsels auditors to adopt a five-pronged approach designed to take advantage of technology, as follows:

- The developing and testing of a survey instrument.
- Developing a list of email addresses of all selected for participation.
- Sending an invitation to participate, including a hyperlink to the survey in question.
- Survey completion, with automatic data capturing and tabulation.
- Analysis, interpretation and report writing.

He further suggests that the entire process could be completed within 4 weeks. While this may be over-optimistic, it is undoubtedly true that the audit process is now much simpler, and therefore cheaper, than even a short time ago.

Analysis and action phase

A report is now prepared, which comprehensively describes and evaluates communication practices. It should be noted that this period presents both opportunities and dangers. Audits arouse increased interest and expectations. As a general rule, people recognize that everyone likes to sing loudly about their successes, while remaining mute about their mistakes. Thus, if an audit is followed by silence it will be widely assumed that managers are busy burying dreadful secrets in the basement. A key principle when confronted with bad news, if this is what emerges, is that it should be shared openly and quickly, thereby enabling those involved to at least gain credit for their honesty (Payne, 1996).

The results of the audit are, in the first instance, presented to the top management team, orally and in writing. Later chapters in this book explore the various challenges and difficulties that also abound during this phase of the audit process. For example, Chapter 10 considers how 'bad news' should be presented, to both senior managers and the wider organization. The results then need to be circulated widely, by whatever means are most appropriate. Action plans should also be publicized. In this way, the process of audit, as well as whatever changes to which it gives rise, helps achieve significant strides forward in open and clear communication.

THE UTILITY OF COMMUNICATION AUDITS

Based on this review, it can be concluded that communication audits have the following methodological strengths:

- They permit auditors to identify the subjective interpretations of reality held by all important actors in organizational life. This extends to customers and clients, increasingly recognized as having a vital contribution to make to the business planning process.
- Depending on the method utilized, people are permitted to voice their views and feelings in their own words, while also recording on objective measurement scales their responses to communication issues, which can be analysed extensively. By one means or another, audits explore individual perceptions of communication. Such perceptions sometimes disclose a harsher communication reality than senior managers had hoped or planned for (Tourish and Robson, 2003). However, in the long run, organizational effectiveness is impossible without positive feelings towards the communication processes within the organization concerned, and with the external publics it serves. Audits bring the reality of how people feel to the fore. In many cases, this will be overwhelmingly concerned with acknowledging the existence of excellent communication. Where problems are revealed, managers will have the advantage of knowing what obstacles they must overcome to move the situation forward.
- Common understandings of organizational life are identified. Despite the fact that audit participants will inevitably have many different perceptions, they will also agree on enough issues to facilitate the development of a strategy that will lead to improvements in communication climate.
- The understanding that participants have of communication episodes can be compared to formal organizational channels and systems, to explore the gaps that exist between imagined and real practice.

The communication audit approach to measuring and evaluating organizational performance was very popular, and generated a large volume of academic publications, in the 1970s. However, as noted by Hargie and Tourish (2004, p. 238), 'The number of publications declined in the 1980s and was reduced to a trickle in the 1990s.' In essence, the lack of academic interest in audits occurred for two main reasons. First, the primary focus for organizational analysts in this period was on theoretical frameworks rather than applied concerns (Mumby and Stohl, 1996). Second, interpretive approaches were the driving force behind organizational investigation (Scott *et al.*, 1999), influenced by a reflexive philosophical perspective on communicative enquiry (Anderson and Baym, 2004). As a result, the audit approach tended to be perceived as positivist, scientific and prescriptive. It was viewed as being counter to the emergent intuitive approaches, and seen as a pragmatic management tool that would produce few new conceptual or epistemological insights into organizational functioning.

However, although there was a dearth of academic study in the latter part of the 20th century, practitioners were not deterred, and indeed the audit approach became widespread in organizations. To meet this demand, innumerable consultancy companies now offer auditing as a core part of their business (as a search of the internet will reveal). Similarly, the process of auditing has always been included on most organizational communication courses, with students carrying out real-world audit assignments as part of their degree programmes (Scott *et al.*, 1999; Shelby and Reinsch, 1996; Zorn, 2002). In this way, and despite the absence of academic research, the audit momentum was maintained. Perhaps not surprisingly, given this breadth of interest, the academic study of audits gathered pace at the turn of the century. The first edition of this book, published in 2000, no doubt contributed to this. This was followed by a new edition of an established audit text (Downs and Adrian, 2004). Book chapters (e.g. Kazoleas and Wright, 2001; Tourish and Hargie, 2004a), audit research papers (e.g. Fox, 2000; Bilbao *et al.*, 2002; Hargie *et al.*, 2002, 2003; Quinn and Hargie, 2004; Hogard *et al.*, 2005; Hargie and Dickson, 2007; Dickson *et al.*, 2008), and critiques of audit methodologies (Gayeski, 2000; Dickson *et al.*, 2003) followed. One reason for this resurgence of interest is that it was recognized that the audit is not just a positivist and top-down management tool, but that the equally valid interpretations of employees must be fully considered in the design and operationalization of audits. One outcome from this has been the development of collaborative audit approaches (Jones, 2002). The audit was no longer regarded as simply a mechanistic exercise that was 'done to' employees, but rather one that could be 'done with' them as a collaborative venture. We anticipate that both academic and practitioner interest in communication audits will be maintained in the decades ahead.

RESISTANCE TO THE AUDIT PROCESS

Nevertheless, there is often resistance to implementing a communication audit, for many reasons. Managers often feel that their agenda is already overcrowded. They are reluctant to burden it further with issues that are widely regarded as too intangible to be measured, let alone transformed (Tourish, 1996). A war can only be fought on so many fronts before exhaustion and despair claim victory over the main protagonists. In today's marketplace enormous demands are already made on managers' time and energies. Many simply feel that they do not have the space to examine communication issues. The key here is to make an irresistibly convincing case in favour of the benefits obtained through the audit process, while selecting an approach that will not make unrealistic demands on people's time.

Time concerns are reinforced by fear. Once communication has broken down, the fires of rumour, uncertainty and discontent are ignited. Managers have a natural reluctance to get close to such a conflagration, fearful that they may be singed by the flames. The result is that many of them attempt to ignore a crisis, hoping that when the worst of it is over they will be able to salvage something from the debris left behind. Others send in communications experts, who often have insufficient back-up at corporate headquarters to be effective. Again, it is necessary to show how audits function like smoke detectors, alerting organizations to the first whiffs of trouble, when something can still be done about it. Beyond this, a variety of attitudinal and structural obstacles to the implementation of communication audits have been identified.

Attitudinal obstacles

Tourish (1997), Hargie and Tourish (2004) and Robson and Tourish (2005), in discussing resistance to the audit process, identified the following attitudes from managers, which have been widely encountered. In each case, they represent an obstacle to the serious investigation of communication practice. Practitioners need to be aware of them, and consider their likely impact on proposals to audit communication:

1 *'Too much information is commercially sensitive, and if we let it out our competitors will benefit.'*

Accordingly, managers may be suspicious of anything that seems to promise a more open flow of information than what has prevailed in the past. Within this perspective, supply businesses are seen as competitors rather than partners. Customers are noisy, demanding and never satisfied. Employees don't know what they want, but know that they want more of it.

Our argument is that an organization's most important asset is its staff, its suppliers and its customers. Research suggests that loyalty (on the part of employees, investors and customers) is more important in securing profitable growth than market share, scale, cost position or other key business variables (Reichheld, 1996). However, enduring and productive relationships are only possible if people feel valued. They only feel valued if they feel informed. Secretiveness destroys trust, self-confidence and involvement, creates resistance to change and increases uncertainty (Allen *et al.*, 2007). Customers and employees, when kept in the dark, may begin to panic, and then flee.

Within organizations, it has been found that most staff have a deep curiosity about the general management issues that animate those further up the hierarchy (Tourish and Hargie, 1996a, Tourish and Mulholland, 1997). People are not just interested in how they do their job. They are passionately concerned with the broader environmental context in which that job occurs. The more uncertain the external environment, the more important this becomes. Managers can and should turn this to their advantage.

A failure to be open results in a loss of confidence in senior managers. They are assumed to be concealing destructive hidden agendas. Such views are almost invariably exaggerated. However, their impact on relationships, cohesion, and commitment is explosive. In any event, the notion that the decision-making process can be quarantined is a fantasy. As Payne (1996, p. 81) noted: 'There are few secrets in large organisations, and it is rarely possible to contain bad news.' Fax machines spring leaks. Support staff gossip with each other. People click on the 'reply all' option by mistake, when responding to emails. Offices adjoin corridors, and people passing office doors hear what is being said within. In consequence, much of what managers imagine to be top secret is actually routine gossip in the staff canteen. It is also probably being talked of much more negatively than is justified by the facts. Research suggests that negative information about something influences us much more than positive information, thereby enhancing the destructive impact of tittle-tattle and innuendo (Hargie *et al.*, 2004). Further, if people hear about important issues through the grapevine it means that managers have simply exchanged the opportunity to be seen as open for an image of being out of touch. This must rank as one of the worst trades in business!

2 *'Communication might be bad in most organizations, but I communicate very well and things are fine in my organization.'*

Despite this happy conviction, most managers are poor at evaluating their effectiveness as communicators. There is widespread evidence (Dawes, 2001; Fine, 2006) that most of us believe:

- we are more effective in our jobs than the average score of all people doing it (a statistical impossibility),
- our opinions are more correct than they are,
- more people agree with us than actually do,
- we contribute more to group decision making than most other people involved, and
- we are better listeners than is really the case.

People possess Olympian 'reflexes of self-justification', which cause us to recognize weaknesses in the performance of others, but to imagine that we ourselves are doing better than we are. Even poor performers, including some managers, can suffer from delusions of adequacy, or superior performance. Thus it has been repeatedly found that 'managements tend to credit themselves for positive outcomes and blame negative results on the environment' (Tsang, 2002, p. 51). Indeed, there is a view that to 'submit' to an audit is to admit shortcomings in the way one runs one's department. In essence, then, an audit would only tell managers what they already know anyway – that everything is terrific. It is therefore hardly surprising that one national survey in the US found 60% of top management respondents saying they communicated 'frequently' with their employees, while only 30% of non-management staff agreed (Crampton *et al.*, 1998).

In addition, it is well known that people try to influence us through ingratiation – in particular, through flattery (Stengel, 2000). When we attempt to ingratiate ourselves with people who have higher status than us we often tell them what we think they want to hear, rather than what we really feel (Rosenfeld *et al.*, 1995). Unfortunately, the research also suggests that most managers take this distorted feedback at face value. They believe it is genuinely meant, and accurate. They are not alone in harbouring such notions. Most dictators, as they are hustled off the stage of history, can be heard protesting 'but my people love me'. Psychologists have termed this perceptual myopia 'the boss's illusion' (Odom, 1993). Thus, if we seriously want to find out how well our organizations are communicating internally and externally we must employ an objective system of measurement, rather than rely on our own intuitions, contaminated as they are by self-interest. Knowledge is virtue. A communication audit provides managers with an objective account of how well they are doing, and so bypasses those self-serving biases that may have distorted their understanding in the past. It can also inform detailed plans for change within the organization.

3 *'Why do I need to examine my performance in detail? Can't I simply implement examples of good practice from elsewhere?'*

Finding out how well you are doing remains an essential first step towards improvement. Communication programmes need to focus on real problems, rather than on imaginary aches and pains. No one suggests that we should routinely swallow pills for every medical contingency, whether we are ill or not. Indeed, it is not advisable to take someone else's tablets – a practice that may prove fatal. Likewise, it is foolhardy to launch into an all-embracing communication programme without a thorough examination of how well existing systems are functioning. Careful diagnosis is essential, leading to a carefully targeted treatment regime.

4 *'Why should I do something (e.g. ask people how well I am doing as a communicator) that means I will get kicked in the teeth?'*

First, examining current practice focuses the minds of senior management teams on the crucial issues:

- What sort of culture do we want to create?
- What is our management style?
- What behaviours do we pursue that are inimical to our philosophy, and that we can and must change?
- What are the key issues we should be communicating about?
- How are we communicating on these issues?

Clarity on these issues is essential for communication and business success.

Second, negative feedback is not inevitable. Many examinations of communication performance have found extremely positive evaluations towards immediate managers, positive attitudes towards the organization, a strong desire to be involved, and in many cases an appreciation for the extremely difficult job that senior managers perform (e.g. Tourish and Hargie, 1996a). These strengths should be publicized, celebrated and built on. However, every organization has weaknesses. The job of management is not to preside over complacency and inertia. It is to improve the organization's efficiency and effectiveness. This means seizing every opportunity to identify those areas where it is possible for everyone, including top managers, to do better.

Third, a communication review reveals what the dominant mood of the organization or its external publics actually is. This might be news to some managers, but it will not be news to those who have provided feedback. If communication is really poor then most people are already well aware of it, suffer its consequences, talk about it constantly, and are eager for initiatives designed to improve it. An audit merely allows the organization to measure the extent of their dissatisfaction. To think otherwise is akin to believing that drivers can improve their prospects of avoiding collisions by closing their eyes, plugging their ears and driving faster. Measures to review and transform communication also bring therapeutic benefits, by enabling people to ventilate views they are ordinarily compelled to repress. In the process, organizations gain valuable information, and can plan more effectively for the future.

5 *'Perhaps people feel alienated and uninvolved, and think that senior managers don't communicate with them sufficiently. Isn't this to be expected when large organizations have so many people to communicate with? Can I really do anything about it?'*

Such a view suggests chronically low, and disabling, expectations. We have, on occasion, also heard senior managers express the opinion that

'Communication is like the weather. We would all like it to be fine, but there's not much any of us can do to change it.' The reality is that no organization achieves high quality outcomes over an extended period of time if staff or customers feel uninvolved and alienated. People want to feed ideas into the organizations in which they work, and with whom they do business. But our audits, in a variety of organizations, have found that many of them have largely given up on this, feeling that the system is too hierarchical and disrespectful of what those at the coal face have to say and contribute. Intelligent people take steps to anticipate weather conditions and prepare to cope effectively with them. In terms of communication, an organization is like a house, which should be prepared to cope with all weather conditions. Research suggests that high expectations are more likely to lead to quality outcomes (Shapiro *et al.*, 2007). Low expectations become self-fulfilling prophecies, as the nightmare takes physical form, and are eventually punished in the marketplace.

6 *'No matter how much information you give people, they will still complain and say that they need more.'*

This view echoes that of Zimmerman *et al.* (1996), who proposed that a communication metamyth underlies much thinking about organizational communication and strategy. In essence, they argued that no matter how much information people receive they will invariably continue to report that they want more. The metamyth is that by providing more information these needs will diminish or disappear. While there is a need for more longitudinal audit studies to explore this issue, Hargie *et al.* (2002) provide substantial evidence that carefully tailored communication programmes do produce more communication satisfaction, when tracked over a significant period of time. Chapter 11 provides additional information from this case study, clearly suggesting that managers who carefully design communication strategies to address clearly identified weaknesses are likely to find improvements in communication climate.

7 *'What's the point?'*

People who hold this perspective – essentially, one of futility – perceive the entire exercise to be misguided. They believe that audits are in essence worthless, since you are seeking advice from those with no real insight or knowledge base. It is only managers who can see the wider panorama. As a result, any information collected would be misinformed and valueless. One such manager said to us: 'What we would get would be unrealistic suggestions. Employees operate in a narrow world and don't understand the constraints we face.' However, this viewpoint is basically untenable. Employees have an invaluable database of insightful, and individually unique, job-related information. Such knowledge has to be shared for the organization to perform at its optimum level. For this reason, it is increasingly common practice to solicit employee suggestions in the quest for continuous improvement, with many studies suggesting that this approach can dramatically improve performance (Blanchard, 2008). We would argue that a similar mindset should be applied to the communication function.

Structural barriers to implementation

Many barriers prevent managers from acting on the knowledge that they have, to create high performing organizations (Pfeffer and Sutton, 2000). We would suggest that these also underpin the attitudinal obstacles discussed above, and discuss them in this context.

1 *Strategy and financial barriers*

Managers have been schooled to pay more attention to strategy formulation and financial issues, rather than employee or customer relations. In many cases, strategic planning has become ludicrously complex, all-absorbing and self-defeating. One result is that many strategic plans are either never implemented, or fail to achieve their objectives (Finkelstein, 2005). A failure to share information, hierarchically imposed barriers to honesty and departmental segregation are often key culprits. Nevertheless, those trained in number crunching have a tendency to devote their attention to what can be most easily quantified, rather than to such apparently intangible issues as how employees and customers feel about communication. A central argument of this book is that it is much more possible to measure communication effectiveness than most managers realize.

2 *Social barriers (or 'the follow the herd' instinct)*

Many managers have been influenced by macho notions of business leadership, popularized in the anecdotal management literature. In this world, CEOs are invariably pictured with bulging biceps. For example, the cover of the prestigious *Harvard Business Review*'s special issue in January 2007, devoted to 'the tests of the leader', pictured a shirt-sleeved male executive performing press-ups on a boardroom table. The impression is created that everyone behaves this way, in 'the real world'. Thus, managers are influenced by what they think the majority of their rivals are doing. When dysfunctional fads acquire large numbers of enthusiastic disciples, the unconverted are more likely to conclude that there must be something in them. Celluloid fantasies become reality. We have pointed to the fallacy of regarding mass support for an opinion as evidence of its correctness in Chapter 1. Paradoxically, this means that when competitors disregard the subtleties of communication, other companies become inclined to do likewise, rather than seek competitive advantage from behaving differently to their rivals. Thus, if most companies do not audit communication it is more difficult to convince managers that they should buck the trend.

3 Power and political barriers

Once people are used to managing in a particular way, precedent, habit, inertia and a reluctance to admit to mistakes makes it more likely they will continue to behave as they have always done. In management, what has already happened (rather than feedback from the marketplace) often determines what happens next. Furthermore, a great deal of experimental research suggests that concentrating power in management hands produces an exaggerated impression of the quality of the work performed under such conditions (Pfeffer and Sutton, 2006). In other words, once we feel that we have had responsibility for a task or a process we exaggerate the success of what has been achieved. Illusions of indispensability and infallibility then take root. ('*I know I am an excellent communicator.*') This makes it more difficult to reconsider communication practices, particularly if critical feedback is involved and the sharing of power has been proposed. Why change something when you believe that your opinion is more important, and certainly more correct, than anyone else's?

4 Hierarchical barriers

Most people attempt to minimize the possibility of critical feedback, fearing that it will lead to a loss of status. For this reason, performance appraisal is fraught with difficulties (Tourish, 2006). Managers asked to evaluate their organization's communication effectiveness can feel threatened, and respond by challenging the necessity for doing so. Combined with this, human resources in general and communications in particular rarely have a status equivalent to that of other key departments.

Each, or all, of these barriers may have to be confronted before organizations can implement audits successfully. When presenting to senior managers we list the above obstacles, and highlight the fact that some of the managers present may harbour one or more of these thoughts. We then try to overcome these objections with persuasive counterarguments, and have an open debate on the issues involved. A consistent focus on the following themes is therefore helpful:

- *Show how the audit will assist the organization with its current business needs and priorities.* What concrete problems, internally and externally, will it help to solve?
- *Demonstrate the non-judgmental nature of the audit process.* It should be

made clear at the outset that feedback, in the form of final reports, will avoid the 'naming and shaming' of individuals or groups. (This may require strong diplomatic skills at the report writing stage.)

- *Emphasize the involvement of key decision makers in the audit process.* (We have discussed some steps to accomplish this earlier in the chapter.) This will overcome many of the obstacles discussed here, and ensure a more receptive context for the final audit report.
- *Highlight the attitudinal and structural barriers discussed above.* An awareness that bear traps lie ahead helps managers to avoid stumbling around in the dark, and then falling into them.
- *Use the audit to celebrate what the organization does well, as well as discuss where it has problems.* This is more likely to embed the principle of audit in the organization's psyche, and increases the prospects that it will be employed on an ongoing basis. We discuss this issue in more detail in Chapter 10, in the context of how best to draft an audit report.

In a majority of cases this acts as a pre-emptive strike, allowing the audit process to flow smoothly. However, in other instances the auditor may have to complete the exercise knowing that certain people are opposed to it.

Audits can effect profound improvements in communication, internally and externally. This potential will only be realized if the organization is convinced of its potential, and managers show determination to overcome the obstacles that stand in the way. The good news is that the measures necessary to achieve this are quite straightforward. The key is to aim high, start with small steps, and grow bolder with experience.

CONCLUSION

Prioritizing the quality of communication between managers and staff, and between organizations and their customers, yields business dividends. However, new ideas are often turned into planning marathons that produce long, unreadable documents, and an infestation of committees rather than action plans. Many organizations are paralysed by 'working parties' that do no work, 'project teams' that can do nothing until they report to 'project boards' (who are always too busy to meet), and 'briefing sessions' in which nothing is ever brief.

This chapter locates communication audits within a radically different approach. Audits are a means of assessing current performance, in order to devise improvements. Ideally, these should be designed to take account of the communication practices of the best performing businesses in the world. These represent a gold standard, against which the performance of the organization conducting the audit may be compared. In turn, the audit process is an ongoing cycle rather than a single snapshot. The results from one audit can be contrasted with those gained from future audits. In this way, it forms an internal benchmark. These are generally regarded as easier to maintain, and usually consist of more reliable data, than those derived externally (Cox and Thompson, 1998). If meaningful recommendations have been devised and implemented, the measurement indices should show a pattern of continuous improvement. Organizations can then rejoice over real rather than fictitious triumphs. However, we acknowledge that the benefits of a communication audit are not immediately apparent to many managers, and the notion of implementing one certainly does not sell itself. It is vital that auditors focus on what the audit can deliver, in terms of improving both communication itself and the underlying functioning of the organization in which it will be conducted (Hart, 2006).

In addition, communication is an inherently difficult, contested and ambiguous phenomenon, fraught with difficulty at every stage. As Robertson (2005, p. 4) expressed it: 'Modern corporations have become information gluttons, yet they are starving for the kind of communication that fills people's need to share understanding and meaning and foster trust.' Communication audits help to resolve some of this tension, by rendering the intangible tangible, moving communication issues further up the management agenda and, ultimately, improving efficiency and effectiveness in an increasingly competitive marketplace. Subsequent chapters in this book explore the different techniques available in more detail, and offer case studies where they can be seen in action. The final chapter then explores how the audit process fits into the development of a comprehensive communication strategy, which we argue is essential for organizational success.

Part II

Audit methodologies

Chapter 3

The questionnaire approach

Phillip G. Clampitt

INTRODUCTION

Most organizations are enchanted with questionnaires. The lure of a survey lies in the seeming simplicity of the methodology, the ostensive ease of administration and the apparent directness of interpretation. Yet, these are merely illusions based more on the ubiquity of surveys rather than their actual utility. For instance, researchers have shown that what survey respondents say they will purchase is often very different from what they actually buy (Morwitz *et al.*, 1997). Mothers will not readily admit to spending more on dog food than on baby food. But, in fact, many do (Macht, 1998).

Methodological issues are largely a matter of the proper use of well-established scientific procedures. Administering a questionnaire and interpreting the results will require scientific understanding tempered with an artful consideration of organizational politics. The purpose of this chapter is to discuss both the art and science of developing, administering, analyzing, and interpreting surveys.

DEVELOPING A QUESTIONNAIRE

Developing an effective questionnaire requires respect for social scientific conventions and sound judgement. The discussion that follows is presented as a linear step-by-step procedure. Generally, this is a useful way to proceed, but bear in mind that auditors may have to loop back and revisit a previous step.

Step 1: Research the organizational background

Having an understanding of the organization is essential to developing a useful survey. Why? It allows auditors to make reasonable judgements about the inevitable tradeoffs involved in the survey process. For instance, learning that the general education level of employees is low implies that adjustments are necessary in the length and complexity of the questionnaire. Indeed with millions of adults considered functionally illiterate, there are limits on the utility of written surveys. The organizational background also allows auditors to ascertain the best ways to administer the survey. For instance, e-mail might be a good administrative tool for some organizations (Goldhaber, 2002). Finally, the organizational background will aid in the proper interpretation of the data. One audacious student auditor became enamored with data indicating that none of the employees had worked for the organization for more than 4 years. He proceeded to 'illuminate' the company president with the following observation: 'If you can't retain employees for more than four years, you've got a turnover problem of major proportions. This fact alone tells me that employees can't be satisfied with your communication practices.' The president calmly replied that the 'company is only four years old'. Then he thanked the audit team for their efforts and quickly ushered them out the door.

The '100 facts' exercise is one way to gather this background information. The objective is simple: develop a list of 100 facts about the organization. This is merely an exploratory procedure, so the order and level of specificity of the facts are not really important. In a way, this is like a detective doing an initial scan of a crime scene, looking for any kind of information that might provide a useful lead. Box 3.1 provides some categories of facts that might be useful. This information can be gathered in all sorts of ways including interviews with key personnel, observations of organizational practices, and examination of corporate documents (employee handbooks, newsletters, annual reports, etc.). Once the facts are gathered, it is important for the audit team to discuss the implications of their findings: What tradeoffs will we need to make? What are the constraints we will be working under? What are employee expectations regarding the survey? Preliminary answers to questions of this sort provide valuable insights later in the process.

Step 2: Ascertain the purpose

This step may appear to be straightforward, but years of experience suggest that it is not. In fact, it may be the most difficult step of all. The critical

---

Box 3.1 100 'facts': some examples

- Demographic information about employees
- Layers of management
- Communication tools frequently used
- Dates of previous surveys
- Locations of employees
- Departmental structure

question is: After the survey is completed, what does the organization want to happen? Or, as I have asked CEOs, 'How will you assess the effectiveness of this process?' Sometimes organizations only have a vague notion about how they will use the results. Auditors need to help them clarify their desires. There are a variety of objectives including assessing:

- the communication competence of employees
- the conflict management style of employees
- the effectiveness of communication channels (newsletters, e-mail, etc.)
- the adequacy of information dissemination
- the quality of organizational relationships
- employee satisfaction with communication
- employee understanding of major initiatives
- the effectiveness of top management communication.

Each of these may imply a different type of survey or even methodology. Sometimes various parts of the organization have different objectives in mind. The senior management team may only want to 'get the pulse' of the organization, while some managers will use the data to drive specific changes in their departments. Reconciling these often conflicting objectives needs to be done in the planning stages. For example, if managers are not convinced they will receive some benefit from the process, they will not readily encourage their employees to participate.

Step 3: Consider a variety of existing instruments

Questionnaires are often referred to as 'instruments', and with good reason. They are the tools of the trade. Like all tools they are designed for a specific purpose; hammers are for nails and screwdrivers for screws. Unfortunately, there are times when apprentices hammer in the screws; it may work but it is not particularly elegant or effective. For instance, asking employees in a survey about how often they use internal web sites to access corporate information is probably a waste of paper. Counting the number of 'hits' on certain pages is more likely to yield useful information (Sinickas, 1998). This issue is discussed in more depth in Chapter 9.

Organizational communication scholars have used hundreds of instruments. The ones that are routinely used can be classified into two types: process and comprehensive instruments (Downs *et al.*, 1994). The process instruments examine communication at a more micro-level, investigating issues such as conflict management, team building, communication competence or uncertainty management (Clampitt and Williams, 2005). The comprehensive instruments examine communication practices on a more macro-level, such as satisfaction with the communication climate or supervisory communication. Both kinds of instrument have their place, but this section briefly reviews some of the most widely used instruments that are of a comprehensive nature. More extensive reviews of the instrument can be found in the existing literature. In most cases, complete versions of the surveys can be obtained from these sources (e.g. Rubin *et al.*, 1994; Greenbaum *et al.*, 1988; Downs and Adrian, 2004). These instruments have generally proven to be reliable, valid and useful in a vast range of organizations.

Communication Satisfaction Questionnaire (CSQ)

When Downs and Hazen (1977) developed this instrument, they were investigating the relationship between communication and job satisfaction. They were successful. Generally the more satisfied employees were with communication, the more satisfied the were with their jobs. However, certain types of communications, like those with the supervisor, tended to be more important than others. After extensive testing, Downs and Hazen (1977) isolated eight key communication factors: communication climate, relationship with supervisors, organizational integration, media quality, horizontal communication, organizational perspective, relationship with subordinates, and personal feedback. Other scholars have generally confirmed the reliability and validity of the instrument (Hecht, 1978; Crino and White, 1981; Clampitt and Girard, 1987, 1993; Pincus, 1986). For example, scholars from The Netherlands found 'evidence of criterion-related validity, indicating that CSQ results can provide insight into aspects of the organization's internal communication system that significantly influence employees' overall level of communication satisfaction' (Zwijze-Koning and de Jong, 2007, p. 279). The survey consists of 40 core questions, with five items devoted to each of the eight factors. In addition, there are six questions about job satisfaction and productivity. A databank exists that can be consulted for comparative purposes (see www.imetacomm.com/CME3 – 'Research Database' tab). It is relatively easy to administer and can be completed in less than 15 minutes. The CSQ may not provide all the details necessary for specific action plans. For example, it does not directly address top management communication and decision-making (Zwijze-Koning and de Jong, 2007). However, it does provide an effective overview of potential problem areas that can be further investigated.

ICA Audit Survey

Gerald Goldhaber led a team of scholars from the International Communication Association in the development of a package of instruments designed to assess organizational communication practices (Goldhaber and Rogers, 1979; Goldhaber and Krivonos, 1977; Goldhaber, 1976; Downs, 1988). In 1979, the ICA ended official sponsorship of the project but the methodology lives on in the public domain (Goldhaber, 2002). Many people still refer to it as the 'ICA Audit'. After over 8 years of development, one of the principal diagnostic tools that emerged from this collaboration was the 'ICA Audit' Survey or the Communication Audit Survey. The questionnaire consists of 122 questions divided into eight major sections:

1   Amount of information received about various topics versus amount desired.
2   Amount of information sent about various topics versus amount desired.
3   Amount of follow-up versus amount desired.
4   Amount of information received from various sources versus amount desired.
5   Amount of information received from various channels versus amount desired.
6   Timeliness of information.
7   Organizational relationships.
8   Satisfaction with organizational outcomes.

The first five sections use a similar scaling format. On a 1 (very little) to 5 (very great) scale, employees are asked to rate the amount of information they *'now receive'* on a given topic such as 'organizational policies'. In a parallel scale, respondents are asked about the amount of information they *'need to receive'* on 'organizational policies' or some other topic. Then a difference score can be generated that compares employees' information needs with the amount actually received. Some questions about the validity of the instrument and the utility of the difference scores have been raised (Downs *et al.*, 1981). Subsequent revisions of the instrument have tried to address these concerns (DeWine and James, 1988). In general, this instrument is one of the boldest and most comprehensive attempts to measure all aspects of an organization's communication system. A version of the instrument, adapted by the editors of this book, is included in the Appendix.

Organizational Communication Development audit questionnaire

Osmo Wiio and his Finnish colleagues developed the Organizational Communication Development (OCD) audit questionnaire as part of an assessment package built around the Delphi technique. (This technique is discussed in more detail in Chapter 8.) Their purpose was straightforward: 'determine how well the communication system helps the organization to translate its goals into desired end-results' (Greenbaum *et al.*, 1988, p. 259). The OCD is actually a refined version of an earlier survey (LTT) developed by Wiio in 1972 and administered to some 6000 employees in 23 Finnish organizations. One version contains 76 items that are grouped into 12 dimensions:

1   Overall communication satisfaction.
2   Amount of information received from different sources – now.
3   Amount of information received from different sources – ideal.
4   Amount of information received about specific job items – now.
5   Amount of information received about specific job items – ideal.
6   Areas of communication that need improvement.
7   Job satisfaction.
8   Availability of computer information systems.
9   Allocation of time in a working day.
10   Respondent's general communication behavior.
11   Organization-specific questions.
12   Information-seeking patterns.

More recently refined versions have fewer dimensions and items (Wiio, 1975, 1977). Because of confidentiality concerns, the instrument has not been subjected to some psychometric tests used to assess other surveys (Greenbaum *et al.*, 1988). Yet, the OCD addresses several issues that are not covered by the other instruments.

Organizational Communication Scale

Roberts and O'Reilly (1973) originally developed the Organizational Communication Scale (OCS) while working on research for the US Office of Naval Research. The scale was developed to compare communication practices across organizations. The OCS comprises 35 questions that can be broken down into 16 dimensions. Employees use 7-point Likert scales to respond to items about the following dimensions:

• Trust for supervisor
• Influence of supervisor
• Importance of upward mobility
• Desire for interaction
• Accuracy
• Summarization
• Gatekeeping
• Overload.

Additional questions ask employees about the percentage of time they spend in the following communication activities: upward communication (factor 9), downward communication (10), and lateral or horizontal communication (11). Another series of items ask about the percentage of time using various modes of communication (12–15). A final question (factor 16) asks about employees' general level of communication satisfaction. This instrument is by far the shortest one reviewed in this section. It has a couple of unique content areas like 'summarization' and 'influence of supervisor' that other instruments do not contain. Other scholars have found that variables like this may have an important impact on organizational communication practices. Yet, because the instrument is quite abbreviated, it may be difficult to unearth other issues that may be problematic, such as interdepartmental communication.

The obvious question is: Which instrument is best? That depends on the purpose of the audit and the constraints on the audit process. If, for example, time was limited, it would be difficult to use the ICA Audit Survey. The best advice is to carefully review all the alternatives. There are several works that can aid in that process (e.g. Downs and Adrian, 2004; Rubin *et al.*, 1994; Greenbaum *et al.*, 1988). As a starting point, Table 3.1 provides points of comparison between the surveys reviewed above.

Step 4: Determine the proper instrument – either existing or custom-designed

There are two basic options: choose a pre-existing instrument or develop one. There are benefits and costs to each approach. Pre-existing instruments generally have been scientifically tested and developed by professionals. Therefore auditors can be fairly sure that the survey is valid – it measures what they think it measures. And they can be reasonably certain that the instrument is reliable – the results are stable over time. Typically discussions of reliability and validity can be found in the research literature about the instrument. Moreover, normative data are often available that will allow some comparisons between organizations.

On the other hand there are several potential disadvantages in using a

Table 3.1 Comparison of instruments

	CSQ	ICA	OCD2	OCS
Developer	Downs and Hazen (1977)	Goldhaber and Krivonos (1977)	Wiio (1975)	Roberts and O'Reilly (1973)
Number of items	46	122	76	35
Dimensions	10	8	12	16
Scaling device	Satisfaction level	Likert-type	Satisfaction level	Likert-type others
Open-ended questions	Yes	Yes	Yes	No
Databank available	Yes	Yes	No	No
Average completion time	10–15 minutes	45–60 minutes	30–40 minutes	5–10 minutes

pre-existing instrument. The authors may need to grant permission to use the survey. Some of the questions on the survey may not be applicable to the organization. A few of the most frequently used questionnaires are too long to administer via the internet.

Developing a custom-designed questionnaire poses some unique challenges. Almost anybody can compile a list of seemingly insightful questions. But it is foolhardy to assume that this is what constitutes a useful instrument. There is an art to constructing a useful questionnaire. There are the scientific issues of validity and reliability to consider. For example, the wording of a question can have a significant impact on how it is answered. Consider the following survey item:

> Do you approve or disapprove of enhancing our employee newsletter in order to improve organizational communication?

This particular question introduces a number of problems. First, it is bipolar and offers respondents only two choices. What if employees have an attitude somewhere on the continuum between approve or disapprove? Second, the question makes the dubious assumption that a newsletter will actually improve 'organizational communication' (which may mean something different to every employee). In fact, employees' attitudes about the newsletter and 'organizational communication' may be two separate issues. Finally, what could be done with the results gleaned from this question? In the unlikely event that significant numbers of employees 'disapproved', then what actions are implied? Should the newsletter actually be discontinued? Or are respondents asking for changes in the format of the newsletter? Or are employees upset about the content of the newsletter? These cautions are not meant to discourage but only to warn that it is not as simple as it seems.

If auditors choose to develop a survey, it is important to consult the literature about how to do so (e.g. Edwards *et al.*, 1997; Fink, 2002). This can be useful for a number of reasons. Well-developed custom-designed surveys are often better suited to employees of a particular organization. They tend to use terms familiar to employees. Custom-designed surveys typically target more specific issues than their more generic cousins. For instance, none of the major instruments reviewed in the previous section asks about how effectively management communicates the need to control costs, yet in one company this was the most critical communication issue.

The choice of instruments is critical to the success of the audit process. As a rule of thumb, for those first learning about the process, it is best to use a pre-existing tool and then make adaptations to the instrument.

Step 5: Make appropriate adaptations to the survey

Two types of modifications need to be considered. First, what demographic data are needed? Sometimes the demographic data can be helpful in isolating problem areas. For instance, in one audit there were dramatic differences between the way females and males viewed the effectiveness of the communication system. Second, what departmental or unit breakdowns are needed? This is always a tricky issue. The breakdowns need to be specific enough to isolate areas of concern but not so specific that respondents feel their anonymity is compromised. A good rule of thumb: the smallest group size should be limited to seven people. Demographic and unit breakdown items should be included at the end of the survey. Thus, if employees feel uneasy about providing that information, they will at least answer the substantive questions.

PLANNING THE ADMINISTRATIVE PROCESS

Sound administrative procedures are essential for an effective audit. This section provides a number of guidelines to improve the integrity of the administrative process.

1 Determine the sample size necessary to fulfill the objectives

Auditors have two basic choices: (a) survey everyone who wants to participate, or (b) survey a sample of the population. If possible, opt for the first choice. There are two reasons for this recommendation. First, surveys are often used as a tool to set new organizational agendas, such as changing the performance appraisal system. If a sample is used, then those who did not participate can resist the change by arguing that they 'did not get a chance to provide any input'. In several cases we have encountered employees who said: 'Management picked the employees for the survey. They got just the answers they wanted.' Logical arguments about the statistical reliability of a sample hold little sway with people who feel emotionally isolated because they were not included. Second, surveying the entire population allows auditors to provide specific actionable results for all groups in the company. Results often reveal remarkable differences between various working groups. First-level supervisors may have entirely different issues to address with their groups than the organization as a whole needs to address. Few first-line supervisors would want only one person from their department to represent the views of the entire department. Yet, some uninformed managers misuse the data to draw exactly these kinds of conclusions about a work unit. Technically this problem is known as a *lack of generalizability*. Surveying the entire population can preclude this problem.

That said, there is a place for sampling. Samples are an efficient way to make useful generalizations about the entire population. Samples provide a way to avoid the often cumbersome efforts needed to survey the entire population. There are different kinds of samples that can be used to make sure that the results are reasonably unbiased (Fink, 2002). The critical issue is randomization. That is, everyone has an equal chance of being surveyed. However, some executives are tempted to be a little 'fast and loose' with this principle. So, exercise caution.

2 Develop an administrative protocol

Failure to adequately address administrative issues is one of the more subtle ways to undermine a communication audit. The quality of the data may directly turn on how employees are motivated to participate, and how the survey is distributed. These issues are related to one another and the discussion that follows focuses on how to make the appropriate tradeoffs.

How can employees be motivated to participate?

Most organizations do not make completing a survey a mandatory job requirement. Therefore, auditors are faced with the task of motivating employees. This is becoming increasingly difficult because surveys are almost as common as junk mail. And many employees treat surveys just like another piece of junk mail. There are really two aspects to this quandary. First, how can employees' fears be disabused? Second, how can employees be persuaded that participation is important?

Employees often fear that somehow the results of their survey will come back to haunt them. For instance, an employee who candidly criticizes his or her boss might be passed over for a promotion. Generally, this means that employees need to be guaranteed anonymity. Without that guarantee they are less likely to provide frank responses. This is directly tied to the issue of who should administer the survey. Usually, an outside consultant is the best choice; the supervisor, the worst choice. Even if employees *suspect* that their survey can fall into the hands of supervisors, there can be a problem. That is why interoffice mail is not the preferred method for *collecting* survey data, although the survey could be *distributed* via interoffice mail. When we use survey sessions to administer surveys, we often make a theatrical production of placing completed surveys in a locked box. In fact, we usually destroy individual surveys after the data are coded into the computer.

How the data will be used is another motivational issue. One company used survey results to assign bonuses for supervisors. When the supervisors found out, they actively lobbied their workers for 'votes' on the survey. This is one of the worst uses imaginable of a communication audit. In another situation, we discovered after interviewing members in a unit, that the data on satisfaction with training programs were tainted. Many of the employees admitted that they artificially inflated the ratings on the training questions because they were sick of going to mandatory training classes. Both of these situations highlight the motivational impact of the decisions regarding how the data will be used.

Assuming that employee fears can be minimized, there are a variety of ways to inspire participation. Frankly, some organizations 'bribe' employees with raffles, gifts, and door prizes. Others publicize less direct or tangible rewards such as improvements in working conditions or the 'opportunity to express your opinion'. Either way, the WIFM issue (What's In It For Me?) is being addressed. There are more altruistic appeals that work in some companies, such as suggesting there is a kind of civic obligation to complete the questionnaire. One paper mill appealed to workers' sense of duty by comparing the survey process to maintenance procedures on their machines. Mill workers may not like to do it, but it is necessary to keep the organization running efficiently. These appeals could be characterized as WIFO issues (What's In It For the Organization?). Typically, the WIFM issues prove more effective than the WIFO issues (Clampitt, 2007).

How will the data be collected?

There are several administrative options. One commonly used method is to administer the survey in a group setting. For instance, employees may be scheduled to complete the survey in the corporate training room. This method allows the auditor to brief participants before they take the survey. The briefing generally involves the following elements:

- describing the purpose of the audit
- discussing how the data will be used
- providing assurances about confidentiality
- explaining how to complete the survey
- discussing the feedback process
- answering any questions.

Using this approach often increases employee trust in the process by decreasing their anxiety. Participants are also more likely to be motivated to complete the survey.

There are several potential disadvantages of survey groups. One potential disadvantage is that they can raise employee expectations too high. A synergy may be created by the meetings in which employees may expect management to respond to concerns more quickly than is possible. Another potential disadvantage involves logistics. Can the audit team secure enough rooms to administer the survey? Does the team have enough time to set up the schedule and actually administer the survey? Do the rooms provide sufficient anonymity for participants? These are the kinds of questions that need to be considered when opting for this choice.

Sending the survey through the post or interoffice mail is a common administrative procedure. Typically this maximizes coverage, allowing you to reach employees who are geographically dispersed, who work on different shifts or in different time zones. However, there are some tradeoffs. Confidentiality concerns may be raised if the completed surveys are returned via interoffice mail. It is also more difficult to motivate employees to participate in the process. Consequently, rates of return for mailed surveys are often relatively low when compared to other methods. For instance, one company distributed a survey in the mail to one division, and scheduled survey sessions for a sister division. The participation rates were 25% and 55%, respectively.

Many organizations use internet-based administrative procedures. There are a number of issues that must be addressed with this approach, one being the confidentiality of the data. Employees must believe that they cannot be identified in order for them to provide candid responses. Another issue to address is the length of the survey. Internet-based surveys work fairly well if the survey is short because most users will not fill out a lengthy survey using this medium. As a result, the auditors are restricted to a few relevant questions, forcing them to make some tough decisions about which issues are relevant. Consequently, the results may be less comprehensive than those attained through other procedures.

However, the main advantages of internet-based surveys are the speed and the ease with which results can be tabulated. They are an effective way to check the 'pulse' of the communication system on a routine basis. Auditors can determine the concerns of employees and use the data to quickly address those issues. This is similar to how skilled politicians use opinion polls: they track public opinion on a few key issues and then fine-tune their messages accordingly. One prominent scholar argued that 'this type of survey can be completed (developed and implemented) within 4 weeks at less than one tenth the cost of a traditional survey and with response rates ranging from 60% to 70%' (Goldhaber, 2002, p. 452).

One manufacturing plant with 1000 employees uses this approach quite effectively. This plant creates a 'pulse report' by e-mailing a survey every other week to approximately 50 randomly selected employees (see Box 3.2). Employees are asked eight closed-ended questions and two open-ended questions. They generally complete the survey in less than 5 minutes and are 'rewarded' with a raffle ticket. The company then posts the results and management responses to employee concerns on an electronic bulletin board. The plant uses the data to continually track employee concerns and determine the effectiveness of the managerial communication strategy. This has proven particularly helpful in providing direction for meetings, suggesting articles for the newsletter, and planning for organizational changes.

Some auditors take this approach one step further. For example, they

Box 3.2 Pulse report

Directions: Place an X in the appropriate space below.

Questions	Strongly Agree	Agree	Undecided	Disagree	Strongly Disagree
1. I understand where the plant is headed in the next quarter.					
2. I understand why the plant is heading in the direction it is.					
3. I believe we need to reduce costs in the plant.					
4. I have the tools to do my job effectively.					
5. I am actively trying to control costs in the plant.					

Directions: Place a number between 0–100 in the appropriate space.

Questions	Number 0–100
6. On your last shift, how many people made positive comments about the plant?	
7. On your last shift, how many people made negative comments about the plant?	
8. On your last shift, how many incidents did you witness where someone took an unnecessary safety risk?	

Directions: Please fill in a written response in the appropriate space.

Questions	Please write your response below
9. What is your most important job-related concern?	
10. If you could ask the plant manager one question, what would it be? Why?	

construct a short, eight to ten item survey composed of broad, macro-level communication questions. Issues like the communication climate or decision-making are the focal point of the questions. The computer instantly tabulates the responses and generates follow-up questions based on the employee's answers to the macro-level questions. This type of survey has the potential to provide the kind of depth and breadth necessary for a finely tuned communication strategy.

It is also worth flagging a further issue – that is, the impact of web-based surveys on response rates. One meta-analysis of 45 published and unpublished comparisons of web and other survey modes found that, on average, web surveys delivered a response rate 11% lower than their counterparts (Manfreda *et al.*, 2008). Clearly, there are no perfect data collection methods, and many of the approaches discussed here can be used to ameliorate some of these negative effects, such as taking clear steps to engage people's attention and support. It remains the case that web-based surveys have many advantages, and these must be judiciously weighed against the potential impact on response rates.

3 Test the administrative procedures and questionnaire

This is a particularly helpful step when using a new instrument. You can determine what questions are difficult to understand and those that do not yield important information. Even with pre-existing questionnaires, it is important to pilot test the instrument and administrative procedures. For example, one company selected a survey that made extensive use of the word 'team'. One unit in the company had just been through some poorly conceived and executed training about 'team-based' management. Whenever these employees heard the word 'team', they cringed. Consequently, this particular group systematically rated the survey questions containing the 'T-word' low. In short, the negative connotations trumped the intended denotations of the auditors. Therefore, they decided to replace the 'T-word' with 'work group'.

Testing the survey is typically done in a focus group format. A random selection of employees are asked to complete the survey. A facilitator then interviews the group, asking questions such as:

- What did you like most about the survey?
- What did you like least?
- Were the instructions understandable?
- What questions were difficult to answer? Why?
- Were there any words that you did not understand?

Typically a funnel questioning sequence works best, starting with the general questions and then moving to the more specific ones. Using this approach allows auditors to discover issues they may not have thought of, like readability problems associated with the physical layout of the survey.

4 Decide how feedback will be provided

There are several crucial questions that need to be answered: What format will be used to present the results? What will be the auditor's role in interpreting the results? How will the results be communicated? How will you transition from the results to the next step? This section will address each of these issues.

What format will be used to present the results?

Quantitative data can be reported in any number of different ways and with varying levels of statistical sophistication. Some organizations want graphics, while others prefer simple numeric reporting, typically including the mean, standard deviation, and frequency. While all these decisions do not need to be made before the survey is administered, they need to be discussed.

There are also options in reporting qualitative data. Some companies only want a listing of employee answers to open-ended questions. This is fairly easy to do but it often creates some difficulties. For instance, managers often play the 'who said that?' game when encountering a particularly touching or distressing statement. The focus of the discussion tends to be driven by the poignant or enraging statement. Thus a sense of balance and proportion is often lost. Others prefer that the data be content-analyzed. This approach tends to promote more thoughtful and balanced interpretations of the data. However, it does take a great deal of time and effort to properly content-analyze data.

What will be the auditor's role in interpreting the results?

Some senior executives feel they need little assistance in interpreting data. In fact, they may only hire an auditor to administer the survey and 'crunch the numbers'. This can present an ethical quandary because some executives believe they are qualified to interpret the data, when in reality, they are not. For instance, on one survey, a question asking about employees' satisfaction levels with 'working for your supervisor' yielded the following results:

Department A = 6.2 mean (Scale: 0–10, low–high)
Department B = 6.0 mean

Based on this data, one of these 'qualified' executives drew the dubious conclusion that Department A was much more effectively managed than

Department B. The results were not statistically significant, but the executive insisted that this result provided conclusive evidence to support his interpretation. Because of similar instances, the auditor refused to work with the company on future projects. Clearly, not all executives approach data analysis in this way. Since most organizations need at least some help interpreting the results and to fend off situations such as this, it is important to negotiate up front about this type of situation.

One way to strategically address these issues with the client is to provide sample output, reports, and feedback protocols during the initial negotiations. Then auditors can be sure that the issues are discussed and the client can make any necessary adjustments.

How will the survey results be communicated?

Typically, the results are presented in both an oral and a written format. Generally, senior management receives the report first. In some instances, the process ends here and senior management never release the results to anyone. Long-term, this is counterproductive because participation in future surveys is less likely. More often, the results are then rolled out or 'downloaded' to other levels in the organization (Clampitt and Williams, 2007). Usually a written summary is then prepared for all participants, and at times employees are offered the option of attending open briefing sessions.

How will you transition from the results to the next step?

Clearly senior management need to take some time to process the diagnostic phase of the audit before moving to the 'next step'. There are two basic possibilities:

1   Sometimes senior management want to have all the action plans in place before releasing the diagnostic data to employees. In that case, employees simultaneously receive a diagnostic report from the auditors and a set of responses in the form of an action plan from senior management.
2   Other organizations value employee input and make a clearer distinction between the diagnosis and the prescription. Thus, they present the audit results and then merely outline the procedures that will be used to respond to the diagnosis.

Communicating the audit results is fairly straightforward. A more difficult issue involves discerning the 'action step' in which the following concerns are addressed:

- What are the major issues?
- When should they be addressed?

- How should they be addressed?
- Who should address them?

The key point is to draw a clear line between *diagnosing* and *prescribing*.

ANALYZING THE DATA

How quantitative and qualitative data are displayed has a profound impact on the ultimate interpretations of the information. Information displays influence our reasoning, inform our intuitions, and imply corrective action. Ineffective displays make it difficult to draw proper conclusions and can lead us into discussions of the trivial. Tufte (1983, p. 9) made this compelling argument:

> Modern data graphic can do much more than simply substitute for small statistical tables. At their best, graphics are instruments for reasoning about quantitative information. Often the most effective way to describe, explore, and summarize a set of numbers – even a very large set – is to look at pictures of those numbers. Furthermore, of all methods for analyzing and communicating statistical information, well-designed data graphics are usually the simplest and at the same time the most powerful.

Therefore, auditors need to carefully think about the choices made in displaying the data. This issue is discussed more fully in Chapter 10. With that in mind, consider the following analytical options.

Quantitative data

A variety of techniques, ranging from simple to complex, can be used to present and analyze the numeric data. Some basic options are reviewed below:

Rank-order method

Using the means from each question, rank related items from high to low. For instance, if auditors were using the ICA Audit Survey, then items about the timeliness of information could be ranked in one table. Another table would contain items regarding organizational relationships, and so forth. For the Communication Satisfaction Survey, we usually rank all 40 items in one table. Statistical tests can be used to group the items on the tables into high, medium and low 'zones'. These procedures can aid the auditor in identifying underlying themes or patterns in the data. Items will often appear in some natural conceptual clumps, like a group of items related to 'information dissemination' versus others related to 'supervisory relationships'. The major drawback of the rank-order method is that it forces the identification of strengths and weaknesses. But what if all the means are above (or below) the conceptual midpoint? How do auditors make sense of a situation like that? The next technique addresses that very issue.

Databank comparisons

Most of the commonly used surveys have databanks available. An example of this is the Communication Satisfaction Questionnaire databank, composed of the results of 26 audits (see www.imetacomm.com/CME3 – 'Research Database' tab). This allows other auditors the option to compare their organization's results with those in the databank. Many businesses are particularly keen on this approach because it is a type of 'best practice' comparison. Statistical tests can be used to assess significant differences between the norm and the targeted organization.

The excitement generated by a databank comparison should be tempered by the inevitable problems those comparisons create. First, organizations often differ from one another in significant ways and it may be inappropriate to use the databank as a comparison point. For example, in a business organized around the team concept, a 'good' score compared to the databank may not be good enough. Other organizations that are less dependent on teams could find the same result gratifying. Second, sometimes the databank comparisons reveal seemingly contradictory findings to other analytical techniques. In one organization, the highest ranked items on the survey revolved around supervisor communication, yet even these scores were well below the databank norms. Is supervisory communication a strength or weakness? That, of course, depends on whether auditors take an internal or external focus of analysis. This particular organization was in a similar position to a football team with a 'star' player who was merely average when compared to others in the league.

Factor scores

Most of the standard audit surveys have been tested and reveal various key factors. These are groupings of questions that appear to measure similar underlying issues. Some are easy to spot, like all the questions relating to supervisory communication, while others are more difficult. These require more sophisticated statistical techniques like factor analysis, principal component analysis, and regression analysis. These can often be helpful in determining key relationships between variables. Some auditors use the predetermined factors as the basis for their analysis. Statistically savvy researchers use a variety of techniques to draw their conclusions.

All these techniques are viable options for the preliminary analysis of your data. Often they are used in various combinations. The fundamental point is to recognize both the strengths and the drawbacks of each technique.

Qualitative data

Since many questionnaires contain at least a few open-ended questions, it is important to briefly consider how to scientifically analyze this data. The process is relatively straightforward, yet at times intellectually taxing.

1   One auditor reads over all the responses to a given question and looks for underlying themes. Even though the respondents will use different terms to describe their concerns, usually a stable set of issues will emerge from the responses. Typical categories include 'upward communication', 'quality of information', and 'co-worker communication'. There is no way to determine the ideal number of the categories. However, generally, anywhere from five to ten categories works best. If there are too few categories, it is difficult to make useful recommendations. If there are too many, the reliability becomes questionable. Content analysis is a blunt instrument; one can't put too fine a point on the categories. And there are always some responses that are so idiosyncratic that they defy classification. Best to put those in a category called 'other'.
2   Another auditor repeats step 1 while being shielded from the classification system developed by the other auditor. This, again, is a way to help improve reliability and validity.
3   The firewall comes down and the two auditors meet and share their respective category systems. After some discussion, they agree on a category system.
4   The firewall goes back up. Separately the auditors go back to the original set of responses and tally up the number of responses in each category. Often a respondent will make a comment that falls in two categories. Both should be noted, but auditors should record the number of 'multiple-coded items'. Sometimes the data sets are so large that it is impossible to review all the responses or devote the time of two researchers to the analysis of one question. In these cases sampling techniques are the best option.
5   The firewall comes back down (for the final time). The researchers compare their coding decisions and check the number of agreements. They reconcile any differences. This is the reliability test and should be 75% or better. If not, the category system is flawed and needs to be revised.
6   Based on the data, the auditors construct a chart summarizing their data. There is an example in Chapter 13.

Some clients will insist on seeing the entire list of employee comments. This is fine, if used in conjunction with content analysis procedures, and if care is taken to ensure that the responses remain anonymized. Well executed content analysis helps us to more systematically process these responses as it provides a sense of organization and proportion to the data. The analysis provides a shield from a particularly eloquent statement, venomous remark or catchy comment skewing the interpretation.

INTERPRETING THE RESULTS

Properly interpreting the results of an audit requires discipline, insight, and perspective. Auditors need to be disciplined enough to not jump to conclusions. Insight is required to look beyond the surface and search for deeper patterns. Perspective allows auditors to distinguish the trivial from the important. The dedicated auditor will acquire these attributes with experience. However, heeding the following suggestions can hasten the learning process.

Erect a temporary firewall between the qualitative and the quantitative data

The firewall provides discipline in the interpretative process. Numbers and words may paint different pictures. It is important to see both images before attempting to synthesize them. For instance, in a manufacturing plant, the numeric data pointed to a problem with the general communication climate. Yet, the chief complaint emerging from written questions involved 'trash' and the 'dirty working environment'. If the auditors relied solely on the numeric data, they would have ignored the trash problem. Even if they viewed the qualitative data through the lens of the quantitative data, they would have minimized this important concern. Instead, the firewall allowed them to see that the 'trash' problem was a legitimate concern that the numeric section was simply not sensitive enough to pick up.

If there is a team of auditors, setting up a firewall is easy. Assign one group to examine the quantitative data and arrive at tentative conclusions. The other group does the same for the qualitative data. If this is not possible, then analyze one set of data and put aside the tentative conclusions. Then move to the other set of data.

As a rule of thumb, it is best to start with the qualitative data. Why? Sometimes auditors will unwittingly interpret the quantitative data and then *massage* the qualitative data to *confirm* the original findings.

Anticipate various interpretations of the questions

Professional survey designers scrupulously try to avoid highly ambiguous questions. Despite their best efforts, almost all surveys contain unclear items. Not only can words be interpreted in various ways, there is also the issue of the contextual parameters of the question. One commonly used survey asks employees about their satisfaction with communication regarding 'organizational changes'. In several audits, this item turned out to be a problem area. The question then became, 'What changes are the employees talking about?' The questions simply couldn't be answered with the existing data. As Downs and Adrian (2004) insightfully noted about this dilemma, the main problem is that auditors may generate interpretations that are not faithful to the meanings as intended by the respondents.

There are two ways to address these dilemmas. First, auditors could make a 'best guess' based on other available evidence. Self-deception is always a possibility in this case. Positive thinking can lead us to accept the more benign of the possible interpretations. Second, further research could be conducted using other methods such as interviews or focus groups. Time permitting, this is the preferred alternative. Then auditors can have enough specificity to clearly address the issue.

Discern the difference between *more* and *less* important items

Experienced auditors guided by research findings soon learn that some survey items are more important than others. For instance, the Communication Satisfaction Questionnaire contains the following item: 'Extent to which my supervisor trusts me' (Downs and Adrian, 2004). Previous studies have demonstrated a high correlation between this question and the general communication climate (Clampitt and Downs, 1993). As a rule of thumb, if this item is low, then the satisfaction levels with other communication issues will be low. It is a bell-weather question. Moreover, questions about supervisors tend to be the most important communication items because employees have a high preference for information from their supervisors. On the other hand, items about the corporate newsletter are usually less salient. That is, they usually have less impact on the entire communication climate than other issues. Of course, it is far easier to make specific recommendations to improve a newsletter than it is to restore the trust between employees and their supervisors.

Distinguish between macro- and micro-level concerns

When the stock market takes a tumble, it does not mean that every stock, or even every sector of the market, is on the decline. Likewise, global results about the organization's communication system may not be applicable to all departments and levels. For instance, the general results might indicate a problem with the timeliness of certain kinds of information. Yet, there may be one or more departments in which this is not the primary concern. Identifying these pockets is important for two reasons. First, a pocket may be a place to look for a 'best practice' lesson. If one department has mastered the 'timeliness' issue, it might provide insight into how other departments could do the same. Second, action plans constructed for the entire organization might not be applicable to every part of the organization. In other words, by identifying the pockets you can avoid the 'one size fits all' mentality.

Identifying the pockets can provide specific focal points for each unit or department. Too often, organization-wide problems are quickly dismissed as everyone's problems. Often, if it is *everybody's* problem, then it is really *nobody's*. This means auditors need to be very careful when discussing macro-level problems. Ideally the audit should identify major problems requiring specific actions that can be assigned to particular individuals or departments to solve. But the ideal is usually not the reality. 'Improving trust between management and employees' may be a worthy goal but who really 'owns' that problem? Thus, it is particularly important when talking with senior management about macro concerns to temper the remarks with discussions of 'pocket' differences.

Synthesize the results of the qualitative and quantitative analyses

There are essentially two possibilities:

- *Similar themes.* These are conclusions that all the data sources point to. They tend to be highly salient issues, although they may be stated in somewhat different ways. For instance, employees may make written comments such as, 'I wish I knew how I was doing.' A survey question revealing dissatisfaction with the 'appraisal system' could indicate a similar concern.
- *Dissimilar themes.* Inevitably some themes emerge from one data source that do not emerge from another. This does not mean those issues are unimportant. All data gathering methods have biases and one of the methods may not be sensitive to certain concerns.

Determining which issues to highlight in the report is a challenging task requiring thorough knowledge of the organization and insight gleaned from the organizational communication literature. The quality of this synthesis often determines the value of an audit to the organization.

Contemplate actions that might be taken

Audit results do not necessarily imply specific and direct actions. The ICA Audit Survey has one section asking employees to compare the amount of information they receive on various topics with the amount of information they desire. In several audits, the amount desired exceeded the amount actually received in every topic area. So what? What can be done with these results? We ultimately concluded that the answers to these questions actually constituted a 'curiosity index' (Downs *et al.*, 1981). If more information was provided on all the issues, then employees would be overwhelmed. Therefore, we had to use our judgement to discern where the really significant information gaps were. This meant we had to rely on our knowledge of the particular organizations as well as our general notions about organizational communication practices. For instance, we deemed information about job-related duties as more important than information about 'benefits', even though the benefits issue would have been easier to address.

As auditors enter the rather murky world of action plans, it is best to be tentative. Suggest several courses of actions that might address the issues, then the client can choose those that are most compatible with the organizational culture. Clearly separate the diagnostic results from the prescriptions. This protects the auditor's credibility and allows the client to participate in the decision-making process. The result: a greater likelihood that the decisions will actually be implemented.

CONCLUSION

Scholars have devoted years of their lives to perfecting questionnaires and survey techniques. They have provided us with numerous valuable lessons and tools. In an age when surveys are as commonplace as weather forecasts, few people appreciate the art and science of the process. And like a weather forecast, few people recognize all the effort required to produce a fairly accurate picture of an extraordinarily complex phenomenon – organizational communication.

Chapter 4

The interview approach

Rob Millar and Anne Tracey

INTRODUCTION

The interview is considered to be one of the central tools within internal and external communication audits. Its utility was perhaps best illustrated by Downs' (1988) assertion that, if confined to using just one audit method, he would choose the interview. Some 16 years later that assertion still remained (Downs and Adrian, 2004). Given the nature of many organizations, in terms of numerous employees at different levels, across various departments, perhaps on different sites, and with a wide range of clients and customers, the survey questionnaire is often the first method that comes to mind. It is initially difficult to conceptualize how a method that involves 'talking to people' could possibly provide an accurate and reliable picture of communication in a complex environment. However, just like any other methodology, the secret of its success depends on giving thorough consideration to planning, development, implementation, analysis and interpretation (Payne, 1999). The purpose of this chapter is to identify and discuss those issues crucial to employing the interview as an effective audit method.

INITIAL CONSIDERATIONS

Why is the interview useful?

The interview has been defined by Millar *et al.* (1992, p. 3) as:

> A face-to-face dyadic interaction in which one individual plays the role of interviewer and the other takes on the role of interviewee, and both of these roles carry clear expectations concerning behavioural and attitudinal approach. The interview is requested by one of the participants for a specific purpose and both participants are willing contributors.

This definition emphasizes the social nature of interviews, which is the main distinguishing feature of this method when compared to many others. It is primarily a process of interpersonal interaction set within a particular context and with specific purposes (Hargie, 2006; Hargie and Tourish, 1999). It will have primary goals, secondary goals, and a structure. The two-way flow of communication that characterizes the interview method offers four major advantages over alternative information gathering strategies:

1   It is more likely to elicit unanticipated information and to enable a greater depth and meaning of communication experiences to be explored and recorded (Forman and Argenti, 2005; King, 1994). Studies that limit themselves to questionnaire methods alone may miss crucial and meaningful information regarding communication. For instance, Ghoshal *et al.* (1994) acknowledged that the survey methods used in their study of communication in multinational organizations enabled frequency of communications to be analysed but revealed little about the content or quality of such communication – information that is crucial for auditors, and that also may be crucial for further management strategizing. Likewise, using interviews, Proctor and Doukakis (2003) unearthed information about organizational change that had not been revealed through an earlier questionnaire survey.

2   Meeting with individuals may also enable auditors to get a better sense of the way in which organizational practices and issues are perceived and interpreted by staff, employees and, where relevant, service users.

3   The interview can also serve the need, both for auditors and respondents, for the audit to have a human and social aspect with regard to the discovery of information. The importance of fulfilling this need for both sides is perhaps best illustrated by comparing the audit interview with the employment interview. Despite having questionable validity and reliability in providing accurate and reliable information, the interview is the most frequently used selection tool (Millar and Tracey, 2006). Potential employers and employees are obviously reluctant to accept that a suitable decision could be reached without human interaction. For this reason, the interview has been retained, with recruiters focused on developing procedures intended to minimize its shortcomings. In a similar vein, carrying out an audit without engaging in *any* face-to-face interaction would not be acceptable. One possible consequence of adapting to the needs of respondents may be to create a more relaxing and tension-free climate for the collection of information (Lloyd and Varey, 2003).

4   The interview has major advantages where a flexible approach to gathering information is beneficial, especially where responses may be relatively unknown and the topic requires exploration, and when it is important that all points of view are represented (Bryant, 2006). Such flexibility enables a large number of questions to be included, each of which can be considered in a variable order depending on the respondent (Daly *et al.*, 2003).

Thus, specific procedures have been developed for audit interviews that will enhance the accuracy and reliability of information obtained, while meeting the human and social expectations of participants.

When is the interview useful?

The interview can be used at a number of points during the communication audit:

1   Initial uses include interviewing key personnel to clarify the nature and type of audit that will best meet their needs. These interviews can also help auditors to gain a background to and become familiar with the organization and its general communication practices.
2   Interviews may be used as the first step in developing an audit question-naire to be administered to a large number of respondents. Information obtained from interviewing a sample of members will enable salient, relevant and important areas to be included in the written instrument. Chapter 17 in this volume offers an example of this, wherein interviews with serving police officers prior to an audit in their organization led to a number of changes in the main questionnaire instrument that was eventually employed.
3   They can be used as one of a range of methods of collecting audit data (Forman and Argenti, 2005; Quinn and Hargie, 2004; Tourish and Robson, 2003). Using interviews to complement other methods in the audit process helps to provide a more comprehensive and insight-ful formulation of the communicative climate and process (Zack and McKenney, 1995).
4   Even when auditors use wholly quantitative methods, following data analysis, interviews with a selected sample can be a valuable way of helping them to understand, explain and interpret results (Proctor and Doukakis, 2003).
5   Interviews can be used at differing times during the process in order to serve a variety of purposes. Initial exploratory interviews can help aud-itors to construct an interview guide, to be used in more focused second round interviews. Interviews can also be scheduled to take place before and after interventions, allowing the impact and efficacy of communica-tion initiatives to be evaluated.

PLANNING

The precise nature and depth of information required about communication will strongly influence interview planning. With respect to communication audits, Downs and Adrian (2004) detail a number of purposes for interviews, ranging from initial exploratory functions to the identification and probing of specific issues. None the less, most interviews take one of two forms; that is, *exploratory* where the purpose is to generate issues, or *focused* where the purpose is to obtain specific information on pre-selected subject areas. For example, the aim of surveying the formal communication structures within an organization would be best achieved by conducting highly standardized focused interviews in which each communication structure and channel is covered in a systematic way (Stewart and Cash, 2000). Conversely, if the auditor's aim is to gain a picture in some depth of the experiences of communication from the perspective of employees or service users, the exploratory interview is more useful.

Whatever information is desired it is incumbent on the auditor to maximize the likelihood of it being relevant, reliable, valid and authentic (Brenner, 1981; Gorden, 1987; Seidman, 1998). To this end, there are a number of very important planning decisions and procedures that need to be considered if the efficacy of the interview method is to be assured. The following questions should be given careful consideration and attention.

Who will conduct the interviews?

Given the central role of communication skills in conducting effective interviews, it is essential that all interviewers involved in audits have highly developed skills. In order to ensure that this is indeed the case and to maximize consistency across interviewers and interviews, specific training on the way in which the interview is to be conducted should be provided (van Tilberg, 1998). It is widely acknowledged that training enhances the validity and reliability of information gained through this method (Campion *et al.*, 1997; Pollner, 1998; Sias and Cahill, 1998). Collins (1997) identified two functions that training serves. First, interviewers need to be convinced that a standardized approach is essential. Second, training must, 'develop a uniform level of skill in probing and obtaining information in depth' (p. 81). This training should directly address how to use the interview guide and focus on developing skills in opening, questioning, listening and closing the interview. Research evidence would suggest that the most appropriate and effective medium in this respect is that of communication skills training programmes (Hargie and Tourish, 1994). The procedures and components of such programmes are well established and documented (Dickson *et al.*, 1997).

However, interpersonal skill is only one characteristic of the interviewer and there are additional personal factors that can significantly impact on interview effectiveness, and even on the credibility afforded the audit by the workforce. The influence of interviewer race, culture, gender and age must be given serious consideration (Hargie and Tourish, 1999; Miltiades, 2008). For example:

- Is it likely that communication incidents perceived as sexual or racial harassment will be disclosed to the same degree to any interviewer?
- Will a young inexperienced interviewer obtain a wealth of information from a senior manager?
- Should young white male interviewers carry out interviews of customers in an outlet where the clientele is exclusively female and predominantly Muslim?

As the research evidence indicates that these factors will indeed impact on the quality of interview conducted (Collins, 1997; O'Muircheartaigh and Campanelli, 1998; Padfield and Procter, 1996; Sarangi, 1994), there should be a pool of interviewers with varying characteristics and backgrounds. Ideally, interviewees should be given the opportunity to express preferences, but in the absence of this, the auditor must take such factors into account.

Who will be interviewed?

The gathering together of a pool of participants from which the required information will be collected is of paramount importance for any audit. In working with participants who are members of formal organizations this will necessitate gaining access through 'gatekeepers' who have responsibility for the operation of the site (Seidman, 1998). Those high up in the hierarchy should also provide a public endorsement of the audit, which in turn encourages those lower down to participate fully. Participants need to be representative of the range of different roles (Lloyd and Varey, 2003) and also reflect all levels or grades of the hierarchy (Quinn and Hargie, 2004). Likewise, in external audits, the entire client base should be covered. Furthermore, the final composition of samples should be by random selection across categories, a type of stratified random sampling. However, alternative techniques for acquiring samples have been employed in communication audits, such as snowballing (Bryant, 2006). Some studies using the interview technique have also found that, depending on the precise focus of the audit and its capacity to generate interest among employees, people may often volunteer for additional interviews, thereby expanding the sampling frame beyond what was originally anticipated (e.g. Tourish, 2007b).

The need for close attention to sampling is illustrated by the findings of an investigation into communication within the North Yorkshire Constabulary. Interviews identified several common strands but also revealed the differing views of particular groupings, which included the executive, middle managers, junior ranks and civilian support staff (Green, 1992). It is important to remember that at least two participants from each subgroup are required in order to protect the anonymity of respondents in feedback, and it is normally recommended that all key personnel be included.

There are few concrete criteria to inform decisions about how many participants are enough. Participant numbers vary widely from study to study. Robson and Tourish (2005) interviewed nine participants, Bryant (2006) interviewed 22 and Quinn and Hargie (2004) interviewed 41. Tourish (2007b) interviewed 105 respondents across four organizations, in a study of upward communication from non-managerial staff to managers. However, in following the sampling criteria set out by Green (1992), a figure that represents the minimum number of individuals required can be formulated. The number of people in each subgroup should be sufficient such that reserves are in place if individuals decide not to participate, or for some other reason are prevented from taking part. In terms of the 'What's in it for me?' perspective, the willingness of interviewees to participate – especially in external audits – can be encouraged if incentives are on offer (see Chapter 5). Once this sample has been identified, the decision about whether to increase sample size depends on at least two factors:

1   *The type of communication audit.* If the audit is concerned with the provision only of a general overview of communication, then the minimum sample should be sufficient. However if the audit is a basis for making specific and major changes within an organization, its findings and acceptability would be greatly enhanced by a significant sample from each subgroup.

2   *The time and resources available.* Auditors must realistically estimate whether increasing the sample size is feasible within the audit timescale and the human and financial resources allocated. It is important to remember that interviewing is a very time consuming, labour intensive and expensive form of data gathering. Interviewers will have to schedule appointments, travel to and from interviews and carry out the interviews. For each interview, there is then time for transcribing or writing up the content, and analysis of such data is particularly time consuming (King, 1994). The cost to the organization also increases with sample size as interviews are typically carried out in working hours. Many organizations therefore place restrictions on the number of interviewees that they are willing to make available, and the length of time that will be permitted for conducting the interviews.

There is one final observation that is warranted, and that relates to the verbal demands placed on participants of the interview method. The procedure is strongly dependent on the ability of respondents to be able to articulate their points of view (in response to a variety of questions posed by the interviewer). It has been pointed out that this is a salient consideration for audit interviewers particularly where the requirement is for reflective appraisals and personal judgements (Dickson *et al.*, 2003).

The decision as to the number and type of participants is usually the result of balancing a number of competing demands for resources against the need to produce findings of sufficient reliability, validity and authenticity. It therefore normally entails a degree of compromise.

How long should each interview last?

In practical terms, interviewers must decide on the length of time to be made available for interviewing each participant. To some extent the duration of any particular interview will be closely related to the purpose for which the interviews have been arranged. The length of time scheduled is also dependent on the person being interviewed. Downs and Adrian (2004) offer some advice on this issue where they suggest that managers may require a greater length of time (e.g. around 2 hours) than non-managers (e.g. around 30 minutes). Sias and Cahill's (1998) interviews, which focused on peer relationships at work, lasted an average of 20–30 minutes, whereas Gabriel's (1998) organizational storytelling interviews lasted between 45 and 75 minutes. One hour appears to be a common average length of time (Bryant, 2006; Quinn and Hargie, 2004). However, where in-depth techniques of interviewing are employed, such as the Retrospective Interview Technique, considerably longer periods of time may be required, which in turn places heavy demands on participants (Dickson *et al.*, 2003).

Once a time frame has been decided it is important to inform all potential participants of such a time commitment prior to their agreement to be interviewed. They can then make an informed decision about participation and schedule their time accordingly. Furthermore, the agreed limit must then be adhered to by the interviewer. The temptation to just carry on for a little while longer is not only an unacceptable infringement of the interviewees' time but in general reduces trust in the interviewer (Seidman, 1998), while at the same time inhibiting purposeful communication (Gorden, 1987). Just as it is recognized that developing organizational trust can improve organizational communication (see Chapter 1), so the development of trust within the interview is crucial to the quality of interpersonal communication achieved.

Developing the interview guide

Interviewers must have some form of interview guide or plan in order to ensure that the purpose of the interview will be achieved. The format and nature of the interview guide developed will differ significantly, depending on whether exploratory or focused interviews are being planned. Let us examine each of these.

Exploratory interviews

In the initial phase of the communication audit, there is often uncertainty about what types of information might be available, what range of responses participants are likely to make and whether all areas high in salience have been anticipated. Here, the interview is employed as a method of discovery (van der Jagt, 2005). In such circumstances, it is conceivable that an interview guide would not be used, in order to allow respondents to express their perceptions of important processes spontaneously in the interview. The outcomes of such interviews can usefully contribute to the interview guide for the next phase or the development of a question-naire (Hofstede, 1998).

Nevertheless, even in exploratory interviews, it is useful to have some form of broad guide to the major topics to be covered. For example, van der Jagt (2005, p. 179) explored 'ways of thinking' by asking senior executives 'for their vision on 15 different themes'. If participants raise and deal with the types of issues anticipated by the interviewer then such a guide may remain redundant. However, there is at least the possibility that participants may not mention some concerns that interviewers hoped they would. In these circum-stances reference to the interview guide may remind interviewers to suggest topics and ask questions that hitherto had not been discussed. It also guards against the interviewer being drawn into detailed accounts of irrelevant issues, or the interview turning into a chat.

The main body of the interview guide for exploratory interviews should consist of a list of broad opening questions that can then be followed up depending on the responses of participants. There is no suggestion that all questions need to be predetermined nor asked in any particular set sequence. Indeed, herein lies the flexibility of the interview method. It is only important that all relevant questions be asked at some point during the interview pro-cess. This type of exploratory approach is also useful in the later stages of the audit where explanations for particular findings are being sought.

There are many examples of the successful use of exploratory interview guides in studies that have investigated communication processes across a range of contexts:

- In the medical context, King et al. (1994) employed a semi-structured interview guide that covered specific topics such as information gathering by doctors, their perceptions of uncertainty and risk, details of referral decisions, and doctors' relationships with patients.
- In a study exploring the role of internal communication during organiza-tional change Daly et al. (2003) organized their unstructured interviews into three sections; the introduction, which established the business context; followed by the major section, which dealt with issues pertaining to change management and internal communication; and ending with participants' own perceptions regarding the inter-relationship between internal communication and change management.
- Robson and Tourish (2005) probed participants' attitudes in three broad areas: internal communication in general; their understanding of, and

support for, new organizational structures; and how well they grasped the vision of the top management team.

• In a detailed exploratory interview guide in the organizational sphere, Goldhaber (1993) constructed a list of 11 main questions all of the open type and prefixed by 'What' or 'How' and requests to 'Describe' particular phenomena (see Box 4.1). This latter question type, referred to as a narrative/directive question (Dillon, 1997), can be very useful in that participants are asked to provide concrete details, actual behaviours and specific circumstances.

• In their study of communication in the clergy, Lount and Hargie (1997) asked individual clergy to reconstruct specific situations (or critical incidents) where communication between themselves and parishioners was either effective or ineffective.

• Appelbaum et al. (2003) explored downsizing and the perceptions of a company programme designed to alleviate its impact from the point of view of management and employees; a range of question types were drafted as part of an extensive interview guide that focused on reactions to the announcement and impact of downsizing, the company's efforts to ameliorate the impact and the effectiveness of a company programme. The same questions, phrased appropriately, were posed to all participants.

Although, in each context, questions are used to focus participants on specific aspects of organizational communication (e.g. formal and informal channels, decision-making processes, conflict, organizational change, successful versus unsuccessful scenarios, and interpersonal communication at various levels) participants are free to choose what disclosures to make in their personal responses. What characterizes all these forms of interviews as exploratory is that there is a general notion of subject areas to be covered, but ample opportunity for interviewees to take the lead, openly discuss these areas as comprehensively as they choose, and to raise any additional issues (Forman and Argenti, 2005). As illustrated by the above examples, the exact form of the interview guide to be developed will be largely influenced by the context in which the audit is taking place.

Focused interviews

In circumstances where interviewers are concerned with more factual type information, are time-constrained, or where meaningful quantification and comparability is sought, they may adopt a much more highly structured or standardized approach to their interviews (Collins, 1997; King, 1994; Sias and Cahill, 1998). In the focused interview, most aspects of the interview are rigidly predetermined, from topics, to question types and sequence and even response alternatives (Downs, 1988).

Box 4.1 Exploratory interview questions in an internal audit

1 Describe your job (duties, function). What decisions do you usually make in your job? What information do you *need* to make those decisions and from where should you get it? What information do you *actually* get to make those decisions and from whom? Are there formal (written) or informal policies in your organization which determine how you get this information? Should any policies be added, changed or abandoned?

2 What are the major communication *strengths* of this organization? Be specific.

3 What are the major communication *weaknesses* of this organization?

4 Describe the *formal* channels through which you typically receive information about this organization. What kinds of information do you tend to receive? How often?

5 Describe the *informal* channels through which you typically receive information about this organization. What kinds of information do you tend to receive? How often?

6 How often, if ever, do you receive information about this organization which is of low value or use to you? If and when you do, what kinds of information do you receive? Be specific. From whom do you receive this?

7 What would you like to see done to improve information flow in this information? Why hasn't it been done yet?

8 Describe the way decisions are typically made in this organization.

9 When conflict occurs in this organization, what is the major cause? How is conflict typically resolved?

10 Describe the communication relationship you have with your immediate supervisor. Your co-workers. Middle management. Top management. Your subordinates (if appropriate).

11 How do you know when this organization has done a good or bad job toward accomplishing its goals? What measures of effectiveness are used in this organization?

Source: Goldhaber, G. (1993) *Organizational Communication* (6th edition, p. 362). Madison, WI: WCB Brown and Benchmark. Reprinted with permission.

It is important to remember, however, that the content of such questions will ideally have been generated from exploratory interviews. Focused interviews are characterized by the use of mainly closed questions relating to very specific areas of enquiry. They are typically less time consuming, but not always, and can be very useful in checking out the generalizability of information obtained in the initial phase of an audit. Moreover, responses can be more easily coded and analysed than those derived from exploratory interviews.

There is the danger, however, of exerting considerable direction and control over participants. Seidman (1998) cautions interviewers against manipulating or restricting the responses of participants. Some participants are quite happy being directed through the use of short closed questions, where alternative responses are provided. But others may be considerably less satisfied with this approach. Where participants are particularly garrulous, interviewers may need to impose a higher degree of control and direction on the interview by frequently re-focusing participants through the use of more closed type questions. The key is that interviewers must be sensitive to the interview as experienced by participants.

As has been indicated, the type of interview will exert a powerful influence on the nature of interviewer behaviour that will be appropriate in working towards the purpose of the interview interaction. For example, the types of questions in keeping within the exploratory interview are quite different from those that are more useful in the focused interview. The next section examines considerations that must be borne in mind when interviewers actually come to carry out interviews.

CONDUCTING THE INTERVIEW

Both types of interviews require some form of structure in order to guide the interviewer from beginning to end. Training of interviewers should include practical experience of following the interview guide and conducting the interview in a standardized and skilful way. In our increasingly multicultural society, any reputable training of interviewers should include consideration of effective cross-cultural communication. Such training might raise awareness of cultural differences, challenge commonly held myths and stereotypes, and consider the interpretation of verbal and non-verbal behaviour (Nixon and Dawson, 2002).

All interviews should be planned in terms of three basic stages; namely, (a) the opening, (b) the body, and (c) the closing. Each stage requires that interviewers attend to the achievement of specific functions pertinent at each phase, whether this be establishing a working relationship, providing orientation, developing trust, agreeing a mode of working ethically, gathering relevant information through effective use of questions, or closing the interview sensitively. While the body of the interview will differ significantly in exploratory and focused interviews, conducting the opening and closing will share similar characteristics.

The opening

In any encounter between two individuals it is generally accepted that first impressions count (Hargie and Dickson, 2004). An interview should be held in comfortable surroundings, which ensure privacy for the interaction. The interviewer should seem like someone who will conduct the interaction in a professional manner. The interviewee should be greeted by name and the name and associated role of the interviewer stated. An explanation should be given as to how the respondent was selected. The task of establishing rapport and a trusting relationship is crucial, particularly if collection of sensitive and truthful information is required (Oakley, 1981). It is at this point that issues relating to the welfare of participants should be comprehensively covered. The interview guide should provide interviewers with specific statements that must be included in the opening. These should cover confidentiality, anonymity, rights of withdrawal, request for tape recording, note-taking and the ultimate use of information disclosed. This may simply be a process of reminding participants of assurances given previously, during the recruitment stages.

In addition to the relationship building aspects of the opening phase, there is a more cognitively focused element that Stewart and Cash (2000) and Downs and Adrian (2004) refer to as 'orientation'. Here the interviewer must indicate what the objectives are, propose ideas about how the interview will proceed, and give an indication of the structure, content and duration of the interview.

The body

Following this opening stage, interviewers are normally required to start the interview by asking interviewees one or more questions. Given that participants are unlikely to have developed any significant relationship so early in the interview process, it is normally best for the interviewer to begin by asking for factual or descriptive information. Examples from internal and external audits are:

- 'When did you join the company?'
- 'Could you tell me exactly what your job entails?'
- 'How many times a week would you come here?'
- 'For how long has Goodfolks been your main supplier?'

This gives the interviewee time to settle into the interview, without feeling threatened or interrogated. The implementation of the body of the interview will differ according to whether it is exploratory or focused.

Exploratory interviews

If the objectives of employing the exploratory interview are related to generating an understanding of phenomena that are not well known, or where understanding the experience of others is of paramount importance, open questions are recommended.

These offer considerable freedom, place responsibility on participants to choose what issues to raise and allow interviewees to talk in some depth. Seidman (1998) gave the following illustrations of such broad invitations to talk: 'Take me through a day in your work life', or 'Reconstruct your day for me from the time you wake up to the time you go to bed.' It is also useful to ask participants to recount more specific and limited experiences, such as a critical incident, a turning point or a significant event. Examples of open questions are:

- 'Could you tell me about your job?'
- 'What are the communication strengths of the organization?'
- 'Could you describe a situation where a lack of information affected your job performance?'
- 'Can you recall a positive (or negative) event that affected the quality of communication in the workplace and tell me about it?'

To give an example, Appelbaum *et al.* (2003), in their study of the effects of downsizing, asked participants:

- What reactions did management expect once downsizing was announced and the company started to implement the plan? How was management prepared to deal with these reactions?
- What behaviours or reactions were observed in the post phase of the downsizing? What impact did these have in the workplace and how is management dealing with these?
- How did you and your fellow workers react once the downsizing was announced?

The typical exploratory interview is well described by Lloyd and Varey (2003, p. 198) where:

> interviewees were asked to explain what they believed might be achieved through good communication in a strategic alliance environment, focusing on how it can assist both themselves and other project team members.

It will be clear that many open questions begin with words such as What, How, Why and Where, and request participants to express their particular points of view. In general, the crucial advantage of open as opposed to closed questions is the low level of influence imposed on participants – where they can present their opinions, attitudes, thoughts, feelings and understandings unrestricted by the interviewer.

In exploratory interviews, the sequence of questioning is an important characteristic of effective interactions. The less structured interviews are, the more important it becomes to base questions on preceding material offered by participants. Interviewers often have to think on their feet and make on the spot decisions in the absence of tight structure. Not only does this 'verbal following' contribute to the flow of the interview but it sends a strong signal to participants that interviewers are listening to what they are saying. In this context the interview guide is just that, a guide to assist in accomplishing the focus of the audit. It may suggest areas to be included but does not specify the order or manner in which they are to be covered nor does it exclude exploration of new issues (Forman and Argenti, 2005).

Of course, the utility of asking open questions can be lost if interviewers fail to listen actively to the messages contained in participants' responses. The situation can be further exacerbated where interviewers insist on posing very open questions and then persist in interrupting participants when they are responding. Appropriate use of silence allows interviewees time both to think about responses and to articulate them fully. Where participants are enabled to disclose material to interviewers, who in turn engage in effective listening, it is more likely that opportunities for using probing questions will arise. Indeed, this constitutes one strength of the interview approach.

It can be very difficult to follow what some interviewees are trying to say, what they mean by the words they use, or sometimes even to make any sense out of their replies at all. In such circumstances it is imperative that interviewers acknowledge these difficulties and develop a greater understanding by exploring responses in depth. Such exploration is progressed by extensive use of probing, or follow-up questions. Failure to probe can result in the collection of superficial, ambiguous, vague and relatively meaningless information (Fowler and Mangione, 1990). This leads to the strong possibility that interpretation of the information will require many assumptions to be made by the interviewer, thereby distorting the data obtained.

There are a number of different types of probing question, each of which can be effective in its own way. They should be introduced in a non-threatening manner such as 'You mentioned feeling as if you were kept in the dark about management decisions. I was wondering . . .' Among the more relevant probes are those that:

- seek further *clarification*: 'Could you tell me exactly what you mean by that?'
- ask for *exemplification*: 'Could you give me an example of when you have felt like this?'

- check *accuracy*: 'You have *never* been told of any decisions by your manager?'
- question *relevance*: 'How do you think that this affects the way you do your job?'
- request *further information*: 'Could you tell me a bit more about that?'

By employing such follow-up probes, interviewers invite participants to disclose additional information, which serves to reduce ambiguity, vagueness, and contradictions, to extend the story, and to sharpen detail, meaning and understanding.

The use of effective probing techniques can be problematic for interviewers to acquire, hence the importance of training. According to Collins (1997), where interviewers fail to establish satisfactory relationships with participants, they may either fail to engage in sufficient probing or may give up very easily. Moreover, the ways in which interviewers probe can have a significant impact on the nature of information elicited. For instance, Houtkoop-Steenstra (1996) analysed interviewer behaviour in semi-open research interviews in order to discover the types of probes used. When faced with inadequate responses, interviewers employed a number of probing devices, which included presenting several answer options, suggesting a response, or reformulating the response. It was concluded that the use of such leading probes compromised the validity of the information obtained. Therefore, the use of probes may not necessarily represent acceptable interviewer behaviour – the types of probes used and the way they are used are crucial if participants' responses are to be relied on.

A further issue is worthy of note where the use of probes is being considered. By intent, these seek to delve deeper into the personal world of participants, to find out more details from them and to pin them down. The hope is that probes will invite interviewees, albeit in a rather challenging way, to tell a little more about themselves and whatever context is pertinent. However, there is clearly a possibility that their use may be perceived quite differently by participants. Indeed, they may be seen as means by which interviewers are invading their privacy, threatening their safety, increasing their vulnerability and increasing their need to defend themselves (Fletcher, 1992). So there is a delicate balance to be sought between the needs of interviewers and those of participants.

If interviewers are to meet their objectives it is also imperative that they listen carefully to responses. The type of listening required in the interviewing process generally exceeds that which is witnessed in everyday encounters. For this reason, care must be taken to include breaks between interviews or have other tasks interspersed in the interviewers' schedules. Such listening requires interviewers to give their full and undivided attention to verbal and non-verbal responses (Hargie and Dickson, 2004). Listening is not simply a process of hearing or recording what is communicated but entails the listener engaging in more complex processes of understanding and evaluating the message (Bostrom, 2006). The importance of active listening assumes a pivotal role in the successful elicitation of relevant, reliable and sufficiently detailed information. One very influential way of letting participants know that listening is taking place is to ensure that the types and sequence of questions posed during interviews display strong relationships to interviewee responses.

Focused interviews

Many of the general guidelines included in the previous section will apply in some way here. The major difference between the two is in the dominant question type included in the interview guide. In focused interviews, where the purpose is to collect specific information, question types need to be extremely precise and are typically termed closed. These might include simple recall questions such as, 'Who is your immediate boss?', 'Do you use email?', or 'How often do you use email?' In the case of the latter question options can convert the question into a multiple choice format. Respondents are required to use the alternatives provided by the interviewer in giving an answer to the question. For example, 'Do you think communication is (i) worse, (ii) better, or (iii) the same, as it was 6 months ago?' Where the required information tends to be factual, rapid coding and quantitative analysis are necessary and interview time is very limited, such closed type questions are appropriate. In very highly structured approaches, such as the Retrospective Interview Technique, inconsistencies between interviewers may be greatly reduced as the interviewer is simply administering the protocol (Dickson *et al.*, 2003), rather like administering an objective psychological test.

However, the use of high degrees of structure and predominantly closed questions can present a major danger because of the impositional potential of this approach. As Dillon (1997, p. 120) cautioned:

> The significance is that the questioner who asks closed questions may be specifying categories of thought that are unrepresentative of what respondents think, with the result that respondents confirm our own frame of reference without our even realising it.

This threat will be minimized if the content of the interview guide has been informed by the findings of the exploratory interview phase, and the phrasing of questions adheres to the same criteria as are relevant to the construction of questionnaires (see Chapter 3).

In summary, if auditors engage in active listening, attend to participants, ask appropriate initial and follow-up questions and employ silence skilfully, they will collect relevant, appropriately detailed and trustworthy information in the interviews. This being the case it remains to close the interview.

The closing

In both interview contexts it is important to plan and allocate time for ending the interview as both a business transaction and a social encounter. To achieve an effective closure the ending should be viewed as a stage rather than an event, and be built into the interview guide. The beginning of this closing phase should be marked with an indicator such as 'I'm aware that we only have a few minutes left so could we begin to draw our meeting to a close' (Saunders, 1986). There should also be no doubt when the interview has finally concluded. Examples of concluding remarks would be 'Thanks again for your participation. I hope that things continue to go well for you' or 'Your input has been very helpful and is much appreciated.'

Where a highly focused interview has been conducted there may be little to do but thank participants for their assistance; that is, a *social closure* (Hargie and Dickson, 2004). The inclusion of a social element in closure is not only courteous but also complies with one of the recommendations of Smith and Robertson (1993) for treating all interviewees in a fair and civilized manner. Respondents should leave their interview feeling appreciated. At the end of exploratory interviews, it is important that the interviewer also draws the encounter to a close by creating some coherent sense of the interview. This idea of offering some kind of summary constitutes one aspect of *cognitive closure*. It is a means of seeking agreement from participants that the main themes of the communication have been accurately received and understood. In offering such a summary, participants are afforded an opportunity to dispute or amend the interviewer's perception of what was communicated.

Similarly where personal experiences are explored it is important that participants should not be allowed to leave interviews in any way damaged by the event. For instance, in the case of an internal audit, suppose that when discussing communications with a supervisor, the interviewee discloses an experience of sexual harassment and becomes visibly upset in recounting the incident. What does the interviewer do? Allowing the interviewee to leave the interview in a distressed state would certainly constitute unethical practice (Smith and Robertson, 1993). This type of situation poses clear ethical dilemmas for the interviewer, such as:

- Do you record the incident without comment and if you do, does this imply condonement?
- Do you encourage the employee to report the matter and if you do, is that your role?
- If it is a particularly serious incident, does your assurance of confidentiality preclude you from doing anything about it?

- Will your scheduled interview with that particular supervisor be coloured by this knowledge?

These possibilities illustrate the importance of formulating a very specific ethics and confidentiality policy and including it in the opening of the interview guide.

Some mention should also be made concerning the subsequent use of any information disclosed. During interviews participants are required to respond to a variety of questions posed by interviewers, some relatively factual while others may require deeper levels of self-disclosure. It is possible, as illustrated above, that such disclosure may leave the participant more vulnerable or exposed and quite likely feeling somewhat threatened having made the disclosure. In such circumstances the source of the findings of an audit should not be traceable. Invoking Smith and Robertson's (1993) ethical principles, whereby participants should not be damaged in any way by the experience, and that all information disclosed during an interview should not be misused or used to the detriment of the interviewee, interviewers need to deal with such concerns explicitly, prior to the ending of an interview. Given that such matters are an essential part of the opening phase of interviews, additional reference to them during closure will reinforce the interviewer's desire to assure participants that they will be treated justly and with respect, and that what was agreed will be delivered.

A final aspect of effective closure relates to situations where subsequent follow-up interviews have been scheduled as part of the audit process. It is important to discuss such future links so that participants are clear regarding any future commitments. This may relate both to time and to expectations of the purpose of further interviews and what might be covered with respect to content.

Conducting the interviews, in terms of the opening, body and closing, is therefore not straightforward and certainly involves much more than just 'talking to people'. The preceding section has demonstrated the importance of having appropriate interview guides, and skilled interviewers who can implement them effectively. We now move on to examine issues relating to the recording of interviewee responses.

RECORDING INFORMATION FROM INTERVIEWS

The importance of accurately recording participants' responses cannot be over-emphasized. Indeed, King (1994) recommended that *all* interviews of a qualitative nature should be routinely tape recorded. Recent studies indicate that audio recording and transcription are indeed normal elements of procedure (Bryant, 2006; Quinn and Hargie, 2004; Tourish, 2007b). However, other studies simply talk of 'comments' from participants being analysed (for example, Tourish and Robson, 2003). Tape recording clearly reduces the need to take notes during interviews, a procedure that can be very disruptive to the flow of the interaction. However, if tape recording is adopted then the researcher must take cognizance of the following factors:

1   There must be clear reasons for using a tape recorder. It may be because a complete account of the verbal transaction is required, or that the interviewer is interested in the actual way participants articulate their experiences.
2   Participants must be informed of the reasons for using the recorder, and given a full explanation of why this is being requested, how their communications are to be used, to whom they will be available, to what extent their responses will be identifiable, and when the recordings will be wiped. Issues of confidentiality and anonymity are of considerable importance to participants and should be dealt with at the beginning of the process. They are then in a position to give informed consent or not.
3   Active listening must continue throughout the interview and interviewers should not relax their attention because they know they will have the interview on tape. Audio recordings are not complete accounts of interactions, so interviewers must at all time be vigilant and observant of the wealth of non-verbal messages being communicated.
4   Participants must be offered the opportunity of opting out of a procedure that requires recording, or be able to request that the tape recorder be turned off at any point.
5   There should be a contingency Plan B if the tape recorder fails to operate or where a participant requests that the machine not be used during the interview.
6   Interviewers should be fully familiar with the tape recorder. Technophobes should avoid this medium!

Where tape recording is not possible the auditor must have developed a technique for taking down key words or phrases primarily as memory joggers. Indeed, the practice of routinely taking shorthand notes is useful as there can be no guarantee that the tape recording will be audible. Technology often fails us. Note-taking should be completed in a manner that will not create a tense and distant relationship between participants. It is then imperative that interviewers take time immediately following completion of the interview to reconstruct as much as possible of the content of responses. In this situation there will be implications for the scheduling of interviews in that adequate space must be built into the procedures to allow each interview to be reconstructed prior to any further interviews being conducted. Blind faith in our powers of recall is hazardous. Numerous errors are likely to occur when we rely on memory to reconstruct multiple events.

Downs and Adrian (2004) suggest that an assistant, whose role is purely to take notes as the interview proceeds, could also participate in the interview. The auditor is then free to listen and attend to interviewees and what they have to say. This, of course, has disadvantages. The presence of a second party reduces the likelihood of in-depth interviewee disclosures, adds to costs, and requires additional permission from participants.

ANALYSING INTERVIEW DATA

The purpose of the chapter so far has been to highlight and explore key issues about the interview as an effective audit method. In essence, while interviews have the potential to generate a rich database of valuable information, it is important to consider a range of factors in advance of a communication audit. Whatever form or purpose the interviews take – exploratory or focused – the auditor will want to ensure that this method of investigation produces data that are worthy of the investment of resources (e.g. time and money). Issues such as the nature and purpose of the audit, the interviewers, inter- viewees and the management of interviews need to be well thought through in the planning phase. For example, training for potential interviewers might be an important consideration (Millar and Tracey, 2006).

The interviews undertaken in the audit may produce a large volume of recorded material. The next step in the process is transcription and analysis of the data. The processes involved in analysing qualitative data are now discussed.

The transition from manual to computerized methods

In the past, qualitative researchers had the unenviable task of working with large amounts of data through manual methods. For example, when the tran- scribed interviews were read and theoretical ideas were beginning to form, the transcripts were usually cut up (manually) and separated out into relevant categories or themes (with the help of index cards). This same process applied to all material relevant to the research, such as field notes, memos. As Kelle (1998, p. 5) stated, 'Before the advent of computers, "cut-and-paste" tech- niques were the most widely used methods of organising data material.' When computer-aided analysis programs began to emerge in the 1960s and 1970s, there was reluctance by researchers in the qualitative tradition to accept information technology into their analytic work (Kelle, 1998). While computer programs became 'indispensible' tools for quantitative method- ologists, qualitative researchers regarded such systems as suitable for man- aging numerical not textual data. It took over a decade, and encouragement from experts in the field of research such as Miles and Huberman (1984) and Conrad and Reinarz (1984), before computer software began to be accepted into the field of qualitative research analysis. Now, as Bazeley and Richards (2000, p. 2) have noted 'Qualitative computing has entered the mainstream.' With the advent of computer programs for qualitative data analysis, the 'manual labour of cutting and pasting and retrieving labelled chunks of text is greatly eased by getting the software to do the tasks for you' (Bryman, 2002, p. xix).

Computer software for handling qualitative data is commonly referred to as CAQDAS (*C*omputer-*A*ssisted *Q*ualitative *D*ata *A*nalysis *S*oftware). However, as features of software programs vary so much in terms of inter-face, capacity and applicability, Kelle (1998) warns that analysts need to be informed of the variations before selecting a program for managing unstructured textual data. (A comprehensive review of a range of programs is provided by Prein *et al.*, 1998.)

Considering the range of computer-assisted software that is available, it seemed appropriate to select one as a way of demonstrating how a program might support the analysis of audit data. In this case, Nvivo 7 (N7) (Richards, 2006), has been chosen for the illustrated discussion. Nvivo programs have been devised, remodelled and updated by a team of researchers in Australia over several years. N7, a comprehensive package for managing and analysing qualitative data, offers a range of tools to facilitate the building of themes/ categories through the systematic coding, categorizing, restructuring and reviewing of textual data. The program also allows more complex processes such as model or theory building to be performed (if that is what is required).

Before continuing, it is important to emphasize the following:

- Computerized programs are not designed to *do* the analysis (as some might hope!).
- The analyst interprets the data (does the thinking) and the program 'holds' the interpretations (thinking) throughout the process.
- Nvivo shows a 'bird's eye view' (Bazeley and Richards, 2000) of the textual data and assists with the management of documents.
- Coding of data in Nvivo is used to 'identify topics, themes or issues, and bring together data segments where these occur' (Bazeley and Richards, 2000, p. 23).
- The stages of analysis (previously carried out manually as noted above) can be achieved through the different functions/tools of the program that are activated by the click of a mouse.
- All information stored as a result of coding can be instantly retrieved and read on screen or printed out.
- Regardless of the choice of methodology, all software programs will facilitate basic coding.
- Most software programs are supported with tutorials and manuals for those who wish to increase their knowledge and understanding of how a program works.

Analysing the interview data involves three sequential steps.

Step 1: Become familiar with the interview data

The first stage is for the auditor to become very familiar with the interview material collected. The process of familiarity can be enhanced when interviews and transcriptions are facilitated by the same person (Tracey, 2006). Undertaking both tasks ensures that the data are 'heard' twice, a useful starting point for the analysis. Alternatively, the transcripts can be read and re-read by the analyst. Downs and Adrian (2004) make the point that if the audit is conducted through a team effort then all written material – transcripts, notes and memos – should be available to all other members of the team. The advantage of being familiar with interview material is that some ideas or perceptions of what is going on in the data may have begun to emerge. To keep track of any thoughts and ideas that are occurring, Glaser's (1978) prime rule of 'stop and memo' comes to mind. In the words of Wengraf (2001, p. 211), 'When you are transcribing, when you are coding, when you are sorting, when you are writing up, when you are reading contextual literature', memoing, 'is very important'. In N7, memos can be written and stored like any other document, in the memos folder.

By the time the interview documents are imported into the selected software program, the audit analyst is ready to begin the task of coding the data. In Step 2, coding and categorizing of the data is underway.

Step 2: Search for categories in the interview data

An auditor (or members of the audit team) will want to examine a set of interviews to establish the main themes and categories that are contained in the data through a systematic 'coding system'. The golden rule about basic coding is that it involves the meticulous process of reading the data line by line, sentence by sentence and breaking down or 'fracturing' the data into meaningful chunks (Strauss and Corbin, 1998).

The containers for coding in Nvivo are described as *nodes* (Bazeley and Richards, 2000). Themes or categories are allocated a node title that is representative of the meaning implied by the participants. When a section of data is coded, free-standing nodes are created as new themes/categories emerge in the process and are stored in the nodes folder. The conceptual name for the node can be adopted directly from the text ['in-vivo coding'] or generated through the analyst's own theoretical ideas. As each interview is analysed, the existing nodes are visible on screen, allowing the analyst to conveniently 'code-on' from one interview to the next. Nodes can be easily retrieved and the content explored in N7. The convenience of coding and retrieving data can only be witnessed by first hand use of the program.

Gradually, a 'picture' of data emerges as the analysis progresses. Wengraf

(2001), however, reminds us that 'coding systems' need to be modified and revised and that while caution is needed, 'qualitative-data-processing packages make this process of creative revision feasible' (p. 227). The auditor also needs to guard against the accusation that a particular category of response is simply one idiosyncratic respondent rather than a definite theme.

Towards the end of the first stage of coding, a number of important steps will have been undertaken and completed by the auditor or audit team:

1   Transcripts will be coded into nodes that are representative of the themes or categories embedded in the interviews. Guidelines for theme identification are outlined in the example of an audit discussed in Chapter 15.
2   The themes or categories that are supported with extracts from a large range of interviews will be apparent. In some cases the salience of themes is represented by the frequency with which they occur in transcripts (see for example, Lloyd and Varey, 2003; Tourish and Robson, 2003).
3   The exact number of categories that emerge at this stage may depend on the amount of raw textual data that has been generated. It is difficult to be precise about what this number should be, but more than 10 begins to raise doubts about the reliability and comprehensibility of the system, and too few (say 2/3) is simply too crude to facilitate improved understanding and insight.

Step 3: Make thematic connections within and between categories

As interviews from the communication audit are coded and connections begin to form, the data are shaped into hierarchical families of categories and sub-categories known in Nvivo as 'trees' (stored in the trees folder). As relationships unfold in the analytic process, trees can be re-shaped and re-structured. However, an open mind is essential if an adequate system of categories and linked themes is to evolve. Determining relationships between categories and sub-categories can be achieved by asking pertinent questions ('What connects the experiences of employees interviewed as part of this audit?'), examining responses (look across all employee responses to interview questions rather than being confined to responses to single questions), or by employing a model to gain a perspective on the data (for example, the Paradigm Model, Strauss and Corbin, 1990, 1998). The main aim at this stage of the analytic process is to think about relationships between sub-categories and their categories, and to look for evidence that themes are supported by as large a range of interviewees as possible. Downs and Adrian (2004) offer some useful considerations for the interpretation phase of the process and alert the reader to the pitfalls that can occur. It seems that 'continuous communication' and an integration of ideas through open discussion (with triangulation as a safety mechanism) seem to be the essential ingredients that will ward off contaminators such as 'groupthink'.

Some of the valuable tools in N7 that might assist with interpretations and perhaps contribute to more open and fruitful team discussions are the Modeler and Report summaries. For example, with the use of the Modeler, visual models of the data can be created and retained on the screen or printed off if required. The availability of a concrete visual map of the data allows auditors to explore, discuss and comment on the connections/relationships in an open forum. Additionally, in N7, reports of the data analysis can be readily requested and accessed. For example, a Node Summary Report would provide a list of nodes that emerged in the analysis and an account of the number of times that data were coded to each node. This would provide an overview of the themes that had occurred more than others. In particular, a Coding Comparison Report would allow auditors to check for consistency in coding across team members, a common element in the current manual analytic protocol (Robson and Tourish, 2005; Tourish and Robson, 2003). These easy to access Coding Comparison Reports may fit with what King (1994) calls 'quasi-statistical approaches' where the frequency of themes is recorded. Frequency data can be tested statistically to establish differences between groups or estimate inter-auditor agreement. In the final audit report, statistical evidence can help to provide, at a glance, an estimate of the level of support for categories. As Downs and Adrian (2004, p. 249), noted, 'key statistical data will stand out more if they are presented using some kind of graphic display'. However, if obtaining optimum meaning is the goal, a combination of statistical findings with the words, phrases, and intonations of interviewee responses is preferable.

REPORTING THE FINDINGS

The final task confronting the auditor is to present the findings in a concise but comprehensive form (see Chapter 10 for a full discussion of this issue). A well structured, clearly presented account that both summarizes and provides evidence to support the main themes is more likely to be read and acted on. There are various methods available for reporting findings based on textual data, ranging from paraphrasing respondents' expressions to reporting considerable amounts of text verbatim. However, two important messages regarding the writing and presentation of a final audit report are worth noting. Downs and Adrian's (2004) advice is, 'Manage the Message' in terms of presentation, and if the report is to make an impact then initial impressions are highly salient. Clearly, although it is the final step in the process, writing up the final audit report is a critical part of the process (see Chapter 10). In general, the report of findings should include the following:

- A summary of the main and significant themes in the text.
- Inclusion of extracts from the interviews in the form of illustrative quotes that support the summary of themes.
- A clear and coherent 'story' easily followed by the reader and well evidenced at all points. It may be useful to include larger extracts from selected interviews in addition to smaller chunks alluded to above. The inclusion of such extracts guards against accusations of prejudice and bias, which are more likely when reports are presented solely as paraphrased auditor summaries.
- Data should be reported 'in a descriptive, non-evaluative way' (Downs and Adrian, 2004, p. 249).

Finally, it is important to address concerns experienced by interviewees relating to identification and potential vulnerability. Where their exact words are presented as findings there is the possibility of them being traced as the source. If assurances were provided at the commencement of the process then it is incumbent on the auditor to act accordingly; that is, ethically. In order to ensure anonymity the auditor may be required to omit any details that could be used to trace the identity of an interviewee.

CONCLUSION

This chapter has presented the key stages in the audit interview process. Evidence has been drawn from a range of sources that document a widening variety of qualitative research techniques, including an increasing diversity of interviewing approaches. The status of the interview as a method of conducting communication audits has been supported through the transfer of knowledge and skills from organizational and other related contexts. The interview approach recognizes the richness and authenticity of stories and narratives as a major source of information about organizations. Auditors must have the ability to listen to, understand, analyse and report accurately and sensitively what they are told by interviewees.

Chapter 5

The focus group approach

David Dickson

INTRODUCTION

The success of any communication audit is ultimately governed by the nature, quality and utility of the information that it generates. These data can be obtained in a variety of ways and take different forms. They can be expressed in numbers that represent, for example, how often communication has taken place, how much information has been received from a particular source, or alternatively how it has been judged and evaluated with respect, for instance, to effectiveness. As discussed in Chapter 3, surveys, as a well-established technique for auditing communication, are a common means of gathering material of this type. Indeed, the term 'audit' tends to reflexively trigger images of this type of activity leading to the collection and processing of sets of figures. But audit data can also be non-numeric, captured in the actual words and forms of expression of those whose views and opinions are sought. The value of such qualitative material has been highlighted as part of the auditing process (Downs and Adrian, 2004; Tourish and Hargie, 1996b).

Interviews are an investigative technique associated with generating data in the form of text. The focus group can be thought of as a type of group interview (Freeman, 2006) although this should not be mistaken for merely conducting a sequence of one-to-one interviews involving the facilitator or moderator and each of the participants in turn (Hartman, 2004). Rather, eliciting opinions and points of view through encouraging interaction among members is a unique dimension of the focus group (Webb and Kevern, 2001). Indeed, Boddy (2005) argued that the term 'focus group discussion', rather than 'interview' better captures this essential ingredient, although the latter is the more common nomenclature. In practice, a focus group involves a small number of participants who share certain characteristics of relevance to the research and meet with a facilitator to discuss in some depth a topic, or narrow range of topics, of interest to both parties. The nature of the information created by focus groups is a prime consideration in their use. It affords the researcher profound insights into the meanings and ways of understanding which members of the group bring to their experiences of the issues, events or circumstances forming the substance to the research (Lunt and Livingstone, 1996). Furthermore, by exposing the actual interactive processes at work in the negotiation and joint creation of meaning during the discussion, the researcher can begin to tap into the mechanisms through which, for instance, shared social realities are established in everyday situations (Zorn *et al.*, 2006). As such, focus groups are capable of providing a richness of knowledge that cannot be matched by, for instance, surveys. They serve a different function. Those who have failed to appreciate this fundamental fact have ended up misusing focus groups as a quicker and easier way of collecting surface information, generalizable to larger populations, about the prevalence of habits, practices and points of view. This type of malpractice is one reason why focus group research has acquired a dubious reputation in some quarters and borne the brunt of some barbed criticism (Gaber, 1996).

CHARACTERISTICS OF FOCUS GROUPS

Focus groups are defined by Zorn *et al.* (2006, p. 116) as:

> small groups of people (usually 6–12 participants) who are similar on some demographic dimension (e.g. age or social role) and who are brought together for the purpose of investigating participants' views on a particular issue. Typically, a moderator guides the discussion by focusing participants' attention on various issues related to the topic. Participants respond to both the moderator's questions and other participants' responses.

They are generally regarded as 'a useful tool in understanding what people do and how they think, feel and make decisions' (Beyer, 2008, p. 32). Several identifying features have also been teased out by Millward (2006) and Stewart *et al.* (2007), among others. Accordingly, focus groups:

* serve the purpose of illuminating the experiences, understandings and perspectives of participants
* are held at the behest of a facilitator who may also be part of a research team
* have the topic for consideration initiated by a facilitator whose role it is to stimulate associated discussion
* typically involve recording the discussion in some form to provide a permanent record for subsequent analysis
* often have findings subsequently documented in a report.

In broader terms, key constituents can be captured in several pivotal criteria along lines suggested by Morgan (1998) and Litosseliti (2003). As such, focus groups are:

1   *A way of doing research to collect qualitative data.* The key purpose of the exercise is to produce information primarily to satisfy the needs of the researcher. This sets the focus group apart from other types of group involvement established to satisfy the needs of the participants (e.g. self-help groups, group therapy).

2   *A lens for directing attention onto a narrow topic or issue.* An important starting point is in the framing of a well-defined and clearly delineated purpose. It is one of the responsibilities of the group facilitator to ensure that the discussion does not overspill the topic boundaries so specified, but to do so in a way that does not place an uncompromising straight-jacket on the talk or erode its general informality. Focus groups are also focused in the sense that a considerable amount of information can be gathered in a relatively short, condensed period of time.

3   *A method of generating research data through relatively informal group discussion.* Indeed, Webb and Kevern (2001, p. 800) observed that 'all definitions of focus groups centre on the use of interaction among participants as a way of accessing data that would not emerge if other methods were used'. Unlike the individual interview, the emphasis is not just on interaction between the interviewer and the respondent, but rather on the interchanges among the participants as they compare, debate, challenge or support, but ultimately extend, the personal meanings and experiences that each contributes as they explore the topic.

In addition to experiences, attitudes or opinions forming the content of talk, focus groups offer data of a different kind, of communication-as-process, that may be of interest to the researcher. As noted by Lunt and Livingstone (1996, p. 85) the focus group is a social event in its own right, which may involve those present engaging in the sort of social tasks that form part of routine life. They explained how we can think of what happens during the discussion as, 'a simulation of these routine but relatively inaccessible communication contexts that can help us discover the processes by which meaning is socially constructed through everyday talk'. Likewise, Zorn *et al.* (2006, p. 121) drew attention to the capacity of focus groups to simulate 'naturalistic meaning construction processes'. This dimension, of course, may well be of interest when seeking insights into how communication functions in organizations as part of the auditing task, although in practice attention has been more commonly paid to attitudes and opinions as products of interaction (i.e. to content) rather than to interactive processes per se (e.g. Dickson and Hargie, 2006; Tourish and Hargie, 1996b).

Several additional characteristics of focus groups are mentioned by Vaughn *et al.* (1996). They make the important point that it should not be part of the overall intention to obtain data with a view to making firm generalizations to broader populations. This issue will be returned to shortly in the discussion of the focus group as qualitative research.

Other information-gathering procedures that, while sharing common-alities, have been contrasted with focus groups, include the nominal group technique, the Delphi technique, leaderless discussion groups, brainstorming and synectics (Boddy, 2005; Stewart *et al.*, 2007). Points of demarcation hinge on, in the case of the focus group, an emphasis on the primacy of free discus-sion among participants, a person recognizably in the role of moderator or facilitator, and the research-driven, group-generated nature of the informa-tion created.

BACKGROUND TO FOCUS GROUP APPLICATIONS

The focus group, as a social science research technique, is now well estab-lished. Its origins have been traced back to the early work of Bogardus (1926), although they are more commonly attributed to that of Robert Merton and colleagues at the Bureau of Applied Social Research, Columbia University. In the early 1940s, they made use of the technique to gauge reactions to wartime radio broadcasts. Since then it has evolved through growth and development in market research settings to its present popularity, gained particularly over the past two decades across a range of areas of application (Kidd and Parshall, 2000; Morgan, 1998; Puchta and Potter, 2004). These include academic enquiry, market research, advertising, health-care and family planning, political campaigns, training evaluation, pro-gramme and campaign assessment, and organizational research (Brooks, 2002; Quible, 1998). The contribution of the focus group to improving cor-porate communication is a more recent application. Here it can be utilized in various ways and at different stages of the auditing process (Downs and Adrian, 2004) to:

• make an initial assessment and diagnosis of difficulty
• provide a preparatory stage to the subsequent formulation of a survey
• help interpret findings from surveys or other quantitative sources
• establish participants' anticipatory reactions to proposed change
• evaluate new programmes and procedures once they are put in place.

As a mark of the growth of interest in the technique it was estimated that by the late 1980s some 700 specialized facilities for conducting focus groups were available (Goldman and McDonald, 1987). While the vast majority of these were in the USA, Fletcher (1995) observed the number in the UK to be growing rapidly. Furthermore, in addition to an estimated 200,000 market research group interviews in the USA costing some $160 million per annum

(Bristol and Fern, 2003), it was reckoned by Morgan (1997) that over 100 articles a year featuring this technique could be found in academic journals alone. A review by the present author in 2007 using the search engine 'ProQuest' to trawl for focus group journal articles in business and management unearthed over 900 'hits'. Similarly, a search of the International Bibliography of the Social Sciences, together with PsychINFO, using Ovid Online with focus groups as the keyword, unearthed over 500 hits for journal articles in 2006. The publication of key texts (e.g. Greenbaum, 2000; Krueger and Casey, 2000; Morgan, 1998; Puchta and Potter, 2004; Stewart *et al.*, 2007) represents further significant benchmarks in the establishment of the approach. Increasingly, the focus group is also becoming not only the method but also the subject of investigation. An empirical basis for decision making about the efficacy of the technique, and how best to operationalize it, is emerging to complement the traditional reliance on the experience and intuition of practitioners (Fahy, 2006; Kidd and Parshall, 2000; Stokes and Bergin, 2006).

Reasons for this burgeoning interest in the focus group are multifarious and include:

- a well-established pedigree in market research circles
- a flexibility that makes it readily adaptable to academic tasks
- an increasing acceptance of qualitative research perspectives in tracts of the social sciences with a tradition of scepticism about this methodology
- generating data that differ in nature from those of one-to-one interviews, coupled with the recognition that, for certain topics, no acceptable quantitative research alternative may be available
- a belief, in some quarters, of being cheaper and quicker than other methods such as surveys. This belief is contested, nevertheless, being labelled by Barbour (2005, p. 745) as: 'One of the common myths surrounding the use of focus groups.' In any case, such a criterion should not be the prime consideration in making decisions about methods. Furthermore, beliefs such as these have led to cases of focus groups being used injudiciously and consequently disparaged for being 'cheap and nasty'.

While traditionally focus groups have involved participants in face-to-face discussion, telephone-mediated variants have been described by Greenbaum (1998) and used by White and Thomson (1995) to explore aspects of family physicians' contacts with their external publics. The internet has opened up a whole new set of focus-group possibilities, the most common of which are synchronous, or 'real-time', and asynchronous variants (Sweet, 2001). While in both cases groups are 'virtual' (i.e. members never physically come together), in the case of the former, participants are at least online at the same time. Comparable findings were reported by Roy *et al.* (2006) when 'real' and online synchronous groups were used to explore factors that facilitated and inhibited healthy weight maintenance among young adults. Fahy (2006) also reported broad consistencies in actual patterns of interaction during face-to-face and online group discussions (although not specifically in a focus group context). Nevertheless, a relative lack of negative socio-emotional engagement typified the latter medium.

It would be misguided to assume that the mechanics of operating a traditional focus group (which will be discussed later in the chapter) can be successfully transferred as they stand to the virtual environment. Issues raised by the computer-mediated environment together with adaptations to be considered, including ways of creating rapport, are discussed by such as Sweet (2001) and O'Connor and Madge (2003), both useful sources of further information for those considering online applications. In addition to the online medium, other recent developments in focus group deployment include involving natural groups or communities, and holding sessions in familiar environments such as homes or work sites (Stewart *et al.*, 2007).

USES OF FOCUS GROUPS

Focus groups can be configured in three contrasting patterns of information-gathering described by Morgan (1997) and Millward (2006). They can be deployed in a complementary arrangement with several other techniques, serve in a subsidiary role to the main information-gathering instrument, or be used as the sole approach to exploration.

First, they can be included as one of a number of investigatory techniques in a multimethod strategy in which each contributes to the overall richness of the data gathered. It has been argued that this approach maximizes the potential of the focus group and furnishes a fuller understanding of the topic than could be gleaned from the technique on its own (Agar and McDonald, 1995). The strategy has also been commented on favourably with specific reference to auditing communication (Downs and Adrian, 2004). Triangulation, as a well-established research protocol, is based on bringing several methods to bear on an issue (Cohen and Manion, 1980). By illuminating the subject from more than one vantage point, its textured richness and complexity can be captured in greater detail. In so doing, each technique can be used as a form of validation of the others. In an investigation conducted by Dickson *et al.* (2004), focus groups were used alongside in-depth interviews and a communication audit questionnaire to investigate relationships, with particular emphasis on potential sectarian negativity, among the workforce of a large private sector organization in Northern Ireland. Likewise, in the commissioning of an audit on external communication, for instance, there may be distinct advantage in cross-referencing (a) what sales staff say they do when dealing with customers, as represented by self-report data, (b) the more insightful meanings that they attach to their experiences as elicited by focus groups, and (c) actual behaviour, together with levels of displayed interpersonal skill, revealed by observational techniques such as videotape analysis or mystery shoppers.

Second, focus groups can be included in a subsidiary role to another information-gathering technique that carries the burden of the data generation. Employed in this way, they can feature during the exploratory stage of a project in a relatively uncharted area as a source of initial ideas and hypotheses, to be subsequently investigated by other means. Many regard focus groups as giving of their best when put to use in this exploratory role (Hartman, 2004; Stokes and Bergin, 2006). Indeed, this was the primary purpose that Merton envisaged for them back in the early days: 'for us, qualitative focused group-interviews were taken as a source of new ideas and hypotheses, not as demonstrated findings with regard to the extent and distribution of the provisionally identified qualitative patterns of response' (Merton, 1987, p. 558). Additionally, when included during the initial phases of a study they can be employed to obtain background information, identify issues, and perhaps locate problems or matters of concern, to be followed up with a more extensive survey of a larger sample of respondents. As little was known about the issue, Herington *et al.* (2005) selected the focus group as the method of choice in their exploratory study of the strength of relationships between the firm and its employees, from the latter's perspective, in a sample of medium to large regional and national Australian companies.

Commencing a communication audit with an initial focus-group stage can help to establish how (and why) channels and modes of communication within the organization, and between it and its external publics, are perceived and utilized by different sections of the workforce or groups of service users and customers. Additional advantages of the preliminary use of focus groups are not only that topics of relevance can be more precisely targeted in subsequent investigation, but that specific forms of expression peculiar to those groups can be reflected in the framing of questions when designing the subsequent questionnaire (Vaughn *et al.*, 1996).

An alternative follow-up arrangement involving the focus group in a secondary role, switches attention to the other end of the investigator process. Here findings emerging from the major observation-based or, perhaps, survey-based part of the audit are examined in greater detail. The researcher may be keen to find out why particular patterns of communication observed on videotape are perpetuated, or why discrepancies emerged between the evaluations of certain modes of communication by different groups of staff. According to Morgan (1998) there is always room for a focus group perspective when an understanding of diversity is sought. Focus groups are a useful way of tapping the actual meanings that participants attach to obtained observational or questionnaire responses.

Third, the researcher may rely on the focus group on its own as the technique of choice. Caution has been advocated, though, in considering this 'stand-alone' option (Downs and Adrian, 2004; Kidd and Parshall, 2000). Care must be taken to ensure that the strategy is congruent with the goals of the investigation. As mentioned, the strength of focus groups lies in their ability to uncover the meanings, experiences and attitudes of participants relating to the subject or event at issue. Estimating how often staff in the organization use email or whether members receive sufficient information about the company, concerns typically addressed by communication auditing protocols, is essentially the forte of more quantitative procedures.

PHILOSOPHICAL ISSUES

Focus groups are firmly sited within the broad qualitative research tradition (Hartman, 2004) while refusing to pay particular allegiance to any specific instantiation, be it grounded theory, phenomenology or ethnography (Kidd and Parshall, 2000). Any attempt at a comprehensive account of the onto-logical, epistemological or axiological undergirdings of the qualitative approach to thinking about and doing research lies well outside the remit of this chapter. Nevertheless, a proper appreciation of the focus group, its uses and abuses, requires some level of acknowledgement of this background. Qualitative research defies a simple, universally accepted definition. For our purposes, though, it can be thought of along lines suggested by Denzin and Lincoln (2005, p. 3), as involving 'an interpretive, naturalistic approach to the world. This means that qualitative researchers study things in their natural settings, attempting to make sense of, or interpret, phenomena in terms of the meanings people bring to them.' In this sense qualitative research is juxta-posed with quantitative investigation.

Classically, quantitative research derives its inspiration from the natural sciences. Grix (2004) distilled its defining attributes to include the quest to identify variables and concepts representing phenomena of interest that can be isolated, operationalized and measured, thereby revealing patterns among them, unearthing cause–effect relationships, and enabling predictions to be made, hypotheses tested and theories developed. Five key points of demarca-tion between the qualitative and quantitative traditions have been itemized by Denzin and Lincoln (2005). These are:

1   *Positivism.* Quantitative researchers readily embrace a positivistic stance, whose *raison d'être* is the discovery of absolute truths about objective phenomena in the world that have an independent, detached reality. Emphasis is placed on the accurate measurement of objective phenom-ena in an independent, value-free way, thereby enabling firm cause–effect relationships to be established and generalized beyond the immediate confines of the enquiry in the form of steadfast, universal laws. By

contrast, the position of qualitative enquiry is that the phenomenon that is to be studied is essentially subjective and socially constructed. Here the nature of the research process is, through interpretation, to unravel the meanings and understandings that participants bestow on their experiences.

2 *Postmodernism*. While quantitative researchers tend to adopt fixed positions on the correct approach to investigation leading to the one correct outcome, many of those working in the qualitative tradition are quite comfortable with postmodern ideas that are accepting of alternative, but equally valid, methods that unearth contrasting, but equally legitimate, narratives.

3 *The participants' perspective*. Qualitative research places the researcher in an altogether different and more egalitarian relationship with the participant whose role is elevated from that of passive 'subject' and whose perspective becomes the unavoidable object of enquiry. As a corollary, the 'gathering of non-numeric data is deemed to be desirable within this paradigm because it frees researchers to explore, and be sensitive to, the multiple interpretations and meanings which may be placed upon thoughts and behaviour when viewed in context' (Henwood and Pidgeon, 1995, pp. 115–116). This is not to say that qualitative researchers eschew all attempts at quantification. Some present their findings using numbers, but they tend to be less seduced by inferential statistics, avoiding the typically complex, multivariate analytical procedures that have become the hallmark of their quantitative counterparts.

4 *Contextual constraints*. Those conducting a qualitative study are more cognizant of the exiguities of everyday life impinging on participants and their relationship with the researcher. Qualitative research tends to be idiographic rather than nomothetic in orientation, although there is no logical requirement that it must be so (Smith *et al.*, 1995). Idiographic investigation is directed at an intensive understanding of the individual and the particular, considered in its own terms. Nomothetic research, by contrast, operates at the level of the collective, with individual data sacrificed to the group statistic in deriving universal laws. Ironically, such laws may afford little depth of understanding of any specific individual or case. Furthermore, qualitative research and focus group applications tend to produce data that are emic rather than etic, drawing on the distinction made by Kippendorf (1980). Emic data emerge in 'natural' form in the sorts of uncontrived situations where they are normally found. Etic information, on the other hand, is shaped by the impositions of the researcher and his/her views of the situation. While both are 'pure types', data in the form of respondents expressing their views and preferences in their own language are more emic than those collected, for example, by ticking boxes in a researcher's questionnaire.

5 *Gathering rich data.* Qualitative researchers place greater value on the richness of the accounts garnered from participants.

Despite the focus group being firmly encamped amid qualitative methods, some researchers who have made use of it have been accused of approaching the task with essentially positivist mindsets. Freeman (2006) distinguished between realist and constructionist, and Millward (2006) between essentialist and constructionist, perspectives. Unlike constructionists, realists/essentialists:

- tacitly assume that focus group findings inform a single external, objective reality
- are interested in the individual contributions of participants in analysing qualitative data and presenting results
- look for consensual positions on issues
- spend little time illuminating the group processes through which attitudinal positions or constructed histories are shaped by those present
- derive their data exclusively from the content of talk.

Tourish and Hargie (1996b) made a cogent appeal for a greater use of qualitative research in conducting communication audits. While this should be in a complementary role to quantification, they argued that there is a need to permit staff within organizations to freely and directly express, in their own terms, their views and opinions on the communicative aspects of their work, 'rather than invariably [seeking] to reduce them to quantitative categories' (p. 40).

To what extent, though, can qualitative and quantitative research co-exist? The response depends on whether an epistemological or a merely technical question is being posed. As expounded by Bryman (1988) the epistemological version of the qualitative/quantitative debate leads inextricably to profound issues of the fundamental nature of social science, the ontology of its subject matter, how enquiry should be pursued and what counts as valid knowledge. At this level, the two positions tend to be dialectically cast as paradigms in irreconcilable opposition. Nevertheless, many communication scholars have increasingly argued that the assumption of paradigmatic incommensurability between orientations towards research (such as positivism versus social constructionism) has been overstated, and that a judicious blend of elements drawn from both is more likely to illuminate the phenomenon under investigation. Those interested in exploring this issue further will find much stimulating debate from many of the contributors to Corman and Poole's (2000) edited text on organizational communication, devoted largely to this issue. Those who address the qualitative/quantitative bifurcation in more technical terms, on the other hand, are prepared to make choices between qualitative and quantitative techniques on largely pragmatic rather than epistemological/

ontological grounds. As such, investigatory procedures selected, once stripped of possible doctrinal baggage, are those felt best suited to the particular research issue at hand. If need be, this may result in the utilization of a judicious combination of qualitative and quantitative procedures, with a suspension of the dialectic around fundamental assumptions underpinning both. Many researchers use focus groups in this complementary way, as we have already seen in the section dealing with uses of focus groups, and argue the advantages of so doing (Manfredi *et al.*, 1997).

CONDUCTING FOCUS GROUPS

Many publications offer detailed guidance on the 'how-to' aspects of organizing and operating focus group research (e.g. Greenbaum, 2000; Krueger, 1998a, 1998b; Krueger and Casey, 2000; Litosseliti, 2003; Morgan, 1998; Puchta and Potter, 2004; Stewart *et al.*, 2007). These sources will be drawn on extensively in this section. It should be noted, however, at the outset that while systematic enquiry into the technique and its efficacy is increasing (e.g. Dickson *et al.*, 2003; Fahy, 2006) a large proportion of the received wisdom on how best to make use of focus groups is still epistemologically sourced from the experiences and assumptions of practitioners (e.g. Breen, 2006). Prescriptions are often buttressed by theory and research imported from cognate areas including small group dynamics and interpersonal communication.

Planning and preparation

For Wilkinson (2003) sound preparation is one of the pillars of a successful focus group research application. The old adage 'well begun is half done' is not unique, of course, to this type of study. It is important that a vision of the project in its entirety be framed from early on (Morgan and Scannell, 1998). There are a range of points to consider at the outset, including:

- What are the questions that the project seeks to answer?
- Are focus groups the most suitable approach?
- Who should be included as participants?
- How can they be recruited?
- How many will be required?
- How can the group interviews be conducted to best effect?
- Where will discussions be held?
- How should they be recorded?
- What is to be done with the recordings once they are made?
- How detailed does the final report have to be?
- How long will the audit take?

What are the objectives of the research?

Downs and Adrian (2004), in discussing focus group protocols in auditing communications, asserted that the first move should be 'to analyze your objectives and identify the organizational issues that you wish to understand more thoroughly. Everything flows from this initial statement' (p. 216). The essential purpose of focus group research has already been explained but deserves repeating. It is basically to illuminate the meanings and interpretations that others place on their experiences: to appreciate how they make sense of the communication systems and processes of the organization together with their functions and utilizations. Why does a particular group of junior managers, let's say, find weekly meetings of little benefit, according to the questionnaires that they have completed, when most other staff generally appreciate this channel of communication? Focus group research offers a path to get 'inside' the shared experiences of others and to begin to appreciate events from their perspective.

If the intention, on the other hand, is to make convenient use of the focus group as an easier or quicker way of gathering information, the strategy needs serious reconsideration. The chances are that the details garnered will not really enable the sorts of questions posed to be conclusively answered. That apart, while the information-gathering stage of focus group research can be completed relatively quickly, subsequent transcription and analysis, if thorough, can be much more time-consuming than other techniques, such as small-scale surveys (Morgan, 1998). The point though is that cost should not be the primary concern. Ensuring the method is fit for purpose is much more important.

Who should be involved in the audit?

The four main stakeholders in the typical focus group audit are the commissioning organization, the research team, the moderator (who may or may not be an integral part of the team), and the participants. Deciding on whether the research should be conducted 'in-house', by employees of the organization such as the personnel department, or bought in from outside, is one of the first steps to be taken. Apart from issues of expertise, having the audit carried out by a section of the company can introduce the perception (if not the reality) of a 'political agenda' that may seriously compromise the enquiry and the extent to which employees are prepared to contribute fully and openly (Greenbaum, 1994). Employees may be reluctant to speak their minds on company policy, practice or personnel if they know that what they say in the focus group discussion will be ascribable to them personally and brought to the attention of management (Ettorre, 1997).

Selecting a suitable moderator is regarded by Downs and Adrian (2004) as one of the most crucial decisions to be taken during planning. The depth of group discussion and the richness of the information yielded ultimately depends on the competencies of this pivotal individual. In addition to the more specialized skills of guiding group discussion, the moderator must be acceptable to the participants, be familiar with the auditing process, have a firm grasp of the issues to be explored, and be cognizant of the organizational background to the particular investigation. The moderator should also contribute to the preparation of the interview guide for the focus group session. Additionally this person usually has a central part to play in the subsequent analysis of the data. Depending on the expertise and skill mix of the commissioned research team, it may be sensible to buy in the services of a moderator with acknowledged expertise who can be briefed on the background to the particular audit.

Matters to do with identifying participants are also part of planning, but for convenience these will be discussed, together with those of recruitment, as the next stage of conducting focus group research.

Where should the sessions be conducted?

The two most telling considerations in relation to location are, first, convenience for participants (Breen, 2006) and, second, comfort (Millward, 2006). Conducive focus group facilities can often be hired and are used extensively by market researchers. They typically offer an appropriately sized room with good acoustics, furnished with a table and suitable chairs, together with an adjoining observation room beyond a one-way mirror. Resources for providing refreshments are an additional factor, given that sessions may last from 1 to 2 hours.

The observation room can be used by other members of the research team and, if necessary, messages passed to the moderator to pursue issues raised during the discussion. CCTV equipment is an acceptable substitute for the lack of a one-way mirror, permitting the interaction to be monitored from outside the conference room. Recording equipment is also required. While audio-recording is the most common, video facilities enable non-verbal detail also to be included in any subsequent analysis. Furthermore, it can be easier, on occasion, to identify the speaker from video, especially during instances of overtalk (Kidd and Parshall, 2000). Clear and distinct sound quality, though, is more important than visuals. This means using a room with good acoustics and quality equipment. The microphone has been described as the most important tool of all (Krueger, 1998c) and having more than one strategically placed may be a requirement, especially with larger groups. Indeed, operating several recording machines, in crucial cases, is a hedge against gremlins spoiling the whole enterprise.

Whilst customized facilities have distinct advantages, they are far from essential. Most focus groups are carried out in lesser surroundings. Indeed a case has been made, particularly by those from a constructionist background interested in group process aspects of the discussion, for organizing the focus group where participants are normally found, whether it be in the workplace, or their own homes (Kitzinger, 1994).

How should the focus group be organized?

Drawing up the moderator guide is a further planning task. This contributes a basic template for the session, specifying topics, framing possibly questions, and affording some degree of commonality across groups, where this is looked on as being important. For the most part, though, the moderator guide should not be thought of as a tightly prescribed set of specific primary and secondary questions that must be posed verbatim and adhered to religiously. It is less like a questionnaire in this sense and more a reasonably relaxed framework for containing the discussion. What attracts many researchers to focus groups in the first place is that they 'allow people to give their views in their own way and in their own words' (Puchta and Potter, 2004, p. 47). In addition to specifying topics and/or questions for the session, the guide should earmark introductory procedures, cater for ways of getting the group relaxed in the situation and with one other, as well as including steps for bringing the discussion to an end (Vaughn *et al.*, 1996; Greenbaum, 1998).

Anticipating analysis

The output of focus groups is talk (together possibly with non-verbal communication, if this has been collected). A final part of planning covers what to do with this material. During most discussions the moderator, or an observer, will keep notes on what takes place. If the purpose of the focus group is simply to tune into the typical terms and forms of expression used by a particular group when talking about a topic in their everyday language, for instance in preparation for carrying out a survey, it may be possible to achieve this simply by relying on recall of the discussion, bolstered by these field notes. Anything more than this most basic processing requires recording of the discussion on audio or videotape for subsequent transcription and more systematic analysis.

Identifying and recruiting participants

Identifying participants includes the tasks of deciding who best to include and how many to select. As far as the first is concerned, the aim is to involve those who have the most pertinent information to offer and are prepared to do so. Given that the object of the exercise is not to generate findings that are generalizable to broad populations, any attempt at scientific sampling is unnecessary. Sampling is done instead on theoretical grounds (Millward,

2006). A systematic strategy is often applied, particularly by investigators taking a realist/essentialist perspective, in order to segment the overall collective into categories that are internally cohesive in respect of some characteristic that is conceptually significant to the audit. Categories should be distinguished from each other on these terms. For example, in the case of an internal communication audit, it may make sense to initially stratify the workforce from junior shop-floor staff through to senior management. Morgan and Scannell (1998) cautioned that it is almost always unwise to combine workers and supervisory staff in a single focus group. Existing group dynamics and embedded relationships make it unlikely that either of these groups would be completely frank and open with their views in the presence of the other. It may also be desirable, depending on the purpose and background to the investigation, to group staff that work together on some distinct task, or perhaps share a geographical location. According to the logic of segmentation, the rule of thumb is to divide up the collective in such a way as to create homogeneity within but heterogeneity between groupings (Morgan, 1997). Initial screening of recruits may be necessary to ensure that they satisfy these criteria. That said, there should still be sufficient gradation of perspective on the topic within groups to fuel discussion and debate (Krueger and Casey, 2000).

Discussions are conducted in groups of from six to 12 members (Millward, 2006) although Herington *et al.* (2005) referred to mini-focus groups of from four to seven participants that were used in their study of relationships between the firm and its employees. Discussions usually last from 1 to 2 hours. Most audits require from three to four focus groups, the principle being that group discussions are continued until information saturation is reached, with no new material forthcoming from additional interviews. Segmentation means that three to four groups may therefore be needed per segment of the collective participating.

Once identified, potential members have to be recruited. This task tends to be more straightforward with internal publics. Recruiting from external publics can throw up different challenges. For a start, there may be no obvious way of locating members, although customer lists can help massively in this respect. Making cold telephone calls to screen for suitable participants is a worst-case scenario. Once contacted, these people may be less prepared to participate, making it necessary to introduce incentives in the form of direct payments, free meals, gifts, paid trips, or overnight accommodation to take part. On the other hand, Lanigan (1997) pointed to the biasing effects of 'groupies' or 'professional respondents' who keep turning up at focus groups, often lying about personal details in order to be recruited.

As a way of maximizing the chances of having the desired number attend as and when required, it is common practice to 'over-recruit' by arranging for one or two more than are actually needed to come along. Even so, a system of telephone reminders is also prudent, particularly with external publics.

Moderating and recording the group interview

The personal skills and attributes of the moderator have considerable bearing on the nature and quality of the data collected (Sim, 1998), and are a key consideration in deciding who should fill this pivotal role (Litosseliti, 2003). According to Krueger (1998b, p. 4) the task should be 'to guide the discussion and listen to what's said but not to participate, share views, engage in discussion, or shape the outcome of the group interview'. The specific moderating style adopted is tailored by the purpose of the focus group and the degree of structure envisaged, placing an emphasis on either content alone or additional process aspects of the interaction (Millward, 2006). In general, though, the style should be one that conveys genuine interest in and respect for members and what they have to offer. It is they and their views that should take centre stage, with the moderator staying largely in the conversational background, becoming more actively involved only to keep the discussion going, guide it back on track or gently encourage the reticent to take a fuller part.

Despite the fact that they are examples of group interviews, focus groups operate most effectively when the moderator concentrates on keeping participants discussing among themselves in a general atmosphere of relaxed informality, rather than engaging in a question-and-answer session with each in turn (Puchta and Potter, 2004). The advantages of the technique stem from the discursive element of the group encounter. This can also be promoted by presenting objects, pictures, and materials to stimulate debate (Stewart *et al.*, 2007).

In addition to general style and sets of skills around information exchange, there are particular sub-tasks that have to be taken on board by the moderator. These include effecting introductions, establishing ground rules and 'setting the scene', easing the members into free and easy interchange and, once the discussion has run its course, negotiating closure (Loeb *et al.*, 2006).

Good quality discussion that is not captured in a good quality recording is often so much lost opportunity. For any other than the most rudimentary of analyses, a permanent record of what was said is indispensable. As already pointed out, this is usually done on audio or videotape.

Analysing the data and reporting outcomes

Analysing focus group output can be the most difficult and time-consuming part of the auditing exercise. There is no one best or commonly accepted way to carry out this task (Wilkinson, 2003). Some approaches are much more rigorous and involved than others. The one opted for will depend on the goals of the research and the thoroughness of the report required. Krueger and Casey (2000) mentioned four broad strategies for analysis based on memory, notes, tapes and transcripts. Using the first and least rigorous, the moderator relies on mere recall of what took place. Shortcomings include all the vagaries and distortions of memory to which even the most experienced researcher can be prone. However, when the interview has been watched by other members of the research team, some of these idiosyncrasies can be countered to a certain extent. If the focus group was held to simply get a feel for the words and types of expression used by groups of workers, as a preparatory step to a more detailed enquiry, this option may suffice. Nevertheless, it precludes anything other than the most cursory of analysis. In the case of the second option, raw memory is supplemented by field notes in an attempt to capture the substance of the discussion.

With the third possibility, the researcher relies on careful listening to the tape recording, perhaps alongside an abridged transcript, to extract and interpret the essential findings. The permanence of the record facilitates a more involved examination of interchanges. However, it is the fourth option, transcript-based analysis, which is the most common and affords the greatest depth of scrutiny. It is virtually obligatory, particularly when the focus group has been used as the sole method. Here recordings are transcribed in their entirety for subsequent analysis, alongside field notes. Transcribing is a time-consuming business. A group discussion lasting just 1 hour can take more than 4 hours to transcribe and yield some 20 to 25 pages of text. It may take a further 12 hours for even an experienced researcher to complete the analysis and document the findings (Morgan, 1998).

The particular interests and general research assumptions of the investigator that underpin the focus group study may point towards capturing only the content of the discussion or, additionally, the interactive processes that evolved. Some form of content analysis tends to be the preferred option in the former case, while those interested in the latter turn to approaches such as conversation or discourse analysis. It is also possible to include both approaches in a single study, although this is rare. The transcription requirements of each differ. Content analysis is by far the most common approach to analysing focus group data as part of a communication audit (Downs and Adrian, 2004) and will be concentrated on here. Attempting an overview of approaches based on conversation or discourse analysis is well beyond the scope of this chapter. Interested readers are directed to useful sources elsewhere (e.g. Coyle, 2006; Gee, 1999; Puchta and Potter, 2004; Willig, 1999; Wooffitt, 2001).

Content analysis has been defined by Kippendorf (1980, p. 21) as 'a research technique for making replicable and valid inferences from data to their context'. Three main forms of content analysis noted by Millward (2006) are qualitative, quantitative and structural. Although all three have much in common, qualitative content analysis is concerned with revealing robust themes or patterns of meaning through imposing or unearthing appropriate categories and codifying the data accordingly. The quantitative variant involves the analyst in carefully allocating units derived from the text to often mutually exclusive groupings for subsequent numeric representation as frequencies, percentages, or similar descriptive statistics. These units can range from single words (e.g. words indicating respect for management) to the number of lines of text given over to specific topics (e.g. accounts of how different communicative media are used at work). For Morgan (1997), 'Descriptive counting is especially useful in research projects that compare distinctively different groups to determine how often various topics are mentioned' (p. 61). Being seduced by the allure of numbers in this way, though, has been criticized, with Barbour (2005) even suggesting that if it is felt to be necessary to represent focus group outcomes in figures then this method of investigation most likely is being misused.

Finally, structural content analysis extends the previous two by examining 'the relationships between response elements in the target material' (Millward, 2006. p. 294). This may be a useful thing to do in exploring 'complex systems of which naturally occurring focus groups are an excellent example' (p. 294).

Content analysis comprises both mechanical and interpretative components, the two being closely linked (Kippendorf, 1980). The former has to do with the physical task of selecting relevant elements and sub-dividing the text into units to be systematically organized into categories: the latter with divining meaning and creating an internally coherent system of categories that have significance within the context of the enquiry. In the research undertaken by Dickson *et al.* (2004) into inter-communal relations at work, and already referred to, these categories took the form of broad themes and associated sub-themes such as levels of sectarianism in the organization, management's handling of sectarian incidents, tolerance among the workforce, and dealing with sectarian grievances. Analysis unfolds through iterative cycles of coding and sorting units, as categories are extended or refined based on reading and re-reading the text. Richards (2005, p. 86) describes coding as being 'like the filing techniques by which we sort everyday information and ensure access to everything about a topic'. To continue with Richards' (2005) simile, if coding is like filing, then categories are the files.

Categories can be largely pre-established on the basis on theory, prior knowledge, or the particular requirements of the research. Alternatively, they may be allowed to emerge from the actual data in a 'bottom-up' fashion (Boyatzis, 1998; Downs and Adrian, 2004). It is here that the process most resembles what Krueger (1988) called 'detective work': 'One looks for clues, but in this case the clues are trends and patterns that reappear among various focus groups' (p. 109). It is important that the researcher be thorough, working systematically by defining categories and establishing rules for coding units. As analysis progresses, certain groupings may no longer be sustainable, resulting in sub-division or perhaps amalgamation. In any case a more refined and internally coherent system than can accommodate all units in reasonably discrete categories is the objective. Nor should it be thought that the analyst must work towards a consensual position in respect of the group findings. Rather it is quite often within the range and diversity of significant positions exposed by the focus group approach that the richness of the resulting data is fully harnessed and a comprehensive understanding revealed of the issues under exploration in the communication audit (Downs and Adrian, 2004).

While the task of analysing content can still be completed physically through 'cut and paste', a variety of computer software packages are available to ease data management. These are particularly useful in larger projects where the challenges of manual data handling can be daunting. The most popular of these computer-assisted qualitative data analysis systems (CAQDAS), some of which are capable of handling data in formats other than mere text and including video, include Nvivo (and its predecessor, NUDIST), ATLAS.ti, ETHNOGRAPH, and HyperRESEARCH. Overviews of their various features, benefits and shortcomings are provided by, for example, Disko (1998), Kidd and Parshall (2000), Padgett (2004), and Silverman (2005). The reader interested in CAQDAS applications is referred to these sources for further detail. Many of these packages are also supported by extensive websites where much useful information about the specific product can be accessed, including, in some cases, free sample application downloads.

Approached particularly from a realist/essentialist perspective, and given the potential for personal bias and idiosyncratic interpretation to creep in, establishing that the outcome of the analysis is not merely the figment of the creative imagination of the analyst becomes a crucial issue. Procedures for establishing the degree of agreement, in the form of a numeric index, between the codings of two analysts, include Cohen's Kappa (Cohen, 1960), which represents consistency as a coefficient value, taking chance agreements into account. Vaughn et al. (1996) specified a stage of category negotiation in the steps that they recommend for handling the data. Here two members of the team working independently, along the lines already described, come together to compare their coded output and reconcile differences that may emerge.

CONCLUSION

Focus groups are a way of doing qualitative research, using group discussion. They are concerned not so much with establishing how extensive something is or how often it happens. That is essentially the domain of quantitative enquiry, which places a premium on the generalizability of findings from a sample to the population from which it was drawn, utilizing inferential statistics. The function of focus groups is rather on uncovering the meanings and interpretations that individuals, in their own terms, place on their experiences. It may also be of interest for some who are interested in more than just the content of the debate, to explore the interactive, discursive processes through which attitudes and opinions become established in talk. This line of enquiry is much less common, though, in communication auditing applications.

Focus groups have enjoyed substantial growth in popularity, particularly in market research, health and social sciences research. They have much to contribute to the communication auditing process, particularly in combination with other techniques. As such, they can be used in the initial stages when investigating an issue about which little is known, as a way of generating preliminary ideas and hypotheses. Alternatively, they can identify areas of concern to be explored more systematically by means of quantitative procedures. As a follow-up to a survey, on the other hand, focus groups are an effective approach to illuminating the significance of existing numeric findings. The focus group has, therefore, the potential to unearth quality data of value in conducting a comprehensive audit of organizational communication. While not without its detractors (e.g. Gladwell, 2006), the method has been characterized by Barbour (2005, p. 744) as 'reaching the parts that other methods cannot reach'.

Chapter 6

Data collection log-sheet methods

Owen Hargie and Dennis Tourish

INTRODUCTION

This chapter focuses on two audit methods, both of which use a system of data collection log-sheet (DCL) to collect information. The DCL is a structured form on which specific items of detail have to be completed. The information content being sought, and the method of entry (tick box, Yes/No, Likert scale, open comment, etc.) are carefully determined, and the DCL is thoroughly field-tested prior to the audit exercise. This method differs from the questionnaire approach in that here the respondent measures and evaluates *actual* communication experiences immediately after they have occurred. With questionnaires, the respondent is asked to reflect back on, and evaluate, past general communication trends and patterns, rather than focus on the specific here-and-now.

In audits, DCLs can either be completed by the member of staff, or by an outside observer. Indeed, the two main approaches presented in this chapter differ on this dimension. In the first, diaries and logs, the respondent is responsible for the completion of DCLs. In the second, undercover auditing, an independent evaluator fills these in after an interaction with the person being secretly observed.

DIARIES AND LOGS

As defined by Thiele *et al.* (2002, p. 2) the diary method of data collection requires 'respondents to record information about their subjective experiences, cognitions, behaviors and social interactions linked to a temporal framework'. Analysis over time is therefore a key determinant in deciding to use this approach. If a 'snapshot' is required then other methods, such as questionnaires, are simpler and easier to apply. However, if the objective is to study communications across a set period, then the use of a systematic 'diary' or 'log' may be more appropriate.

Although the title of this section suggests that what we all know as traditional diaries should be scrutinized and audited, this in fact is not the case. While the well known and much loved 'Dear Diary' can be a fascinating storehouse of information and opinion about communication with others, it is at best a subjective and erratic source of data. For example, King George V who died in 1936, had spent 25 years on the throne through some very turbulent and violent periods. It was hoped that his diaries would offer an opportunity to carefully study the deepest insights of a key player. However, in fact the King only kept a diary for the first few days of each year, during which time he merely recorded less than enthralling impressions of the weather, in terms such as 'Rainy' and 'Cold'. Likewise, at the time of the Russian revolution, when seismic changes were sweeping the country, the diary of Tsar Nicholas II was not exactly analytical or perceptive. In those tumultuous times, when most people in his circle were panic stricken, typical diary entries read: 'Got dressed and rode a bicycle to the bathing beach and bathed enjoyably in the sea' and 'Walked long and killed two crows. Drank tea by daylight.' More insight into the nature of the period could be gleaned from reading tea-leaves than from the Tsar's entries. One reason for the disparity between experiences and diary entries may be that, as explained by the Scottish writer J.M. Barrie (1891), 'The life of every man is a diary in which he means to write one story, and writes another.'

On the other hand, there are detailed diaries that have informed and inspired generations, a prime example being the poignant record kept by Anne Frank in her terrifying and brief life under Nazi occupation in Amsterdam. Although certain diarists are assiduous in maintaining a daily record of events, and indeed some do so with a view to publication (e.g. Campbell, 2007), their entries vary greatly in structure, length, focus and depth of analysis, and in the honesty and frankness with which they address key issues. Thus, although personal diaries are an interesting form of historical record and social artefact, and can be studied as forms of social science data in their own right, they are not really useful as audit tools within organizations. While they can provide an overview of who people have interacted with, how often, about what topics and for what duration, the problem is that in the organizational context it is usually only formal meetings and contacts that are entered into diaries, and so other information will not be included.

Diary methods have been used in research studies to chart the behaviour and experiences of individuals in fields such as health (Cheng et al., 2007), nutrition (Ashfield-Watt et al., 2004), and travel and tourism (Axhausen et al., 2007). Depending on the nature of the research, different types of diaries are employed. The audit diary method described in this chapter involves obtaining written responses from participants on a carefully prepared pro-forma or data collection log-sheet (DCL), on which they itemize and evaluate communicative activities over a set period. The International Communication Association Diary (Goldhaber and Rogers, 1979) provides a useful DCL template that can be adapted to meet particular requirements (an example of this is given in Chapter 11). While audit texts (e.g. Goldhaber and Rogers, 1979; Downs, 1988) make a distinction between 'diaries' and 'network analysis', in essence these both use variations of the DCL method. The main difference is that the former, also known as 'the duty study' (Goldhaber, 1993), involves detailing one's *own* communications, while the latter entails an estimate of how the respondent interacts with *others*. Chapter 7 contains a detailed examination of network analysis.

Advantages and disadvantages of diaries

There are both pros and cons in using diaries. The advantages are as follows.

1   *They are ubiquitous*. The diary is a familiar, user-friendly, artefact for most people and so the task of keeping one is viewed as fairly unproblematic. Respondents understand and accept the notion, and the validity, of keeping a personal record. While precise instructions, and in some cases training, about exactly what is required are important, half the battle is won through familiarity with the diary concept. As noted by Fu (2007, p. 196) 'Compared with observations and interviews, the diary approach is normally more familiar, natural, and unobtrusive to respondents.'

2   *They provide information about the temporal sequence of events*. Structured diaries give the auditor specific detail about the source, recipient, nature and perceived effectiveness of each individual communication. A very wide range, depth and variety of information can be gathered. Such data would be very difficult to obtain through other means.

3   *Where repeat information is required from respondents over a period of time, it is a cost-effective approach*. Once respondents are fully informed and understand exactly the nature of the assignment, they can be left to get on with it. The auditor does not have to be on site to collect the material. This is carried out at the end of the observational period (or at interim intervals if the time-scale is long). However, if diaries are to be completed over a prolonged period, at least one motivational reminder letter from the auditor is useful.

4   *Classification is made by the person doing the job*. As noted by Finch *et al.* (2008, p. 89): 'Diaries represent an effective means of obtaining detailed and accurate personal data from respondents.' By contrast, observers may not have access to, or fully comprehend, the full range of interactions engaged in by members of staff. Their perspective is also that of 'outsider' while the diary is completed from an 'insider' frame of reference (Weinshall, 1979).

The disadvantages are:

1   *It relies on staff to conscientiously complete the logs – the auditor has no*

real control over how well this is done. As expressed by Breakwell and Wood (1995, p. 296) 'getting people to remember to make entries at the right time about the right things can be difficult, even when they have goodwill towards the research and every intention of complying with your instructions'. Downs and Adrian (2004, p. 192) concurred with this, pointing out that the main problem is that 'employees soon tire of this assessment process, and the authenticity of collected data becomes quickly suspect'. Obviously, the likelihood of regular completion diminishes in direct proportion to the extent to which respondents have doubts or are unconvinced about the value of the exercise. Goldhaber and Rogers (1979) described how they faced resistance to the diary method from individuals in organizations, owing to its time-consuming nature, or to a lack of conviction about its validity. They cited the case of how in one instance they received initial commitment from a hospital to use this approach. However, at the training session for staff one surgeon baulked at the task. As Goldhaber and Rogers explain: 'One doctor told us, "when I come out of an operation with blood on my hands, just how do you expect me to get serious about this diary"' (p. 30).

Some years ago, one of our university colleagues decided to carry out a study into temporal variations in sexual intimacy. As part of this project, he issued diaries to staff in the faculty and requested that they enter a tick in the relevant day each time the person had sexual intercourse. Anonymity was guaranteed and diaries were to be returned through the internal mail. Not surprisingly the results were erratic. The return rate was very low, and some individuals who did return their diaries seemed to have an impossibly prodigious rate of sexual activity! The study was abandoned. Interestingly, as a substitute method, he carried out a daily count of the number of condoms that appeared in the sedimentation tanks of the Belfast city sewage plant. After monitoring activity for a period of 333 days he produced his results, which showed a weekly rhythm as well as seasonal fluctuation in mating frequency (Tittmar, 1978).

2   This latter study reveals a second problem, namely *the veracity of what is reported*. It is difficult to know whether respondents are reporting truthfully, or whether they have embroidered or reconstructed the actuality. The accuracy of self-reports in general has therefore been widely questioned, since self-justification biases can cause people to exaggerate the frequency of behaviours that enhance their self-image and downplay or misinterpret those incidents that may cause them to lose face or that conflict with how they view themselves (Travis and Aronson, 2007). For this reason, diaries are best used in conjunction with other audit methods, the data from which serve as a source of evidence for reliability checks.

3   *Another drawback is that what is termed 'sample maintenance' is low*. In other words, there is likely to be a high drop-out rate and hence a low

level of returns. This increases in line with the complexity and duration of the observation period.

4   The auditor needs to be aware of the possibility of *reactance*, which refers to the process whereby a research intervention can affect the subject. Reactance is not peculiar to this method, but the ongoing nature of the diary approach means it is more likely to occur. Thus the very task of having to complete a diary and analyse communications may in itself influence the respondent's thoughts, perceptions, feelings and behaviour. Breakwell and Wood (1995) gave as one example Freud's study of his dreams. When he started recording these, he found that he began to wake at points in the sleep cycle where he was able to remember the dream. In this way, the act of logging his dreams changed his sleep patterns. When respondents begin to complete a diary, it can become a significant part of their daily activities. They may, for example, begin to initiate communications with others in order to be able to make more entries in their log. It can also make them very aware on a moment-by-moment basis of who is communicating with them, and to what effect. The act of recording and rating past communications may, in turn, affect the nature, purpose and content of future interactions. As Duck (1991, p. 153) put it: 'subjects' recall of communication influences their approach to those interactions by providing opportunities to recapitulate, ponder, or plan for the future'. The extent and impact of reactance are almost impossible to determine, but the auditor should take steps to minimize its effects. Respondents should be made aware of this phenomenon and encouraged to respond as naturally as possible. In audits of a prolonged duration, a reminder of the possibility of reactance should be included in mid-audit 'motivational' communications from the auditor to all respondents.

Optimizing diaries

In order to gain the maximum benefits from this method, the following points should be borne in mind.

- As with all audit methods, *planning is very important*. The auditor has to decide *who* is to be included, *what* issues are to be investigated, and *how* data are to be recorded.
- Where numbers dictate that it is impossible to collect diaries from all staff, *a consistent sampling frame must be devised*. Some audit researchers argue that randomization in this type of exercise is necessary to ensure a valid data set, and that 50% of respondents in each work group should be audited (Porter, 1988). However, an alternative view was proposed by Goldhaber and Rogers (1979), who argued that purposive (or judgemental) sampling is a viable alternative to randomization. There is

no hard and fast rule here. In essence, the sampling method used will be determined by the objectives of the audit. Frequently, it will also be determined by what is actually possible or tolerable within the organization where the audit is being conducted. Audits often present a conflict between what is *ideal* and what is *possible*: it is wise to side with the latter.

- *The content of the diary DCL should clearly reflect, and directly measure, the goals of the audit.* These can range across various issues, such as how often certain sections of the organization communicate, what channels tend to be most and least used, the duration of communications, and so on.

- *Choose the most appropriate recording system for the target group.* More complex systems may be suitable for senior managers, or for office workers, but for shop-floor workers in a more industrial setting the method for recording data should be kept as simple as possible. In all cases, the layout of the DCL should look professional, and provide enough space for the data that have to be entered in each row/column. Another important factor is that the DCL must not appear daunting or off-putting to respondents. An initial 'gulp' response to first viewing of the sheets can set respondents to believe that the exercise is unrealistic and very difficult. The DCLs should therefore be thoroughly pilot tested and modified to meet specific requirements before being shown to respondents.

- *Staff should be given as much preparation and training as possible in how to complete the logs.* The ideal is to have a training session with all respondents, during which one or more dummy runs are carried out. In fact, most sources regard training as an essential prerequisite to using this method. As expressed by Goldhaber and Rogers (1979, p. 30) 'The major lesson we have learned is to only use the diary when there are very good reasons, when specialized training is provided, and when adequate controls are possible.'

- *Accompanying instructions should be carefully designed and pilot tested.* These should be readily comprehensible and at a level appropriate for the target audience. It is important to provide a contact telephone number (help-line) and e-mail address, which respondents can use to clear up any queries they have.

- *It has been said that one picture is worth one thousand words and one example is worth one thousand pictures.* For this reason, it is useful to give respondents an example of a completed DCL, to illustrate what exactly is required. However, care should be taken to emphasize that this is not an exact template and that variations are acceptable.

- *Entries should be made as soon as possible after each communicative episode.* Delays in completing the logs tend to result in inaccuracies, since respondents then rely on memory (a notoriously faulty faculty!).

For example, research into what is known as 'imagination inflation' has established that the more people try to imagine something the more likely they are to inflate it into an actual memory, irrespective of whether it really occurred, while adding further convincing details in the process (Loftus, 2004; Mazzoni and Memon, 2003). Retrospective diary accounts, which require respondents to imagine or reconstruct what they think occurred, may be prone to this problem. Delays also result in a higher number of incompletions, and an increased drop-out rate. One early attempt to circumvent such problems was employed by Hinrichs (1964), who supplied his subjects with a pocket alarm set to go off five times during the day. Respondents were requested to record details about their communications each time the alarm went off.

- *Regular contact with respondents is useful.* It helps to improve sample maintenance, and allows the auditor to answer any queries about the exercise.
- *Incentives, in the form of payments or inclusion in a prize lottery, also facilitate sample retention.* In a review of diary methodology, Fu (2007, p. 206) concluded that 'monetary incentives encourage the informants to maintain their diary-keeping routine'.
- *If the objective is to obtain very detailed information on logs, it has been shown that it is best to use what is known as a foot-in-the-door approach* (Hargie *et al.*, 2004). This involves asking initially for brief details and then increasing the amount required once respondents have been involved for a period. So the tactic is to begin with a relatively brief diary and then up the ante. When presented with what seems a very difficult task at the outset, the respondent drop-out rate is high. However, once they are committed to the audit exercise a request for some more detail may not seem so unreasonable.
- *Given the demands of this method, DCL audits should be time-limited.* In our experience, if respondents are asked to complete detailed forms for any more than 1 week, the drop-out rate becomes unacceptable. This time period has been confirmed by Zwijze-Koning and de Jong (2005, p. 437) who point out that: 'Because the task of keeping track of all communication activities places a high burden on the employees of an organization, a diary-based study will have to be restricted to a short period of time.' One possibility is to spread the task over a period of time. For example, Johnson *et al.* (1998) used the diary method to have managers record all of their activities over a period of 3 weeks; however, this task was spread out so that managers completed the task for 1 week at a time over a total research period of 18 months.
- Finally, given the nature of this method, *diaries are more appropriate for use with the upper echelons of an organization.* Managers are used to form-filling and record-keeping and for them filling in log sheets is more likely to become just another administrative task. However, shop-floor

workers are less familiar with such bureaucratic niceties. If diaries are to be used with the latter group their level of complexity should be kept to a minimum.

The data obtained from diary analysis can be most insightful, since they provide patterns of typical communicative encounters engaged in by relevant sections of the organization (see Chapter 12). In their review of this approach, Bolger *et al.* (2003, p. 580) pointed out that 'A fundamental benefit of diary methods is that they permit the examination of reported events and experiences in their natural, spontaneous context.' The results from this audit system are probably as close as it is possible to get to obtaining an overall picture of the pattern of communication within any organization. How the results are analysed depends on the exact purpose of the audit, and the precise nature of the information that has been gathered. Usually, both quantitative and qualitative analyses are possible. Furthermore, temporal, sequential and reciprocal matrices can be developed to provide a communication network analyses from the results. For auditors who require intensive numerical investigation, a range of detailed and specialized statistical analyses are available for analysing and interpreting diary-type data (see Norton, 1980; Porter, 1988; von Eye, 1990).

Example of a diary audit

One audit that we conducted was concerned with the quality of communication across senior levels of the national health service (NHS) in one region of the UK. Specifically, the audit examined communication at senior management levels between staff in the Region (R), District (D), and the Trusts (T) within that district. As part of this audit, DCLs were sent to all managers in order to chart communication patterns. These requested respondents to provide details of all communications received during a 1-week period from the other two relevant sources (see Box 6.1 and Figure 6.1). Thus:

- T staff completed DCLs regarding their communications with R and D
- R staff completed DCLs regarding their communications with D and T
- D staff completed DCLs regarding their communications with T and R.

Respondents were asked to list the source of the communication, the topic, the channel, the length or duration, whether it was one or two way, and finally to rate the effectiveness of the communication. A total of 40% completed DCLs were received from D staff, 64% from T staff, and 76% from R staff. These figures were fairly representative of levels of communication between these three areas, with a high proportion of D staff indicating that they had no communication whatsoever with T or R during the week of the audit. The satisfactory level of returns in this investigation was facilitated by two

Box 6.1 Communication analysis sheets

Instructions for completion

On the sheets attached please record all communications received by you during the week **24–28 April**, inclusive, from other staff within the Organization. Please list each communication in a separate numbered row. Give details under each heading as follows:

Source — State whether the communication was from a middle manager, a senior manager or another member of staff. If the communication was not from management please specify the occupational group concerned.

Topic — State the purpose of the communication.

Channel — State the communication channel **(face to face; telephone; e-mail; fax; letter; memorandum; etc.)**

Length/duration — State either the length of the communication (e.g. **2 page** memorandum) or the duration (e.g. **5 minute** telephone call).

Feedback — State whether the communication was **one way** and you were simply a recipient, or **two way** in that you were expected to respond with your views or give information.

Evaluation — Please rate how effective you feel each communication episode was from your perspective, using the following ratings:

7 = Totally effective
6 = Very effective
5 = Quite effective
4 = Neither effective nor ineffective
3 = Quite ineffective
2 = Very ineffective
1 = Totally ineffective

strongly supportive letters sent to all staff from the Chief Executive Officer. One was delivered before the data collection period, and the second on the first day of the audit week.

An example of the type of results from this part of the audit is shown in

NAME..   LOCATION..

	SOURCE	TOPIC	CHANNEL	LENGTH/ DURATION	FEEDBACK	EVALUATION
1						
2						
3						
4						
5						
6						
7						
8						

Figure 6.1 Communication analysis sheet.

Table 6.1. Communications recorded by T staff revealed an overall total of 195, of which 151 (77%) were in writing, 31 (16%) by telephone and 13 (7%) face-to-face. While T staff rated communications as between 'quite' and 'very' effective, those with D received a higher score than those from R. The results showed that a much larger proportion of the T communications were in writing and the average length of document dealt with was also lengthier at 4.3 pages (compared to 2.8 for R and 2.3 for D). Furthermore the T staff indicated that the bulk of these communications were one way with no feed-back required (whereas both R and D recorded a higher proportion of two-way communications). In fact, the lowest level of face-to-face contact was indicated by T staff, with only 13 (7%) of their total communicative episodes via this channel (as opposed to 39% for D and 27% for R).

The interpretation of the results from the DCLs was further informed by the anticipated levels of contact, given the organizational structure, together with the responses to an accompanying detailed questionnaire. One picture to

Table 6.1 Results of DCLs completed by T staff

	R	D
Total communications	162	33
Average evaluation	5.2*	5.6*
Total two-way communications	83	
Total one-way communications	112	
Number/duration of communications	Telephone n = 31 Average duration = 4.9 minutes	
	Face-to-face n = 13 Average duration = 112 minutes	
	Written n = 151 Average length = 4.3 pages	

* *Scoring key:* 1 = Totally ineffective; 2 = Very ineffective; 3 = Quite ineffective; 4 = Neither effective nor ineffective; 5 = Quite effective; 6 = Very effective; 7 = Totally effective.

emerge from the results of this audit was that of T staff constantly communicating at length in the written medium, with a minority of their communications involving no response from others. We recommended that this finding be further investigated, given the potential for isolation raised by such a *modus operandi*. An overall analysis of the total of 364 communications recorded by all staff revealed that 197 (54%) of these were written, 105 (29%) were by telephone, and 62 (17%) were face-to-face. Another of our recommendations therefore was that attention be paid to methods whereby the latter channel of communication could be more widely employed.

Thus this diary method unearthed some very interesting findings and provided a rich seam of data. The results allowed senior managers to appraise their existing patterns of communication, and indicated areas of serious concern as well as existing strengths to be built on.

ECCO

Another example of a DCL method is what has been termed 'Episodic Communication Channels in Organization (ECCO) Analysis', initially developed by Davis (1953). This is a DCL that is specially designed 'to analyze and map communication networks and measure rates of flow, distortion of messages, and redundancy' (Goldhaber, 1993, p. 374). The ECCO is used to monitor the progress of a specific piece of information through the organization. The information to be tracked should be (1) true, (2) expected to be widely known by most if not all staff, (3) basic and straightforward, (4) recent, and (5) released through a specific channel.

Downs and Adrian (2004) pointed out that in an ECCO, respondents should be asked to list on a DCL:

1   whether or not they know all or part of the information
2   if they know about it, to cite the parts they know

3   if they know about it, when they first learned of it
4   where they were when they first became aware of it
5   by which channel (e-mail, phone call, memo, etc.) the message was delivered
6   what was the source (manager, colleague) of it.

An analysis of completed ECCO DCLs provides a picture of whether or not communication is flowing well, how long it takes information to reach certain destinations, which media seem to be most effective in disseminating messages, and where there appear to be problems. The ECCO questionnaire is brief and can be easily completed in a few minutes. This means that it can be administered to a large sample of staff. Among its disadvantages are that some staff may be reluctant to identify sources, while others are loath to admit that they are in ignorance of what will then be perceived to be an important piece of information.

The ECCO technique has several advantages:

- It is cost-effective, as it does not involve a great deal of employee time to complete the ECCO questionnaire – usually no more than a few minutes (Zwijze-Koning and de Jong, 2005).
- It is a flexible method that can be tailored to investigate specific aspects of employee knowledge. While initially developed as a measure to track the progress of one specific message within an organization, the adaptability of the ECCO approach means it can be applied across a wide range of situations and for a variety of purposes, including the evaluation of existing systems and the diagnosis of shortcomings in communication channels. For example, Stevenson and Gilly (1991) used a variant of this technique to track the handling of patient complaints within a hospital setting. They found that managers were more likely to rely on informal relationships than on formal procedures when dealing with such problems.
- It gauges the precise level and depth of existing employee knowledge and highlights deficits that should be remedied.
- The questionnaire facilitates benchmarking, in that future ECCOs can be carried out to chart specific improvements, or decrements, in employee knowledge.
- It highlights recurring problems and pinpoints difficulties in communication, thereby facilitating change interventions.
- It can generate findings that are unexpected. For example, Power and Rienstra (1999) carried out a study of a major division within a City Council in Australia in which they used an ECCO to evaluate the impact of a new initiative aimed at promoting the career interests of females within the organization. They found that although the information dissemination was effective, in that it reached 88% of the target group, over

50% of respondents were apathetic or distrustful about the initiative itself.

- On a wider scale, by carrying out parallel ECCO research studies across a range of organizations, it is possible to make broader conclusions about the general state of organizational knowledge in a particular realm. Thus, Hargie and Dickson (2007) used the same ECCO questionnaire in a major study of four organizations in Northern Ireland, in which they investigated employee knowledge of policies and procedures for dealing with grievances of a sectarian nature. They found a consistent lack of knowledge of these policies and procedures in all companies. While the result of each individual ECCO was useful for the specific corporation, the combination of findings enabled Hargie and Dickson to make general recommendations about how organizations in Northern Ireland could take steps to improve their communications in this domain.

The disadvantages of the ECCO are that:

- It can be a time-consuming procedure for the auditor, involving considerable liaison with managers, and careful pilot testing with employees, to ensure that the ECCO really measures what it is intended to measure.
- There can be suspicion by employees of what they may see as a 'test' of their ability. The questionnaire has to be presented in such a way that it is clearly viewed by respondents as an opportunity for them to give feedback rather than as a form of assessment.
- Like all self-report methods, it relies on the accuracy of respondents and so can be subject to memory distortion and response biases. As mentioned earlier, one problem is that respondents may be reluctant to admit to a lack of knowledge of what is perceived to be important information.
- It can be difficult to persuade respondents to complete the questionnaire. As highlighted by Downs and Adrian (2004, p. 185), 'ECCO's greatest weakness is the high nonresponse rate.'
- As a quantitative method, it produces numerical data but does not provide any accompanying respondent interpretation or explanation.

An example of an ECCO DCL based on one we used in an actual audit is presented in Box 6.2. The information had in this case been communicated through the company newsletter. The results enabled us to conduct various analyses. Interestingly, we found that some 6% of respondents did not know that Sue Bloggs had been head of customer services, let alone that she was leaving or that a new structure was in place (see Box 6.2). However, over 60% of staff claimed to have heard all parts of the information and most had received it from the newsletter, with the next most common channel being a colleague. The one part of the message that had failed to penetrate was the final one relating to the fact that the head of communications was now in

Box 6.2 Example of an ECCO DCL

Gender: ❑ Female   ❑ Male

Age: ❑ Under 20 years ❑ 21–30 ❑ 31–40 ❑ 41–50 ❑ Over 50 yrs

Post: ❑ Full-time ❑ Part-time ❑ Temporary full-time
         ❑ Temporary part-time

How long employed: ❑ Under 1 year ❑ 1–5 yrs ❑ 6–10 yrs
                              ❑ 11–15 yrs   ❑ Over 15 yrs

Present position: ❑ I don't supervise anyone ❑ First-line manager
                         ❑ Middle manager   ❑ Senior

Other (please specify) _____

What is your job? _____

Please tick the box beside each of the statements below if you knew this information before you completed this Questionnaire. If you did not know it, please leave the box blank. If you leave all boxes blank do not complete any more of the Questionnaire.

❑ Sue Bloggs is leaving
❑ Sue Bloggs is going to Head Office
❑ Sue Bloggs was Head of Customer Services
❑ The post of Head of Customer Services will not be re-advertised
❑ The new Head of Communications is Davinder Patel
❑ Davinder Patel will now be responsible for customer services

From what *source* did you first hear or read about this information (please tick only one box)

Written medium   Talking medium
❑ Company newsletter   ❑ Colleague
❑ Notice on staff board   ❑ Line manager
❑ Formal memo   ❑ Senior manager
❑ E-mail   ❑ Overheard someone
Other (please specify) _____

Through which *channel* did you learn about this information?

❑ Staff meeting   ❑ Informal conversation
❑ Company video   ❑ Telephone call
❑ Written communication
Other (please specify) _____

When did you first learn about this information (please circle only one)?

Days ago   Today   1   2   3   4   5   6
Weeks ago   1   2   3   4

Where were you when you first learned about this information?
- ❏ Staff canteen   ❏ At my normal working location
- ❏ While visiting another department   ❏ At a formal staff meeting
- ❏ Outside of the company

Other (please specify) _____

charge of customer services – less than 30% of the workforce claimed knowledge of this. As a result, the next edition of the newsletter carried a main feature on Davinder Patel and his role in the company.

UNDERCOVER AUDITING

One audit approach that has developed rapidly in recent years is that of 'mystery-customer research' (MCR). This technique, also known as 'mystery shopping', 'service shopping', 'secret shopping', 'phantom shopping', 'anonymous consumer shopping', and 'covert observation', has been defined as 'the process wherein trained marketing research personnel go to establishments and evaluate their service standards and identify problem areas' (Burnside, 1994, p. 32). It involves observers (or 'shoppers') visiting (or telephoning) a location and 'acting' as consumers, while carefully noting the behaviour of the service provider. As the title of this section indicates, it is a form of 'undercover audit' wherein the assessor poses as a consumer and actually experiences the service. MCR is therefore a type of covert participant observation.

This approach has been termed 'the "moment of truth" when the customer meets the salespeople' (Holbert and Speece, 1993, p. 93). MCR is now ubiquitous, operating in a wide range of both private and public sectors including, inter alia, finance, automotive, food, hotel, leisure and tourism, retail, telecommunications, the utilities, and local government (Miller, 1998). Indeed it has also been employed in the Christian church, where non-churchgoing 'mystery worshippers' visit churches to assess aspects such as the welcome received, the sermon, and the comfort and appearance of the church (Gledhill, 2007). MCR is a major industry, with an estimated $1.5 billion per year spent on this service worldwide (Calvert, 2005). One reason for this is that the bonuses of management and staff in many companies are increasingly being linked to MCR measures of customer satisfaction (Tuzovic and Bruhn, 2005). For example, at some companies, 40% of employees' quarterly bonus pay is directly related to MCR results (Estell, 2001).

Historically, MCR has its roots in the field of cultural anthropology, where anthropologists lived as part of a tribe in order to gain an in-depth insight into their patterns of living (Wilson and Gutmann, 1998). The key aspect here was that the researcher actually *experienced* what was happening.

Similarly, the important dimension of MCR is that the person acts just like a 'real' consumer and plays out the entire scenario in this role. Only afterwards are detailed notes taken. Usually some form of data collection log-sheet (DCL) is used to structure the audit. This is not displayed in the location, but is completed immediately following the visit. Increasingly, the DCL is electronic, in the form of a hand-held computer into which the results are entered, since this can facilitate rapid analysis. The exact nature of observation depends on the context. In a sales context it would include questions such as:

- How long was it before a salesperson approached you?
- Did the salesperson offer a greeting or other welcoming remarks?
- Did the salesperson engage in eye contact throughout the interaction?
- Did the salesperson close the encounter with a friendly comment?

In the banking sector (Leeds, 1995) the investigator scrutinizes actions such as whether the member of staff:

- shakes hands
- smiles
- offers a seat
- presents a business card
- asks relevant questions
- recommends the best product to meet the presented needs
- asks for the business
- helps in completing the application form
- offers a follow-up service.

In other locations the mystery shopper will observe situation-specific aspects such as whether:

- shelves in a supermarket are well stocked
- a sales assistant in a fashion store offers help within 2 minutes
- bar staff open an interaction with a greeting and smile
- a librarian asks 'Is there anything else I can help you with?'
- background music is being played in a restaurant
- prices are clearly displayed in a car showroom
- all ticket machines in a train station are in working order
- a telephone call to a company is answered within six rings.

Part of the inspection may involve a request being made (e.g. seeking assistance, asking a specific question about a product) followed by careful monitoring as to how it is dealt with. Alternatively, the assessor may be sent to an outlet to audit an entire procedure, such as going to a bank and opening an account, visiting a local tourist attraction, or actually purchasing a specific item from a shop. In the latter case, this will apply only if the cost is not prohibitive. For example, if the investigation were into the standard of service in a luxury car showroom, then obviously a purchase would not be feasible. In such instances, the evaluator backs off just before the point of commitment.

Cobb (1997) identified a number of key objectives served by MCR (Box 6.3), while Cramp (1994) enumerated four operational fundamentals of the process (Box 6.4). In fact, the following key steps are essential to promote an effective mystery shopping process (Biere, 1998; Leeds, 1995).

1   *Define clearly the specific goals of the process at the outset.* Also, determine in advance how problems will be resolved if and when they are identified. To fail to prepare at this stage is to prepare to fail.
2   *Design the programme specifically to meet the set goals.* The standards

---

Box 6.3   The main purposes of MCR

To:

1   identify the extent to which consumer needs are being met
2   chart precise strengths and weaknesses in current practice
3   assess whether new initiatives have been implemented on the ground
4   check for consistency of standards across outlets
5   inform performance incentive schemes and guide the payment of bonuses
6   evaluate the effectiveness of staff training programmes
7   enable managers and staff to improve overall performance.

Box 6.4   Four main fundamentals of MCR

1   *Realism.* It should mirror reality. Thus, if 80% of consumers are couples, then two evaluators should visit the location together.
2   *Unobtrusive.* The shopper should not create a scene or pose unusual difficulties for the person being assessed.
3   *Objectivity.* The main purpose of the evaluation should be to check measurable aspects of the service. While some subjectivity may be permissible, this should be kept to a minimum.
4   *Consistency.* Shoppers should receive rigorous training to ensure consistency of evaluation across outlets. Everyone should be measuring the same things in the same way.

against which personnel are to be judged need to be clearly delineated. These should then be explained fully to staff so that they know exactly what is expected of them. They should also be as specific and objective as possible. For example 'Was your meal served within 20 minutes of being seated?' is high in objectivity, whereas 'Were the staff friendly?' entails an element of subjectivity. Questions such as the latter need more detailed specification ('Did the waiter smile?' 'Were you asked if you were enjoying your meal?' etc.). Assessment drives effort. But if staff do not know what benchmarks are being employed, they cannot endeavour to shape their behaviour in this direction. These standards must be agreed and supported by staff – this is absolutely essential. Ideally, staff should be involved in their identification.

3   *A DCL measurement system that is simple, yet robust, should be developed, and fully pre-tested to ensure it is both reliable and valid.* For example, Burnside (1994) describes how Victoria Wine actively involved both customers and staff in the eventual identification of 34 key service aspects for measurement across all outlets, in its 'Working Together for Customers' quality programme. Following initial testing, a weighting process was applied to ensure that different types of outlet were judged fairly in relation to one another. Results from visits were quickly fed back to staff who then demonstrated a commitment to improving service through a range of identified actions.

4   *Select the appropriate type of auditor for the location being assessed.* Some organizations recruit evaluators from their own client base rather than using professional contract ones. This has a number of advantages. It means that feedback comes from a 'real' user's perspective, that staff are less likely to identify auditors (since these are actual clients), and it is usually more cost-effective than employing outside consultants. In selecting auditors, Cobb (1997) recommended that they should:

- represent the same geodemographic spread as actual consumers – thus if consumers are both male and female, auditors of both gender should be employed.
- possess qualities such as good retentive memory and high levels of visual and aural observation skills. While there is evidence that females are more accurate in this type of evaluation, it is also the case that males and females are often dealt with differently, and so males need to be used as evaluators and may require more extensive training (Morrison *et al.* 1997). In some instances two mystery shoppers are employed, one to engage in the interaction and the second to observe and record the outcomes (e.g. McKechnie *et al.*, 2007).
- not be over-aggressive personalities – professional complainers are not appropriate!
- behave appropriately. The objective is to allow staff to perform to

their optimum level, not to put them under stress. It is certainly not the role of the auditor to be an *agent provocateur*, deliberately creating difficulties for the service provider. As stated by one manager in a study by Wilson (2001, p. 727) the mystery shopper 'shouldn't be trying to catch the service provider out'.

5 *Tell staff that they will be 'shopped' (but not exactly when or by whom).* Staff may initially display negative reactions and these have to be handled sensitively. The exact purposes of the programme should be explained, and the actual DCL to be used should be given to all staff. The positive aspects (e.g. incentives and rewards) should be highlighted. Reassurance needs to be given that, when analysing and interpreting the audit findings, the emphasis will be placed on overall trends, and that the results will not be used as an employability criterion.

6 *Thoroughly train the auditors.* Inform them fully about the exact goals of the exercise (e.g. compliance with set procedures, part of a bonus payment initiative). If it is to be reliable, then evaluators need to receive extensive training in observation and recording methods. There are well-documented cognitive processes, including attentional focus, attitudinal biases, conformity pressures, knowledge base, and expectancy effects, which influence the extent to which the observer will be objective and therefore effective (Morrison *et al.*, 1997). Training can help to overcome these contaminating factors. It is especially important where a team is employed to simultaneously investigate different sites within the same organization. All assessors should receive the same standardized training, and preliminary reliability checks should be made to ensure that their reports are comparable and compatible.

7 *Implement an ongoing programme of evaluations.* There is research to show that performance gains are significantly greater where regular consumer auditing, rather than sporadic or one-off appraisals, takes place (Biere, 1998). The aim should be that of a continuous improvement cycle. An infrequent system of evaluation provides only a limited insight, and perhaps even an inaccurate or unrepresentative snapshot, of performance (anyone can have an 'off-day').

8 *Link the results of mystery shopping directly to incentive schemes to motivate and reward staff.* It should be clear that exceptional performance will be rewarded, so that carrots rather than sticks are very much in evidence. What gets measured and rewarded generally gets done, hence the effectiveness of this method. Some organizations actually link their surveys to employee contests complete with accompanying rewards for 'winners'. These rewards range from letters from senior management, through 'congratulations' notices (e.g. employee of the month) prominently displayed, to actual monetary rewards. Care needs to be taken here, however, since the introduction of such performance-related rewards

may result in jealousy or resentment, and so be counter-productive to the fostering of good team spirit. Indeed, the available evidence suggests that performance-related pay demotivates staff, does not help organizations keep their best people or get rid of their worst performers, and generally creates a feeling of injustice (Hargie *et al.*, 2004).

9 *Provide detailed results in a concise, comprehensible and actionable format, highlighting both strengths and weaknesses.* The objective is not just to collect data, but rather to allow the information gathered to be converted into action plans, which will then effect improvements in performance.

10 *As part of the MCR process, it is important that supervisors as well as first-line staff receive briefings and training* (Wilson, 2001). This should include training in how to interpret findings and be cognizant of their implications.

The mystery shopper method provides a more direct, detailed, scientific and structured approach than simply asking consumers to recall their experiences (Hague and Jackson, 1995). As summarized by Chisnall (1997, p. 46) 'when undertaken with sufficiently large samples and systematically organized MCR can provide valuable insights'. In addition, there are bottom-line benefits. Biere (1998) describes how financial institutions that implemented MCR raised their performance levels by some 20% inside 15 months. In noting such developments, Miller (1998, p. 27) argued that 'Mystery shopping is finally shedding its cloak-and-dagger image and has become a mainstream market-research technique that companies cannot afford to ignore.'

MCR as espionage

A variation on this theme is that of 'competitor mystery shopping', where an assessor from one company visits rival outlets to note how well they handle consumers, and to learn from them if possible. In other words, this method is a form of industrial 'competitor espionage' (Jesson, 2004). It has been employed in this way for years by consumer magazines such as *Which* and *Money Magazine* to report to subscribers on the performance of different businesses. The technique has witnessed an ever-increasing usage. Indeed, the US Society for Competitive Intelligence Professionals (SCIP), which is concerned specifically with enabling businesses to acquire information on competitors using legitimate methods, has witnessed a 40% annual growth in membership (Curtis, 2001).

Holbert and Speece (1993) illustrated how before the hotel chain Marriott launched its subsidiary, the Fairfield Inn chain, they sent a team on a 6-month intelligence mission to gather information on existing hotels with whom they would be competing in the same price band. Strengths and weaknesses of all aspects of the competitors, from check-in to sound-proofing in bedrooms, toiletries in the bathroom, and through to check-out, were carefully itemized.

As a result, the design and service standards of the Fairfield Inn chain were based on solid research evidence. The success of this chain proved that the investment was worthwhile. Interestingly, Chris West, managing director of Competitive Intelligence Services, has reported that the most effective method for obtaining information from competitors is to employ females with French accents, arguing that 'people are often more tempted to talk to a young woman with an attractive voice' (Curtis, 2001, p. 28).

Another variant here is 'matched pair' auditing. In this procedure, two auditors, similar in most respects, but with at least one vital difference, both visit the same location to investigate whether or not there is discrimination in the administration of services. Thus, a matched pair of assessors (e.g. one African American and one non-minority) will separately visit a company. The results from their experiences are checked and compared for differences, and if any occur further evaluations are then carried out to check for a possible pattern of differential treatment. A similar matched pairs procedure can be followed to determine bias in the treatment of those of different gender, age, and so on. Research using this method has unveiled gender and ethnic discrimination in employment recruitment practices (Darity and Mason, 1998), and in housing and car sales (Yinger, 1998).

Finally, in the medical sphere there is what is known as the 'pseudo patient' method. This was used in an early study by Rosenhan (1973). He and seven of his students had themselves admitted to different mental hospitals. They each said they had heard voices and were diagnosed as schizophrenic. The average length of stay was 19 days. None of the staff spotted the fact that they were being deceived, although about a third of the patients did. The psychiatrists did not change their initial diagnoses, but marked the case notes of the 'patients' as 'schizophrenia in remission'. Among the interesting findings from this study was that when a patient and psychiatrist met casually the latter only made eye contact on 29% of the occasions. When casual meetings between strangers were surveyed, eye contact always occurred.

In the sphere of general hospitals, mystery shopping also occurs (Meyer, 1997). Here, a pseudo patient checks into hospital, and, posing as a patient with a specific complaint, undergoes everything from X-rays to blood tests. Over a typical 2-day stay a detailed check is made of the behaviour of staff in admissions, the emergency department, nursing, human resources, security and maintenance, as well as other facilities such as car parking, food services and housekeeping. This approach has also been employed to assess the effectiveness of information and medication given by community pharmacists to patients (Alte et al., 2007).

Ethical issues

There are several ethical dilemmas surrounding the MCR audit method (Cramp, 1994). First, staff time and effort are wasted in dealing with a fake client. Thus, in the hospital example cited above, the valuable skills of health professionals are spent dealing with a phoney patient, when they could have been devoted to genuinely sick individuals. Furthermore, where a worker's pay is linked to bonuses (e.g. in the automotive trade) this wasted effort is especially unfair, and some would argue morally untenable, since it literally costs the person part of their wages.

Second, there is a strong odour of dishonesty about the entire process. Since it entails 'undercover testing' (Leeds, 1995), it is a form of secretive inspection regime that smacks of sneaking, snooping and subterfuge. This raises concerns about the validity of the entire exercise. As summarized by Jesson (2004, p. 617): 'Not only do we have a snapshot of an interaction between two people that is false, one person is lying and the data are decontextualized.' Is it really justifiable for management to send incognito assessors on the sly to check up on their personnel? Companies respond to this criticism by arguing that they always inform staff that MCR will be taking place, and that the evaluations then occur with their informed consent. Indeed, some organizations regularly use mystery shoppers, and so staff know that at some stage the person in front of them will in fact be a 'spy'. In other cases, the company tell staff that within a set time frame (e.g. 3 months) they will be audited by a trained evaluator posing as a real client. However, this 'informed consent' is not consent at all. Staff cannot really refuse to be investigated. In some instances the process of MCR actually forms part of the contract of employment. If you want the job you accept the assessment – it is not negotiable. An interesting point of speculation here is how managers would feel if trade unions adopted mystery shopping methods to monitor management performance! Another issue is whether those who deem it ethical to engage in deception in their mystery shopping role will be trustworthy enough to report their findings truthfully (Norris, 2004).

Third, there are reservations about the effects of the procedure on the evaluators. Rawlins (1998, p. 376) notes the dangers of a system where: 'Cloaking oneself while scrutinizing others, the detached observer achieves a sense of vicarious social connection, without assuming any obligations to other persons or for mutually beneficial comportment.' Indeed, it can be argued that the mystery shopper is a relative of the paid informer. Where undercover operations are for the wider good of society they are morally acceptable. However, when they are designed primarily to improve the profit margins of a corporation they are at the very least ethically questionable. The assessors are at the cutting edge of the entire process and are likely at some stage to have qualms of conscience about their activities.

Fourth, the ramifications of MCR for those being assessed have to be considered. The knowledge that someone will eventually appear and pose as a consumer is bound to affect staff behaviour. There is an inevitable (if not always conscious) grain of ingratiation, coupled with a sprinkling of suspicion as consumers are dealt with. This was humorously depicted in the classic sitcom *Fawlty Towers* by the behaviour of the hotel owner Basil Fawlty, as he reacted towards guests he viewed as possible hotel inspectors. His behaviour towards those he viewed as potential inspectors could most politely be described as grovelling, in marked contrast to the contempt he reserved for 'normal' guests. MCR is regularly used to monitor the performance of service staff who are already under severe pressure because of what has been termed 'emotional labour'. This term is used to describe the form of employment in which the employee is expected to constantly display a certain type of affect (e.g. the friendly, smiling, hotel receptionist). Prolonged emotional labour can be exhausting (Martínez-Iñigo *et al.*, 2007), and this is exacerbated by the effects of being spied on intermittently. As expressed some years ago by Selltiz *et al.* (1976, p. 218)

> the investigator who proposes to enter a situation without revealing his research purpose has an obligation to ask himself whether there is any possibility that his disguised activities will harm any of the people in the situation and if so, whether the potential results of his research are valuable enough to justify their acquisition under these circumstances.

There is a growing and worrying trend towards what has become known as 'the surveillance society', including the use of a variety of surveillance techniques in the workplace (Sewell and Barker, 2006). The Surveillance Society Network has produced a report to illustrate the pervasive nature of surveillance on most aspects of our lives (www.ico.gov.uk/upload/documents/library/data_protection/practical_application/surveillance_society_full_report_2006.pdf).

This is manifested in what has been termed the 'Big Brother syndrome' in organizations (Milne, 1999). Employers are increasingly checking on all aspects of the work of staff, by logging telephone calls, checking e-mails and internet sites visited, and monitoring behaviour on hidden spy cameras. This, in turn, can lead to an erosion of the workforce's individual and collective autonomy (Ford, 1999). The use of MCR is another example of this surveillance mindset. What managers need to remember is that employees who perceive themselves to be not trusted will be less loyal. They are also likely to rise to the perceived challenge of devising ways of beating the surveillance system (Webb and Palmer, 1998).

Several suggestions have been made (e.g. Dawson and Hillier, 1995; Carrigan and Kirkup, 2001) to help reduce the ethical problems associated with MCR. Indeed, organizations such as ESOMAR, the world organization for market research (www.amai.org/docs/ESOMAR_guidelines_2005.pdf), the Mystery Shopping Providers Association (www.mysteryshop.org/ethics/), and the UK Market Research Society (www.mrs.org.uk/standards/downloads/revised/active/Mystery%20shopping%20guidelines.pdf) have produced guidelines for those carrying out mystery shopping. For example, ESOMAR make a clear distinction between mystery shopping *research*, where all data are treated as strictly confidential and no one is personally identified, and a mystery shopping *project*, where the data are collected as part of an assessment of staff. It has been argued that there are fewer ethical problems associated with using this methodology for research as opposed to for commercial assessment (Norris, 2004), as it is possible to ensure the anonymity of participating organizations and individuals.

Among the key recommendations for those using MCR are:

- Disciplinary action must not be taken on the basis of MCR. Another manager in the Wilson (2001) study stated: 'It is important that we make clear that mystery shopping is not used as simply another stick for managers to beat employees with' (p. 729).
- Staff must be informed in advance during exactly which period MCR will be occurring.
- The objectives of the exercise should be fully explicated.
- Staff should be clearly informed if reporting will be at an outlet or an individual level.
- If staff are to be identified individually this should be part of their contracts.
- Clearance should also be sought from unions or other relevant staff associations.
- The results should not be used to discipline staff.
- Staff should not attempt to 'evaluator spot', to avoid any interference with genuine customers.
- Evaluators should be thoroughly trained.
- The assessor should spend no longer than a normal consumer in any outlet or on any telephone call.
- Staff should be told if visits or telephone calls are to be recorded, and if so who will have access to the recordings and what will happen to them.
- An item should be purchased where possible.
- No follow-up action should be requested.
- Visits should not be made at busy periods.
- No more that one visit per quarter should be made.

While these ethical guidelines, if fully implemented, help to offset the concerns about MCR, they have their limitations. In practice, they are often ignored (Ng Kwet Shing and Spence, 2002). For example, in her analysis of the area, Miller (1998) cited the positive views expressed by industry personnel from various fields. One of these sources states that: 'One of mystery shopping's benefits is that you often get recordings of people doing wonderful jobs which you can use as an example to others.' So much for the ethical principle above, about no use of recordings! Also, one wonders what usage is made of these when a member of staff is not perceived to be doing a good job. Similarly, Leeds (1992, p. 25) in discussing the need to optimize MCR outcomes, argues that supervisors need to be trained 'to interpret the mystery shopper's findings, how to correct mistakes, and how to discipline'. Again, such advice flies in the face of the above ethical guideline that MCR should *not* be used as part of the discipline process. We personally know of organizations that check on how their staff respond to telephone enquiries by recording calls from mystery shoppers. These recordings are then used as part of the ongoing feedback and discipline cycle with staff.

Clearly, there are strengths and weaknesses associated with MCR. A major drawback is the lack of hard evidence as to the effectiveness of this approach. As noted by Morrison *et al.* (1997, p. 351) 'Published data on the accuracy (reliability and validity) of mystery customer research appear to be non-existent.' While it may have initial short-term effects in terms of employee performance, there are serious doubts about the long-term effectiveness of this approach – in essence the novelty effect tends to wear off and staff revert to their former behaviour (Wilson, 2001). Furthermore, MCR may be able to effect changes in specific practical features (e.g. how clean the facilities are, whether up-to-date magazines/newspapers are available, duration of wait time) but the extent to which it can impact on deeper systemic elements (e.g. level of trust in the company, degree to which consumers feel they really matter, ability of employees to empathize with customers) is more problematic (Finn and Kayandé, 1999; Van der Wiele *et al.*, 2005).

However, MCR is widely used, popular across a wide range of sectors, and when rigorously implemented does seem to produce performance improvements. It is therefore not likely to disappear. Detailed research is needed into all aspects of the process, including the design of DCLs, and the effects of age, gender, race, and other geodemographic variables on the assessment procedure.

There is also a need for a strict ethical code to determine its use. In analysing some of the issues involved, Miles (1993) quoted one person involved in the business of MCR as saying 'We are trying to find a compromise between high moral tone and pragmatism.' The worry, of course, is that in the world of business, pragmatism usually wins. It may be for these reasons that some European countries are less enthusiastic about MCR than their UK and US counterparts. Thus trade unions in Germany and France regard mystery shopping as a threat, and in the former country objections have been raised on data protection grounds. In Australia, if employers wish to conduct covert surveillance on employees they must obtain permission from a magistrate.

Anyone using this audit approach treads a fine line between the desire for hard data about how clients are actually being dealt with, and an awareness that such information arrives in questionable ethical baggage. MCR is more acceptable when the audit is at outlet level, and the results do not 'finger' specific individuals. Problems can then be dealt with by local management in a low-key rather than a high profile manner. In general, it is our view that auditors should only use MCR if there are no viable alternatives, and when they do so they should ensure that proper ethical safeguards are put in place – and adhered to.

CONCLUSION

In this chapter we have reviewed two separate types of audit method, both of which have been employed extensively in many differing contexts. They are similar in that the core methodology involves the completion of carefully designed log-sheets. A major difference is that in one case the process is one of self-report by the individual involved, while the other involves a covert evaluation of a member of staff by a trained observer. The first, diaries and logs, requires that staff analyse their own communications on a preset sheet as soon as possible after they occur. In the second, undercover auditing, an observer pretending to be a consumer engages in an interaction with a member of staff and immediately afterwards fills in an assessment form.

Although the DCL methods described in this chapter do not analyse behaviour *in vivo*, in the absence of video or audio recordings they are as close as it is possible to get to charting the topography of organizational communications. Both methods have strengths and weaknesses. Self-reports are prone to inaccuracy. We all reconstruct to some extent when asked to recount our experiences – and we usually do so to show ourselves in a better light. Bias in diaries is therefore to be expected and anticipated. With proper pilot testing of the DCLs, coupled with preparation and training of respondents, such effects can be minimized. In the case of MCR, there are problems of intra- and inter-observer reliability, but again these can be lessened by rigorous field testing and training of auditors. A more serious issue here is the dubious nature of the ethics of using subterfuge to collect data, unbeknown to the person being investigated.

Chapter 7

Communication network analysis

Menno D.T. de Jong and Karen H. Zwijze-Koning

INTRODUCTION

This chapter focuses on network analysis as a communication audit technique. Network analysis differs from most other audit methods, as its primary focus is on the relationships between employees rather than their personal experiences or judgements. Network analysts try to evaluate the quality of organizational communication by assessing the structural patterns in the relationships among staff. All kinds of relationships between employees may be studied. In an audit context, two types of relationships predominate: (1) affective relationships (e.g. employees' feelings of friendship, trust, or appreciation), and (2) various kinds of information exchange relationships.

Over the years, network analysis has become an important research tool in the social sciences, used to answer many different research questions, both in organizations and outside them. Specialized books are available that describe the essentials of network analysis in detail (e.g. Wasserman and Faust, 1994; Scott, 2000). Furthermore, an extensive terminology has been developed to characterize networks, network relationships, and the role of individual actors (Brass, 1995; Monge and Contractor, 2001).

In this chapter we describe the utility of network analysis as a communication audit tool. First, we discuss the network perspective on organizations, arguing that it is impossible to think of an organization without networks, and that an evaluation of the networks may contribute significantly to the outcomes of a communication audit. After that, we give an overview of the various data collection methods that can be used to conduct a network analysis. Finally, we address the analysis of network data, together with some practical examples from our own research.

NETWORK ANALYSIS AND COMMUNICATION AUDITS

Every organization can be seen as a complex combination of networks. First, there is the formal organization structure, which prescribes the position that individuals and organizational units have in the organization. In addition, there are also formal communication structures that predefine who in the organization should interact with whom on various matters. Over time, the formal structures of organizations have become increasingly complex, and when companies merge even more challenges are placed on organizational networks. Formal organization and communication structures are by no means infallible, as is underlined by the many reorganizations that occur in practice.

Furthermore, it is important to recognize that formal organization and communication structures are only part of the story. In their work, employees develop preferences for interacting with certain colleagues while avoiding others, and communication and sometimes even decision-making may depend strongly on the informal circuit (the so-called grapevine). Every organization will thus develop an informal communication system. Many different factors play a role in the emergence of such network relationships (Monge and Contractor, 2003), and these do not necessarily coincide with considerations for the overall effectiveness of the organization. Employees may develop network relationships to optimally satisfy their own needs (or those of their departments); they find out which colleagues are willing to share important information, how organizational decision-making can be influenced most effectively, or which coalitions will be most beneficial to them. Network relationships are also affected by (physical) proximity and (physical or mediated) accessibility. Most employees will have experienced how dislocation of organizational units can obstruct communication lines, and how moving their office or workplace from one place to another affects their contacts within the organization. At the same time, modern methods of communication can help to maintain social networks over time and space (Larsen, 2008). Similarity in personal and demographic characteristics also appears to be important for forming new network relationships (the so-called homophily principle).

A network analysis is included in a communication audit to evaluate the functioning of the formal and informal networks in an organization. Going beyond the individual perceptions of employees, a network analysis can shed light on the organization as a whole, on specific relationships, and on the position of individual employees, subgroups or departments.

Though various research questions may be addressed through the use of this technique (see Zwijze-Koning and de Jong, 2005), all network analysis research in communication audits focuses on uncovering *communication patterns* within an organization. The analysis shows which communication lines are present, and which are not, making it possible to detect and diagnose whatever 'information blocks' are hampering communication effectiveness. Closely related to this, the network analysis may also uncover *communication roles* of employees. It may become clear that certain individuals play a crucial role in the dissemination of information, whereas others are rather isolated. A network analysis may also identify *subgroups*, either functional groups or informal cliques. Employees in these subgroups might have similar attitudes towards their jobs and the organization, as reflected in constructs such as job satisfaction, communication satisfaction, organizational identification, and organizational commitment. By uncovering these groups, network analysts can help to explain these organizational phenomena (Lucius and Kuhnert, 1997).

It is important to distinguish between various types of networks. Although more fine-grained distinctions are imaginable (and may be useful in particular organizations), we propose that a network analysis in a communication audit focuses on at least three different types of communication:

- The strategic network: information exchange relationships regarding organizational policy and decision-making.
- The operational network: information exchange relationships regarding daily work routines.
- The personal network: friendships and personal interactions within the organization.

Each of these three networks focuses on different aspects of the organizational communication, and a comparison of the characteristics of the three networks is often very informative, as we demonstrate later in this chapter.

DATA COLLECTION FOR NETWORK ANALYSIS

In this section we discuss four data collection techniques that are frequently used to map communication networks: sociometric questions, observation, the small world technique, and archival analysis. In addition to these four techniques, network analysts may also use diaries and an ECCO analysis, but these techniques, which both have broader applications, are described in Chapter 6. For each of the four techniques we give examples of their use and address some reliability, validity and feasibility issues.

Sociometric questioning

Sociometric questioning is by far the most frequently used technique for studying communication networks (e.g. Bovasso, 1996; Feeley, 2000; Friedkin and Slater, 1994; Human and Provan, 1997; Ibarra and Andrews, 1993; Rice and Aydin, 1991; Schwartz and Jacobson, 1977). When researchers use sociometric questions, respondents are asked to indicate their frequency of contact with other members of the organization. In some cases, the communication network is mapped based on a single question, as is the case in the International Communication Association (ICA) network analysis instrument, where respondents are asked to react to the statement, 'During a typical workday, I usually communicate about work-related matters with the following people through the following channels' (Goldhaber, 1993, p. 363). In this way, respondents describe the information exchange relationships around them; the result is called an 'ego-centred network'. Another option is to use more than just one overall sociometric question and to formulate a series of more specific questions that together map the network of information exchange within an organization (e.g. 'With whom do you talk about problems that you encounter in your daily work?' 'With whom do you discuss the progress you make in your work?' and so forth).

In a similar way other types of exchange relationships may be studied, for example friendship relationships ('Whom do you consider to be your friends within this organization?'), advice relationships ('To whom do you go for advice within this organization?'), or relationships of material aid ('With whom do you sometimes exchange books within this organization?'). Other types of exchanges that may be studied are trust, social support, or influence relationships, all depending on the type of network under study.

Sociometric questions can take many forms. Data may be collected by means of questionnaires or during interview sessions (face-to-face or by telephone). Respondents may be asked to freely recall all of their network contacts, or fill out a roster containing the names of all of their colleagues (recognition). Different answering scales may be used, ranging from drawing a line (the longer the line, the more frequent the contact), to answering on predefined scales relating to frequency of contact (often, sometimes, never), or having respondents indicate how often they meet each network member (X times a week, X times per day, etc.). Respondents may be asked to name a fixed number of network contacts (e.g. a maximum of five), or they may be allowed to name as many contacts as they can recall. Sociometric questions can cover different time frames, such as network contacts during a typical working day, or interactions during the past week, month or even year. Finally, different aspects of the relationship may be examined, such as the strength, duration, quality, or importance of the relationship.

Sociometric questions usually result in network configurations that represent the relatively stable patterns of communication within the organization. Analysis of the data may reveal groups, and communication-related roles may be exposed – such as network stars (opinion leaders), liaisons, bridges, gatekeepers and isolates (for a description of these roles, see the 'Analysis of network data' section). Sociometric questions can cover different types of information exchange or different types of relationships, which can reveal varying network configurations. They seem to reliably identify the (informal) communication links within the organization (Brewer, 2000). However, it has been shown that more specific sociometric questions (such as 'With whom do you communicate about problems regarding your work?') produce more reliable results than more general questions (such as 'With whom do you communicate about work-related matters?') (Barrera, 1980). In addition, when respondents are asked to freely recall their network contacts, this produces a more stable range of names than when a roster is used (e.g. Ferligoj and Hlebec, 1999).

However, the validity of sociometric questions is threatened by the fact that respondents may give socially desirable answers when asked to name their network contacts. Respondents may feel threatened and consequently name the contacts they think they are supposed to have (as indicated by the formal organizational chart), rather than those that they actually have. Respondents may also name more network contacts than they actually have in order to present themselves as important to the organization. Brewer (1995) showed that the status of network contacts (e.g. being an executive) positively affects the extent to which these employees are recalled in a network analysis. He also showed that proximity influences employees' recollection of their network contacts. People will more easily remember the contacts they have with immediate colleagues who work nearby. Bailey and Marsden (1999) found that the vagueness of sociometric questions clearly affects their validity. They conducted a think-aloud study in which participants were asked to verbalize their thoughts while answering sociometric questions. Their results showed that respondents may think of different things when asked, for example, to name the people with whom they discuss important matters. Many respondents thought of work-related issues (naming colleagues as their network contacts), while others named people with whom they had discussed personal problems (naming family members). Finally, Ferligoj and Hlebec (1999) showed that when respondents are asked to use a roster to generate their network contacts, they will name more network contacts, and will also include more 'weak ties'. Weak ties are co-workers with whom employees interact infrequently. Such ties have proved to be important for the diffusion of information in organizations, since they often provide new information to employees (Granovetter, 1973).

Regarding the feasibility of sociometric questions, the efficiency of the technique stands out. Sociometric questions are relatively easy to administer and so a large number of respondents can usually be incorporated in the study. As a result, sociometric questions are very popular and frequently used by network researchers.

Observation

Observation is frequently used in the social sciences, mostly as a qualitative research technique for studying such things as small group behaviour, the behaviour of experts, or the process of work within an organization (e.g. Beyer and Holtzblatt, 1998). However, it is sometimes also used as a quantitative research technique for studying communication networks in organizations (Atteslander, 1954; Freeman *et al.*, 1989; Zack and McKenney, 1995). Since observation is labour-intensive and usually time-consuming, the technique is mostly used in small-scale organizational settings or for studying more qualitative aspects of communication networks in organizations, such as the behaviour of network members during meetings (Hanlon, 1980; Slack and Rowley, 2001; Vinten, 1994).

Observation research can take many different forms. Researchers may participate in the work process during the period of observation (participative observation), or they may watch employees from a distance as they perform their work duties. Employees may be informed about the aims and scope of the research (overt observation), or they may be left unaware of the fact that they (and their interactions) are being studied (covert observation). Observation studies may also vary in their level of detail. For example, a video camera may be used to record meetings or other relevant moments of interaction. This permits the researcher to study such things as the tone of voice used during interactions or non-verbal communication employees use during information exchange. Researchers may take notes of these moments of interaction and compare and discuss their notes afterwards.

Sometimes researchers are instructed to note any aspect of the interactions that they consider important (unspecified observation), though in most cases a pre-structured format is used (e.g. an interactio-gram; Atteslander, 1954), which specifies exactly which characteristics are to be observed and noted. For use as a network analysis technique, this variation of observation seems the most appropriate, since it would be almost impossible to note every aspect of every observed interaction. Therefore, researchers usually specify in advance and on the observation sheet, which features of the interaction are to be incorporated: for example, (1) the names of the members exchanging information, (2) the duration of the interaction, (3) the place of the interaction on the work-floor. This is complemented by more qualitative data such as non-verbal communication signals or even the content of the interaction.

When the number of observed interactions is sufficient, observation research may shed light on communicative patterns in organizations and also on groups and communication-related roles in the organization. Where more qualitative data are incorporated in the study, observation research can also help us understand the communication styles used by individual network members or even the types of information that are exchanged during meetings or at other moments of interaction.

Of course, network observation has serious drawbacks. First, the studied time frame is usually limited. Researchers may, for example, study the interactions of employees during 1 week, or during a small number of meetings (2–5). These few days or meetings are not necessarily representative of the 'normal' communication process in the organization; it is possible that employees' communication activities vary during the year as a consequence of varying organizational activities. Second, observation also has a 'place' restriction: it would be impossible to observe all relevant moments of inter-action during a day or a whole week. This is why observation research is mostly used to study the communicative behaviour of important individuals. In such studies, the researchers stay with these individuals during a certain period of time and record all their interactions and certain communicative features associated with these interactions. Finally, when observation is used to study more qualitative aspects of communicative interactions (such as the communication style used), there are reliability issues regarding the researcher's interpretation. Inter- or intra-coder reliability is commonly cal-culated when such qualitative data are used, but it has proved difficult to attain a sufficiently high level of reliability (Potter and Levine-Donnerstein, 1999).

As far as validity is concerned, the situation is more positive. Observation research does not depend on self-reporting, which means that there is no problem of employees misunderstanding questions or forgetting to name certain network members. Employees are also no longer able to give the socially desirable answers. Of course, the so-called 'observer's paradox' means that respondents may be inclined to adjust their (communicative) behaviour because of the presence of an observer in their work environment (as was the case in the famous Hawthorne studies conducted by Roethlisberger and Dickson, 1939), in which case the normal communication situation will not be accurately represented. Differences between observer and observed (e.g. in race, gender, age) can exacerbate the observer's paradox. Finally, it may be hard for observers to avoid interacting with employees, which threatens the validity of the research. For example, Schwartzbaum and Gruenfeld (1969) found that employees tend to communicate with the observer, even when they are asked not to do so.

Ultimately, the major drawback of observation research is its feasibility. Both training observers and collecting the data is very time consuming.

Small world technique

Another technique to study information exchange relationships within organ-izations is the small world technique, originally developed by Milgram (1967). Essentially, the small world technique focuses on the nature of the communi-cation lines between employees: is there an immediate relationship or are they connected to each other by one or more colleagues? As such, the technique sheds light on the degrees of separation and on the path length between employees or departments.

While it has not been widely used in the context of a communication audit, it seems a useful approach for studying the flow of messages within an organization (Rogers and Argawala-Rogers, 1995). Depending on the research questions, there are many possible variations of this technique. However, usually the respondents are given a folder presenting an imaginary problem. They are then asked to send this folder to a predefined target person (chosen by the researcher). If the respondent does not personally know this target person, he or she is asked to send the folder to someone whom they think is more likely to know the target person. Employees who receive the folder are asked to fill out a questionnaire covering several personal characteristics as well as characteristics of the person to whom they send the folder. These questions will vary, depending on the research questions of the study. Respondents may, for example, be asked to name the co-worker's job position, describe their relationship, or explain exactly why they gave the folder to this particular colleague. Researchers who have used this technique (e.g. Stevenson and Gilly, 1991, 1993; Travers and Milgram, 1969; Lundberg, 1975) have investigated the number of links between the first respondent and the target person, the type of relationships that were used to forward the message, and the routes by which the message travelled through the organization.

The small world technique seems mainly suitable for uncovering communication-related roles in an organization, such as sociometric stars or gatekeepers. Employees who are frequently asked to forward the message to the target person may be seen as central to that communication network, or may even be gatekeepers in the communication system as a whole. By analysing the routes the folders take, it becomes clear how the real and informal communication system functions, in contrast to the organization's formal communication system. A unique feature of the small world technique is its ability to map bottom-up communication routes in the organization. For example, the number of links between production line employees and top management can be studied, indicating how effective internal communication lines are and how effective employees are in finding their way in the organization.

There is one major concern with the reliability of the small world technique. It is still unclear how many messages need to be included to warrant stable and reliable results about the organization's communication system and the specific communication network under study. This applies to the number of problems per network, as well as the number of folders per problem, and the number of target persons to include. It is likely that the response will decrease as the number of problems that are presented to the respondents increases.

There are also some problems with the validity of this technique. First, the response rate can be low (Stevenson et al., 1997). In addition, folders may get lost in the organization, which indicates the existence of communication problems, but without providing the data to diagnose these problems. Respondents may also forget to return the questionnaire (attached to the folder), which makes it more difficult to analyse the routes by which the information travelled through the organization. Finally, if respondents think of the assignment as a kind of game, they may treat the issue less seriously.

The effort required of most respondents in a small world study is minimal and thus the feasibility of the technique seems rather favourable. However, the technique does place a considerable burden on the target persons in the study and on 'stars' or gatekeepers in the communication network.

Archival analysis

A final technique for studying communication relationships in organizations is the analysis of archival data. Three types of archival data may serve as the input for a network analysis: internal mail records, phone records and e-mail exchanges. All three make it possible to identify the specific actors involved (in the case of mail and e-mail, it is even possible to distinguish between sender and receiver), date and time of the messages exchanged and in some cases the topic of the messages (Danowski and Edison-Swift, 1985). For the use of network analysis, these moments of information exchange are coded as observed interactions (Zack and McKenney, 1995).

The method is restricted to some specific types of mediated communication; communication in face-to-face situations is neglected. It can be maintained that the method yields insights into the communication patterns regarding the particular media, but it seems questionable whether such findings may be generalized to overall communication patterns. Given this limitation, it does not seem justified to draw inferences about subgroups within the organization or communication roles of employees on the basis of archival network data.

With respect to the reliability of this type of data, there are few concerns. Since data can be gathered unobtrusively, many reliability threats can be ruled out. Data may be gathered during a longer period of time or across several time intervals. However, when the content of the message exchanged is taken into account, there may be problems regarding intercoder reliability (Lombard et al., 2002).

The validity considerations about archival data resemble those described under observation. On the one hand, archival data do not depend on employees' self-reports, which rules out the possibility of socially desirable answers, or misinterpretation of the questions asked. On the other hand, when employees are informed about the (goals of the) study, there is a chance of reactivity: they may change their behaviour to what they think is desirable.

The major concern regarding the feasibility of this type of data collection is the issue of privacy (this is even more important when the content of the message is also analysed). Second, when data are collected during longer periods of time or across more time intervals, the amount of data collected may become considerable and data management can become a problem (see for example Eveland and Bikson, 1987). On the positive side, this type of data collection does not place a high burden on employees and is therefore very feasible in practice.

ANALYSIS OF NETWORK DATA

Network measures

There is not usually just one communication network within an organization, but several (varying by type of information exchange or type of relationship). Network auditors try to discern which networks are most important or problematic for the organization and study employees' relationships concerning these networks. A network analysis can thus result in a huge amount of data and entangled network configurations (especially when the organization has many employees). To reduce the complex data resulting from network analysis, network scholars have developed a range of measures that help describe the relationships and patterns of relationships among network members (Brass, 1995; Monge and Contractor, 2001). Examining these measures can help us evaluate the network data. Three different types of measures can be identified.

First of all, there are measures that describe the *relationships* between actors in a network: for example, the frequency of contact between network members, the strength of a relationship, its multiplexity (the extent to which actors have more than just one type of relationship with each other), or the symmetry of a relationship (the extent to which both actors acknowledge the relationship). Auditors may find it useful to learn about the strength of relationships in an organization or even their multiplexity, since these measures indicate strong influence relationships between employees.

Second, there are measures that describe individual employees' *position* in the network. The most basic measures for employees' positions in a communication network include their in-degree (the number of incoming links) and out-degree (the number of outgoing links). Three more comprehensive measures may be used to detect or diagnose communication problems in an organization:

- Employees' degree centrality (the number of colleagues they have a network relationship with) indicates to what extent they have a central position in the organization's network (compared to other members in the network). This measure helps a communication auditor to distinguish between employees who are very active in the network and employees who do not sufficiently participate in the network.
- Employees' closeness centrality (the total distance, in terms of links, to all other colleagues) indicates to what extent employees can easily reach other members in the network. This is important within a communication

audit context, since it shows an auditor where 'the action is' in the network. Employees who have a high closeness centrality have very short communication lines to other members of the network and can thus easily communicate with other employees.

- Employees' betweenness centrality (the number of times an employee has an intermediary position between two colleagues in the network) indicates their importance in the communication flows within the organization. Employees with a high level of betweenness centrality are positioned frequently between two other employees in the network. In this way, they can mediate the communication between these two colleagues. For a communication auditor, these actors are important because their position gives them some degree of control over the information that reaches other members in the network.

There is also a terminology to characterize the roles people have in the network. A *star* is an employee with a central position in the network and can often be characterized as an opinion-leader. Opinion-leaders are important to identify, because they may play a crucial role in intervention programmes. A *liaison* is an employee who links two or more otherwise unlinked groups, without being a member of either group. As such, this person functions as an important communication link between the groups. A *bridge* is an employee who not only links two groups, but also is a member of both groups. A *gatekeeper* is an employee who is positioned between two or more parts of the network. Because of this position, a gatekeeper can easily control the type and amount of information that flows from one group of employees to another. Finally, an *isolate* is an employee with few if any links to colleagues. Isolates are often employees who feel detached from the organization as a whole and may be bottlenecks in the organization's communication system.

Third, there are also measures that describe the *entire network*. For the interpretation of these measures, it is recommendable to compare different networks in an organization (e.g. the strategic versus the operational versus the personal network), or to compare the same type of network across similar organizations (e.g. the strategic network of organization A versus the strategic network of organization B). Three measures may be indicative of the extent to which there are communication problems in the organization:

- *Inclusiveness* involves the extent to which all employees participate in the network. It shows the auditor whether certain networks function organization-wide, or whether certain (groups of) employees are not included.
- *Density* represents the extent to which network members are connected with each other. It is calculated by dividing the total number of ties in the network by the total number of possible ties. It gives an indication of the

number of communication lines in the network and of the degree of participation in the network by all employees.

- *Centralization* involves the extent to which the network members are dispersed. When a network is highly centralized, there are only a few individuals who have many relationships with each other. This may be important, as some networks (for instance when decision-making is involved) might benefit from a more decentralized network structure, and a high level of centrality can thus lead to employees' dissatisfaction with decision-making processes in the organization.

Network visualization

Another way to analyse network data, is to visualize the communication network. When analysing network data this way, it is important to keep an open mind and look for surprises (Porter and Adrian, 2004). It may be useful to examine specific characteristics of groups and individuals in the network – for example, the communicative distance between sites and/or departments. It seems logical that two departments that are working on the same product (e.g. Engineering and Marketing & Sales) need to work closely together in order to be successful. However, if there is little contact between the two departments, this obviously represents a communication problem that needs attention.

It would also be interesting to compare the position of employees holding the same type of job in a network (such as all managers, members of the support staff, executives, or line personnel). When a specific functional group is missing from a network (e.g. concerning strategic discussions), this may cause problems for the way decisions are made in the organization. Similarly, one could look at individuals who hold special positions (indicated by their number of relationships regarding a specific topic). For example, an individual may be the only actor connecting two departments, which gives this person a unique gatekeeper position and subsequent control over the amount and type of information flowing between the two departments. Finally, it is important to look for unexpected or noteworthy relationships with individuals at other sites or in other functional groups. Sometimes, network analysis reveals central individuals (communication 'stars'), who maintain contact (e.g. with managers or executives) through unique relationships, which in turn helps integrate these individuals and their direct colleagues into the organization as a whole.

In addition to studying individuals or groups within one network, it seems equally important to compare different networks within an organization. Comparing these different networks can reveal important differences in their configuration (such as their level of centralization, or inclusiveness), as well as differences in the positions of individuals in the networks (such as in their level of centrality, or closeness).

Of course, visualizing network data can help to confirm the findings based on network measures, and in turn the network measures can help to confirm results based on the visualization.

UCINET and NETDRAW

Various software packages are available for analysing and visualizing network data. UCINET (Borgatti *et al.*, 2002) is a relatively user-friendly program in which actor-by-actor matrixes can be constructed that reflect employees' relationships to one another (see Figure 7.1). Within these matrixes, a 1 represents the existence of a relationship between two employees, and a 0 represents the absence of such a relationship. The program calculates the most important network measures (see above) and visualizes the communication relationships that employees have with one another using NETDRAW (the network visualization package that comes with UCINET).

Case example 1: Network visualization

Figure 7.2 shows the result of an actual network study that we conducted. The figure represents the overall communication network of relationships between employees of a large school (teachers, managers, staff members). A single line (an arrow pointing in one direction) represents communication of a particular employee with another colleague on a regular basis. When the line is reciprocal (an arrow pointing in both directions), both employees claimed to have had contact with one other on a regular basis during the past year.

	TCH1	TCH2	TCH3	TCH4	SS1	SM1	MM1	TCH5
TCH1	0	0	0	1	0	1	0	
TCH2	0	0	0	0	0	1	1	
TCH3	0	0	0	0	0	1	0	
TCH4	0	0	0	0	0	0	0	
SS1	0	1	0	0	0	1	0	
SM1	0	1	1	0	0	0	1	
MM1	0	1	0	0	0	1	0	
TCH5	0	0	0	0	0	1	0	
BM1	0	0	0	0	0	1	0	
TCH6	0	1	0	1	0	1	1	
SS2	0	1	0	0	0	1	1	
MM2	0	1	1	0	0	1	1	
TCH7	0	1	0	0	0	0	0	
SS3	0	0	0	0	0	1	0	
TCH8	0	0	0	0	0	1	0	
TCH9	0	0	0	0	0	1	0	

Figure 7.1 Actor-by-actor matrix in UCINET.

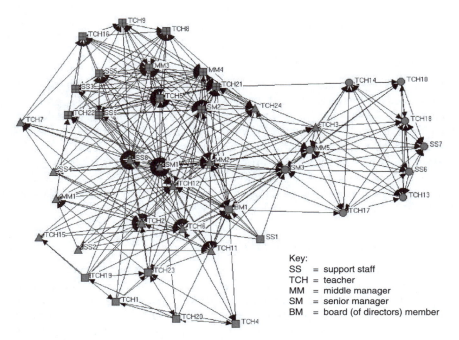

Figure 7.2 The overall communication network of a large secondary school (the shapes of the nodes represent the various sites of the school).

When we look at this network, one of the first things that stands out is the separate position of one of the sites of this school: it is clearly separate from the other locations. Many teachers and staff members at this site have few or no contacts with employees at other sites. Only the managers of the separate site (SM3 and MM5), as well as one teacher (TCH3), uphold strong relationships with members of the organization at the other sites. From a management perspective, it seems undesirable for an organization to have a group of employees who have few or no relationships with colleagues at other sites. The separate position of these employees within this organization may easily result in decreased levels of employee identification with the school as a whole and impede school-wide collaboration and the mutual exchange of ideas.

Another remarkable feature of this network visualization, which is related to the problem mentioned above, is the special role of the senior and middle manager working at the isolated site. Given their position in the communication network, these managers appear to be very influential in the organization's communication system. For the employees working at the separate site, these managers form the only direct information route for information flowing from other sites, as well as from the board of directors. The managers seem to have so-called gatekeeper positions, and as such hold control over the type and amount of information that reaches subordinates at their site. They may easily enforce their opinion about school-wide events (or even important superiors) on their subordinates. There was also one teacher at the remote site who maintained contact with colleagues at the other sites, linking employees who would otherwise not have been linked to their direct counterparts. In this way, this person performed an important liaison role, representing an extra communication link between employees at the isolated site and those of the school as a whole, a link not based on the hierarchical communication structure.

From this example, we see the unique value of network analysis as a communication audit tool. Both the isolated position of the one site and the specific communicative roles of the two managers and the one teacher represent communication problems that might well have been overlooked, had we not performed a network analysis. Other audit techniques, such as for example the critical incident technique and the Communication Satisfaction Questionnaire (see Zwijze-Koning and de Jong, 2007), focus on employees' perceptions of communicative behaviour and are less likely to detect that there is no information exchange between two entities, or that communication links are missing, especially when they do not perceive this situation as problematic. When responding to a communication audit, it is not easy to consider non-existing behaviours or the absence of communication lines, simply because the goal of most audit techniques is to evaluate current communication lines and the actual behaviour of employees. Network analysis, however, can uncover these problems, and appropriate recommendations can be made.

Case example 2: Network measures

Network data may also be evaluated by examining the various network measures based on that data. More specifically, one can examine employees' scores within a particular network (e.g. strategic discussions), or across different types of networks (comparing particular employees across, for example, the strategic, operational and personal networks of the organization).

Examining the network measures in one of our own studies, we found an employee with a betweenness centrality score of 26.62 (in the operational network), where the average index score was only 2.54. Looking more closely, we learned that this staff member had particularly strong relationships with the board of directors, as well as with many managers of the sites of this organization. It was a most remarkable position, because none of the other staff members had such a high centrality score, and also because this person seemed to maintain such strong relationships with the school's management team. We looked at responses from the more qualitative data collection techniques for an explanation. From these data we learned that this particular employee was responsible for the school's financial administration and that he worked as a first assistant to the board of directors. During the time of the study, the school was dealing with serious financial problems and this staff member was frequently asked to gather information from all school sites concerning such things as the exact number of students or salary costs, and report this to the management team. From these qualitative observations, we learned that this situation was only temporary and thus did not call for any structural adjustments in the communication system. However, it did raise some doubts about the current situation in this organization, since it seems undesirable for a board of directors to depend so much on one individual employee. Were this individual to be absent for a longer period of time during this period of financial crisis, the organization would be confronted with a serious communication problem.

It is also sometimes useful to compare employees' positions (or the position of certain groups) across different types of network. This was demonstrated when we once compared the position of the principal of a school across the three different networks within that school (the coordinative, strategic, and personal). When we compared his betweenness centrality index score for the various networks with the average index score for these networks (see Table 7.1), his score showed remarkable deviations. The principal appeared to be very central in the strategic network of the school, and was thus highly involved in discussions concerning the school's identity, future plans, or how new policies were to be implemented. However, his centrality score for the personal network appeared remarkably low, which meant he did not participate in personal conversations with employees, for example about their home situation or daily news items. Apparently, the principal had many relationships within the school (hence his central position in the strategic network and to a lesser extent the operational network), but he seemed to take little time to discuss personal matters with his subordinates. This observation corresponded with the more qualitative data we had gathered from the employees. While employees experienced a lack of involvement from all members of the management team, they made it clear that this applied most strongly to the principal. Employees mentioned several critical incidents

Table 7.1 Normalized betweenness centrality index for the principal and other employees

	Principal's betweenness centrality index*	Average betweenness centrality index*
Strategic network	2.22	1.58
Operational network	0.96	1.08
Personal network	0.45	1.43

* Based on symmetrized networks.

where he had handled issues that were important to the employees in an impersonal manner, and they also mentioned his lack of personal attention for teachers and managers of the school. Some employees described how the principal would not greet them in the hall as he passed them on his way to a meeting. In this way, the qualitative data supported the data gathered on the basis of the network analysis.

CONCLUSION

In this chapter we have explored the utility of network analysis as a communication audit tool. We have demonstrated how data collection methods such as sociometric questioning, observation, the small world technique and archival analysis are all useful sources of information with their own unique strengths and weaknesses. Within a communication audit, different types of network measures as well as the visualization of communication networks can help to detect and diagnose important communication problems in organizations.

The contribution of network analyis lies primarily in its ability to map communication patterns in organizations and to uncover groups and communication-related roles of employees. As such, a network analysis may help a communication auditor to detect and diagnose problems that remain unnoticed when the audit only focuses on individual perceptions and experiences of employees. Compared to most other audit techniques, network analysis focuses relatively strongly on actual behaviours (instead of perceptions). Furthermore, it gives a detailed image of the communicative behaviour of individual employees and organizational units.

Within a communication audit, a network analysis may have three functions. First, it is possible to use network analysis as a primarily descriptive technique. The method is then used to give an overview of the way people communicate within the organization, but does not necessarily have to lead to problem detections itself. The results serve as background information to help interpret the results of other audit techniques. Second, network analysis may be seen as an independent source of information about communication problems in an organization. Although the translation of network data into problem detections is not always straightforward, it is sometimes possible to detect and diagnose communication problems on the basis of network analysis alone. This will often require a comparison of network data against an ideal model of the organizational networks, or a comparison with the network data of different (but similar) organizations. Third, network data may be used to support the findings of other audit techniques. This form of triangulation works in both directions. Network data may be used to corroborate or explain the feelings of dissatisfaction employees express in critical incidents, surveys or interviews. It will also be fruitful to verify whether problems found through network analysis are also acknowledged in employees' self-reports.

In all, network analysis provides a unique and important perspective on an organization's communication system; a perspective that only network analysis can bring to a communication audit.

Chapter 8

Auditing professional practice

Owen Hargie and Dennis Tourish

INTRODUCTION

The audit principle is now very familiar in all professions. As noted by Jamtvedt *et al.* (2008, p.1) 'Audit and feedback continues to be widely used as a strategy to improve professional practice.' Financial audit, medical audit, clinical audit, organizational audit, and so on, are all commonplace terms (Baker *et al.*, 1999). Likewise, the concept of communication audit is accepted by most professional bodies, and has been recognized as having a key role to play in evaluation (Hogard and Ellis, 2006). It is also consistent with a more general focus on consulting professionals during analyses of professional practice (Hogard, 2007). Within this context, the audit approach has developed rapidly in relation to the analysis of the interpersonal performance of a wide range of professionals. Much of this development was initiated in the 1980s, a time when huge changes were sweeping through the professions. Prior to this, as Marinker (1986, p. 15) pointed out:

> professional standards were very much a matter for the professions themselves ... The move from private to public accountability is ... best understood in relation to the growth of information in society, and a new sophistication among members of the public.

As the public demanded better service from professionals, methods had to be found to satisfy this demand. As summarized by Reid (1988, p. 230), 'The evaluation of professional practice is central to every aspect of the organisation, delivery and quality of services.'

Audits of professional practice occurred at all levels. An example of a small-scale audit was one conducted by Markar and Mahadeshwar (1998) into written communications between two professional groups – GPs and psychiatrists – in relation to the outpatient assessment of patients with learning disabilities. In a more comprehensive audit study, Skipper *et al.* interviewed all health professionals associated with a particular clinic in a large hospital (see Chapter 12). At a general level, government-backed audits were also implemented. Thus, in the UK the Audit Commission has for some years regularly investigated the effectiveness of public services in the fields of health, housing, local government and criminal justice, and it continues to produce detailed reports on their findings (see www.audit-commission.gov.uk/). To take but one example, in 1993 the Audit Commission carried out a detailed, influential and widely quoted audit of acute general hospitals in England and Wales. This set standards as to what patients were entitled to expect in hospital, and measured these against the actuality. This audit examined, *inter alia*:

- patient information leaflets
- hospital notice boards and signposts
- telephone communications with patients
- written communications from hospitals to patients
- the discharge process
- the main problems experienced by patients – both practical in terms of being in hospital and clinical in relation to their consultations with health professionals
- patient complaints and how hospitals deal with them
- how the specific problems faced by non-English-speaking patients are handled.

The utility of the Audit Commission's approach can be illustrated by examining only one small part of the 1993 hospital audit. This investigated the treatment received by female outpatients with breast lumps who were referred to hospital for clinical examination. Eight key treatment standards were formulated and 12 consultant surgeons were then audited on these. As shown below, the results revealed few surgeons using each standard, as indicated by the numbers in brackets.

1   Written information used (n = 1)
2   Discussion of radiotherapy before a decision taken on surgery (n = 2)
3   Patient dressed on meeting the surgeon (n = 2)
4   Nurse included in the discussion of treatment (n = 3)
5   Patient dressed for discussion of the prognosis (n = 4)
6   Patient invited to bring a companion (n = 6)
7   More than one chance to discuss the treatment (n = 6)
8   Consultant working with a breast nurse (n = 7)

One surgeon did not score on *any* of the standards, three scored on only one, and the best score was one surgeon who used seven out of the eight. Furthermore, the Audit Commission found that the clinical protocol usually involved the patients arriving at hospital, being asked by a nurse to strip naked, medical staff arriving and not introducing themselves by name, conducting the entire procedure – including medical history, reasons for referral, clinical examination, and treatment options – all with the patient undressed and usually lying on the treatment couch with only a sheet to cover her. The conclusion was that such a 'way of conducting the consultation strips patients of their dignity as well as their clothes, and because it increases their feelings of vulnerability, makes it even more difficult for them to focus on what is being said and questions to ask' (1993, p. 26). Not surprisingly, when interviewed, patients expressed considerable dissatisfaction with their treatment. This audit had a substantial impact on the way in which patients were treated in hospitals.

Various audit methodologies have been employed in studies designed to monitor, evaluate and improve the communication performance of professionals across a broad spectrum. Indeed, all of the methods covered in the previous chapters are relevant. Questionnaire surveys, in-depth interviews, focus groups, diary logs, and undercover methods have all been utilized to gauge information about professional practice. For example, in the pharmacy profession alone, questionnaire surveys (Koo et al., 2003) and interviews (Olsson et al., 2002) have been conducted to determine consumer views, pharmacist self-report measures of performance have also been employed (e.g. Latif, 2000), and the undercover approach has been utilized to test pharmacist responses to patients presenting with specific problems (e.g. Chiang and Chapman, 2006).

This chapter examines three further methods for examining professional practice, namely the critical incident technique, constitutive ethnography, and the Delphi technique.

CRITICAL INCIDENT TECHNIQUE

This is a specific methodology that is used to educe concrete instances of effective and ineffective behaviour in any context. It is an inductive approach, in that all of the data emanate from the respondents. The critical incident technique (CIT) is based on the view that internal feelings of satisfaction or dissatisfaction with a person, profession or organization are the result of actual experiences. In particular, the way in which events that are 'out of the ordinary' are experienced is central to judgement formation, and leads to the eventual attribution of positive or negative attitudes towards the source. These attitudes then influence how future encounters are 'seen', categorized, and responded to. This perspective was neatly summarized by the former British Prime Minister, Benjamin Disraeli: 'Experience is the child of Thought, and Thought is the child of Action.' We are therefore using the word 'critical' in a very particular sense, to indicate an event or experience that has a special importance for the respondent, rather than one that is necessarily negative in nature.

When asked for a 'critical' example, it is argued, the experience that is chosen reflects a wider general view about how the person feels – the incident is retrieved from the relevant memory 'file'. An exploration of what individuals see as important experiences, or incidents, therefore provides pertinent information about their attitudes to a particular group of people, or to an organization in general. It also offers practical insight into key areas of both good and dysfunctional performance. As a simple example, we expect things to progress normally when we go to a restaurant for a meal. But what happens when the waiter spills a glass of red wine over your new suit? How such a 'critical' incident is handled by the manager and staff will have a key impact on your attitude to the restaurant. In summarizing the reasons why they used this approach in their study of adverse sedation events in children undergoing surgery, Coté *et al.* (2000, p. 805) explained: 'We used critical incident analysis because this is the most efficient way of studying rare events to determine what went wrong and why', with the further benefit that one can, 'interpret the events as a rational guide to systems changes that could prevent similar incidents in the future'. Equally, it is important to chart those instances where clients have had exceptionally positive, value-enhancing experiences, above and beyond what they would have normally expected, as these have been shown to produce dramatic increases in consumer satisfaction and loyalty (Füller and Matzler, 2008).

In essence, the CIT taps into the cognitive schema of individuals (Kressel *et al.*, 2002). A schema is a cognitive structure that provides the individual with readily accessible information about what to do in a particular situation. Schemas are built up and developed over time, as a result of increased experience of a situation. Thus by adulthood we have formulated schemas for a huge variety of situations, such as dining in a restaurant, checking into a hotel, greeting friends, and so on. These schemas enable us to behave 'without thinking'. So when we enter a restaurant we don't have to consciously think about what to do – we just automatically engage the relevant schema and related script for 'restaurant mode'. However, if something unexpected occurs (either a positive or negative event) then the auto-pilot is switched off and we become mindful of our responses. As a result, such events become more memorable. By then examining these exceptional events we can learn more about how to deliver positive experiences and how to avoid negative ones.

The critical incident method was pioneered by Colonel John C. Flanagan (1948, 1954), who, as Director of the Division of Aviation Psychology first used it to investigate the specific competencies of air pilots in the Second World War. He asked experienced pilots to reflect back on the last time they saw a trainee pilot do something that was effective or ineffective (i.e. the 'critical incident') and then to answer three main questions:

- What led up to this situation?

- What exactly did the man do?
- Why was it effective/ineffective?

Based on their responses it was possible to identify actual instances of positive and negative behaviours, which in turn led to a compilation of key pilot competencies. Following the early pioneering work of Flanagan, thousands of investigations have been carried out using various forms of the CIT approach (Gremler, 2004). As described by Urquhart *et al.* (2003, pp. 63–64): 'The critical incident technique . . . is regarded as a flexible set of principles, to be modified for the situation under study.' However, although variations have been suggested to the critical incident technique (Roos, 2002; Lundberg, 2008), and differing terminology has been used to describe this method (Butterfield *et al.*, 2005), the central approach remains much as initially developed by Flanagan. Thus Mallak *et al.* (2003) noted the three core aspects that need to be investigated:

1   a description of the situation and events that led to the incident
2   the actions of the central people involved
3   the outcomes from the incident.

In the organizational sphere, Davis (2006b) recommended a fourth issue:

4   the possible future implications for the organization arising from the incident.

In essence, CIT involves three main phases.

1   *Defining the target population.* The main issue here is how precise to be in setting the parameters for inclusion. There is a tradeoff between exclusivity of focus and generalizability of findings. This is known as the 'bandwidth-fidelity problem' in research (Singh, 2004). It means that methods that measure a broad span are by their nature less precise than those that focus on a narrow area, while the latter produce a more limited spread of understanding than the former. For example, in a study of the key skills of lawyers the researcher would have to consider the types of specialism and range of functions of different members of the profession. Decisions would then have to be taken about whether to include all qualified lawyers in a single (broad) study, or to have separate (narrow) studies for those specializing in specific areas (corporation, litigation, etc.). Other decisions would have to be made, for instance about whether prosecuting counsel and public defenders should be studied separately.
    The next issue is who to employ as the 'subject matter experts' (SMEs) (Anderson and Wilson, 1997), who will identify and analyse the incidents. In most studies this is usually restricted to experienced practitioners and

instructors. However, consumers and other professional groups can also provide informed insight. For instance, in one study of the role of the cancer nurse, the expertise of patients, carers, nurses and doctors was all gleaned and combined to identify key competencies (Cox *et al.*, 1993). A related aspect is the number of SMEs that should be utilized. There is no set answer here. Indeed, in his review of 141 CIT research studies in the service sector, Gremler (2004) found that the number of SMEs used in different studies ranged from 9 to 3852.

2   *Obtaining the description of incidents.* In obtaining accounts of incidents, two factors need to be considered. First, how many incidents in total should be collected? Second, what method should be used for collecting them? There is no definitive answer to either question. In relation to overall number, Caves (1988, p. 206) noted how in most studies 'the usual practice has been to seek refuge in large numbers of incidents'. However, the larger the sample size, the fewer the incidents required from each person. In general, between two and four incidents seem to be the upper and lower limits of studies that have used CIT (Dunn and Hamilton, 1986; Lount and Hargie, 1997). In relation to the method for collecting data, there are two main alternatives, questionnaires and interviews (see Chapters 3 and 4 for a full review of each method).

Where interviews are utilized, SMEs need to be notified well in advance about what is expected of them. They should have identified and thought carefully about the incidents *prior to the interview or questionnaire completion.* Interviews should be recorded for later transcription and analysis, with the role of interviewer being that of guide, facilitator and listener. Anderson and Wilson (1997) recommended using workshops to collect CIs. They advise that each workshop should last for 3 hours, the first 30 minutes of which is devoted to training; there should be 10–20 SMEs per session, with each individual attending only one workshop. The advantage of this group approach is that it saves time – one explanation of the CIT methodology suffices for up to 20 SMEs.

Regardless of which approach is adopted, the guidelines identified by Dickson *et al.* (1997) (Box 8.1) provide a useful data collection template. When asked to select a critical incident, SMEs should be told to select an example that (a) deviates significantly in either a positive or negative fashion from the norm, and (b) can be described in detail (Bejou *et al.*, 1996). During CIT interviews, as a rough rule of thumb, Edvardsson and Roos (2001, p. 253) recommended the exploration of 'cause, course and result'. In other words, subjects should be asked to explain exactly what caused the incident, precisely how it progressed, and what the perceived outcomes were. They also argue that an incident can be regarded as 'critical' when it has important consequences for the organization under study.

3   *Identifying the competencies.* This is a very important stage of the

---

Box 8.1 Identification of critical incidents in practice

Think of one or more occasions recently where you witnessed good or poor communication practice. Under each of the following headings, describe *exactly* what happened.

Where did the event take place?

Why was the interaction considered to be effective/ineffective?

Who were the people involved?

What features of the individuals were important in the interaction?

What actually occurred in the interaction?

What was the outcome?

What are the implications of this incident for future practice?

---

process. It involves careful content analysis to convert the data obtained into discrete and clearly distinguishable competencies. In practice, this task is almost always completed by the researchers, both because of its time-consuming nature and the data analysis skills required. However, Caves (1988) strongly advised that the SMEs should also be involved at some stage, ideally to help to validate the content validity of the final list of competencies. In other words, the 'insider' knowledge of professionals is useful to complement the more 'objective' perspective of the researcher.

A case study will help to illuminate the discussion at this point. In their study of the priesthood, Lount and Hargie (1997) used the CI technique to identify key interpersonal skills of Catholic priests. Having negotiated access with the bishop of one diocese in Ireland, they randomly selected 33 priests, representing 25% of the total number of priests in the diocese. These SMEs were contacted by telephone and, having agreed to participate, were asked to think in advance about personal experiences of what for them were important communication incidents in their work. This procedure was employed to give the priests time to reflect on key experiences and so reduce the likelihood of trivial incidents being selected. The priests were then interviewed by the researchers in the former's environment and were assured of absolute confidentiality. The standard format for this type of interview was followed (see Box 8.1).

A total of 184 critical incidents were obtained from the interviews. Analysis of these showed that they included 84 different types of people (from an architect to an undertaker), and 15 main categories of problem. The most frequently reported problem dealt with was that of marital disharmony, followed by bereavement. In dealing with such problems, priests used a total of 89 different interpersonal skills. A list of the 25 most reported skills was then compiled and sent to all 135 priests in the diocese, who were asked to rate each skill on a 5-point scale, and then to identify and rank order what they considered to be the five most important skills. The analysis of this data then allowed the researchers to compile a final schedule of the key skills as perceived by priests themselves. Of these, the top five were listening, understanding, honesty, confidentiality, and showing care/concern. These data formed part of an overall audit of professional practice in the priesthood.

The simple, yet robust, nature of the CIT method has led to its widespread usage across a wide variety of contexts, including, *inter alia*, dentistry, nursing, teaching, social work, marketing, university lecturing, speech therapy, counselling, medicine, surgery, pharmacy, the priesthood and management (Butterfield *et al.*, 2005; Lount, 1997). The exact purposes of research studies employing this methodology vary far and wide. For example, in the professional sphere it has been used to:

- identify effective conflict handling and mediation skills used by healthcare managers to deal with disputes in a hospital setting (Kressel *et al.*, 2002)
- chart those effective and ineffective communication behaviours of virtual team workers that are regarded by team members as central to the success or failure of the team (Dekker, 2007)
- compare effective and ineffective approaches to handling incidents of a sectarian nature in the workplace (Dickson *et al.*, 2003)
- investigate the perceptions of health professionals, residents of old people's dwellings and their families, as to the most important dimensions in the care of the aged (Cheek *et al.*, 1997)
- identify and assess the competence strengths and weaknesses of entrepreneurs (Mulder *et al.*, 2007)
- chart the factors taken into consideration by professionals working in family courts when they make their final decision about where a child should reside (Banach, 1998)
- identify effective and ineffective approaches employed by healthcare professionals when breaking bad news to patients (Dickson *et al.*, 2002)
- measure the quality of coordination in the construction industry (Darshi De Saram *et al.*, 2004)
- ascertain how and in what ways nurses respond to the spiritual needs of their patients (Narayanasamy and Owens, 2001)

- survey training directors of APA-accredited programmes in the USA and Canada about the exact nature and implications of ethical transgressions made by psychology graduate students (Fly *et al.*, 1997)
- examine facilitative and inhibiting spouse behaviours in relation to patients with heart problems (Broström *et al.*, 2003; Martensson *et al.*, 2001)
- identify factors that affect the competence levels of nurse supervisors (Arvidsson and Fridlund, 2005).

The method can also be used to audit external publics. For example the CI method has been used to:

- discover the impact of negative and positive shopping experiences on customers in the retail sector (Wong and Sohal, 2003)
- ascertain patient satisfaction or dissatisfaction levels with various aspects of their care (Pryce-Jones, 1993)
- identify the precise factors that provoked customers of service firms to switch their patronage from one outlet to another (Roos, 1999)
- determine the effects of service failures on customer attitudes to airlines (Bejou *et al.*, 1996)
- distinguish situations in which the emotional needs of patients attending a cancer unit were not met by staff (Kent *et al.*, 1996)
- investigate 'welcoming' and 'unwelcoming' experiences of disabled consumers in retail outlets (Baker *et al.*, 2007)
- detail the impact that the presence of other customers has on individuals in a shared service environment (Grove and Fisk, 1997)
- chart the specific business-to-business context of problems experienced by buyers in retail wine outlets (off-licences, pubs, hotels, restaurants, etc.) in their dealings with wine suppliers (Lockshin and McDougall, 1998)
- investigate the effects of service guarantees on service recovery in the hotel industry (Lidén and Skålén, 2003).

Using the critical incident technique within organizations

In the specific communication audit context, the CIT method has been widely employed. This is not surprising, given that it 'provides detailed insight into the communication processes within the organization' (Zwijze-Koning and de Jong, 2007, p. 265). As noted by Downs and Adrian (2004, p. 158) 'The technique is well respected, and it can be a valuable audit tool'; however, interestingly, as a result of practical experience in their audits they changed the term 'critical incident' to ' communication experience'. This was after receiving negative feedback from senior management who baulked at the connotations associated with the term 'critical', perceiving it to be an appeal to respondents to record only negative experiences. Others have also suggested changing the name, with Keatinge (2002) recommending 'Revelatory Incident'. We have also witnessed a negative response to the term from senior staff with whom we have worked on audits, coupled with confusion from respondents about the exact meaning of 'critical' (particularly when conducting audits in the health sector!). As a result, and while the method remains exactly the same, we recommend that auditors use the term 'Communication Experience' to gather data about critical incidents (see the main questionnaire in the Appendix).

The data gleaned from this part of the questionnaire (see the Appendix) reveal some very important information (Tourish and Hargie, 1996b). First, a comparison can be made of how many reported instances are effective and how many are ineffective instances of communication. This then provides a rough measure of the overall communication climate. If the vast proportion of reported examples are overwhelmingly negative, then there are clearly problems with communications. In organizations where communications are functioning reasonably well, one would expect an effective/ineffective ratio of at least 50/50 to prevail. Higher or lower ratios provide a useful barometer of communication pressures, particularly if the technique is used to chart the progress of communication over a prolonged period of time. Second, the sources of effective or ineffective communication can be delineated. A detailed examination of responses will reveal exactly where these high and low pressure points are located. For example, in one audit we found that the overwhelming source of dissatisfaction was not with working colleagues or managers, but with a service department within the company. We were therefore able to identify the exact department and the precise reasons for dissatisfaction. In essence, what the service department viewed as priorities did not concur with the views of staff in the recipient departments. Consequently, new standards of service were agreed and monitored to overcome the problem.

While, in general, this method is used to give respondents complete freedom to select whatever example they wish, in some audits the focus is narrowed to specific areas. For instance, SMEs may be asked to focus specifically on a staff group (such as communication with managers, or with staff from other sites), or a communication medium (such as telephone or e-mail), and restrict their example entirely to that category. In fact, the original ICA Audit Questionnaire had a 'critical incident' sheet attached to *every* section, so that respondents had to provide a separate incident relating to channels of information, sources of information, and so on. However, in our experience this amounts to overkill, and the time and duplication required to complete all of these incident sections meets with resistance from managers and staff alike. Response rates can therefore fall precipitously when people are faced with requests for far too much information. On the other hand, the inclusion of a single incident allows respondents the freedom to select from all of their experiences what they consider to be most typical of communication in their organization. As a consequence, this one section often acts as a form of thermometer, identifying hot and cold areas of organizational communication temperature.

Points for consideration

In evaluating the CIT technique, the following points should be borne in mind.

Face validity

The notion of providing a personal example of communication makes sense to most people, who will readily concur with the following sentiments of the Scottish philosopher Thomas Carlyle (1860, p. 299):

> What is all knowledge too but recorded experience, and a product of history; of which, therefore, reasoning and belief, no less than action and passion, are essential materials?

We all spend a fair proportion of our lives telling family, friends and colleagues about things that have happened to us in our dealings with others, what we said or did, and how we felt. Not surprisingly, therefore, many respondents relish the opportunity to complete this section of a questionnaire, or interview, detailing their key experiences.

Respondent-centred nature

Since the method brings to centre stage the frame of reference of respondents, it is free from the 'designer bias' that can contaminate the quantitative sections of questionnaires. The incidents, and how they are reported, are created by respondents – this section of the questionnaire is left open for them to select and describe freely what they wish. Of course, if interviews are used to collect the incidents these can result in bias if they are not conducted properly (see Chapter 4). Another problem here is that CIT depends on the capability of the respondent to remember and relate the incidents accurately. The possibility of response bias and distortion in the accounts of interviewees needs to be recognized (Michel, 2001). Memory is a constructed process and over time we can reconstruct experiences to fit with our existing cognitive schemas. On the plus side, CIT produces a wealth of insight into the complexities and subtleties of the issue under analysis, and provides a depth of understanding of the underlying meanings that would be difficult to achieve by other methods (Keatinge, 2002).

Methodological reservations

The qualitative nature of this method has produced some criticisms about the reliability and validity of the results – mainly along the lines that it does not allow for statistical analyses. However, when implemented in a systematic and consistent fashion, the CI approach has been shown to be a sophisticated data collection methodology (Zwijze-Koning and de Jong, 2007; Schluter *et al.*, 2008), and one in which the advantages far outweigh any disadvantages (Johnston, 1995). It provides an in-depth analysis of what respondents perceive to be the main issues, and allows them to describe these in detail. In an organizational context, this can serve to put flesh on the bare bones of quantitative data gathered in the main body of a questionnaire. As expressed by Pryce-Jones (1993, p. 95) 'Quantitative methods are designed to produce numerical statements of effects (numbers of opinions held) without identifying primary causes. Critical incident technique pinpoints individual causes of dissatisfaction.' In other words, the main body of the questionnaire may reveal that staff are very unhappy with senior managers. However, it does not reveal *why* this is the case – the CIT approach will be much more likely to provide this detail. In essence, number crunching methods produce a picture of the event under scrutiny, but it is often a monochrome image – the addition of qualitative methods can help to convert this into full technicolour.

Illumination of minority views

If recurring causes of deep dissatisfaction are found across even a small minority of respondents, then this can be very significant. In quantitative sections of the questionnaire such insight may be lost, since the majority of respondents will not have rated this as a problem – and so its overall rating will be at least in the 'satisfactory' band. For instance, most people may be happy with the company intranet, yet a few people in one part of the organization may feel that it is missing important information from their area. The CIT section will bring this to light, and detail the specific reasons why this is the case.

Inclusion of rating scores

While the CIT method is primarily qualitative, it also allows for a certain degree of quantification. For example, counts can be made of the number of times specific incidents recur, or particular issues are mentioned. An additional approach is to have respondents rate various aspects of the incidents. These ratings can then be used to measure different dimensions of the issue under investigation. Thus, in their study of wine retailers' experiences with wholesale suppliers, Lockshin and McDougall (1998) asked respondents to rate the following on a scale of 1 to 10:

- how serious the identified incident was
- the way in which the problem was dealt with
- how frequently this particular problem occurred
- how important this supplier was to the respondent's business
- their overall level of satisfaction in their dealings with this supplier.

These ratings provided additional insight into the views of retailers. They revealed that respondents were less satisfied with the way in which routine as opposed to non-routine incidents were handled. This suggests that clients expect normal procedures to be followed as a matter of course and can get annoyed if this is not the case, but where a problem that is more unusual occurs they will be more tolerant in their expectations of the time needed to resolve it. In terms of recovery strategy, or how the problem was dealt with, if it was solved after one telephone call as opposed to two or more calls, ratings of satisfaction with the way it was handled and with the supplier per se were higher, the problem was rated as more minor, and the product line was viewed as more important to the business.

Time and labour

As with most qualitative techniques, the CIT method can be very demanding. If interviews are used, these in themselves are time consuming. The content analysis of results is then a laborious and slow process, involving detailed scrutiny of either written or tape-recorded responses. Thus it is by no means an inexpensive audit methodology.

Positive models

Because CIT asks for effective as well as ineffective instances of communication, it identifies and illuminates existing best practice. Many managers (and indeed staff) may initially see the audit as a form of Spanish Inquisition. However, audits produce many good news stories, and these can serve as useful role models for the promotion of best practice. The CIT approach allows the auditor to provide detailed insight into exactly where, why, and with whom, satisfaction with communication is high. When these are highlighted in the audit report (see Chapter 10), it becomes clear to all that, far from an inquisition, the audit can be an excuse for a celebration.

CONSTITUTIVE ETHNOGRAPHY

The nature, implementation and identification of the central components of expert performance represent a complex field of study (for a full review of this area see Ericsson and Smith, 1991). Indeed, a salutary warning was sounded by the former British Prime Minister, Lord Salisbury, when he advised as long ago as 1887: 'No lesson seems to be so deeply inculcated by the experience of life as that you should never trust experts'! Different perspectives are held on the best way of accessing the behavioural components of expertise. For example, one view is that social scientists have the necessary training, knowledge and skills to identify and analyse interpersonal performance. The corollary perspective is that this is not the case, but that rather only those who practise within a given situation or profession are capable of charting the core components, since only they can fully understand both the central context and the subtle nuances involved. The latter view largely guides the technique known as constitutive ethnography (CE), although this methodology also recognizes the role of social scientists in navigating the procedure.

The term 'constitutive ethnography' was first coined by Mehan (1979), who developed this research approach as part of his investigations into teacher–pupil interactions in school classrooms. As he summarized it: 'A description of the interactional work of participants that assembles the structure of these events is the goal of this style of research' (p. 8). Mehan was particularly concerned with an examination of the social organization of interpersonal encounters – in his case classroom lessons. In describing this methodology, he noted: 'constitutive ethnography requires that three criteria be met: first, the organization described by the researcher must, in fact, be the organization employed by the participants; second, the analysis must be retrievable from the materials; and third, the analysis must be comprehensive' (p. 35).

This approach was later further developed and refined by Saunders and Caves (1986) and Hargie *et al.* (2000), who tailored it to meet the specific requirements of skill identification in professional contexts. The important part of these refinements was that the professionals themselves were moved to centre stage in the overall research methodology. The main function of this later form of CE is that of 'analysing and identifying aspects of interpersonal behaviour which occur in social interactions in order to chart those skills and strategies that go to producing skilled performance' (Dickson *et al.*, 1997, p. 197). It uses an 'expert-systems approach' within what has been termed the 'consultative' research paradigm (Caves, 1988). In other words, consultation is central to the whole ethos, with professionals playing a key role as 'experts' in investigating their own practice. As noted by Crabtree (1998, p. 100) the goal here is that of 'mapping the *primary* concepts constitutive of practice'.

Variations of this approach have been used in research studies. For example, Tallman *et al.* (2007) employed 'grounded ethnography' in a study where they video-taped 92 adult primary care consultations and then had the doctors and patients separately view the recording of their own consultation. They then audio-taped interviews with patients and physicians based on their reactions to the video recordings. In addition they obtained measures of ratings of patient satisfaction for each of the doctors in the study. The researchers then analysed the video recordings to identify the skills used by doctors, and related these to the post-consultation comments of both physicians and patients, and to the ratings of patient satisfaction. As a result they were able to develop a profile of effective and ineffective physician consultations in terms of communication skills.

The form of CE relevant for audits involves obtaining video recordings of actual interactions between professionals and clients, and then subjecting these to detailed peer analysis. As Mehan (1979, p. 19) pointed out: 'Constitutive studies employ videotape and film . . . because they preserve data in close to their original form. Videotape serves as an external memory that allows researchers to examine materials extensively and repeatedly.' It is therefore useful at this stage to briefly examine some of the issues relating to this medium.

Video recording

Cameras are now ubiquitous. They are to be found, *inter alia*, at sports grounds, in stores, in pubs and hotels, in city centre streets, on main arterial routes, in university computer rooms, and in hospital corridors. The UK is the country with the greatest number of cameras per head of population. Thus, someone walking in the city of London will be filmed by some 300 surveillance cameras within a 30-minute period (Litterick, 2006). Indeed the UK has 4.2 million public cameras (one for every 14 citizens) and the average person will be recorded on camera 300 times per day (Rogers, 2006). In an era of spy satellites, and television exposé programmes featuring hidden cameras, we no longer find it unusual to think that someone might be watching us. Since 1975 cameras have been used in stores to study the buying behaviour of customers (Chisnall, 1997). For example, how long are customers in the store before they make a purchase? What areas of the store are they most likely to walk through? Do they read the information on labels before they buy a product? Are they more or less likely to purchase following an approach by a member of staff?

In the UK, the Market Research Society's code of ethics states that consumers should not be filmed unless they are in a location where they could reasonably expect to be seen or heard. This rules out, for example, the use of cameras in changing rooms. However, as Gumpert and Drucker (1998, p. 414) point out: 'The act of entering a bank, office building or housing complex implies consent to photograph, videotape, or both in order to prevent crime.' The notion of surveillance, and its acceptance by the general public, is now widespread. Despite this, and especially in research studies, Dowrick (1991) highlighted the importance of consent in the use of video. He argued that subjects should sign a consent form that:

1   communicates the purpose of the project and whether or not it is for research or other purposes

2   gives the reason/need for recording the participant
3   presents the steps that will be taken to ensure confidentiality
4   states the absolute right of the subject to withdraw at any time and for any reason
5   describes what will happen to the tapes and when they will be erased.

However, it is not always possible to secure the informed consent of every participant on an individual basis. For example, the Hargie *et al.* (2000) study described below involved an overall total of 105 hours of video recording actual pharmacist–patient consultations. The pharmacists in this study (who owned their stores) did not want their customers to be approached by a researcher, either before or just after entering the shop, to be informed about the nature of the research project. It was felt that such 'interference' by the researchers might lose them potential business. As a result, the method of individual informed consent could not be employed.

To enable the study to continue, an alternative method was adopted, which used the generic approach of having large posters displayed prominently on windows, doors and around all areas of the shop for one full week leading up each video-recording session. These described the nature and purpose of the project, assured individuals that all recordings would only be seen by the research team, and that tapes would be erased at the end of the study. Posters were 'updated' on the days of recording, stating clearly that video-taping was taking place that day. The camera was placed on a tripod at the side of the counter so that patients would be aware visually of its presence. This method has been used in other similar studies (Wilson *et al.*, 1989; Smith *et al.*, 1990).

Constitutive ethnography in practice

Once recordings have been obtained, professionals then analyse these in depth, both individually and in groups, in order to identify and describe the *constituents* of effective and ineffective performance. It is behaviour analysis by those involved in the actual interactions and so is *ethnographic* in design. The pattern of analysis involves building from individual opinion and analysis through to group sharing and pooling of knowledge. This results in the eventual itemization of the verbal and nonverbal behaviours deemed essential for effective professional communication.

This method can best be explained by reference to an actual study. A major investigation of community pharmacy practice using this methodology was carried out by Hargie *et al.* (2000). In this investigation, 15 pharmacists agreed to have their consultations with patients video recorded for later analysis. A total of 20 consultations were recorded for each pharmacist. These were then analysed in four stages.

Stage 1: Individual analysis

Here, pharmacists were given an analysis form on which they had to judge whether each consultation (episode) was effective or ineffective, and give reasons for their choice (Box 8.2). They then had to view their tapes and select their five most effective and five most ineffective consultations, and complete a more detailed written assessment of their performance on these 10 episodes, including comments on the specific professional situation depicted, and the frequency with which it typically occurred (Box 8.3). They also recorded any

---

Box 8.2 Classification of recorded episodes

Instructions to pharmacists

During this individual viewing session we would like you to view each of your recorded episodes and broadly classify whether, in your opinion, your communication with patients was **effective** or **ineffective**, stating briefly the reason for your choice.

Format of individual viewing session record sheet

Episode no.	Effective	Ineffective	Reason
1			
2			
3			
4			
5			
6			
7			
8			
9			
10			

Box 8.3 Schedule used for selection of effective/ineffective episodes

Instructions to pharmacists

During this individual viewing session you are requested to select the 10 episodes of your own communication with patients for further analysis by the study group. We would like you to select 5 episodes that in your opinion are examples of **effective** communication and 5 that you think are **ineffective**. Please complete the following details as fully as possible.

Name   Episode no. [ ]

What is the situation?

This is an example of **effective/ineffective** communication because

In my view, the communication in this situation is **effective/ineffective** because

I would consider this situation to be a rare occurrence: Yes[ ]   No[ ]

I would deal with this situation: once a day[ ] once a week[ ] once a month[ ] once a year[ ]

Points to be borne in mind from the tape (not immediately obvious) when assessing the communication in this episode are:

What I would do differently to improve communication in this situation would be:

---

background detail that, while perhaps not obvious from the video, was in their opinion relevant to the assessment of communication. This information then facilitated discussion at Stage 2. Finally, they made suggestions about how the communication could have been improved. Since at this stage participants in CE were watching recordings of their own interactions for the first time, issues relating to self-viewing need to be borne in mind. The project team must be sensitive to participants as they assimilate their own self-image, and allow time for this process to bed down, only after which can meaningful behaviour analysis occur (see Dickson *et al.*, 1997 for a review of this area).

Stage 2: Triad sessions

At this part of the analysis, pharmacists met in groups of three to share their expertise and evaluations and also to scrutinize the consultations of each other. They were asked to review their own 10 consultation episodes and the 10 identified by each of the other two in the group, their task being to consensually select the most effective and least effective consultation for each individual (see Box 8.4). The triad then completed a schedule for each of these six episodes (Box 8.5). This required them to clearly identify seven behaviours of the pharmacist that were instances of good pharmacist–patient communication. In addition, they were instructed to identify any behaviours that the pharmacist could have taken to improve the consultation.

Box 8.4 Instructions for triad selection of core episodes

Now that everyone has completed Stage I of the project we are interested in generating some discussion about what constitutes effective and ineffective communication within community pharmacy practice. During this triad session we would like you to view your selected episodes again along with the 10 episodes from the other members of your group, and for the triad to select one effective and one ineffective episode per pharmacist. These will be included in the 'pool' of episodes that will be seen by the entire study group. We would like you as a triad to complete the 'selected' episode sheet provided so that at this session we have a completed viewing sheet for each of the 3 effective and 3 ineffective episodes selected by the triad. For the purpose of the exercise you should appoint a coordinator and secretary for each pharmacist.

For your 6 selected episodes please try to identify 7 different actions of the pharmacist that are, in your opinion, instances of effective pharmacist–patient communication. If this task seems rather abstract, make it more concrete by imagining that you have a pre-registration pharmacist beside you. Use the tape to point out to the inexperienced pharmacist instances of communication that they would do well to attend to. We would like you to describe what is going on in such a way that what you put on paper would be meaningful to someone who has not seen the video-tape.

In column I we would like you to write down what the pharmacist did (actions) that, in your opinion, made the interaction either effective or ineffective. In column II we would like you to describe the message(s) that the action(s) listed conveyed (meaning). Finally, in column III we would like you to indicate whether the action was an example of in-effective or effective communication for both the pharmacist and the patient. e.g. As a triad you might analyse the action described in the following way.

I. Action	II. Meaning	III. Effective(E)/Ineffective(I)	
		For the pharmacist	For the patient
1. Pharmacist interrupts their conversation with patient, to ask assistant to lock up	Pharmacist wants to get away (after all it's 5.30 pm)	E (as they wished, brought interaction to a close)	I (obviously had more to say but pharmacist closure meant no opportunity to express feelings)

We appreciate that you may want to include more than one definition of the pharmacist's action and correspondingly, more than one meaning. However, having reached consensus within your triad we would like you to provide **only one** definition of every action and meaning in each episode. Please provide a minimum of 7 listed actions.

Box 8.5 Triad viewing sheet

Name_____   Episode no. _____

This episode was chosen as example   Effective communication (E) [ ]
of   Ineffective communication (I) [ ]

The 7 actions that, in our opinion, are instances of **good** pharmacist–patient communication in this episode are as follows:

I. Action	II. Meaning	III. Effective(E)/Ineffective(I)	
		For the pharmacist	For the patient
1.			
2.			
3.			
4.			
5.			
6.			
7.			

Stage 3: Categorization of behaviours

After the triad sessions the next task was that of classifying all of the identified behaviours into categories and labelling them. Given the very time-consuming nature of this part of the project, the social scientists on the research team carried out this initial categorization task. While ideally this would be carried out by the professionals themselves, in practice this is unrealistic. However, to emphasize the consultative nature of the study, the initial categorizations were presented as a tentative first step, to be subjected to detailed analysis by the pharmacists. Following further discussion, an eventual list of effective communication categories and related sub-categories was agreed. All 30 recorded consultations were then viewed by the project team who were asked to evaluate each using this category list. This process led to further discussion and refinements, resulting in a final agreed classification.

Stage 4: Individual ratings of essential behaviours

In this final phase, pharmacists individually viewed the 30 consultations again and rated on a 6-point Likert scale the extent to which each of the identified communication skills was essential for effective pharmacist–patient communication in that context. In addition, pharmacists were asked to indicate on a separate scale the extent to which they felt that each of the skills was essential for effective pharmacist–patient communication *as a general rule*. This allowed an estimate to be made of the perceived contribution of specific skills to effective pharmacist–patient interaction generally. These ratings were then used to weight the relative importance of the identified skills and sub-skills.

Following all of these stages, it was possible to compile a detailed list of 45 key communication behaviours, which were in turn categorized into 11 main skill areas. The two most important skill areas identified were those of rapport-building with, and explanation to, patients, Similar projects using the constitutive ethnographic framework have been carried out in the fields of speech therapy (Saunders and Caves, 1986), physiotherapy (Adams *et al.*, 1994) and university lecturing (Saunders and Saunders, 1993a).

Points for consideration

In evaluating the CE approach, the following points should be borne in mind.

Logistics

Since professionals themselves are at the heart of CE, it necessitates considerable commitment from them. Methods have to be found for recruiting sufficient numbers to make the investigation viable (allowing for a potential drop-out). A range of material and other resources are also needed, including time, finance and technology. In the study described above, research funding was obtained to pay for locum cover to release the community pharmacists from their work and to purchase specialized audio-recording equipment. Inevitably, however, the pharmacists had to devote more time than the locum cover paid for. Their goodwill and personal commitment were therefore necessary to ensure the successful completion of the study. The arrangements for video recording and timetabling of viewing sessions are also time consuming, sometimes quite complicated, and inevitably demanding. This all takes place before any data analysis can occur, so this method is not one for the faint-hearted auditor! In practice, therefore, CE is a method usually employed in well-funded research investigations.

Face validity

The results obtained from CE have very high face validity within any profession. This is primarily because identification of skills comes directly from members of the profession – they are neither imposed nor invented by others. It is possible for social scientists to follow much of the CE protocol described above, but then to carry out the analysis and interpretation of data themselves (see for example Rackham and Carlisle, 1978). However, this is open to the criticism that the analysis has been conducted by 'outsiders' and so lacks an 'insider' view of what is happening, and the interpretations are therefore less relevant.

Generalizability

One criticism is that CE only represents the views of a small number of people, who may or may not be representative. In reality, and given the commitment expected of them, the professionals who take part will be volunteers. It is not possible to randomly select them. In discussing this issue in relation to the recruitment of community pharmacists in their study, Hargie *et al.* (2000) recognized that one of the most difficult problems they faced was the recruitment of the sample of pharmacists. Since participation would necessitate allowing the research team to video record all of their interactions over a set period and would then require a substantial time commitment to the ensuing analyses of these recordings – often in the evenings – it was clear that it would not be possible to randomly select a set number of pharmacists and request that they participate.

Rather, to recruit pharmacists, what they did was to publicize the study widely, both with direct mail shots and media publicity, and ask for volunteers. What must also be remembered here, of course, is that CE is a qualitative research methodology, and so issues of statistical relevance are not centre stage (see Chapter 5 for a discussion of this issue).

Expertise

Where possible, attempts should be made to identify 'expert' professionals, and also to consider specialized areas of sub-expertise, in recruiting the sample. Thus, in their study, Adams *et al.* (1994) asked senior physiotherapists to nominate 'expert' therapists within the specialist fields of neurology, obstetrics, outpatients and paediatrics, whom they thought should be included. Likewise, Saunders and Saunders (1993b) in recruiting 37 lecturing staff to take part in their investigation into effective university teaching skills, asked the deans of the seven faculties at the selected university to nominate appropriate lecturers across the main discipline areas within their faculties. What constitutes an expert will, of course, vary across contexts. For instance, in their investigation into the skills of effective negotiators, Rackham and Carlisle (1978) used three criteria to select expert negotiators, namely that they:

- had a track record of significant success over time
- were rated as effective by *both* sides
- had a high incidence of implementation success in reaching agreements that proved to be viable.

Analytical ability

Another criticism is that professionals may not have the requisite skills to carry out meaningful evaluations of the behaviour of themselves and their colleagues. This is where the role of the social scientist is essential. Training and guidance may be needed at various stages, and the progress of each participant must be monitored on an ongoing basis.

Professional-centred nature

The client's perspective is not really taken into account in CE. While professionals may be asked to consider this perspective, this is very different from accessing it first hand. This means that in order to gain a complete picture of professional–client communications, other audit approaches (client interviews, focus groups, questionnaire surveys, etc.) need to be used to supplement CE in terms of gauging the client's perspective.

DELPHI TECHNIQUE

This method was developed in the USA in the early 1950s by Olaf Helmer and his colleagues (Helmer and Rescher, 1959). Their work at the Rand Corporation, on 'Project Delphi', concerned an analysis of the probable targets and outcomes of a possible Russian bombing campaign (Dalkey and Helmer, 1963). As noted by Reid (1988) it may therefore be viewed as one of the positive spin-offs from the Cold War. The technique is named after Apollo's Delphic Oracle, an ancient Greek myth that purported that a 'chosen one' living on the island of Delphi could predict the future with infallibility. The oracle was supposed to have a network of informants, and so could combine data from a range of sources. Using a similar rationale, the researchers at Rand argued that if a consensus could be obtained from a number of experts, their decisions were likely to have high validity. The problem, of course, was in obtaining objective and true consensus. The experts could not simply be brought together in a discussion group, since there are many problems therein: the most forceful individuals tend to impose their views on others, more introverted people are less likely to state their ideas in a public forum, conformity pressures mean that group members acquiesce with the majority view rather than state their dissent, and so on. As a result, a process of anonymity was developed so that all opinions could be given equal weight. The views of all participants would be considered and fed back to everyone involved for consideration. These three features of anonymity, maximum expert involvement, and feedback, are the central planks in the Delphi platform (Gordon, 1994).

The approach is similar to CE in that it elicits the views of a panel of experts in a procedure that involves building from individual perspectives to reach an eventual overall group consensus (Linstone and Turoff, 1975, 2002). The main difference is that under the rubric of the main Delphi technique (DT) the participants never actually meet. In fact the DT has five defining features:

1   *A panel of 'experts' are recruited to conduct the analysis.* As discussed
    earlier, the notion of 'expert' is in itself a moot topic, and in reality panel
    members are usually selected on the basis of what has been vaguely
    referred to as their 'reputations' (Dickson *et al.*, 1997). In her review of
    the DT, Powell (2003) highlighted two key criteria for the selection of
    experts: (a) credibility with the target audience, and (b) experience in the
    field. Clayton (1997, pp. 377–378) raised a third criterion, namely that the
    experts involved in DT should have responsibility for the implementation
    of findings: 'Because Delphi is a tool to aid understanding or decision-
    making, it will only be an effective process if those decision-makers who
    will ultimately act upon the results of the Delphi are actively involved
    throughout the process.' In terms of numbers involved, the size of panels
    has varied widely, ranging in number across studies from 10 to 1685; in
    essence, the larger the panel the higher the drop-out rate, with panels of
    20 and under more likely to retain all their members (Reid, 1988).

2   *The experts never meet face to face.* All information is sent to them
    individually in writing and they return their written responses directly to
    the central source. Participants are guaranteed complete anonymity. The
    reason for this is to encourage openness and honesty – people are more
    likely to express their real opinions in private than in public. It also
    removes those psychological influences, such as dominant personalities
    and status differentials, that influence committee-style discussions. While
    in theory it also gives respondents the time to give considered views, a
    down side of anonymity is that it can also lead to hasty, ill-judged opin-
    ions and a lack of accountability. As a result, modifications to the original
    DT have been proposed. For example, what has been termed 'quasi-
    anonymity' has been recommended, where respondents know who else
    is involved in the overall exercise, but all individual contributions
    remain strictly anonymous (Rauch, 1979). Further along this continuum
    is the 'nominal group technique' (NGT), which in essence is face-to-face
    Delphi. Using the NGT, the group members are actually all in the
    same room but they make their contributions in writing individually
    and independently of the others present (MacPhail, 2001). As with the
    DT these individual contributions are then collated and presented (on a
    flipchart or screen) for further individual scrutiny – no discussions occur.
    Another variant of the DT, known as 'wideband modified delphi'
    (Boehm, 1981), actually includes stages of communication and discus-
    sion among the experts. Here, while the decisions are made anonymously
    they are preceded by meetings to agree the main parameters for analysis.
    Initial decisions are followed by a discussion of existing consensus and
    disagreements, and then the experts make their final decisions individually
    and anonymously.

3   *The exercise is conducted in writing, with the project leader coordinating
    the whole process.* The advent of e-mail has facilitated this part of the DT

procedure (Marsden *et al.*, 2003). Indeed Linstone and Turoff (2002) distinguished between *conventional Delphi*, where paper and pencil is used, and *real-time Delphi*, where the process is mediated by computer technology, thereby ensuring that feedback can be given rapidly. Within an organization, the process can easily be completed using the intranet. There is some evidence that the use of computer-mediated methods can improve initial response rates (Ladner *et al.*, 2002). The fact that respondents do not have to be brought together for discussions reduces many of the logistical and resource problems associated with CE. It also means that a Delphi analysis can accommodate participants who may be spread over a wide geographical area (Mayfield *et al.*, 2005). One drawback of the DT is that, given the ongoing demands of involvement, the response rate can drop off significantly after the first round. McKenna (1994) found that using face-to-face interviews in this first stage significantly increased later returns; this is not surprising since the development of a personal relationship has been shown to increase commitment to a task (Hargie *et al.*, 2004).

4   *Two or more 'rounds' take place, in between which the project leader sends a summary of the results of the previous round to panel members.* The full range of opinions is fed back, together with an indication of the extent of consensus on each, and a request for further evaluation and comment on each item. A 5- or 7-point Likert scale with a zero (neutral) mid-point is often employed, with respondents being asked to rate each item. This allows a numerical analysis of consensus to be computed.

5   *An eventual identification of final areas of concordance and discordance is compiled at the end of the process.* The final goal of the DT is a more rounded decision based on the judicious use of expert opinion. In this sense, this approach 'can be viewed as a constructive effort in building knowledge by all who share in the process' (Kennedy, 2004, p. 505). As expressed by Jeffery *et al.* (1995, p. 48), 'After three to four rounds of discussion, opinions and revision, a much better defined opinion, one with high consensus, is the result.' However, there is no set definition of what 'consensus' actually means in DT, either between 'rounds' of the process, or in terms of the final decision (Greatorex and Dexter, 2000). Thus, when do we know that a final or 'best' agreement has been reached? Setting a percentage level seems to be the most common approach, although in different studies researchers have been shown to set varying standards ranging from 100% agreement down to as low as 55% concurrence (Powell, 2003). It is also important to ensure that the initial questions given to the experts are comprehensive, since one of the most common failures of the DT is that certain important areas are omitted from the analysis (Miller, 2001). In fact the task of developing an accurate questionnaire at the outset has been recognized as one of the main problems in employing the DT (Franklin and Hart, 2007).

The DT can be used to examine what key 'players' agree to be the most important communication issues in any profession or organization. It continues to be employed in a range of studies in different professions including, for example, public relations (Watson, 2008), tourism (Kaynak and Cavlek, 2007), dentistry (Lightfoot *et al.*, 2005), nursing (Keeney *et al.*, 2006), health nutrition (Hughes, 2004), midwifery (McKenna *et al.*, 2002), distance education (Thach and Murphy, 1995), library and information sciences (Baruchson-Arbib and Bronstein, 2002), counselling (Vázquez-Ramos *et al.*, 2007), marital and family therapy (Blow and Sprenkle, 2001), education (Hunt *et al.*, 2000; van Zolingen and Klaassen, 2003), medicine (Broomfield and Humphris, 2001), occupational therapy (Atwal and Caldwell, 2003), and pharmacy (McBride *et al.*, 2003; Mackellar *et al.*, 2007). It has also been used widely in organizational contexts (Fairley, 2002), including for the identification of training needs (Somers *et al.*, 1984). Varney (1990) carried out an interesting study using DT in which a random selection of organization development (OD) professionals on the OD Network Roster were asked to first identify and then evaluate the significance of key books and articles in the OD field. This led to the production of a list of what were viewed to be the key publications central to this area. Also in the OD domain, Reid *et al.* (1990) identified the potential applications of DT as including an examination of:

- how staff view the future of the organization
- role definition and clarification regarding exact responsibilities and duties
- goal setting and the determination of key organizational priorities
- the resolution of conflicts and differences between staff
- the identification of current information and communication concerns.

As summarized by Reid *et al.* (1990, p. 40):

> The Delphi Technique has been widely used by organizations as an aid to decision-making. Its features and several of the applications which have been reported in the management and planning literature . . . suggest . . . many potential uses in activities which are essential to the work of organization development.

CONCLUSION

To improve practice it is necessary to audit existing levels of performance, identify areas of strength and weakness, and devise action plans to remedy identified deficits. In the professional sphere, as noted by Reid (1988, p. 232): 'The challenge is to find some means of evaluating professional practice that is both acceptable and credible with the professions, and which has some scientific standing and will produce hard data.' In fact, the techniques employed to audit professional communications will be dependent on a range of factors, including the expertise of the auditors, the time and resources available, and the motivation of the professionals themselves. For example, in relation to the latter point, Goldhaber and Rogers (1979) found that their attempt to use a diary method with hospital staff was thwarted by the resistance of surgeons to what they saw as a time consuming and seemingly pointless methodology (see Chapter 6). Thus, the method chosen needs to be one that has high face validity with those who will be required to implement it.

In this chapter we have examined three such methods, the critical incident technique, constitutive ethnography, and the Delphi technique. While all three methods have different procedures and formats, what they have in common is that they can all be employed to carry out an in-depth investigation of professional communication. They are also all flexible enough to allow for some modifications to meet the demands of particular areas or specific resource limitations. The templates as covered in this chapter can therefore be adjusted depending on objectives and circumstances. This issue is discussed in more depth in Chapter 20.

Chapter 9

Auditing electronic communication

Paula O'Kane, Owen Hargie and Dennis Tourish

INTRODUCTION

The world of work in the 21st century has witnessed vast developments within and around its communication systems. In the first edition of this book the current chapter was entitled 'Auditing the communications revolution', reflecting the ground-breaking electronic (e)-communication media that were then just beginning to become mainstream. However, email and the Internet are now well established and widely utilized. Newer tools such as blogs, wikis, instant messaging, podcasting, and so forth (see Box 9.1) have moved to centre stage in our quest for innovative communication techniques. At the same time, many of the opportunities and challenges posed by these formats remain similar to those of email and the Internet.

The abundance of communication devices generally, and in organizational life specifically, has led to the coining of the term 'multicommunication' (Turner and Reinsch, 2007). This term is derived from the concepts of multi-tasking, parallel processing and polychronicity, and describes the process of interacting with multiple persons through a variety of channels simultaneously. Such multicommunication is now a fact of life (Lee *et al.*, 2005). However, digital natives (those who grew up with computers) find it easier to adapt to this multicommunicative style than digital immigrants (older people born before the digital revolution who had to enter this new world later in life). Nevertheless, continual change in this domain is endemic since 'in the world of technology, there is always the Next Big Thing lurking just around the corner' (Beaumont, 2008, p. 21). Where once the typical office executive had a briefcase with pen and paper, diary and a packet of post-it notes, these office aids have been replaced with electronic gadgets such as the smart mobile phone, blackberry or palmtop.

Given this continued progress, the present chapter begins by focusing on how business communication systems have developed in recent years. It then proceeds to provide an overview of the two key tools of email and the Internet, which still underscore most of our e-communications, and examines how corporations can best audit these. Within this, it considers both the

---

Box 9.1 Workplace electronic communication tools and terms

Communication tool	*Organizational application(s)*
Email	Personal communication using Internet technologies to individuals or groups of colleagues and/or clients, suppliers and other organizational stakeholders.
Internet	Mass communication with the public, including media, competitors, suppliers, as well as customers and clients. Recent advances have enabled individuals to customize websites to meet their specific needs.
Intranet	The internal Internet of the organization providing a central storage area in which information relevant to all employees, or a group therein, can be stored and retrieved for simultaneous, instant access.
Extranet	An extranet expands the capabilities of the intranet to allow the organization to communicate with external clients at remote sites and permits access to specific information relevant to them.
E-Business	This all-encompassing term represents the use of Internet and other related technologies to 'do business'.
E-Commerce	The use of electronic channels to buy and sell products and services.
E-Tailing	Electronic retailing refers to the purchasing of goods and services using the Internet as the facilitator and is normally associated with business to consumer purchasing.
E-Human Resource	The use of the Internet or intranet to facilitate on-line transactions related to Human Resources such as updating personal details, querying employee information and making decisions without the need for Human Resource Department interaction.
E-Recruitment	The use of Internet and/or email to advertise and/or select candidates for jobs within an organization.
Podcasts	The term comes from a combination of the acronym 'pod' for 'portal on demand' and 'broadcasting'. Podcasting technology is used to deliver audio and audio-visual messages internally and externally within an organization in both real time and non-real time for

	replay on personal computers or portable media players.
Blogs	A blog (weblog) enables individuals and groups to communicate via the Internet using mainly text, but also with images and video about topics important to them or, more often than not, an online diary. Others can post comments to their blog.
Wiki	A group of web pages that users can create and update to build a body of knowledge within an specific area of interest, for example Wikipedia. Can be used as a organizational knowledge tool.
Instant Messaging (IMing)	Real-time synchronous text-based conversations between two or more people using e-communication systems such as the Internet and mobile communications.
Video-Conferencing	A method of communicating through audio-visual aids between groups at two different locations via communication technology such as the Internet or phone line.
Telephone	Used to transfer voice messages, usually between two people, across analogue or digital networks all around the world. Most recent manifestation is the mobile phone which supports wireless conversations.
Blackberries	Wireless handheld devices that support not only mobile telephone conversations, but the sending and receiving of emails, surfing the web and other electronic services.

external and internal organizational environment and the upsurge in techno-logically enabled communication. Crucially, some of the core aspects of both legal and corporate governance in regard to e-communication are then explored. In addition, issues relating to the founding father of technological communication devices, the telephone, are reviewed and processes specific to auditing both customer and colleague telephone conversations are dis-cussed. In the final section the role of electronic auditing – using technology to facilitate the audit process – is highlighted.

THE GROWTH OF E-COMMUNICATIONS

With the explosion of e-communication in the new millennium, both in the workplace and at home, corporate websites have become an essential means of communicating with customers. People now expect organizations to have user-friendly websites and efficient email systems. Furthermore, interactive and audio-visual interaction is becoming increasingly popular, thanks to the success of companies such as YouTube. Social-networking sites like facebook.com and myspace.com provide the public with methods of communicating with both people they know and others who are unknown but share similar interests, or perhaps work for the same company. This latter application opens up a new world of communication opportunities for employees to get to know each other and discuss and debate organizational issues.

To access these and other Internet and email applications successfully a broadband connection is an essential piece of apparatus. In the UK business sector, the number of organizations with broadband connections grew from 29% in 2003 to 77% in 2006, representing a 265% increase, and reflecting the increasing reliance that workplaces place on e-communication. The level of e-commerce transactions has also increased among business enterprises. Within the EU, in 2006 Denmark had the highest proportion of business orders conducted over the Internet, with the UK in second place. Central to the recent upsurge in e-commerce activity is Internet access in the home. This facilitates both information retrieval and online transactions. In 2006, 52% of households in the EU had Internet access at home, with highest levels evident in The Netherlands (80%) and the lowest in Greece at 23% (Forrest and Leaver, 2007). In the US the percentage of adults who accessed the Internet grew from 15% in 1995 to 71% in 2007, with 56% of users accessing the Internet on a daily basis (Pew Internet and American Life Project Surveys, 2007).

This volume of usage will inevitably grow. For example, one offshoot of the advances of both wireless and Internet technology is the increased access to communication tools within developing countries. Where the infrastructure for telephone wires was limited in the past, mobile communication has provided an alternative for organizations to access their contacts, and Internet technology has opened up a whole world of information and communication. Similarly, email supersedes the need for an efficient postal service, something often absent in developing nations.

Internet connections facilitate email contacts. There were 1.2 billion email users worldwide in 2007 (The Radicati Group, 2007). Within the business environment, Ferris Research (2006) estimated the number of email users to be around 780 million. The scale of traffic here is shown in the fact that in 2006 some 183 billion emails were sent worldwide each day (The Radicati Group, 2006). Clearly both Internet connections and email communication now far outweigh the number of telephone calls, face-to-face (F2F) inter-actions and written documentation in the workplace. The importance of understanding these mediums cannot be underestimated.

An area which is often under-researched in relation to new technologies is the small–medium enterprises (SMEs) sector. In relation to the use of mobile phones for business purposes, only 51% of SMEs were mobile active in the UK in 2005, while 79% had Internet access and 68% utilized broadband services (Ofcom, 2005). This sector may well have the most to gain from the future of Internet technologies, as their business world is further opened up in terms of suppliers, customers and links with other organizations. The Internet has reduced the cost of communication and research and therefore opened up a new communicative world to smaller businesses.

Given the increased potential that these applications have brought to organizations, we begin by reviewing the two core tools of email and Internet technology.

THE BEGINNINGS: EMAIL

Where a few years ago to have an email address on one's business card was considered to be the height of professionalism and modern business acumen, it has now become standard practice. But the extensive use of email brings a set of emerging issues, each of which needs to be considered within the work-place. The precise content and scope will depend on the extent to which the organization has utilized email and how and in what ways the corporation views its email system, for example from an essential to a supporting role. Ten core issues relating to email communication need to be taken into consideration when auditing this medium:

1 *Overload.* The incidence of overload, that is more data than a person perceives he or she can deal with within a specific period of time, has been exacerbated through the everyday use of email (Dawley and Anthony, 2003). Some of the key reasons for email overload include:

- not optimizing the technology available to reduce spam and filter information
- an organizational culture in which people are encouraged to communicate all information rather than using personal filtering judgement
- as detailed below, the misuse of the email system for personal purposes.

Sillince *et al.* (1998, p. 238) confirmed this when they found that one of the core drawbacks of email was the creation of 'large unnecessary quan-tities of information'. Much of it is non-job-essential and some of it is spam, yet time has to be spent reviewing it (and deleting, replying, etc.). However, perceptions of overload vary from employee to employee: what one person finds interesting and important may be regarded as unnecessary, in the same context, by another (Edmunds and Morris, 2000). This poses difficulties in terms of making decisions about what exactly constitutes load. Thus a clear picture of the actual extent and consequences of load has to be established. The perception of overload creates further problems since people may feel unable to trawl through all their received emails to isolate important or urgent information. One line of research has sought to reduce overload through the design of a tool that helps to manage an employee's inbox by combining task management software with an email client, demonstrating a role for both employee self-management and systems design in improving email communication (Bellotti *et al.*, 2005). By gaining an understanding of what employees view as unnecessary information through an audit, organizations can begin to put procedures in place to reduce overload.

2 *Interruptions*. The 'ping' sound that announces the arrival of new mail and the little envelope appearing in the bottom right-hand corner of our computer alerts us in a somewhat romantic *You've Got Mail* way to the arrival of what might be an urgent or exciting message in our in-box. With trepidation we tentatively navigate to our email, only to find it's a link to YouTube and 5 minutes of distraction. The familiarity of this scenario is often the cause of a loss in concentration, sometimes welcome but often unwelcome and unproductive. Jackson *et al.* (2003) found that, on average, new email was opened by employees within 1 minute 44 seconds of receiving notification of its arrival, and that the majority of emails were actually opened within 6 seconds. This suggests that employees are leaving their current tasks to deal with perhaps unimportant issues, resulting in a concentration loss and possibly creating an unwanted distraction in their working day. Interruptions can be minimized by a combination of email management rules and guidance and training. These issues are discussed further below.

3 *Misuse*. At its basic level the function of email is to send and receive information between individuals and groups. However, the system can be abused by individuals pursuing personal goals. Three distinct areas can be delineated here. The first relates to 'back-covering', in which email is used to send information to those who do not necessarily need it, so that the sender can ensure that all possible bases are covered. The second is concerned with 'appearing diligent'; wherein unnecessary emails are sent to significant colleagues to confirm or appear that the sender is working hard. Finally, email can be used as a tool for 'negating responsibility'. Here, an employee quickly forwards emails containing work requests to encourage colleagues to take responsibility for tasks that are not actually part of their remit; by so doing the sender is also disclaiming

personal responsibility for the work (O'Kane, 2004; O'Kane and Hargie 2007).

4   *Cyber harassment.* Email, in particular, can be used as a method for harassing or bullying colleagues, either overtly or covertly. The occurrence of cyber harassment has increased in recent years (Whitty and Carr, 2006). The lack of F2F contact in email appears to give people the courage to articulate themselves in offensive and insulting ways, which they would avoid in social interaction (this is further discussed later, in terms of 'flaming'). This gives potential harassers and bullies an unchallenged method of offending others. It also presents the opportunity for miscommunication or misinterpretation, which can result in meanings being perceived that were not intended. The upside of this, for the person who feels harassed, is the evidence trail that email leaves (see below). This enables cases to be fully investigated with all information being available. However, such evidence is usually only called into play once a formal complaint has been made. Many victims of harassment are initially unwilling to report a colleague for this kind of activity.

5   *Netiquette.* This term is a derivation of 'network etiquette' and refers to the setting of guidelines with respect to the way in which email (along with other forms of e-communication) is used in both the workplace and social settings. Most organizations do not have an acceptable use policy that provides employees with an overview of what e-activity is acceptable in the workplace (Whitty and Carr, 2006). This can cover issues such as how an email should be written, within what timeframe a reply should be sent, advice about acceptable attachment sizes, how to use the priority status appropriately, and when to begin and end an email dialogue. In other words, at what stage an email is considered to be too long, when it is deemed urgent, and who should actually make these decisions. Much of the debate here surrounds the level to which an organization should dictate employee use of email. Audits of email communication can be used to ascertain employee opinions on these issues in order to inform an acceptable use policy, and also to assess the extent to which existing netiquette policies are being adhered to.

6   *Working relationships.* In terms of relationship building, some employees find that being able to initiate contact with colleagues via email (or other e-communication tools) is much simpler (and perhaps more importantly, less intimidating) than using the telephone or introducing themselves in person to someone in a different department or site (Hacker *et al.*, 1998). In a study of external communication, Leek *et al.* (2003) illustrated how IT was allowing suppliers and buyers to form new contacts and relationships. Bishop and Levine (1999) interviewed 17 employees in a high-tech company and found that email provided them with the ability to contact other like-minded colleagues in order to conduct their work more effectively. Both these groups of people therefore developed

relationships through email, which may not otherwise have occurred. Similarly, employees can readily maintain contact with people they have met within the company through email exchanges. For example, in an investigation of email use in a university, participants reported feeling more 'in touch with others', because prior to email they had found themselves becoming distanced in their expanding workplace (Romm *et al.*, 1996). This consequently also increased their general communicative confidence with both known and unknown colleagues. To understand the role of email within work relationships it can be useful to carry out a social network analysis in which both formal and informal links between employees are identified and explored (see below).

7   *Flaming.* Flaming is defined as 'a tendency for people to communicate irate or negative emotions in emails, which would have been less likely to be expressed through other media' (O'Kane *et al.*, 2007, p. 311). Email is now widely perceived to be a casual communication medium in which users do not have to take the time to carefully consider and reconsider what they communicate to others. This can lead to both intentional and unintentional conflict, with a strong potential for conflict escalation (McGrane *et al.*, 2005). This dynamic is largely created by virtue of the way in which emails are written. Friedman and Currall (2003) noted that inherent features of the technology, not encountered in F2F communication, such as reduced social cues, diminished feedback, the asynchronous nature of email, lengthy emails, and excessive reviewing, can lead to higher levels of conflict. They also suggested that some responsibility must lie with the user of the technology and that the encouragement of greater self-awareness can help to reduce the negative effects. Sallis and Kassabova (2000) studied the email traffic in a newsgroup and found that, in conjunction with poor grammar, vocabulary, and written expression, informality led to ambiguity. This, in turn, could create misunderstandings and lead to increased conflict.

8   *Knowledge.* The concept of managing knowledge within an organization has become a key element of business success (Bontis *et al.*, 2003; Gadman and Cooper, 2005). Inherent in the use of email in the workplace is the ability to transfer huge volumes of information. The challenge for both the individual and the organization is to ensure that this information is useful. All too often information is transferred for the wrong reasons (see 'misuse' above). Effective communication has long been associated with knowledge creation (Connelly and Kelloway, 2003; Peters and Fletcher, 2004), but research has also suggested a growing role for email as a day-to-day information management and social interaction tool that can improve knowledge construction (Levin and Cross, 2004; McFadyen and Cannella, 2004). New organizational knowledge and understanding is not only acquired and transferred but also constructed and explicated when employees take part in an ongoing interactive email

process (O'Kane *et al.*, 2007). Within this, there is a two-way interaction between information and relationship management, which assumes an important role in relation to knowledge construction. If a good relationship is present between two or more people then the information transferred will be enhanced; equally, in order to create relationships people must be willing to disclose and share information, and in essence trust the other person (Tardy and Dindia, 2006). Once these two factors are combined and assessed, knowledge creation becomes much more of a reality within the organization.

9   *Reputation.* Further external issues relate to the way in which employees communicate with external publics. An email that emanates from a corporate address is seen as part of that organization and its content is thereby associated with the reputation of the company. Corporations must devote time and energy to training employees in acceptable email usage and ensure that they are aware of the possible negative implications of what they communicate. An acceptable use policy again plays an important role here.

10   *Contact.* With the increase in online interactions, many companies provide only an email address through which external publics can contact them. However, such a policy may not be acceptable to the time-poor, Generation Y digital natives, who insist that their queries be answered both immediately and satisfactorily. In a sense it harks back to the past, when complaints and queries were dealt with by writing a letter or telephoning and waiting for a response. At the same time, email has advantages over both the telephone and traditional written communication (snail mail). First, the ability to autogenerate a response allows people to understand when their query might be dealt with, when they can expect a response, and also confirms that it has been received. Second, the writer of the email can compose and send it much faster than snail mail, thereby providing a sense of completion and achievement. However, if a client's email disappears into a black corporate hole and no reply is received then the company's image is damaged. By ensuring that email queries are dealt with quickly and efficiently, companies not only save money but also create satisfied customers.

Each of these issues sheds light onto what needs to be investigated when auditing the effectiveness of email usage within the virtual workplace.

THE INTERNET ... AND INTRANET ... AND EXTRANET ...

The Internet is a system of networked computers that had its beginnings in the 1960s in the form of the ARPANET (Advanced Research Projects

Agency Network), commissioned by the Department of Defense to promote the sharing of super-computers among researchers in the United States. In the early 1990s it metamorphosed into what was initially termed W^3, now known as the world wide web (www) (Berners-Lee *et al.*, 1992). This technology has become an almost indispensable source of information globally. As can be seen from Box 9.1 the Internet and its associated technologies form the basis of many other communication tools. The two that map Internet technology most closely are the intranet and the extranet. These use the Internet platform to deliver information to specific chosen audiences, internally in the organization for the intranet and externally to selected stakeholders for the extranet. There are two key types of Internet design: static, in which information remains relatively stable; and, dynamic, in which the content is constantly evolving and changing either from the client side (user) or the server side (organization) (Perriss *et al.*, 2006). In designing and auditing the utility of either type of application, or any of the web interfaces, the following aspects should be reviewed:

1   *Design.* The Internet is often the first point of contact an external person has with the organization. In this sense it acts as a public relations tool, not only for relationships with the general public but also with journalists and other researchers attempting to discover key corporate information (Callison, 2003). Therefore, it is essential that the site is designed in such a way that it is user friendly. Although the future holds many challenges through such propositions as 'Clean Slate Design', in which a total rethink of Internet architect would occur (Feldmann, 2007), the current generation of tools need to be both robust and user friendly. Internet designers must ensure that the site has a clear and logical structure in which information can be found and assessed quickly. A general 'three-click rule' applies here (Feather, 2000), in that users should find what they are looking for on the screen within three clicks of the mouse. Ivory and Megraw (2005) studied the development of websites over the period 2000–2003 and, while acknowledging that design principles changed over time, identified the following core website design issues:

   •   Amount of page text: This was found to be dependent on both the function of the page (e.g. if it is a home page it should be shorter) and the growing availability of increased bandwidth. While there are no hard-and-fast rules here, ultimately designers should ensure that the usability of the page is maintained.
   •   Length and quality of link text: This refers to the hyperlinks used to navigate to different pages. It is suggested 2–4 words is an appropriate length for hyperlink text.
   •   Number and types of links: Ivory and Megraw found that the number of links on web pages had increased between 2000 and 2003 and

those that were most effective were grouped together into clusters (or navigational bars). Their study identified graphical links as confusing because users found them difficult to recognize. Additionally, they indicated that the repetition of links is effective. This was reinforced by Lorenzo and Gómez (2007) in their study into e-tailers when they found that users preferred 'free-network' design; that is, the inclusion of multiple links on every page.

- Number and types of graphics: Graphics should be minimized to improve download speed and, as those that contain text can be confusing, they should be avoided. Animations take longer to load and can be distracting so they need to be both limited and appropriate.
- Use of font styles and sizes: Sans serif fonts are considered the most legible. Recommendations of size vary, with a maximum of 14 pt, but it is worth bearing in mind that users can change view sizes.
- Use of unique colours and colour combinations: Good web pages were found to use one to four colours for body text and up to three for headings, as well as high contrast colour combinations, for example black text on light green, white, medium-beige, medium-green and light beige backgrounds.
- Consistency across pages: Good pages should demonstrate consistency in page layout to help users with navigation, but titles should clearly be different from page to page to help users keep track of their current page.

Any audit of the utility of an organization's website should consider each of these core issues.

2   *Download time.* Surfers expect pages to load within 2 seconds and will grow frustrated and potentially abandon the page if this does not occur (Nah, 2004). This is especially true of digital natives who have grown up with the 'twitch speed' of technology. Koiso-Kanttila (2005, p. 67) argued that 'perceived time scarcity is closely interwoven with the benefits and concerns of the Internet'. To avoid time delays, the layout should provide the surfer with a sense of consistency and ability to quickly and logically draw their eyes to the content (Begbie and Chudry, 2002). In this sense, it is important to keep the site simple but effective. The user should not get lost in all the detail provided, and must be able to quickly locate all the relevant information.

3   *Currency.* The Internet, in its many guises, provides an unprecedented method of delivering up-to-date information to employees, customers and other stakeholders. When this is not the case the utility of the site comes into question and with it the reputation of the organization. If the material is out of date it not only provides surfers with the wrong information but also creates a situation in which people are unwilling to trust the content of the site and may not make use of it in the future.

4   *Propaganda*. One of the stated benefits of the Internet (and intranet) when it was first introduced was to reduce organizational hierarchies and provide effective communication. The concept that all employees would have access to the same information at the click of a button at the same time, and also have open access to other people in the corporation, was thought, in the beginning, to be a positive move. Although it has achieved this to a certain extent, the use of passwords to protect information from particular people has moved the goalposts. The higher echelons can then control what appears on the site, and so create a one-way tool for company propaganda or impression management both for external communication through the Internet and internal through the intranet (O'Kane, 2004). In this way, the organization, and its key employees, can exert control over how they present themselves (Döring, 2002). Auditing both employee and customer attitudes in relation to Internet access can help to facilitate more two-way communication options.

5   *Cyberslacking*. The Internet brings with it the possibility of excess surfing for purposes other than work, known as cyberslacking (Whitty and Carr, 2006). This use and misuse of the Internet for personal reasons costs the organization in terms of time and money, but can be difficult to quantify and monitor. Although sites visited can be analysed, this information does not always reflect the reasons and rationale for the time spent on the Internet. It is even suggested that overly high levels of Internet use could be classified as an addiction or psychiatric disorder (Yellowlees and Marks, 2007). Here, again, corporations can help to counteract any uncertainties by introducing an acceptable use policy, and auditing the extent to which this is effective.

6   *Corporate reputation*. The growing use of the Internet to communicate with the public and present a positive company image also paradoxically provides the potential for damage to the corporate reputation. Take the case of the emergency crash landing of a British Airways (BA) Boeing 777 at Heathrow airport in January 2008, an incident that unsurprisingly dominated the news bulletins and newspapers for several days. The chief executive of BA featured on the media throughout the day of the incident, and referred customers to the BA Internet site, where passengers could, in real time, check the status of their flights and discover where to find out further information. But the downside of this real-time synchronous communication is the lack of control organizations have over who else can post information about them. For example, in the BA case, within hours an MSN (Microsoft Network) blog was created to discuss theories about the crash.

Many of the issues identified in the review of email and Internet communication can also be mapped into the newer communication tools, and it is to these that we now turn.

INTO THE FUTURE...

Newer communication tools such as blogs, podcasting, social networking and instant messaging have also been embraced by organizations for interacting with key stakeholders. Many of the issues that surround their use are extensions of those found in email and Internet communication, but nevertheless need to be investigated in their own right.

Blogs are used by individuals to record their opinions and ideas in relation to a specific topic, which can be as far-ranging as a running report on a gap year world trip to opinions about a new working practice. The number of blogs tracked by Technorati, a blog-indexing site, mushroomed from a few hundred thousand to more than 50 million within the 3-year period 2005 to 2008. Each day sees the creation of 175,000 new blogs and the addition of 1.6 million new posts to existing blogs (Hamel, 2007). Sifry (2004) described corporate bloggers as people from a company who may blog in either an official or a semi-official capacity, or are connected with the company in such a way that even though they are not official spokespeople they are clearly affiliated. Within PricewaterhouseCoopers such key people as the global chief accountant, Richard Keys, updates his online blog regularly (Keys, 2008), while in a different context, Coca Cola used blogs to discover employees' opinions about key company values (Culhane, 2008). Interestingly, Hamel (2007, p. 190) noted that:

> while many organizations solicit ideas via some sort of electronic suggestion box, or run online discussion boards that facilitate knowledge sharing, few companies invite employees to publish hard-hitting internal blogs or host open-to-all online discussions on key decisions.

Kelleher and Miller (2006), in their study into the relational outcomes of using organizational blogs as opposed to corporate websites to communicate key messages, found blogs to be perceived as more conversational than websites and this in turn positively correlated with organizational relationships. What this tells us is that corporate blogs, when used appropriately by the correct people, can provide an alternative method of developing a closer relationship to both employees and the public, and in this sense provide a more democratic form of communication that can empower stakeholders to make suggestions and discuss key issues (Hamel, 2007). The downside of blogs is that they can also be used to discredit the reputation of an organization by disgruntled employees, competitors, or customers who have had a perceived bad experience. For example, *The Times online* cited disgruntled owner Adrian Melrose's blog about the Land Rover Discovery (www.haveyoursay.com) as one of the top 50 blogs in their 2007 list (Blakely, 2007). Technorati.com enables organizations to measure the return on investment (ROI) by typing in the name of their blog and gaining a report on the number of links, comments and backtracks that take place in blog conversations. This provides an indication of the extent to which blogs are utilized. Alternatively, companies can measure click-through rates from blogs to corporate websites to understand the level of sales or leads they are generating. The impact of blogs on corporate reputation can be monitored using software developed by organizations such as www.marketsentinel.com (Delahaye-Paine, 2007).

Podcasting is used to facilitate audio-visual communication via the Internet. Its prevalence is increasing as the technology to produce and broadcast podcasts becomes mainstream through websites such as YouTube. In an organizational context managers can utilize podcasts as a method of communicating key messages. For example IBM uses them to update staff, investors and the media about their recent business developments (Ellson, 2006), while PricewaterhouseCoopers regularly place freely available podcasts on their website in relation to topics such as new UK immigration rules (December 2007) or tax accounting (September 2007). Other purposes include conference sessions, presentations, training and knowledge sharing (Strategic Direction, 2006). The benefits of using the podcast medium can be seen in the sound and vision element, which enables businesses to provide a richer message that may be more likely to be watched than reading a press release or annual address. Coupled with this is the ability to download the podcast to a computer or MP3 player to review at a time that suits the individual. Unlike blogs (which facilitate two-way communication) podcasts provide a medium, much like the corporate website, that companies can use to control the message they communicate to their employees or the public. Its potential can be extended by facilitating real-time interactive podcasts in which viewers can ask questions and make comments. Linked to this innovation in audio-visual technology is the new generation of Internet technologies, known as Web 2.0, that are being designed to base this communication around audio-visual interaction. The value of a podcast can be measured through traditional auditing tools (such as questionnaires and interviews), as well as monitoring the number of downloads of the podcast by employees or the public.

Instant messaging (IM) enables employees to 'talk' to each other using a text-based tool. It has become an invaluable method for facilitating informal communication in the workplace and is often used for 'scheduling, negotiating availability and maintaining awareness' (Huang *et al.*, 2004, p. 279), as well as decreasing the cost of communication and enhancing collaboration over organizational boundaries (Cameron and Webster, 2005). It is estimated that IM is used in either a formal or an informal sense in 90% of offices (Dwan, 2004). In order for it to become a valuable tool within the organizational environment it is crucial that there is a critical mass of users interacting and communicating through IM. On the downside, IM is seen as lacking the cues prevalent within F2F communication and is charged with interrupting employees in their work schedule (Cameron and Webster, 2005). The extent to which employees use IM can be measured using software that tracks the time they spend on it, but this does not reflect how effective the interaction is. To understand this, employees can be surveyed about their opinions on using the e-communication tool, or a content analysis could be carried out on IM conversations to assess their relevance and utility. The latter method raises ethical issues, which we discuss later in the chapter.

Electronic services are also growing. With the integration of the Internet (and its inherent applications) into many business practices there has been a trend in the emergence of 'e' applications. At its very forefront is the all-encompassing term 'e-business'. This is a difficult term to qualify but has been broadly defined by Li (2007, pp. 1–2) as employing the Internet and associated technologies

> to integrate and redesign an organization's internal activities, processes and external relations, and create new ways of working that are significantly different from, and very often far superior to, what was possible (or conceivable) in the past.

Within an organizational environment, this can take forms such as e-recruitment, e-human resources, e-mentoring, e-communication, e-tailing and so on (see Box 9.1). Each of these presents challenges for businesses to optimize their use in the workplace, while auditing to ensure that the level of personal contact is appropriate for employees and clients.

Introducing virtual communication tools is only the beginning for an organization. They must subsequently ensure that these are being used appropriately, legally and effectively in the workplace. One way of so doing is to incorporate a review of them within a communication audit.

AUDITING E-COMMUNICATION

The unique characteristics of e-communication open up a minefield in terms of auditing the capabilities of these tools. To begin with, the organization needs to have clear audit objectives. This will ensure informed decision-making about the best data collection tools to utilize. The range of data collection methods that can be employed is extensive, from the traditional methods of questionnaire, interview and focus groups through to data-monitoring software and social network analysis. This section identifies the core issues to be audited. It then reviews how both traditional and new audit tools can be embraced in the networked environment, and finally concludes by reviewing the audit trail created by e-communication devices.

What to audit

Volume of emails sent and received

There are two key ways in which the volume of email communication sent by an employee can be monitored. First, users can be asked to self-report their email usage. For example, Dabbish and Kraut (2006, p. 434) asked their respondents to answer three key questions:

- How many new email messages have you received in the past 24 hours?
- How many new email messages have you read in the past 24 hours?
- How many email messages have you sent in the past 24 hours?

Although self-report can provide a quick method for ascertaining levels of email communication, as noted in Chapter 6 it can be subjective and open to distortion. In order to provide a more objective measure, software can be used to record the level of email activity within a given timeframe (see below). Although this provides a ball park figure in relation to the usage of email, it does not allow the appropriateness of the communication to be measured. To do this the organization may need to access and assess individual email content. Such a process poses important ethical and practical issues.

It should be acknowledged, first, that significant surveillance of employees' use of e-communication technologies already takes place. Pfeffer (2007) cited a number of studies to show that 60% of US employers were using software to monitor incoming and outgoing email. Nearly one quarter had fired people for violating existing policies, while 65% used software to block access to some websites. The ethical issue here is that accessing employees' email content may violate their privacy, by creating an environment in which individuals are effectively being spied on. This can make honest communication about workplace issues impossible. Moreover, the dividing line between private and public lives has become increasingly blurred, as workloads have intensified and people work longer hours. E-technologies have not only enabled many to work from home but have made such off-site work an expectation in many jobs. This has further squeezed people's ability to deal with non-job-related issues when away from the workplace, and forced many to conduct what is strictly private business, including sending personal emails, from work-based systems. Among the ethical questions posed is this: Is it reasonable for companies to expect their staff to work longer hours and, increasingly, to do so from home, while insisting that no element of their personal lives should ever intrude when they are in their formal workplace?

In practical terms, it may also be that such an approach is counterproductive. Organizational surveillance can make it very difficult to create a climate of trust. Additionally, psychological reactance theory postulates that prohibited behaviours become more desirable, thereby increasing resentment at our inability to perform them (Brehm and Brehm, 1981; Miller *et al.*, 2006). This can spark various forms of resistance responses that do more damage than the behaviour the surveillance is designed to check. We would therefore urge managers to consider very carefully the tradeoffs involved in investigating such issues as email content, and above all to be quite explicit about whatever policies are eventually implemented.

Email appropriateness and relevance

What the figures on email usage do not tell is how relevant the content of the emails is, if the information is useful, and whether it assists employees to do their job better. In order to obtain this level of detail the organization needs to employ a methodology that allows the items listed in Box 9.2 to be assessed.

Internet and intranet surfing

One of the key problems associated with Internet usage is the potential for employees to surf for activities other than those that are strictly work-related. We would reiterate the ethical issues we flagged above in our discussion of email audits. Beyond that, however, corporations have an obligation to prevent damaging or illegal Internet activities, such as accessing child pornography websites and storing associated material on company computers. Thus clear guidelines should be in place regarding the extent to which

---

Box 9.2 Criteria for auditing email

- Is the email a form of SPAM?
- Was the user able to identify the content from the 'header' information and subsequently make a quick decision about its relevance?
- Was the receiver's email address in the 'copy to' (cc – to indicate for information only) or the 'to' (to indicate for action) line?
- Was the information relevant to the employee?
- Was the communication task-related, organization-wide or personal?
- Was the email of high priority and did it include an appropriate priority status?
- Did the content of the email strengthen or damage relationships?
- Did the email assist in improving horizontal, vertical or diagonal communication?

personal access is allowed. This provides a benchmark from which employees can be assessed on the appropriateness of their surfing. Given that this is clearly understood, once again software monitoring tools can be used to establish how long employees are spending on the Internet and what sites they are accessing. The challenge from this is to be clear as to the relevance of the website visited and how closely related it is to the job. Some organizations take this a step further by denying access to particular commonly used sites such as Ebay or Facebook to prevent some level of misuse, while others designate time, such as the lunch break, in which employees may engage in personal usage. As will be seen below, this raises several questions in relation to trust.

Load

One of the most common complaints relating to email, as detailed above, is the overwhelming volume of information that can be contained in the in-box. It is important to understand whether the information included in an email, or through an intranet site, could have been communicated through other means. This enables organizations to establish whether overload, or indeed underload, is occurring. Dabbish and Kraut (2006) measured the impact of email load using seven items on a 5-point Likert scale:

1   I can handle my email efficiently.
2   I have trouble finding information in my email.
3   I can easily deal with the amount of email I receive.
4   I sometimes miss information or important messages.
5   I reply quickly to the message I need to.
6   Dealing with my email disrupts my ongoing work.
7   I find dealing with email overwhelming.

Each of these could be adapted and applied to other elements of e-communication.

Whether emails frequently become flame mails

It may be necessary to train people to reflect on the messages they write before they send them, and consider whether other channels are more appropriate for dealing with particular problems. Protocols for the effective and civilized use of emails are increasingly being developed and should be circulated to staff (O'Kane et al., 2004). By investigating the content of emails through a diary analysis (see Chapter 6) or critical incident technique (see Chapter 8), negative email patterns can be identified.

How e-communication complements or substitutes for other channels of communication

It is vital that e-communication does not entirely replace F2F interaction between colleagues, or between managers and their staff. As a rule of thumb, if the audit shows that email has become the predominant channel of communication for dealing with important issues it is likely that too many 'human moments' are missing. This will weaken the prevailing organizational culture. It may therefore be time to revisit first principles. As part of this process, it might also be helpful to create special opportunities for F2F communication. Hallowell (1999), for example, cited a CEO who required all employees working from home to come into the office once a month for some unstructured face time. More research is needed into the effects of such initiatives.

Return on investment

A basic premise of any communication strategy is that it should strengthen business performance. Without this, the side effects (i.e. costs) outweigh any gains obtained from the treatment. They might even become toxic. Thus Internet, intranet and extranet applications should improve sales, productivity and competitiveness. En route, their effectiveness can be judged by whether they deliver improvements in areas such as:

- order management
- inter-departmental collaboration
- customer service
- database access
- inventory management.

Each organization should select its own performance indicators and measure intranet effectiveness by these yardsticks.

How to audit

Given the above overview of the key e-communication tools and the issues to be measured, the next step is to choose an appropriate audit tool to meet the specific measurement objectives. The precise approach adopted, as so often, depends on the needs of the organization, the time allowed for the audit and the resources available.

Questionnaires

Many questionnaires have been developed to measure different aspects of e-communication (see Table 9.1). Each of these can be employed or adapted

Table 9.1 Electronic communication questionnaires

Area	Scale	Author
Adaptation of existing communication scales	International Communication Association's Audit Survey Communication Satisfaction Questionnaire	Goldhaber and Rogers, 1979 Downs and Hazen, 1977
Technology scales (measures how comfortable users are with e-communication)	Usage Perceived Ease of Use (PEU) Perceived Usefulness (PU)	Davis, 1989; van Schaik and Ling, 2005
Computer scales	End User Computing Satisfaction Instrument (EUCSI)	Doll and Torkzadeh, 1988
	Computer Self-Efficacy Scale	Murphy et al., 1989; Barbeite and Weiss, 2004
	Computer Attitude Scales	Nickell and Pinto, 1986; Loyd and Loyd, 1985
	Computer Anxiety Scales	Marcoulides, 1989; Heinssen et al., 1987; Barbeite and Weiss, 2004
Overload	Email Overload	Dabbish and Kraut, 2006
Intranet/website scales	Intranet Effectiveness	Murgolo-Poore et al., 2003; Murgolo-Poore et al., 2002
	Intranet Self-Efficacy Scale	Torkzadeh and Van Dyke, 2002
	Website Scale	Bunz, 2001a
General e-communication	Computer–Email–Web (CEW) Fluency Scale/Computer-Mediated Communication Competency Scale	Bunz, 2001b, 2003

to meet individual organizational needs. Additionally, as with all question-naires, the organization can develop a survey to meet specific needs, but this can be a time-consuming process (see Chapter 3). A good alternative is to use a modification of an existing audit instrument such as the Communication Satisfaction Questionnaire, or the ICA Communication Audit instrument (see the Appendix) in which users can be asked to identify how much information about specific topics or tasks they send and receive through email, the Internet and other e-communication tools. Market research questionnaires can also be used to understand how customers view both the organization's website and their email interaction. Additionally, by using an ECCO questionnaire (see Chapter 6), an organization can obtain specific details about the way in which information is being communicated through e-channels.

Interviews

Interviews (see Chapter 4) can also be employed to evaluate e-communications. Thus O'Kane *et al.* (2007) used a sample of targeted in-depth interviews to audit email within a large aeronautical company. They argued that this technique enables the auditor to get below the surface manifestations to 'build "thick descriptions" of the relevant themes' (p. 313) emerging from interviewee responses. Of course, combinations of techniques are also useful. For instance, O'Kane and Hargie (2004) used a combination of a specially designed questionnaire and deep-probe interviews to audit the email and intranet systems in a Norwegian manufacturing company. They found that the two methods complemented one another, and together provided data that an individual method would not have produced.

Diary analysis

Diary analysis can enable employees to reflect in depth about their daily email and Internet usage (see Chapter 6). This would facilitate an analysis of issues related to timeliness, overload, relevance and ease of finding information. In conjunction with this, participants can be asked to attach copies of key emails that are then content analysed to identify how and in what ways email is being utilized.

Mystery shopping

Mystery shopping can be adapted to the email context (see Chapter 6). Here, a mystery emailer sends a number of messages to an organization. Responses can then be measured along dimensions such as timeliness, informativeness, relevance and friendliness. In the context of the Internet, mystery shoppers log on to discover specific information and report on site appeal, ease of usage, any broken links, or information that is inaccurate, out-of-date, or irrelevant.

CIT

The critical incident technique (see Chapter 8) allows companies to assess examples of exceptionally good and bad email communications, and enables an analysis of these to form the basis of an acceptable use policy. Likewise this technique can be used to assess users' positive and negative experiences with aspects of the company's Internet and intranet.

Social network analysis

Email and the Internet (specifically social networking sites and blogs) enable new informal relationships to develop. These can alter our daily patterns of interaction, and may play a role in determining the organizational structure. In order to understand this, a social network analysis can be conducted (see Chapter 7). In fact, specialized software can analyse the email communications of employees to identify where stronger and weaker relationships lie (e.g. www.trampolinesystems.com/). This has been used to interrogate the Enron database, with interesting results regarding who was speaking to whom about what topics. Once again, such analysis opens debates in relation to trust, monitoring and the law (discussed below).

Software tools

In their study of email interruptions, Jackson *et al.* (2003) utilized remote recording of employee screens using Windows Virtual Network Computing (Win VNC), to obtain their reaction and response times. Specifically, they were able to use the information gleaned to assess how quickly employees reacted to email communication, the time they spent reading the email and how long it took them to resume their previous activities after dealing with the email. Other software can identify objectionable Internet sites and unusual email activity, capture offensive words, and so on (Urbaczewski and Jessup, 2003). Although such monitoring raises many dilemmas (see below), it does provide the organization with a picture of the time spent reacting to and dealing with email communication during working hours, as well as an indication of what employees are discussing. However, it gives no indication of the importance or urgency of the email messages. Other methods reviewed above may be best placed to do this. In relation to the content of Internet sites, software can be used to identify broken links and any unauthorized activity.

Given these final two methods of analysis in relation to monitoring it is necessary to consider the audit trail created by e-communication.

The audit trail

E-communication leaves a clear and present audit trail that not only the organization but, if necessary, governmental bodies can use to investigate and monitor activity that has taken place. Not only can e-communications be monitored and archived, so too can telephone conversations. Recent developments have seen the introduction of software designed to enable corporations to identify employees who may be potential saboteurs, industrial spies, data thieves, or even whistle-blowers (Marks, 2007). By identifying key words and phrases that appear frequently or are ominously absent from email communications, the system can identify those who may pose a threat to the company or who feel alienated. By taking the information inherent in email use, as well as in blogs and IM conversations, and feeding it into a software program, the results can make interesting reading.

Yet again, this poses fundamental ethical issues. While such technology can be used to promote good behaviour, it can also be used to punish it, while insulating malefactors from the consequences of their actions. Enron serves as a good example. When fed the 250,000 emails sent between employees of the doomed Enron corporation, the software identified employee Sherron Watkins as being both alienated and having clandestine sensitive interests. She turned out to be the Enron whistle-blower (Marks, 2007). The information was used by top managers, who were eventually convicted of criminal activities, to safeguard their positions for a further period, during which they continued to swindle their employees and customers. This brings to the fore a number of key issues.

The law

Using the audit trail as a form of assessing e-communication brings with it a myriad of difficulties, which vary from country to country and organization to organization. At a primary level, legal constitutions control how email information can be used. In the United States any business-related email and Internet information is considered to belong to the company, to be used and monitored as they please. This goes further when we consider the case of Enron. Since its collapse the emails that circulated in the period prior to this have been put in the public domain and can be searched and analysed. In contrast to this, in the United Kingdom, although it has to assume responsibility for the content of their emails, an organization cannot monitor its employees' email usage unless the individual is under investigation in relation to a crime in which e-communication has played a role. Employees must also be informed that their communications are being monitored, and there has to be a legitimate business purpose for so doing (Mason, 2005). Therefore, companies need to be aware and take into consideration the legalities of how they audit e-communications.

Corporate governance

Coupled with this is the governance system internal to the organization. It is best practice to issue an acceptable use policy that outlines what is and is not acceptable in relation to e-communication use, together with penalties for misuse (Urbaczewski and Jessup, 2003). This provides employees with demarcation lines within which they can use the electronic systems, while putting measures in place to prevent them from being sued for harassment and/or slander (Mason, 2005).

Privacy, ethics and trust

A third issue is the ethics of monitoring employee email and Internet usage. By placing embargos and telling employees that their email may be monitored, the corporation is both suggesting mistrust and also invading their privacy in relation to what they do on the Internet or might write in their IM conversations or blogs. Companies therefore have to tread a fine line between trusting employees and checking on them.

Having analysed the key features involved in auditing e-communications, it is now important to consider audit aspects relating to the original, and still extensively used, mediated communication system, the telephone.

A CASE IN TIME: TELEPHONE COMMUNICATION

It is perhaps paradoxical that we are ending our analysis of communication technology by briefly examining business ramifications of the telephone, the invention of which launched the first major communication revolution in the late 19th century. Indeed, the wiring of the world began with the telephone. Recent years have seen this invention much over-shadowed by the Internet and its offspring technologies, but the telephone is still an integral part of all businesses and their transactions. For example, some 80% of all financial transactions are enacted via the telephone, and customers are five times more likely to telephone a company than to write to them (Hargie *et al.*, 2004). In auditing telephone communication its recent manifestations also need to be considered. The first, mobile telephones, is often viewed as the bane of modern society, but in business communication it is invaluable as it enables employees to be contacted at any time and for the most part, in any place in the world. Indeed, the surge in telephone communications was stimulated by mobile phone usage. For example, in 1985 there were only 25,000 mobile phone users in the UK, but by 2003 this figure had risen to the saturation level of 50 million users. In 2008 there were 2 billion mobile users worldwide. The second VOIP (Voice Over Internet Protocol), such as Skype, uses Internet technologies rather than traditional telephone wires and has reduced call charges to a fraction of the price of traditional telephone tariffs.

The telephone is used for many different purposes within organizations, from communication between employees, to call centres that concentrate on sales, or in dealing with customer queries. In fact 50 billion minutes per year are spent on the phone to call centres, and there are over 5000 of these in the UK alone. More worrying, 18% of people abandon companies because of poor telephone experiences. Some of the core areas in which the public find problems with business telephone services (Hargie *et al.*, 2004), and so need to be audited, include:

1   a delay in calls being answered
2   being left 'hanging on' for a long time
3   being greeted by voicemail rather than being dealt with in person
4   entering a 'voicemail jail' system, wherein the caller is constantly instructed to press various buttons to access a wide array of options, many of which are of no interest
5   being put through to the wrong person
6   leaving a message on voicemail and no-one returning the call.

There are various ways and levels at which an audit can be carried out into telephone usage. For example, organizations should have a pro-forma for taking messages, which lists the name/address/phone number of the caller, date/time of call, main points of the message, and when the person is available for a call back (see Box 9.3). The auditor should conduct a content analysis of these pro-formas over a set period (e.g. 1 week), to ascertain the extent to which all information has been logged, and where improvements are required.

At another level, electronic call logging systems give accurate information about how many calls are made to and from each extension number, how long before incoming calls are answered, whether a call was dealt with in person or transferred to voicemail, the duration of each interaction, what the cost to

---

Box 9.3 Telephone messages pro-forma

Message for _____   Date/Time _____

Caller's name _____   Designation _____

Caller's tel. no. _____   Fax _____   Email _____

Times when caller will be available to take a return call:

_____

Main reason for the call _____

_____

Message:

_____
_____
_____
_____
_____
_____

   Message taken by _____

the company is of each external call, and to whom it was made. This information is important in informing task analysis (e.g. what percentage of a worker's time is spent on the telephone), and in attributing costs to relevant departments. However, while it produces an accurate measure of the dimensions of the artefact, such analysis gives no information about its quality.

In order to assess quality of service, customer surveys and interviews can be employed in external audits. For example at the end of a telephone interaction organizations often give customers the option to complete a survey either on the current telephone conversation or by going to the website to complete it. However, the most common method used to assess this field is that of mystery shopping. Here, a 'pretend' client makes the call and checks how it is dealt with against a range of criteria. We summarize some of these in Box 9.4.

Box 9.4 Criteria for auditing telephones

- Was the call answered within three rings (or 4 seconds)?
- Did the person sound genuinely pleased to be taking the call?
- Did the person begin with a greeting, followed by location, name, and position (i.e. 'Good afternoon, Booking Office, Jane Hodges, Client Executive speaking')
- Was an offer of help made? (e.g. 'How may I help?')
- Was your name ascertained at the outset?
- How often in total was your name used?
- Were your needs and requirements established at the outset?
- Were these checked for fulfilment at the end?
- If relevant, was the call transferred swiftly to the right department (within 10 seconds)?
- If you were left hanging on, was an explanation given as to why?
- Was your permission obtained for this (e.g. 'Could you excuse me for a few seconds, while I get that file?')
- If the person could not deal with the enquiry immediately, was a reason given?
- Did the person explain precisely what would happen next?
- Were you told when someone would return the call?
- Were key points fed back to you during the call to show concerted listening, and to check that these were your main concerns?
- Were regular signals of active listening used (e.g. 'Ah ha', 'Right', 'Yeah', 'OK').
- Was action reassurance given about the timeframe within which relevant issues raised would be dealt with?
- If making a complaint were you given time to ventilate without interruption? Did the person speak gently? Did they acknowledge

> your emotions (e.g. 'I can understand that you feel very strongly about this')?
> * Were the main points summarized at the end of the call?
> * Were you rewarded for calling (e.g. 'Thank you for calling', 'I'm glad you let us know')?

Finally, we end this chapter by examining the concept of electronic auditing, where email and the Internet are used to administer audit instruments (such as questionnaire surveys) and collect data.

ELECTRONIC AUDITING

The key focus of this chapter was to reflect on e-communication tools and create an understanding of their unique dimensions that need to be reviewed and assessed within any organizational setting. But not only do these tools raise new communication challenges and opportunities for businesses, they also provide alternative methods for collecting audit data.

Online questionnaire

Traditionally surveys are administered using either mail, telephone or personal administration (Murphy, 1997). In recent years, there has been a growth in computer-based administration, which can involve both email and web technologies. Many studies have addressed the differences in response rates, bias, and so on, between traditional and electronic administration (Shih and Fan, 2008). Thus Goldhaber (2002), comparing intranet data collection and traditional paper-based surveys, found that intranet data collection led to faster completion rates, administration was about a tenth cheaper, and there was a greater response rate. Hayslett and Wildemuth (2004) investigated response rates from mail surveys, web announced by mail, and web announced by email. They found that although replies were received more speedily through the web, mail surveys produced a greater response rate. Email, as opposed to snail mail, announcement was more effective at encouraging respondents to complete online. They found no sampling bias or difference in the content of responses. Similarly, Klassen and Jacobs (2001) reported higher item completion rates for web-based surveys, but lower response rates. They concluded that with the cost-efficiencies associated with web-based distribution, this was likely to become more popular, and the lower response rates reported could be offset by the ability to survey more people.

In terms of email-based surveys, Schaefer and Dillman (1999) discovered that returns were quicker but response rates similar between email and snail-mail surveys. Additionally they also found that item non-responses were lower, and more complete answers were given to open questions through email surveys. They recommended that an option to return by mail should also be included. As with the Hayslett and Wildemuth (2004) study, an email invitation to complete was found to be more effective than a mail one. Schaefer and Dillman foresaw the move to web-based surveys (from email) as increasing the effectiveness of computer-based data collection in the future, although Shih and Fan (2008), in their meta-analysis of 35 studies, concluded that mail-based surveys still attracted a greater response rate. This could be attributed to the survey sample being more carefully targeted as expenses are higher.

In conclusion, there appears to be some contradiction in studies of the response rates between computer-based and mail surveys, with the majority reporting that response rates decreased in computer-based surveys, but this can be attributed to larger, less targeted sampling procedures. However, there is agreement that with computer-based formats administration is faster, an email invitation works more effectively than a snail-mail one, item-completion rates are better, and there does not appear to be any response bias.

Online focus group (forum)

Rather than conducting the traditional focus group in a F2F environment, an online focus group provides an alternative that can bring people together from geographically dispersed regions at different times, thereby removing some of the limitations of traditional focus groups (see Chapter 5). Reid and Reid (2005) compared the differences between these two mediums and discovered that although Computer-Mediated Communication (CMC) groups contributed less to the discussion within a set timeframe, overall the number of ideas generated was similar between the two groups, suggesting that, given the nature of the sample and their dispersion, online or CMC focus groups could provide a viable alternative. Three core issues that need to be given careful consideration are the design of the focus group, developing rapport, and the selection of an appropriate virtual venue (O'Connor and Madge, 2003).

CONCLUSION

Taking stock of all of the information that can be communicated through cyberspace produces a myriad of decisions and a maze of options for organizations. It is important to remember that it is not always appropriate, ethical or indeed possible to attempt to audit all employee e-communications. The organization needs to make a judgement call about what it thinks is important for effective communication and operational efficiency. The matter of tradeoffs has to be considered. For example, an employee might spend 20 minutes in the afternoon booking flights or researching the best mortgage deals, but may then spend an hour in the evening at home working online on a key business issue that needs to be resolved. These dynamics make evaluating e-communication difficult and ethically challenging.

Overall, this chapter has reviewed a number of e-communication technologies and has highlighted issues associated with auditing their usage. It has also illustrated how such technology can be employed to facilitate the administration of communication audits. The field of e-communications has grown exponentially in recent decades: there is every reason to suppose that the growth in technologies will continue in the future. As with organizational communication scholars in general, communication auditors will be stretched to stay abreast of the opportunities and challenges that are posed. But one thing is clear: communication audits must increasingly take such issues into account, in order to present anything like a rounded account of life in the virtual domain of the modern workplace.

Chapter 10

Crafting the audit report

Dennis Tourish and Owen Hargie

INTRODUCTION

Once the audit has been implemented, and the data collected and analysed, there is then the key task of presenting the results in the form of a report. This is a defining point in the whole exercise. Considerable care may have been devoted to the implementation of the audit, but if this is not reflected in the final written presentation, all the planning, script conferences and dress rehearsals will have stopped short of a convincing public performance.

For example, it is possible to:

- over-emphasize the difficulties that lie ahead
- baffle the organization with an over-abundance of statistics
- outline a sweeping change agenda, which inspires panic rather than action
- deal summatively with the audit's main findings, generating lethargy rather than energy.

We have also encountered audit reports written by some consulting firms, in which the recommendations have been principally framed to avoid offending anyone, and so lose the firm future business. The consequence is that they are of little use as a guide to action for the organization concerned. (Incidentally, we have found that most organizations *prefer* a frank rather than a diplomatic appraisal of their communication climate.)

Our goal in this chapter is to enable readers to avoid these pitfalls. Accordingly, we propose an overall structure for a typical audit report and outline what each section is intended to achieve. Given that a report will present both positive and negative findings, and that the latter may be threatening for some people, we discuss how 'bad news' can best be broken. A good deskside manner is as vital for auditors as a bedside one is for medics. In particular, we pay close attention to developing the recommendations that should flow from the audit findings. Furthermore, we argue that, if such recommendations are to take root, wide constituencies of opinion must be persuaded of their benefits, so that they become motivated and committed to seeing them through. In consequence, we outline some of the key levers of persuasion suggested by the research literature that seem particularly pertinent in this context, and explore how they can be employed in the course of constructing an audit report.

STRUCTURING AN AUDIT REPORT

Reports are 'used to inform, analyze, recommend and persuade' (Lamb, 2006, p. 19). They are a systematic evaluation of options available to an organization, given goals, constraints and resources (Baake, 2007). Effective reports can therefore be viewed as 'a guide to action'. All other issues (e.g. the amount of detail required, statistical sophistication, and literary style) are subordinate to this clear imperative. Additionally, people have a particular expectation that an audit report dealing with communication will be an exceptionally crafted demonstration of good communication practice. As Downs and Adrian (2004, p. 247) argued, this means that 'the final report must be a superb form of communication about communication'.

The defining traits of effective reports are widely agreed (e.g. Messmer, 2003; Hargie *et al.*, 2004). Typically, excellent reports are assumed to be:

1 *Timely:* This refers to both the production of the report and its contents. Ideally, it should arrive before it is due (but certainly no later), and contain the most up-to-date information available on the problem at hand. An audit report should display an awareness of the most current and relevant techniques in the field, combined with an acute focus on the current business needs of the organization involved. It should answer today's problems rather than yesterday's, while preparing everyone for the challenges of tomorrow.

2 *Well written:* The report should be clear, concise, and interesting; it should grab the reader's attention and hold it throughout; it should avoid errors in grammar, spelling, punctuation and factual content. One factual error damages the credibility of your whole case, much as a single lie shatters a manager's reputation for honesty. It should be characterized by short words, everyday English, short sentences (of between 15 and 20 words), and active verbs (Scammell, 2006). Above all, it should be driven by a bias towards action, which solves a problem, identifies the next steps the report's readers can and must take, and be directly related to the underlying business objectives of the organization.

3 *Well organized:* A good report is designed to be read selectively, so that the reader can pay attention only to its most necessary parts. Most reports have multiple audiences, and will have few readers interested in its entire content. For this reason, an executive summary (listing main findings and recommendations) is obligatory. Surprisingly, compiling such a

summary is often the most difficult part of the exercise, since it implies a careful identification of the most important themes and a judicious selection of the most relevant supporting details. Perhaps this process explains Mark Twain's fabled comment to a friend, on sending him a lengthy letter. Twain complained that that he hadn't had time to write a short letter, so a long one would have to do.

4   *Attractive:* It should be clearly labelled, arrive in good condition, and be presented with an attractive typeface and layout. Graphics, bar charts, pictures and diagrams present data in an accessible format, simplify the job of the reader and also enhance the attractiveness and impact of a report. However, to achieve this they must be presented effectively. Frownfelter-Lohrke and Fulkerson (2001) identified the following deficiencies often found when data are presented in graphical form, together with some means of avoiding them:

- *Inadequate chart titles and labels*: There should be clear, detailed and thorough labelling that describes what the data represent.
- *Obtrusive backgrounds; no clearly defined borders*: Highly coloured or pictorial backgrounds may look attractive on a computer screen, but often distract the reader from the information that is contained in the graph. Backgrounds and colour should be unobtrusive in order not to draw attention from the graph. They are there to assist understanding, rather than seize centre stage.
- *Optical illusions and major design variations*: For example, three-dimensional displays can distort a reader's interpretation of the graph.
- *Inappropriate colours*: In particular, a large number of colours create confusion and make it difficult for readers to compare like with like.
- *Trendy visual effects ('chartjunk')*: Simplicity is the key to better comprehension, and recall.

Figure 10.1 provides an example of a pie chart from one of our audits, summarizing a breakdown of the staff that were surveyed, to illustrate the point. Figure 10.2 provides the same data as a histogram. First impressions count. They shape expectations about the overall import of the report. Thus a professional cover and good binding are also essential. A well presented report projects a favourable impression of the audit exercise, and creates an aura of attractiveness around its central recommendations.

5   *Cost effective:* The report's recommendations should be designed to solve real problems facing its readership, and should be clearly explained, possible to implement, and cost effective. Although there are no guidelines on the maximum number of recommendations the report should contain, it is important to remember that an organization with 40 priorities

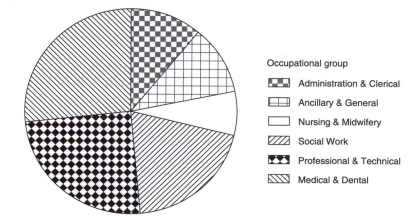

Figure 10.1 Breakdown of the sample (1).

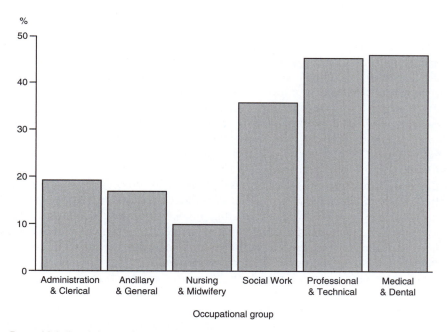

Figure 10.2 Breakdown of the sample (2).

in reality has none. On the other hand, a small number of key proposals are known as an action plan. We return to this issue later in this chapter.

6 *A report begins before the beginning*, with the terms of reference set for its production. These identify the problem(s) it will be expected to solve, set

explicit limits on the range of issues to be addressed, and identify specific outcomes towards which the report should aspire.

Standard formats exist for the structure of a report, and in general retain their validity in the case of communication audit reports. It has been suggested (Hargie *et al.*, 2004) that they should normally contain the following:

- Title page
- Contents
- Acknowledgements
- Executive Summary
- Introduction
- Methodology
- Findings/Conclusions
- Recommendations
- Appendices
- References

The *Acknowledgements* are an opportunity to identify important change agents within the organization who have participated in the most important aspects of the communication audit exercise. This, of course, suggests that such people will have been involved in designing the audit process, or collecting data, and that key findings will have been shared with them as they emerge. It is certainly unhelpful to present senior people with a nasty surprise at the end of the audit, and then expect their enthusiastic support (Barrington, 1992). By involving them, and sharing the credit in the eventual report, auditors will gain a valuable reputation as team players, and establish that the entire exercise has been rooted in the business needs of the organization. Such an approach also has the added advantage of spreading responsibility for awkward issues raised and difficult decisions proposed: it is harder for people to reject the audit conclusions outright, if the Chief Executive has been identified as a key figure in drawing up the team's terms of reference, gathering the data and devising the recommendations.

A further reason for this, suggested in the research literature on persuasion, is that the credibility of a message source is a key factor in determining a message's persuasive impact (Miceli *et al.*, 2006). One of the key dimensions of credibility is *power* (Poggi, 2005). Top executives in an organization are likely to possess *legitimate power* (i.e. their hierarchical position possesses innate authority and confers extra legitimacy on the office holder's perceptions and actions); *coercive power* (i.e. they are perceived as having the ability to enforce their will by having the ability to apply sanctions); and *expert power* (i.e. their recognized expertise or in-depth knowledge can directly persuade another of the value of a particular course of action). Associating the report with powerful and hence credible figures, capable of exercising these and other forms of power, is an important means of enhancing its persuasive impact.

The *Summary* should outline both the main findings and recommendations. Typically, a report will have multiple audiences, with vastly differing information needs (Lamb, 2006). Therefore, most people will read only this section. One research investigation, into the efficacy of a particular approach to report writing, found that three quarters of readers merely skimmed the report, with only one quarter reading it thoroughly (Stallworth and Roberts-Gray, 1987). Likewise, most readers tend to read only the abstracts that appear at the beginning of articles in academic journals, much as those of us who write them would like to think otherwise. Given that the end purpose of the audit exercise is to promote action and change, this reinforces the need for a cogent, comprehensive summary.

However, the rest of the report lends authority to the summary. Readers who query a particular finding or recommendation can delve into the appropriate section in more depth, to reassure themselves that the audit has been rigorously conducted, data genuinely representative of communication transactions within the organization collected, and that the report's recommendations are based on solid evidence. Otherwise, it may be assumed that they are either a wish fulfilment list drawn up by alienated malcontents, or a top manager's ideal image of what should be rather than what is. Such supporting testimony is excised from the summary, which needs to combine brevity with a comprehensive account of the most salient issues.

The *Introduction* should explain who commissioned the communication audit, who was responsible for the overall conduct of the exercise, and the purpose of the report. It should briefly outline the method of inquiry that was adopted and the terms of reference that were set. It should also explain how the data have been assembled and arranged, how the report is structured, and whatever general background factors are considered to be most crucial. In general, this means identifying the importance of communication to the organization at this stage. The temptation here is to assume that, since the issue is by now over-familiar to the audit team, it will be equally familiar to everyone else, and that there is no need to discuss basics.

The *Methodology* outlines, in detail, the steps taken to assemble the audit data. It is generally agreed (Downs and Adrian, 2004) that the key issues that must be explained include the following:

- What techniques were employed in the audit?
- Why were these techniques selected, in preference to any others?
- How, and by whom, was the data collection carried out?
- How many staff, clients or customers were audited?
- How were they selected?
- If everyone was not included, what percentage sample was used?

It is also useful to provide a summary table, which describes the total break-down of the sample. We provide an example in Table 10.1, derived from an audit conducted by us in an NHS Trust. The data it contains were presented earlier in this chapter, in the form of a pie chart and a histogram (Figures 10.1 and 10.2). Readers can compare the two, and decide which they feel presents the data in the most striking and accessible form. For many datasets, histo-grams, bar charts and pie charts are a more striking and hence preferable mode of presentation, and are now widely used.

The *Findings/Conclusions* section details precisely what you have discovered. It should also analyse the importance of your findings. If 80% of the organ-ization's employees are satisfied with information received from top man-agement, what precisely does this mean for the organization's communication strategy? What are the implications for trust, loyalty and commitment? How well does it compare to previous surveys, or contemporaneous surveys in other organizations within this business area? Does it mean that plain sailing lies ahead, or are there storms on the immediate horizon?

The *Recommendations* section of the report is where you most clearly link data to action. Abundant research in many contexts shows clearly that feedback by itself changes nothing (Tourish, 2006): the kind of feedback delivered, how tightly it is tied to doable action plans, and the degree to which support for implementation exists are crucial. In particular, Thornbory and White (2007) emphasized that recommendations should never come as a sur-prise to the reader. In the first instance, they should be *implicit* in the report. Thus the recommendations should relate directly to key problems that have been heavily flagged in its main body. They should emerge clearly from the findings, rather than appear unheralded in the middle of the conclusions. Second, emergent recommendations should be discussed informally with key people during a lengthy process before the report is formalized. The principal finding (judged by its importance to the organization, and as iden-tified in the terms of reference) should attract the most emphasis in the recommendations.

Table 10.1 Breakdown of the sample

Occupational groups	Staff in post	Sample size	Percentage of occupational group
Admin. and clerical	53	10	18.8
Ancillary and general	84	14	16.6
Nursing and midwifery	332	33	9.9
Social work	28	10	35.7
Professional and technical	9	4	44.4
Medical and dental	11	5	45.5
Total	517	76	14.7% of workforce

To capture attention, an audit report should expend most of its energy in outlining the particular difficulties that communication problems are creating for the organization at present, rather than potential difficulties to which current practices might give rise in the hypothetical future. As the famous economist John Maynard Keynes once famously remarked, 'In the long run, we are all dead.' Managers are therefore biased in favour of addressing immediate problems rather than distant tornadoes, which they hope might pass them by. As two early researchers in this area emphasized, managers tend to use communication as a corrective rather than a preventive process (Greenbaum and White, 1976). Consequently, recommendations are more likely to attract attention, and support, when they focus overwhelmingly on real and present dangers.

An important question is how many recommendations the report should contain. We have scrutinized audit reports where the number of discernible recommendations has varied from 3 to 43! There are no absolutely clear-cut rules or research findings in this area. However, research into change management suggests that an excessive number of action points produces paralysis rather than action, by preventing a consistent focus on the clear vision that is a precondition for success (Kanter, 1991). As O'Shea *et al.* (2007, p. 108) noted: 'Bringing about change in a large and complex organization is a difficult task.' There has also been such a blizzard of change in most workplaces over recent years that both managers and employees have struggled to adjust, or change their behaviour before the next wave of change renders their last effort redundant (Pfeffer and Sutton, 2006). This kind of disruption sparks increased uncertainty, in spite of the fact that uncertainty reduction is a driving force behind many interpersonal communication episodes (Field *et al.*, 2006), and is characteristic of an organizational context capable of sustaining successful innovation (Pearson, 1991).

In short, when faced with a call for action on every front, people find it difficult to discern clear priorities or to focus their energies on any one issue, to the point where they can see it through to completion. An overwhelming agenda also makes it difficult for managers to track and hence benchmark the impact of particular initiatives. Given what is known about human memory, and the limited attention span of the average TV viewer, it was probably wise for God to give Moses 10 commandments, rather than 110. In our experience, and we acknowledge the need for further research into this question, 10 major recommendations are sufficient to stimulate both action and further reflection within any organization.

Kramlinger (1998) has argued that, in constructing a message people can easily learn, it is vital to address employees' real concerns, and make a connection to whatever values are shared throughout the organization. Clearly, recommendations that promote actual change must assume a simple form that people can memorize, become inspired by, act on and convince others to respond to. The eminent psychologist B.F. Skinner (1954) concluded that the two most powerful reinforcers are *success* and *an awareness that progress has been made*. This suggests that an audit report should talk about the strengths of action plans as well as the weaknesses they are designed to address, thereby (in marketing parlance) promising the organization a clear set of benefits.

It is vital that recommendations are relevant to the organization that has been audited, and that managers will be able to implement them. Good generals know never to give an order that cannot be obeyed. Nothing erodes a leader's authority faster than failure. Recommendations that may have worked in other organizations in the past might be impractical in a different context. Suggesting that they be implemented when this is likely to be a stretch too far does not facilitate action, or improvements in communication.

It is useful if the recommendations seek to build on positive behaviours that at least some sections of the organization are already displaying, rather than if they represent an entirely new set of values, behaviours and relationships that everyone will have to learn from scratch. In these terms, and selecting from suggestions made by Kramlinger (1998), it is vital to frame recommendations so that they tell people:

- Why were we doing different and perhaps wrong things before?
- In what way is this change consistent with previous changes?
- What, if anything, will remain the same?
- How is this change grounded in our values and commitments?
- What will the organization look like in a year?
- What will individuals gain or lose?
- What support will be provided to make the change work?
- What will top managers do to make sure the change is effective?

The cardinal question to be addressed is: What can the organization do differently to that which it already does, and how will this make a difference to the main problems that it currently faces? We list below a number of recommendations that have been implemented in a wide variety of organizations, to give a flavour of what is possible:

- The use of additional formal communication channels, such as newsletters, bulletin boards, new meeting structures, e-mail, the Internet and the intranet.
- Development of communication goals, objectives and policies, and the disclosure of these to relevant publics.
- Open disclosure policies on certain issues. Frequently we have found that people imagine managers to be more secretive on a range of issues than they are. We have therefore recommended that a 'A Freedom of Information Act' be announced, which explicitly declares that managers can be approached on a number of identified issues and will be prepared to provide any information available on them.

- Better upward input solicited by top management to improve the planning process. Frequently this has involved intensive follow-up effort to transform team briefings into a system for promoting two-way communication and hence involvement.

This is by no means a definitive inventory of likely recommendations, which always relate to the unique findings of the audit that has been conducted. The case study chapters contained in Part III of this book discuss particular organizational interventions to which various audits gave rise, and that should enable readers to begin a debate into the most relevant changes that seem pertinent to their needs.

The *Appendices* contain supporting material that is important to the overall case but does not belong logically in the main body of the report. These include examples of data collection instruments (e.g. questionnaires, survey instruments, observation schedules), tables that are of interest to some readers but are marginal to the main issues being explored, or more lengthy extracts from interviews with people who have been surveyed. Few readers will explore this section in depth. However, the knowledge that they are there reassures people that the report's diagnosis is based on a rigorous methodology, solid evidence and hard work.

The *References* is a list of main sources cited in the text – books, reports, newspaper articles, journal articles or official statements. Again, this reassures readers that the methods, findings and recommendations contained in the report rest on a tangible body of research and experience, rather than the sort of inspiration born of missed or impending deadlines. There is no need for a huge number of references – a report is a guide to action, rather than an academic masterpiece. A small number of references (probably in the region of about 10) should be sufficient to enable anyone who wishes to explore a particular issue in more detail to do so. Such follow-up is also likely to strengthen their interest and hence commitment to the issues raised in the report. This reinforces the report's credibility. Credibility is central to successful persuasion, and hence to change.

A number of other key issues in writing an audit report are now considered.

THE SIGNIFICANCE OF STATISTICS

Stephen Hawking, in the acknowledgements to his best selling *Brief History of Time* (1988), wrote: 'Someone told me that each equation I included in the book would halve the sales' (p. vi). He therefore includes only one equation in his book – that for relativity ($E = mc^2$). A similar approach to statistics in reports is vital. Investigations of teachers and administrators in schools explored precisely this question (Brown and Newman, 1983). They found that teachers and administrators were:

- much more receptive and supportive of recommendations emerging from short reports that contained no statistics
- slightly more supportive if frequency data and percentages were included
- more likely to reject the same set of recommendations if the report contained notations for type of statistical analysis and significance levels.

In part, as has been well documented, this is because most people have a poor grasp of statistics, and the laws of probability (Fine, 2006). This explains the popularity of national lotteries, once defined as 'a tax on stupidity'. However irrational it may be, most of us tend to place more trust in stories and individual experiences that we can recall vividly, than we do in statistical averages. Anecdotal evidence therefore has significant influence when we are making decisions (Christie, 2007). For this reason, smokers find the fact they know someone who has survived the habit a convincing reason to continue with it, while pooh-poohing the epidemiological evidence that it damages health. Additionally, many of us distrust those who wield figures in argument, recalling Mark Twain's famous comment that 'there are lies, damned lies and statistics'.

It is clear that statistics require careful presentation. Above all, readers are more likely to make use of them in making decisions when they are presented simply and in ways that they can relate to through their real experiences (Brase, 2002). Thus statistics are useful to provide evidence – that is, as an indicator of what the main trends in communication are, and as a means of persuading people that certain changes are necessary. However, although statistics are important in this endeavour, it has been pointed out that the most effective persuaders

> supplement numerical data with examples, stories, metaphors, and analogies to make their positions come alive. That use of language paints a vivid word picture and, in doing so, lends a compelling and tangible quality to the persuader's point of view.
>
> (Conger, 1998, p. 90)

It is therefore necessary to integrate statistical findings with the actual words of real people in the organization, who can explain in the language of individual experience what the facts and figures really mean.

In addition, many readers of the report will approach any and all findings with trepidation, fearing that their reputation or that of their departments is in some way on the line. They may therefore be inclined to exaggerate or understate precisely the most important findings, in the service of internal political agendas. People may also attack the statistical tests used, metamorphosing within seconds into mathematical geniuses, intent on recruiting adherents to the good old cause of the status quo. A communication audit report should minimize the scope for such misunderstandings and gamesmanship. This means that its authors should consider such issues as:

- If a score of 4.1 is achieved on a 5-point scale (such as that utilized in the ICA instrument, and discussed in Chapter 3), what does it *mean*? Is the communication climate freezing cold? Or, on the contrary, has springtime arrived early?

- If 80% of staff are moderately dissatisfied with communication, should this be a cause for panic? Or does it compare favourably with levels achieved by other competitors in this industry?

- What are the sub-group scores within the organization? Do most group-ings feel the same, or are there pockets either of great satisfaction, or of total alienation? Where, in other words, is the greatest need for rapid action, and where can we encourage people to immediately celebrate their achievements?

- What are the optimum scores that can be achieved with the particular research instrument employed in this investigation? It is rare, in our experience, for organizations to achieve scores above 4 when a 5-point scale has been used. Central tendency would suggest that scores tend to settle on a mid-point range. This puts what might appear to be initially low scores in context.

- It is also helpful to compare present scores with those for the same or similar items on previous surveys, either within this organization or in audits conducted in other organizations (Downs and Adrian, 2004). For example, we worked with one organization in which senior managers were initially depressed at an overall satisfaction score of 3.7, on a 5-point scale. It was necessary to point out that in this particular sector of industry 3.7 was actually in the upper quadrant of organizations that we had surveyed, and close in any event to what experience suggested was the maximum that could be achieved.

- Consider carefully how to report issues of statistical significance. The problem is that managers often become obsessed by what is statistically rather than what is practically significant. The difficulty, and one possible solution, is neatly summarized as follows by Edwards *et al.* (1997, p. 130): 'because statistical significance tests are affected by sample sizes, surveys conducted with samples of several hundred or several thousand respond-ents may obtain significant results even with group differences as small as .1 or .2 on a 5-point scale'. They go on to point out that, although statistically significant, these differences, may have little or no practical application for the organization. One suggestion they make is for a 10 percentage point predetermined level of practical significance. Thus, if a 5-point scale is converted to percentages, 10% would represent a value of 0.5, which these guidelines suggest could be used as a measure of practical significance.

BREAKING BAD NEWS

A communication audit report should be an *honest* and *accurate* account of the communication climate found within the organization concerned. However, this general imperative does not exhaust the vexed question of how to present what might be termed bad news to senior managers. We have already alluded to the difficulty of interpreting data, particularly of a statistical kind. People are especially sensitive to negative input – what has been termed the automatic vigilance effect (Pratto and John, 1991). This reflexive action is consistent with threat-rigidity theory, which postulates that, 'a threat to the vital interests of an entity . . . will lead to forms of rigidity' (Staw *et al.*, 1981, p. 502). One of our most fundamental needs, in most relational contexts, is to present a positive face to others, and to be reassured that the positive light in which we see ourselves is widely shared. Critical feedback may appear to threaten face needs, and hence be perceived as an attack on vital interests (Tourish and Robson, 2006). Thus, when managers are faced with such feedback, they are more likely to retreat into well worn patterns of behaviour than to stay open to new ideas or encourage challenges to existing practices.

People faced only or mostly with criticism also feel powerless to effect change, imagining that there are no instances of effective practice for them to build on. Consistent negative feedback, and the absence of positive reinforcement, promotes the conviction that things can only get worse, whatever people do. This syndrome is known as 'learned helplessness' (Peterson *et al.*, 1993). Moreover, rigidity effects are reinforced by a natural desire to avoid blame and confusion (Barnett and Pratt, 2000). In essence, a sense of proportion and the provision of balanced feedback are vital (Audia and Locke, 2003). Thus, one study found that managers who received a small number of unfavourable, behaviour/task-focused comments improved in their performance more than other managers, but the performance of managers who received a large number of unfavourable, behaviour/task-focused comments declined more than that of other managers (Walker and Smither, 2004).

Reports should therefore draw attention to both the strengths and the weaknesses of communication. Otherwise there is a possibility that the entire report may be rejected. Where the audit results are bad, of course, there is always the possibility of managerial reactance. As Quirke (1996, p. 203) noted:

> It is remarkable how . . . senior managers suddenly become experts in research methodology, asking questions about statistical validity, phrasing of questions in the questionnaire, individuals selected for interview, five-point scales and false positives.

Such resistance to uncomfortable findings can manifest itself in heated questions about the audit procedures employed. The upshot is that the findings are summarily dismissed as invalid or inaccurate, and any possibility of positive change vanishes in the red mist. Employees are then portrayed as whingers, malingerers or trouble makers – as the audit findings are rejected (Wilmot and McClelland, 1990).

We have conducted 'repair' work with one organization where precisely this occurred in a particularly disastrous form. An internal audit team had carried out its work with great energy, determination and enthusiasm – but neglected to keep the senior management team informed of its progress. When they presented modestly critical findings, in an oral presentation to the top management team, their methodology was queried, the validity of the findings rejected and the group disbanded in disgrace. In consequence, a highly talented and important group of people became demoralized, while 2 years passed before the organization dared to re-examine its communication practices again. It was necessary to start work with both the group and senior managers from the very beginning, while placing an enormous stress on the importance of ongoing communication between the two.

How can such disasters be averted? Fundamentally, we would argue that many of the principles that apply when breaking bad news to employees (Ilgen and Davis, 2000), or providing them with critical feedback more generally, also hold in this context (Cannon and Witherspoon, 2005). A number of suggestions are offered here, based on what the research literature suggests to be most effective:

- When positive and negative feedback have to be communicated about a person, object, process or organization the message recipient is more likely to believe the message when it begins with the positive comment (Jacobs et al., 1973). This may be because a variety of self-serving biases cause most of us to routinely exaggerate our personal proficiency (Sutherland, 1992). Drivers often appear to imagine that the roads would be safe, providing everyone else stayed at home: a recent survey of British drivers found that 95% rated themselves as better than the average driver (Hargie et al., 2004). Likewise, most people seem to believe that they could communicate perfectly, if only there was no one else around to get in the way. In consequence, a message that begins by confirming what we think we already know (i.e. *what I am doing well*) has a greater intuitive validity for most people, and leaves them more favourably disposed to accept what follows. A report should begin by accentuating the positive, in the form of stating whatever good news it honestly can.
- Indicate how the findings compare with surveys of this kind in other organizations, or how much further improvement could be realistically expected at this juncture of its history (Morris and LoVerde, 1993). Context is vital to promote understanding and facilitate action.
- The report should be written in non-inflammatory and neutral language, offering solutions rather than a grievance list (Badaracco, 1988). It

should be sensitive to the internal politics, language and values of the organization concerned. Rather than identify scapegoats, responsibility for problems should be shared as widely as is honestly possible, thereby encouraging a collective determination to do something about them. Naming and shaming leads to aggravation, conflagration and retaliation.

- Reinforcing the previous point, it is vital that critical feedback be constructed as non-judgementally as possible (Murray, 1989). Feedback that appears as a personal attack or denigrates a person's character, rather than focusing constructively on either their behaviour or the situation in which they find themselves, tends to provoke strong defensive emotional reactions (Moss and Sanchez, 2004). This means that communication auditors should avoid negatively labelling the people involved in any communication problems they have identified (e.g. 'human resources in this organization is causing communication blockages for every other department, and therefore creating nothing but trouble'). On the other hand, an emphasis on detailed behaviours that can be changed is likely to be perceived as helpful feedback, and spur further change (Cannon and Witherspoon, 2005). Thus, a report *could* usefully say: 'Employees require more information about the impact of the reorganization plan on job security. We recommend that a short statement be prepared by human resources on this issue, in conjunction with communications staff.'
- Managers will also be faced with a difficult decision if the report has uncovered a great deal of bad news. Should they circulate it, or try to keep it quiet? Auditors may well be called on to make recommendations on this point also. It is worth remembering that widespread feedback to all employees of the main audit findings is correlated with increased faith in the possibility of the audit leading to meaningful change (Tourish and Robson, 2003). Some years ago Edwards et al. (1997) cited findings in one organization, where only 11% of people who received feedback felt that survey results would not be used well. This figure rose to 84% among those who were not in receipt of such feedback. It makes sense to hold employee feedback sessions, which management may or may not attend, that are designed to achieve the fullest possible dissemination of both critical and positive audit findings. In this context, it is worth noting the finding from other research to the effect that when managers openly accept critical feedback, rather than seek only positive strokes on their performance, their stature actually rises (Ashford and Tsui, 1991). A further study by Tsui et al. (1995), involving a survey of almost 3000 managers, peers, superiors and subordinates found that exerting extra effort and explaining decisions was positively associated with managers being viewed as effective. Thus feedback sessions should openly acknowledge the difficulties faced by the organization in terms of communication, as well as celebrate its strengths.

INFLUENCING AND PERSUADING TO EFFECT CHANGE

As mentioned several times in this chapter, the ultimate purpose of an audit report is to persuade the organization concerned to implement the recommendations that the report outlines. Persuasion has been defined as: 'The skill that is most fundamental to persuasive success is that of adapting messages to audiences. Skilled persuaders adapt their messages to those they seek to influence' (O'Keefe, 2006, p. 323). Wells and Spinks (1996, p. 27) proposed that persuasive messages should therefore seek to:

(1) attract attention;
(2) arouse psychological needs;
(3) present persuasive information showing the receiver how to satisfy those psychological needs;
(4) present evidence to support claims;
(5) urge action.

We have, in several instances, pointed to particular levers of persuasion (e.g. the use of power as a means of enhancing credibility) that can serve to accomplish these goals. All of these should be employed to lay out clearly the strength of the evidence on which the persuasive appeal or report recommendations is based (Walton and Reed, 2002). Additional levers of persuasion that could be employed include the following.

Threat/fear

This tactic involves the use of fear-arousing messages and the threat of negative outcomes, in order to secure compliance with a desired course of action (Pratkanis, 2007). The success of this strategy is dependent on three critical elements (Hargie *et al.*, 2004). First, the magnitude and severity of the negative outcome. Second, its probability of occurring if nothing is done to avoid it, and third, the effectiveness of the recommended response to remove the threat. For example: 'Successfully implementing these recommendations will transform the communication climate within this organization. Failure to do so will see a further deterioration, and the prospect of industrial action during the forthcoming pay round. We believe that these proposals can avert such a danger.'

Logical argument

An appeal to reason and logic is the cornerstone of many persuasion efforts (Perloff, 2007). It is therefore useful to examine strategies that can maximize the impact of this approach. There are well established features of arguments, and of the way they are delivered, which increase their persuasive power:

- The message should be fully *comprehensible* – the meaning must be clear and unambiguous. As argued earlier, adding clear interpretation to audit findings reduces ambiguity and accomplishes this goal.
- The report should be *shared* with a few key people inside the organization before it is finally printed. This enables them to identify obvious factual mistakes, or suggest areas that might require further analysis, if the logic of the recommendations is to be readily apparent to readers. Handled carefully, such a process of consultation adds force to the report's arguments and credibility to the efforts of the audit team. Care should be taken to ensure that it does not become a means of top executives enforcing a whitewash job, in which all sins become virtues and each disaster is described as 'a rapidly accelerating, upwardly mobile learning curve'. A report that celebrates every Little Bighorn as the organization's finest hour will have no credibility, and will spur cynicism rather than action.
- The important aspects of the argument should be *emphasized* to underline them. Bearing in mind that the report will be read in its entirety by only a few people, this suggests that the main findings should be repeated at several points, particularly in the summary and conclusion.
- The *advantages* of the recommended course of action, and the *disadvantages* of the alternatives, should be firmly stated and supporting evidence cited. This is referred to as *sidedness* in message delivery. Two-sided messages while emphasizing the positive aspects of the message also recognize negatives, whereas one-sided ones are partisan and only accentuate the positive. In general, the former are more effective (Pratkanis, 2007). Thus an audit report can acknowledge the difficulties in implementing particular recommendations and perhaps concede that there may be parts of the organization not yet ready for a particular approach.
- Reports benefit from the use of *vivid examples*, which have been shown to be a powerful technique for effecting influence. For example, the communication audit questionnaire reproduced in the Appendix of this book contains a section asking respondents to identify an example of communication that most typifies the quality of communication inside their organization. They are then asked to indicate whether this experience was positive or negative. A communication audit report can use this data in two ways. First, it can tabulate the ratio of positive to negative examples offered. The higher this is in favour of positive examples the healthier the communication climate is likely to be. (Examples of this are provided in Chapter 11, reporting an audit in an NHS Trust.) Second, the report can extract representative comments from the examples, to buttress the auditors' case. For example, a major finding that people feel

under-informed about a key change issue could be supported by a representative sample of quotations. These strengthen the argument in favour of the audit team's recommendations.

- Clear *conclusions* should be evident to the report's readers. The evidence here is clear: 'messages with explicit conclusions are more persuasive than those with implicit conclusions' (O'Keefe, 2006, p. 334). In a meta-analysis of research in this field, Cruz (1998, p. 228) found that one reason for this is simply that: 'The more explicit the conclusions to a persuasive message, the better the conclusion is comprehended.' Thus the reader should have no doubt about the overall nature of the findings, and be fully aware of the main action points being proposed.

DELIVERING THE REPORT ORALLY

Finally, the audit report will normally be presented orally to the top management team. This is frequently the most challenging, and decisive, part of the whole exercise. Many managers will have only skimmed the report. In particular, they will have been looking for issues that relate directly to their part of the organization's function. It is therefore essential that the presentation provides a summary of the audit's overall main findings. In addition, as noted earlier, it is important to recognize that if critical comments have been made, some managers who feel most directly affected may well arrive in attack mode, and anxious to ridicule the entire project. Rather than wearing a crash helmet and flak jacket, the best defence is the shield of top-class presentational skills. Unfortunately, these are generally the exception than the rule. As Etherington (2006) has noted, most audiences and presenters in a business context share only one objective – and that is to get out of the room as quickly as possible. There are many excellent texts that advise on how to avoid this and deliver professional, persuasive presentations (e.g. Bradbury, 2006), and we do not intend to dwell on the point here.

In essence, how a message is delivered is often as crucial in determining its impact as the nature of the message itself. Hence, the well-known aphorism that the medium is the message. Confidence, clarity and a focus on essentials are vital. The audit team should practise the presentation as much as possible. In particular, at least one member of the team should play the role of critical evaluator, anticipating as many objections to the report as possible. The objective is to ensure that no question will be asked that has not been thoroughly prepared in advance. As with the whole nature of the audit report, the presentation should be conducted in a professional manner. Audio-visual aids are now standard, and their use is expected. However, PowerPoint is often used poorly, leaving an audience 'overwhelmed by the dense packages of data and text that requires them to intuit the story the speaker wishes to share' (Hentz, 2006, p. 426). A key danger is overuse. Careful thought, selectivity, imagination and the ability to talk around the subject matter rather than read from a screen are all crucial determinants of success (Friedman, 2007).

It is therefore also vital that presenters monitor people's non-verbal behaviour, looking for signs of drift, hostility or boredom, and adjust the content, length or style of delivery accordingly (Taylor, 2008). However much the presentation has been planned, an audience provides real-time feedback. Plans need to be changed if the context in which the presentation is occurring has shifted.

Above all, and as with the audit process in general, the presentation must show that the team appreciates the organization's strengths, has accurately diagnosed its weaknesses and has, in partnership with all those it has worked with, devised a clear programme of action that will solve its problems.

CONCLUSION

This chapter has outlined a structure for compiling a communication audit report, a process for persuading key people of its merits, and suggestions for the widespread dissemination of the report's main findings and recommendations. Too many reports languish on shelves, or find themselves instantly consigned to that filing cabinet of lost hope – the nearest waste-bin. Our main point has been that audit reports can avoid these fates if they are planned as an integral part of the audit process, and if they are designed as a guide to action. It is vital that senior managers are on board throughout. This can be accomplished by, for example, getting them to respond to draft surveys, reports and recommendations, or otherwise commenting on the nature of the findings.

Thus, attention must be paid to:

- Producing accurate data.
- Achieving a balance between negative and positive findings.
- Devising recommendations that address real problems, and that are 'doable'.
- Persuading the organization at large of the merits of the audit team's proposals.

Communication audits can make a major contribution to organizational success. But the audit itself does none of this. In the final analysis, the audit report is the most visible product of the audit team's efforts, and hence the most potent factor of all in determining the impact the exercise will have within the organization concerned.

Part III

Audits in action

Chapter 11

Charting communication performance in a healthcare organization

Owen Hargie and Dennis Tourish

INTRODUCTION

The National Health Service (NHS) is by far the largest employer in the UK and one of the largest in the world, with over one million employees. It was formed in 1948 to provide health services free of charge to all citizens. Not surprisingly, the demand for these services rose rapidly. The pressures produced by this resultant demand, coupled with the logistics of running such a huge, nation-wide organization, soon led to an obsession with administrative structures and costs. Inevitably, given its scale of operation and budgetary demands, government is centrally involved in the affairs of the NHS (Milewa *et al.*, 2002; Bate *et al.*, 2004; Redman, 2008). When the impact of political changes enforced by the diametrically opposing ideologies of Conservative and Labour governments about how healthcare should be delivered is sprinkled on, the NHS mix becomes highly unstable. Indeed, the management structure of the NHS is rather like flat-pack furniture – difficult to put together, the instructions received by the person expected to manage the activity often appear to make little sense, the bits do not always fit neatly, and it never seems to be designed to last. This has meant that staff working in this field have tended to live in very uncertain times with regard to how NHS facilities are organized and managed. As illustrated by Henderson (2005) in the USA, and Rentsch *et al.* (2003) in Switzerland, similar communication problems can be found in the healthcare organizations of many countries.

When we were first approached by the NHS Trust about auditing their communications, our initial step was to arrange a meeting with the Chief Executive and the Head of the Corporate Communications Department, to gain some insight into the organization itself and their objectives for the exercise. It soon became obvious that we were dealing with two disciples wishing to spread the gospel of the importance of effective organizational communication. What they wanted to achieve in the first instance was an objective and accurate picture of existing strengths and weaknesses, to enable them to build on areas of identified best practice while implementing changes to rectify deficits. What they needed, but did not have in place, was a coherent communications strategy, and the audits led directly to the construction of one. The problems they faced can best be appreciated by examining the nature of the facility they have to manage.

THE ORGANIZATION

This was a large organization providing health and social services across eight main programme areas:

- Child Health
- Family and Child Care
- Elderly
- Mental Health
- Learning Disability
- Physical and Sensory Disability
- Health Promotion and Disease Prevention
- Primary Care and Adult Community.

The scale of operation was reflected by the fact that the organization:

- had an annual budget of over £100 million
- employed 4000 staff
- spanned a geographical area of 1149 miles, covering a diverse mix of urban and rural areas
- provided health and social care services for a population of some 320,000 people
- ran 90 different health and social care facilities, such as residential child care units, centres for adults with learning disabilities, residential care homes for the elderly, and a major psychiatric hospital
- arranged care for 8000 people in their homes each day
- engaged in a total of 700,000 contacts per year with patients and clients
- employed the complete spectrum of health and social care professionals (consultants, doctors, nurses, occupational therapists, radiographers, speech therapists, social workers, etc.), together with the related swathe of administrative, estates, clerical, secretarial, technical and ancillary staff.

The total of 4000 staff included some 800 home helps. These are workers who are employed, mainly on an hourly basis, to provide help (cleaning, cooking, shopping, etc.) to the elderly and infirm in their homes. The questionnaire employed in the main phase of this audit (see below) was inappropriate for this target group, since it addressed a wide range of issues that were largely irrelevant to the communication issues faced by them. Accordingly, home helps were audited by an open-ended questionnaire, in which they were asked to list three main strengths and three main weaknesses in the way people communicated with them, and to suggest any changes that would improve current communication practices. In this chapter we do not have space to present the findings from the home help audit, but rather will concentrate on the main body of the workforce who completed the full audit questionnaire.

OBJECTIVES

Following the initial discussion with the Chief Executive and Head of Communications, a series of detailed planning meetings were held with the Communications team to work out how, and in what ways, an audit could best be carried out. Given the geographical spread and the wide range of staff groups involved, it was eventually decided that a depth questionnaire would offer the most detailed picture of the communication. A Communications Workshop was then run by the authors, at which time the proposal for an audit was presented to the Senior Management Team (SMT). The rationale for the exercise, the proposed questionnaire methodology, and the broad aims of the audit were explained. As a result of concerted deliberations and debate, the key issues about which the Trust should be communicating were formulated and agreed for inclusion in the questionnaire. The exact objectives for the audit were also delineated.

This Workshop served to ensure that all members of the SMT were fully apprised of the audit and had the opportunity to help form its final shape. This involvement served to increase their commitment to the exercise. Since they would also be involved in organizing the release of some of their staff to complete audit materials, it was vital that they fully understood its importance and were able to cascade this down the hierarchy. Given that participation is a proven tool for effecting influence in organizations (Hargie *et al.*, 2004), we would commend to auditors that they involve as many key players as possible in the initial stages of the audit exercise.

An important output from the detailed planning sessions with staff from the Corporate Communications team, and the consequent feedback from the SMT, was that six objectives were agreed for the first audit (Audit1) and carried forward to the second audit (Audit2):

1 To examine in depth the attitudes of staff towards internal communications.
2 To use a depth validated questionnaire to gauge the views of a 5% sample of the total staff population, stratified across staff groups and geographical locations.
3 To identify key issues current within the Trust for specific inclusion in this questionnaire.

4   To produce qualitative and quantitative findings to guide related action plans and act as a benchmark for future audits.
5   To separately investigate the view of home helps, using an open format postal questionnaire and to produce a set of recommendations relating to the findings.
6   To produce a report on all of the main findings from the audit, to also contain a set of recommendations for action.

For Audit2, and again following the same planning and consultation cycle, an additional seventh objective was formulated:

7   To compare and contrast the findings from the present audit with those obtained from the audit conducted 2 years previously. (Audit1 therefore provided benchmarking standards against which progress was measured 2 years later.)

THE AUDIT INSTRUMENT

Once the planning cycle had been completed, it was clear that what the Trust both wanted and needed was an organization-wide analysis of communication. No previous such systematic evaluation had occurred, and so no information was available regarding the state of communications generally or in specific locations in particular. As explained above, it was therefore agreed that a comprehensive questionnaire should be employed as the main instrument.

The questionnaire utilized in this audit was an adaptation of the ICA Questionnaire. This instrument has a sound conceptual framework and has been shown to have validity, reliability and utility in auditing organizational communication (see Chapter 3). It produces a great deal of quantitative data and thus provides benchmarks against which to measure future performance. It also includes open questions that allow respondents to freely express their views about aspects of communication. The original ICA Questionnaire was modified by us, following audits we conducted in a range of NHS sectors (see the Appendix). Four main changes were made:

1   The language was modified to reflect the norms of the NHS sector. As a simple example, the term 'middle management' was used rather than 'immediate supervisor'.
2   We added an open-format first question, asking respondents to list three main strengths and three main weaknesses in the way other staff communicate with them. This allows respondents to reflect generally on their own views about what is good or bad about current practices, before being 'set' in any way by the standard questions that follow.

3   The original ICA instrument had a 'critical incident' sheet alongside every page (see Chapter 8). We found that staff viewed the completion of these sheets as a very time-consuming and tedious task. As a result we reduced this, while retaining the concept, by requesting respondents to give *one* critical incident of their choice that was most typical of communication within the organization. We made this the penultimate question.

4   A final question was added asking respondents to recommend three changes that would improve communication. We have found that the responses to this question produce a wealth of useful suggestions. This gathers in valuable information that would otherwise be lost.

In addition, the questionnaire has a section devoted to what are considered to be the main issues facing the organization at the particular time of audit. In this audit some of these issues remained the same from Audit1 to Audit2, while others changed.

THE AUDITS

An identical procedure was followed in both audits. All staff were informed by a letter from the Chief Executive that an audit would be taking place in the near future. The main objectives of the audit were explained and it was pointed out that some staff would be chosen at random to participate. The next step was to select the survey sample.

This type of audit necessitates selecting a sample population genuinely representative of key sub-groups as the basis for data collection. In theory, an organization comprising 600 staff could be audited by surveying 10% of the staff (n = 60) selected at random. However, in practice most organizations have a range of discrete occupational groups and managerial levels, all performing different roles, and with possibly very different perspectives on communication effectiveness. Furthermore, some of these groups may be small in number, yet of key importance. Since a 10% sample of 10 staff would mean that only one person would be audited, a simple crude percentage approach will result in such influential groups being under-represented. This means that a weighted stratified sampling technique is needed. Where numbers are over 100, a sample of 5% is usually sufficient. When less than 100, we have used the following weightings as a basis for sampling within a number of audits:

Number in sample	% surveyed
90+	10
60–89	15
40–59	25
30–39	30

Number in sample	% surveyed
20–29	45
15–19	60
10–14	80
1–9	90

Using this sampling frame, and bearing in mind other important consider-ations such as gender and managerial level, a randomly selected, stratified, cross-section of staff were then chosen by us from the Personnel Information Management System (PIMS) print-out. Thus the gender balance in both audits was 80%F:20%M, reflecting the staffing complement; likewise the proportions of staff at various levels of management, and on full-time or part-time contracts, were representative. Staffing categories and audit totals are shown in Box 11.1, and again these figures were in proportion to overall staffing numbers.

As previously explained, the Trust has seven main sub-regions. Question-naires were distributed in person by the authors in a suitable room at each of these seven main central locations. The selected staff were given 1 hour off work to engage in the exercise. This method of administration was adopted for several reasons. It allowed us to:

1   Explain that we personally selected staff at random and that no one was chosen by the Trust to take part.
2   Make it clear that we were university researchers and so independent of the organization.
3   Give a personal assurance that all information would be treated in the strictest confidence, that completed questionnaires would only be seen by us, and that no names were to be put on the questionnaires.
4   Emphasize the fact that since a fairly large number of staff had been given an hour off work to complete the audit, their views were clearly of importance to the Trust.

Box 11.1 Categories and numbers of staff audited

	Audit1	Audit2
Administrative and Clerical	34	42
Works and Maintenance	4	2
Ancillary and General	14	16
Nursing and Midwifery	37	44
Social Work	20	16
Professional and Technical	14	12
Medical and Dental	14	8
Other	23	16
Totals	160	156

5   Carefully describe the questionnaire and answer any queries regarding its completion.

6   Raise the response rate well above that which would have been achieved by a postal administration.

An attendance list was taken for each administration so that we could track and follow-up any missing staff (this was explained to respondents). Once the first set of completed audit questionnaires had been obtained from the locational distribution, a postal drop was then carried out to reach those staff who had not been able to attend. As a result, a final total of 160 Audit1, and 156 Audit2 questionnaires were obtained, representing over 5% of the total staff (excluding home helps) in both cases.

RESULTS

The questionnaire is divided into a number of sections, each dealing with a different aspect of communication (such as *information received, information sent*, and *action taken on information received*). The sections contain a number of very specific questions, and respondents are asked to rate each, using a 5-point scale, along two dimensions that in essence measure 'how it is now' and 'how it should be' (see Table 11.1). This allows for comparisons regarding staff views about current (real) and desired (ideal) communication practices (see the Appendix). The totals for each section are then summed to give overall scores for that aspect of communication. Scores in the questionnaire can then be converted into percentage satisfaction scores. For example, as can be seen from Table 11.1 showing the information being sent, the total Audit2 score for 'information received now' was 2.5 as opposed to an 'information needed' score of 3.3 (Table 11.1). These scores are converted into percentage scores by multiplying by a factor of 20 (given the 5-point scale used). Thus, the percentage satisfaction score of 2.5 for 'information received now' in Audit2 represents 50% satisfaction as opposed to a desired score of 3.3, or 66%. To put it another way, there was a 16% shortfall between perceptions of amount of information actually received as compared to what is perceived to be needed.

In addition, the differences between the scores for each of the items and the overall totals can be tested for significance using the Wilcoxon signed ranks test. Although the Wilcoxon test employs median scores, in our audit reports we present mean scores (as in Table 11.1), since we have found these to be the most readily understood and digestible measure of central tendency. The average individual understands the notion of average scores, whereas medians and modes can cause indigestion for many people.

Overall levels of 'satisfaction with communication' scores are calculated by summing each individual's raw scores for each item for communication as it

Table 11.1 Amount of information being sent (Audit2)

Topic area	Information received now	Information needed	Rank
Performance appraisal systems	2.0	3.2*	1
How decisions that affect my job are reached	2.6	3.6*	2
Promotion opportunities	2.2	3.2*	2
Staff development opportunities	2.5	3.5*	2
Important new service developments	2.1	3.1*	2
The goals of the organization	2.2	3.2*	2
Major management decisions	2.4	3.3*	7
Improvements in services, or how services are delivered	2.4	3.3*	7
How my job contributes to the organization	2.8	3.6*	9
Specific problems faced by the organization	2.3	3.1*	9
Pay, benefits and conditions	2.1	2.9*	9
Things that go wrong in my organization	2.7	3.5*	9
My performance in my job	3.0	3.5	13
The total range of services offered	2.9	3.4	13
How problems that I report in my job are dealt with	3.4	3.8	15
What is expected from me in my job	3.0	3.4	16
Mean total	2.5	3.3*	

Scoring key: 1 = very little; 2 = little; 3 = some; 4 = great; 5 = very great.
Note: * $p < .01$ (Wilcoxon). Rankings based on differences between means for information sent and needing to be sent.

'is now' (in sections with two columns, this is the left-hand column scores) and dividing by the total number of items in the questionnaire. Cross-tabulations are carried out between these overall satisfaction scores and background information criteria, using chi-square tests. The objective here is to determine whether a correlation exists between levels of satisfaction with communication and factors such as gender, location and occupational grouping. Let us now turn to the main findings of the audit.

Audit1–Audit2 comparisons

Cross-tabulations

In Audit1 the only significant difference to emerge was between geographical locations, with three of the seven regions recording significantly lower satisfaction scores than the other four. As a result, we ran focus groups at these three locations to tease out why such differences existed. We asked three main questions:

- How do you feel in general about communications between staff and managers within the Trust?
- What are your main views about communications within the area where you work – what are the main strengths and weaknesses?
- What specific additional measures would you like managers to take to improve communication in your area?

We found that staff in these areas did not have specific grievances, but rather they felt more strongly about those issues that were generally perceived to be problematic by all respondents. In Audit2 no significant differences were found between satisfaction scores and background information criteria, indicating that any locational problems that may have existed had been overcome.

Overall satisfaction levels

As the figures in Box 11.2 illustrate, there was a definite overall improvement in the scores for Audit2 as compared to Audit1, with an overall mean improvement of 0.3 (6% increased approval rating). On almost every section of the questionnaire, the Audit2 results were an improvement on the findings from Audit1. Other important findings in relation to satisfaction were as follows.

Box 11.2 Comparison of scores for main questionnaire areas

	Audit1	Audit2	Change
Information received	2.4	2.8	+0.4 (8%)
Information received on important issues facing the Trust	2.1	2.4	+0.3 (6%)
Information received from various sources	2.6	3.0	+0.4 (8%)
Information received through various channels	2.4	2.7	+0.3 (6%)
Timeliness of information received	3.2	3.5	+0.3 (6%)
Information sent	2.5	2.5	0
Action taken on information sent	2.9	3.1	+0.2 (4%)
Information sent on important issues facing the Trust	1.8	1.8	0
Working relationships	3.4	3.7	+0.3 (6%)
Overall satisfaction score	2.6	2.9	+0.3 (6%)

Information received

The largest change scores were for information received. Following the finding from Audit1 that there was a problem with the amount of information being received by staff, two of our recommendations were that: 'More information should be disseminated about all aspects of the work of the Trust, and the key management concerns that are current' and 'There should be more face-to-face communication between senior managers and staff.' As a result, the Trust put in action a plan to improve its performance on this aspect of communication. Three main strategies were introduced:

1   A monthly letter was sent by the Chief Executive directly to all staff at their home addresses in which he presented up-to-date information and itemized the main decisions made by the Trust Board. A point of contact was also included for feedback from staff.
2   A Trust Newsletter was introduced and again sent to all staff at home. This Newsletter was used to inform staff about the results of both audits, and to provide details about the communications strategy that would be introduced to meet identified deficits. It was also used to publicize the fact that Audit2 would be taking place.
3   The Chief Executive initiated a series of regular visits to all sub-regions at which he met with staff, listened to their views and explained current policy.

These actions clearly produced positive results, as measured by the improvement scores of between 6% and 8% for satisfaction with the amount of information received in general, information on important issues facing the organization, and information from various sources and different channels (Box 11.2).

Information sent

Conversely, there was no change at all in the figures for amount of information sent, although there was a slight improvement (4%) regarding action taken on any information that had been sent (Box 11.2). This indicated that an important task for the organization following Audit2 was to explore ways in which staff participation in its operation could be increased. In making our recommendations we pointed out that the desire of staff to send more information (see Table 11.1) indicated their willingness to become involved, and strongly advised that this should be built on. To facilitate this, one of our Audit2 recommendations was that the system of team briefings be reviewed to include a *requirement* that staff list items they wished to have referred up the line to more senior managers. Another was that plans should be drawn up to foster greater interdepartmental communication and involvement in the work of the organization.

The results from Table 11.1 also highlight the importance of audits to be timely. At the time of Audit2 the Trust was introducing a new system of staff appraisal, and the questionnaire data showed this to be the area of greatest concern for respondents. Indeed the 1.2 (24%) shortfall here between information received and that needed was one of the largest deficits in the entire audit. Our actual recommendation here was that 'The Trust should investigate why the issue of performance appraisal is causing concern, and should engage in more communications with staff about this aspect of their work.'

Working relationships

Following Audit1 it was evident that one of the solid building blocks on which to erect a firm communication edifice was the fact that working relationships among staff were good. People on the ground expressed high levels of trust for colleagues and line managers, with somewhat lower levels for middle and senior managers. These bonds were further strengthened by Audit2, with an overall 6% increase in relational satisfaction (Box 11.2), and this rate of increase was consistent for colleagues and managers. Thus, as communications improved, working relationships were perceived to be better. Following the rule that good news should always come first in audit reports (see Chapter 10), our first recommendation in Audit2 was that 'The Trust should ensure that this level of harmony is maintained and enhanced.'

Comparison of difference scores

As previously explained, on most sections of the questionnaire there are two columns. In the first column, respondents rate on a 5-point scale their actual level of satisfaction with communication at present. In the second column they rate their ideal satisfaction level. The difference between these two scores then represents a score for current level of satisfaction or dissatisfaction. Box 11.3 presents comparisons between the *difference* scores obtained in the two audits. The lower these change scores, the more satisfied staff are with communication – an ideal difference score would be '0'. As can be seen, there was again a definite overall improvement in Audit2 across all areas, with a total improvement score of 0.4 (8%). The mean score for satisfaction across all respondents in Audit2 was 2.9, as opposed to 2.6 in Audit1 (Box 11.2). This indicated that respondents felt that while internal communications were on an upwards trend, there was still room for improvement. The target overall ideal satisfaction score, as set by respondents in both audits, was 3.5. This indicated that staff wished communications to be functioning at a moderately good level. In our experience, organizations rarely achieve scores of above 4.0. We recommended therefore that a realistic general communication target score for the next audit was 3.2.

Box 11.3 Comparison of difference scores for main questionnaire areas

	Audit1	*Audit2*	*Change*
Information received	1.5	1.0	0.5 (10%)
Information received on important issues facing the Trust	2.0	1.4	0.6 (12%)
Information received from various sources	1.1	0.8	0.3 (6%)
Information received through various channels	1.2	0.7	0.5 (10%)
Information sent	0.9	0.8	0.1 (2%)
Action taken on information sent	0.9	0.7	0.2 (4%)
Information sent on important issues facing the Trust	0.9	0.7	0.2 (4%)
Overall mean difference scores	1.2	0.8	0.4 (8%)

Satisfaction with managers

The questionnaire can be used to measure satisfaction with various levels of management. Thus, in Audit2 the scores in Box 11.4 for colleagues and managers were obtained by combining the ratings from various sections of the questionnaire for each source and then calculating the mean score for each. The interesting aspect of these audit results is that these converted scores are realistic in two senses. First, they are close to the actual targets set by many large corporations that audit on a regular basis. Second, staff recognized that middle and senior managers, and the Chief Executive, cannot be expected to achieve satisfaction scores as high as colleagues or immediate managers. It is worthy of note here that an important advantage of the questionnaire used in this audit is that it quantifies communication in terms of communication scores, so that targets can be set for managers at all levels to improve their current satisfaction scores. For example, an examination of Box 11.4 suggests that a realistic target for immediate managers to achieve in Audit3 would be 3.9 (78%).

Communication examples

As part of the questionnaire, respondents are asked to select and describe one effective or ineffective experience that is for them most typical of communication within the organization (see the Appendix). Perhaps the most striking feature of comparison between the two audits was the ratio of positive to negative examples cited (Box 11.5). As discussed in Chapter 8, the 'critical incidents' that staff report as being typical of communication provide insight into whether they feel positive or negative about the organization as a whole. Where communication is functioning at a reasonable level we would expect a

---

Box 11.4 Actual and ideal satisfaction scores: Audit2

	Actual satisfaction score	Ideal satisfaction score	Shortfall
Colleagues	4.0 (80%)	4.3 (86%)	0.3 (6%)
Immediate managers	3.7 (74%)	4.2 (84%)	0.5 (10%)
Middle managers	3.3 (66%)	3.8 (76%)	0.5 (10%)
Senior managers	3.0 (60%)	3.7 (74%)	0.7 (14%)
Chief Executive	3.0 (60%)	3.5 (70%)	0.5 (10%)

Box 11.5 Comparison of examples

Year	Positive examples	Negative examples
Audit1	19	96
Audit2	63	61

---

positive/negative ratio of at least 50/50 to be reached. However, the ratio in Audit1 was 5:1 in favour of negative examples. By Audit2 this had been transformed, with positive examples outnumbering negative ones. This was a considerable achievement, and another clear indicator that the communication strategies introduced after Audit1 had effected positive change during the intervening 2 years. A closer examination of these examples revealed that in both audits some two-thirds of all positive examples related to communication with line managers, illustrating the key role they play in ensuring organizational effectiveness.

Open questions

The questionnaire includes three other open questions, which ask respondents to give examples of: (1) three main communication strengths, (2) three main weaknesses, and (3) suggestions for improvement in communications. These questions produce a mass of information that, when content-analysed, revealed recurring trends, together with some fascinating comments about organizational functioning. In both Audit1 and Audit2 the open-question results confirmed the direction of findings from the quantitative section of the questionnaire. For instance, in terms of specific cited strengths of communication, the two main changes from Audit1 to Audit2 were *the Chief Executive's direct communications* and *the Newsletter*. It will be recalled that these were both initiated following Audit1, and the comments from staff in the open sections were a clear indicator that these innovations had been well received.

The other strengths mentioned in both audits confirmed the good working relationships with colleagues and line managers. Furthermore, in Audit1 a commonly stated weakness was the lack of information from senior managers, but this was not a main theme in Audit2, again confirming the success of these initiatives.

A final issue that emerged in both audits was that of the problems faced by the split-site operation. This included communication difficulties for staff working within the same occupational grouping but across different sites; concerns regarding the fact that some departments who provided important services were located some distance away; and general communication problems such as difficulties with internal mail and telephone. Staff also repeatedly expressed a wish to meet and share more with colleagues working on other sites. Our recommendation here was that 'The Trust should therefore develop plans to foster greater interdepartmental communication.' Given its geographical spread, there were no easy solutions to this. However, as ways in which distal contacts could be facilitated, we recommended that:

- important meetings (including SMT meetings) should be rotated around the different locations
- technological communication channels be given priority
- cross-site conferences and training days be organized on a regular basis
- the criterion of cross-site location be a key consideration in the formation of task forces, working teams, and so on.

The fact that staff expressed such a strong desire for contact with colleagues in other sites suggested a strong sense of corporate identity and we also recommended that this should be fostered.

CONCLUSIONS

Like people, all audits are different, although with some commonalities. The experienced auditor must be able to tailor general audit measures to meet the specific needs of particular organizations. For the reasons stated, a depth questionnaire was the most appropriate measurement tool in the two audits reported in this chapter. It allowed the Trust-wide communications picture to be brought into sharper focus. Like an X-ray, it showed up areas where problems were located while also illustrating the healthy regions of the organizational body. The check-up after 2 years using identical measurement tools also enabled the progress of organizational health to be directly charted. The precise diagnostic nature of the questionnaire allowed an informed prescription to be made to treat areas of dysfunction. The fact that more than one method can be usefully employed was illustrated in

Audit1, when focus groups were used to investigate a specific area of difference identified from the questionnaire.

In this audit we followed the recommended template as presented in Chapter 2, which can be summarized as follows:

- The support and enthusiasm of the Chief Executive was confirmed at the outset.
- The Senior Management Team were fully involved in the early planning decisions.
- Clear audit objectives were delineated.
- All staff were informed that the audit would be taking place and its purpose was fully explained.
- The same audit tool was employed to diagnose initial problems and measure progress – in other words like was compared with like.
- The auditors were external to, and independent of, the organization.
- The results of the audit were disseminated to all staff.
- A set of achievable recommendations was drawn up, together with related action plans, and these were also explained to staff.
- Following Audit1 an overall Communications Strategy was formulated for the Trust and this was used to guide and direct policy and practice in this area.

The findings from this case study illustrate clearly the contribution that audits can make to improved performance. Once areas of weakness have been identified through auditing, an action plan can be put in place to rectify identified deficits. Follow-up audits then allow the success or otherwise of the intervention to be accurately tracked. The results from this audit also help to nail the myth that no matter what you do, staff will simply ask for more. We found that when staff realized that senior management were making a concerted effort to improve communications, there was a tangible increment in overall ratings throughout the questionnaire, coupled with realistic expectations of the levels at which managers could be expected to perform.

Chapter 12

A communication audit of a hospital clinic

Myra Skipper, Owen Hargie and Dennis Tourish

BACKGROUND

The previous chapter described an internal audit of staff within the National Health Service (NHS). This chapter is also concerned with an audit of communications in the NHS, and again the audit has a 'research' impetus (see Chapter 20) in that it was intended that the results would be of interest to the wider health community. The focus of this audit is on a Swallowing Clinic operated by a small team of designated staff, but sited within a large hospital. While the core team of Clinic staff was small, its operation necessitated ongoing communications with health professionals from other hospitals and patients from across a wide geographical spread. The audit of the Clinic therefore had to encompass an analysis of both internal and external communications. It also used three main tools to evaluate communication:

- depth interviews
- diary analysis
- analysis of video recordings of interactions.

Staff in the NHS are employed in regional facilities, with a clear line management structure to whom they are immediately answerable. However, most are also members of professional groups with whom they have a strong allegiance (doctors, nurses, speech and language therapists, etc.), all with specific aims, roles and responsibilities. Furthermore, the way in which different groups perceive the exact nature of the roles and responsibilities of their own and other professions often varies, making communication and relationships somewhat problematic (Dickson *et al.*, 1997). A main stated aim of the NHS, to 'shape its services around the needs and preferences of individual patients' can at times be difficult to effect given such a context (www.nhs.uk/aboutnhs/CorePrinciples/Pages/NHSCorePrinciples.aspx – accessed 2 February 2008).

The Swallowing Clinic operated within this real-world NHS setting. The Clinic had been in operation for a period of 4 years, and while the numbers attending were initially small they had been gradually increasing as knowledge of the facility grew. It was a relatively new service using a technique called 'videofluoroscopy', which records moving X-ray images onto videotape. Here, the patient swallows a small amount of food together with barium and this enables images to be filmed at all stages in the swallowing cycle. The purpose of the Clinic was to assist in the treatment of the condition known as 'dysphagia' – disorders of swallowing at any point between the ingestion of food into the mouth and its arrival in the stomach. At its most serious dysphagia is life-threatening since it becomes impossible for food to be eaten by the patient without risk of aspiration (the passage of ingested material into the lungs with the consequent risk of choking and infection). The main benefit of videofluoroscopy is that it facilitates accurate diagnostic treatment decisions to be made with greater safety and speed.

The Clinic was located within a large teaching hospital with 600 beds, situated within the Belfast conurbation. The videofluoroscopy assessment method described above had not been previously available, and no similar facilities were offered anywhere else in Northern Ireland (NI). Thus, as well as serving the immediate urban catchment area of some 250,000 people, the Clinic served the entire country. Referrals were accepted from a range of different professionals in other hospitals and practices elsewhere, with the regional speech and language therapists acting in a gatekeeper role. This meant that the accurate flow of information to and from the Clinic was a key aspect of its functioning.

All patients attending the Clinic were experiencing swallowing difficulties, the majority as a result of neurological damage following stroke. However, since the hospital was the main centre for surgical intervention in NI for patients with head and neck cancer, the Clinic also served this patient group. Others with progressive neurological disorders, such as Parkinson's disease and motor neurone disease, were also referred. At the time of audit, the Clinic was staffed by a team of three professionals all specializing in dysphagia: a speech and language therapist, a dietician and a radiologist. Part-time secretarial/administrative support was also provided.

The key challenge to Clinic staff was to make information easily understood and quickly accessible to all those involved. However, some communication problems had been identified by staff. As time passed, it became increasingly evident that communications did not appear to be as effective as they should have been, with the result that the work carried out was not offering maximum benefit to patients. The perceived problems included:

- Expressed confusion by some professionals about the Clinic's services as compared to the services provided by the radiology department.
- An apparent lack of clarity about the role of different professions in the assessment procedure.
- The fact that advice given seemed to be sometimes ignored by other staff.
- The receipt of information by the Clinic was often inadequate, and staff

were unsure about whether the messages they transmitted to patients and other professionals were effective.

In relation to the latter point, there is considerable evidence in the literature that patients have a wide range of needs (Rutten *et al.*, 2005), and often feel their concerns are not addressed (Sanson-Fisher *et al.*, 2000). In addition, information between professionals is frequently fraught with problems (Robinson and Cottrell, 2005). The extent to which these factors were prevalent in the operation of the Clinic was unclear. The health professionals within and external to the Clinic were undoubtedly caring and competent individuals all working for the best interests of their patients. However, good intentions are but essential raw materials – they need to be shaped and coordinated to produce optimum outputs (in this case the highest quality of patient care). It was in this area of coordination and communication that there seemed to be room for improvement. At the same time, problems are often only in the eye of the beholder, and while difficulties had been identified by staff, it was not clear if these concurred with those perceived by those using the Clinic. Indeed, no formal attempt had been made to ascertain the views of clients, or to investigate the communicative functioning of this facility. Accordingly, a decision was taken to initiate a formal audit.

THE COMMUNICATION AUDIT

Following discussion and collaboration with staff, the following objectives were agreed for the audit, namely to:

1   Examine the extent to which the appointment and referral system between the Clinic and its clients was effective.
2   Gauge the views of all professional staff and patients who used the Clinic.
3   Analyse the actual interaction patterns that occurred during the assessment procedure itself.
4   Identify strengths and weaknesses in communication practices and make recommendations about how existing procedures could be improved.

The pilot study

The interview format and schedule were tested, and minor modifications made prior to the main audit. In terms of areas of focus, it became clear that the following themes were important for patients:

- prior expectations of the assessment and its outcomes
- exact reasons for the assessment

- advice given, by whom, and how comprehensible it was
- relationships with health professionals
- expectations and hopes for the future
- anxieties and how they are handled
- their overall role in the assessment procedure.

These themes therefore formed the core of the interviews. In addition, from interviews with patients at different stages of their condition, it appeared that their perspectives may well change over time. As a result, it was decided to interview patients on two occasions: immediately following the assessment, and then some 4 weeks later.

In relation to staff interviews, the core recurring themes to emerge were:

- the nature and purpose of the assessment itself
- perceived advantages of the procedure
- the pressures of time in relation to competing demands
- relative knowledge and experience of different staff
- emotional issues surrounding the swallowing domain – for both staff and patients
- perceptions of the roles and responsibilities of different professional groups
- organizational issues surrounding the operation of the Clinic.

Following pilot testing, the main audit was implemented. Over a period of 9 weeks, all communications with the Clinic were charted and analysed. The methods used, and total numbers involved in each, were as follows:

- Data collection log-sheets (n = 63) were kept so that all communications with the Clinic could be logged.
- Clinic assessments were video recorded (n = 22) and analysed to determine interaction patterns.
- Interviews were conducted with all professionals (n = 61) who had contact with the Clinic.
- Two interviews were conducted with patients (n = 35) – the first immediately following assessment and the second 4 weeks later.

AUDIT FINDINGS

The audit produced a large amount of data, and we will here summarize the main trends in each phase.

Data collection log-sheets

In order to chart the flow of communications to and from the Clinic, a diary method was employed (see Chapter 6). A data collection log-sheet was devised. This required Clinic staff to detail all their contacts in terms of who initiated the communication, what channel was used and whether the reason for it was to do with organizational matters (e.g. dates of appointment) or substantive issues of information (e.g. feedback of assessment results). After pilot testing, all staff were trained in the use of the log-sheet prior to the audit.

A separate log-sheet was completed for every patient by each member of the Clinic team (Figure 12.1). All communications with each patient, and with professionals associated with the patient, were logged daily from the time the patient was first referred until the final Clinic assessment was sent to the referring agent. Though simple in its format and conception, this method provided a comprehensive list of everyone involved with each patient, and gave important details about the exact nature of Clinic communications.

The log-sheet findings (Table 12.1) demonstrated that speech and language therapists were key players. They were in communication with the assessment team more than any other professional group, although their actual numbers were comparatively small (e.g. less than half that of medical staff). They also initiated contacts with the Clinic more frequently than any other group. Dieticians were identified as another important profession – for example they initiated contact with the Clinic twice as frequently as nursing staff. The results also showed that the written channel was the main method for communications with the medical profession, unlike nursing where the primary medium was face to face. In the case of dieticians the telephone predominated. For speech and language therapists, the phone and face to face were both important channels, and they also at times received a video recording of the assessment in addition to the written report.

These results paint an interesting picture. There is growing evidence to show that most people prefer face-to-face communication, followed by telephone, and that the written channel is least preferred (Hargie *et al.*, 2004). Levels of intimacy, warmth and commitment decrease across these three. Yet, face to face is the most time-consuming medium, followed by phone and then written methods.

The source of over three-quarters of all communications was the assessment team. Further analysis revealed the primacy of the role of the speech and language therapist, in that 77% of the Clinic staff communications were actually initiated by her, and she also directly received 68% of all outside contacts with the Clinic. A similar pattern emerged in relation to contacts with patients and their relatives, where again the speech and language therapist was the prime mover. The data further revealed that only a very small proportion of contacts (4%) were initiated by patients and relatives, and that

Page _____   Name of patient: _____

Number _____   Completed by: _____ Position _____

Period covered: From…………… to…………….

Communication with	Consecutive communications										
	1	2	3	4	5	6	7	8	9	10	11
Initiated by											
Self											
Other											
Channel used											
Face to face											
Telephone											
Written											
Video											
Type of communication											
Organization											
Information											

Figure 12.1 Data collection log-sheet.

Table 12.1 Data collection log-sheet results for communications between staff

Communication with	Method				Total	Initiated by	
	Face to face	Phone	Written	Video		Clinic staff	Other
Speech therapist (n = 10)	24 (34%)	25 (35%)	15 (21%)	7 (10%)	71	49 (69%)	22 (31%)
Dietician (n = 9)	4 (17%)	13 (54%)	7 (29%)	—	24	18 (75%)	6 (25%)
Doctor (n = 30)	9 (14%)	12 (19%)	43 (67%)	—	64	49 (76%)	15 (24%)
Nurse (n = 18)	36 (64%)	13 (23%)	7 (12.5%)	—	56	49 (87.5%)	7 (12.5%)
Occupational therapist (n = 2)	1 (33%)	1 (33%)	1 (33%)	—	3	3 (100%)	0
Physiotherapist (n = 5)	5 (45%)	5 (45%)	1 (10%)	—	11	9 (82%)	2 (18%)
Radiographer (n = 5)	10 (42%)	12 (50%)	2 (8%)	—	24	22 (92%)	2 (8%)
Secretary (n = 1)	12 (44%)	7 (26%)	8 (30%)	—	27	18 (67%)	9 (33%)
Total communication	101 (36%)	88 (31%)	84 (30%)	7 (3%)	280	217 (77.5%)	63 (22.5%)

these were primarily face to face. This finding suggests that the patient played a passive role in the process.

In relation to substantive matters, communication with radiographers and the secretary largely concerned the organization of the Clinic (80%). By contrast, contacts with other health professionals related mainly to information dissemination (78%). With relatives, again the main content was to do with the exchange of information, although organizational issues were also important.

Overall, the results revealed that a core 'gate-keeping' and information-giving role is played by the speech and language therapist. The primary method of communication was face to face, except in the case of doctors where over two-thirds of communications were written, and dieticians who used the telephone for the majority of their communications. These log-sheet findings helped to map the topography of the Clinic. On the higher ground were doctors who tended to send messages from a distance. Lower down the slope was the base camp where the communication patterns were face to face and where the other health professionals could be found talking directly with the clinic team about patients (Table 12.1). Scaling across all of the terrain was the speech and language therapist, who had the full picture and was at the centre of the operation.

Video recordings of the Clinic

Prior to their arrival at the site Clinic, patients were informed by their speech and language therapist (who had been fully informed about the nature of the audit) that the assessment would be video recorded if they gave permission. Each patient was given a consent form on which the details of the study were outlined, and which was signed if permission was given for recording. No patient refused consent for this part of the study.

Two fixed cameras were placed on the wall in such a way that they covered the entire room. No attempt was made to hide these, since everyone knew that the session would be filmed. However, as they were above head height it was usually a case of 'out of sight out of mind' and both staff and patients reported that once the 'action' started they forgot about the cameras. As the assessment procedure itself took place in different parts of the room, a mixer system was installed to allow the recorded view to be switched from one camera to another. Pilot testing revealed that this procedure eliminated blind spots and captured the entire procedure. Piloting also revealed that to overcome the noise from the X-ray equipment, two microphones were required. One was placed above the lead screen to record intra-staff interactions, and the other was suspended from the ceiling in the area where the patient was seated.

The video recordings were analysed in relation to talk-times, number and source of questions, and the information and instructions given. The results showed that patients' talk-time accounted for just over 12% of the total (Table 12.2). It was also found that the amount of time taken by relatives increased when patients were unable to communicate verbally themselves. Thus, relatives of non-speaking patients had almost 19% of the talk-time, as compared to 6% for the other group of relatives. However, the largest proportion of talk was filled by the Clinic team members, with the speech and language therapist herself accounting for over one-quarter of the total.

In terms of the source of communication, when the total figures in Table 12.3 are converted into percentages, it transpired that the Clinic team was responsible for initiating 80% of communications, accompanying professionals for a further 6%, patients initiated 11% of the interactions, and the remaining 3% came from relatives. A total of 46% of interactions was directed to the assessment team as compared to 42% to the patients, 7% to visiting professionals and 5% to relatives. Again, the central figure was the speech and language therapist who was responsible for initiating 39% of all communications.

In line with the emerging picture, the Clinic speech and language therapist was again centre stage. She was involved, as source or recipient, in sequences comprising a total of 434 questions, 801 information-giving interactions and 329 instructions. In fact, she asked the highest number of questions, and gave the highest amount of information and instructions (Table 12.3). As confirmation of the findings from other research in the health context (Hargie and Dickson, 2004), the patient played a subsidiary role, asking few questions but receiving many, and being given a high proportion of instructions and information.

Patient interviews

Two interviews were planned with each of 21 patients. The first took place immediately after the assessment and the second some 4 weeks later. Owing to the increased illness and incapacity, or death, of some patients, follow-up was not possible in seven cases. Thus a total of 35 interviews were audio recorded. Content analysis revealed a number of core themes.

Table 12.2 Percentage talk-times in the Clinic

	Speech therapist (C)	Radiologist	Speech therapist (O)	Patient	Relative	Dietician	Nurse (O)
Percentage of talk-time	25.6	17.4	13	12.4	12.2	11.7	7.7

S&LT (C) = Clinic speech and language therapist
S&LT (O) = Speech and language therapist from outside the Clinic who was accompanying the patient
Nurse (O) = Nurse from outside the Clinic who was accompanying the patient

Table 12.3 Source and recipient of questions, information and instructions

	Source of:				Recipient of:			
	Questions	Information	Instructions	Total	Questions	Information	Instructions	Total
Speech therapist (C)	259	477	312	1048	175	324	17	516
Radiologist	102	333	156	591	107	202	28	337
Dietician	212	156	133	501	67	136	213	416
Patient	93	194	12	299	329	511	316	1156
Speech therapist (O)	21	83	7	111	21	59	11	91
Relative	19	67	9	95	20	77	34	131
Nurse (O)	29	30	10	69	16	31	20	67
Totals	735	1340	639	2714	735	1340	639	2714

S&LT (C) = Clinic speech and language therapist
S&LT (O) = Speech and language therapist from outside the Clinic who was accompanying the patient
Nurse (O) = Nurse from outside the Clinic who was accompanying the patient

Although the procedure had been explained by the speech and language therapists prior to attendance, patients reported *differing expectations of the assessment* and had varying levels of *understanding of its nature*. Thus, 18% said they had 'no idea' what the exact purpose of the examination was, with the same percentage (18%) being confused about the videofluoroscopy. The two main reasons proffered by patients for their Clinic assessment were the general and vague ones that staff wanted to 'see what is happening' (41%) and 'confirm all is well' (24%). It was also clear that patients *with language problems* in addition to their swallowing difficulty had *greater difficulties in understanding*. They were less certain of what to expect, less clear as to who the various members of the Clinic were, and more unsure about the reason for the assessment. This finding underlined the need for specific and concerted attention to be devoted to explaining the purpose of the Clinic visit carefully to this group of patients both before and during the assessment.

In general, patients were *positive about their experience* in the Clinic. Although they generally felt that no unanswered questions remained, they still expressed *concerns about receiving conflicting advice*. Interestingly, these were not voiced at the time of assessment. This indicated that a step needed to be placed in the procedure where the patient would be encouraged to express such worries and have them answered. They also felt that *the assessment was required by staff* and it was *their place to comply*, or, as expressed by one respondent, 'do what you are told'. This confirms their 'subservient' expectations, as found in other parts of the audit, and highlighted that the matter of patient empowerment was in need of development. The importance of this can be illustrated by one respondent who said that he did not feel able to query the textures used in the Clinic, although the fact that he felt they were unrepresentative of what he had been attempting to eat on the ward made him severely doubt the validity of the result.

Overall, 61% of patients indicated that the assessment had made a difference to the action taken by themselves and others, but 22% indicated that the results had not done so. It is also interesting to note here that while the evidence from other parts of the audit consistently highlighted the major role of the speech and language therapist, patients were almost totally unaware of this. Some 11% commented that her role was concerned with speech, 9% said she played very little part in the assessment and the remaining 80% had no comment to make about her role. The doctor and dietician were seen as the main operators. This suggested that speech and language therapists needed to convey more clearly to patients the core role they played in the entire procedure.

Staff interviews

From the 80 staff identified as having involvement with the Clinic, 61 were interviewed from across the full range of professions (Table 12.4). No one

Table 12.4 Health professionals involved in interviews

Profession	Staff based at the Clinic Hospital site	Staff based at other sites
Doctors		
Consultants	5	8
Registrar	2	–
SHO	1	–
JHO	2	2
GP	–	2
Total	10	12
Nurses		
Sisters	3	–
Staff nurses	6	3
SEN	–	1
Student	1	–
Total	10	4
Others		
Dieticians	5	5
Speech and language therapists	2	7
Physiotherapists	3	1
Occupational therapists	1	1
Total	11	14
Overall total	31	30

refused to take part and the sample atrophy was caused by staff moving jobs, being on leave, or unable to fix a time because of work schedules. The results revealed that the majority of respondents *were positive about the Clinic*. They felt *it had influenced their perceptions of the assessment and management of swallowing problems*, and *provided information not available by other means*. It was also found that *medical staff in the site hospital had a clearer understanding of the procedure than those from outside*, a difference that was less evident with therapists. Likewise, the degree to which swallowing was seen as a priority differed considerably among the staff groups, with the site respondents not surprisingly believing it to be more important than those from elsewhere.

Concerns relating to communication were felt most keenly *by speech and language therapy staff, who expressed the view that the procedure was not fully understood by other professional groups*. They also were worried that *the assessment results might not be accepted by other groups*. A common theme in the interviews was that staff overwhelmingly *recognized the importance of ensuring patient understanding of the process*. Yet, as we have seen, in reality this was not achieved, revealing a communication crevice in need of repair.

A final communication issue was *the different perspectives held by respondents of the roles and responsibilities of their own and other professionals, and of the problem itself.* In relation to the latter, one junior doctor with limited experience, expressed the view:

> Swallowing problems is not anything major or anything like diagnosis of cancer and I feel that even the junior staff can speak to the patients or a relative about a swallowing problem.

This was in sharp contrast with the views of a nurse with considerable experience of patients with swallowing disorders who commented:

> It's a big handicap and it can ruin your life . . . just about everything is affected by it . . . It's a big nursing problem and a big problem for the patient.

This was reflected in the responses of various professionals to the roles of one another. One speech and language therapist in noting the discrepancies that existed said:

> You could have a lot of people working on the problem but not necessarily as a team, so they would be giving conflicting advice.

The need for coordination and consistency was also recognized by a doctor who in recognizing that staff may be unaware of what others have told patients and relatives concluded:

> It is a question of communication, and this I think is perhaps the most difficult and most neglected area.

Thus there was a clearly expressed need *for greater team-work and collaboration to be developed* and fostered among all those dealing with patients with dysphagia. This is reflected in the general literature where problems of inter-role conflict have been well documented (Lui *et al.*, 2001; Sorensen and Iedema, 2008).

CONCLUSIONS

This audit used a combination of three main methods – diary analysis using data collection log-sheets, interviews and video recordings – to obtain a complete picture of the operation of a Swallowing Clinic. This triangulation of methods provided a panorama from these different but equally important perspectives. The main findings were:

- The speech and language therapist played a central role in organizing referrals to the Clinic and in the assessment procedure itself.
- Although this role was accepted by most staff it was not recognized by patients.
- Doctors differed from other professionals in that their communications about patients were mainly in writing.
- The patient's perceived role was that of being cooperative and compliant.
- There was a lack of patient understanding of the assessment procedure, and this was particularly marked among patients with language difficulties.
- Even when they did not understand, patients felt unable to express this openly.
- There were differing views among professionals about roles and responsibilities, and a feeling that more team-work was needed.

Following the audit, the findings were disseminated through a series of presentations to different professional groups in both formal and informal settings. This allowed the results to be shared, but also served as useful forums to publicize the need to rectify the above-listed findings, and especially the need for greater inter-professional collaboration. The results influenced the conduct of the Clinic in specific ways. For example, it became standard procedure in the acceptance of referrals to ask the referring agent how any change in management would be dealt with if the need for such changes was indicated by the results. This highlighted the issue of management options, allowing the Clinic to have a clearer understanding of the perspective of those involved. It also prevented patients from having to cope with the stress of the assessment if no benefit was going to accrue for them. A signed referral form was required so that it was clear to all those involved that agreement to proceed was made on this basis.

Report writing was also influenced by the finding that the import of the assessments were not always understood by all staff. Feedback was altered to underline to all involved that recommendations were based on a specific set of factors and that the patient could be put at risk if, for example, larger amounts of food or different consistencies were given. In light of their identified key role, it also became policy to insist on the involvement of a speech and language therapist, so that the necessary monitoring could continue after the assessment.

Following completion of the study, other Clinics were introduced in NI, and staff who gained their experience through attendance at the site Clinic were centrally involved in their organization. An important aspect of this audit was not only that it sought to examine the functioning of one Clinic through a multifaceted approach, but also that it attempted to establish its representative nature so the results could be applied in a wider setting.

Chapter 13

A communication audit of a paper mill

Phillip G. Clampitt and Laurey Berk

INTRODUCTION

The intern readily admitted that her telephone call was a 'shot in the dark'. She was phoning all the local universities to see if 'anyone there knew how to create a world class communication system for a paper mill'. She was not having much luck until she stumbled into our voice mail system. When we finally contacted her, she was vague about what she wanted but eager to have us talk with the members of the mill's 'communications task force'. We agreed. Assembled around the table were the mill manager, the human resource manager, several supervisors, an hourly worker, and the intern. With some trepidation we began by asking about the issues they were hoping to address. The mill manager simply said, 'We want to develop a world class communication system. How do we do that?' He was disturbed by climate survey results that consistently indicated employee concerns with the communication system. This was the conversation that eventually led to a series of communication assessments and other related projects.

In this case study, we discuss how assessment results can be used to continuously improve communication systems and practices. Figure 13.1 reveals

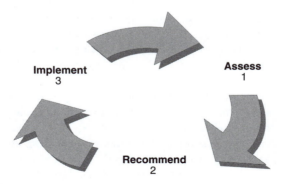

Figure 13.1 The audit process.

the process we used. Step 1 involved assessing the communication system by researching current practices, administering a survey and interviewing key personnel. Based on the assessment we made specific actionable recommendations (step 2). We then assisted the organization with implementing some of the recommendations (step 3). To check on the progress, we repeated the process. Cycling through the process became an institutionalized way of ensuring that the communication systems and practices were constantly improving. We discuss the details of this process and the outcomes in the following sections.

BACKGROUND

Like any good detective, we started by gathering relevant facts about the mill. We examined past survey data, employee publications, corporate reports, and bulletin boards. We interviewed key members of the staff. The result was a disjointed list of over 100 factual statements about the mill (see Box 13.1).

At the time of the first assessment, the mill employed over 600 employees working around the clock in four rotating shifts. Most of the employees were middle-aged males with strong family values. The mill manager was held in high esteem by both union and non-union employees. In order to improve relations with the union, he set up a joint labor–management (JLM) team that met every fortnight to discuss issues of mutual interest. The mill was one

---

Box 13.1 100 facts about the mill (partial listing)

The numbers

- 650 employees
- 4 shifts
- 26 departments
- 73% male

Communication channels

- E-mail
- Electronic bulletin boards
- Postings on dozens of regular bulletin boards
- Monthly employee newsletter
- Joint labor–management (JLM) meetings
- Monthly report for supervisors (on productivity, safety, quality, etc.)
- No regular mill-wide meetings

of several mills and plants that comprised a company that was, in turn, owned by a multinational corporation. The mill was regarded as the 'cash cow' of the corporation, which was having some difficulties with its European operations.

COMMUNICATION ENVIRONMENT

The mill made several attempts to improve the communication system. The Executive Team had developed a 'Communications Bill of Rights' (see Box 13.2), which was a document to stir conversations about communication effectiveness by the senior staff. The document was instructive on several accounts. First, it identified some of the issues the staff were trying to address. Second, it pointed to some of the underlying problems that the senior staff unwittingly spawned. The most obvious was that the Bill of Rights focused entirely on communication *rights* with no mention of *responsibilities*. The underlying assumption was that the senior staff bore almost total responsibility for the effectiveness of communication. Indeed at the root of much of their frustration was that they put enormous resources

---

Box 13.2 Communications Bill of Rights

We the people, recognizing the advantages of a successful communications program at the Mill, do hereby declare that all employees have the right:

1   To clear, understandable, and unambiguous communication.
2   To ongoing communication – not just in times of crisis or need.
3   To information before, not after, important events.
4   To give feedback on issues and have all two-way horizontal and vertical communications lines open and clear.
5   To be told about issues affecting their company, their jobs, and their responsibilities.
6   To be recognized for their accomplishments and achievements so they feel like 'somebodys' on their job every day.
7   To know why the company adopts its policies and procedures and to know about changes in the business and social environment the company works in.
8   To an explanation of the company's community relations activity and to share in the responsibility for civic and community projects.
9   To a continual overview of successes and failure with products or services, and company growth and vision.

into communicating 'properly' but had very little to show for their efforts. Fortunately, the Bill of Rights was never adopted and circulated to employees. It was, however, an exquisite example of senior management's thinking. To their credit, the team recognized that 'something was askew'.

So much for the mind-set of the management team. What were the key components of the communication system? In addition to the typical departmental meetings, the plant relied on the following communication channels:

- *E-mail system:* The system was widely used by administrative employees to communicate with one another. They assumed that this was also an effective tool to communicate with hourly employees. All administrative employees had dedicated computer terminals at their desks; hourly employees had to share terminals.
- *Bulletin boards:* The boards were scattered throughout the plant. Some had designated functions like 'safety information' or 'job postings' but most were under departmental control. Even though the boards were considered one of the mill's most important communication channels, they were unevenly maintained and updated.
- *Newsletter:* The newsletter was distributed once a month and contained the following regular features: union news, birthdays and work anniversaries, safety updates, general mill information and personal interest stories. The general consensus was that the newsletter enjoyed a wide and thorough readership. Assessment results would confirm this perception.
- *Joint labor–management meetings (JLM):* Union representatives and management discussed major issues in these meetings. The hope was that union representatives would share relevant information with their fellow union brothers and sisters.

Senior management often communicated key messages via all four channels.

However, data from an organizational climate survey conducted 2 years prior still indicated there were problems. In particular, the management team was worried about two survey items:

- Over 80% of hourly employees felt that 'employees responded (negatively) to formal and informal communications from mill management personnel'.
- Over 80% of hourly employees felt negatively about the 'extent (to which) mill management shares organizational information' with them.

These results, coupled with the frustrations wrought by the management team's musings regarding a 'Bill of Rights', prompted a strategic change in approach. They decided to seek professional assistance in dealing with the communication issues. Thus, their strategic goal for the year was clear:

'Conduct a professional survey on communication. Determine what a world class communication system looks like.'

THE FIRST COMMUNICATION AUDIT

After the communications task force agreed on the basic assessment process, we sought input from several key groups, including other members of the top management team, union officials, and a number of supervisors. Our aim was to have these opinion leaders shape the assessment process and thus motivate others to fully participate. Accordingly, we asked how the process could be beneficial to them and sought their advice on various audit procedures. Although we used the Communication Satisfaction Questionnaire developed by Downs and Hazen (1977) as the centerpiece of the audit, we encouraged union officials, supervisors, and employees to add other appropriate questions. This proved particularly helpful in motivating these opinion leaders. We also ended up adding 13 questions to the survey to target certain specific concerns.

Other important issues arose during this initial consultation:

- Could the results be used to seek retribution against dissatisfied employees?
- Would the results be used to promote or demote supervisors?
- Would the administration of the survey place even more burdens on supervisors?

These were all legitimate concerns that we addressed in three ways. First, we were very clear about the purpose of the assessment process. All our messages to employees about the process highlighted our central objective: to improve communication processes at the mill. We assured employees in face-to-face meetings that the focus was organizational *processes*, not *personalities*. Second, we guaranteed the anonymity of employee responses. Being an outside consulting firm, we – not the company – were able to control the data. In fact, we even mentioned to employees that after the data were coded into the computer, their individual surveys would be shredded. This also signaled to supervisors that we would be doing most of the work. Third, we assured employees that we would not report results of groups containing fewer than seven employees. These measures apparently alleviated most of the employee concerns.

Components

After the initial consultation with these groups, we developed an assessment package that included the following:

- *Communication satisfaction survey:* The survey consisted of 46 standard questions and 13 items unique to the mill. The survey also contained four open-ended questions that allowed us insight into some of the 'big picture' issues. At the end of the survey, employees were asked to provide various demographic data and indicate a shift and departmental code.
- *Channel assessment:* Content analysis was performed on the three of the most frequently used channels: bulletin boards, monthly employee newsletter and monthly report for supervisors. Our purpose was to empirically study the *actual* messages sent through formal channels. Those data were compared to the *intended* messages of the senior staff.
- *Follow-up interviews:* After a preliminary assessment of the survey data, we randomly interviewed 43 employees. Our objective was to confirm tentative conclusions drawn from the quantitative data and to probe for more details on certain issues of concern.

The communications committee then reviewed and approved the 'final' package. In addition, we presented a flow chart of all the activities involved in administering the package and providing feedback to the various groups. The last step before the administration was pre-testing the survey with a group of volunteers. Based on their feedback, we made a few minor wording changes to the instrument.

Promotion and administration

Since the communications committee determined that participation would be voluntary, we felt that motivating employees to participate was critical. Therefore, we publicized the process with bulletin board and paycheck announcements (see Box 13.3) as well as personal communications to

---

Box 13.3 Sample publicity for the survey sessions (this was inserted with the employee paychecks)

We need your help

As part of our commitment to continuous improvement, we will be evaluating the strengths and areas for improvement in our communication system within the mill. We will be looking at the effectiveness of various means of communication such as memos, bulletin board announcements, the employee newsletter, and verbal communication. To conduct the evaluation, *we need your help*. We need to know your views on how well we communicate with one another. We have asked Metacomm, a consulting firm specializing in internal organizational communication, to coordinate the evaluation.

Here's how we will proceed:

- Metacomm will be administering a brief survey to all employees. **All responses will be completely confidential**.
- The surveys will be taken in groups of approximately 30 employees.
- Metacomm will conduct these sessions in the Assembly Room and will collect the surveys at the end of a 30-minute session.
- Sign-up sheets will be posted on the entryway wall the week of July 20th.
- All employees will receive a summary of the findings in November.

Special times have been designated for each shift. For those on vacation, a confidential mail-in survey will be provided.

Here's the schedule . . .

We are aiming for 100% participation. Your input is vital. In appreciation for your participation, a door prize will be given out at each session. The door prize will be on display at the mill entrance. If you have any questions about the survey process, please feel free to call Paul M. at ex. 2348.

supervisors. This process was a bit paradoxical since we had to use the very communication system we were auditing to inform employees about the audit. Some incentives proved useful. Hourly employees were paid overtime wages to participate. In addition, a raffle for coolers and gift certificates was held for those who completed the survey.

Twelve survey sessions were scheduled around the clock to administer the questionnaire. When employees arrived, we orally briefed them about the objectives, guidelines, and the feedback process (see Box 13.4). When they completed the survey we again reminded them that the 'next steps' would include random employee interviews and briefings over the results.

RESULTS

Over 55% of employees participated in survey sessions. Thirty-six percent of the respondents were salaried and 64% were hourly. The salaried were somewhat over-represented as respondents as they comprised 23% of the mill employees. During follow-up interviews we found that many of those who chose not to participate reported that they were suffering from 'survey fatigue'. That is, they had filled out too many surveys that yielded too few benefits. This is a fairly common complaint in many organizations (Management Decisions Systems, 1993).

Box 13.4 Survey session introduction

1 Objectives of the survey
2 Responses are **confidential**
3 No right or wrong answers
4 Background on survey

- History
- Approximate completion time

5 Follow-up

- Interviews
- Report findings

6 Instructions

- Scale
- Department codes

Table 13.1 Rank order and norms of survey items

Rank	Question	Mill mean	Metacomm norm	Significance
1	Job satisfaction	6.69	6.79	
2	Supervisor trusts me	6.62	7.45	*
3	Right amount of supervision	6.53	7.14	*
4	Information on policies and goals	6.47	5.73	*
5	Activity of grapevine	6.41	6.39	
6	Subordinate responsive to directives	6.23	6.88	*
7	Compatible work group	6.11	7.07	*
8	Subordinate anticipates my information needs	6.10	6.53	
9	Effectiveness of employee newsletter	6.05	na	
10	Supervisor open to new ideas	6.01	6.69	*

Notes: The numeric survey questions are ranked in descending order according to respondents' satisfaction with the following factors on a 0–10 scale (0 represents no satisfaction, 5 represents average satisfaction, and 10 represents high satisfaction).
* $p < .05$

We prepared a table that rank-ordered all the quantitative results and also showed a comparison to our databank norms (see Table 13.1). The databank norms were drawn from assessments conducted in 26 companies (see www.imetacomm.com/CME3 – 'Research Database' tab). Initially, we looked for trends based on the mill results alone. Then we used the databank norms to analyze the data from a broader perspective by examining how this mill compared to other companies. In addition, we prepared tables based on the content analyses of the open-ended questions, the channel assessment, and interview data (see Table 13.2). All of these tools were used to draw conclusions about the general communication issues faced by the mill. We also prepared more specific tables breaking down the results by department and shift.

We made a clear separation between data analyses and conclusions. In fact, two separate booklets were prepared. One contained all the charts discussed above. The other was a report that synthesized the results, providing tentative conclusions and recommendations. Our strategy was to secure everyone's agreement on the basic analyses before suggesting any specific conclusions or recommendations. Indeed, we reviewed the data booklet with the staff first.

Table 13.2 Sample content analysis of interview data
'What do you think are the greatest communication strengths of the mill?'

Rank	Category	%	N	Sample comments
1	Climate: openness/keeps us informed	45	27	• 'Open atmosphere, sharing.' • 'More open – information given freely.' • 'Open about business conditions and how company is doing; open to customer feedback.'
2	Leadership of top management/downward communication	17	10	• 'Bob D. has good presentations; good general information – everyone knew about the No. 7 paper machine project.' • 'Leadership is good; no secrecy.' • 'Bob D. comes down on floor and talks with us – open climate.'
3	Channels/accessibility	17	10	• 'PA system throughout mill, notices on changes sent to everyone, have many information meetings.' • 'Accessibility to people – voice mail, pagers that maintenance and supervisors carry . . .'
4	Good intentions/attempts at improving	12	7	• 'Improving – used to be secrecy.' • 'They're trying – there's still not a precise way of getting communication around.'
5	Miscellaneous	9	5	• 'Communication with union is great – especially regarding injuries.' • 'Educational programs have improved.'

Note: Reliability = 97%; Responses = 59; Respondents = 42.

Our strategic tentativeness paid off in a number of ways. First, it allowed the senior staff to shape the action plans. This, in turn, provided them more motivation to implement the plans. Second, the senior staff made a number of perceptive observations about the raw data that we simply overlooked because we lacked intimate knowledge of the mill. Third, it boosted our credibility as auditors because it demonstrated that we were unlike many 'vendors' who used surveys to sell training programs.

We formed our conclusions by integrating our quantitative and qualitative data. For example, we found that the fourth highest ranked survey questions involved satisfaction with 'information about policies and goals'. Additionally, the ratings for these questions exceeded the Metacomm norm (see Table 13.1). Other related items were also highly rated. These findings closely corresponded with the highest-rated category from the interviews on the mill's greatest communication strengths (see Table 13.2). Therefore we concluded that the 'mill-wide communication climate' was a strength (see item 3 below). We used a similar method to reach the following conclusions:

1   Satisfaction with *supervisory communication* was strong at the mill. The second most highly rated survey item was employee satisfaction with the extent to which 'my supervisor trusts me'. Employees also felt satisfied with the amount of supervision they were given and that their supervisors were open to new ideas.

2   Employees were also highly satisfied with their *work groups*. They often mentioned a 'family theme' when describing their work groups. Employees like the friendship and camaraderie with their co-workers.

3   Employees felt that a great strength was the *mill-wide communication climate* of 'openness' and accessibility to information. However, while information was accessible, people often mentioned that the information was not understandable and they did not know how to use it.

4   There was a relatively high level of satisfaction with the *employee newsletter* and *bulletin boards*. However, our studies revealed that each could be used more effectively.

5   Employees expressed dissatisfaction with *feedback* about how they were being judged, recognition of their efforts and information on their job progress. Feedback was often mentioned to be infrequent, inconsistent or non-existent.

6   There was dissatisfaction with the flow of *routine information*. Employees felt the greatest weakness of the communication system was that they were not kept informed on daily operations and that they did not receive their job information on time.

7   There was dissatisfaction with *interdepartmental communication*. Comments such as 'one hand doesn't know what the other is doing' were common.

8   Many employees did not see how they fit into the '*big picture*'. They felt

like a 'missing puzzle piece'. There was confusion about what important committees were doing and how their decisions were made.

9   Employees felt that improving *problem solving* with their supervisor could increase their satisfaction and productivity. There was a feeling that superiors did not understand job problems and that problems in 'my job' could be handled better.

The senior staff basically agreed with these findings.

We used a cascade approach to provide feedback. In the first meeting, the senior management team was orally briefed on the mill-wide results and given the booklets to peruse at their leisure. In a following meeting, the various department heads were briefed on the mill-wide and their specific departmental results. Finally, we prepared a two-page summary of the major conclusions that was distributed to all employees. The mill manager attached a written response to our summary that outlined the next steps. In addition, we held a couple of open meetings for employees who wished to review the results in more depth.

NEXT STEP

When it came to action plans, we were venturing into unknown territory. Diagnosing problems is one thing, knowing what to do about them is another matter altogether. As we discovered, the analysis was the easy part. Nevertheless we accepted the challenge and continued to work with the mill by attacking some of the root problems. Interestingly, one of the key issues was redefining the senior staff's view of communication effectiveness. Recall the 'Communications Bill of Rights'. After further discussions, the staff began to see the inherent problems of that approach. We reoriented the staff's thinking by suggesting that a 'World Class Communication System' had five key attributes:

- The leadership team has a *strategic commitment* to effective communication.
- Employees at all levels have the appropriate *communication skills*.
- There is a proper *infrastructure of channels* to meet mill objectives.
- There are proper *communication policies and procedures* to meet mill objectives.
- *Information is managed* in a way to meet mill objectives.

This strategic view of communication, while not perfect, reoriented the discussion around a system of interlocking issues rather than exclusively focusing on the needs of employees (see Box 13.5). We were trying to challenge the notion that senior management was solely responsible for the effectiveness of

Box 13.5 Attributes of a world class communication system

Strategic commitment

1 There is a strategic commitment from top management to promote and practice effective communication. This means:

   - There is a clear vision of the objectives of the communication system.
   - There is a compelling desire to continually improve the system.
   - There is a commitment to provide the financial resources necessary to enact the vision.

2 There is a commitment by management and employees to uphold ethical stands for communication.

Communication skills

3 Top management has the ability, desire and means to inspire a vision in the employees.
4 Managerial employees have superior communication skills.
5 All employees have above-average communication skills.
6 Employees know how they are performing against recognized standards of performance.

Channel infrastructure

7 The organization has an effective infrastructure of channels to meet three communication challenges:

   - quickly handle emergencies
   - disseminate day-to-day information
   - present a realistic vision of the business environment.

8 Channels used by communicators are congruent with employee needs, management's objectives, and the message capacity of the channel.

Communication policies and procedures

9 Employees know how they fit into the 'big picture' and believe they are empowered to carry out the organizational mission.
10 Dynamic programs are in place to make sure employee concerns are heard and acted on.
11 Departments interact with one another effectively.
12 The communication system is routinely evaluated.

Information management

13   Employees have relatively easy access to all information they deem necessary, with some minor exceptions.

14   Active measures are in place to make sure that employees receive relevant and timely information but not more than necessary.

15   There are safety valves built into the communication system to circumvent communication breakdowns.

Table 13.3 Core issue ratings

Core issue	Rating
Strategic commitment	High
Communication skills	Medium
Channel infrastructure	Medium
Communication policies and procedures	Medium-low
Information management	Medium-low

the entire communication system. Hourly employees and newsletter editors also had responsibilities. Even the taken-for-granted ways of communicating needed to be challenged.

We used these core strategic issues to filter the results and weigh the significance of issues raised in the audit. In fact, we even rated the mill on each of the core issues using a 'meter' with 'low', 'medium', and 'high' ratings (Table 13.3). Even though we readily admitted that our analysis at this point was somewhat subjective, the leadership team agreed and actually found it a useful way to prioritize action plans. There is an intuitive element to auditing; expertise is not totally based on facts and figures.

With this new strategic approach to communication, we attacked the core problems with the following specific projects:

- *Redesign the employee newsletter:* We suggested a realignment of information priorities and the inclusion of regular standing columns based on the priorities. Given the organizational culture, employee recognition and personal interest issues would remain, but visionary commentary from top administrators and stories that celebrate mill values would take on added importance.

- *Introduce a new channel: quarterly 'State of the Mill' address:* This channel would enable top management to more effectively link individual employees' efforts and roles with the mill 'big picture'. This oral channel would allow for discussion of key industry trends and the organization's responses to the trends. Likewise, it could be a forum to download and discuss key organizational decisions (Clampitt and Williams, 2007).

- *Change the format and content of the 'Monthly Report':* This report, intended for mill-wide distribution, resembled a 'grab bag' because of the inclusion of so many different components (key indicators, future directions, key external events, ongoing projects) that were often buried in one paragraph. We suggested clarifying the core audience for the monthly report (hourly workers) and organizing the report around the mill values (productivity and cost, quality, service and safety), with key indicators measuring each value. To help authors in preparing and submitting information for inclusion in the monthly report, we also developed a more user-friendly 'feeder report'.
- *Develop leadership skills:* The survey and interviews revealed that this was an area in need of further development. We developed training sessions on enhancing communication effectiveness in the areas of conflict management, problem solving, listening, feedback, recognition, and channel selection.

The senior staff also decided that after these projects were underway, we should conduct another assessment in a couple of years to determine the effectiveness of the changes. This approach merged nicely with the mill's basic commitment to 'continuous improvement'. If the assessment revealed that the projects did not address the problems, then we would try something else.

THE SECOND AUDIT

Most of the action plans discussed above were implemented. However, on the second go-around, the parent company decided to expand both the size and the scope of the audit. They asked us to survey all the mills and plants in the company and expand the content to include a vast array of other issues. Our intent, therefore – to determine the effectiveness of our communication projects at the mill – was compromised a bit. Nevertheless, we were able to compare the results for the mill on several items. We used the same 0–10 satisfaction scale (0 representing low satisfaction, 10 representing high satisfaction) for many of the items. The results were as shown in Table 13.4.

There were positive changes for many of the results. One of the first projects we implemented after the initial assessment was to introduce a new channel, the quarterly 'State of Mill' address by the mill manager. It was gratifying to see improved satisfaction levels with information on finances and major changes, which were areas that this channel addressed. The modest decline for 'communication with top management' may appear puzzling, but interview data revealed that when most employees answered this question, they were referring to the senior leadership of the *company*, not the on-site *mill manager*.

Several projects, such as the format changes in the newsletter, were completed just a few weeks prior to the second assessment. In fact, because

Table 13.4 Comparison of audits 1 and 2

Item	Audit 1	Audit 2
Information on finances	5.5	6.4
Information on major changes	5.6	6.0
Communication with top management	5.6	5.2
Effectiveness of employee newsletter	6.0	5.9
Clarity of written communication	5.7	5.8
How conflicts are handled	4.6	4.6
Interdepartmental communication	4.8	4.2

change is often resisted, we would not have been surprised by a modest decrease in related items (Clampitt and Berk, 1996; Peltokorpi, 2008). So it was not terribly surprising to discover that satisfaction with 'the effectiveness of the employee newsletter' remained stable. Likewise, satisfaction with the 'clarity of written communication' showed little change. The changes in the format and content of the monthly report had only been recently introduced. After discussing this item in more depth, we decided that this was partially a skill issue based on the writing abilities of managers. This discussion was particularly instructive because it reminded us once again of how difficult it is to correctly interpret some survey items and subsequently develop an appropriate response.

Although we had several projects in the works dealing with leadership development, these had not been rolled out in all areas of the mill. Thus the results on certain items, while disappointing, were not terribly surprising. For instance, employee satisfaction with 'how conflicts are handled' was virtually unchanged while satisfaction with interdepartmental communication declined. Interdepartmental communication typically is a particularly vexing issue (Clampitt, 2005). In this case the issue was compounded by the fact that over 50 employees were added to the mill in the intervening years.

We included several special items in the second survey. On an agree/disagree scale (1 representing strongly disagree and 7 representing strongly agree), we asked a question directly focusing on the monthly report: 'The new monthly report is better than the former.' The mean of 5.1 showed significant agreement with the statement.

In general, these were encouraging findings. Changes in the channel infrastructure were particularly well received. However, the results also indicated the difficulty in making significant changes in a well-entrenched communication system.

SO WHAT?

There are many lessons to be learned from these assessments. First, we hope it illustrates more specifically the procedures discussed in this book (questionnaire survey, interviews, etc.). These procedures can be adapted to virtually any company. Second, this illustrates how the classic notion of continuous improvement can be used to enhance a communication system. In particular, the leap between the diagnostic and prescription phases is one that is rarely discussed in the literature. In fact, since this assessment, we have developed more specific procedures for addressing common communication problems (Clampitt, 2005; Clampitt and Berk, 1996). Yet we believe the key is to maintain a strategic tentativeness in regard to actual solutions. However, we should note that this sentiment is not one shared by all consultants. Many believe that their role is to 'solve' the problems. We take a more interactive view and believe that our role is to act as a catalyst for developing appropriate responses. Finally, the case demonstrates the importance of having a firm understanding of organizational communication theory. Without that theoretical basis, we never could have answered the 'world class communication system' question. Intuition, tempered in the organizational communication literature, allows auditors to go beyond the data provided by the inherently limited investigative tools and suggest new approaches to novel issues. In short, we learned that effective auditing is both a science and an art.

Chapter 14

An interpretive audit case study

Naheed Tourish, Rita Marcella, Dennis Tourish and Owen Hargie

INTRODUCTION

Organizations are often viewed as solid, almost physical entities, whose legitimacy is rarely open to question, and which are amenable to fairly straightforward managerial interventions. Within this framework, communication consists of an exchange of information in and out of an organization. By contrast, in the communication perspective developed by Saludadez and Taylor (2006, p. 37), organizations are conceptualized as being 'grounded in a social process of interpretation . . . Organization is created and recreated . . . in and through the everyday sensemaking activities of its members.' They are therefore socially constructed phenomenon, and sites of struggle, domination, resistance, negotiation, accommodation and power.

This means, as Boje (1995, p. 1001) argued, that they can be understood as

> a plurality of stories and story interpretations in struggle with one another . . . More important, organisational life is more indeterminate, more differentiated, more chaotic, than it is simple, systematic, monological, and hierarchical.

This has tremendous importance from the standpoint of how auditors approach the audit process and their own role within it. Jones (2002, p. 469) has argued that the auditor should be 'a skilled and committed listener to, and within, organizational communication processes' as opposed to 'an outside expert, a diagnostician of communication problems'. She challenges the notion that any observer can achieve total objectivity – or that what has been dubbed as 'immaculate perception' (de Cock, 1998, p. 3) exists in reality, unlike the idealized accounts of research that are sometimes published. An interpretive audit conceptualizes the auditor as an intrigued and enquiring voyager, with the members of the organization as conductors or guides. Interpretivism is less of a designated method (e.g. it could consist of interviews, textual analysis, participant observation, etc.), and rather more of a mindset and theoretical orientation. It is one that accepts ambiguity and uncertainty as ever-present features of human communication, and seeks to explore the paradoxes, contradictions and deep structures that lurk beneath the surface of interaction. This chapter is a case study of one communication audit conducted from within this framework.

RESEARCH ISSUES, METHODS AND ORGANIZATIONAL CONTEXT

The study reported here was part of a wider research investigation into upward communication in organizations (Tourish, 2007b). As with many audits, it was therefore concerned with one aspect of the communication process rather than the whole. Nevertheless, upward communication is attracting greater attention, and the degree to which robust systems exist to promote it can be regarded as an important ingredient of effective communication strategies. This issue is discussed in more detail in Chapter 20.

Despite this, employee silence is a common problem (Milliken and Morrison, 2003). Mute employees mean an invaluable source of feedback is curtailed. Based on an extensive literature review into these issues, key variables were identified for further study in the communication audit reported in this chapter, including:

- employee silence
- ingratiation (i.e. the extent to which employees honestly communicated their feelings, or exaggerated the degree to which they agreed with management decisions)
- power, size and hierarchy
- wider managerial strategies that affected people's willingness to speak up.

In essence, we wanted to explore the sensemaking processes employed by employees when they were communicating with those of a higher status, particularly when their views were critical of organizational orthodoxy, and we wanted to examine how such communication processes were impacted by wider managerial strategies and actions (see Chapter 19 for a further discussion of sensemaking).

Organizational context

The organization where this audit occurred was a regional European airport. It was one of Europe's busiest commercial heliports – serving about 3 million passengers a year and offering flights to around 35 destinations. The months during which the audit was carried out were exciting times for the organization; within the next 10 years alone, this fairly large company of about

240 people planned to invest around £50 million on improvements to its terminal and airfield. A near doubling of passenger numbers was expected by 2030. The Managing Director (MD) spoke of his hope that it would become 'Europe's most successful regional airport . . . promoting social and economic prosperity for all.'

Two internal communication surveys had been conducted within the space of 18 months. The first survey, henceforth called Survey A, discovered that employees were not satisfied with the existing communication dynamics. A many-pronged and all-encompassing communication strategy was launched forthwith; this was pronounced extremely successful by the senior management team. A second survey, called Survey B, appeared to support this contention.

The new communication strategy emphasized how the organization would 'recognize and value . . . staff as essential participants in the business and as such, value their feedback' and would 'therefore encourage them to make their opinions known on issues that affect them directly'. Innovative catch-phrases, tags and slogans were engineered to impel the workforce and vibrant in-house publications were designed to energize them. Selected employees were given the title of 'Ambassador'. A £5 reward voucher was offered for every helpful suggestion given by an employee. Suggestions were provided in writing, through a typical and simple 'suggestion box' system.

Yet, the company was engaged simultaneously in a process of downsizing – a process that much previous research has shown adversely affects morale, motivation, productivity and communication (Tourish and Hargie, 2004c). Interestingly, the communication strategy dealt with many general management issues, but did not once mention the issue of downsizing. The general tenor of the strategy is demonstrated by the excerpts in Box 14.1.

A number of preparatory meetings for the audit were held with key people in the organization, particularly its MD and Director of Human Resources (HR). During these, the HR Director selected the names of 20 employees to be interviewed, across various management levels and drawn from the disparate functions within the organization, including its fire service, administrative functions, and security team. However, during the early stages of the audit, an involuntary snowball effect occurred and many more employees volunteered to be interviewed. This resulted in a total sample of 37 semi-structured interviews.

The 37 interviews were held over a period of 5 weeks in a variety of quiet rooms at the office of the organization, made especially available for this purpose. Each interview, except the one with the MD, was about an hour to one and a half hours long. In line with the main audit focus identified above, these were designed to explore upward communication. Sample questions are included in Box 14.2.

The confidential and anonymous interviews were tape recorded and then transcribed. Finally, the interviews were analysed in detail. Since an

Box 14.1 Excerpts from organization A's communication strategy

'[The Organization] believes it is essential that their staff are informed on the progress, policies, plans and financial stability of the Organization. We recognize and value our staff as essential participants in the business and as such we value their feedback and will encourage them to make their opinions known on issues which affect them directly. In pursuing an effective communication policy, we aim to help staff achieve a better understanding of our objectives and policies and to gain your commitment to them.'

'We firmly believe that an informed employee is an effective employee. So we take very seriously the question of communication in all its aspects. We want our employees to be in the picture about their work, how they fit in, how well they are doing, what the Organization is doing and where it is going.'

Channels of communication:

- *Your supervisor/manager*
- *PC access to all*
- *Open communications events*
- *Intranet site*
- *E-mail to MD*

It was specifically mentioned at the end of the strategy document that the 'direct e-mail account to the local MD gives staff the opportunity to put questions directly to [the Managing Director]. This creates a channel for upward and downward communication for the MD.'

interpretive approach guided the audit, it was decided not to use Qualitative Analysis Software such as Nvivo or N6. Such tools are useful in interview analysis (see Chapter 4). However it can be argued that they are less relevant for interpretive methodological frameworks. Data analysis software technology, however sensitive and sophisticated it might be, is not a substitute for intuitive and interpretive thought. Indeed, in terms of interpretivist frameworks, it may be viewed as a barrier that can prevent the researcher from becoming fully immersed in the data. Therefore, framework analysis (Swallow *et al.*, 2003) was used as the base note for the analysis. The raw data were charted and tabulated on Excel sheets, before being sifted and distilled through the process of interpretive analysis.

Thus the interviewees were indexed. They were given codes that contained key information about them: their place in the hierarchy of the organization, their tenure with the organization and their gender. The raw data were

---

Box 14.2 Sample questions from interview schedule

- Tell me how communication works in the organization.
- Describe the communication strengths of the organization.
- Describe the communication weaknesses of the organization.
- What is the greatest unresolved communication issue or problem in the organization?
- Have there been any significant changes in upward communication lately?
- What could be done to improve communication from non-managers to senior managers?
- What is the main obstacle to this being achieved?
- If there are barriers to upward communication, how do you deal with them?
- Could you think of a critical issue, or an example, when you find yourself suppressing your ideas and opinions?
- Do you sometimes exaggerate how much you agree with the opinion of your boss?
- How did your supervisors react when you advanced a critical opinion about the organization?
- How responsive is management to employee ideas?

---

categorized in detail into variables (e.g. silence/ingratiation/impression management), departments within the organization, and levels within the hierarchy. Based on the variables, our analysis was then developed.

AUDIT RESULTS

Three main, inter-related themes emerged from the analysis of interview data. We discuss these next.

1 The contaminating effects of downsizing

An interpretive audit approach means that the auditor must be guided by the responses of the interviewees. Although we had been informed in advance that downsizing was taking place at the time of our intended audit, we did not know precisely how it would impact on communication, or the general morale of employees. However, it quickly became apparent that it was the primary topic that people were keen to discuss – whatever question they were asked. For example, when asked about upward communication in general most interviewees rapidly related this to downsizing, without any prompting from us.

Thus, and typical of most interviewees, this was how a young manager summed up the state of upward communication in the company:

> There is none at all . . . because downsizing would be the biggest influence on that . . . and there is silence because people are so nervous of what is going to happen next . . . But people don't do it [communicate upwards]. It just doesn't function. They have downsized to a certain point where it no longer functions . . . with the insecurity and uncertainty that it creates, when you do wish to talk with your supervisor about an important issue, you think twice about saying anything. You don't want to endanger your situation.

He continued:

> People are scared of it [downsizing]. Everyone is scared for their jobs. Security [the department] hasn't had their turn yet but it's coming eventually. Jobs will be lost in security. So you don't want to speak out of turn and then be the one who has to go.

Illustrating this, a customer service officer reported:

> I think it is fake to have this fantastic communication stuff and then people made to go . . . My team is constantly wondering when the axe is going to fall . . . I think it's a very uncertain organization we are in at the moment. It comes from the top – our MD is a new thinker apparently.

On a similar note, a member of the airfield security team sighed:

> There is no procedure, no policy. [The organization] still doesn't have an official redundancy policy. They assess you . . . They offer you packages and give people a chance to go . . . So, it could be people who speak up who are chosen to go. Oops! Sorry! There goes your head! So, people are scared – they sit in the meetings and say nothing then get outside and say what they really think. Everyone is scared for their jobs. So you don't want to speak out of turn and then be the one who has to go.

Upward communication had almost ground to a halt. The preceding quotations illustrate that this was directly affected by the downsizing process.

Certainly, the organization received a great deal of favourable publicity in the local media. It was perceived as a highly successful, modern, well-managed business, with a phenomenal rate of growth. However, was the incredibly dynamic MD being led, in part, by his desire to secure future advancement for himself? This was certainly a common perception. As a security guard iterated:

> [The MD] is a bean-counter. He sees the savings . . . We are simply finan-
> cial units. If he [the MD] has to get rid of eight financial units, he will.
> He doesn't care who they are. He will take that opportunity and that's his
> way to the top.

Such attitudes extended across the organization. The Fire Service is a vital
unit of any airport. Downsizing was also expected here. One firefighter
reported the communication effects as follows:

> Yes, it's not every day we speak about it [downsizing] but much more
> frequently than we used to. We are all aware of it – it's a concern. They
> [management] are even looking to fundamentally review the fire service –
> our pay-scales and roles and responsibilities. I appreciate there might be a
> need for some change. But the managers employed them and thought
> they were suitable – why should we have to apply for our jobs again? But
> they are looking at getting us to apply via the development centre to be
> reassessed – and then probably many of us asked to go. They want more
> and more for less and less.

Interestingly, an entirely different view was held by the MD. When asked
whether the downsizing had had any impact on employee morale or upward
communication he remonstrated tersely:

> But, but . . . what has the restructuring got to do with morale or
> upward communication!? . . . We have never done so splendidly . . . I have
> launched many [new communication initiatives] and all my employees
> have been very responsive to that. I don't think that the downsizing has
> had any impact whatsoever on communication within the organization.
> They are two totally unrelated issues . . . Now, if you don't mind, I have
> another appointment.

It was a brief interview, with an abrupt end.

On the other hand, the HR Director shed further light on the rationale
behind the downsizing:

> The difficulty in communication is particularly bad with the older mem-
> bers of staff who have been here for a long period of time, who just don't
> understand why things have to change from how they were years ago . . .
> The MD's reaction to some of this is, 'Well, just get rid of them.' He
> frequently will come to me with a list of names and say, 'Just get rid of
> these people!' I have to remind him that we do have employment law and
> need to be fair. I don't agree with his style but guess I do understand the
> whole philosophy of – why invest your time with people who are never
> going to be on the train we are going on – I guess they are left on the

platform somewhere. Last month, the lady who won [the suggestion scheme award] was made redundant the following week! I thought you really don't want to win this! We genuinely didn't know that was going to happen . . . I felt so bad.

Despite the communication strategies that the MD launched, with much fanfare and pizzazz, there was one topic on which they had had no discussion whatsoever – and that was the subject of downsizing. A junior manager explained:

I think [the MD] makes an effort in the [communication workshops] to make things easy to understand, like budgets and so on. But he does not make an effort to explain the much bigger concepts . . . It's left to [name of line manager] for instance to handle the downsizing.

How an organization communicates about such issues is not an easily forgotten trifle. Talking about the restructuring going on in the customer service department, where the employees of the information desk were being reassessed (with a view to eliminating their positions and installing an automated system in their place) a young security guard explained:

I think they [senior management] don't think we are smart enough or aware enough of what is going on in the big picture. [The organizational newsletter] mentioned about the passenger information desk being changed and they put a positive spin on it – which I found quite funny, but in a *bad* way, because it is not funny. People will be let go. But it would be better if they just came clean, but they won't do that.

A young manager summarized the bewilderment and confusion within the workforce:

In my perception there are three factors at work here. On one hand you have the big profits – 30% or 35% up in the last quarter they said. On the other side, there are [the MD's new communication initiatives]. And yet people being made to go . . . To me these three don't work together. I get squashed! I think there will always be that perception in the grassroots people of why are they cutting staff when we are making profits? Our passenger numbers are up this year as well. But we are still cutting back and it is extremely difficult to understand why and no one seems to have the answers.

2 The effect on loyalty

It has been widely recognized that loyal employees make extra efforts in their work, and can be positive public relations representatives in the external world (Organ, 1988). However, research into the effects of downsizing has shown that it damages loyalty, creates a fearful expectation of imminent further restructuring, and generates concern about communication, consultation, resources and training (Tourish and Hargie, 2004c). The climate of this company also bears out this analysis. As an interviewee from the customer services department explained:

> There is a lot of disillusionment. A loss of morale . . . When I started here I thought I was very lucky. The first two and a half years I loved it. After that it changed. I am still here as I have a mortgage and my job isn't too labour-intensive . . . Very few people would feel free to speak up here. They will speak among themselves and sometimes hope you will overhear and pick up on it. They feel powerless. They don't think they can change anything.

Such attitudes also have a direct bearing on the social capital of the organization on which communication is built. Social capital has two main components: associability and trust (Leana and Van Buren, 2000) and refers to the capacity of people to work together amicably in groups and organizations (Coleman, 1988). Trust refers to the willingness of people to engage in affiliative behaviours with each other. Clearly, social capital is central to organizational success and trust is the energy that holds people in these organizations together. Given that people's perception of how fairly or otherwise they are treated impacts on how trusting they are willing to be (Othman, 2008), it is scarcely surprising that both social capital and trust are adversely affected by downsizing, to a far greater extent than most other management initiatives. Reflecting this insight, a member of the airfield security team said:

> I wish management would explain what's going on . . . Surely we have a right to know? Everyone is very apprehensive at the moment so it would be good to understand why the organization is doing what they are doing. Just now there is so much speculation and unease. The stress and sickness levels are high. Morale is low . . . They are robbing Peter to pay Paul. We have lost the personal touch.

3 Dearth of upward communication

The morale of the employees within the organization was low; they were anxious, frightened and insecure. This impacted on the manner in which they communicated with their superiors. The communications strategy encouraged employees to communicate directly with the MD. However, as a young security guard said, 'He says his door is open, but from what I have heard, I wouldn't risk it.'

Furthermore, during the audit conducted within Company A, it became obvious that it was commonly believed that the results of Survey B were not accurately portrayed. As one of the security staff said:

> The problem I have with this survey they [management] did last year . . . they said 75% said they were happy with their job and 73% preferred to remain silent. But, if you are happy you would speak up, wouldn't you? I think the answers were cherry-picked.

Moreover, the Financial Manager, who was retiring shortly and was very outspoken, confided:

> I don't think the communication initiatives are happening. The numbers are being made up. I talk to people and they don't seem to know what's going on. I think there's some lies happening. The MD thinks its working but that's not what I hear.

The downsizing was obviously a sensitive, uncomfortable issue. Most employees admitted to being cautious, circumspect and guarded in their communications with their superiors. This resulted in two parallel upward communication kinetics. First, there was amplified ingratiation and impression management behaviour from employees as they communicated with their superiors to tell them what they thought they would like to hear, and so evince great faith in their strategies and communication initiatives. Second, a thick mist of employee silence developed, born of cynicism and insecurity. Speaking about this, a junior manager said:

> The people whose departments [are being downsized] are being affected right now . . . They have lost interest which is understandable. It's difficult. This used to be a place where you had a job for life and it's not now. Everyone wonders when their day will come . . . This affects how people communicate; they'd be more guarded and cautious . . . Just say what the boss wants to hear . . . maybe even just stay quiet.

From the perspective of a security guard, the outlook was as follows,

> Yes, I see a lot of arse-licking or . . . the conformity thing, when you go to these [communication workshops of the Managing Director]; they show you how great the organization is doing. There are two pictures – one for the Stock Exchange but there is a second one for the employees. They can't give you a pay rise and there will have to be cutbacks and

redundancies – doom and gloom. But for the [Stock Exchange], everything is rosy in the garden; profits are high, there is growth, the organization is so successful . . . and we know that's the case because we read the papers.

Overall, our data paint an unflattering picture of upward communication in this organization. There was plentiful evidence of fear and insecurity. Employees also believed that ingratiation and silence were widespread, and showed little faith in data produced by management to suggest the opposite. Moreover, our interviews showed that these concerns were shared by some senior managers themselves (for example, the well-respected but soon to retire Finance Manager). Stories abounded of people being penalized for dissent, while all communication issues were widely interpreted through the lens of the downsizing initiatives being implemented. In terms of sensemaking, the responsibility for the resultant problems was laid at the door of the MD, who was seen as being focused overwhelmingly on 'the numbers', and his own rosy future, to the detriment of the well being of his people. The MD, meanwhile, seemed resistant to critical feedback and determined to pursue his strategy. It was, however, abundantly clear that his behaviour had set an unhelpful tone for the organization's internal communications. It was suffused with paradox. On the one hand, he organized brilliant communication workshops. On the other hand, the core issue animating staff – downsizing – was not addressed. In addition, the listening behaviours required to promote a real climate of communication exchange were absent. There are lessons in this for all who aspire to a leadership role in organizations. Thus, while these findings have a particular significance for the organization in question, as we now discuss, they also have a much wider significance.

STRATEGIES AND AUDITS IN CONTEXT

Communication is not an isolated function, unaffected by the overall climate in which it occurs. Rather, it determines, and is determined by, the ambience of the organization, the values of its leaders and the behaviours and strategies that they employ to achieve their goals. Communication audits evaluate a multitude of different communication issues, as various chapters in this book demonstrate. This chapter, conducted within an interpretive paradigm, illuminates how communication strategies can intersect with and be affected by such wider initiatives as downsizing. In particular, people were too frightened about being selected for downsizing to openly voice their feelings to managers, and identify the negative effects that it was having. They were correspondingly cynical about communication, negating many of the positive intentions that lay behind the organization's formal communication strategy. As a senior member of the fire brigade explained:

Staff are a bit confused; although you go to the [communication work-shops] and he [Managing Director] blows his own trumpet, but there are people there who think, 'Well I've just had a letter asking if I want to reapply for my job or take redundancy.' It's hard to get your head around . . . The morale here is not very good just now. When I come to work now I don't like it much. It's not the same. I think a lot of people are scared. I know I am. There's a lot of uncertainty. People say they could come in tomorrow and it [downsizing] could happen to them.

Undoubtedly, some of these issues would have surfaced if investigated by other means, including surveys. But it is worth noting that, in many organiza-tions, 'talk itself increasingly *is* the work, not just a means to an end' (Jones and Stubbe, 2004; p. 188). Ambiguity, uncertainty and paradox are therefore ever-present features of workplace communication. Consequently, we do not believe that surveys would ever capture the full strength and depth of people's feelings, the stories that they share with each other, or the sensemaking heur-istics employed in their construction. On the other hand, a more interpretivist approach has great value in taking researchers deeper into the hidden depths of organizational life. It is in these depths that the most interesting insights often lie, waiting to be discovered.

Thus this audit clearly reveals the relationship between communication and management behaviour more generally. Communication is clearly an import-ant ingredient of organizational success, as discussed in Chapter 1 of this book. How it is used during, and is affected by, downsizing is a vital issue (Pfeil *et al.*, 2003; Tourish *et al.*, 2004). But razzle dazzle communication practices cannot overcome the problem of management messages that appear to threaten people's most vital interests, and of a management philosophy that states that people are an important asset, combined with actions that suggest the opposite.

This audit was primarily a research investigation, rather than a service for the organization. We were not therefore mandated to produce a report or recommendations designed to improve practice. One might, however, have imagined that the company would have requested this. Indeed, part of its rationale for facilitating the research was that the data could supplement some of the findings in their own second survey (Survey B). However, as a final detail about the audit process, this did not happen. Our main HR con-tact, who had been helpful in making the arrangements for the audit and who had been most interested in its progress, was herself downsized. Given that the audit was always a research investigation, and the organization had not commissioned it specifically to inform the development of its communication strategy, there was also a correspondingly lower interest by the MD in its findings. In any event, and in line with the interview data summarized here, the MD appeared, overall, to show only a moderate interest in such issues as employee morale and engagement, and in the effects on people of his strategy.

GENERAL AUDIT LESSONS

There are general lessons here for those conducting communication audits within an interpretivist perspective. The main ones are:

- *Interpretive audits require flexibility.* Interview schedules are important. So is the identification of key variables that the audit team wishes to analyse. However, the process is driven as much by the actual environment that one encounters within the organization concerned as it is by pre-determined research questions and the needs of the audit team. Listening to what interviewees are telling us means that we must, on occasion, shift focus, add fresh questions to our original design, and if necessary take extra time to listen respectfully while people divulge information about issues that may have been peripheral to our original purpose. Thus the process is iterative: interpretive auditors need to adjust prior research designs and protocols in light of emergent findings and issues.
- *Interpretive audits help us to understand how communication processes relate to the general strategy of a given organization.* Survey methods constrain the responses that people can give. In many cases, this may be what researchers need to do. But interpretive approaches open people up. They will go beyond purely communication issues, and discuss how such issues intersect with everything else in the workplace. A fuller picture of organizational life will be created.
- *Auditors need to prepare for the unexpected.* In this case, we had several such experiences. The first was the 'snowballing' that occurred, as more and more people volunteered to participate. But the second was the sudden withdrawal of the Managing Director from his previously agreed interview, in the face of questions that conflicted with his existing perception of the climate within his organization. It was necessary to work even more closely with the HR Director, to ensure that the audit could be completed. No doubt these events also sent a communication message throughout the company.
- *Auditors need to be prepared to handle strong emotions.* Many of our interviewees were highly distressed at discussing the issues we were raising. On occasion, we allowed people to talk much longer than scheduled as they ventilated their feelings. Empathy skills are essential.
- *Confidentiality is critical.* This is, of course, true in all audits, but we felt that it was particularly vital in the context in which we were operating. Many interviewees appeared to forget that their words were being taped, and made statements that could easily have damaged their careers. Interpretive auditors have a heightened ethical responsibility for those with whom they meet.

Mintzberg (2005) has argued compellingly in favour of imagination, insight and discovery in the process of theory development. As he noted, this means that research needs to provide rich description. Whatever their other virtues, large-scale surveys do not do this. But rich description is precisely what interpretive audit approaches can generate. They are probing, creative, iterative, imaginative and challenging. It is therefore not surprising that more interpretive audit studies are now being published (e.g. Jacobs, 2006). We believe that they are important for both consulting and research in communication, and urge their wider application in our field.

Coda

Without exception, the most critically minded and outspoken employees who were interviewed lost their jobs further down the line, in the downsizing process. A year and a half after the completion of the audit, the MD moved on to a more senior position within a larger company.

Chapter 15

Auditing the annual business conference of a major beverage company

Cal W. Downs, Albert Hydeman and Allyson D. Adrian

INTRODUCTION

External audits identify areas of interdependence and collect vital information from many sources. They are crucial to business success, and to the creation of a rounded picture of the communication climate facing a given organization. In this chapter, we provide a case study of an external audit conducted by means of deep probe interviews. Before exploring exactly what was done, it is useful to look at a rationale for external audits, which have often been neglected in favour of their internal counterparts.

1 They complement internal audits in significant ways

Auditors of internal communication often assume that if communication processes are working internally, then the whole company is working well and the bottom line will be productive. However, internal audits focus on the preferences, wishes, and reactions of the people inside the organization, rather than on how interdependent agents such as clients and 'customers' react to what goes on. There is a need to extend audits to a larger group who are not on the organization chart but who play a very significant role in determining the outcomes of business processes.

For example, we once worked with an advertising agency which started to re-engineer its structure. There was widespread hope and enthusiasm that this restructuring would improve things. And internally, there was no great problem. Externally, however, a crisis emerged when clients were not pleased with the changes and threatened to take their business elsewhere if the changes were not reversed. Note that the changes had not caused any major problems internally, but they wreaked havoc with those people on the periphery.

2 They provide a standard against which the internal operations can be assessed

As the advertising example above demonstrates, outcomes for most organizations are determined by their intermediary clients and organizational representatives. When the effectiveness of outcomes is determined through interaction with other parties, it is vital to include those external relationships in assessments of company processes. Moreover, advances in technology in recent decades have increased the opportunities that have always existed for interaction between firms and customers, between customers and between firms (Ramani and Kumar, 2008). In other words, internal company processes do not operate in a vacuum; the external relationships provide a contextual backdrop that must be taken into account when assessing internal effectiveness.

3 *External audits measure outcomes that are significant to the organization*

Organizations generally exist to facilitate some product or service for other people. Often the connection between the organization and the ultimate client or customer is mediated through some other level that is attached to the organization but that is not technically an integral part of it. The external audit is an attempt to measure outcomes as far as this middle group is concerned. How well are their needs being addressed? What problems do they see with the way the main organization is functioning? The success of the external, interdependent agents is reciprocally related to the success of the primary organization. For that reason, auditors must take into account the outcomes of these external mediating agencies. Acknowledging the reciprocal relationships between the parties forces auditors to investigate the complexities of organizational situations and also increases the likelihood of finding useful information that leads to relevant recommendations.

4 *External audits are a form of environmental monitoring*

Every organization must continually make sense of what is happening around it in terms of economics, politics, society, and legalities. Subtle social changes in fads and trends often affect business. The audit also permits auditors to compare consumer attitudes toward an organizational culture with what employees think is an ideal culture. Often, employees and those on the periphery are at odds because their vested interests are different.

5 *Technology is changing the ways organizations communicate with their suppliers, vendors, business partners, and consumers*

Any such change can have important ramifications for the organization, and managers should want to keep abreast of the impact of those changes. For example, Rowley (2006) illustrates how organizations are increasingly called on to provide customers with access to information resources. It would seem, then, that the lines between internal and external organization parts are growing thinner (Tourish and Hargie, 2004b). Furthermore, technologies are costly, and the audit is one method to collect information that helps measure the return on communication investment.

6 *Audits do not only provide information about the focal organization, but they can also be designed to provide sensitivity to competitive threats*

Those on the organization's periphery are probably bombarded with information about competitors. Therefore, their comments are likely to be given from a frame of reference in which they know what the competition is offering. In other words, the focal organization is rarely the 'only game in town'.

PRELIMINARY ISSUES

External audits, before they get off the ground, have to confront a number of preliminary issues or dilemmas. Some of the most common decisions this throws up include the following:

1 *Whether to assess via quantitative or qualitative data*

A case can be made for each, depending on what one wishes to do with the data. Many businesses prefer quantitative data. Bottom lines are determined by the numbers. Polls are taken by the numbers. People like numbers because they like what they know. Similarly, businesses are most familiar with questionnaires and interviews that sample opinions about their products and services. Consider how J.D. Power and Associates have popularized the quantitative information they get from consumers to tell us which airline the respondents preferred in terms of satisfaction, which car is the most popular, and so on. This information can be valuable and is used to create great marketing strategies. Such sampling of opinion is useful – as far as it goes. We can count how many people like the organization, but quantitative data do not normally tell you *why* they like it. Auditors often leave the explanations behind the data to assumptions and inferential statistics.

Within the context of quantitative and qualitative data, there are many different forms for collecting this information. Three of the most prominent data collection methods include questionnaires, interviews, and focus groups (see Chapters 3, 4 and 5 in this book). And there are several contrasting methodologies that can be explained for each one. The auditor makes a choice, and sometimes there is value in triangulation of the different methodologies (Downs and Adrian, 2004).

One of the factors to be included in the choice is what your desired respondents will favour.

2 *Determining the people from whom to collect information*

As in any investigation, it is desirable to have (a) a representative sample so that conclusions can be generalized to the whole group, and (b) a stratified sample based on important demographic differences. However, in external audits, what constitutes the boundaries of the organization is already less clear. It is harder to talk about getting a certain percentage of respondents or a certain type of stratification. Instead one has to identify the sources of interdependency among the primary organization and its collaborating entities. In this chapter, we discuss these issues as they apply to conducting a qualitative audit.

3 *What skills the auditor has that can provide meaningful data*

We have chosen to demonstrate in the following case study how deep probe interviews can be used to yield promising data for external audits. In fact, it is uniquely adaptable to external audits because of the problems thrown up by the geographical distribution of respondents. For example, it may yield some of the same data as focus groups, but it is difficult to assemble some of the respondents we would want in the same place for a focus group. But they are often easily accessible by telephone. Let us now turn to the case study itself.

INDUSTRY BACKGROUND

The beverage industry generates billions of dollars in the United States each year. The industry has seen growing competition spurred by two developments. First, until recently, there were a few central breweries that dominated sales. However, this pattern is changing and microbreweries are becoming increasingly popular and offer more competition. This marketplace has seen a proliferation of mini-brands, serving to erode marketshare dominance of all the major competitors. Second, globalization has made it much easier to ship products across national boundaries.

The market is now highly competitive with significant brand diversification. Acquisitions are playing a major role in building market dominance. The overall US brewing marketplace has less than five companies controlling an overwhelming majority of marketshare. An intensely competitive atmosphere requires increasingly shrewd operation, marketing, and distribution strategies. Above all, a company needs to maintain the commitment of its distributor network.

THE COMPANY

Sigma (a fictitious name) ranked in the top three beverage manufacturers and distributors in the world at the time this audit was conducted. An international beverage maker, it employed over 6000 people domestically, including corporate, plant operations, field, and management, staff. Additionally, there were over 400 domestic distributors who were intensely interested in company developments.

Structurally, it had developed a somewhat decentralized corporate structure with headquarters in the midwestern United States. Yet within its divisions it remained very hierarchical. The primary divisions included Sales, Marketing, and Operations, with product distribution through exclusive business contracts. There was also a strong Department of Corporate Communication. The primary responsibilities of the corporation included production, development, quality control, management, and distribution of various beverage brands. Additionally, the corporation developed and executed all national and international advertising.

Exclusive distribution contracts were awarded and administered by the corporation through 20 market area management offices placed locally for more direct interaction with the distributor network. For a number of years, the company had been moving toward more decentralization, with a greater focus on local issues.

COMMUNICATION AND STRATEGY

Internal and external communication were similar to the prevalent patterns for most organizations. First, key executives had meetings and exchanged written communication with department heads within functional lines. Second, market areas' field representatives were responsible for managerial interactions between Sigma and individual distributorship leadership. Third, the primary personnel from each distributorship included the principal owner, general manager, sales manager, and operations manager; they had a communication set-up among themselves, and also with the field representatives.

One of the principal forms of communication was an annual national meeting of distributors, called the National Sales Meeting. It generally lasted 2 days and included a series of general sessions ending on the final evening with a large awards banquet. In the past, the content had always been a general attempt to impart a sense of enthusiasm for the upcoming marketing campaign and the announcement of distribution promotions. The assumption was that great enthusiasm would result from a fun-filled, entertaining presentation of the general topics. In fact, their field representatives had at one stage been requesting a 'big bang' of a show, a party to celebrate a 'brand new day' that would win over the distributors to the fact that little had changed following recent management changes at Sigma. The traditions set for these meetings were very strong indeed.

But the company had experienced a change of top level leadership in critical areas. The new team valued communication and desired a more strategic approach to how it was managed. This increased awareness led to the choice of a new communication consultancy to produce a national communication event in lieu of the more entertainment-oriented type of event that been employed in the past. These new consultants had a policy of encouraging all clients to audit their audience via a standardized protocol prior to embarking on the development of new forms of national meetings.

THE AUDIT RATIONALE

It is important to note that the audit described in this chapter was not initiated as a response to a diagnosed problem. The company did not ask the consultants to 'fix' anything. There was no communication Band-Aid or surgery to be performed. Rather, they felt that they had an opportunity to improve the national event and to communicate more intelligently. The new managers appreciated the strategic role of communication, and they just wanted to adopt a 'smarter' approach.

Prior to the launch of the audit an announcement was transmitted to all distributors via the computer network that was routinely employed for the dissemination of important announcements. The bulletin gave a general overview of the rationale and proposed benefits for the audit. However, the audit was not going to be directly relevant to most of the internal personnel. Thus the announcement was given just as a courtesy to keep them informed.

In the final analysis, this external audit was a form of environmental monitoring, based on the premise that the company needed to listen to the concerns of the distributors and then design a sales meeting that addressed those concerns.

THE AUDIT TECHNOLOGY

The basic technology used in this audit was a deep probe interview called DORA, or Direct Open-end Response Analysis. Such interviews yield rich data, not about performance, but about *attitudes*, *opinions*, *emotions*, and *expectations*. These are the processes that cause people to perform in the ways they do.

Initially, the business team had to be convinced of the value of this approach because most businesses, as we discussed above, are more comfortable with quantitative data. But DORA is not based on quantities. It discovers themes, feelings, and expectations.

Audit objectives

The general goals were to chart the attitudes and opinions of distributors who had attended previous meetings, and to identify their expectations of and recommendations for the next event. In the long term, it was hoped to establish trends by tracking some baseline questions. The two specific object-ives were therefore to:

- assess expectations and satisfaction with regard to advertising, core brand focus, local market involvement and the Sigma management team
- sample distributor recommendations for future National Business Conferences.

Preliminary planning

Prior to the survey, the auditors assisted the Executive Management Team to generate a list of assumptions with regard to this audience. This was performed as part of the preliminary phase of establishing their perceived objectives for the national meeting. Among the assumptions identified were the following:

1   Distributors look forward to a good show every year.
2   The meeting is considered a chance to see the new advertising.
3   The distributor audience is easily bored and does not come to the meeting for in-depth information or details.
4   Most distributors trusted the corporate leadership and were suspicious of the new executives.

The sample

As part of the audit process, the general population pool was separated into six geographic sample sets. A random sample of 30% nationally was selected. Researchers conducted interviews only with day-to-day managers of distributorships, who personally attended the National Business Conference. These samples were further subdivided as shown in Table 15.1 between the large and small distributorships.

Table 15.1 Interview sample population

Sample area	Large distributors	Small distributors	Region
I	27	8	California
II	68	20	Northwest and Southwest
III	33	10	Texas
IV	192	58	Midwest
V	61	18	Northeast
VI	122	37	South and Southeast

In a prior telephone call, an appointment was made for a call back to have the interview at a time convenient for the respondent, and they were told approximately how long the interview would take. In many cases, respondent interest led to longer interviews.

Telephone interviews

For the sake of accuracy and reliability, the interviews were conducted by previously arranged telephone conversations, and they were subject to the following controls:

- Acquisition of responses in the same time period ensured that current events that may influence attitudes were shared among the respondents. On each day of the survey, an equivalent proportion of respondents was interviewed from each of the geographical regions.
- The purpose of the survey was explained in depth, and confidentiality was assured.
- The interviewers made notations of tone and manner of the responses as well as verbatim accounts of responses. Tone is an important aspect of any message because it shades the meaning of the word. Notations were made as to whether the comment was hostile or helpful, serious or flippant. Note was also made of hesitations, long pauses, laughter, or cynicism.
- Interviewers were never allowed to use synonyms or to whitewash the language in any way. What was actually said was recorded.

THE SURVEY

Protocol

The interview protocol included specific directions to the interviewers for introducing the purpose of the interview as well as for delivery of questions, recording of responses, and ending the interviews. Particularly, interviewers were cautioned against voicing their own opinions or commenting on any answer. 'Thanks' or 'OK' were used as transitions to the next question. The objective of the protocol was to ensure that the interviews were conducted as uniformly as possible.

Questions

Thirty-four questions were ironed out with the Sigma liaison executive group to form a standardized survey interview, consisting primarily of open-ended questions. The interview guide was organized in a 'script' format with key words highlighted. When an interviewer was asked for clarity regarding an item, the interviewer could rephrase the item, making certain to include the key words.

Listed below are sample questions from the 34-question standardized interview guide:

- Why did you attend the National Business Conference last year?
- Why will you attend the meeting this year?
- What do you feel is the corporate purpose for holding a national meeting?
- What should be the corporate purpose for holding a national meeting?
- On a scale of 1–10 (with 1 representing very poor, and 10 representing very good), how would you rate the last National Business Conference overall? Why did you give this rating?
- For you, what was the most important message of the morning General Business sessions?

Probes

In an attempt to facilitate complete answers, interviewers were given pre-established probes on their interview guides. Setting these probes required considerable planning and a thorough testing of the questions.

Pilot phase

A test phase had been conducted to monitor questioning and recording techniques for the purpose of assuring consistency. Following this pilot phase, problems with ambiguity and awkwardness were addressed prior to commencing the data collection.

THE ANALYSIS

Individual information was kept in strictest confidence, as had been promised to the respondents. The primary tool used for the analysis of responses to the deep probes was content analysis, using ad hoc categories or themes that were identified by the consultants. A listing of all responses for each question was printed out, or the data were transferred to 'DORA for Coding and Responses', which allowed theme development and coding on screen. The protocol called for an initial pass, theme consolidation, and then final coding.

Themes were developed by analysing responses to one question at a time, before progressing to the next question. The researcher read each response, classified the themes, and refined and modified the themes as they progressed. Once 'a pass' through all responses had been completed, the researcher made an attempt to consolidate the themes, limiting the number as much as possible without jeopardizing the meaning of the responses. Then, to ensure that the theme arrangement 'worked' well, the researchers went through each response a second time, doing a manual coding of responses.

Since two researchers analysed responses to each question, the resultant themes were compared. Where major differences occurred, themes were reviewed by both researchers and the wording was refined.

Listed below are key guidelines for use in assigning themes and applying codes. It was emphasized continually that there is a difference between identification/distinction and judgement, and the auditor was to refrain from personal bias and judgement at all times.

Theme identification criteria

The following criteria were used:

- A theme is a response to the question, not mere dialogue.
- A theme is a complete thought, not necessarily a complete sentence.
- A theme can be a common thread of thought within the dialogue and may not be stated overtly.
- A single response may yield multiple themes.

Coding criteria

The researcher was required to read the complete response and ask: 'What is the most dominant point?' If the response contained multiple themes, yet no clear dominance, coding proceeded by choosing the first theme mentioned and then coding the other themes later. For example, the following themes were generated from the exemplar listed responses to the question: 'What was the most important message of the morning General Business sessions?'

Consolidation

'Probably the most significant thing in the morning was the clear statement that there will be wholesaler consolidation; in other words, an overall reduction of wholesalers in the US.'
'I would say the consolidation issues.'
'Oh, it was pretty obvious: consolidation.'
'The message on consolidation [*laughed slightly*].'

Continued focus on core brands

'Just that the . . . uh . . . core brands are picking up and are doing better, and the surprise was the depth of their interest in consolidation.'

'That we are going to focus on core brands and packages for next year.'
'It would be um . . . um . . . their umm . . . commitment to the continu-
ation of the core brand strategy.'

One-hour meeting

'I am not sure that an hour is really enough . . . I felt there was not
the enthusiasm . . . and love and sincerity for the business coming from
the top.'
'I guess the general sessions were to be one hour to maximize distributors' abilities to attend several seminars.'
'I came away feeling I was just going to have to make it on my own.
Not enough time was spent.'

Other themes identified in response to the question were:

- Times are tough.
- New distributor agreements.
- There is a future for us.
- New advertising.
- Marketing plans.

Finally, themes were then assigned to the demographic sub-groups of (a)
geographical region, and (b) size of distributorship, so that comparisons
could be established.

THE REPORT

Before any meaningful analysis could be completed, the auditors needed
to understand the basic characteristics of the business and its culture,
their nomenclature, and their objectives. Once the initial coding and tabulation was completed, it was useful to employ the assistance of the company's leadership to refine research insights and observed relevance of the
themes.

Reports on the 34 questions generated an extensive document that followed
the basic format for each question of:

- data on a chart
- item analysis
- thematic review and observations.

These were then followed by presentation of Final Observations and
Conclusions.

A major thrust of this report was oriented toward the purpose of, and expectations for, the national meeting. Below, we show some of the main themes identified in response to particular interview questions.

- Item analysis: *Why did you attend the meeting last year?*

Two main themes emerged, as Chart 15.1 shows. The fact that 22.5% of the sample rated the mandatory nature of attendance as the lead reason suggested a somewhat low valuation of the potential benefits of the meeting.

The inverse correlation between the stratified samples for these top two themes was noted. It clearly indicated great interest in advertising, plans, and strategies by the larger, more successful distributors whereas the smaller distributors' perspectives were somewhat less optimistic.

Perhaps the most interesting of the emerging themes was the desire for interaction with other distributors. A comparison of the weight of this theme against the one referring to information from the corporate executives revealed a clear preference for information acquired from peers rather than corporate leadership.

It was important to note that data from the previous year indicated the reasons for attendance were as follows:

41%   To obtain general information
34%   It is simply a matter of business

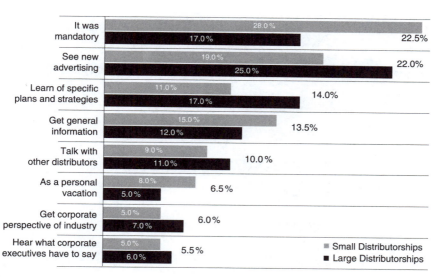

Chart 15.1 Question 1: Why did you attend the meeting last year?

Note: Individual and average scores have been rounded to the nearest percentage point.

33%   Attendance is mandatory
14%   To meet the new management
14%   To hear future plans
11%   To see other distributors

A review of the data revealed a shift from a mandatory, matter-of-business purpose for attending in previous years, to a far greater focus on information gathering and learning.

• Item analysis: *Why will you attend the meeting this year?*

This item proved an excellent follow-up probe to Question 1. Once again, two themes emerged as dominant and, as with the precedent item, there was an inverse correlation between large and smaller distributors in terms of importance (Chart 15.2).

The first theme (favoured by the smaller distributors) was obviously motivated by the recent changes in top management. Two of the five top executives had been replaced with heretofore unknown individuals. The lower weight given this theme by the larger distributors was explained by the content of their responses. These larger distributors referred to a series of smaller meetings that had been held to inform them about these new leaders.

The second theme (greatly favoured by the larger distributors) indicated an increased value for peer level interactions possible at the national meeting. Again, this too was more than likely a result of the changes in leadership. In

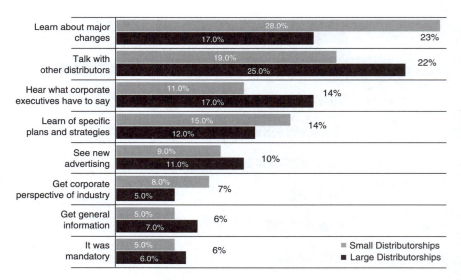

Chart 15.2 Question 2: Why will you attend the meeting this year?

Note: Individual and average scores have been rounded to the nearest percentage point.

terms of the larger distributors, they had met the new guys but wanted to hear their fellow distributors' opinions as well as explore the possible implications.

This probe item also showed a clear interest in more specific information regarding corporate plans and strategies. The distributors' reasons for attending this meeting versus past meetings had definitely changed, moving from moderate indifference to active anticipation. No longer was the mandatory aspect to the meeting so important.

In general, this population was looking to the meeting with a heightened awareness of its potential for the acquisition of information important to their business.

• Item analysis: *What do you feel is the corporate purpose for holding a national meeting?*

Much like Question 1, responses to this question were somewhat unexpected (Chart 15.3). When first asked, many expressed a personal interest of their own. Virtually all respondents had to think for some time before responding, often with an answer they clearly considered a guess. Very few appeared to respond with any sense of authority.

The same curious pattern of inverse correlation between the two subgroups occurred. The large distributors perceived the unveiling of new advertising as the primary corporate purpose for the national meeting. The smaller

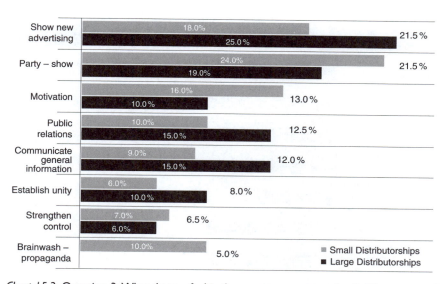

Chart 15.3 Question 3: What do you feel is the corporate purpose for holding a national meeting?

Note: Individual and average scores have been rounded to the nearest percentage point.

distributors felt that the party or show was an end in itself. The smaller distributors saw a general attempt to *motivate* the masses as another main purpose for holding the national meeting, whereas the larger distributors viewed *public relations* as a general purpose.

The subordinate themes revealed some underlying attitudes that may also impact on how the meeting was perceived. Both sub-groups seemed to feel the purpose of this meeting was to exert control over the distributors. The smaller distributors went further, in speculating that the leadership was interested in furthering an agenda of covert influence.

Overall, the audience seemed to consider the meeting as a 'party' or 'show' that communicated an agenda of corporate messages. These distributors considered the communication that took place at this meeting to be, for the most part, one-way. All in all, this response was not a very healthy message.

• Item analysis: *What should be the corporate purpose for holding a national meeting?*

Like Question 2, this item seemed quite welcome. Most respondents seemed enthusiastic about the opportunity to give their opinions (Chart 15.4).

The comparison between themes for Questions 3 and 4 revealed some remarkable differences. The purposes cited as those *intended* by the corporation were clearly one-way and routine. The themes that emerged here as

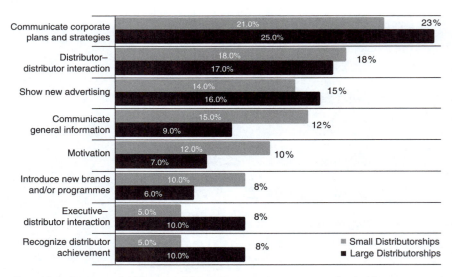

Chart 15.4 Question 4: What should be the corporate purpose for holding a national meeting?

Note: Individual and average scores have been rounded to the nearest percentage point.

to what the purpose *should* be for the national meeting were interactive and dynamic. Several aspects of this array are really quite remarkable:

- Both sub-groups seemed united in how they weighed the importance of these themes.
- These themes incorporated Advertising, Information, and Motivation.
- Approaching the meeting as a 'show' or 'party' was gone entirely. Despite the fact that a 'show' was seen as the corporate intent, it was the last approach this audience would prefer.
- This group was intensely interested in learning of the plans and strategies of the corporation.
- Distributor interaction with peers was viewed as of primary importance, to the degree that it should be an express purpose to the meeting itself.

FINAL OBSERVATIONS AND CONCLUSIONS

The pre-assessment survey provided the corporate leadership with some critical insights that allowed them to provide their distributors with a more productive meeting while avoiding some pitfalls of misunderstanding. And it was important to note how similar themes occurred in answering different questions.

From apathy to opportunity

The comparison of themes under Questions 1 and 2 clearly indicated an enhanced interest in the upcoming meeting. The corporate leadership had believed that the distributors had always embraced these national meetings as previously designed. However, the results clearly indicated not only a history of ineffective meetings, but new opportunity in the fact that this audience was keen on hearing what the new executives had to say.

The corporate assumption that the distributors trusted the former leadership was questionable. Also wrong was the assumption that the new executives would not be trusted. On the contrary, it appeared there was more receptivity than in past years as a result of the introduction of fresh blood. These executives seemed to represent a new hope for trust in the leadership. Although the jury was out, this was undoubtedly an opportunity to be seized.

Change in strategy

As a result, more time was devoted to presentations from the new executives. The agenda was changed to include more detailed information rather than just broad general comments. The leadership decided to unveil more than just the advertising but also the tactics and strategies behind the advertising

and marketing. At the event, the audience responded in a very obvious manner with more spontaneous laughter and applause than any of the previous
show-like meetings of the past. The increased detail prompted distributors to
seek out corporate employees between sessions, engaging them in impromptu
information-gathering conversations, eventually leading to more business
opportunities.

Venue for interaction

The leadership was aware that there was a lot of 'visiting' going on at the
meetings, but they were completely surprised by the enormous value the
distributors placed on simple sharing of ideas with their colleagues.

Change in strategy

Given that the informal communication channels were so highly regarded,
the planners orchestrated more opportunity for the top leadership to interact
with the distributors in more casual settings. Banquets became buffets and
seating was made more informal. Hallway and lounge areas were furnished
with comfortable seating and more time was set aside for casual interaction.
A series of panel meetings rather than seminar lectures was planned for the
exchange of learning between distributors. These mini-meetings not only
sparked new ideas and approaches for distributors, but allowed the corporate
leadership to record and collect the products of these ad hoc 'think tanks'.

Discovery of a 'Class System'

The data had made it painfully obvious that there was a significant disparity
between the large and smaller distributors. The survey revealed how corporate attempts to target their communications to the larger distributors who
represented the most significant part of the business resulted in a wide difference in attitudes and beliefs, and friction between the two groups.

Change in strategy

The focus on interaction and increase of detail provided at the meeting served
to empower the smaller distributors. Many commented on feeling more 'in
the know' after attending the meeting.

Communication vs. show

Perhaps the most important discovery was dispelling the myth that the distributors came to the meeting to have fun, relax, and party. The traditional
'show' format was shown to be ineffective, unappreciated and a hindrance

to the positive possibilities for the national meeting. Rather than having a motivating affect on the audience, taking the approach of a show or party looked more like smoke and mirrors to the distributors.

Change in strategy

A more formal and dignified design was adopted. The funds formerly spent on singers, dancers and special effects was invested in state-of-the-art speaker support and graphics. This allowed the executives to go into much greater detail while maintaining an effective level of understanding and retention.

The value of recognition

This was perhaps the most obvious tree overlooked as a result of focusing on the forest. These distributors worked hard to succeed, and the national meeting was the perfect place to recognize that achievement. What better way to build trust and loyalty?

Change in strategy

The meeting sessions featured documentary-style videos heralding best practice efforts of selected distributors from around the country. This allowed the audience to feel part of the main presentation and extended the value of interaction and sharing to the presentation itself. The response was overwhelming and was an obvious contributor to increased audience response and participation.

Detail not propaganda

The national meeting was now considered a communication 'event' rather than a 'show' and the focus was on communicating important and useful information. The leadership recognized the value of using this national event as a 'listening post' for new ideas and approaches to the business. The results from the meeting included more than merely furthering a national agenda. This national event now served to further develop and improve on that agenda.

THE RESULTS

The national meetings had been conducted with distributors for many years, following the same party format. It was not until an external communication audit provided detailed information to be used in designing the National Business Conference that it was transformed into an important communication event. The respondents revealed that they were tired of the 'smoke and mirrors' used in prior meetings. They complained of the grand spectacles with no substance that they were confronted with each year at the meeting. They virtually begged for just good information with great detail regarding plans and strategies, without distracting bells and whistles. They considered all the hoopla of the past as just a way to camouflage initiatives that were not necessarily in the favour of the distributors.

In conjunction with the audit consultants, the executives designed a meeting that consisted of well-produced speaker support and provided details of company plans. Plenty of time was set aside for two-way conversation in casual settings. A question and answer session was introduced. The results included a massive swell of support from the individual distributor principals and a reassessment and reorganization of the field representative network, including a more direct channel to the top executives.

Another important result was that the executives were so convinced that the communication audit had benefited them, they used it to plan all of their conventions. They also learned from this external audit that, regardless of how well they interacted internally at Sigma, they could not be successful unless they were successful externally with their vast network of distributors.

GENERAL AUDIT CONSIDERATIONS

Reports of external communication audits in the academic literature remain rare, unfortunately. We believe that this case study demonstrates that they can, and ought, to be a vital part of any serious effort at managing external relationships. There are additional difficulties with such audits, as we have demonstrated. But these can be overcome, using appropriate methods and with due diligence on the part of the audit team. In the modern world, people expect communication to be first class, and increasingly hold organizations to a high standard. This chapter demonstrates that wise organizations take this issue seriously, and can derive significant benefits from doing so.

Chapter 16

Auditing the corporate culture of a large manufacturing company

Donna McAleese, Owen Hargie and Dennis Tourish

INTRODUCTION

This chapter describes an audit of the culture of a large manufacturing firm in the UK. Culture is a dimension of corporate life that has been the focus of considerable research and debate. It has been defined as 'the sets of behaviors, beliefs, values, and linguistic patterns that are relatively enduring over time and generation within a group' (Spitzberg, 2003, p. 96). According to Brown (1995, p. 57), culture may be viewed as the 'cement', or 'glue', that binds an organization together, promoting 'consistency of perception, problem definition, evaluation of issues and options, and preferences for action'. Furthermore, it is now accepted that when individual and organizational values are working in tandem, levels of job satisfaction increase (Cole, 2007; Keers, 2007; Wiley, 2006). Thus it can be said that culture is a useful force for organizational integration and cohesion.

McAleese and Hargie (2004) provided a set of guiding principles for culture management, which senior staff should weigh up in building, maintaining or fine-tuning organizational culture. They contended that five distinct, yet related, elements are essential if culture management is to be successful, and that when all five principles are effectively merged to form one unified whole, the organization should be functioning at optimum level with a fully engaged workforce. These five principles are that the organization should:

1   Formulate an overall 'culture strategy'.
2   Develop 'cultural leaders'.
3   Share the culture by communicating effectively with staff.
4   Measure the cultural performance.
5   Communicate the culture in all dealings with customers.

In relation to recently appointed employees, or neophytes, research has highlighted that organizational entry is a demanding time, and acquisition of information is pivotal to enable them to fit in to their new environment (Wolfe Morrison, 2002). One way of reducing tension is to glean information from those with whom we have formed relationships. A key element of this study therefore was to investigate how communication between employees transmits the culture of an organization to its newest recruits.

COMPANY BACKGROUND

In order to protect the anonymity of the organization, it will be referred to as Company X. The firm is part of a large multinational corporation that employed 6500 staff at the commencement of the study. The workforce was segmented into two main sections: operations and support functions, which were further divided into 14 departments. The history of the company has been far from problem-free. In the decade preceding this study, a combination of factors such as major job losses, industrial action, disputes with management and problems with communication (internally and externally) had resulted in a defensive and suspicious workforce. Two thousand job losses had been declared, with no prior warning to employees. Unrest over the announcement was further intensified when, after lengthy negotiations, 60% of workers rejected a pay offer, opting instead for a course of industrial action. An intense period of discussion between management and trade unions resulted in stalemate, and industrial relations at the company suffered. While this backdrop could be perceived by some as an obstacle to the collection of sufficient information on culture and communication, the process of doing so offered, in reality, a therapeutic outlet for many employees who felt the need to express their views and opinions on the current status and performance of the firm. Conducting the study during such turbulent times also served to:

- pinpoint problems in the existing culture of the company
- identify practical strategies that could be employed to enhance performance and improve staff morale
- highlight (to managers) the preferred ideal culture chosen by employees
- provide in-depth information on the effects of the transmission of the current troubled culture to new staff.

OBJECTIVES

The objectives of the study were as follows:

1   To empirically examine the current culture of a major corporation in terms of the behavioural norms through which it is manifest.
2   To qualitatively investigate three key levels of culture – artefacts, espoused values and basic underlying assumptions – using ethnography and semi-structured interviews.

3   To ascertain aspects of ideal organizational culture as identified by current employees.
4   To uncover the means by which culture is disseminated to new employees.
5   To establish how, and in what ways, new employees develop an awareness of organizational culture through communication.

THE AUDIT

This study was guided by Schein's (2004) model of the 'Three levels of culture'. Schein segmented analysis down into manageable layers (see Figure 16.1), which progress from an examination of the superficial aspects of culture, through the manufactured company philosophies, strategies and goals, to the ingrained, taken-for-granted values and assumptions that guide the daily functioning of the organization. This method of enquiry was deemed most suitable, as it channelled the project throughout the progressively deeper stages of investigation. Five methodologies were employed in data collection:

- an ethnographic study that analysed artefacts at level 1
- two questionnaires: one examined espoused values at level 2, while the second measured the ideal culture to which employees aspired
- a series of semi-structured interviews to explore basic underlying

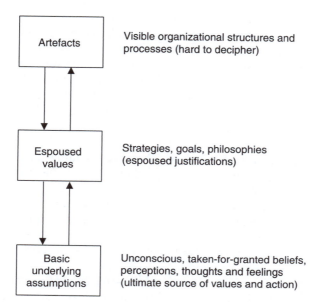

Figure 16.1 Three levels of culture analysis.

assumptions at level 3, as well as investigating the link between communication and culture dissemination.

Five departments were selected for inclusion in the study on the basis that they contained the highest number of most recently employed staff. Three of the sections were used for distribution of questionnaires, and semi-structured interviews were conducted in the remaining two sections. The sampling method used for the questionnaires was stratified random, which involved dividing the population into groups, each containing subjects with similar characteristics (in this case length of time in service), after which a random sample was drawn for each stratified list. Purposive sampling was used for the semi-structured interviews so that participants were selected according to their length of time employed. As one of the objectives of the study was to examine the extent to which communication facilitated the transmission of organizational culture to new staff, there was a higher weighting of members employed for less than 3 years in this sample.

Questionnaires

Two quantitative instruments were used to measure the current culture and the ideal culture. In relation to current culture, the Organizational Culture Inventory (OCI) (Cooke and Lafferty, 1989) was employed. This measured the behavioural norms and expectations associated with aspects of culture such as shared values and beliefs. This questionnaire presents a list of statements that describe some of the behaviours and 'personal styles' that might be expected or implicitly required of organizational members. Some of the cultural norms measured are positive and supportive of constructive interpersonal relationships, effective problem solving, and personal growth; others are dysfunctional and could lead to unnecessary conflict, dissatisfaction, and symptoms of strain on the part of organizational members. The OCI measures 12 different cultural norms, as described in Box 16.1, organized into three general types of culture:

- *Constructive cultures*, in which members are encouraged to interact with others and approach tasks in ways that will help them to meet their higher-order satisfaction needs.
- *Passive/defensive cultures*, in which members believe they must interact with people in defensive ways that will not threaten their own security.
- *Aggressive/defensive cultures*, in which members are expected to approach tasks in forceful ways to protect their status and security.

A special form of the OCI – the *OCI Ideal* – measured the ideal culture of Company X that employees desired. This was used to create a vision of the culture that the company should encourage to maximize its long-term

Box 16.1 Description of 12 culture types and styles

Constructive styles

An **achievement culture** characterizes organizations that do things well and values members who set and accomplish their own goals. Employees set challenging but realistic goals, establish plans to achieve them, and pursue them with enthusiasm. Achievement organizations are effective; problems are solved appropriately, and clients and customers are served well.

A **self-actualizing culture** characterizes organizations that value creativity, quality over quantity, and both task accomplishment and individual growth. Employees are encouraged to gain enjoyment from their work, develop themselves, and take on new and interesting activities. While self-actualizing organizations can be somewhat difficult to understand and control, they tend to be innovative, offer high-quality products or services, and attract and develop outstanding employees.

A **humanistic-encouraging culture** characterizes organizations that are managed in a participative and person-centred way. Members are expected to be supportive, constructive and open to influence in their dealings with one another. This leads to effective organizational performance by providing for the growth and active involvement of members who report high satisfaction with and commitment to the organization.

An **affiliative culture** characterizes organizations that place a high priority on constructive interpersonal relationships. Members are expected to be friendly, open, and sensitive to the satisfaction of their work group. This can enhance organizational performance by promoting open communication, cooperation, and the effective coordination of activities. Members are loyal to their work groups and feel they 'fit in' comfortably.

Passive/defensive styles

An **approval culture** describes organizations in which conflicts are avoided and interpersonal relationships are pleasant – at least superficially. Members feel that they must agree with, gain the approval of, and be liked by, others. Though possibly benign, this type of work environment can limit organizational effectiveness by minimizing constructive 'differing' and the expression of ideas and opinions.

A **conventional culture** is descriptive of organizations that are conservative, traditional, and bureaucratically controlled. Members are expected to conform, follow the rules, and make a good impression. This can interfere with effectiveness by suppressing innovation and preventing the organization from adapting to changes in its environment.

A **dependent culture** is descriptive of organizations that are hier-archically controlled and non-participative. Centralized decision mak-ing leads members to do only what they're told and to clear all decisions with superiors. Poor performance results from the lack of individual initiative, spontaneity, flexibility, and timely decision making.

An **avoidance culture** characterizes organizations that fail to reward success but punish mistakes. This leads members to shift responsibilities to others and to avoid any possibility of being blamed for a mistake. The survival of the organization is in question since members are unwilling to make decisions, take action, or accept risks.

Aggressive/defensive styles

An **oppositional culture** describes organizations in which confrontation prevails and negativism is rewarded. Members gain status and influence by being critical and thus are reinforced to oppose the ideas of others and to make safe (but ineffectual) decisions. While some questioning is func-tional, a highly oppositional culture can lead to unnecessary conflict, poor group problem solving, and 'watered-down' solutions to problems.

A **power culture** is descriptive of non-participative organizations structured on the basis of the authority inherent in members' position. Members believe they will be rewarded for taking charge and control-ling subordinates (and being responsive to the demands of superiors). Power-oriented organizations are less effective than managers may think; subordinates resist this type of control, hold back information, and reduce their contributions to the minimal acceptable level.

A **competitive culture** is one in which winning is valued and members are rewarded for out-performing one another. People operate in a 'win–lose' framework and believe they must work against (rather than with) their peers to be noticed. An overly competitive culture can inhibit effectiveness by reducing cooperation and promoting unrealistic stand-ards of performance (either too high or too low).

A **perfectionistic culture** characterizes organizations in which perfec-tionism, unproductive attention to detail, and hard work 'for hard work's sake' are valued. Members feel they must avoid all mistakes, keep track of everything, and work long hours to attain narrowly defined objectives. While some amount of this orientation might be useful, too much emphasis on perfectionism can lead members to lose sight of the goal, get lost in details, and develop symptoms of strain.

effectiveness. Consisting of the same number and type of questions as the instrument used to examine the current culture, questions are worded so that employees list behaviours that should be expected in order that the company performs to its full potential.

One hundred audit 'packages' were distributed via internal mail, each containing the OCI. A smaller number (20) of the OCI Ideal surveys were distributed in the same way to provide a snapshot of the culture to which current employees aspired. Participants were given an initial 2 weeks to return completed questionnaires (again via internal mail) before a reminder was sent by e-mail along with a final deadline for submission. A further 2 weeks were granted to maximize responses.

Ethnography

Schein (2004) maintained that the most salient point to bear in mind when dealing with organizational artefacts is that, at this level, culture is easy to observe but very difficult to decode. Researchers may report on what their senses pick up but without experiencing culture at the deeper level (of its values and assumptions) there is no guarantee that their interpretation of findings will be correct. Schein therefore suggested that a comprehensive and accurate analysis at level 1 is essential before progressing to the more 'hidden' layers at levels 2 and 3. Accordingly, ethnography was considered the most appropriate method of analysis at level 1 in this investigation. At its most basic, ethnography is a social science research method that involves three main types of data collection: interviews, observation and analysis of documents. Information obtained via these means is then scrutinized to produce a written description of the features of a particular culture (Harris and Johnson, 2000; Moore and Rees, 2008). Much thought was then given to the method of observation and it was decided that non-participative (overt) rather than participative (covert) techniques would be employed. Reasons for this choice were two-fold:

1   We wanted to obtain an overview of cultural artefacts as they first appeared to visitors or new employees. In this sense participant observation was not necessary as artefacts sought were directly observable.
2   As stated earlier, Company X was in a state of unrest during the course of the research and staff were suspicious and defensive of management. Accordingly, we felt that an open and honest approach to data gathering (e.g. during interviews), would foster relationships based on trust and mutual respect from the outset – resulting in frank and candid responses.

Permission was obtained from senior management to observe employees in their work environments. Because of Health and Safety regulations, the auditor was accompanied at all times by a member of the Communications staff during data gathering. The ethnography was conducted over a 3-day period during which information was gleaned from a range of sources using dialogue (short informal interviews), direct observation of employees and their environments, and analysis of written material produced by the firm.

Findings were then applied under seven main categories of artefact as recommended by Brown (1995) – material objects; physical layout; technology; language; behaviour patterns; symbols; and rules, systems, procedures and programmes.

Interviews

It could be argued that the most salient parts of culture are virtually undetectable, as they encompass thoughts, feelings and insights that are only discernible to those living the culture every day. Consequently, it was decided that the most effective method of obtaining the personal experiences of employees in relation to culture was through in-depth semi-structured interviews. In considering the need to balance the degree of autonomy offered to the interviewer with the content and depth of information required for this study, the interviews were partially structured into six main themes. These examined the views of participants on induction, artefacts, being a new-comer, culture type, communication and culture transmission. The research commenced with distribution of the qualitative instruments (OCI and OCI Ideal) in order that preliminary findings could be developed during the ethnography. The 20 deep-probe interviews were then conducted after analysis of the surveys and the ethnography in order that important issues could be further investigated.

RESULTS

Results are presented in this section in the same order that data were collected; that is, quantitative data, followed by the ethnography and interview findings.

Organizational culture inventory

In total, 86 respondents (out of 100) completed the OCI. The demographic details are reported in Table 16.1. The OCI examined the culture of Company X under three main factors: Constructive, Passive/Defensive and Aggressive/Defensive, which were further subdivided into 12 main types or styles of culture (Table 16.2). Raw scores for the 12 culture styles were totalled, providing an overall tally for each cultural factor. Results from the OCI highlighted that the Constructive cultural factor scored highest (132.1) in comparison to the Passive/Defensive (106.5) and Aggressive/Defensive (105.1) factors. This indicated that staff within Company X perceived their current culture to be primarily Constructive in nature.

On further examination of these findings (under each cultural factor) it is clear that the achievement culture style obtained the highest score (34.8) in

Table 16.1 Background information on OCI respondents

Category	Sub-category	Frequency	%
Gender	Female	23	27
	Male	63	73
Age	<39	25	30
	40–49	31	36
	50–59	15	17
	>60	15	17
Education	Non-degree	30	36
	Degree and above	56	65
Organizational level	Non-management	63	73
	Management	23	27
Years with organization	Up to 4 years	39	45
	5–10 years	13	15
	10 years or above	34	40
Occupation	Office-based staff	31	36
	Technical staff	25	29
	Production	30	35

Table 16.2 Results of OCI current culture

Cultural factor	Culture style	Score
Constructive	Humanistic-encouraging	32.6
	Affiliative	34.0
	Achievement	34.8
	Self-actualizing	30.7
	Total 132.1	
Passive/Defensive	Approval	24.5
	Conventional	29.6
	Dependent	30.6
	Avoidance	21.8
	Total 106.5	
Aggressive/ Defensive	Oppositional	24.7
	Power	25.5
	Competitive	24.1
	Perfectionistic	30.8
	Total 105.1	

the Constructive cultural category. This suggested that employees considered a culture that is both effective and values members who set and accomplish their own goals to be prevalent in their organization. The three remaining styles in this sector: humanistic-encouraging, affiliative and self-actualizing, also scored above average for the 12 types (average 28.64).

The Passive/Defensive cultural factor is based on the premise that employees must interact with people in defensive ways that will not threaten their own security. It consists of four culture styles (approval, conventional, dependent and avoidance), and the dependent culture style emerged with the highest score in this category (30.6). Again, this pointed to the fact that employees considered this type of culture, which denotes a hierarchically controlled and non-participative organization, to be manifest on a daily basis.

The third cultural factor (Aggressive/Defensive), expects staff to tackle problems in forceful ways to protect their status and security. The highest scoring culture type in this sector was perfectionistic, in which employees must pay strict attention to detail – avoiding mistakes and working long hours towards goals that are poorly defined. The remaining three styles under the Aggressive/Defensive category scored below average: oppositional (24.7), power (25.5) and competitive (24.1), indicating that the perfectionistic culture type was more readily observable for many organizational members than others under the same heading.

Overall, these results highlighted that employees considered the Constructive factor to be indicative of the current culture in their organization. In other words, staff considered the culture of the firm to be presently one in which members are encouraged to communicate with others and approach their jobs in ways that will help them to meet their satisfaction needs. However, while this result was positive (from a managerial perspective), findings from the remaining two cultural factors were less encouraging. The dependent style appeared dominant (in its category) as did the perfectionistic type, indicating that employees also perceived the culture of Company X to be hierarchically controlled, non-participative and one in which long working hours are expected if mistakes are to be avoided.

OCI Ideal

All 20 OCI Ideal surveys were returned (see Table 16.3 for information on respondents). Results for the OCI Ideal (Table 16.4) highlighted that, again, the Constructive cultural factor scored highest (157.8) in comparison to the Passive/Defensive and Aggressive/Defensive categories, which scored 93.0 and 95.1 respectively. These findings suggested that staff within Company X believe that their ideal culture should be principally Constructive in nature.

While an overview of the three cultural factors is beneficial, further scrutiny of the culture styles under each of these headings also provides useful information. For example, Table 16.4 highlights that under the Constructive cultural factor, the humanistic-encouraging type scored highest (41.1). This indicates that employees believed that Company X should be more supportive of a culture that encourages employee growth and active participation, which, in turn, would lead to increased job satisfaction and commitment to the firm. Table 16.4 also highlights results from the affiliative, achievement and self-actualizing culture styles, which scored 40.6, 40.1 and 36.0 respectively. These types are closely connected, as they all focus on 'healthy' aspects of organizational life, where employees are content, innovation and creativity are encouraged, and constructive interpersonal relationships are paramount.

Table 16.3 Background information on OCI Ideal respondents

Category	Sub-category	Frequency	%
Gender	Female	10	50
	Male	10	50
Age	<39	5	25
	40–49	5	25
	50–59	5	25
	>60	5	25
Education	Non-degree	8	40
	Degree and above	12	60
Organizational level	Non-management	9	45
	Management	11	55
Years with organization	Up to 5 years	4	20
	6–10 years	4	20
	10 years or above	12	60
Occupation	Office-based staff	8	40
	Production	12	60

Table 16.4 Results of OCI Ideal

Cultural factor	Culture style	Score
Constructive	Humanistic-encouraging	41.1
	Affiliative	40.6
	Achievement	40.1
	Self-actualizing	36.0
	Total	157.8
Passive/Defensive	Approval	23.2
	Conventional	24.1
	Dependent	28.1
	Avoidance	17.6
	Total	93.0
Aggressive/Defensive	Oppositional	23.3
	Power	23.7
	Competitive	21.7
	Perfectionistic	26.4
	Total	95.1

In considering the remaining two cultural factors, Passive/Defensive and Aggressive/Defensive, the latter scored slightly higher in the OCI Ideal. In the Passive/Defensive category, the dependent culture style ranked highest – a result that would conflict with earlier findings from the Constructive factor, as a dependent culture depicts an organization that is hierarchically controlled and non-participative. Results in the Aggressive/Defensive category were consistent with those obtained for the OCI (on current culture) in that the perfectionistic type obtained the highest score in its section (26.4). However, this finding clashed with responses from the Constructive factor as, on one hand, employees seemed to favour a culture in which cooperation was encouraged and staff approached tasks in ways that facilitated job satisfaction, while, on the other, they showed preference for a culture that stifled individuality and autonomy in the workplace.

Overall, employees indicated that their preferred (ideal) culture for the organization was Constructive in nature. Within this factor, the humanistic-encouraging style scored highest, highlighting that a culture in which employee development and participation is promoted would be welcomed by staff. Analysis of the Passive/Defensive and Aggressive/Defensive factors again revealed that the dependent and perfectionistic styles scored highest in relation to others in the same categories. When results of the OCI and OCI Ideal in Company X are considered jointly, it would appear therefore that the current culture is not far removed from the model culture to which employees aspire.

Ethnography

The findings here are reported in relation to the seven main categories of artefact mentioned earlier – material objects; physical layout; technology; language; behaviour patterns; symbols; and rules, systems, procedures and programmes.

Material objects

All employees received an induction folder during the orientation programme on their first day. Additionally, some departments produced their own welcome packs for new staff. Similar to others designed by the company for schools and visiting parties, each of these contained a CD-ROM holding a wealth of information, such as the company mission statement, rules and policies, codes of ethics and company history. However, many had no idea what the packs contained, with one person commenting:

> I took it home the day I got it and stuffed it in a drawer . . . If I needed to know something when I started I asked someone, whether the answer was in the pack or not.

Office-based employees had access to a wide range of company information through regular meetings, an internal television system (which broadcasts messages from the Corporation to all sites) and the intranet (from which they could print policies and procedures if necessary). Despite the fact that the mission statement was on the intranet (as well as on leaflets that were available to new staff during induction), very few employees were aware of what it actually contained. One commented:

> Oh, the mission statement. Hmm, I have seen it on the wall somewhere. I haven't a clue about what it says though. That's how much notice I took of it.

Only one mission statement was observed during the 3-day observation period, framed on a wall in one of the company's conference rooms. The company does not design any advertising material. However, other written materials are produced, such as the internal monthly magazine for staff and the annual report for shareholders.

Internal magazine

An A3-size monthly publication, the company magazine provides a full-colour outlet for delivering corporate communication. It contains information on product development as well as departmental and individual staff achievements. Articles are also included on wider issues that affect the company in general.

Annual report

Over 100 pages long, the design is sleek and full-colour, comprising sections ranging from financial summaries to details on health and safety. Descriptions of company values on issues such as human resources and social responsibility are also given and a full section is devoted to describing how the firm can 'make a difference', through its dedication to employees, the community and the environment. However, staff frequently remarked that the company did not live up to their promises:

> Oh, yes, management say that they listen and maintain that they want to hear our views and opinions, but when it comes down to it, they don't give a damn.

Observable around the company were professional and often stunning photographs of the main product both in production and in operation when finished, which provided workers with a view of what they aim to produce. These seemed to produce a sense of corporate pride in employees. During informal discussions, these photographs were frequently brought to the attention of the researcher. There was evidence of personal possessions on the desks of office-based employees. Interestingly, because of the nature of tasks in the factory, health and safety issues, and the fact that manual workers did not have 'workstations' per se, such individual belongings were absent from the shop floor.

Physical layout

On approach, the site of the company is extensive. Security guards meet visitors and staff at the main entrance and direct them to one of three types of car parks: directors, staff or visitors. After parking, guests have to sign in at security and obtain a visitor's pass, which cannot be removed for the duration of the visit. Access to administration is obtained only through the use of 'swipe' cards, which are issued to employees when they join the company. In this way, visitors (and the auditor) are restricted from offices unless accompanied by a member of Company X. The Communication manager accompanied the researcher on a tour of the administration building and factory floor, during which the following points were noted:

- Offices were private in some areas and open plan in others. They were equipped with desks, personal computers and telephones for each member of staff. Photocopiers, fax machines, etc. were communal and were located centrally within each section. Some staff were satisfied with the office layout and others were unhappy, with one stating:

  > There are 12 people in this room alone. I know there is enough space, but we have no privacy. Someone is always looking over my shoulder to see what I'm doing or listening to my phone calls.

  Additionally, some remarked that they were disappointed when they joined the company that no desk, phone and computer were initially provided. While a few sought out their own equipment, the remainder waited 5 weeks until the basics were provided. The wait, one employee claimed, added to the stress of starting a new job:

  > It made life really awkward and very stressful for me. I had to share with another member of staff who resented the intrusion.

- There were kitchens in the main building where staff could gather to have lunch, and vending machines provided snacks throughout the complex. Televisions were scattered in key areas throughout the administration building only to broadcast internal communication messages. This medium was absent for other sections, e.g. operations.
- The workplaces of senior management were located down a separate corridor, which veered off from the rest of the staff. There was a door at

the top of the hallway that, when opened, revealed that the area was very quiet. All doors to individual offices on this corridor were closed. When asked about this corridor, one group of employees stated that they thought it was 'funny', as each door in this area was taller than average, giving the illusion of height, grandeur and power to those housed there. Employees stated that to a newcomer this hallway appeared very threatening until, as one remarked:

> You see a really short, unimportant-looking person coming out from behind one of those grand doors and you say to yourself, 'Oh, maybe that corridor isn't as scary as I thought!'

- The operations or factory side of the business was situated in a huge building separate from administration. The factory itself was very impressive in terms of size, deafening noise and sheer numbers of employees (the majority of whom were male). Informal interactions revealed that the majority of office staff had been on the shop floor. However the reverse was not the case. Very few of the factory workers had been in the administration building and none had been given a tour of the rest of the site. One employee commented:

> I don't think anyone I have ever worked with has been given a proper tour of the rest of the company. Some of us had to run messages to the offices at times and we'd have seen a little then, but other than that, we never got a chance to see where 'the suits' work.

Technology

The area in which technology was most evident was in the factory. This was full of large pieces of heavy machinery, such as cranes, and sections of the manufactured product were instantly observable. The 'swipe' system for access was regarded by some employees as an inconvenience, but others noted that when they forgot their cards and were in another department, asking to borrow a card gave them a chance to interact with other staff.

Language

Employees used a 'technical' language, replete with acronyms, with the result that new staff or visitors were generally unable to comprehend what was being discussed. This 'language' was difficult for a newcomer to learn as existing employees took it for granted that the terms were known:

> When I started, I hadn't a clue what they were talking about and when I asked a colleague, he looked at me as if I was stupid! In fact, when I cast my mind back, I don't think he even told me the answer. If

I remember correctly, I think he directed me to the list of acronyms on the intranet.

Further dialogue with members in the factory also uncovered that existing employees were loath to divulge information *of any kind* to new staff who joined the firm straight after leaving a large neighbouring manufacturing company. Remarks indicated that competitiveness was rife between the company and its neighbour, even though they manufactured different products. When staff were made redundant from the neighbouring corporation, it was clear that their skills could be adapted to accommodate Company X. Thus when these new staff arrived employees were resentful and, in many cases, efforts to be unhelpful were palpable. One member remarked:

> I couldn't actually believe how other men treated me when I came here and, for a while, I thought it was personal. It was only after I had been here for a while that I realized that they were only standoffish to people who came from [name of company]. To other new starts, they are helpful and try to make them feel at home.

Another point raised through informal discussions with employees was that staff are sometimes 'cliquish', forming exclusive groups of like-minded individuals who prefer to interact solely with other group members.

Behaviour patterns

In terms of company events, it emerged that the company invests heavily in acknowledging and rewarding staff for efficient performance. Such rewards have become the norm in the organization and are 'expected' by staff. Examples include:

- A prize night, which is hosted annually to recognize achievement.
- Celebrations for long-term staff. Employees are awarded 'service pins' from 5 years onwards and, at 25 years of service, they receive a gift of their choice and an outing.
- An annual family day.
- Christmas lunches.

Informal conversations revealed another interesting factor in relation to behaviour patterns in that office-based staff are 'expected' to work after hours. Despite the fact that they are contracted to work a set number of hours per week, it is taken for granted that they stay longer. In fact, according to one employee:

> It is actually frowned upon for you to leave on time. In my younger

days, I saw myself having to make excuses to leave on time ... Now I can see the younger employees and especially new employees are still doing that.

Symbols

According to Brown (1995), this is a very general category that encompasses material objects, physical layouts, and one-off actions by employees made to demonstrate a point. Material objects and physical layouts have been fully discussed earlier in the chapter. In terms of one-off actions, one striking example that occurred was that employees went on strike, causing major disruption to production. Management eventually met the demands for a pay increase after contracted negotiations. However, this action, and the breakdown in trust and relationships that it signified, certainly changed the operational culture of Company X.

Rules, systems, procedures and programmes

The first point of contact with employees is on their induction day, therefore management use this medium to convey the most relevant information. For instance, during orientation, it is the responsibility of the human resource department to inform staff on:

- Organizational development – e.g. staff appraisal, training needs analysis and the performance management programme.
- Policies – such as alcohol and drugs, smoking, dress code, mobile phones, company collections, and so on.
- Recruitment – information on internal applications.
- Absenteeism – general guidance on how to report illness.
- Health and safety – provision of a handbook and advice.
- General company rules – through provision of an employee handbook.

Again, however, there was a collision between formal and informal cultures. Discussions with employees revealed that staff appraisal was given particular attention by the company, with a 15-page booklet available on the intranet. However, in reality many employees did not see it as very important:

> Oh appraisal, it's just an annual chat with my boss. Really it's nothing more than that. It's certainly not something to be worried about anyway.

Interviews

The schedule drawn up prior to commencement of the interviews was semi-structured in that it covered topics related both to the research objectives and to the initial findings from the ethnography and questionnaires. Analysis of the interviews produced valuable information on induction, cultural artefacts, being a newcomer, culture type evident in Company X, and communication. Sixty-five per cent of respondents stated that they learned much of the culture of their new firm through talking with colleagues. Five main themes emerged from an analysis of interviewee responses: accuracy of information about organizational culture, the provision of insight about expected behaviour, the unhelpful nature of communications, the importance of communication in information seeking, and avoiding unnecessary errors.

Accuracy of information about culture

One interviewee pointed to the *'rehearsed'* nature of the induction procedure and the fact that the *'real'* culture of the firm could only be experienced when the job had actually been undertaken:

> I would say a lot of the culture is passed on that way, sort of informally, you know. I mean, everybody knows that induction is all rehearsed and laid out. I suppose the only way to find out the real culture is to start working in it.

Other respondents stated:

> Well, when I think back, I learned so much from my colleagues that I'd have to say it had a huge effect on the way I found out about the culture of the firm.

> I would say that talking to people and getting to know how the company really worked was the main way I found out about the culture of this place. I mean, induction is only a spiel – management tell you what they want you to hear and when you start to actually work, things couldn't be more different.

Provision of insight about expected behaviour

Respondents highlighted the benefits of learning the company culture through informal communication. For example, they found out how to behave, what was expected of them and were able to avoid making mistakes as a result of others' revelations:

> Talking about my new job to other people was a great way for me to find out what was expected of me in here. After all, the induction was good and all, but it doesn't explain or show you what way you need to do your individual job does it?

I think that people telling me about this company – about what to do and what not to do, was the real way I found out how to conduct myself. As far as induction went, in terms of getting the culture message across, the only purpose it served was to let us know that we should join the union.

These findings are important when viewed in relation to extant research, which generally purports that the initial period of employment in organizations proves critical in shaping the attitudes and behaviours of employees (Kammeyer-Mueller, 2002; Wiley, 2006).

The unhelpful nature of some communications

A minority of interviewees did not feel that colleagues' revelations aided them in any way (in fact, they considered them unhelpful), and others felt that culture dissemination through communication from colleagues was both an advantage and a disadvantage when settling into Company X. As exemplified by two respondents:

Yes and no. Sometimes I heard stuff I didn't want to. When personalities clash, people sometimes don't get on very well . . . and I found that some staff tried to 'warn' me against other people. I didn't personally find that very useful.

I'm not too sure about that. I suppose it helped me to a large extent although I'd have to say that a lot of information that was passed on informally was not very helpful. I remember being told things about people, negative things, and they only made me form a bad opinion of them before I had even had any dealings with them. That kind of thing just passes on a bad culture instead of being helpful.

The importance of communication in information seeking

The notion of information seeking was a core factor in this investigation. Indeed, research has highlighted that the more frequently newcomers ask for information the more effectively they will master their jobs (Saks and Ashforth, 2000). One participant drew attention to the fact that so much new information was necessary in order for him to function when he joined the company that it was impossible to ask all the questions he wanted to. In this respect, information from other employees was very helpful:

Well, on the shop floor, you have to ask how to do your job, you know, all the procedures and that might be hard to find out if you didn't ask. From my own point of view, if I had asked everything I needed to know,

I'd never have shut up. So it was really helpful for me when people volunteered stuff.

Avoiding unnecessary errors

A final theme was that communications from fellow employees enabled neophytes to avoid unnecessary errors:

It was great because I could avoid making mistakes before situations even arrived.

When I look back people telling me their own experiences of this place was really helpful to me. People say you learn by your mistakes, well I learned from others' mistakes too.

These results are significant for managers in Company X for several reasons:

1 They provide evidence that informal channels of communication are operative in the organization.
2 They indicate that the majority of staff sampled found communication from existing employees advantageous on arrival.
3 The fact that the bulk of staff found revelations beneficial provides an opening for managers to utilize this medium to transmit culture.
4 Findings also highlight the negative consequences of such communication on the process of socialization and the transmission of culture.

DISCUSSION

The main aim of this study was to establish how, and in what ways, culture was transmitted to new employees. The difficulties inherent in measuring culture and the array of views and opinions on what approaches should be adopted are myriad. According to Burchell and Kolb (2003, p. 51) 'A range of qualitative and quantitative methods is available for cultural studies, each with their own advantages and disadvantages.' However, one way to avoid the extremes of these trade-offs is to use mixed methods (Martin, 2002; Moore and Rees, 2008). Accordingly, this audit employed a blend of qualitative and quantitative approaches to generate findings that were both relative and sensitive to the deeper aspects of culture.

One possible limitation of the OCI as a research tool is that the instrument assesses behavioural norms only. Corporate culture has several layers, two of which are behavioural norms and organizational values (Rousseau, 1990). In an attempt to offset the exclusion of corporate values from the audit, appropriate questions were incorporated into the qualitative interviews. In relation to the use of deep-probe interviews, participants were asked to comment on their experiences when they joined the firm. When interviewees recall past events, they often recreate incidents differently in their minds, resulting in a misrepresentation of experiences (Dickson *et al.*, 2003). The auditors addressed this dilemma in two ways:

1   By ensuring that the interview sample varied in terms of length of employment. In this way, experiences as a newcomer were more vivid for some than others.
2   By making sure that not all questions were memory-based. The interviews gathered data on present as well as past events, so that the validity of findings did not rest entirely on accuracy of recall.

In considering the effectiveness of ethnography as a method of culture analysis, the auditors found that observing and recording cultural artefacts was relatively straightforward, but translation and interpretation were rather more complex. By working covertly (using participant observation) to experience the culture, first-hand 'insider' knowledge could have been heightened. However, this latter approach is time-consuming and carries with it a range of ethical issues (deWalt and deWalt, 2002). One limitation that could not be overcome during the ethnography was that the auditor had to be accompanied at all times while in the organization. Ideally it would have been preferable to record data without this supervision but this was not possible in the present audit.

Overall, analysis of the OCI and OCI Ideal indicated that a culture that promotes communication, interaction, innovation and constructive interpersonal relationships was indicative of both the current and the preferred culture of employees in the firm. However, two underlying culture styles, which supported non-participation, top-down communication and inflexibility, also emerged from these analyses. In relation to the ethnographic study, findings highlighted that communication practices in Company X were not operating to their full potential. In particular, a 'them and us' attitude existed between lower level employees and management, resulting in a dearth of information flow up the chain of command.

The majority of interviewees learned much of the culture of their new firm through communications from fellow employees. Participants also claimed that gaining knowledge of the company culture through this informal medium had advantages and disadvantages. For example, while they gained an awareness of acceptable behaviour and customary practices, and found out how to avoid making mistakes, they also acquired knowledge of disagreements between individual employees and/or departments. So what are the implications of this for Company X?

The need for change in business, be it minor or major, is seldom far away. Organizations are not stagnant. To survive they must regulate and fine-tune their policies, systems and procedures to cope with environmental changes and the needs of employees (Faull *et al.*, 2004). Studies have highlighted various considerations that must be borne in mind, should management decide to make amendments (Chen, 2004; Higgins *et al.*, 2006). In particular, Hodge *et al.* (2003) pointed to two possible approaches that managers can utilize: top-down and bottom-up. However, in light of the culture in Company X, it is difficult to see how either of these methods could be successfully employed. Evidently, organizational members mistrusted senior executives and were suspicious of middle management. Those on lower levels were also frightened of losing their jobs, morale had been depleted, and many were loath to voice their concerns on any of these matters to anyone (both inside and outside the firm). Consequently two fundamental recommendations were put forward:

1   The company should embark on a change programme for organizational culture. The set of guiding principles that should be employed in fine-tuning organizational culture as identified by McAleese and Hargie (2004) were recommended as a template. It was therefore advised that managers: formulate an overall 'culture strategy', develop 'cultural leaders', share the culture by communicating effectively with staff, measure the cultural performance, and communicate the culture in all dealings with customers.

2   The power of informal channels of communication needed to be harnessed. Organizations frequently assert that one of their most important assets is their staff, yet they often fail to put this mantra into practice. However, securing employee loyalty is only possible if people feel valued – and they only feel valued if they are well informed. Essentially, an effective balance must be struck between what managers *think* employees should *know* and what staff themselves *believe* they should be *told*. Bottom-up communication is therefore central in ensuring that employees feel valued and play active roles in communicating a positive company culture.

Several key issues emerged from this audit. First, a unique 'way of life' will inevitably develop over a period of time within any company, resulting in the adoption of set rules, systems and procedures that employees learn and use to accomplish both organizational and individual goals. To that end, no one method of culture analysis may be applied universally. Rather, methodologies should be carefully selected in light of specific organizational factors and constraints. Second in considering the application of Schein's (2004) model of culture analysis, it could be argued that, while it is possible for artefacts (level 1) and espoused values (level 2) to be examined from a newcomer's perspective, analysis of basic underlying assumptions (at level 3) would be more problematic, as knowledge at this level is acquired over time, which a new recruit may not have served in the company. Essentially then, this highlights that analysis of culture using neophytes as a sample would require a new framework.

Finally, the intrinsic difficulties in observing and measuring organizational culture have been widely discussed, and it would appear that past research projects have concentrated mainly on the development of instruments that effectively addressed these concerns (Wilkins and Ouchi, 1983; Louis, 1985; Smircich, 1985). Consequently, the issues surrounding the transmission of culture are not as widely investigated and, in particular, analysis from a newcomer's perspective has not been widely researched. Importantly, while Schein's (2004) theory of culture analysis was considered effective in terms of offering guidance and providing a logical model for analysing organizational culture in Company X, this audit has also highlighted the importance of measuring the extent to which culture is disseminated to neophytes via informal (verbal and non-verbal) channels.

Chapter 17

Auditing a major police organization

Dennis Quinn, Owen Hargie and Dennis Tourish

BACKGROUND

This study describes a communication audit of a major UK policing body. Police organizations are not solitary entities, but rather are part of the larger UK public service sector, funded and monitored by government. In exercising governance, the need for quality of communication between user and provider has been identified by the Audit Commission as essential for all elements of the public sector. Likewise, communication is perceived as essential and necessary for optimal efficiency in all sectors of the criminal justice system, of which the police are an integral part (Greene, 2000). It has also been shown that effective communication is a crucial aspect of the core business of policing (Kim and Mauborgne, 2003). For example, ensuring the receipt of the correct information by the right person at the optimum time is not only paramount for major crime investigations, but also for the operational needs of the organization in providing a day-to-day service to the public.

The effects of poor communication have been noted, particularly as a cause of stress within the police service (Stinchcomb, 2004). Although there is some evidence of a changing culture (Feltes, 2002), police organizations often tend to reflect hierarchical management structures, synonymous with quasi-military or paramilitary lines (Cochran and Bromley, 2003; Toch, 2008), and the one studied in this audit was no exception. The potential problems that can be created by this type of structure have been evidenced through the identification of cultural gaps; for example, the bifurcation between 'street cops' – operational police officers, and 'management cops' – police officers in a managerial role, and feelings of 'them and us' by junior officers in their relationship with senior officers (Perlmutter, 2000; Cope, 2004). However, while the need for good communication has been identified, the lack of research into or establishment of communication strategies in UK police bodies has also been noted (Collier *et al.*, 2004). This was also the case with the organization under focus here, where no concerted attempt had been made at the time of the audit to intensively measure communication.

THE ORGANIZATION

This was a large police organization of just over 12,000 officers. As there are diverse roles, ranks, departments, branches and units, provision of an all-inclusive study of the whole organization would have entailed accounting for a mass of variables. This would have been prohibitively expensive and time consuming. It was therefore decided to select a specific section for analysis, particularly one that would be indicative of the communication of the overall organization.

The point of service for the police is that provided by the uniformed officer, and these were managed in a basic unit of management known as a sub-division – a geographical area managed by a senior officer, usually a superintendent. It is at this level that management impacts most on the organization. The number of officers employed at this level is approximately 68% of the total. Managerial policies and practices influence officers on the ground, and interpretation of these policies and practices is reflected in the service to the public. In addition the sub-divisional unit of management was reflective of the overall structure and establishment of the organization. It was in essence a microcosm of the hierarchical structure of command and management, and being the basic unit of management and representing some two-thirds of all police personnel, reflected the working culture of the wider corporate body. Selection of the sub-divisional level meant that the data collected from the study were reflective of the perceptions of officers delivering a service to the public. A small civil workforce provides administration support at this level, and while the study was concerned with the police element of the organization, and civilian staff were not included as a core part of the study, they were to a limited degree accounted for as part of the management system.

Three sub-divisions were selected for inclusion in the audit. One was large and geographically responsible for both urban and rural environments, while the other two were smaller – one policing within a rural environment and the other within an inner city context. These three sub-divisions employed 600 officers, representing some 5% of the total organization.

SELECTION OF AUDIT TOOLS

Given that the organization had not previously been studied holistically in terms of communication, comprehensiveness was regarded as an important aspect of the methodology. Selection of a small number of audit tools that can be manageable yet comprehensive enough to render valid data to ensure objective measurement is a recommended means of achieving comprehensiveness (Tourish and Mulholland, 1997). The audit therefore utilized three tools for data collection, namely, face-to-face interviews and two separate questionnaires. While interviews take time and can be costly they allow for in-depth coverage of topics (see Chapter 4). Interviews, which were carried out in police stations, provided the opportunity to assess in detail the perceptions of those at the level of service delivery. The interview utilized in this study was an adaptation of the Explanatory Interview Guide (Downs and Adrian, 2004). A quota sample of 20% of officers (n = 41) within one sub-division was selected, with each interview lasting 35–40 minutes. The sample spanned the hierarchical levels from constable to inspector. Interviews were audio recorded, transcribed and content analysed.

Two questionnaires were employed in the audit. The first was an adaptation of the International Communication Audit (ICA) Survey (Goldhaber and Rogers, 1979). This was employed to measure communication in general. The questionnaire utilized was a modified version of the instrument presented in the Appendix of this book. At the end of the questionnaire, subjects were requested to record details of one communication incident, whether effective or ineffective, and were also asked to provide suggestions as to how they felt communication could be improved. The second questionnaire was the Organizational Culture Survey (Glaser et al., 1987). The canteen culture of the police with its cohesive and defensive nature, and reluctance to change, has been highlighted (Kiely and Peek, 2002). This suggests that police bodies are culture bound, and so the effect that culture has on organizational perceptions was regarded as an important aspect of the audit.

QUESTIONNAIRE ADMINISTRATION

Prior to administering the questionnaires each superintendent sent a letter of introduction, support and request for cooperation for the audit to each officer. This had the potential for being both positive and negative. On the one hand it provided senior managerial validation for the audit, but on the other it had the potential to be viewed as being part of just another management objective. Given the formal structure of police organizations, the stamp of 'higher authority' was necessary to ensure full access and cooperation with middle management in administering the audit. This is a common issue in many audits, since middle managers are generally key gatekeepers. In practice, their consent is essential for auditors to obtain access. It means that additional steps must be taken to reassure respondents of the auditors' independence. The key means of doing so is to offer assurances of confidentiality – and live up to them.

In this case, all members of staff received a questionnaire and an addressed return envelope. A covering note provided guidance for its completion and gave an assurance of confidentiality. While management provided access and support there were factors that could have militated against the achievement of a successful audit. These included survey fatigue, cultural reluctance to change, and the gap between management and lower ranks. Each of these had the potential to be audit barriers; that is, the survey could be seen as a management-originated exercise, could be seen as resulting in potential change within the organization and negatively impacting on their own roles in particular, or could be perceived as just 'more bureaucratic paperwork'.

To counter this, we made a deliberate point of briefing each section, unit and office in person, presenting the rationale for the audit, the safeguards of autonomy and confidentiality, and the security provided in submission of the questionnaires. This personalization of the audit was aimed at providing assurance and understanding of the exercise. One of the authors was a member of the organization and in a middle management position, and this had both positive and negative impacts. At one level, he could be seen as being a colleague, but on the other he may have been perceived as a member of middle management seeking further 'management cop' advancement. Given this backdrop, it was emphasized that the audit offered advantages in terms of the potential for people to be heard on issues important to them, and thereby to help change the communication climate. This proved to be quite successful in that the overall response rate for questionnaires was 33%.

AUDIT RESULTS

Interviews

Several themes emerged from the content analysis:

- **Bureaucracy**. A large number of interviewees raised this issue. Bureaucracy included the transmission of irrelevant material and an overdependence on 'unnecessary paperwork'. Formal channels were perceived to be the main means of communication, the bulk of which was written: *'there must be miles and miles of trees chopped down in the rainforest in Brazil for the paper that's generated through this job. Unbelievable.'* Indeed one officer wryly remarked *'a lot of paperwork is piled up due to the unnecessary paperwork'*.
- **Satisfaction with immediate managers**. All respondents reported a positive relationship with their immediate supervisor, seeing them as being willing to share information and being open to new ideas.
- **Communication with senior management**. While a majority of officers perceived communication with local senior management as positive, e.g. *'If they wanted us to know something they would tell us'*, a significant minority felt there was a gap between staff and management and that more contact was needed, i.e. *'It would be useful for them just to come down and say how things are going.'*
- **Need for more informal channels**. There were numerous references to the

need for more informal communications between units/sections, and greater personal interaction as a strategy for achieving objectives: '*To me there's nothing beats going and talking to somebody.*'

- **Communication and organizational change**. Almost all interviewees raised the fact that the organization was facing major change, and most felt that they did not receive enough information about this, and would like to be kept informed, since: '*it's always nice to know what's happening to you*'. Likewise, all interviewees had received some information via the grapevine and indicated that they believed some aspects of these rumours.
- **Communication problems with other departments**. Over one-third of respondents raised the problem of communications with other departments, particularly CID (Criminal Investigation Department), and several officers mentioned that there were 'conflicts' in this relationship.

Questionnaires

ICA Survey

The interviews were completed before, and informed, the ICA questionnaire part of the audit. In addition to assessing the climate of the sub-division it was clear that the questionnaire would need to reflect the terminology and levels of management and departments/units found within sub-divisions. It was therefore adapted to reflect these and clearly delineate what was meant by each question – for example, 'co-workers' were separated into specific groups. This took particular note of the differences identified by the interviewees with regard to their perception of specific departments. For example, CID were specifically mentioned as an individual group with whom uniform staff had identified a communication problem, while members of other departments were grouped together. In addition, civilian administrators were identified as a specific group in relation to information flow. This recognized their potential influence on the communication climate of the sub-division.

The average total scores for each of the questionnaire sections are as shown in Table 17.1. In the questionnaire, timeliness and general organizational satisfaction are rated by respondents in one column, which allows respondents to offer their perspective on these aspects at that time. The other eight areas are rated along two columns, allowing respondents to state what they feel is happening now in respect of each area (actual) and what they feel should be happening (ideal). A 5-point Likert scale is used for all sections and mean totals can then be derived for each area. Differences were tested using the Wilcoxon signed rank test, and a significant shortfall was found for each section of the questionnaire.

The mean total scores for information received in general (and through various channels and on important issues) and information needed, indicated that respondents felt they were receiving between 'little' and 'some', but

Table 17.1 Mean scores for ICA questionnaire sections

	Present	Desired
Information received	2.5	3.6
Information received through various channels	2.8	3.5
Information received on important issues	2.7	3.7
Information sent	2.8	3.5
Information sent on important issues	2.1	2.8
Timeliness of information received	3.3	n/a
Working relationships with colleagues	3.2	4.0
Working relationships with supervisor	3.8	4.2
Working relationships with management	2.8	3.9
Level of satisfaction obtained through working in organization	2.9	n/a
Overall mean scores	2.9	3.7

Scoring key: 1 = very little; 2 = little; 3 = some; 4 = great; 5 = very great.

wanted a 'great' amount of information. The greatest shortfall here related to the item *How decisions that affect my job are dealt with.* Interestingly, respondents felt they needed to receive *less* information via the grapevine than they were presently receiving. In terms of information sent, the difference between the total means was 0.7, indicating that officers felt that they should also be sending more information. In particular it was felt that more information needed to be sent to *Colleagues in CID.* The scores for timeliness showed that information was between 'sometimes' and 'mostly' on time, although satisfaction scores for immediate managers were much higher than for senior managers. Interestingly, the scores for working relationships showed a greater satisfaction level with immediate supervisors than with colleagues. Satisfaction scores for 'working in the organization' were just below average at 2.9.

Critical incident analysis

The responses to this part of the ICA questionnaire were limited, with only 25% of respondents fully completing this section. Of these, 64% recorded a negative experience while 36% cited a positive one. The ineffective experiences related more to management and other departments in comparison to the effective experiences. In terms of the type of communication encountered, nine mentioned the way in which they were communicated with by some form of management. Examples included the lack of consultation with respect to transfer, being questioned by management without the person introducing themselves, and those in command not transmitting intentions during a period of stress. The overall analysis tended to show similar findings to the interviews and the other ICA questionnaire items, with specific problems identified in relation to downward communication between management and staff. The majority of ineffective experiences (43%) related to those in management roles, while only 17% indicated effective encounters with management. This again reflects a problem with communication between management and staff.

SUGGESTIONS FOR IMPROVEMENT

There was a 37% response rate to this part of the audit, providing a total of 105 suggestions for improving communication within the sub-divisional unit. The suggestions confirmed the trends emerging from the other parts of the audit, as exemplified in the following themes:

'Suggestion for improvement' theme	*Number*
More communication from management	23
More information needed in general	19
More informal approach to communication	17
More regular briefings needed to inform people	14
More openness in decision making	11
More involvement/consultation	6
Less bureaucracy in communication	6

ORGANIZATIONAL CULTURAL SURVEY

This instrument is designed to test six culture dimensions: Teamwork, Morale, Information flow, Involvement, Supervision and Meetings. The means for each item and sub-area are shown in Table 17.2. These scores reinforced the findings from the interviews and the ICA questionnaire, with greatest satisfaction expressed for teamwork and supervisors. The highest mean total related to Supervision (3.3), and an examination of the individual items that go to make up this sub-scale showed that the highest score (3.7) was for *approachability of supervisor*. The second highest rated survey item (3.6) was within Teamwork: *People I work with function as a team*. In contrast, the two lowest frequencies for the survey related to *My opinions count in this organization* (2.1) and *I know what's happening in sections/units/departments outside my own* (2.2), reflecting the two lowest sub-scales, which were Involvement and Information flow respectively.

DISCUSSION

Police bodies, like all organizations, need to measure and evaluate their effectiveness, and a communication audit facilitates this process. This audit illustrated that there was considerable room for improvement. The need for

Table 17.2 Scores for organizational culture survey sections

1	People I work with are direct and honest with each other	2.6
2	People I work with accept criticism without becoming defensive	2.8
3	People I work with resolve disagreements cooperatively	3.2
4	People I work with function as a team	3.6
5	People I work with are cooperative and considerate	3.4
6	People I work with constructively confront problems	3.3
7	People I work with are good listeners	3.2
8	People I work with are concerned about each other	3.3
	'Teamwork' mean	**3.2**
9	Staff and management have a good working relationship	3.0
10	This organization motivates me to put out my very best efforts	2.9
11	This organization respects its workers	2.5
12	This organization treats people in a consistent and fair manner	2.5
13	Working here feels like being part of a family	2.7
14	There is an atmosphere of trust in this organization	2.7
15	This organization motivates people to be efficient and productive	2.5
	'Morale' mean	**2.7**
16	I get enough information to understand the big picture here	2.6
17	When changes are made the reasons why are made clear	2.3
18	I know what's happening in sections/units/departments outside my own	2.2
19	I get the information I need to do my job well	2.7
	'Information flow' mean	**2.5**
20	I have a say in decisions that affect my work	2.3
21	I am asked to make suggestions about how to do my job	2.3
22	This organization values the ideas of workers at my level	2.3
23	My opinions count in this organization	2.1
	'Involvement' mean	**2.3**
24	Job requirements are made clear by my supervisor	3.1
25	When I do a good job my supervisor tells me	2.9
26	My supervisor takes criticism well	2.9
27	My supervisor delegates responsibility	3.5
28	My supervisor is approachable	3.7
29	My supervisor gives me criticism in a positive manner	3.5
30	My supervisor is a good listener	3.5
31	My supervisor tells me how I'm doing	3.0
	'Supervision' mean	**3.3**
32	Decisions made at meetings/briefings get put into action	2.8
33	Everyone takes part in discussions at meetings/briefings	2.6
34	Our discussions in meetings/briefings stay on track	2.6
35	Time in meetings/briefings is well spent	2.7
36	Meetings/briefings tap the creative potential of the people present	2.6
	'Meetings' mean	**2.7**
	Overall mean total	**2.8**

Scoring key: 1 = very little extent; 2 = little extent; 3 = some extent; 4 = great extent; 5 = very great extent.

effective communication was even more important since this particular police body was facing major structural and corporate changes, leading to high levels of staff uncertainty. In such a context, effective communication from management is paramount. This audit provided the organization with valuable and valid data relating to its effectiveness in this area. The use of interviews as an initial step in the audit process allowed for identification of the main issues and factors affecting organizational communication. The interview findings also assisted in the design of questions for the next part of the audit, enabling a more bespoke ICA questionnaire to be developed for the organization.

The triangulation approach used, combining two questionnaires with in-depth interviews, provided validity for the findings, as the same problems emerged from each part of the audit. Furthermore, the fact that these issues recurred over the three different sub-divisions audited, strongly indicates that they were likely to be representative of the organization as a whole.

The audit revealed that, in particular, the perceptions of staff below the level of senior management (superintendent) reflected a position of being less than 'somewhat satisfied' with communication. The problems associated with communications with senior managers and specialist departments, specifically CID, were especially acute. Officers also expressed a wish for greater openness and directness. There was a thirst for more information than currently received about what was happening in the organization. The preferred medium for this was face-to-face contact, a channel also felt to be under-utilized, rather than the more widely used and 'bureaucratic' written communications. These results confirm previous findings from research in other police organizations in terms of gaps between management and street cops, and between the CID and uniform personnel. This commonality of gaps over a period of time reflects a possible systemic resistance to change by the police profession and a need for communication strategies that incorporate continuous evaluation.

However, despite the overall finding of general dissatisfaction, some positive aspects emerged from this audit. There was a much more positive view of communications at section or unit level. In particular officers were happy with their immediate line managers. Indeed, satisfaction levels for communication with supervisors were higher than those for colleagues. This is important, as first line supervisors are in many ways a touchstone for effective organizational relationships. For example, problems between employees and immediate managers are related to stated intentions to leave the organization (Hargie, 2007).

The results for each of the three individual parts of the audit were fed back to the operational manager (superintendent) of each particular sub-division. In addition, the overall findings were made available to the senior management team of the organization itself. In this way, the audit could inform the ongoing process of evaluation and change within this police body. Organizational change is always complex and difficult, requiring effort, expertise, and time (Dawson, 2004). As noted earlier, the quasi-military nature of police bodies also creates a culture of attachment to established structures and rituals, replete with rules and regulations and definitive line management. This makes change very difficult indeed. For an organization as old as the police, there is a natural tendency to treat established procedures and processes with reverence. The fact that police organizations have not been good at moving away from the pyramid type structure and 'management by edict', reflects the problems facing those who may want to change to a more open style of management (Lumb and Breazeale, 2002).

For change to occur, and be successful, accurate information is required at all stages of the change process, and that is where the audit is especially useful. The results of this particular audit provided comprehensive and detailed information about a wide range of positive and negative issues surrounding communication across all levels of the three sub-divisions audited. In this way, it helped to chart the topography of this particular organization and provided valuable data for the managers responsible for its operation.

Chapter 18

Auditing a major retail chain

Judy H. Gray and Heather M. Laidlaw

INTRODUCTION

Key changes in the retail sector have led to the restructuring of labour arrangements in retail organizations. Supermarkets rely heavily on part-time employees (who work under 35 hours per week) to work the 'unsocial' hours at stores, which in some cases are open 24 hours a day, 7 days per week. While these staffing arrangements have provided companies with functional, numerical, and financial flexibility, the impact on internal organizational communication has often been overlooked.

This chapter describes a communication audit that was conducted in a major Australian retail organization. The audit was part of a broader study that investigated the relationship between communication satisfaction of employees and their commitment to the organization. The brief was to gain an understanding of the complexities of organizational communication at the store level so that changes could be made to improve the informational and interpersonal aspects of communication.

Traditionally, employees engaged in work arrangements other than full time tended to hold unimportant jobs that had little impact on organizational success. However, this has changed in such a way that even supervisory and managerial positions, which were formerly considered only suitable for full-time employees, are often held on a part-time basis (Delsen, 1998). In retail organizations, part-time workers tend to perform the same work tasks and hold the same responsibilities as full-time workers (Stamper and Van Dyne, 2003). Success in retail organizations is highly dependent on providing high quality customer service delivered by front-line staff, many of whom are employed on a part-time basis.

In the absence of any internationally accepted definition of part-time work, two approaches are evident in classifying workers in terms of their full-time or part-time status. The first is based on the number of hours worked, where full-time workers usually work 35 hours or more per week, while the second approach classifies workers according to their self-assessment. In order to be consistent with the methods used by the Australian Bureau of

Statistics in gathering census data, both criteria were used in the current study. Around 61% of employees in the Australian retail sector are employed on a part-time basis (Australian Bureau of Statistics, 2007).

Part-time workers can experience quite different working conditions from full-time workers. For example, they may miss out on critical information-sharing events during their scheduled time off work (McComb *et al.*, 2003). A study conducted by Sherer and Coakley (1999) in the US of employees who moved from full-time to part-time employment reported that part-time workers felt isolated and outside the mainstream of information dispersion. Thus part-time workers may be at a disadvantage compared to full-time workers through being less involved in communication networks. Consequently, the present audit aimed to investigate employee perceptions of organizational communication based on the premise that favourable organizational outcomes depend on all employees being actively engaged in effective organizational communication systems.

THE AUDIT

The retail organization involved in this audit has a total of over 10,000 store-level staff in more than 70 supermarkets within the metropolitan area of Melbourne, Australia. Conducting a census of all store staff would have been very time-consuming and expensive, and so the organization supported the alternative of a preliminary audit study based on cluster sampling of stores within a geographical sub-region. A sample of 10 stores within the south-eastern area of Melbourne was selected according to accessibility and the degree of cooperation. Management at seven of those stores gave permission for questionnaires to be distributed to all of their staff over the age of 18 years. While 539 questionnaires were supplied, 118 were returned undistributed. A total of 127 useable responses was received (30% response rate).

Given the geographical spread, a survey was considered the most efficient way of gathering data at a number of sites. The Communication Satisfaction Questionnaire (Downs and Hazen, 1977) was used to investigate employee perceptions of their satisfaction with various aspects of communication in the workplace. In addition, several open-ended questions were included in the survey. The questions were generated by conducting informal interviews with employees from the organization who worked at stores other than those being surveyed. The interviews provided an insight into what the employees considered to be the main issues central to communication. Their responses were used to develop the open-ended questions that were then pre-tested and modified to improve clarity. The final questions were:

- Overall, how satisfied are you with communication at work?
- What suggestions do you have to improve communication at work?

Most respondents (n = 103: 81%) provided comments in response to these open-ended questions.

The survey also asked respondents to indicate their gender, age, education, employment status (full time, part time), length of service in the organization, and current position. Respondents' positions were classified according to 'manager', 'supervisor' and 'operative'. 'Manager' included store managers and department managers, 'supervisor' included any other respondent who was in a supervisory position such as management trainees and shift supervisors, and 'operative' included any non-supervisory position.

Participants were assured of anonymity, confidentiality and that their participation was completely voluntary to protect them from possible discomfort or embarrassment. This was confirmed in the cover letter to participants, which was short and written in a straightforward manner. University letterhead was used to give the study credibility and importance and to indicate independence from the company being surveyed. In addition, respondents were given the option of returning their surveys either to a box at their workplace or by using a reply-paid envelope provided to post the survey back to the researchers at the university.

The audit instrument

The Communication Satisfaction Questionnaire (CSQ) (Downs and Hazen, 1977) is a 40-item instrument with a reported overall reliability of .94 (Greenbaum *et al.*, 1988). It rates communication satisfaction using a 7-point Likert scale ranging from 1 = very dissatisfied to 7 = very satisfied. The aspects of communication investigated were:

1   *Horizontal communication*: the extent to which communication with co-workers and informal communication is accurate and free flowing and includes perceptions of the grapevine.
2   *Subordinate communication*: the communication by managers with their subordinates (only managers and supervisors responded to these items).
3   *Media quality*: the extent to which meetings are well organized and written directives are short and clear.
4   *Organizational perspective*: information about the organization as a whole including notifications about changes, overall policies and goals of the organization.
5   *Organizational integration*: the degree to which individuals receive information about their immediate work environment.
6   *Communication climate*: the extent to which communication motivates and stimulates workers to meet organizational goals.
7   *Personal feedback*: information concerning how workers are being judged and how their performance is appraised.

8   *Supervisory communication*: the upward and downward aspects of communicating with superiors.

Pretesting the survey

Pretesting of the questionnaire to check for readability and to create a more meaningful survey was conducted by administering the complete survey to employees in retail organizations other than the participating one. The results suggested that respondents had some difficulty in understanding several of the questions of the CSQ. For example, they suggested that the item: 'extent to which I do not have information overload' was difficult to understand. The wording was confusing and open to misinterpretation, and the item was subsequently omitted. Other changes to the wording of several items were made to improve comprehension. For example, the term 'subordinate' was replaced with 'people I supervise'. Care was taken not to change the meaning of the items.

The sample

The sample was almost identical to the organization's population distribution of 52% males and 48% females. Over half (54%) were aged between 20 and 29 years of age. Department managers represented 29% of respondents, 21% were supervisors, and 50% were operatives. While 45% worked full time (compared to 24% of the company's retail staff), 55% worked part time (compared to 76% of the company's retail staff). Consequently, there was an over-representation of full-time workers in the sample, and therefore an under-representation of part-time workers.

In terms of length of service to the organization, 25% of full-time and 17% of part-time workers had worked for less than 1 year, 31% of full-time and 51% of part-time workers for between 1 and 5 years, while 44% of full-time and 32% of part-time workers had worked for the company for at least 5 years. Around half the sample (52%) were studying at post-secondary level, while nearly one quarter (22%) had not completed secondary school, and over one quarter had completed secondary school only (26%). A high proportion of part-time workers (70%) were undertaking or had completed post-secondary education compared to 32% of full-time workers.

In summary, older respondents had been with the company longer and tended to hold higher positions in the organization, while lower positions were held by part-time workers, which is typical in the industry. However, younger respondents on average were better educated than older respondents and part-time workers were better educated than full-time workers. Typically, the young, better educated part-time respondents were students who were prepared to work short, split-shifts, and unsociable hours over the short term prior to pursuing other careers.

RESULTS

Overall communication satisfaction

Table 18.1 presents the mean communication satisfaction scores for the eight factors and compares the mean scores for full-time and part-time respondents. In summary:

* The mean scores varied from the lowest of 3.53 to the highest of 4.78 on a scale of 1 to 7. These results indicate that the mean scores were clustered around the middle of the scale (4) indicating that, overall, respondents were neither satisfied nor dissatisfied with communication.
* The highest levels of satisfaction were reported for *supervisory communication*, concerning communication with superiors (mean = 4.78), *subordinate communication*, concerning managerial communication with subordinates (4.73), and for *horizontal communication*, concerning the extent to which informal communication was accurate and free flowing (4.53). These results suggest that the interpersonal relationship aspects of communication were the source of slightly higher levels of satisfaction than the informational aspects relating to the amount and quality of organizational communication. Only respondents at managerial level (*n* = 63) responded to items concerning *subordinate communication*. As the items relate to communication initiated by managers, the results may be inflated through managers wanting to create an impression that their communication with subordinates is satisfactory. Items from the instrument indicate that for respondents to be more satisfied with interpersonal communication, supervisors would need to listen, pay more attention to

Table 18.1 Mean communication satisfaction factors by work arrangement (N = 127)

Communication satisfaction factors	Mean (N = 127)	Mean full time (n = 57)	Mean part time (n = 70)	Mean diff.	t
Horizontal communication[a]	4.53	4.74	4.35	0.39	1.74
Subordinate communication[a,b]	4.73	5.46	4.01	1.45	4.09**
Media quality[a]	3.89	4.17	3.65	0.52	2.10*
Organizational perspective[a]	4.12	4.63	3.69	0.94	3.74**
Organizational integration[a]	4.40	4.62	4.23	0.39	1.63
Communication climate[a]	3.68	4.01	3.41	0.60	2.14*
Personal feedback[a]	3.53	3.80	3.32	0.48	1.74
Supervisory communication[a]	4.78	5.12	4.50	0.62	2.18*

Notes:
a 1 = Very dissatisfied, 2 = Dissatisfied, 3 = Slightly dissatisfied, 4 = Neutral, 5 = Slightly satisfied, 6 = Satisfied, 7 = Very satisfied.
b Only managers and supervisors (n = 63, full time = 41, part time = 22) responded to these items.
* $p = < .05$; **$p = < .001$

workers and provide more guidance for solving job-related problems. Higher levels of satisfaction with informal communication would depend on respondents perceiving communication with other workers as accurate and free flowing which also relates to how compatible they are with other members of the work group.

- The aspects rated least satisfying, with mean scores classified as 'slightly dissatisfied', were *personal feedback*, concerning the workers' need to know how they were being judged and how their performance was being appraised (3.53) and *communication climate*, concerning communication which motivates workers to meet organizational goals (3.68). The results for *personal feedback* are in contrast to the relatively high satisfaction that respondents reported with other interpersonal aspects of communication, namely *supervisory* and *horizontal communication*. Yet supervisors and, to a lesser extent workers at the same level, are the people involved in providing feedback. Consequently, the results highlight particular aspects of interpersonal communication which are the source of dissatisfaction (i.e. feedback). To improve satisfaction with *personal feedback* would require supervisors to communicate clearly that they understood the problems faced by workers and for supervisors to provide constructive and timely feedback on subordinate performance.

Work arrangement and communication satisfaction

Further analysis of the data was conducted using *t*-tests to determine if there were significant differences between the means for full-time compared to part-time respondents for each communication satisfaction factor. Table 18.1 indicates that there were significant differences between full-time and part-time workers for *media quality* concerning the extent to which meetings are well organized and written directives are short and clear, and the degree to which the amount of communication is about right ($t = 2.10, p < .05$); *organizational perspective* concerning information about the organization as a whole including notifications about changes, policies and goals of the organization ($t = 3.74, p < .001$); *communication climate* ($t = 2.14, p < .05$); and *supervisory communication* ($t = 2.18, p < .05$). For each of these factors, part-time workers recorded significantly lower levels of communication satisfaction than full-time workers. All four factors predominantly focus on the level of satisfaction with the content and flow of information within the organization. The results therefore indicate that part-time workers were less satisfied with the information they received than full-time workers.

The lower scores for part-time workers for *organizational perspective* are consistent with the results from a study conducted by Markey *et al.* (2002). This examined Australian workplaces with a significant degree of part-time employment (over 26% of the total workforce). In these organizations, there was a greater incidence of top-down forms of communication and a reduced likelihood of workers being informed about issues of concern to them compared to other organizations. Similarly, another study of management and part-time staff found that communication deficiencies (in particular, a lack of information sharing and limited opportunities for training) were considered the major disadvantages of working part time (Skinner, 1999). The lack of information may contribute to the sense of isolation that often accompanies part-time work status, as identified by Sherer and Coakley (1999).

The lower mean scores for part-time workers for *organizational climate* suggest that they were not as motivated as full-time workers to meet organizational goals. Again, this is consistent with other research. According to Stamper and Van Dyne (2003), part-time workers accrue fewer benefits than full-time workers and therefore have fewer reasons to perform tasks that require extra effort beyond what is required to perform their job. In addition, part-timers may want to keep their involvement in work to a minimum so that they have time for other activities and responsibilities.

Gender and communication satisfaction

There were no significant differences for mean scores between males and females for any of the communication satisfaction factors ($t = 0.01$, $p > .05$). There is little or no theoretical grounding to suggest that levels of communication satisfaction would vary significantly according to gender.

Age and communication satisfaction

Analysis of variance was calculated to see if there were significant differences among mean scores where respondents were classified in more than two groups. Younger workers aged 21–29 years were less satisfied than older workers aged 30–39 years with *organizational integration* ($F = 4.61$, $p < .001$), *communication climate* ($F = 2.80$, $p < .05$), *personal feedback* ($F = 5.15$, $p < .001$), and *supervisory communication* ($F = 3.76$, $p < .01$). Older workers had generally been employed in the organization longer so they may have been more aware of what was expected of them. According to Akkirman and Harris (2005), more mature workers are likely to be more comfortable with the process aspects of communication and therefore are likely to be more satisfied with the communication climate and organizational integration aspects than younger employees.

Education and communication satisfaction

Table 18.2 indicates that more highly educated respondents ($n = 62$) were significantly less satisfied with all aspects of communication satisfaction than respondents who had not undertaken post-secondary education. Most of the workers undertaking or who had completed post-secondary education worked

Table 18.2 Mean communication satisfaction factors by education (N = 120)

Communication satisfaction factors	Education			F	Sig. diff. groups
	Secondary not completed (1) (n = 28)	Secondary completed (2) (n = 30)	Post secondary undertaking or completed (3) (n = 62)		
Horizontal communication[a]	4.97	4.73	4.29	3.78*	1–3
Media quality[a]	4.74	4.53	3.51	10.56***	1–3
					1–2
Organizational perspective[a]	4.66	4.47	3.78	6.47**	1–3
					1–2
Organizational integration[a]	4.51	4.71	4.04	3.55*	2–3
Communication climate[a]	4.44	4.32	3.22	9.62***	1–3
					2–3
Personal feedback[a]	4.11	4.07	3.23	5.39**	1–3
					2–3
Supervisory communication[a]	5.13	5.23	4.41	4.70*	2–3

Notes:
a 1 = Very dissatisfied, 2 = Dissatisfied, 3 = Slightly dissatisfied, 4 = Neutral, 5 = Slightly satisfied,
   6 = Satisfied, 7 = Very satisfied.
* $p = < .05$;
** $p = < .01$;
*** $p = < .001$
Subordinate communication has been omitted. Only managers and supervisors (n = 63) responded to
these items.

part time (75%). Educated respondents may have had higher expectations to
be kept informed and to be engaged in effective work relations. On the other
hand, they may simply have been more willing to express their dissatisfaction
with aspects of communication given that, for most of them, working in retail
did not represent a long-term career commitment and so they were free to
express their ideas without fear of jeopardizing their position.

Position and communication satisfaction

Table 18.3 compares the mean scores for communication satisfaction according to the three position levels in the organization (manager, supervisor, and
operative). Managers had the highest mean scores for *horizontal communication* (4.77), which differed significantly from the mean for supervisors (4.01, *F*
= 3.12, *p* < .05). Managers also had the highest mean scores for *organizational
integration* (4.71), which differed significantly from the mean for operatives
(4.05, *F* = 3.05, *p* < .05). The results indicate that managers were more satisfied with communication concerning their immediate work environment than
operatives. This may indicate that managers received more information
regarding their work environment, and that their job role was clearer than for
operatives.

Table 18.3 Mean communication satisfaction factors by position (*N* = 121)

Communication satisfaction factors	Position			*F*	*Sig. diff.* groups
	Manager (1) (n = 35)	*Supervisor* (2) (n = 25)	*Operative* (3) (n = 61)		
Horizontal communication[a]	4.77	4.01	4.61	3.12*	1–2
Subordinate communication[a,b]	5.21	4.64	–	2.33	
Media quality[a]	4.32	3.74	3.96	1.28	
Organizational perspective[a]	4.51	3.97	3.98	2.20	
Organizational integration[a]	4.71	4.31	4.05	3.05*	1–3
Communication climate[a]	3.99	3.64	3.68	0.56	
Personal feedback[a]	3.86	3.55	3.50	0.68	
Supervisory communication[a]	5.02	4.49	4.72	1.04	

Notes:
a 1 = Very dissatisfied, 2 = Dissatisfied, 3 = Slightly dissatisfied, 4 = Neutral, 5 = Slightly satisfied, 6 = Satisfied, 7 = Very satisfied.
b Only managers and supervisors responded to these items.
* $p = < .05$

Communication satisfaction comments

Comments were classified according to the communication satisfaction factors discussed previously and provided further insight into respondents' perceptions of various aspects of communication.

(1) *Horizontal communication* included the following key words and phrases: *gossip, the grapevine, hearing things second hand, casual communication,* and *hearsay.* There were a total of nine comments (seven by part-time respondents), including:

> The grapevine runs rife as it's the major communication tool.
> (Male, full-time department manager)

> You always hear things second hand, but then again I'm not actively seeking communication. I'll do my job and that's it.
> (Male, part-time department manager)

Many of the comments provided evidence that workers depended on communication with peers for information. Such informal channels of communication often fill the gaps that formal communication fails to address. Thus, the reliance on informal channels may indicate that workers were not obtaining sufficient information through formal channels to satisfy their communication needs.

(2) *Subordinate communication* included: *not feeling intimidated to approach management, a good listener, encourage teamwork,* and *receptive to workers' needs.* There were a total of seven comments (five by part-time respondents) in this category including:

> It seems a lot of information is forced down the ranks but not much goes back up.
>
> (Male, full-time department manager)

The comments included in this category were made by workers in managerial and supervisory positions and generally reflect an awareness of the need for open communication with subordinates. However, several, particularly part-time, respondents expressed frustration concerning the volume of directives coming from higher up the hierarchy and recognized the lack of upward communication. The comments suggest that while full-time managers and supervisors were under pressure to undertake their duties, part-time managers and supervisors were under even greater pressure to cope with the same duties but within a reduced timeframe.

(3) *Media quality* included: *more written instructions, more meetings, too much paperwork,* and *communication varies from too much to none at all.* There were a total of 42 comments (31 by part-time respondents) in this category including:

> Memos are left around like litter and nobody takes any notice of team talks.
>
> (Male, part-time customer service assistant)

Many respondents identified aspects of communication that could be improved, by providing a range of channels to inform all staff. In terms of the adequacy and availability of communication, comments ranged from *none at all* to *information overload.*

Almost half of the respondents who made comments did so about aspects that were classified in the *media quality* category. Given that almost all the comments were negative (just a few respondents provided constructive suggestions), it seems that these aspects could provide a starting point for introducing strategies to improve the informational aspects in the communication process. The high proportion of comments made by part-time workers suggested that they were particularly frustrated by these aspects.

(4) *Organizational perspective* included: *outside* [the store] *'experts' are not really able to offer practical advice, bigwigs from State Office* [are] *not helpful,* and *the company puts profits before its workers.* There were a total of nine comments (two by part-time workers) in this category including:

Communication should work down the company hierarchy. At this store it stops at management and the people it concerns are not made aware of changes.

(Male, part-time operative employee)

Most of the comments here were made by respondents who were managers and probably had more contact with the organization outside the actual store compared to operative staff. The comments suggested that specific strategies needed to be implemented if organization-wide messages concerning policies and changes were to reach all staff.

(5) *Organizational integration* included: *orders, leave instructions for part-timers too, communication is too late, part-timers miss out on team talks and new procedure memos*, and *put notices near clock-on/off point*. There were a total of 12 comments (10 by part-time respondents) in this category including:

[We need a] newsletter every week or two distributed with pay cheques to update prices, practices, new products.

(Female, part-time operative employee)

The comments suggested that respondents were identifying a lack of adequate and timely information. The comments here support existing evidence to show that this could have a negative impact on workers being able to make sense of their work environments and roles (Anderson and Martin, 1995; Rod *et al.*, 2008).

(6) *Communication climate* included: *any communication would be helpful*. There were a total of three comments (two by part-time respondents) in this category including:

I feel the company does not provide any incentives for good work performance, leaving staff lacking in motivation and decreasing the overall performance.

(Female, part-time operative employee)

The comments highlighted an important aspect of communication satisfaction identified by Argenti (1998): that where employees are well informed, they are more likely to be motivated to do a better job, to advance in their positions, and to further the goals of the organization itself.

(7) *Personal feedback* included: *positive and negative feedback, praise, recognition, congratulations, tell staff how they are going, notice extra effort*, and *constructive comments*. There were a total of 13 comments (six by part-time respondents) in this category including:

The only communication is about poor performance and threats of getting the sack.

(Female, part-time service assistant)

If people noticed the work and extra effort we put into the company and gave positive feedback [it] would make me more satisfied with communication.

(Male, full-time operative employee)

The responses suggested that workers wanted recognition and information about their performance. This is scarcely surprising, and is consistent with other research. Thus the importance of staff recognition has been demonstrated in a study of labour turnover in the retail industry where lack of recognition was considered a major driver of staff turnover among part-time staff (Hendrie, 2004).

(8) *Supervisory communication* included: *speaking to employees as adults, pressure from state managers, management should listen, managers are reserved, approachable supervisors, one-way communication, receptive to workers' needs, provide a means to communicate with managers directly*, and *requests are not heard*. There were a total of 37 comments (22 by part-time respondents) in this category including:

Communication is scarce and when problems arise that I give suggestions for or ask assistance with, I feel my comments are largely ignored.

(Female, part-time operative employee)

In such a large bureaucracy our concerns are often voiced but little is done about remedying problems.

(Female, full-time operative employee)

The comments suggested that respondents expected that the communication they provided to their supervisors should not only be listened to, but also acted on. The findings demonstrate how a lack of supervisor receptivity and responsiveness to subordinate communication may reduce employee communication satisfaction. Again, this empirical finding is consistent with other research. For example, the importance of communication as a two-way process was also demonstrated in a study by Hendrie (2004) where 'not being listened to' was given as one of the top reasons for part-time staff leaving a retail organization.

Overall, most comments were critical of the organization. This may have been expected, given that respondents were asked to provide suggestions concerning how to improve communication. However, both full-time and part-time respondents appeared to take the opportunity to raise a wide range of issues that were openly critical of existing management practices and the lack of satisfaction was clearly evident for both groups. At the same time, many of the comments provided practical suggestions that, if implemented, would at least demonstrate management's commitment to listen and respond to suggestions for improvements.

Responses to the open questions provided additional insights that augmented the quantitative data. For example, the comments concerning *personal feedback* elucidated the lack of satisfaction with this aspect of interpersonal communication. Providing feedback gives supervisors the opportunity to engage in empathic communication that involves sharing feelings, and giving praise and criticism. A study by Mayfield and Mayfield (2006) concluded that leader motivating language was positively related to job satisfaction for both full-time and part-time workers. In addition, motivating language was positively related to worker performance but for full-time workers only. These conclusions have implications for the current study. It follows that developing strategies to improve the quality and timeliness of feedback given by managers and supervisors could improve interpersonal communication satisfaction for full-time and part-time workers. However, additional strategies to provide clear information about the immediate work environment need to be devised and implemented to improve part-time worker performance.

Communication satisfaction and customer service

The low levels of communication satisfaction for respondents in the current study, particularly for part-time workers, may have consequences in terms of employee communication with customers. Communication satisfaction contributes to overall job satisfaction (Trombetta and Rogers, 1998), which in turn enhances employee loyalty and teamwork (Sharbrough *et al.*, 2006) and has been closely aligned with customer satisfaction in service organizations (McComb *et al.*, 2003). Consequently, taking action to improve employee communication satisfaction could have a positive effect on customer communication satisfaction.

THE FINAL REPORT

The final report to the Human Resource Management division of the company emphasized the following:

- Part-time workers appeared to be at risk of being marginalized in terms of formal communication processes.
- Supervisors needed to be aware that part-time workers may be missing out on important information. Strategies to ensure that information is

received by part-time workers needed to be devised and implemented so that all workers were included in the communication loop.

- Better educated workers were generally more dissatisfied with communication. To retain educated staff and gain their cooperation and contribution, the company needed to focus on improving all aspects of informational and interpersonal communication at every level.

- In designing programmes and strategies to improve communication, the company should draw on the many practical suggestions of store-level staff.

- Supervisors needed to understand the importance of giving personal feedback to full-time and part-time staff and should undertake training to develop skills in the use of motivating language (see Sharbrough et al., 2006).

- Improving levels of communication satisfaction could to lead to overall improvements in job satisfaction, staff morale, organizational commitment, and customer service and reduce staff turnover.

CONCLUSION

This audit of communication satisfaction in a retail organization was designed to chart any shortcomings in the communication process at store level so that improvements could be identified. The CSQ instrument was a valuable tool for identifying particular deficiencies in the internal communication process. Data gathered using this instrument, together with the comments provided by respondents to open questions, produced a rich bank of information to develop an effective information-sharing system in the company. Although the results are limited by the company-specific nature of the sample, other large organizations in the retail and service industries, particularly those with a high proportion of part-time staff, could benefit from taking note of the findings in this audit.

It was anticipated that effective implementation of the recommendations from the audit would assist management in improving communication at the store level and, in particular, would demonstrate management commitment to all staff, including part-time workers. In other words, the audit provided an opportunity for management to demonstrate that they were willing to respond to upward communication. The report was submitted to the Human Resource Management division as requested, to be disseminated to staff at stores. The research contract meant that the researchers were not permitted to report the results to staff at store level or to have an ongoing role in monitoring the implementation of recommendations. As a result, the extent to which the recommendations were implemented is unclear. Nevertheless, the audit as described in this chapter illustrates how communication can be measured and monitored in the retail sector, and highlights the benefits therein for the corporation.

Chapter 19

A case of making sense of organizational communication

Colleen E. Mills

INTRODUCTION

Communication is the lifeblood of the organization, the fundamental way by which organizing occurs (Albrecht and Bach, 1997; Cooren *et al.*, 2006). A day in the life of an organization contains literally thousands of communication events, each building on previous ones and setting the stage for future ones. Communication is so intrinsic to organizational life that some would say that these events provide much more than the means for organizing. They actually build, maintain, and activate the intentional and unintentional dimensions of the organization (Weick, 2001).

The centrality of communication to organizational experience is revealed when stakeholders such as employees, company directors, customers and suppliers describe an organization and how it operates. No matter what the organization makes or does, stakeholders invariably end up describing an organization's communication, or more precisely, the sense they make of this communication, when they refer to *the* organization. We can test this by asking a few people to describe the organizations they work for and then account for these descriptions. What is particularly interesting is that when we ask people employed by the same organization we encounter a combination of convergent and divergent ideas. Even people who work alongside each other doing the same task, such as sorting produce as it passes on a conveyor belt in a food processing factory or answering telephone calls in a call centre, provide inconsistent descriptions of their organization and its communication. Although an inevitable consequence of the vagaries of human perception, this finding warrants further consideration. This is because these somewhat incongruent descriptions signal different understandings and these understandings inform people's work-related decisions and subsequent actions. If managers can audit these meanings effectively they can take action to increase the alignment of meaning both between employees and between employees and the company (i.e. its aims, goals and policies). In other words, they can operate as data-driven strategic sensegivers. The power of sensegiving in organizations is well illustrated in Gioia and Chittipeddi's (1991) study, which shows how a new leader's sensegiving communication initiated and then facilitated the achievement of organizational change in a university, and in Maitlis and Lawrence's (2007) exploration of the mechanics of sensegiving.

These sensegiving studies are a tiny corner of an extensive literature that includes studies of sensemaking in such varied organizations as tertiary education institutions (Brown and Humphreys, 2003; Gioia and Thomas, 1996; Eisenberg et al., 1998), a food processing factory (Mills, 2000), a telecommunications company (Bean and Eisenberg, 2006), a clothing company (Rouleau, 2005), an engineering and consulting group (Pikka-Maaria and Vaara, 2007), an oil company (Stensaker and Falkenberg, 2007), and a hospital (Bartunek et al., 2006). The foci of sensemaking studies are equally varied, including such diverse topics as online financial information (Herrmann, 2007), sexual harassment (Dougherty and Smythe, 2004), the impact of flooding on the environment (Sellnow et al., 2002), school principal succession (Ogawa, 1991), ways of working (Bean and Hamilton, 2006), and university search processes (Eisenberg et al., 1998). This diversity no doubt reflects the observation that 'people can make sense of anything', which means there is an infinite range of objects of sensemaking for those who wish to study this phenomenon (Weick, 1995, p. 49).

Building on this extensive and diverse foundation, this chapter introduces the idea that a sensemaking approach can be used to audit organizational communication. It then presents the findings from a study of sensemaking about communication during an organizational change process that shows what can be learnt from using such an approach.

A SENSEMAKING APPROACH

The task of the sensemaker is to make his or her experiences into an intelligent reality (Weick, 2001). The reality produced does not mirror some objective truth that exists independently of the sensemaker, however. Rather, from a sensemaking perspective, reality is contingent on what the sensemaker attends to, how they do this, what they choose to represent, and their representational tools. A sensemaking approach to investigating organizations does not assume that organizations and the people within them operate by accessing objective truths. Rather, it assumes that they operate on meanings that are judged to be sensible or plausible (Weick et al., 2005). These subjective truths or sensible rationalizations are what we call 'sense'. According to Weick (1995, p. 57):

> the strength of sensemaking as a perspective derives from the fact that it does not rely on accuracy and its model is not objective perception. Instead, sensemaking is about plausibility, pragmatics, coherence, reasonableness, creation, invention, and instrumentality.

It is about creating meanings that are defensible rather than 'getting it right' (Weick *et al.*, 2005, p. 415).

Weick (1995) describes the relative truths or sensible rationalizations produced by sensemaking as ongoing achievements. By doing so, he is referring to the way that sense is always being refined in the face of current circumstances, subsequent actions, and further information and so is inevitably situational and emerging. This, according to (Weick, 1995, p. 43), is because we are always in the middle of something and this 'something', which he describes as projects, changes constantly so the sense made will reflect this changing landscape. This accounts for the way our stories about past events change from one telling to the next. The sense we create each time we tell a story reflects the projects that we are engaged in at the time of telling the story. For instance, on one occasion, you might be depressed or angry because current projects are not going well, while on another occasion you might be upbeat and happy because projects are going well. Your story telling, and hence the sense expressed in your story, on each occasion, will reflect this project-related mood variance.

Weick (1995, pp. 17–62) details other properties of sensemaking in addition to being 'driven by plausibility rather than accuracy' and 'ongoing'. These include the suggestion that sensemaking is also grounded in identity construction, retrospective interpretations of past events, and enactive of sensible environments (i.e. we create what we can then make sense of), social (i.e. involves shared meanings, common language and social interaction), and focused on and by extracted cues (i.e. familiar structures that provide a simple focus around which sense is developed). These properties mean that when data are collected and analysed from a sensemaking perspective the researcher focuses on sensemakers' understandings of who they are, the organizational environment and its social processes, and the way in which stimuli are bracketed off from the stream of stimuli in which they are embedded, and retrospectively given meaning. When the stimuli are communication events and processes, a sensemaking approach provides an effective mechanism for auditing employees' subjective meanings about organizational communication and understanding the factors that shape them.

'Researchers taking a sensemaking approach study the idiosyncratic and intersubjectively created meanings that people attach to their experiences' (Allard-Poesi, 2005, p. 176). In line with this, the sensemaking approach used to produce the case study in this chapter required the researcher to collect subjects' explanations for the communication they observed or engaged in. This moved the research focus from describing organizational communication to understanding the meanings that communication generates, how these meanings are arrived at, and how they subsequently influence an individual's communication behaviour. To achieve this, the researcher asked questions like:

- 'Why do you think that happened?'
- 'How would you explain that?'
- 'Why do you think that?'
- 'What response did you have and how do you explain this response?'

A literature search reveals that many research approaches fall under the general rubric of a 'sensemaking approach'. These vary according to how the researcher believes sense is represented. Most prevalent are the cognitive approaches (e.g. Gioia and Thomas, 1996; Isabella, 1990; Weber and Manning, 2001), which assume sense lies in individuals' mental processes and 'the micro-logics and activities between people' (Allard-Poesi, 2005, p. 178). Those who have departed from this tradition include Helms-Mills (2003), who contends that context and activity need to be considered in order to understand the intersubjective nature of the sensemaking process. This idea is extended by Weber and Glynn (2006), who in their theoretical article suggest that the connections between sensemaking and institutional context have not been fully explored. They argue that instead of merely constraining sensemaking activity or being the product of sensemaking, the institution can be the 'feedstock for sensemaking' (p. 1655). They propose three mechanisms (priming, editing, and triggering) as means by which sensemaking can be 'fed' by the institution. By doing this, these three mechanisms introduce the organizational context into the sensemaking process.

The pre-eminent writer in the sensemaking field, Karl Weick (Weick, 1995, 2001, 2007; Weick *et al.*, 2005), offers limited guidance on how to research either the process or the outcome of sensemaking. He is first and foremost a theorist, who interprets and integrates the work of others and weaves these into a powerful theoretical tapestry. However, he does note that, 'People who study sensemaking pay a lot of attention to talk, discourse, and conversation' (Weick, 1995, p. 41), which is consistent with his description of sensemaking as a social process. Examples of sensemaking studies that involved the examination of talk, discourse and conversation include studies of how workers in a Norwegian company made sense of a change from traditional office work to nomadic work (Bean and Hamilton, 2006; Bean and Eisenberg, 2006) and Laine and Vaara's (2007) study of how employees in an northern European engineering and consulting group discursively constructed sense using contrasting strategy discourses.

Sensemaking does not occur in a vacuum. Rather, it always has an object – something that the sensemaker is endeavouring to make sense of. Making sense of something is contingent on the sensemaker's personal, organizational, and societal contexts and how these are brought to bear on the object's context. These are revealed in the sensemaker's accounts of their sense and how it is achieved. Various types of analyses are used to reveal the personal, organizational, and societal contexts. If the researcher is working from an interpretive perspective they will be seeking to understand them from the sensemaker's perspective and so will pay attention to the ways sensemakers express their sense and how it was arrived at. Data can be in the form of written text, graphic representations, oral accounts, stories, and discourses, as well as symbols and actions. Other parties will inevitably be involved in the sensemaking process, either directly as sensegivers and collaborators in collective sensemaking, or less obviously through their contributions to the development and maintenance of discourses and social processes. The researcher therefore needs to have a broad lens in order to capture the richness and complexity of the sensemaking event (Weick, 2007).

When the objects of sensemaking activity are specific communication events and practices, a sensemaking approach brings special challenges because of the complicated and often reflexive nature of the contingencies that apply to the social realm. This is most evident when we are looking at the sense people make of their own communication behaviour. They are both the observer and the observed. The challenge is to work out what to attend to in order to capture the nature and outcome of the sensemaking process. What are the contingencies that, when examined, produce sufficient insights to allow the sensemaker's experience to be understood?

Findings from the author's studies suggest that there are general categories of contingencies that apply to sensemaking about communication, regardless of the communication event or practice being made sense of. These include the issue climate, the social context, the communication environment, and the available interpretive discourses. When linked in terms of their relationship to the sense created by organizational actors, these categories give rise to a procedural model of sensemaking that provides a valuable basis for both auditing the communication environment and strategically planning communication practices in an organization (see Mills, 2005, 2006, for a fuller discussion of this model).

This chapter draws on a study of how employees in a New Zealand research company made sense of the change communication associated with a Chief Executive Officer (CEO) succession process. The study was in the first instance a study of sensemaking but by virtue of the object of the sensemaking – change communication – it produced a comprehensive audit of the organization's communication from the participants' perspectives. This chapter confines its attention to those findings that reveal:

- The nature of organizational communication during the change process.
- The values and beliefs employees revealed in their accounts of this communication.
- What was revealed about employees' experience of the organization's internal communication environment.

THE ORGANIZATION

The organization is a New Zealand research institution, governed by a Board of Directors drawn from both the public and private sectors. It is one of several similarly governed institutions that undertake research that is largely funded by the state. The employees, who are among the best in their respective fields, are very well educated, with many holding tertiary qualifications at Masters or PhD level. They include a range of scientists, technical and administrative support staff, and managers. These occupational distinctions are not always easy to apply to the company's employees, however, as some managers engage in research or have done so in the past and so identify themselves as both managers and scientists.

The range of research is extensive, addressing aspects of the natural environment and humankind's interaction with it. This general focus on the natural environment accounts for the company's prominence among those New Zealand organizations with a strong commitment to environmental protection and the sustainable management of natural resources. Employees express views that suggest their attitudes and values are strongly aligned with this commitment to the wellbeing of the natural environment.

The company's employees are distributed across a multi-site operation throughout both of New Zealand's two main islands. The size of sites ranges from the company's headquarters with several hundred employees to a sole charge operation in a remote part of the North Island.

The company is very technology savvy and this is reflected in its communication technology use. Most employees are able to communicate by intranet, internet, video-conference facilities, fax and telephone. These mechanisms provide the primary means by which the company achieves its goals of communication openness and accountability. Some employees undertake considerable travel to reach the sites of their field research and to engage in face-to-face meetings with other colleagues and external agencies. Some of this travel is seasonal because of the nature of the research.

An annual 'roadshow' is a company tradition. During this the CEO travels from site to site presenting his views of the past year's achievements and future activities, and engaging in discussions with staff. These face-to-face encounters are valued by staff and well attended. Often such events are reported or summarized on the intranet and may also be addressed on the Chief Operating Officer's (COO) regular electronic newsletter. It was at one of these roadshows that the CEO formally announced his decision to resign from his position.

The organizational structure at the time of the study was a complicated matrix arrangement formed by a combination of hierarchically arranged management sections (e.g. science management, human resources, facilities management, finance, informational and communication technology) and research project teams. As both management and research team members could be resident at any one of the nine sites and an employee could be involved in more than one project team at a time, the communication and reporting lines were complicated. Whether the employees recognized it or not, for most of those studied a large part of their work day was invested in communication activities.

When the study commenced the organization was led by its founding CEO, who established the company from the remnants of a government department. Many of the staff had been employees of this previous organization but new appointments and retirements over the company's 12-year existence had gradually diluted the links to the previous organization. Longstanding professional and friendship relationships dating back to the earlier organization were still common, however. This meant that some networks had members who shared a long history and were still influenced by expectations about communication rooted in the past.

THE SENSEMAKING APPROACH IN ACTION

While there is an established literature on CEO succession planning, and related organizational outcomes (see Giambatista *et al.*, 2005; Kesner and Sebora, 1994; Poulin *et al.*, 2007), only a few studies have addressed sensemaking during CEO succession (e.g. Friedman and Saul, 1991; Ogawa, 1991). This is despite CEO succession being one of the most common changes that organizations encounter. The present sensemaking study of CEO succession communication was therefore timely. It was longitudinal, spanning the period from the CEO's announcement of his intention to leave the organization to 3 months into the new CEO's tenure (just over 2 years). Its intention was to reveal how employees made sense of the communication associated with the succession process and to see how this compared to the model of sensemaking about communication that had emerged from the author's previous studies of sensemaking about communication during change (Mills, 2000, 2002, 2004, 2005, 2006).

Participants were drawn from across the organization from seven of the nine company sites and included science and non-science staff and managers from all levels of management. Participant selection was not random. A small initial sample, spanning the occupational classes and sites, was selected. Findings from the analysis of data from this initial group then guided the remainder of the sample selection, which was chosen to ensure all types of position and staff from different site sizes were included. This approach was taken as the author's previous studies had shown that position and site size in a company were significant factors in sensemaking behaviour.

In total 34 people were interviewed. Most were interviewed three times, first, in the period immediately after the CEO formally announced his intention to retire, second, after the announcement of his successor, and third, immediately after the successor commenced his employment with the company.

Data were collected using in-depth semi-structured interviews that lasted from 30 to 100 minutes. While a few of these were undertaken by telephone, the vast majority were conducted face to face. Participants were asked to reflect on the communication they had observed or engaged in that was related to the CEO succession process. They were asked to describe their interpretations of this succession-related communication and to then account for their interpretations. Questions sought to encourage participants to present their reasoning about communication rather than to merely describe the communication they experienced. Typical questions included:

- 'What did you make of that?'
- 'Why did you think that?'
- 'How do you explain your response?'

By answering such questions, participants disclosed more than the nature of their workplace communication. They revealed the sense they made of specific communication events and practices, the nature of their sensemaking process, and the way this shaped subsequent action.

The interviews were taped and then transcribed to allow the researcher to examine not only what was said about the organizational communication and the accounts given for it but the language used. This made literary and linguistic analyses possible and reflects the researcher's view that language is more than a neutral vehicle for conveying ideas. It is an integral part of the idea and so to understand the ideas people have about communication it is necessary to study how these ideas are expressed. Agar (1994, p. 89) expresses this notion well when he states, 'When people use words, they do more than just hammer out a sentence. Different words signal a different mentality, a different way of looking at things.' This has important effects on all aspects of organizational decision making. Thus it has been argued that people's mental words or the frames that underpin their sensemaking activities 'influence the way the world is perceived within the organization, as well as critical decisions with respect to perceived external and internal demands' (Basu and Palazzo, 2008, p. 129).

The data collected created a comprehensive database on the nature and sense made of both planned and unplanned succession-related communication. This communication included telephone calls, video and audio conferences, mail exchanges, intranet information and publications, and face-to-face public, group and dyadic communication. It was accounted for in terms of a complex array of personal and organizational dimensions, including personal style, personal priorities, position in the company, employment history, networks, types of science activity, funding processes, the communication climate, geographic location, the matrix structure, and the CEO's style. Woven into the accounts were concepts and conceptual tools that provided anchors for the sense expressed. Several of the latter will be described in this chapter.

THE PREVAILING COMMUNICATION ENVIRONMENT

While the company had some commercial research contracts, it relied heavily on research grants for its revenue. This meant that the preparation of funding applications and the reporting processes associated with managing these grants had a powerful effect on the organization's operations and shaped its internal and external communication. The funding process not only provided a focus for communication, it necessitated researchers accounting for time so that it could be charged to specific research projects. This generated both sensitivity to time demands and a very instrumental approach to the use of time that extended to those who provided technical and support services. The result was a time-pressured and pragmatic communication environment.

Participants attributed their high communication loads to various factors. One was the large number of senior managers. This was a consequence of the CEO's succession-planning strategy. He had established management positions to provide more staff with opportunities to develop managerial skills that would allow them to be considered for the CEO position. The perception was that more managers produced more communication.

The high communication load participants often reported was also attributed to the organization's practice of providing multiple sources for the same information. For instance, meetings would be held and then summaries of the business circulated by email or posted on the intranet. Participants reported not attending some events because they knew post-event summaries would be available. They also reported employing quite radical sorting heuristics at times to cope with high volumes of communication in order to limit its impact on their 'core business' of doing or supporting research. For instance, one scientist reported employing an email sorting heuristic. This involved attending to science-related emails first, then those emails demanding a response that would generate more email if a response wasn't immediately forthcoming, and leaving 'company' emails to the end of the day if there was time. Company emails loosely equated to those dealing with management matters and were the ones most likely to be skim read if read at all. CEO succession emails fell into this category. The categorization of emails was often made based on a combination of subject line and sender's identity.

The irony was that employees described the organization's communication environment as open and providing high information accessibility, yet these characteristics actually worked against the achievement of information accessibility by producing communication overload for many individuals. This led to the emergence of techniques such as the use of heuristics like the one described above to reduce the amount of information accessed and processed.

Another common sorting technique involved relying on a third party (e.g. a team leader) to indicate which messages needed attention. Some employees took this one step further and relied on a colleague or superior to engage in communication activities and then provide feedback on their sense of the event. The rationale for using this technique was couched in terms of impact, a central explanatory concept in the study. Where the communication event was assumed to have little potential to have a personal impact, a third party was likely to be used to make sense of the event.

THE CEO SUCCESSION COMMUNICATION

The succession communication included both formal and informal communication. Table 19.1 compares these two general forms of communication. Except for the informal use of personal networks, participants reported that the form of the succession communication was predictable, suggesting it was not atypical of the organization's communication about company-wide matters.

Table 19.1 Comparing formal and informal succession communication

Formal	Informal
Top down	Lateral, upwards and downwards
One way – informing, updating	*One way* – informing, updating
Two way – invited questions and comments	*Two way* – trading, comparing, joking, evaluating, speculating, hypothesizing, reassuring, collaborative interpretation
Used existing regularly used channels	Used both regularly used informal channels and less used networks
Mainly mediated	Mainly face to face but also mediated
Roadshow, visioning exercise, Chair of Selection Committee's email updates on process, video conference update and question opportunities, farewells, site 'meet and greet' sessions	Cafeteria conversations, email exchanges, casual 1-on-1 exchanges, April Fool's Day intranet article, fact-finding conversations, exchanging info from Google searches on new CEO

The CEO succession process involved three overlapping phases:

1 the departing CEO's disengagement phase
2 the announcement of the new CEO
3 the new CEO's engagement phase.

The participants' accounts of the communication across these phases revealed that while the sense made of the communication at each stage was in some respects individual, there was considerable 'common sense'. This common sense varied from phase to phase as summarized in Table 19.2. It is useful to examine each phase's communication in more detail.

Table 19.2 Sensemaking about succession communication across the three phases

Phase	(1) Pre-announcement	(2) Announcement	(3) Post-announcement
Communication climate	Cursory interest	Curiosity	Concern
Assessment	Can I have any impact/input? If not, then what evidence is there in this communication that the Board is acting appropriately?	What can I find out that I don't know?	How will this new CEO impact on me?
Focus of communication assessment	Agency and trust	Novelty	Personal impact
Level of engagement in succession-related communication	Low after visioning exercise	Sharp peak	High for those with high personal impact assessments
Main communication activities	Scanning	Collecting Comparing Speculating Predicting	Collecting Comparing Speculating Predicting, Interpreting CEO-related information
Expressed communication needs	Involvement and/or information	New information	Reassurance

The notion of impact, mentioned earlier, and its assessment, is a key dimension in the model of how people make sense of communication during change processes that is emerging from the series of sensemaking studies that the study described in this chapter is a part of. Participants in many studies report deciding which communication events they will attend to and their level of engagement in terms of potential impact assessments. The following comments from scientists at separate sites capture how impact, or in this case perceived lack of potential impact, was used to make sense of the lack of interest and participation in the succession communication:

> Yeah it's all happening out there as far as I'm concerned and because it's at levels that don't really impact on site staff too much then the only interest I have is basically just keep track in a very cursory way of what's actually happening within the company and who's going to fit into what slot and who ends up being impacted by the decision.

I guess you look at change and try and figure out how it's going to affect you or the people that you're responsible for or the outcomes that you're interested in. So if I had been in a lower you know, sort of a technician sort of role in which I was not responsible for any of the science or responsible for getting funding for myself or other people around me then I may have paid less attention to it [succession process] because there's nothing really that I could do. On the other hand if I had been in a role of responsibility for more people then I might have felt like that would influence those people for which I'm responsible for and therefore I would maybe try and have been more interested in the way in which the people were going to be affected.

An interesting finding in the study of a research company described here was that the assessment of potential impact included considerations of whether the sensemaker could have an impact on the change process (i.e. succession process). For example, the work of scientists in the company encouraged them to develop a sense of personal agency. The following comment from one of them captures how considerations of personal agency (i.e. the opportunity to have an impact on the succession process) influenced the level of attention (and sense) made of succession communication:

It's not a process that I see I can have any significant contribution to so I just feel it's not a great way to spend my time in terms of worrying about something I have little impact on.

Where participants judged they could not have an impact they reported taking less interest and relying on others to make sense of the succession communication and to alert them if there was something that was worthy of their attention. The following excerpt contains a technician's account of how she responded to emailed documents relating to the succession process. It illustrates how third parties were used to make sense of the succession process and its associated communication when the impact of the communication was judged to be low:

You know at some stage you're gonna talk to someone about it and get a feel for the process. You know looking at documents is more likely for me to be, when I'm talking to someone and they say, 'Oh do you know about this?' And so you go and refer to it but I don't think I – I don't think I've sat down and read any of them.

The following sections look at the form the organization's communication took across the three phases of the succession process. This is followed by summary of what this revealed about the organization.

THE DISENGAGEMENT PHASE

Comments made by the CEO over an extended period of time created an expectation among employees that he would soon announce his intention to relinquish leadership of the company. Therefore, participants reported little surprise when he formally announced the date of his intended departure from the company at a roadshow 18 months in advance of this date. The announcement was made sense of in terms of past communication, prevailing patterns of communication, and the expectations these generated. The following comment illustrates this:

> The CEO has been very open about his ambition to depart and he comes to our site once a year to give a road show presentation – the state of the company. I think it was as much as two years ago that he indicated that he would be leaving. So that's certainly been no surprise . . . I think it was quite nice that he stands up in front of you and tells you his plans. I mean the purpose of his road show is to give a much longer term outlook of the company so it seemed an appropriate venue to do it [announce intention to leave the company].

Lack of novelty in the message or the means by which it was delivered meant little energy or activity was expended making sense of the formal announcement. There was little surprise to trigger the quest for an explanation, one important condition for sensemaking (Weick, 1995). Many employees merely responded to the departure announcement by concluding that it was logical that the CEO should want to move on to pursue new challenges. After 12 years he was the longest serving CEO among similar research organizations in New Zealand. He had established the company and was attributed with having provided clear and clever leadership, which had secured a sound future for the company that employees identified strongly with. Employees accepted that he would want to move on, so the announcement was not treated as contentious or unfortunate. That it was given so far in advance of the event was seen to confirm his image as a strategic operator and planner. Thus his profile was used to interpret his behaviour.

The decision of a CEO to leave his or her post signals the beginning of a period where the governing body, in this case a Board of Directors, crosses the governance–management divide and becomes engaged in the management of the operational activities associated with CEO recruitment. In the case here, the Board had little operational visibility through the early stages of the disengagement phase because of the long lead-in time. Thus for many staff the disengagement period was experienced as 'business as usual'. They reported being much more concerned with the realities of funding applications and doing or supporting research activities than with the succession process. As a result, the CEO succession did not feature in their communication except for occasional informal conversations speculating about who might apply for the CEO position and what input employees might have once the recruitment process commenced. When asked to account for their lack of succession-related communication, participants reported that the process was not having any impact on them and that it did not appear that they would be able to have any impact on the process. Thus they reported just keeping a watchful eye on any announcements by the chairperson of the selection committee. The sensemaking behaviour centred first on assessing if they could have an input and, if this was judged to not to be an option, then finding evidence from the formal communication that the Board was conducting the succession process in an acceptable fashion.

As the disengagement phase progressed the Board became more active, communicating both formally with all staff through emails and occasional networked video and audio conferences, and informally with some staff in one-on-one conversations. Also during this time the Board engaged with the staff in a 50-year visioning exercise designed to establish a long-term vision of where the company was heading and what it sought to achieve. Many staff considered this communication process to be an integral part of the CEO's disengagement and a sign that he was working with the Board to ensure a clear framework was in place to guide and protect the company under the new leadership. It was treated as evidence that the Board was informed about both the internal stakeholders' activities and priorities, and the value of continuing on its current trajectory. It became an important reference point when participants accounted for their level of engagement with the succession process and its associated communication. This, plus an emailed reassurance from the chairman of the selection panel that radical change was not to be expected, meant that many employees reported only a cursory interest in the formal succession communication from the board. They considered life in the organization was unlikely to change radically once the new CEO was appointed.

Clearly, the sensemaking behaviour revolved around a concern about the possibility that the CEO change would bring change. This concern explained why some communication was attended to and other communication was not. It wasn't the only concern though. Employees also reported being concerned about the pressure of work, claiming they were too busy to pay much attention to the succession process. As a result, attendance at video/audio conference updates was not high and formal emails reporting on progress were often just scanned and deleted. However, occasionally something in these emails caught the reader's attention and provided the catalyst for informal comment during a tea break in the cafeteria or in a casual corridor conversation. One such instance was the announcement that the two short-listed candidates would be subjected to psychological testing. This generated discussion because it was considered novel by some as it seemed to be rather late in the succession process to be doing such testing. These three different concerns or issues (i.e. the possibility of change, workload, and novelty) determined what was bracketed off for attention from the stream of communication.

THE ANNOUNCEMENT PHASE

Not surprisingly, the attendance at the announcement video/audio link was the highest of all the video conference events. When asked to account for this, staff indicated that curiosity was their main motivator. They attributed the interest in this communication event to their expectation that they were going to hear information they did not know (i.e. something novel). They reported being curious to hear who their new CEO would be, wanting to find out if they knew the successful candidate, and wanting to establish if one of the rumoured applicants had been successful.

The announcement was made simultaneously across the company using video and audio links. It was made not from Head Office but from the north-ernmost office. Following the announcement, those who were participating were invited to ask questions. This was the most interactive of the formal communication events initiated by the Board. Staff generally welcomed the opportunity to hear the succession news in this way although some found the lack of information about the criteria used to select the new CEO disappoint-ing. They wanted to have the correspondence between the selection criteria and the person profile explicitly explained. They also wanted more informa-tion about the successful applicant. To this end, requests were made for more information and an email was subsequently circulated giving further details about the successful applicant's background.

The sense made of the announcement highlighted how any communication event cannot be understood in isolation from the issue climate and communi-cation history of the participants. For instance, not all centres were able to be linked by video. Those not linked to the video conference heard the announcement via a simultaneous audio link (i.e. teleconference). This was interpreted at the respective sites affected as evidence of their centre's mar-ginality because of size, an issue that was a factor in the sense made of other company-wide communication. The following interview excerpt shows how site size was used to account for the form this communication event took:

Participant: Because we're a small site, ourselves and [another small site] missed out on that. Even though we've got the video con-ferencing [equipment].

Interviewer: So what did you make of the fact that [other sites] were con-nected and you weren't?

Participant: Well what we understood from that was that they were chosen because they had the biggest number of people on site.

The announcement was followed by an intense period of informal communication. Employees reported having corridor and cafeteria conversations for several days after the announcement. These took many forms and varied in tone from serious to jovial encounters. They were fuelled by the outcomes of some employees' information-gathering activities. Many employees reported doing Google searches to uncover information on the new CEO. Others contacted colleagues the new CEO had worked with at another research organization, or individuals known to have links with such people. The information gained from these 'fact-finding' activities was fed into group conversations. This provided the data against which hypotheses were tested and contributed to an emergent rumour-based profile of the new CEO. This profile became a key tool for making sense of the new CEO's communication. It provided the framework that guided attention and data-gathering behaviour – a framework for extracting cues.

The profile was a collective achievement, drawing on and revealing the company's social sensemaking mechanisms. In the first instance, the profile was a site-based creation with its characteristics emerging from informal face-to-face discussions in small groups and dyads. Characteristics in each site's profile quickly spread through the company, aided by the complicated mesh of communication lines created by the matrix structure. Two characteristics of the rumour-based profile created a lot of comment and came to shape subsequent communication behaviour and sensemaking activity. These were the new CEO's supposed conservatism and his experience as a change manager.

The first of these rumoured characteristics was captured in an April Fool's Day intranet announcement, supposedly from the Board of Directors, detailing a new dress code. This code proposed that the company's current casual dress style would be replaced by much more professional personal presentation style 'to portray a more professional image to our shareholders, stakeholders and the general public'. This would require employees to adhere to strict guidelines on facial hair, trouser length, footwear, and, in the case of male staff, wearing ties when on company business. Women, it stated, would have to wear a skirt and blouse. It also asserted that alcohol consumption on company premises would not be tolerated. This, participants in the study believed, linked to a third rumoured characteristic of the new CEO; that he was a teetotaller.

The second rumoured characteristic, that the new CEO was a change agent, prompted employees to undertake individual survival ratings on themselves. This process generated considerable affective engagement among those who gave themselves a poor survival rating. This in turn stimulated informal conversations where people discussed their fears and sought opinions and reassurance from others. It also generated scepticism towards the Board because they had provided reassurance that significant change was not going to occur. Thus, the formal announcement of the identity of the new CEO created a spike of informal communication that generated two sensemaking tools (i.e. a rumour-based profile of the new CEO and a personal survival rating) that then framed subsequent communication and sensemaking activity.

The rumour-based profile could be seen in action in the way participants approached the 'meet and greet' sessions that followed the announcement of the new CEO. These sessions were held around the company so people could welcome the new CEO, and were well attended. Attendance was accounted for in terms of the desire to gain information on 'what he was like'. These formal, although causal, encounters prompted considerable informal discussion where people shared their impressions and collaboratively tried to establish the significance of these impressions in terms of the rumour-based profile. The same pattern as was noted earlier was reported; a formal communication event prompted a spike of informal communication that provided the opportunity for participants to engage in collaborative sensemaking about the elements of the formal communication and their significance. It showed how people relied on social processes to shape, confirm or elaborate on the sense they made of communication, as well as the nature of these social processes. Social networks and individuals' roles within these networks were revealed.

Personal networks forged by years of personal interaction and shared interests were often tapped. When asked to account for this, participants attributed their choices to the high level of trust they had for longstanding network members. These people had proven to be discrete and reliable information sources and sounding boards. People 'close to the action' were also used as sensemaking collaborators. This highlighted the way proximity to decision-makers and those deemed to be insiders was assumed to increase the likelihood of access to accurate and detailed information. It also explained why those in outlying centres were less likely to be consulted for information than those at Head Office. This finding illustrates how the social resources accessed to make sense of communication reinforced the prominence and influence of certain members of informal networks and contributed to their identity maintenance or formation.

THE ESTABLISHMENT PHASE

The new CEO embarked on a series of site meetings once he commenced his employment. These were preceded by an email where he provided an outline of what he wanted to achieve and the format for these meetings. This email prompted planning meetings where groups discussed the presentations they would make. After the meetings ad hoc analyses occurred in offices, corridors, and in the morning tea rooms and cafeterias. The same pattern that was observed in the previous two phases where formal communication prompted a spike of informal communication was evident again in relation to these meetings.

The formal meetings with the new CEO served several purposes, some to do with communication and others to do with making sense of the succession process and its outcome. Participants reported using these communication events as opportunities to gather data to compare with the rumoured profile of the new CEO. They then engaged in informal exchanges to compare their analyses with others and collaboratively speculate about the implications of the collective conclusions. However, compared to the disengagement phase, the informal communication in this phase was much more sophisticated, with much higher levels of engagement reported. How, when, where and to whom the new CEO communicated were all discussed.

The extent of the discussions varied from site to site in ways participants attributed to the special communication environments and issue climates that existed at each of the sites. For example, at one site where the lease on the buildings was due to expire and could not be renewed, the issue of continued operation in that town was woven into the collaborative speculations. The form the speculations took was considered to be consistent with how communication usually occurred. Those who typically played information broker, joker, 'doom and gloom' merchant, or passenger (i.e. someone who doesn't participate and just goes along with others' views) played this role in this instance. Thus the CEO succession also allowed existing patterns of interaction and the associated roles to be reinforced and the prevailing sub-cultures at each site to be sustained. This alerts us to the fact that there is never just one thing going on when sense is being made. The collaborative acts that contributed to individuals' sensemaking about the CEO succession process were simultaneously establishing or confirming employees' sense of the social order in the workplace and personal identities. In so doing, the study provided an example of how sensemaking inevitably involves identity construction and maintenance (Weick, 1995).

REVELATIONS ABOUT THE ORGANIZATION'S COMMUNICATION

The study revealed much more than simply the nature of the succession communication in this company. It provided an audit of the way communication operated and was made sense of by internal stakeholders, which has implications beyond the context of the study. Specifically the study revealed that:

- The way formal communication was approached and the goals of openness and information accessibility created a highly dissemination-oriented communication environment in the company that was at odds with employees' expectation that they should have input into communication processes about things that could affect them. Participants recognized this tension between communication environment and expectations yet actively contributed to the maintenance of the environment through their own communication behaviour. This highlights what has been characterized as the untidiness of sensemaking (Weick, 2001).

- Informal communication was used to provide the procedural and content elements not present in the formal communication (e.g. engagement, collaborative action, and information richness). This was illustrated by the spike of informal communication that surrounded formal succession communication.
- Even the sense made of the simplest communication event or practice drew on a complex array of personal and environmental considerations.
- Sensemaking about communication activated historical interactional issues and was fed by current ones. This suggests that to understand communication we should understand the aspects of interactional history that the sensemaker considers salient.
- Employees' values, beliefs, and attitudes were enacted and reinforced in the process of making sense of organizational communication. For instance, employees in this company valued having input and so tended to disengage or show less engagement with those communication events where no input was possible. This was particularly evident when the event was judged as unlikely to provide new information.
- Having the latitude to take independent action was intrinsic to most employees' sense of themselves and their organizational identities, so the opportunities for, and barriers to, their engagement with the succession process spoke directly to their identities. From an auditing point of view, the accounts given for the level of engagement positioned the informant in the social milieu of the organization.
- The succession-related communication provided a vehicle for individuals to undertake 'identity work' and for the organization to do 'cultural maintenance work'.
- The greatest engagement occurred when employees assessed that the communication or its outcome had the potential to impact on them personally or on aspects of the company with which they identify.
- Employees' impact assessments and the emotion these generated drove the sensemaking about the change communication and any subsequent sensemaking-related communication. This suggests that if we are auditing communication, we need to interpret the data provided in terms of the providers' personal impact assessments and their affective states.
- The organization had the capability to engage in highly sophisticated forms of mediated communication, yet face-to-face (i.e. unmediated) small group and dyadic communication were often used to make sense of this communication. This suggests that any audit should take care to examine the informal face-to-face processes because these appear to be an integral part of the sense made, and impact of, mediated communication processes, especially formal ones.

- Informal communication was not merely a response to insufficient or poor quality formal communication. As noted above, it provided the means to make sense of formal communication, suggesting these two forms of communication should be treated as complementary and part of the same communication event.
- When we explore sensemaking about communication we inevitably end up studying a whole lot more than the communication event or process that is the object of a sensemaking episode.

CONCLUSION

A sensemaking approach, particularly when it is used in a longitudinal study involving multiple data collection points and the same participants, produces a rich database for understanding organizational phenomena. When communication is the phenomenon studied, as was the case here, this allows the researcher to tap into the meanings that both drive and are created by organizational communication. This is because a sensemaking approach such as the one described in this chapter uncovers not only the communication people notice but how they label it, what assumptions they make about it, what conceptual tools they use to frame and interpret it, what actions they take to facilitate interpretation, and how they justify these actions, and the sense that emerges from their sensemaking process.

Such an approach has its challenges, however. First, it is time consuming. Second, it requires a skilled interviewer who can encourage participants to reveal their reasoning about communication without providing pre-emptive conceptual frameworks. Third, the interpretation of the rich and extensive amounts of qualitative data generated requires a skilled analyst who can examine data from different perspectives (i.e. sociological, psychological, linguistic, rhetorical) and move beyond rich description to produce explanatory frameworks that fit the data and create an 'intelligent reality'. To read more about sensemaking methodology, including the argument that it paradoxically seeks to objectify the subjective, see Florence Allard-Poesi (2005).

In the case described here, the communication associated with a CEO succession provided an excellent framework for revealing the way employees focus on communication changes, what drives this change of focus, and how it in turn shapes the communication that occurs. The value in auditing communication by focusing on a specific organizational change seems to lie in the way the change process, in this case a CEO succession, provides specific communication events and processes that served as points of attention. The employees are more engaged with the organizational communication that is occurring around them than during more certain times, and are therefore more inclined to invest energy to make sense of it.

This is possibly because change introduces uncertainty, ambiguity and interruption. When these relate to things that are perceived to matter to an individual this stimulates sensemaking activity (Weick, 1995). Thus, in this case, the possibility of change led to assessments of potential personal impact that caused employees to bracket off succession-related communication for interpretation. This interpretation often involved social processes such as engaging third parties or participating in collective information-sharing and analysis sessions, causing the web and complexity of sensemaking-related communication to expand.

A sensemaking approach, by virtue of the properties it alerts us to, ensures rich data are obtained about organizational phenomena such as communication. These data are multi-level. As sensemaking always has an object, a sensemaking approach produces data on the sensemaker's understanding of that object (e.g. a communication event such as a meeting). In this respect, it produces findings that mirror those produced by other research approaches – see Cooren's edited (2007) text of the analysis of one management meeting from multiple perspectives, for a good example of precisely this point. What distinguishes a sensemaking approach from others, however, is that it takes data gathering to another level by focusing also on the process of creating these understandings. In other words, a sensemaking approach examines the generative processes that account for these understandings. It reveals the representational tools used to create meaning and how these are applied. In this case, we saw several examples of these tools, including the impact assessment process, the rumoured profile, and the survival rating. These cognitive tools both accounted for what was noticed and gave meaning to this, capturing the reflexive relationship between stimuli and interpretation and the way the sensemaker creates the object he or she then makes sense of (i.e. enacts sensible environments).

To conclude then, a sensemaking approach directs the communication auditor's attention to the multi-faceted, multi-level and ongoing process of making sense of interactive experiences in a way that ensures the interplay between the communication object, the sensemaker, and contextual contingencies can be appreciated. It assists the auditor to create his or her own 'intelligent reality' from the idiosyncratic realities of others. Thus an awareness of, and sensitivity to, sensemaking dynamics adds enormously to the interpretive armoury of those engaged in communication audits, and has the potential to generate rich insights into communication processes.

Part IV

Final considerations

Chapter 20

Strategy, research and pedagogy
The role of audits

Dennis Tourish and Owen Hargie

INTRODUCTION

This book has explored the contribution that audits can make to the evaluation, and then transformation, of both internal and external communications. A great deal of evidence has been presented to show that high quality communication is a crucial indicator of organizational health. Those organizations that neglect it are hampered by poor fitness levels, and bedevilled by injury problems. This hinders their ability to compete in the marketplace. A variety of methods have been proposed that will enable organizations to monitor what they do more accurately, in order to effect substantial improvements. The case study chapters in Part III testify to the opportunities for organizational development afforded by a rigorous scrutiny of current practice.

Four substantive issues remain, which we will address in this chapter. These are:

1 The nature of a communication strategy, and how audits can fit into its development.
2 How auditors can choose between the different techniques that have been discussed in this book.
3 The role of audits as a research tool.
4 The contribution of communication audits to the teaching of organizational communication.

Each of these areas is discussed below.

AUDITS AND STRATEGIC COMMUNICATION

Audits are a vital ingredient of attempts to fashion a coherent communication strategy. However, there is no obvious consensus on what the term 'communication strategy' means (Tourish, 1996). This terminological uncertainty means that there are three main traps to avoid in approaching the issue.

First, managers may anticipate that they should be able to predict all their organization's information needs, internally and externally, over an indefinite time frame. False conceptions (of stability, predictability and uniformity) lie behind many of the major problems that have become associated with the disappointing results of most strategic planning (Mintzberg, 2007). The word 'strategy' is often little more than a synonym for bureaucracy, and the absence of tangible outcomes. Thus attempts to develop a strategic perspective in communications can become mired in the same bureaucratic sludge that has enveloped many corporate headquarters, exterminating all known life forms.

Second, attempts may be made to separate the communication function from the other vital roles of management, such as finance, human resources and R&D. Managers can end up paying less attention to communication, because someone else is paying more. This distancing process is often camouflaged, albeit temporarily, by the production of thick (but slick) documents, labelled 'communication strategies'. Their primary purpose is to avoid the painful need to transform internal and external relationships. Thus inaction is concealed behind a frantic paper chase, while the act of being busy is confused with achievement. In general, an under-focus on relationships, and an over-emphasis on the technical aspects of information transmission ('How much colour should we include in this brochure?'), held back the contribution of communication programmes to corporate competitiveness for many years (White and Mazur, 1995). For this reason, we would urge the wider use of the term 'communications management', rather than the ubiquitous and somewhat discredited nomenclature 'public relations'.

Third, and from the point of view of what has been defined as sensemaking in organizations (Weick et al., 2005), many accounts of corporate decision making are retrospective constructions, which attempt to explain and justify that which has often occurred by serendipity. As noted by Sonenshein (2007, p. 1026): 'Research shows that individuals frequently develop subjective interpretations of issues that go beyond objective features (assuming, for now, that such features exist) of those issues because of their expectations and motivations.' It goes against the grain to admit that something that turned out well could have occurred by accident, or even in spite of our best laid plans. We therefore construct myths and stories in which most successes are credited to our own brilliant insights, while corporate failures are the result of someone else's screw-ups. Success has many fathers, while failure is an orphan. We then seek reassurance about what comes next by producing detailed written 'strategies', which attempt to predict the future with the same accuracy as we can predict the past. The outcome is a beautifully crafted written strategy, which nevertheless stifles initiative and bears but a feeble resemblance to emerging reality.

Tourish and Hargie (1996c, p. 12) conceptualize a communication strategy in an entirely different manner. They define it as:

A process which enables managers to evaluate the communication consequences of the decision making process, and which integrates this into
the normal business planning cycle and psyche of the organisation.

Four main consequences flow from this:

1 *Instead of attempting to force communication to the top of management's
already crowded agenda, it should be linked to what is already dominating that
agenda.*

As Potter (2006, p. 85) put it: 'organizational communicators must contribute
significantly and measurably to strategic management. They must think, act,
and manage communication programs strategically, recording measurable
results that contribute to the accomplishment of the organization's mission.'
At each stage, the connection between business priorities and communication
issues needs to be made explicit, concrete, and turned into objectives that can
be measured.

   This approach also addresses another problem. It is a commonplace to find
researchers urging that corporate communicators should be members of top
management teams, or at least represented during their discussions (e.g.
Durutta, 2006). However, as Cornelissen (2008) noted, one problem with this
is that many corporate communicators lack a broader strategic awareness of
the key business issues facing their organizations, and thus possess a limited
capacity to contribute to the strategy development process. Linking communication priorities explicitly to business goals is one key means of over-
coming this obstacle.

2 *A communication strategy should be a means of transforming existing
management practice, rather than an additional activity on top of everything
else that managers already do.*

Responsibility for communication lies with management, rather than with
an isolated individual secreted in a separate office far away from where line
managers do their daily work. Communication has often been neglected,
while managers lavish attention and resources on their other more favoured
children. Neglect makes dysfunctional behaviour inevitable. Where specialist
expertise is needed, its main role should be to support line management and
complement its efforts, rather than act as a substitute for it.

3 *Strategy is not an event, but a process.*

That is, a communication strategy is not something dreamt up by planners
in a room; it is an ongoing activity, involving the entire organization.
Essentially, *strategy is what gets done* (Mintzberg, 2007). It is what people

do, rather than what anyone imagines they do, what they ought to do, what they intend to do, or what they have been told to do. Thus a communication strategy seeks to describe the business challenges that exist, their relationship to communication variables, and the best practices the organization is attempting to employ. A focus on changing behaviours is central to the process. Inevitably, personal example is the key to success. The leaders of the organization must embody proactive communication in their day-to-day work, and model appropriate behaviours for each tier of the organization.

An example makes the point. When Lawrence Bossidy was appointed CEO of Allied Signals the company was earning annual revenues of $359 million but losing money. Three years later it was in profit and with an annual income of $708 million. A focus on communication was central to accomplishing the turnaround. Here is what Bossidy did (Tichy and Charan, 1995, p. 70): 'I travelled all over the company with the same message and the same charts, over and over. Here's what I think is good about us. Here's what I'm worried about. Here's what we have to do about it.' In 60 days, Bossidy talked to 5000 people, in groups of 500. He noted the need to keep the information simple: 'Go to the people and tell them what's wrong. And they knew. It's remarkable how many people know what's really going on in their company.'

As this example shows, a key step in formulating strategy is for managers to decide on a clear set of messages, and then communicate them consistently to all employees (Wadman, 2006). Such messages should address the core concerns of employees, rather than spray an indiscriminate amount of information in all directions about all aspects of every issue (Zhu *et al.*, 2004). Effective leaders never simply assume that everyone shares the same definition of terms that the leader regards as important – such as 'vision', 'loyalty' and 'accountability' (Hamm, 2006). A communication strategy therefore needs to develop a common understanding. It tells employees 'how a decision was made, why it was made, what alternatives were considered, how the decision fits into the organizational mission and vision, how it will affect the organization and how it will affect employees' (Clampitt and Williams, 2007, p. 79). This means planning what messages to send, announcing them, monitoring people's reactions, and responding to their concerns. Neither internal nor external audiences have an unlimited capacity for processing information, or an infinite interest in what an organization or its leaders is doing, thinking or feeling (Christensen, 2002). Message selectivity is therefore crucial. This is strategy as action, engagement and dialogue. Many organizations still think of communication in terms of glossy brochures and press handouts – in short, as a one-off event that will forever remove the possibility of problems. In reality, communication is what happens to organizations while they are busy making other plans. Its occurrence is inevitable – the challenge is to manage it. Thus an emphasis on *process* focuses attention on the ongoing management of relationships, and helps root the notion of a communication strategy in the managerial ethos of the organization concerned.

4 *Measurement should begin with results.*

Many change initiatives fail because the process by which they are introduced is evaluated on such dimensions as satisfaction by those participating rather than bottom line business returns (Hargie and McCoy, 2007; McCoy and Hargie, 2001). For example, public relations practitioners have tended to measure success by the amount of publicity their campaigns attract, rather than their impact on broader business outcomes (McCoy and Hargie, 2003). We are recommending that explicit links should be made between communication and organizational outcomes by all business units. This means habituating managers and staff to address the following questions:

i   *What are the key problems that arise through poor communication?* It should be noted that this is a different proposition to the identification of communication problems, important as this is. Rather, it is to suggest a focus on the deeper business problems that are caused by the organization's communication difficulties. This ensures that the underlying thrust of a communications review (*to improve business performance*) remains in focus.

ii *Flowing from this, what are the organization's major communication problems?* What changes in behaviour are required to eliminate these problems? How specific can we be about these changes? How will we know when they have occurred?

iii *What targets can be set to eliminate the problems that arise from communication failure?* What targets can be set to eliminate communication failure itself? This provides a robust framework for evaluating the new communication process. In addition, staff satisfaction with communication is important for its own sake. If existing communication practice has been thoroughly evaluated, then targets can also be set for:

- increased and sustained knowledge
- high levels of goodwill and credibility
- a regular flow of communication
- accurate expectations about future milestones in organizational development (i.e. fewer toxic shocks), and
- satisfaction with levels of participation.

Ongoing audit research tracks the progress of all these factors.

Changing management and employee communication behaviours

Communication is central to all change management. For example, a study into leadership behaviour during a change management process in the Royal

Air Force in the UK found that managing resources, engaging communication and empowering others were the three most powerful factors in determining success. As the authors conclude: 'people-related dimensions of leadership are the most important for the RAF if it seeks successful change' (Wren and Dulewicz, 2005, p. 308). In parallel with this, it is also widely argued that, in order to effect deep-rooted organizational change, top managers must lead by doing and showing, transforming their own behaviours to model new business imperatives (e.g. Bruch *et al.*, 2005). Leadership is 90% example. Managers must therefore consider how to change their own communication behaviours, in order to model the climate, culture, values, behaviours and beliefs that they wish to see more widely adopted.

However, it is important to recognize that new behaviours, and mind-sets, on the part of employees are also required. Organizations are complex, interdependent social systems. Within that framework, leadership can be viewed as a reciprocal process whereby leaders and followers co-construct meaning through their mutual interaction, and in so doing build trust and create appropriate conditions for change (Fennell, 2005). Thus, if only managers change, then nothing will change. Our own audits have found that many people are comfortable with the notion of a hierarchy, enjoy blaming managers for every real and imagined problem (past and present), avoid accepting responsibility for their own contribution to communication breakdowns, and are profoundly reluctant to contemplate changes in their own communication styles. Other researchers have highlighted the same phenomenon (e.g. Argyris, 1994). Auditors need to be on the look out for this, and show a preparedness to engage with it. Box 20.1 lists a number of recommendations, derived from a variety of research findings, which suggest some steps towards addressing the problem.

Implementing a communication strategy

Flowing from this, what concretely must managers do to develop a communication strategy? Four key stages have been identified (Tourish and Hargie, 1996c). These encompass the process for auditing communication that we discussed in depth in Chapter 2, and are therefore only summarized briefly here:

1   Secure senior management commitment.
2   Identify current practice.
3   Set standards to measure success.
4   Incorporate this process into the business planning cycle (and psyche) of the organization.

A genuine communication strategy means involving all managers and ultimately all staff in identifying goals, standards of good practice, methods of evaluation, and the key channels that will be employed (Jaccaud and Quirke,

Box 20.1 Transforming communication behaviours

- Top managers must model the approaches concerned, encourage others to imitate their behaviour and reward those who do.
- Training in effective communication should be extended into the furthermost recesses of the organization.
- Such training should include the issue of how to give upward feedback.
- Managers also need training in how to respond to criticism and ideas from the shop floor.
- Performance review, at *all* levels, needs to take account of communication performance.
- Reward systems, again at all levels, need to do likewise.
- Targets should be set for interdepartmental cooperation. Many organizations now encourage this as part of the normal business planning cycle.
- Staff should be given the opportunity to work elsewhere in their organizations, rather than in their everyday environment. This breaks down interdepartmental barriers, encourages organizational learning and knowledge dissemination, and facilitates horizontal, diagonal and vertical communication.

2006). The starting point is the requirement that when business plans are being drawn up the communication consequences of these are considered. We return, also, to a previous point: strategy is what gets done, not what gets written in policy manuals.

It is therefore suggested that, at this stage, managers and staff routinely address, in a very non-routine way, the following issues:

- *What are the communication or information implications of the decision-making process?* It is feasible to consult staff at all levels on this issue. The threats and opportunities posed by decisions should also be considered.
- *What will people need to know about the implications of a given policy/ decision?* This could encompass internal and external publics.
- *Who is going to be responsible for transmitting the information concerned – what source is most appropriate?* Communication is primarily a management responsibility, but need not and should not involve only managers.
- *How will this information be communicated* – face to face, through written memorandum, through group meetings, or by other media?
- *What is the absolute essence of the information that will be required by a*

designated audience? (i.e. What is the nature of the message that we will be disseminating?)

- *What can we do to celebrate our achievements and honour people?* One example is that *Fortune* magazine has regularly nominated Southwest Airlines as the best company to work for in America. It is also one of the most profitable. The airline publishes stories of employee accomplishments and exploits in various newsletters. One of its publications is a tabloid style magazine called *Plane Tails*, which seeks to publish 'shocking stories about sensational employees'. It also prints tributes from customers, and more 'normal' company information.

- *What personal behavioural changes can managers make right away to facilitate a new pro-communications culture?* How should managers be facilitated to identify their own strengths and weaknesses as communicators, motivators and, ultimately, leaders?

- *How effectively is two-way communication integrated into decision making?* It is often assumed that the role of communication is to put the best possible spin on decisions that have already been made by managers (Rubin, 1996). The notion is one of decision making followed by communication, rather than one that sees it as integral to problem solving in a team-oriented workplace. More recent approaches to communication emphasize that it is fundamentally 'a two-way process that is interactive and participatory at all levels' (van Ruler, 2004, p. 130). Thus, a communication strategy should also plan, encourage and reward participation in decision making and problem solving – a notion that is gaining greater currency in the research literature. In particular, Tourish (2005) proposed 'ten commandments' designed to institutionalize an upward flow of critical information to the top management team. These included: experimentation with upward and 360-degree appraisal; subjecting positive feedback received from employees to the same or greater scrutiny than is applied to negative feedback; promoting formal and informal contact at all levels; creating 'red flag' mechanisms for the upward transmission of information that cannot be ignored; seeking honest, two-way communication by establishing informal contact with staff at subordinate levels; training managers in how to be open, responsive and receptive to employee input; and eliminating obstructive and hierarchical status differentials.

- *What training needs arise?* In our experience, top leaders often resist the idea that they need further training. The story frequently advanced is that they are too busy, too trained already, or too clever to require it. None of these are convincing rationales. An engaged and proactive workforce cannot be developed without considerable effort and fresh thinking. New skills are needed, while some old habits have to be discarded. Kelley (2006) described vividly a communications programme and strategy that involved training leaders in how to set the tone by crafting compelling stories; how to lead daily 15-minute meetings ('performance huddles'); how to share accurate, performance-based information; how to create real-time information and feedback (or 'scoreboards'), which allowed people to understand their personal role in shaping organizational performance; and how to conduct informal site visits. Most people, senior managers included, require training to improve how well they deliver on these varied fronts.

The strategy should be finally codified into a communication plan, defined as 'a written statement of what communication actions will be taken to support the accomplishment of specific organizational goals' (Potter, 2006, p. 85). In essence, the communication plan deals with how the corporate strategy will be communicated to key stakeholders. This is a critical issue. The effective communication of corporate strategy builds employee morale, enhances shareholder satisfaction, encourages the involvement of investors and analysts, and increases the confidence that various stakeholders place on the ability of management to lead the organization (Gao *et al.*, 2008). A communication plan therefore needs to cover such issues as:

- the main challenges the organization faces
- a situation analysis
- a statement of the overall key messages to be communicated
- an identification of the key publics at which these are aimed
- a clear outline of how such messages will be disseminated
- a budget
- an outline of how the effectiveness of the communication strategy will be monitored and evaluated.

Within this framework, and assuming top management involvement, a basis can be laid for transforming patterns of communication, organizational structures, levels of involvement and, ultimately, key business outcomes.

WHICH AUDIT TECHNIQUE IS MOST APPROPRIATE?

Once an organization decides to implement an audit, and develop a communications strategy, the unavoidable question is raised: which method should it employ? In Chapter 2, we proposed an audit process, characteristic of good practice, which we argued should normally be followed. Beyond this, numerous data collection techniques are available. The most important of these have been discussed, in detail, in Part II of this book. Choosing between them is no easy matter. Each audit should be tailored to the unique context in which it occurs. The challenge is to be clear about the needs of the organization, compare those needs with the audit tools available and then select whichever approach seems most appropriate. Auditing is both a science *and* an art.

To assist with this analysis, Box 20.2 summarizes the most widely used audit approaches, the time they take to implement, their general costs, the type of data collected and the amount of disruption they cause. This offers a pen portrait of each technique contained in earlier chapters of this book. Although intended to stimulate thinking, it is not a substitute for a close analysis of the context in which the audit is being conducted. The following issues should be considered, during such a process:

1 *Does the organization require benchmarks against which future progress can be measured?*

If so, questionnaires have many advantages (see Chapter 3). The data obtained can be readily quantified. Future audits will then show the extent to which the communication climate has improved or deteriorated. Chapter 11 provides a case study of an audit, and a follow-up, where precisely this form of evaluation occurred. Many questionnaires also contain open questions, allowing auditors the opportunity to collate illuminating anecdotes and other expressions of how people feel. The Appendix presents an example of such a questionnaire in detail. We have frequently found that a few colourful comments from audit respondents influences management thinking more than a zillion tables of hard data. (This is in line with the research evidence on the impact of statistics, discussed in Chapter 10.)

Sometimes extra effort has to be expended in interpreting such comments. For example, one audit respondent attempting to express her appreciation of a line manager's open communication style, commented: 'My line manager always does his best to keep me informed, even when he doesn't know what's going on himself.' We think we know what she meant! However, forensic examination does not always yield meaning. For example, another respondent in one of our audits commented delphically: 'I never talk on the telephone, only listen.' Interviews and focus groups are much more difficult to use in benchmarking (see Chapters 4 and 5). However, if resources permit, they can be used to supplement the data obtained by the questionnaire method, cross-check its validity, and explore problems identified in more depth. Whether multiple methods are employed will often depend on such constraints as time, money and human resources.

Questionnaires are not the most useful form of data collection for all populations. Some researchers in the United States have found that Chief Executive Officers are much more willing to participate in face-to-face interviews than they are to complete questionnaires (Wasserman and Faust, 1994). Our own experience corroborates this finding. Thus the nature of the sample population must also be considered when determining the most appropriate form of data collection.

Additionally, and perhaps surprisingly, some researchers have found that postal questionnaires attract a significantly higher response rate than those distributed via e-mail (Mavis and Brocato, 1998). This may be because paper questionnaires remain on desks for longer and stay within sight. However, the 'delete' option is available on most computer screens, thus e-mail surveys can be binned at the click of a mouse, and instantly forgotten about. It remains the case that securing satisfactory response rates is one of the most difficult challenges of data collection. Some researchers have suggested that people's willingness to participate in surveys is falling, with one noting that 'falling response rates is perhaps the greatest threat survey researchers have faced in the past 10 years' (Tourangeau, 2004, p. 791). However, Goldhaber (2002) has countered that internally administered e-mail surveys, particularly if backed up by management support and frequent reminders, can overcome this problem, at least partially (see Chapter 2). In addition, Reichheld (2006, p. 79) wisely noted that: 'As surveys grow to thirty or forty questions or more, the cost per survey creeps up, response rates drop, and sample size shrinks.' Results become unreliable. There is therefore a trade-off between what might be ideal (i.e. a survey that covers *everything*), and what is possible (i.e. a survey that people will actually complete). However, longer questionnaires may be used effectively in certain situations, where for example the organization has agreed to participate in the survey, senior managers are enthusiastically on board, staff have been primed to participate, and completion is scheduled to take place during working hours. It is vital to strike the right balance. Once again, pilots are indispensable as part of this process.

2 *Is the audit one of internal or external communication?*

In general, it is more difficult to use questionnaires for external audits. Internally, forums can be created where staff turn up, receive a detailed explanation of the audit process, and fill in materials under the auditors' supervision. Alternatively, they can be followed up through direct contact, by mail or by e-mail. However, customers, clients and suppliers have less motivation to complete questionnaires. This increases the possibility that only those with a particular axe to grind will get involved, thereby skewing the results. Several methods of dealing with this, to improve response rates, are discussed throughout this book. The mystery shopping technique has its origins in customer research, and allows for quantitative analysis, if this is required. In terms of evaluating direct communication with customers in locations such as shops, this is the most widely employed approach, as discussed in Chapter 8. A number of ethical issues pertaining to this method have also been raised, which should be taken into account. Alternatively, direct observation, interviews and focus groups might be a suitable choice.

Box 20.2 Evaluating audit tools

Tools	Time	Costs	Data collected	Disruption
Questionnaires	30–40 minutes	Main costs are respondents' time; those responding externally may need to be paid; cost of questionnaire analysis and analytical time of auditor	Standardized; quantitative data. Some questionnaires also contain open questions, yielding qualitative data (see Appendix)	Time spent completing questionnaires
Interviews	30–60 minutes	Interviewer time/ interviewee time (for external audits, interviewees may require fee)	Perceptions of employees/ customers/suppliers. Probing permits deep coverage of topics	Time interviewees spend away from their normal tasks
Focus groups	1–2 hours	Staff time; customers (or others) may require payment	Qualitative accounts/ summaries of respondents' opinions	Time participants spend away from their work
Communication diaries	Normally at least 1 day and no more than a week	Used internally; expensive in terms of employee time	Identifies sources of information, channels used and communication networks	High; most respondents find it intrusive; low completion rate
ECCO	5–10 minutes	Used internally; costs limited to employee time	Identifies amount of information known; sources and channels from which it is derived	Minimal
Mystery shopper	5–30 minutes (per transaction)	Employees diverted from 'real' customers; payment of 'shopper'	Quantitative and qualitative data	Minimal, although may change behaviour of staff

Method	Time	Costs	Data	Intrusiveness
Video recording	Indeterminate	Costs of video equipment; some technical help may be needed	Quantitative and qualitative	Minimal; does not tend to disrupt interaction
Critical incidents/experiences	Normally a standard part of questionnaires	No extra costs incurred; often part of data collection technique already being employed	Lively, positive and negative examples of communication processes	Minimal
Constitutive ethnography	4–20 hours of professionals' time	Expensive; professionals may require payment, or hiring of replacements while analysis occurs	Expert insights into dynamics of communication	High; professionals taken away from normal job
Delphi	1–3 hours of participants' time	Moderate: cost of participants' time	Evaluations of communication by experts	Moderate: small numbers suffice
Direct observation	No minimum/maximum normally specified	Low. Time used is that of observer, rather than staff/customers	Data from group interaction, dyadic episodes	Minimal, providing observer succeeds in being unobtrusive
Archival analysis	Indeterminate	Researchers' time	Mail record, phone records, e-mail records, etc.	Moderate
Network visualization	Indeterminate	Researchers' time	Identifies gatekeepers, communication stars, patterns of communication	Moderate

3 *Is the organization already aware of its communication problems, and simply needs to know people's opinions in more depth?*

In this context, further quantitative data, gained from questionnaires, may be as redundant as a third leg. We have faced this situation in many of our audits. An overall picture has emerged. Managers may then wish to clarify:

- Why a particular department is more dissatisfied than others.
- Why people in one location always feel badly informed, while those elsewhere are up to speed on key issues.
- What exactly customers want to know about a given issue.
- Why Department X is refusing to talk to Department Y, but won't make its reasons clear.

In such circumstances, we have conducted follow-up focus groups and interviews to supplement quantitative data. As Downs and Adrian (2004) and Zwijze-Koning and de Jong (2007), among others, have noted, there are many advantages to using more than one method of data collection. More fine-grained analysis is one of them. Denzin (1978, p. 291) introduced the notion of triangulation, which he defined as 'the combination of methodologies in the study of the same phenomenon'. This technique of triangulation is now widely employed, since it allows researchers either to confirm their findings or to discover contradictions that require further analysis (Onwuegbuzie and Leech, 2007).

4 *Has a massive crisis just occurred, requiring rapid analysis?*

We have worked with organizations that have been severely traumatized by unforeseen public relations disasters, often involving a complete breakdown in communication with customers. Invariably, the media have rushed to the scene, cameras at the ready, and sought to pillory both the individuals involved and the wider organization. Under such an onslaught, the careful designing of questionnaires followed by lengthy analysis is impracticable. A small number of skilfully run focus groups, or interviews, generate some rough and ready data, permitting a quick discussion of the way forward. These data are never ideal, or complete. However, a fuzzy picture is more useful than a blank screen. Once the immediate tension has eased, a more in-depth analysis can be undertaken.

5 *Does the audit need to focus closely on a small sub-set of a wider organizational system?*

We worked recently with a public sector organization, reeling from a blitz of bad publicity surrounding a particular incident. This suggested that vulnerable members of the public were ill-informed about some of its key services. Furthermore, the conduit from organization to public was through one professional sub-section of its staff. The objective of the audit was to find out precisely what this grouping knew and didn't know about the service in question – and what it was doing to communicate relevant information to the people who needed the service. Plainly, standardized instruments (which tend to measure global aspects of communication) were of limited use in such an investigation. We therefore devised our own questionnaire, with a special emphasis on open questions, and conducted a number of focus groups, with depth interviews as a follow-up. An 'off the shelf' approach is not always practicable. Another scenario occurs when the objective is to thoroughly audit a particular organizational system in great detail (see Chapter 12 for an account of such a project). Under those conditions, a wide range of audit materials can be justifiably employed, depicting communication practices from multiple perspectives.

6 Is the audit being conducted as part of an organizational development programme, or as pure research?

In the latter case, the primary consideration is likely to be the gathering of plentiful data, in which both depth and breadth are of crucial importance. Here, the data must answer to the most rigorous standards of academic practice, and prove capable of testing complex hypotheses. As with audits in general, the most appropriate method will depend on the research object-ives that have been set. Despite the sometimes polarized nature of the debate (see Donaldson, 2003; Hatch and Yanow, 2003) qualitative research is now attracting considerable attention in academic circles (Onwuegbuzie and Leech, 2007). Increasingly, researchers take a broad view of what constitutes data, and employ both quantitative and qualitative methods in their work (Stablein, 2006). There is an increasing recognition that no one method is appropriate for investigating all problems (e.g. Eisenberg, 2000). Thus, it is entirely possible that such tools as focus groups will help to meet a number of research objectives, either on their own or in conjunction with more posi-tivist inspired methodologies. On the other hand, Chapters 6 and 8 discuss some approaches (e.g. the Delphi technique; video recording of professional/client interaction) that are very labour intensive, and are therefore mostly employed during in-depth research investigations.

7 Is the audit being conducted in house, or by external consultants?

Either way, a whole raft of issues are raised. The first step is to clarify the audit's objectives. Is benchmarking required, or is a rough picture of emerging trends sufficient? If the audit is in house, an honest evaluation of the audit team's expertise should be conducted. For example, does the team have any knowledge of statistics? If not, quantitative approaches aimed at benchmarking would be ill advised. Will it be trusted to treat questionnaires confidentially, or are leaks within the organization the norm? Do the team members have a reputation for independence, or are they viewed as management stool pigeons? A small number of focus groups, interviews and some forms of direct observation are a possible alternative. Worries about confidentiality will remain. However, it should be possible to provide plentiful assurances about confidentiality, and so collect at least some data. We are aware of some attempts to use questionnaires during in-house audits, which attracted pitifully low response rates, and included many questionnaires only partially completed. On the other hand, if the internal audit team is well trusted, is perceived as standing apart from the top management team, and has experienced auditors as members, these problems will be much reduced – and a wider range of choices will be available.

If the auditors are external, and fully conversant with the organization's needs, then the best professional advice should be forthcoming. We recognize that the task of finding trustworthy consultants, tuned into the organization's situation, is itself a challenge. This task is enormously simplified if the organization has a clear view of its own needs.

In general, we believe that the balance of the argument favours involving external consultants. The main reasons for this are as follows:

- *External consultants, carefully chosen, are more likely to have the requisite expertise, and the time, to be fully and professionally engaged with the audit process.* Inevitably, internal audit teams are pulled in several directions at once. Their members still have day jobs to attend to. Frequently, it proves next to impossible to convene even something as simple as a planning meeting. They rarely have the time to consider audit data dispassionately or objectively, and often lack vital interpretive skills.

- *It is useful to seek an outside perspective on what the organization is doing.* External auditors bring to bear experiences gained from elsewhere, including examples of best practice. As the famous German Chancellor, Otto von Bismarck, remarked in the 19th century: 'Only a fool learns from experience: I learn from the experience of others.'

  Internal auditors may also be handicapped by the fear of offending vital constituencies with whom they must work once the audit is completed. How, for example, do you tell your boss, on whom you depend for your bonus, that his diplomatic skills have created an internal climate reminiscent of the Cold War? Organizations should look for external consultants prepared to honestly discuss problems such as these, rather than those whose main aim is to apply liberal helpings of whitewash – while pocketing a hefty fee. A glowing report that fails to reflect reality will be of no use in effecting improvements. Such reports are often produced as a means of telling managers what they want to hear, in the hope of securing further consultancy business. Their main effect is to undermine management's credibility in the eyes of staff, who (as we discussed in Chapter 10) tend to be only too well aware that problems exist.

• *The cost of hiring external auditors has to be set against the demands on the time of internal auditors, which also costs money.* There may also be training needs for internal auditors. A related difficulty is that internal auditors rarely have the time required for comprehensive audits, and end up rushing data analysis. This is a false economy. As computer specialists often point out, 'Garbage in equals garbage out.'

RESEARCH VERSUS AUDIT

While audits can be used in research, not all audits are research. They are often simply used to evaluate the application of research findings in a given context (Malby, 1995). Their purpose is to answer questions such as: Is communication in this organization at an acceptable level of competence? Are our customers receiving the information they need, or not? Exploring these issues does not constitute research. Research is generally concerned with one or more of the following: developing and testing hypotheses; generalizing from one or more studies, to set the standards for what constitutes good practice; exploring new and novel ideas; constructing grand narratives and stories that explain an underlying phenomenon; and contributing to the development and refinement of theories about wider social systems (Smith and Hitt, 2005). Box 20.3 lists the main characteristics of audits and research, indicating where they overlap and diverge. It is clear that audits have the potential to become a well respected and useful addition to the toolkit of those pursuing research into organizational studies. Here, we suggest various areas where this applies.

A wide range of research strategies and tactics are already employed in business and management research (Clegg *et al.*, 2006), which has shown great ingenuity in adapting methodologies originally developed for different purposes. Audits can be used in longitudinal or cross-sectional studies. In other words, they may be employed in an organization(s) over a period of years, or used in a representative sample of cases to give an immediate snapshot telling researchers 'this is how it is'. They are particularly useful in the forms of research discussed below:

• *Action research.* In this, data are collected about a system, results are fed back into the system, variables are manipulated in response, and the consequences are evaluated by the collection of more data. The main emphasis of most recent work in this area has been 'to inform action and transformation *in the local organizational setting* where the research is

---

Box 20.3 Characteristics of audits and research

Audit	*Research*
Compares actual performance against standards	Identifies the best approach (e.g. what communication style most helps with customer retention), and so sets the standards
Sometimes conducted by those who work within the organization being studied	More often conducted by independent, outside researchers
Usually initiated and led by the needs of the organization	Usually initiated by researchers, to explore wider issues
Involves access to information (e.g. employee classification system) by those normally entitled to access it	Requires access to information and databases by people who are not normally entitled to such access
Results designed to be setting-specific	Results intended to be generalizable to other settings
Uses already validated and usually well-established approaches to conduct investigation	May be concerned with testing efficacy of given approach, and developing new ones
Uses already tested hypothesis to check standards, and set internal benchmarks	Develops testable hypotheses, based on audit data; and tests hypotheses based on audit data

---

taking place' (Eden and Huxham, 2006, p. 390). It has therefore been particularly employed in research designed to improve professional practice (Blenkin and Kelly, 2001). Insofar as communication audits enable researchers to manipulate organizational variables (e.g. information flow; channel utilization; source frequency), they are of particular use in this form of research.

- *Case studies*. This is an umbrella term for approaches that look at a particular real-life event, organization or sub-system, and eventually seek to generalize the findings to more substantial populations (Langley and Royer, 2006). These authors argue that case studies should not exclude any form of data. In addition, the case involved can be a person, an event, a process, a problem or anything that in some sense forms a bounded entity (Stake, 2000). The argument is advanced that their in-depth nature, and emphasis on situationally embedded processes, justifies subsequent causal inferences (Lee, 1999). A great deal of such research, using communication audits, has now been published, and is widely referenced in this text. Several examples are also included in Part III.
- *Focus groups*. Here, evidence is collected from specialized and carefully selected groups of individuals. Given the popularity of focus groups

in communication research, they have been thoroughly discussed in Chapter 5 of this book.

- *In-depth interviews*. Typically, such approaches attempt to extract a great deal of evidence from a relatively small number of informants. Such research can be conducted from within two main theoretical paradigms. It can be positivist in orientation – that is, researchers may be primarily concerned with the exploration of causal relationships by means of quantitative analysis. Accordingly, frequency counts can be employed, in such techniques as content analysis. Alternatively, it may be more phenomenological in nature – that is, researchers are primarily concerned with the deeper meanings that respondents attach to communication, or with the values that underpin their behaviours. Chapter 4 discusses interviews in more detail, while several case study chapters also demonstrate their usefulness.

- *Large scale surveys*. Audit questionnaires can be employed to evaluate practices across a significant number of organizations. These can share a greater or lesser number of characteristics, depending on the research objectives or hypotheses being investigated. Chapter 3 explores such issues in more detail. Surveys can also be used in a more localized organizational context. For example, Chalmers *et al.* (2006) reported on the survey results obtained from a large academic library. Typically, large scale surveys require respondents to complete questionnaires in which various constructs such as personality, stress or communication satisfaction are measured (Stablein, 2006). Such surveys assume that, for example, respondents will respond truthfully, and without reporting attitudes that are socially desirable rather than what they really feel or think (Sloan *et al.*, 2004); that the items in the survey will be understood as the researchers intend them (Tourangeau, 2000); and that those responding will be able to make whatever judgements the survey requires (Schaeffer and Presser, 2003). These assumptions may not always be correct. For example, what may appear as minor variations in the response alternatives given to respondents have been shown to dramatically affect judgements and hence responses (Tourangeau *et al.*, 2004). Nevertheless, large scale surveys are common in the social sciences, and in communication audits. Such tactics as piloting the survey instrument, and triangulating this approach with more qualitative methods, can help to ease some of the interpretive difficulties identified here.

- *Participant observer approach*. In this case, a researcher joins the group of individuals under discussion and engages in their activities, but maintains a primary role of observing how the group functions (Remenyi *et al.*, 1998). It is argued that 'By observing people's actions as well as their words, the researcher may gain a broader understanding than might be obtained through other methods' (Riley *et al.*, 2006, p. 1209). The mystery shopper technique is one form of this activity.

Corman (2006) has argued strongly against the trend within organizational communication scholarship towards abstract metatheorizing, divorced from organizational context, and urged more studies of actual communication behaviour. It is a perspective that we share. In our view, communication audits are particularly applicable to the realization of this goal. Beyond this, audits are helpful in the exploration of a wide range of research questions. By means of illustration, Goldhaber (1993) identified six main categories for grouping major research questions that audits could help researchers explore. We discuss these below, and add our own research items to those raised by Goldhaber. We also add a seventh category of our own:

1 *Homophily studies*

These explore the extent to which various phenomena are similar or dissimilar, and their connection with communication. Key research issues here would include:

• Is perceived similarity between a message source and recipient a determinant of communication needs, or likely levels of satisfaction?
• Can communication frequency be predicted by homophily?
• Are highly cohesive teams more or less likely to require high information inputs from people outside the group?

2 *Apprehension studies*

These are concerned with the interaction between levels of anxiety that people feel about where they work, or the businesses they deal with, and their corresponding feelings about communication. Thus:

• Do measures of apprehension predict frequency of interaction, its quality, and consequences?
• Can anxiety about communication be reduced, either through the process of audit, or as a result of the interventions to which it gives rise?
• Contrariwise, to what extent is communication anxiety inevitable in large organizations?
• What role does job seniority play in determining apprehension about communication?
• What is the relationship between group cohesiveness and communication anxiety? (Groups may create a strong support environment that reduces anxiety, or reinforce each member's hostility to the outside world, thereby enhancing it.)

3 Credibility studies

These explore the relationship between credibility and the quality of communication. Thus:

- Does information that emanates from sources with high credibility produce greater overall communication satisfaction?
- What is the relationship between interpersonal trust and the quality of information flow? We have frequently found low levels of interpersonal trust between staff and managers, combined with strong information deficits on key issues.
- What determines credibility in the eyes of customers, who possess limited contextual information about the source they are dealing with?

4 Contingency theory studies

These explore the extent to which effective communication depends on (i.e. is contingent on) such variables as age, gender, ethnicity, status, and length of employment. Thus:

- Do any of the above variables contribute to levels of satisfaction with communication?
- Do different cultures possess different communication needs?
- Can organizational culture be manipulated to resolve the problem of securing accurate upward feedback? Or is it inherently difficult to get people to speak their mind?
- Does extending communication skills training throughout an organization increase overall levels of satisfaction with the communication process? (Some of our own audits suggest that it does, but more research is required to answer this question definitively.)

5 Network studies

These explore the connection between group affiliations and people's ability to sustain networks and their view of communication. Thus:

- To what extent is information about effective or ineffective communication episodes involving customers shared within local communities? Through what channels, and with what effect, is such information exchanged?
- Do people identified as isolates have a heightened perception of communication difficulties?
- Does a strong identification with a particular team, or sub-section of the workplace, enhance or reduce overall levels of company loyalty?

6 *Communication and organizational effectiveness studies*

These look at the extent to which internal and external communication impact on organizational effectiveness. Thus:

- Does customer satisfaction with communication strengthen organizational practice, or produce complacency, inertia and lost competitive edge?
- Do employees with high satisfaction levels have lower levels of absenteeism, sickness and turnover? Are they more productive and innovative than their colleagues?
- Are low levels of communication satisfaction a cause or a consequence of organizational malaise?

7 *Communication technology change studies*

These are concerned with the impact of communication technologies (as discussed in Chapter 9) on organizational functioning. Accordingly:

- What is the impact of specific new technologies on existing patterns of communication?
- Will the preference for face-to-face communication subside in virtual companies?
- Do intranet, internet and telephone technologies help organizations improve their profits? How?
- What standards and protocols can be suggested for the most effective use of such technologies?

COMMUNICATION AUDITS AS PEDAGOGY

Leipzig and More (1982) argued that communication audits bring both a theoretical and a pragmatic perspective to the study of organizational communication. In other words, their use creates a testing ground for theories that purport to explain how humans interact within organizations. For this reason, many academics, ourselves included, have used audits as a standard teaching instrument for a number of years.

Three major pedagogic goals have been suggested as being served by the audit (Shelby and Reinsch, 1996):

1   It connects classroom theory to workplace practice. Given the ambitions of most students on organizational communication courses, this connection enhances motivation, participation and learning.

2   The audit requires students to practise communication skills in a real-life environment. They must:

- form themselves into teams, agree ground rules, and manage interpersonal relationships
- seek contact with interested organizations
- negotiate access
- secure the cooperation of significant gatekeepers, employees and/or customers
- implement the audit, having selected the most appropriate technique
- draft reports
- make oral presentations.

The learning opportunities from such a range of activities are enormous.

3   Students are normally required to develop and then defend decision recommendations. Their diagnostic, diplomatic and rhetorical skills are sharpened.

Given this, Scott *et al.* (1999, p. 67) argued pointedly that 'the communication audit provides a unique educational tool that few other activities can equal when it comes to teaching experientially certain key aspects of business communication'. It is a position that we share. A number of steps in integrating audits into the curriculum have been suggested by these authors, and also by Conaway (1994) and Shelby and Reinsch (1996). These are discussed and supplemented by us as follows.

Team formation

Pierce (2007) outlined an approach to maximizing student learning from group projects that is consistent with our own practice, and that we have also found to be helpful. In essence, we encourage students to be as self-managing as possible. They themselves decide who will belong to the team. We encourage teams to have five members, providing enough resources to manage the task, but no more than seven, thereby minimizing opportunities for social loafing or role confusion. They are then charged with devising appropriate ground rules that address such issues as attendance at team meetings and how rapidly the team will respond to e-mail messages from each other or people outside its ranks. We have also adopted a system of allowing the group to determine if one or more of its members is underperforming and should be fired. Pierce (2007) suggested that before this extreme eventuality, and in line with normal organizational practice, the team must first issue a written warning, and copy it to the course instructor. It is also made clear that everyone must eventually complete an audit project – either in their original team, alone, or in collaboration with other fired team members. Our own experience has been that these empowering tactics, and the possibility of sanction from one's peers, is sufficient to avert such extreme outcomes.

Project initiation

Having been formed into teams, the students are then required to identify organizations with which they want to work. Barring wholly exceptional circumstances, we insist that they look outside the university environment. This further enhances their ability to negotiate the scope of a given project, persuade people of its benefits and gain access to invaluable real-world experience.

Planning

The key aim here is to ensure that projected audits are manageable in size. Small scale studies are normally all that can be realistically accomplished, given the students' limited expertise, time and other resource constraints. We encourage them to clearly identify the sub-set of the organization or its external publics to be audited, and delineate the range of topics to be investigated. This analysis will also determine the audit methodology that they employ. Different groups are required to use varied methods. This ensures that whole-class learning can occur when the feedback stage is reached at the end.

Data collection

This is the 'practice' phase of the audit, in which the methodology is implemented. Typically, we find that students have a tendency to underestimate the difficulties it will bring. As Fichman and Cummings (2003, p. 282) noted: 'Missing data are a common problem in organizational research.' People can block access to information, curtail interviews, go on holiday at inappropriate moments, or depart for other jobs. In our experience, most students are comically unprepared for the stresses and strains of real-world research, and are unduly dismayed when a wheel falls off their cart. As with all research, they are best advised, when faced with a conflict between the desirable and the possible, to side with the latter. It is also frequently necessary to restrain the overenthusiasm of some students, who seek to employ so many methods that the organization would find itself paralysed in an endless round of interviewing, form filling and focus groups, were it to take up their well-intentioned offers of assistance.

Analysis

This is a typical problem-solving phase, during which the data are subject to intense scrutiny. At this point, many students tend to become mesmerized with issues of statistical significance. This results from a veneration of 'hard' data, quickly acquired in a university environment, combined with a panic-stricken conviction that the subject is hideously complex, and far beyond their analytic abilities. Paralysis ensues. The problem is compounded by a tendency to over-focus on problems, rather than on also identifying strengths. As we have discussed throughout this book, a balanced approach on such issues is vital, and the need for this must be communicated to students.

Recommendations and report writing

The difficulty for students here is one shared by experienced auditors. On the one hand, recommendations should be based on best practice standards, and on relevant theory and research. On the other, it is also necessary to consider the existing value system of the organization – and hence what it is capable of. In our experience, students have a tendency to rush their recommendations by selecting a small sample from what they know of the instructing profes-sor's work, and then trying to apply them irrespective of local circumstances. Most noticeably, they urge a vast increase in information flow (more newslet-ters; more videos; more team briefing; more everything), without considering the need to target specific information on particular groups, through carefully selected channels. The assumption is that one colour scheme suits all houses. In short, what emerges at the end is rarely (on first attempt) calculated to meet the business needs of the organization with which they have been working. Corrective input, and challenges to the students' perceptions, are essential. Chapter 10 in this book discusses the process of writing reports in detail.

Feedback

This takes two forms. First, we encourage students wherever possible to pres-ent their report in writing, and orally, to those they have audited. This lends further 'edge' to the assignment. Second, we require them to present it orally to their colleagues. This ensures that the pros and cons of different method-ologies are widely aired, stimulates learning, and takes advantage of the competitive instincts of the students, who want to impress their colleagues.

Throughout, clear protocols and guidelines are essential. Students need to be advised of what is expected from them in terms of final reports, presenta-tions, and use of methods. We endorse the view of Shelby and Reinsch (1996, p. 107), who pointed out that the lecturer should put the onus on students to:

> assume direction and responsibility for their own audits, and know when and when not to intervene . . . the instructor must value process above product, while insisting on products that a working professional may read and will find potentially useful.

Audits as a pedagogic tool offer an invaluable means of exploring many wider issues in organizational communication – such as the role of hierarchy, democracy, power and organizational citizenship. Additionally, they equip students with 'hard' real-world skills that they can use to sell themselves at interviews. Overall, with some encouragement and assistance, most students respond well to the challenge of utilizing communication audits, and derive significant benefits from the process.

CONCLUSION

The central purpose of this book has been to explore research, theory and practice in the field of communication audits. Practitioners, researchers and students of organizational communication can all benefit from a wider use of the audit approach. We have therefore proposed an action framework that integrates audits into the process of developing communication strategies in organizations. We have also illustrated their wider use as research and pedagogic instruments. Earlier chapters in this book outlined many audit tools, and we have made suggestions here designed to help auditors chose from among them.

There are a number of main lessons that we think stand out:

- *Transforming communication requires time and resources.* There is little point in paying lip service to the need for a positive communication climate unless this is accepted. No one can compete in a race without making an effort, and being prepared to turn up for regular training sessions. If improving communication is a priority, effort has to be invested in transforming behaviours, so that the organization can leave behind the present and reach a future, more ideal state.
- *People generally welcome the opportunity to discuss their own communicative performance.* They also learn, and their performance improves, when this is contrasted with best practice models derived from elsewhere.
- *A communication strategy should focus overwhelmingly on changing the behaviours of key people.* Mostly, and contrary to popular opinion, it is the deed that is father to the thought, rather than the other way round. A communication strategy should therefore seek to change *behaviour*, in the expectation that *relationships* and *attitudes* will follow.
- *Feedback is the key.* Open communication without feedback is like a ladder without rungs. It will never move organizations from where they are to where the marketplace tells them they need to be.
- *Persistence and fresh vision are vital.* There are no 'final solutions'. Keeping the channels of communication in good repair is like painting the Golden Gate Bridge. No matter how much you have done, there is always more to do.

- *Measurement is indispensable*. Measure attitudes, measure performance, measure outcomes. Then devise relevant rewards – and measure their impact.

Communication is increasingly recognized as a crucial variable in determining organizational success, and as a vital issue requiring further research. How people interact with each other remains one of the most fascinating and elusive topics to attract study. We discussed a number of research issues earlier in this chapter where audits can be of particular help. As this suggests, there is still so much about which we know so little. The voyage of discovery has barely begun. The methods and tools discussed in this book will facilitate the work of researchers and practitioners prepared to explore the exciting world of human communication, in the still largely unfamiliar territory of organizational life.

Communication Audit Questionnaire

The International Communication Association developed an audit questionnaire in the 1970s, widely piloted in the United States. This questionnaire is discussed in Chapter 3, and is alluded to at other points of this book (see, for example, Chapters 10, 11 and 17). It is generally regarded as a milestone in the development of organizational communication research instruments. Further work was conducted by the editors of this book, using the ICA questionnaire as a basic template, to check its reliability and validity as we entered the new millennium.

As a result, the ICA instrument was substantially revised. A number of new items were added at various points, and old ones omitted. For example, the original instrument when investigating channels asked respondents to identify how much information they received about their organization through various national media. By the same token, given the period during which the instrument was devised, it did not itemize e-mail or the intranet generally. The present questionnaire updates the original in these respects. We also added more qualitative sections (including Section 12). The intention was to produce an instrument that continues to yield meaningful quantitative data, while also providing auditors with more of the insights and benefits normally obtained from focus groups and interviews.

We also identified other areas in which the original ICA questionnaire could be shortened. For example, the original contained many more sections that asked for critical incidents concerning each of the dimensions of communication explored. We reduced this to one critical incident, designed to secure examples from respondents of an incident that most typifies communication for them in their organization. In addition, the explanatory guide for respondents that opens the questionnaire describes what follows as a 'staff survey'. Since the 1970s, audits have been extended into many areas of organizational life, and have come to acquire judgemental connotations for many people. In our experience, describing the process in terms of a staff survey carries a reduced feeling of threat and improves response rates.

Having conducted extensive work with the revised instrument, a sample of 500 cases was analysed to determine the internal reliability of the items within each section of the questionnaire and also to ascertain the degree of relevance of each item to the overall theme as represented by the section topic. Internal reliability scores for each section were consistently high, with an overall Cronbach's alpha value of .84.

STAFF SURVEY

This Questionnaire has been designed in order to find out your views about the effectiveness of communication within [name organization]. It therefore contains a number of questions relating to the sending and receiving of communication. The purpose of this survey is to allow you to openly and honestly tell us how you feel about the way people communicate with you within the [name organization].

The Questionnaire is completely confidential, so do not write your name on it. However, to help us carry out a full analysis of the results we would ask you to provide some background information by answering the questions on the next two pages.

For most of the remainder of the questions you are asked simply to select and circle a number that best reflects your opinion regarding a particular issue. Please answer all of the questions.

Finally, there is one open question at the beginning and two at the end of the Questionnaire. These allow you: first, to describe an actual example of communication within [name organization]; second, to identify strengths and weaknesses in communication; and finally to make suggestions for future communication improvements.

BACKGROUND INFORMATION

This questionnaire is anonymous so please do not write your name on it. However, the following information is necessary to help us analyse the findings in more detail. Please circle the relevant number in each case.

What is your gender?

1. Female
2. Male

What is your age?

1. Under 20 years old
2. 21 to 30 years old
3. 31 to 40 years old
4. 41 to 50 years old
5. Over 50 years old

Do you work:

1. Full-time
2. Part-time
3. Temporary full-time
4. Temporary part-time
5. Job-share

How long have you been employed here?

1. Less than 1 year
2. 1 to 5 years
3. 6 to 10 years
4. 11 to 15 years
5. More than 15 years

How long have you held your present position?

1. Less than 1 year
2. 1 to 5 years
3. 6 to 10 years
4. 11 to 15 years
5. More than 15 years

What is your present level of managerial responsibility?

1.   I don't supervise anyone
2.   First-line manager
3.   Middle manager
4.   Senior manager
5.   Other (please specify) _____

Where are you employed?

_____

What professional group do you belong to?

1.   [List
2.   the
3.   various
4.   professional groups
5.   found within
6.   the organization
7.   being audited]
8.   Other (please specify) _____

How much special training specifically to improve your communication skills have you had?

1.   No training at all
2.   Little training (attended one seminar/workshop/course)
3.   Some training (attended a few seminars/workshops/courses)
4.   Extensive training (attended a large number of seminars/workshops/ courses)

SECTION 1: Strengths and weaknesses in communication

List below what for you are the three main strengths in the way people in [name organization] communicate with you:

1. _____
_____
_____

2. _____
_____
_____

3. _____
_____
_____

List below what for you are the three main weaknesses in the way people in [name organization] communicate with you:

1. _____
_____
_____

2. _____
_____
_____

3. _____
_____
_____

SECTION 2: How do you feel about the amount of information you are receiving?

KEY FOR SCORING ITEMS:

VL = VERY LITTLE; L = LITTLE; S = SOME; G = GREAT;
VG = VERY GREAT

For each area listed below please *circle* the number that best represents the amount of information you are receiving now and the amount you feel you need to receive to do your job most effectively.

Topic Area	This is the amount of information I receive now					This is the amount of information I need to receive				
	VL	L	S	G	VG	VL	L	S	G	VG
My performance in my job	1	2	3	4	5	1	2	3	4	5
What is expected from me in my job	1	2	3	4	5	1	2	3	4	5
Pay, benefits and conditions	1	2	3	4	5	1	2	3	4	5
Things that go wrong in my organization	1	2	3	4	5	1	2	3	4	5
Performance appraisal systems	1	2	3	4	5	1	2	3	4	5
How problems that I report in my job are dealt with	1	2	3	4	5	1	2	3	4	5
How decisions that affect my job are reached	1	2	3	4	5	1	2	3	4	5
Promotion opportunities	1	2	3	4	5	1	2	3	4	5
Staff development opportunities	1	2	3	4	5	1	2	3	4	5
How my job contributes to the organization	1	2	3	4	5	1	2	3	4	5
Specific problems faced by the organization	1	2	3	4	5	1	2	3	4	5
Major management decisions	1	2	3	4	5	1	2	3	4	5
Important new service/production developments	1	2	3	4	5	1	2	3	4	5
Improvements in services/ production, or how services/ production are delivered	1	2	3	4	5	1	2	3	4	5
The goals of the organization	1	2	3	4	5	1	2	3	4	5
The total range of services offered by my organization	1	2	3	4	5	1	2	3	4	5

SECTION 3: How do you feel about amount of information
you are receiving from the following sources?

KEY FOR SCORING ITEMS:

VL = VERY LITTLE; L = LITTLE; S = SOME; G = GREAT;
VG = VERY GREAT

For each person or source listed below, circle the number that accurately
indicates the amount of information you *are* receiving and the amount of
information you feel you *need* to receive to be able to your job well.

Source	This is the amount of information I receive now					This is the amount of information I need to receive				
	VL	L	S	G	VG	VL	L	S	G	VG
Staff who are accountable directly to me	1	2	3	4	5	1	2	3	4	5
Immediate work colleagues	1	2	3	4	5	1	2	3	4	5
Colleagues in other departments	1	2	3	4	5	1	2	3	4	5
People in other departments who provide services for my area	1	2	3	4	5	1	2	3	4	5
Immediate line manager	1	2	3	4	5	1	2	3	4	5
Middle managers	1	2	3	4	5	1	2	3	4	5
Senior managers	1	2	3	4	5	1	2	3	4	5
Team briefings	1	2	3	4	5	1	2	3	4	5
Special talks given by middle managers	1	2	3	4	5	1	2	3	4	5
Special talks given by senior managers	1	2	3	4	5	1	2	3	4	5
The grapevine (by random word of mouth)	1	2	3	4	5	1	2	3	4	5

SECTION 4: How much information are you receiving through these channels?

KEY FOR SCORING ITEMS:

VL = VERY LITTLE; L = LITTLE; S = SOME; G = GREAT;
VG = VERY GREAT

The following questions indicate a variety of *channels* through which information is sent to employees. Please circle the number that accurately represents the amount of information you *are* receiving through that channel now and the amount of information you *need* to receive to do your job most effectively.

Channel	This is the amount of information I receive now					This is the amount of information I need to receive				
	VL	L	S	G	VG	VL	L	S	G	VG
Face-to-face contact between myself and my managers	1	2	3	4	5	1	2	3	4	5
Face-to-face contact among people in my work area	1	2	3	4	5	1	2	3	4	5
Telephone calls from my managers	1	2	3	4	5	1	2	3	4	5
Written communications from my managers (memos, letters, etc.)	1	2	3	4	5	1	2	3	4	5
Policy statements	1	2	3	4	5	1	2	3	4	5
Notice boards	1	2	3	4	5	1	2	3	4	5
Internal publications (magazine, newsletter, etc.)	1	2	3	4	5	1	2	3	4	5
Internal audio-visual material (videos, films, slides, etc.)	1	2	3	4	5	1	2	3	4	5
With your pay slips	1	2	3	4	5	1	2	3	4	5
E-mail	1	2	3	4	5	1	2	3	4	5
Intranet	1	2	3	4	5	1	2	3	4	5

SECTION 5: How do you feel about the amount of information you are sending?

KEY FOR SCORING ITEMS:

VL = VERY LITTLE; L = LITTLE; S = SOME; G = GREAT;
VG = VERY GREAT

For each topic listed below please circle the number that accurately represents the amount of information you are sending now and the amount you feel you need to send to do your job most effectively.

	This is the amount of information I send now					This is the amount of information I need to send				
Topic Area	VL	L	S	G	VG	VL	L	S	G	VG
Reporting my successes and achievements	1	2	3	4	5	1	2	3	4	5
Reporting problems in my work	1	2	3	4	5	1	2	3	4	5
Expressing my opinions about my job	1	2	3	4	5	1	2	3	4	5
Asking for information essential for my work	1	2	3	4	5	1	2	3	4	5
Giving my opinions about the performance of my immediate manager	1	2	3	4	5	1	2	3	4	5
Requesting clearer work instructions	1	2	3	4	5	1	2	3	4	5
Reporting mistakes or failures that occur in my work area	1	2	3	4	5	1	2	3	4	5

SECTION 6: How do you feel about the action taken on information you are sending?

KEY FOR SCORING ITEMS:

VL = VERY LITTLE; L = LITTLE; S = SOME; G = GREAT; VG = VERY GREAT

Indicate, by circling the appropriate number, the amount of *action* that is taken on information you send to the people listed below. Please also indicate the amount of action that you feel *needs* to be taken on this information.

Target People	This is the amount of action taken now					This is the amount of action needed				
	VL	L	S	G	VG	VL	L	S	G	VG
Staff who are accountable directly to me	1	2	3	4	5	1	2	3	4	5
Immediate work colleagues	1	2	3	4	5	1	2	3	4	5
Colleagues in other departments	1	2	3	4	5	1	2	3	4	5
People in other departments who provide services for my area	1	2	3	4	5	1	2	3	4	5
Immediate line manager	1	2	3	4	5	1	2	3	4	5
Middle managers	1	2	3	4	5	1	2	3	4	5
Senior managers	1	2	3	4	5	1	2	3	4	5

SECTION 7: How quickly do you get information from the following sources?

KEY FOR SCORING ITEMS:

N = NEVER ON TIME; R = RARELY ON TIME; SOT = SOMETIMES ON TIME; MOT = MOSTLY ON TIME; A = ALWAYS ON TIME

Indicate, by circling the appropriate number, the extent to which information from each of the following is usually timely (i.e. you get information when you most need it).

Source	N	R	SOT	MOT	A
Staff who are accountable directly to me	1	2	3	4	5
Immediate work colleagues	1	2	3	4	5
Colleagues in other departments	1	2	3	4	5
People in other departments who provide services for my area	1	2	3	4	5
Immediate line manager	1	2	3	4	5
Middle managers	1	2	3	4	5
Senior managers	1	2	3	4	5

SECTION 8: Working relationships

KEY FOR SCORING ITEMS:

VL = VERY LITTLE; L = LITTLE; S = SOMETIMES; O = OFTEN;
A = ALWAYS

In terms of people in [name organization], please circle the number that accurately describes how much you trust each of the following in terms of working together.

I trust the following:	VL	L	S	O	A
Staff who are accountable directly to me	1	2	3	4	5
Immediate work colleagues	1	2	3	4	5
Colleagues in other departments	1	2	3	4	5
Immediate line manager	1	2	3	4	5
Middle managers	1	2	3	4	5
Senior managers	1	2	3	4	5

SECTION 9: How much information do you receive on important issues* facing your organization?

KEY FOR SCORING ITEMS:

VL = VERY LITTLE; L = LITTLE; S = SOME; G = GREAT;
VG = VERY GREAT

There are a number of important issues facing your organization on which you may be receiving information. For each issue, please circle the number that most accurately indicates how much information you are *receiving now* and the amount of information you feel you *need to receive*.

Topic Area	This is the amount of information I receive now					This is the amount of information I need to receive				
	VL	L	S	G	VG	VL	L	S	G	VG
The current financial climate	1	2	3	4	5	1	2	3	4	5
The impact of everything that is happening on jobs	1	2	3	4	5	1	2	3	4	5
How other bodies buy our services	1	2	3	4	5	1	2	3	4	5
The appraisal system	1	2	3	4	5	1	2	3	4	5
Training and development opportunities	1	2	3	4	5	1	2	3	4	5
The structure of the organization	1	2	3	4	5	1	2	3	4	5

SECTION 10: How much information do you send on important issues* facing your organization?

KEY FOR SCORING ITEMS:

VL = VERY LITTLE; L = LITTLE; S = SOME; G = GREAT;
VG = VERY GREAT

There are a number of important issues facing your organization on which you may be sending information. For each issue, please circle the number that most accurately indicates how much information you are *sending now* and the amount of information you feel you *need to send*.

Topic Area	This is the amount of information I send now					This is the amount of information I need to send				
	VL	L	S	G	VG	VL	L	S	G	VG
The current financial climate	1	2	3	4	5	1	2	3	4	5
The impact of everything that is happening on jobs	1	2	3	4	5	1	2	3	4	5
How other bodies buy our services	1	2	3	4	5	1	2	3	4	5
The appraisal system	1	2	3	4	5	1	2	3	4	5
Training and development opportunities	1	2	3	4	5	1	2	3	4	5
The structure of the organization	1	2	3	4	5	1	2	3	4	5

SECTION 11: Communication experience

It would be helpful if you could describe below *one* communication experience in your organization. This experience should be one which for you is most typical of communication within your organization. Please answer the questions below and then give a summary of the experience.

To whom does this experience primarily relate? (circle one)

1.   Person accountable to me
2.   Immediate colleague
3.   Immediate line manager
4.   Middle manager
5.   Senior manager
6.   Person in a department that provides services for me

Was the communication (circle one)

1.   Effective   2. Ineffective

Describe the communicative experience, what led up to it, what the other person(s) involved did that made her/him an ineffective or effective communicator, and the consequences of what the person did.

_____

_____

_____

_____

_____

_____

_____

_____

_____

_____

_____

SECTION 12: The challenges ahead

1. What do you think is the greatest challenge that faces this organization during the coming year?

_____

_____

_____

_____

2. What is your own biggest priority in the workplace during the next 12 months?

_____

_____

_____

_____

3. What do you think your managers most expect from you in terms of performance and priorities right now?

_____

_____

_____

_____

SECTION 13: Suggestions for making communication better

List below three changes in the way people communicate with you that would make communication better in [name organization]. Be as specific as possible.

1. _____
   _____
   _____
   _____
   _____

2. _____
   _____
   _____
   _____
   _____

3. _____
   _____
   _____
   _____
   _____

THANK YOU FOR COMPLETING THIS QUESTIONNAIRE

*EXPLANATORY NOTE ON SECTIONS 9 AND 10

Obviously, the issues of most importance at any given time vary from organization to organization. We recommend that the senior management group be facilitated by the audit team to identify the top half dozen or so issues that they believe to be of most importance at the time of the audit, and that these be included here. In Sections 9 and 10 we give an example of some issues from a recent audit conducted by us.

References

Adams, N., Bell, J., Saunders, C. and Whittington, D. (1994) *Communication Skills in Physiotherapist–Patient Interactions*, Northern Ireland: University of Ulster.

Agar, M. (1994) *Language Shock: Understanding the Culture of Communication*, New York: William Morrow.

Agar, M. and McDonald, J. (1995) Focus groups and ethnography, *Human Organization*, 54, 78–86.

Akkirman, A.D. and Harris, D.L. (2005) Organizational communication satisfaction in the virtual workplace, *Journal of Management Development*, 24, 397–409.

Albrecht, T. and Bach, B.W. (1997) *Communisation in Complex Organizations: A Relational Approach*, Fort Worth, TX: Harcourt Brace.

Allard-Poesi, F. (2005) The paradox of sensemaking in organizational analysis, *Organization*, 12, 169–196.

Allen, J., Jimmieson, N., Bordia, P. and Irmer, B. (2007) Uncertainty during organizational change: Managing perceptions through communication, *Journal of Change Management*, 7, 187–210.

Alte, D., Weitschies, W. and Ritter, C. (2007) Evaluation of consultation in community pharmacies with mystery shoppers, *The Annals of Pharmacotherapy*, 41, 1023–1030.

Amernic, J., Craig, R. and Tourish, D. (2007) The transformational leader as *pedagogue*, *physician*, *architect*, *commander*, and *saint*: Five root metaphors in Jack Welch's letters to stockholders in General Electric, *Human Relations*, 60, 1839–1872.

Ancona, D. and Bresman, H. (2007) *X-Teams*, Boston, MA: Harvard Business School Press.

Anderson, C. and Martin, M. (1995) Why employees speak to coworkers and bosses: Motives, gender, and organizational satisfaction, *Journal of Business Communication*, 32, 249–265.

Anderson, J. and Baym, G. (2004) Philosophies and philosophical issues in communication, 1995–2004, *Journal of Communication*, 54, 589–615.

Anderson, L. and Wilson, S. (1997) Critical incident technique, in D. Whetzel and G. Wheaton (eds) *Applied Measurement Methods in Industrial Psychology*, Palo Alto, CA: Davies-Black.

Appelbaum, S.H., Lopes, R., Audet, L., Steed, A., Jacob, M., Augustinas, T. and Manolopoulos, D. (2003) Communication during downsizing of a telecommunications company, *Corporate Communications: An International Journal*, 8, 73–96.

Argenti, P. (2007) *Corporate Communication* (4th edn), London: McGraw-Hill.

Argenti, P.A. (1998) Strategic employee communications, *Human Resource Management*, 37, 199–206.

Argyle, M. (1987) *The Psychology of Happiness*, London: Routledge.

Argyle, M. (1994) *The Psychology of Social Class*, London: Routledge.

Argyris, C. (1994) Good communication that blocks learning, *Harvard Business Review*, 72, 77–87.

Argyris, C. (1998) Empowerment: The emperor's new clothes, *Harvard Business Review*, 76, 98–105.

Arnold, W. (1993) The leader's role in implementing quality improvement: Walking the talk, *Quality Review Bulletin*, March, 79–82.

Arvidsson, B. and Fridlund, B. (2005) Factors influencing nurse supervisor competence: A critical incident analysis study, *Journal of Nursing Management*, 13, 231–237.

Ashfield-Watt, P., Welch, A., Day, N. and Bingham, S. (2004) Is 'five-a-day' an effective way of increasing fruit and vegetable intakes?, *Public Health Nutrition*, 7, 257–261.

Ashford, S. and Tsui, A. (1991) Self-regulation for managerial effectiveness: The role of active feedback setting, *Academy of Management Journal*, 34, 251–280.

Atteslander, P.M. (1954) The interactio-gram: A method for measuring interaction and activities of supervisory personnel, *Human Organization*, 13, 28–33.

Atwal, A. and Caldwell, K. (2003) Profiting from consensus methods in occupational therapy: Using a delphi study to achieve consensus on multiprofessional discharge planning, *The British Journal of Occupational Therapy*, 66, 65–70.

Audia, P. and Locke, E. (2003) Benefiting from negative feedback, *Human Resource Management Review*, 13, 631–646.

Audit Commission (1993) *What Seems to Be the Matter: Communication between Hospitals and Patients*, London: HMSO.

Australian Bureau of Statistics (2007) *Labour Force Australia*, Cat. No. 6291.0.55.003, Canberra: AGPS.

Axhausen, K., Löchl, M., Schlich, R., Buhl T. and Widmer, P. (2007) Fatigue in long-duration travel diaries, *Transportation*, 34, 143–160.

Axley, S.R. (1984) Managerial and organizational communication in terms of the conduit metaphor, *Academy of Management Review*, 9, 428–437.

Baake, K. (2007) Decision-making in a quasi-rational world: Teaching technical, narratological, and rhetorical discourse in report writing, *IEEE Transactions on Professional Communication*, 50, 163–171.

Badaracco, C. (1988) The politics of communication audits, *Public Relations Quarterly*, Fall, 27–31.

Bailey, S. and Marsden, P.V. (1999) Interpretation and interview context: Examining the general social survey name generator using cognitive methods, *Social Networks*, 21, 287–309.

Baker, R. (1999) The role of clinical audit in changing performance, in R. Baker, H. Hearnshaw and N. Robertson (eds) *Implementing Change With Clinical Audit*, Chichester: Wiley.

Baker, R., Hearnshaw, H. and Robertson, N. (eds) (1999) *Implementing Change with Clinical Audit*, Chichester: Wiley.

Baker, S., Holland, J. and Kaufman-Scarborough, C. (2007) How consumers with disabilities perceive 'welcome' in retail servicescapes: A critical incident study, *Journal of Services Marketing*, 21, 160–173.

Banach, B. (1998) The best interests of the child: Decision-making factors, *Families in Society*, 79, 331–340.

Barbeite, F. and Weiss, E. (2004) Computer self-efficacy and anxiety scales for an Internet sample: Testing measurement equivalence of existing measures and the development of new scales, *Computers in Human Behavior*, 20, 1–15.

Barbour, R. (2005) Making sense of focus groups, *Medical Education*, 39, 742–750.

Barnett, C. and Pratt, M. (2000) From threat-rigidity to flexibility: Toward a learning model of autogenic crisis in organizations, *Journal of Organizational Change Management*, 13, 74–88.

Barrera, M.J. (1980) A method for the assessment of social support networks in community survey research, *Connections*, 3, 8–13.

Barrie, J.M. (1891) *The Little Minster*, London: Cassell and Co.

Barrington, G. (1992) Evaluation skills nobody taught me, in A. Vaux, M. Stockdale and M. Schwerin (eds) *Independent Consulting for Evaluators*, Newbury Park, CA: Sage.

Bartunek, J.M., Rousseau, D.M., Rudolph J.W. and DePalma, J.A. (2006) On the receiving end: Sensemaking, emotion, and assessments of an organizational change initiated by others, *Journal of Applied Behavioural Science*, 42, 182–206.

Baruchson-Arbib, S. and Bronstein, J. (2002) A view to the future of the library and information science profession: A Delphi study, *Journal of the American Society for Information Science and Technology*, 53, 397–408.

Basu, K. and Palazzo, G. (2008) Corporate social responsibility: A process model of sensemaking, *Academy of Management Review*, 33, 122–136.

Bate, P., Bevan, H. and Robert, G. (2004) *Towards a Million Change Agents. A Review of the Social Movements Literature: Implications for Large Scale Change in the NHS*, London: NHS Modernisation Agency. Accessed 29 February 2008 from http://eprints.ucl.ac.uk/archive/00001133/01/million.pdf

Bazeley, P. and Richards, L. (2000) *The Nvivo Qualitative Project Book*, London: Sage.

Bean, C.J. and Eisenberg, E.M. (2006) Employee sensemaking in the transition to nomadic work, *Journal of Organizational Change Management*, 19, 210–222.

Bean, C.J. and Hamilton, F.E. (2006) Leader framing and follower sensemaking: Response to downsizing in the brave new world, *Human Relations*, 59, 321–349.

Beaumont, C. (2008) The shine comes off social networking, *The Daily Telegraph: Review Section*, 26 January, 21.

Bedien, A. (1980) *Organizations: Theory and Analysis*, Hinsdale, IL: The Dryden Press.

Begbie, R. and Chudry, F. (2002) The intranet chaos matrix: A conceptual framework for designing an effective knowledge management intranet, *Journal of Database Marketing*, 9, 325–338.

Bejou, D., Edvardsson, B. and Rakowski, J. (1996) A critical incident approach to examining the effects of service failures on customer relationships: The case of Swedish and US airlines, *Journal of Travel Research*, 35, 35–40.

Bellotti, V., Ducheneaut, N., Howard, M., Smith, I. and Grinter, R. (2005) Quality versus quantity: E-mail-centric task management and its relation with overload, *Human–Computer Interaction*, 20, 89–138.

Berners-Lee, T., Cailliau, R., Groff, J. and Pollermann, B. (1992) World Wide Web: The information universe, *Electronic Networking*, 2, 52–58.

Beyer, A. (2008) The beauty of focus groups, *Marketing Matters*, January, 32–33.

Beyer, H. and Holtzblatt, K. (1998) *Contextual Design. Defining Customer-Centered Systems*, San Francisco, CA: Morgan Kaufmann.

Biere, A. (1998) Solving mystery shopping, *Bank Marketing*, 30, 30–34.

Bilbao, A., March, C. and Prieto, R. (2002) Ten contributions to the use of qualitative methodology in an audit of internal communication in primary care, *Revista Española de Salud Pública*, 76, 483–492.

Bishop, L. and Levine, D.L. (1999) Computer-mediated communication as employee voice: A case study, *Industrial and Labor Relations Review*, 52, 213–233.

Blakely, R. (2007) The 50 best business blogs, *The Times Online*, 13 June. Accessed 1 February 2008 from http://business.timesonline.co.uk/tol/business/industry_sectors/media/article1923706.ece

Blanchard, D. (2008) Lean in for a smooth ride, *Industry Week*, January, 38.

Blenkin, G. and Kelly, A. (2001) *Action Research for Professional Development*, London: Chapman.

Blow, A. and Sprenkle, D. (2001) Common factors across theories of marriage and family therapy: A modified Delphi study, *The Journal of Marital and Family Therapy*, 27, 385–401.

Boddy, C. (2005) A rose by any other name may smell as sweet but 'group discussion' is not another name for 'focus group' nor should it be, *Qualitative Market Research*, 8, 248–255.

Boehm, B.W. (1981) *Software Engineering Economics*, Englewood Cliffs, NJ: Prentice Hall.

Bogardus, E. (1926) The group interview, *Journal of Applied Sociology*, 10, 371–382.

Boje, D. (1995) Stories of the storytelling organization: A postmodern analysis of Disney as 'Tamara-Land', *Academy of Management Journal*, 38, 997–1035.

Bolger, N., Davis, D. and Rafaeli, E. (2003) Diary methods: Capturing life as it is lived, *Annual Review of Psychology*, 54, 579–616.

Bontis, N., Fearon, M. and Hishan, M. (2003) The e-flow audit: An evaluation of knowledge flow within and outside a high-tech firm, *Journal of Knowledge Management*, 7, 6–19.

Borgatti, S.P., Everett, M.G. and Freeman, L.C. (2002) *UCINET for Windows: Software for Social Network Analysis*, Harvard, MA: Analytic Technologies.

Bostrom, R.N. (2006) The process of listening, in O. Hargie (ed.) *The Handbook of Communication Skills* (3rd edn), London: Routledge.

Bovasso, G. (1996) A network analysis of social contagion processes in an organizational intervention, *Human Relations*, 59, 1419–1435.

Bowen, D., Gilliland, S. and Folger, R. (1999) HRM and service fairness: How being fair with employees spills over to customers, *Organizational Dynamics*, 27, 7–23.

Boyatzis, R.E. (1998) *Thematic Analysis and Code Development: Transforming Qualitative Information*, Thousand Oaks, CA: Sage.

Bradbury, A. (2006) *Successful Presentation Skills* (3rd edn), London: Kogan Page.

Brase, G. (2002) Which statistical formats facilitate what decisions? The perception and influence of different statistical information formats, *Journal of Behavioral Decision Making*, 15, 381–401.

Brass, D.J. (1995) A social network perspective on human resource management, *Research in Personnel and Human Resources Management*, 13, 39–79.

Breakwell, G.M. and Wood, P. (1995) Diary techniques, in G.M. Breakwell, S. Hammond and C. Fife-Shaw (eds) *Research Methods in Psychology*, London: Sage.

Breen, R.L. (2006) A practical guide to focus-group research, *Journal of Geography in Higher Education*, 30, 463–475.

Brehm, S. and Brehm, J. (1981) *Psychological Reactance: A Theory of Freedom and Control*, New York: Academic Press.

Brenner, M. (1981) Skills in the research interview, in M. Argyle (ed.) *Social Skills and Work*, London: Methuen.

Brewer, D.D. (1995) Patterns in the recall of persons in a department of a formal organization, *Journal of Quantitative Anthropology*, 5, 255–284.

Brewer, D.D. (2000) Forgetting in the recall-based elicitation of personal and social networks, *Social Networks*, 22, 29–43.

Bristol, T. and Fern, E. (2003) The effects on interaction on consumers' attitudes in focus groups, *Psychology and Marketing*, 20, 433–444.

Brooks, K. (2002) The influence of focus group feedback on the three organizational levels of an international retailer, *Journal of European Industrial Training*, 26, 204–208.

Broomfield, D. and Humphris, G. (2001) Using the Delphi technique to identify the cancer education requirements of general practitioners, *Medical Education*, 35, 928–937.

Broström A., Strömberg, A., Dahlström, U. and Fridlund, B. (2003) Congestive heart failure, spouses' support and the couple's sleep situation: A critical incident technique analysis, *Journal of Clinical Nursing*, 12, 223–233.

Brown, A. (1995) *Organizational Culture*, London: Pitman Publishing.

Brown, A.D. and Humphreys, M. (2003) Epic and tragic tales: Making sense of change, *Journal of Applied Behavioral Science*, 39, 121–144.

Brown, N. (2006) The development of a questionnaire assessing metacognitive patterns of students majoring in accounting in higher education, *Accounting Education*, 15, 301–323.

Brown, R. and Newman, D. (1983) An investigation of the effects of different data presentation formats and order of arguments in a simulated adversary evaluation, *Educational Evaluation and Policy Analysis*, 4, 197–203.

Bruch, H., Gerber, P. and Maier, V. (2005) Strategic change decisions: Doing the right change right, *Journal of Change Management*, 5, 97–107.

Bryant, M. (2006) Talking about change. Understanding employee responses through qualitative research, *Management Decision*, 44, 246–258.

Bryman, A. (1988) *Quantity and Quality in Social Research*, London: Unwin Hyman.

Bryman, A. (2002) Series editor's foreword, in G.R. Gibbs (ed.) *Qualitative Data Analysis: Explorations with Nvivo*, Buckingham: Open University Press.

Buckingham, L. and Cowe, R. (1999) We'd rather not go to the shops, *The Guardian*, 3 April, 26.

Bunz, U. (2001a) *The Internet Fluency Scale: Development, Results, and Application*, Paper presented at the National Communication Association Convention, Atlanta, GA.

Bunz, U. (2001b) *Usability and Gratifications: Towards a Website Analysis Model*,

Paper presented at the Annual Conference of the National Communication Association, Atlanta, GA.

Bunz, U. (2003) Growing from computer literacy towards computer-mediated communication competence: Evolution of a field and evaluation of a new measurement instrument, *Information Technology, Education and Society*, 4, 53–84.

Burchell, N. and Kolb, D. (2003) Pattern matching organizational cultures, *Journal of the Australian and New Zealand Academy of Management*, 9, 50–61.

Burnside, A. (1994) In-store spies snuff out poor service, *Marketing*, 28 April, 32–33.

Butterfield, L., Borgen, W., Amundson N. and Maglio, A. (2005) Fifty years of the critical incident technique: 1954–2004 and beyond, *Qualitative Research*, 5, 475–497.

Callison, C. (2003) Media relations and the Internet: How *Fortune* 500 company web sites assist journalists in news gathering, *Public Relations Review*, 29, 29–41.

Calvert, P. (2005) It's a mystery: Mystery shopping in New Zealand's libraries, *Library Review*, 54, 24–35.

Cameron, A. and Webster, J. (2005) Unintended consequences of emerging communication technologies: Instant messaging in the workplace, *Computers in Human Behavior*, 21, 85–103.

Campbell, A. (2007) *The Blair Years*, London: Hutchinson.

Campbell, M. (1982) The business communications audit: Evaluating and improving business communications, *Montana Business Quarterly*, 20, 15–18.

Campion, M.A., Palmer, D.K. and Campion, J.E. (1997) A review of structure in the selection interview, *Personnel Psychology*, 50, 655–702.

Cannon, M. and Witherspoon, R. (2005) Actionable feedback: Unlocking the power of learning and performance improvement, *Academy of Management Executive*, 19, 120–134.

Carlyle, T. (1860) *Critical and Miscellaneous Essays*, Vol. II, Boston, MA: Brown and Taggard.

Carnall, C. (2007) *Managing Change in Organizations* (5th edn), Englewood Cliffs, NJ: Prentice Hall.

Carrigan, M. and Kirkup, M. (2001) The ethical responsibilities of marketers in retail observational research: Protecting stakeholders through the ethical 'research covenant', *The International Review of Retail, Distribution and Consumer Research*, 11, 415–435.

Caulkin, S. (2007) What sort of boss gives a monkey's about his staff?, *The Observer Business Supplement*, 28 January, 8.

Caves, R. (1988) Consultative methods for extracting expert knowledge about professional competence, in R. Ellis (ed.) *Professional Competence and Quality Assurance in the Caring Professions*, London: Croom Helm.

Caywood, C. (1998) Taking an outside-in approach, *Strategic Communication Management*, February–March, 21.

Chalmers, M., Liedtka, T. and Bednar, C. (2006) A library communication audit for the twenty-first century, *Libraries and the Academy*, 6, 185–195.

Chartered Institute of Personnel Development (CIPD) (2006) *Working Life: Employee Attitudes and Engagement*, London: CIPD.

Cheek, J., O'Brien, B., Ballantyne, A. and Pincombe, J. (1997) Using critical incident technique to inform aged and extended care nursing, *Western Journal of Nursing Research*, 19, 667–682.

Chen, L.Y. (2004) Examining the effect of organization culture and leadership behaviours on organizational commitment, job satisfaction, and job performance at small and middle-sized firms of Taiwan, *Journal of American Academy of Business*, 5, 432–439.

Cheney, G., Christensen, L., Zorn, T. and Ganesh, S. (2004) *Organizational Communication in an Age of Globalisation: Issues, Reflections, Practices*, Prospect Heights, IL: Waveland Press.

Cheney, G., Straub, J., Speirs-Glebe, L., Stohl, C., DeGooyer, D., Whalen, S., Garvin-Doxas, K. and Carlone, D. (1998) Democracy, participation, and communication at work: A multidisciplinary perspective, in M. Roloff and G. Paulson (eds) *Communication Yearbook* (Vol. 21), New York: Sage.

Cheng, S., Olsen, W., Southerton, D. and Warde, A. (2007) The changing practice of eating: Evidence from UK time diaries, 1975 and 2000, *British Journal of Sociology*, 58, 39–61.

Chiang, P. and Chapman, S. (2006) Do pharmacy staff recommend evidenced-based smoking cessation products? A pseudo patron study, *Journal of Clinical Pharmacy and Therapeutics*, 31, 205–209.

Chisnall, P. (1997) *Marketing Research* (5th edn), Maidenhead: McGraw-Hill.

Christensen, L. (2002) Corporate communication: The challenge of transparency, *Corporate Communication: An International Journal*, 7, 162–168.

Christie, C. (2007) Reported influence of evaluation data on decision makers' actions: An empirical examination, *American Journal of Evaluation*, 28, 8–25.

Cialdini, R. (2001) *Influence: Science and Practice* (4th edn), New York: Harper Collins.

Clampitt, P. (2005) *Communicating for Managerial Effectiveness* (3rd edn), Newbury Park, CA: Sage.

Clampitt, P. (2007) Decision downloading, *MIT Sloan Management Review*, Winter, 48(2), 77–82.

Clampitt, P. and Berk, L. (1996) Strategically communicating organizational change, *Journal of Communication Management*, 1, 15–28.

Clampitt, P. and Downs, C. (1993) Employee perceptions of the relationship between communication and productivity, *Journal of Business Communication*, 30, 5–28.

Clampitt, P. and Girard, D. (1987) *Time for Reflection: A Factor Analytic Study of the Communication Satisfaction Instrument*, Paper presented at the ICA Convention, May.

Clampitt, P. and Girard, D. (1993) Communication satisfaction: A useful construct?, *New Jersey Journal of Communication*, 1, 84–102.

Clampitt, P. and Williams, M. (2005) Conceptualizing and measuring how employees and organizations manage uncertainty, *Communication Research Reports*, 22, 315–324.

Clampitt, P. and Williams, M. (2007) Decision downloading, *Sloan Management Review*, 48, 77–82.

Clayton, M. (1997) Delphi: A technique to harness expert opinion for critical decision-making tasks in education, *Educational Psychology*, 17, 373–386.

Clegg, S., Hardy, C., Lawrence, T. and Nord, W. (eds) (2006) *The Sage Handbook of Organization Studies* (2nd edn), London: Sage.

Cobb, R. (1997) Isn't it just common sense?, *Marketing*, 31 July, S16–18.

Cochran, J. and Bromley, M. (2003) The myth(?) of the police sub-culture,

Policing: An International Journal of Police Strategies and Management, 26, 88–117.

Cohen, J. (1960) A coefficient of agreement for nominal scales, *Educational and Psychological Measurement*, 20, 37–46.

Cohen, L. and Manion, L. (1980) *Research Methods in Education*, London: Croom Helm.

Cole, B. (2007) Physician recruitment tactics offer docs peace of mind, *Health Care Strategic Management*, 25, 2–4.

Coleman, J.S. (1988) Social capital in the creation of human capital, *American Journal of Sociology*, 94, S95–S120.

Collier, P., Edwards, J. and Shaw, D. (2004) Communicating knowledge about police performance, *International Journal of Productivity and Performance Management*, 534, 58–67.

Collins, M. (1997) Interviewer variability: A review of the problem, *Journal of the Market Research Society*, 39, 69–84.

Conaway, R. (1994) The communication audit as a class project, *The Bulletin of the Association for Business Communication*, 57, 39–43.

Conger, J. (1998) The necessary art of persuasion, *Harvard Business Review*, 76, 85–95.

Connelly, C. and Kelloway, E. (2003) Predictors of employees' perceptions of knowledge sharing culture, *Leadership and Organization Development Journal*, 24, 294–301.

Conrad, P. and Reinarz, S. (1984) Qualitative computing: Approaches and issues, *Qualitative Sociology*, 7, 34–60.

Cooke, R.A. and Lafferty, J.C. (1983, 1986, 1987, 1989) *Organizational Culture Inventory*, Plymouth, MI: Human Synergistics, Copyright 1989 by Human Synergistics, Inc. Adapted by permission.

Cooren, F. (ed.) (2007) *Interacting and Organizing: Analyses of a Management Meeting*, Mahwah, NJ: Lawrence Erlbaum Associates, Inc.

Cooren, F., Taylor, J. and Van Every, E. (eds) (2006) *Communication as Organizing: Empirical and Theoretical Explorations in the Dynamic of Text and Organization*, Mahwah, NJ: Lawrence Erlbaum Associates, Inc.

Cope, N. (2004) Intelligence led policing or policing led intelligence, *The British Journal of Criminology*, 44, 188–203.

Corman, S. (2006) On being less theoretical and more technological in organizational communication, *Journal of Business and Technical Communication*, 20, 325–338.

Corman, S. and Poole, M. (eds) (2000) *Perspectives on Organizational Communication: Finding Common Ground*, New York: Guilford Press.

Cornelissen, J. (2006) Metaphor and the dynamics of knowledge in organizational theory: A case study of the organizational identity metaphor, *Journal of Management Studies*, 43, 683–709.

Cornelissen, J. (2008) *Corporate Communications: Theory and Practice* (2nd edn), London: Sage.

Cornelissen, J., van Bekkum, T. and van Ruler, B. (2006) Corporate communications: A practice-based theoretical conceptualisation, *Corporate Reputation Review*, 9, 114–133.

Coté, C., Notterman, D., Karl, H., Weinberg, J. and McCloskey, C. (2000) Adverse sedation events in pediatrics: A critical incident analysis of contributing factors, *Pediatrics*, 105, 805–814.

Cox, A. and Thompson, I. (1998) On the appropriateness of benchmarking, *Journal of General Management*, 23, 1–20.

Cox, K., Bergen, A. and Norman, I. (1993) Exploring consumer views of care provided by the Macmillan nurse using the critical incident technique, *Journal of Advanced Nursing*, 18, 408–415.

Coyle, A. (2006) Discourse analysis, in G. Breakwell, S. Hammond, C. Fife-Schaw and J.A. Smith (eds) *Research Methods in Psychology*, London: Sage.

Crabtree, A. (1998) Ethnography in participatory design, in R. Chatfield, S. Kuhn and M. Muller (eds) *Proceedings of the 1998 Participatory Design Conference*, 12–14 November, Seattle. Palo Alto, CA: Computer Professionals Social Responsibility.

Craig, R. (1999) Communication theory as a field, *Communication Theory*, 9, 119–161.

Craine, K. (2007) Managing the cycle of change, *Information Management Journal*, 41, 44–50.

Cramp, B. (1994) Industrious espionage, *Marketing*, 18 August, 17–18.

Crampton, S., Hodge, J. and Mishra, J. (1998) The informal communication network: Factors influencing grapevine activity, *Public Personnel Management*, 27, 569–584.

Crino, M.D. and White, M.C. (1981) Satisfaction in communication: An examination of the Downs-Hazen measure, *Psychological Reports*, 49, 831–838.

Croston, S. (2005) Making BP's figures more compelling, *Strategic Communication Management*, 9, 3.

Cruz, M. (1998) Explicit and implicit conclusions in persuasive messages, in M. Allen and R. Preiss (eds) *Persuasion: Advances through Meta-analysis*, Cresskill, NJ: Hampton Press.

Culhane, D. (2008) Blog logs a culture change, *Communication World*, January–February, 40–41.

Cuno, J. (2005) Telling stories: Rhetoric and leadership, a case study, *Leadership*, 1, 205–213.

Curtis, J. (2001) Behind enemy lines, *Marketing*, 24 May, 28–29.

Cushman, D. and King, S. (2001) *Excellence in Communicating Organizational Strategy*, New York: State University of New York Press.

Dabbish, L.A. and Kraut, R.E. (2006) *Email Overload at Work: An Analysis of Factors Associated with Email Strain*, Paper presented at the Annual Conference of the Computer Supported Collaborative Work (CSCW), Alberta, Canada, 4–8 November.

Dalkey, N. and Helmer, O. (1963) An experimental application of the Delphi method to the use of experts, *Management Science*, 9, 458–467.

Daly, F., Teague, P. and Kitchen, P. (2003) Exploring the role of internal communication during organizational change, *Corporate Communications: An International Journal*, 8, 153–162.

Danowski, J.A. and Edison-Swift, P. (1985) Crisis effects on intra-organizational computer-based communication, *Communication Research*, 12, 251–270.

Darity, W. and Mason, P. (1998) Evidence on discrimination in employment: Codes of color, codes of gender, *Journal of Economic Perspectives*, 12, 63–90.

Darshi De Saram, D., Ahmed, S. and Anson, M. (2004) Suitability of the critical incident technique to measure quality of construction coordination, *Journal of Management in Engineering*, 20, 97–109.

Davis, A. (2006a) Taking communication to the next level at Mayo Clinic, *Strategic Communication Management*, 10, 14–17.

Davis, F.D. (1989) Perceived usefulness, perceived ease of use, and user acceptance of information technology, *MIS Quarterly*, 13, 319–340.

Davis, K. (1953) A method of studying communication patterns in organizations, *Personnel Psychology*, 6, 301–312.

Davis, P. (2006b) Critical incident technique: A learning intervention for organizational problem solving, *Development and Learning in Organizations*, 20, 13–16.

Dawes, R. (2001) *Everyday Irrationality: How Pseudo-scientists, Lunatics and the Rest of Us Systematically Fail to Think Rationally*, New York: Westview Press.

Dawley, D. and Anthony, W. (2003) User perceptions of e-mail at work, *Journal of Business and Technical Communication*, 17, 170–200.

Dawson, J. and Hillier, J. (1995) Competitor mystery shopping: Methodological considerations and implications for the MRS Code of Conduct, *Journal of the Market Research Society*, 37, 417–427.

Dawson, P. (2004) Managing change: Communication and political process, in D. Tourish and O. Hargie (eds) *Key Issues in Organizational Communication*, London: Routledge.

Day, J., Dean, A. and Reynolds, P. (1998) Relationship marketing: Its key role in entrepreneurship, *Long Range Planning*, 31, 828–837.

de Cock, C. (1998) Organizational change and discourse: Hegemony, resistance and reconstitution, *M@n@gement*, 1, 1–22.

de Walt, K. and de Walt, B. (2002) *Participant Observation: A Guide for Fieldworkers*, Walnut Creek, CA: AltaMira Press.

Deetz, S. (1995) *Transforming Communication, Transforming Business: Building Responsive and Responsible Workplaces*, Cresskill, NJ: Hampton Press.

Deetz, S. (2001) Conceptual foundations, in F. Jablin and L. Putnam (eds) *The New Handbook of Organizational Communication*, Thousand Oaks, CA: Sage, pp. 3–46.

Deetz, S.A. (1992) *Democracy in an Age of Corporate Colonization: Developments in Communication and the Politics of Everyday Life*, New York: State University of New York Press.

Dekker, D. (2007) Effective versus ineffective communication behaviors in virtual teams, *System Sciences*, January, 41. Available from http://ieeexplore.ieee.org/xpl/freeabs_all.jsp?arnumber=4076452

Delahaye-Paine, K. (2007) How do blogs measure up?, *Communication World*, September–October.

Delbridge, R., Gratton, L., Johnson, G. and the AIM Fellows (2006) *The Exceptional Manager: Making the Difference*, Oxford: Oxford University Press.

Delsen, L. (1998) When do men work part-time?, in J. O'Reilly and C. Fagan (eds) *Part-time Prospects: An International Comparison of Part-time Work in Europe, North America and the Pacific Rim*, London: Routledge.

Denzin, N. (1978) *The Research Act: A Theoretical Introduction to Sociological Methods*, New York: Praeger.

Denzin, N.K. and Lincoln, Y.S. (2005) Introduction: The discipline and practice of qualitative research, in N.K. Denzin and Y.S. Lincoln (eds) *The Sage Handbook of Qualitative Research* (3rd edn), Thousand Oaks, CA: Sage.

DeWine, S. and James, A. (1988) Examining the communication audit: Assessment and modification, *Management Communication Quarterly*, 2, 144–168.

Dickson, D. and Hargie, O. (2006) Sectarianism in the Northern Ireland workplace, *International Journal of Conflict Management*, 7, 9–28.

Dickson, D., Hargie, O., Brunger, K. and Stapleton, K. (2002) Health professionals' perceptions of breaking bad news, *International Journal of Health Care Quality Assurance*, 15, 324–336.

Dickson, D., Hargie, O. and Morrow, N. (1997) *Communication Skills Training for Health Professionals* (2nd edn), London: Chapman and Hall.

Dickson, D., Hargie, O. and Nelson, S. (2004) Cross-community communication and relationships in the workplace: A case study of a large Northern Ireland organization, in O. Hargie and D. Dickson (eds) *Researching the Troubles: Social Science Perspectives on the Northern Ireland Conflict*, Edinburgh: Mainstream Press.

Dickson, D., Hargie, O. and Wilson, N. (2008) Communication, relationships, and religious difference in the Northern Ireland workplace: A study of private and public sector organizations, *Journal of Applied Communication Research*, 36, 128–160.

Dickson, D., Rainey, S. and Hargie, O. (2003) Communicating sensitive business issues: Parts 1 and 2, *Corporate Communications: An International Journal*, 8, 35–43, 121–127.

Dickson, D., Saunders, C. and Stringer, M. (1993) *Rewarding People: The Skill of Responding Positively*, London: Routledge.

Dickson, M., Resick, C. and Hanges, P. (2006) When organizational climate is unambiguous, it is also strong, *Journal of Applied Psychology*, 91, 351–364.

Dillon, J. (1997) Questioning, in O.D.W. Hargie (ed.) *The Handbook of Communication Skills* (2nd edn), London: Routledge.

Disko, J. (1998) Using qualitative data analysis software, *Computers in Human Services*, 15, 1–19.

Doll, W. and Torkzadeh, G. (1988) The measurement of end user computing satisfaction, *MIS Quarterly*, 12, 259–274.

Donaldson, L. (2003) Organization theory as a positive science, in H. Tsoukas and C. Knudsen (eds) *The Oxford Handbook of Organization Theory: Meta-theoretical Perspectives*, Oxford: Oxford University Press.

Döring, N. (2002) Personal home pages on the Web: A review of research, *Journal of Computer-Mediated Communication*, 7. Accessed 28 February 2008 from http://jcmc.indiana.edu/vol7/issue3/doering.html

Doucouliagos, C. (1995) Worker participation and productivity in labor-managed and participatory capitalist forms: A meta-analysis, *Industrial and Labor Relations Review*, 49, 58–77.

Dougherty, D. and Smythe, M. (2004) Sensemaking, organizational culture, and sexual harassment, *Journal of Applied Communication Research*, 32, 293–317.

Dowling, G. (2006) How good corporate reputations create corporate value, *Corporate Reputation Review*, 9, 134–143.

Downs, C. (1988) *Communication Audits*, Glenview, IL: Scott, Foresman.

Downs, C. and Adrian, C. (2004) *Assessing Organizational Communication: Strategic Communication Audits*, New York: Guilford Press.

Downs, C., Clampitt, P. and Laird, A. (1981) *Critique of the ICA Communication Audit*, Paper presented to the International Communication Association, Minneapolis, May.

Downs, C., DeWine, S. and Greenbaum, H. (1994) Measures of organizational communication, in R. Rubin, P. Plamgreen and H. Sypher (eds) *Communication Research Measures: A Sourcebook*, New York: Guilford Press.

Downs, C. and Hazen, M. (1977) A factor analytic study of communication satisfaction, *Journal of Business Communication*, 14, 63–73.

Dowrick, P. (1991) *Practical Guide to Using Video in the Behavioral Sciences*, New York: Wiley.

Duck, S. (1991) Diaries and logs, in B. Montgomery and S. Duck (eds) *Studying Interpersonal Interaction*, New York: Guilford Press.

Dunn, W. and Hamilton, D. (1986) The critical incident technique – a brief guide, *Medical Teacher*, 8, 207–215.

Durutta, N. (2006) The corporate communicator: A senior-level strategist, in T. Gillis (ed.) *The IABC Handbook of Organizational Communication*, San Francisco, CA: Jossey-Bass.

Dwan, B. (2004) Email errors: The cost of careless messages, *Computer Fraud and Security*, February, 16–18.

Eden, C. and Huxham, C. (2006) Researching organizations using action research, in S. Clegg, C. Hardy, T. Lawrence and W. Nord (eds) *The Sage Handbook of Organization Studies* (2nd edn), London: Sage.

Edmunds, A. and Morris, A. (2000) The problem of information overload in business organizations: A review of the literature, *International Journal of Information Management*, 20, 17–28.

Edvardsson, B. and Roos, I. (2001) Critical incident techniques: Towards a framework for analysing the criticality of critical incidents, *International Journal of Service Industry Management*, 12, 251–268.

Edwards, J.E., Thomas, M., Rosenfeld, P. and Booth-Kewley, S. (1997) *How to Conduct Organizational Surveys*, Thousand Oaks, CA: Sage.

Edwards, P. and Wajcman, J. (2005) *The Politics of Working Life*, Oxford: Oxford University Press.

Eisenberg, E. (2000) The kindness of strangers: Hospitality in organizational communication scholarship, in S. Corman and M. Poole (eds) *Foundations of Organizational Communication: Finding Common Ground*, New York: Guilford Press.

Eisenberg, E., Murphy, A. and Andrews, L. (1998) Openness and decision-making in the search for a university provost, *Communication Monographs*, 65, 1–23.

Ellson, A. (2006) Podcasting holds key message for smaller firms, *The Times Online*, 4 May. Accessed 1 February 2008 from http://business.timesonline.co.uk/tol/business/columnists/article712825.ece

Ericsson, K. and Smith, J. (eds) (1991) *Toward a General Theory of Expertise*, Cambridge: Cambridge University Press.

Estell, L. (2001) A green light for incentives, *Incentive*, 175, 114–115.

Etherington, B. (2006) *Presentation Skills for Quivering Wrecks*, London: Cyan Books.

Ettorre, B. (1997) How to get the unvarnished truth, *HR Focus*, 74, 1–3.

Eveland, T.K. and Bikson, J.D. (1987) Evolving electronic communication networks: An empirical assessment, *Office: Technology and People*, 3, 103–128.

Fahy, P. (2006) Online and face-to-face group interaction processes compared using Bales' Interaction Process Analysis (IPA), *European Journal of Open, Distance and E-Learning*, retrieved from www.eurodl.org/ on 26 April 2007.

Fairhurst, G. (2007) *Discursive Leadership: In Conversation with Leadership Psychology*, London: Sage.

Fairhurst, G.T. (2005) Reframing the art of framing: Problems and prospects for leadership, *Leadership*, 1, 165–185.

Fairley, D. (2002) Making accurate estimates, *IEEE Software*, 19, 61–63.

Faull, K., Kalliath, T. and Smith, D. (2004) Organizational culture: The dynamics of culture on organizational change within a rehabilitation center, *Organization Development Journal*, 22, 40–55.

Feather, F. (2000) *Futureconsumer.com: The Webolution of Shopping to 2010*, Toronto: Warwick Publishing.

Feeley, T.H. (2000) Testing a communication network model of employee turnover based on centrality, *Journal of Applied Communication Research*, 28, 262–277.

Feldmann, A. (2007) Internet clean-slate design: What and why?, *ACM SIGCOMM Computer Communication Review*, 37, 59–64.

Feltes, T. (2002) Community-orientated policing in Germany: Training and education, *Policing: An International Journal of Police Strategies and Management*, 25, 48–59.

Fennell, H. (2005) Living leadership in an era of change, *International Journal of Leadership in Education*, 8, 145–165.

Ferligoj, A. and Hlebec, V. (1999) Evaluation of social network measurement instruments, *Social Networks*, 21, 111–130.

Ferris Research (2006) *The Email Archiving Market, 2006–2010*, 10 May.

Fichman, M. and Cummings, J. (2003) Multiple imputation for missing data: Making the most of what you know, *Organizational Research Methods*, 6, 282–308.

Field, J., Ritzman, L., Safizadeh, M. and Downing, C. (2006) Uncertainty reduction approaches, uncertainty coping approaches, and process performance in financial services, *Decision Sciences*, 37, 149–175.

Finch, S., Lalama, C., Spino, C., Schwartz, H., Wasserman, R., McCormick, M. and Bernstein, H. (2008) Practice-based research network solutions to methodological challenges encountered in a national, prospective cohort study of mothers and newborns, *Paediatric and Perinatal Epidemiology*, 22, 87–98.

Fine, C. (2006) *A Mind of Its Own: How Your Brain Distorts and Deceives*, Cambridge: Icon Books.

Fink, A. (2002) *The Survey Kit* (2nd edn), Thousand Oaks, CA: Sage.

Finkelstein, S. (2005) When bad things happen to good companies: Strategy failure and flawed executives, *Journal of Business Strategy*, 26, 19–28.

Finn, A. and Kayandé, U. (1999) Unmasking a phantom: A psychometric assessment of mystery shopping, *Journal of Retailing*, 75, 195–217.

Flanagan, J.C. (1948) Contributions of research in the Armed Forces to personnel psychology, *Personnel Psychology*, 1, 52–53.

Flanagan, J.C. (1954) The critical incident technique, *Psychological Bulletin*, 5, 327–358.

Fletcher, B. (1995) Not just a room with a view, *Marketing*, 23 March, 27–29.

Fletcher, J. (1992) Ethical issues in the selection interview, *Journal of Business Ethics*, 11, 361–367.

Fly, B., van Bark, W., Weinman, L., Kitchener, K. and Lang, P. (1997) Ethical transgressions of psychology graduate students: Critical incidents with implications for training, *Professional Psychology: Research and Practice*, 28, 492–495.

Ford, M. (1999) *Surveillance and Privacy at Work*, London: Institute of Employment Rights.

Forman, J. and Argenti, P. (2005) How corporate communication influences strategy implementation, reputation and the corporate brand: An exploratory qualitative study, *Corporate Reputation Review*, 8, 245–264.

Forrest, C. and Leaver, M. (2007) *Focus on the Digital Age: ICT in the International Economy*, London: Office for National Statistics. Accessed 17 December 2007 from www.statistics.gov.uk/downloads/theme_compendia/foda2007/Chapter6.pdf

Fowler, F.J. and Mangione, T.W. (1990) *Standardized Survey Interviewing: Minimizing Interviewer-related Type Error*, Applied Social Research Methods Series, Vol. 18, Newbury Park, CA: Sage.

Fox, E. (2000) An audit of inter-professional communication within a trauma and orthopaedic directorate, *Journal of Orthopaedic Nursing*, 4, 160–169.

Franklin, K. and Hart, J. (2007) Idea generation and exploration: Benefits and limitations of the policy Delphi research method, *Innovative Higher Education*, 31, 237–246.

Freeman, L.C., Freeman, S.C. and Michaelson, A.G. (1989) How humans see social groups: A test of the Sailer-Gaulin models, *Journal of Quantitative Anthropology*, 1, 229–238.

Freeman, T. (2006) 'Best practice' in focus group research: Making sense of different views, *Journal of Advanced Nursing*, 56, 491–497.

Friedkin, N.E. and Slater, R.M. (1994) School leadership and performance: A social network approach, *Sociology of Education*, 67, 139–157.

Friedman, K. (2007) Power up your PowerPoint presentations: Rely on more than your slides, *Tactics*, March, 22.

Friedman, R. and Currall, S. (2003) Conflict escalation: Dispute exacerbating elements of e-mail communication, *Human Relations*, 56, 1325–1347.

Friedman, S.D. and Saul, K. (1991) A leader's wake: Organization member reactions to CEO succession, *Journal of Management*, 17, 619–642.

Frownfelter-Lohrke, C. and Fulkerson, C. (2001) The incidence and quality of graphics in annual reports: An international comparison, *Journal of Business Communication*, 30, 337–357.

Fu, Y. (2007) Contact diaries: Building archives of actual and comprehensive personal networks, *Field Methods*, 19, 194–217.

Füller, J. and Matzler, K. (2008) Customer delight and market segmentation: An application of the three-factor theory of customer satisfaction on life style groups, *Tourism Management*, 29, 116–126.

Gabbionta, G., Ravasi, D. and Mazzola, P. (2007) Exploring the drivers of corporate reputation: A study of Italian securities analysts, *Corporate Reputation Review*, 10, 99–123.

Gaber, I. (1996) Hocus-pocus polling: You can get any result you want from a focus group. That doesn't mean it will be right, *New Statesman*, 125, 20–22.

Gabriel, Y. (1998) The use of stories, in G. Symon and C. Cassell (eds) *Qualitative Methods and Analysis in Organizational Research. A Practical Guide*, London: Sage.

Gabriel, Y. (2004) Narratives, stories and texts, in D. Grant, C. Hardy, C. Oswick and L. Putnam (eds) *The Sage Handbook of Organizational Discourse*, London: Sage.

Gadman, S. and Cooper, C. (2005) Strategies for collaborating in an interdependent impermanent world, *Leadership and Organization Development Journal*, 26, 23–34.

Gao, H., Darroch, J., Mather, D. and MacGregor, A. (2008) Signalling corporate strategy in IPO communication: A study of biotechnology IPS on the NASDAQ, *Journal of Business Communication*, 45, 3–30.

Gayeski, D. (2000) From audits to analytics, *Communication World*, 17, 28–31.

Gee, J.P. (1999) *An Introduction to Discourse Analysis*, London: Routledge.

Gergen, K. (2000) *Invitation to Social Constructionism*, London: Sage.

Ghoshal, S., Korine, H. and Szulanski, G. (1994) Interunit communication in multinational corporations, *Management Science*, 40, 96–110.

Giambatista, R.C., Rowe, W.G. and Riaz, S. (2005) Nothing succeeds like succession: A critical review of leadership succession literature since 1994, *Leadership Quarterly*, 16, 963–991.

Gildea, J. and Rosenberg, K. (1979) Auditing organizational communications: Is there life beyond print-outs?, *University of Michigan Business Review*, 41, 7–12.

Gioia, D.A. and Chittipeddi, K. (1991) Sensemaking and sensegiving in strategic change initiation, *Strategic Management Journal*, 12, 433–448.

Gioia, D.A. and Thomas, J.B. (1996) Identity, image, and issue interpretation: Sensemaking during strategic change in academia, *Administrative Science Quarterly*, 41, 370–404.

Gladwell, M. (2006) *Blink: The Power of Thinking Without Thinking*, Harmondsworth: Penguin.

Glaser, B. (1978) *Theoretical Sensitivity: Advances in the Methodology of Grounded Theory*, Mill Valley, CA: Sociology Press.

Glaser, S., Zamanou, S. and Hacker, K. (1987) Measuring and interpreting organizational culture, *Management Communication Quarterly*, 1, 173–198.

Gledhill, R. (2007) Non-believers to sit in judgement on churches, *The Times*, 21 December, 32.

Goldhaber, G. (1976) *The ICA Communication Audit: Rationale and Development*, Paper presented at the Academy of Management convention, Kansas City.

Goldhaber, G. (1993) *Organizational Communication* (6th edn), Madison, WI: WCB Brown and Benchmark.

Goldhaber, G. (2002) Communication audits in the age of the internet, *Management Communication Quarterly*, 15, 451–457.

Goldhaber, G. and Krivonos, P. (1977) The ICA communication audit: Process, status, critique, *Journal of Business Communication*, 15, 41–56.

Goldhaber, G. and Rogers, D. (1979) *Auditing Organizational Communication Systems: The ICA Communication Audit*, Dubuque, IA: Kendall/Hunt.

Goldhaber, G.M., Yates, M.P., Porter, D.P. and Lesniak, R. (1978) Organizational communication: 1978, *Human Communication Research*, 5, 76–96.

Goldman, E. and McDonald, S. (1987) *The Group Depth Interview: Principles and Practice*, Englewood Cliffs, NJ: Prentice Hall.

Gorden, R.L. (1987) *Interviewing: Strategies, Techniques and Tactics* (4th edn), Homewood, IL: Dorsey Press.

Gordon, T. (1994) *The Delphi Method*, AC/UNU Millennium Project Futures Research Methodology, available from www.futurovenezuela.org/_curso/5-delphi.pdf

Granovetter, M. (1973) The strength of weak ties, *American Journal of Sociology*, 78, 1360–1380.

Grant, D., Hardy, C., Oswick, C. and Putnam, L. (eds) (2004) *The SAGE Handbook of Organizational Discourse*, London: Sage.

Greatorex, J. and Dexter, T. (2000) An accessible analytical approach for investigating what happens between the rounds of a Delphi study, *Journal of Advanced Nursing*, 32, 1016–1024.

Green, S.M. (1992) Total systems intervention: Organizational communication in North Yorkshire Police, *Systems Practice*, 5, 585–599.

Greenbaum, H. Clampitt, P. and Willihnganz, S. (1988) Organizational communication: An examination of four instruments, *Management Communication Quarterly*, 2, 245–282.

Greenbaum, H. and White, N. (1976) Biofeedback at the organizational level: The communication audit, *Journal of Business Communication*, 13, 3–15.

Greenbaum, T. (1994) Focus group research: A useful tool, *HR Focus*, 71, 3.

Greenbaum, T. (1998) *The Handbook for Focus Group Research*, Thousand Oaks, CA: Sage.

Greenbaum, T. (2000) *Moderating Focus Groups: A Practical Guide for Group Facilitation*, Thousand Oaks, CA: Sage.

Greene, J. (2000) Community policing in America: Changing the nature, structure, and function of the police, in J. Horney (ed.) *Criminal Justice, Vol. 3: Policies, Processes, and Decisions of the Criminal Justice System*, Washington, DC: National Institute of Justice.

Gremler, D. (2004) The critical incident technique in service research, *Journal of Service Research*, 7, 65–89.

Grix, J. (2004) *The Foundations of Research*, Basingstoke: Palgrave Macmillan.

Grove, S. and Fisk, R. (1997) The impact of other customers on service experiences: A critical incident examination of 'getting along', *Journal of Retailing*, 73, 63–85.

Grunig, J. and Grunig, L. (2006) Characteristics of excellent communication, in T. Gillis (ed.) *The IABC Handbook of Organizational Communication*, San Francisco, CA: Jossey-Bass.

Gumpert, G. and Drucker, S. (1998) The demise of privacy in a private world: From front porches to chat rooms, *Communication Theory*, 8, 408–425.

Gurchiek, K. (2006) Shoddy writing trips up employees, firms, *HR Magazine*, July, 44.

Hacker, K., Goss, B., Townley, C. and Horton, V. (1998) Employee attitudes regarding electronic mail policies: A case study, *Management Communication Quarterly*, 11, 422–452.

Hague, P. and Jackson, P. (1995) *Do Your Own Market Research* (2nd edn), London: Kogan Page.

Hallowell, E. (1999) The human moment at work, *Harvard Business Review*, 77, 58–70.

Hamel, G. (with Breen, B.) (2007) *The Future of Management*, Boston, MA: Harvard University Press.

Hamm, J. (2006) The five messages leaders must manage, *Harvard Business Review*, May, 114–123.

Hanlon, M.D. (1980) Observational methods in organizational assessment, in E. Lawler, D.A. Nadler and C. Cammann (eds) *Organizational Assessment: Perspectives on the Measurement of Organizational Behavior and the Quality of Work Life*, New York: Wiley.

Hardage, G. (2006) Communicating the Southwest way, *Strategic Communication Management*, 10, 4.

Hargie, O. (2006) Skill in practice: An operational model of communicative performance, in O. Hargie (ed.) *The Handbook of Communication Skills* (3rd edn), London: Routledge.

Hargie, O. (2007) Managing your communications: A key determinant of organizational success, in R. Karlsdottir (ed.) *Læring, Kommunikasjon og Lederutvikling*, Trondheim, Norway: Tapir Akademisk Forlag.

Hargie, O. and Dickson, D. (2004) *Skilled Interpersonal Communication. Research, Theory and Practice* (4th edn), London: Routledge.

Hargie, O. and Dickson, D. (2007) Are important corporate policies understood by employees? A tracking study of organizational information, *Journal of Communication Management*, 11, 9–28.

Hargie, O., Dickson, D. and Nelson, S. (2003) Working together in a divided society: A study of inter-group communication in the Northern Ireland workplace, *Journal of Business and Technical Communication*, 17, 285–318.

Hargie, O., Dickson, D. and Tourish, D. (2004) *Communication Skills for Effective Management*, Basingstoke: Palgrave Macmillan.

Hargie, O. and McCoy, M. (2007) The importance of context: How a problem like the evaluation of communication can be solved, *Communication Director*, 2, 80–83.

Hargie, O., Morrow, N. and Woodman, C. (2000) Pharmacists' evaluation of key communication skills in practice, *Patient Education and Counseling*, 39, 61–70.

Hargie, O. and Tourish, D. (1993) Assessing the effectiveness of communication in organizations: The communication audit approach, *Health Services Management Research*, 6, 276–285.

Hargie, O. and Tourish, D. (1994) Communication skills training: Management manipulation or personal development?, *Human Relations*, 47, 1377–1389.

Hargie, O. and Tourish, D. (1996a) Auditing communication practices to improve the management of human resources: A regional study, *Health Services Management Research*, 9, 209–222.

Hargie, O. and Tourish, D. (1996b) Auditing internal communication to build business success, *Internal Communication Focus*, November, 10–14.

Hargie, O. and Tourish, D. (1999) The psychology of interpersonal skill, in A. Memon and R. Bull (eds) *Handbook of the Psychology of Interviewing*, Chichester: Wiley.

Hargie, O. and Tourish, D. (2004) How are we doing? Measuring and monitoring organizational communication, in D. Tourish and O. Hargie (eds) *Key Issues in Organizational Communication*, London: Routledge.

Hargie, O., Tourish, D. and Wilson, N. (2002) Communication audits and the effects of increased information: A follow up study, *Journal of Business Communication*, 39, 414–436.

Harley, B., Hyman, J. and Thompson, P. (2005) The paradoxes of participation, in J. Hyman, B. Harley and P. Thompson (eds) *Participation and Democracy at Work: Essays in Honour of Harvie Ramsay*, London: Palgrave.

Harris, M. and Johnson, O. (2000) *Cultural Anthropology* (5th edn), Needham Heights, MA: Allyn and Bacon.

Hart, R. (2006) Measuring success: How to 'sell' a communications audit to internal audiences, *Tactics*, April, 3 and 19.

Hartline, M. and Ferrell, O. (1996) The management of customer-contact service employees, *Journal of Marketing*, 60, 7–26.

Hartman, J. (2004) Using focus groups to conduct business communication research, *Journal of Business Communication*, 41(4), 402–410.

Hatch, M. and Yanow, D. (2003) Organization theory as an interpretive science, in

H. Tsoukas and C. Knudsen (eds) *The Oxford Handbook of Organization Theory: Meta-theoretical Perspectives*, Oxford: Oxford University Press.

Hawking, S. (1988) *A Brief History of Time*, London: Guild Publishing.

Hayslett, M.M. and Wildemuth, B.M. (2004) Pixels or pencils? The relative effectiveness of web-based versus paper surveys, *Library and Information Science Research*, 26, 73–93.

Hecht, M.L. (1978) Measures of communication satisfaction, *Human Communication Research*, 4, 350–368.

Heinssen, R., Glass, C. and Knight, A. (1987) Assessing computer anxiety: Development and validation of the computer anxiety rating scale, *Computers in Human Behavior*, 3, 49–59.

Helm, S. (2007) The role of corporate reputation in determining investor satisfaction and loyalty, *Corporate Reputation Review*, 10, 22–37.

Helmer, O. and Rescher, N. (1959) On the epistemology of the inexact sciences, *Management Science*, 6, 25–52.

Helms-Mills, J. (2003) *Making Sense of Organizational Change*, London: Routledge.

Henderson, J. (2005) Evaluating public relations effectiveness in a health care setting: The identification of communication assets and liabilities via a communication audit, *Journal of Health and Human Services Administration*, 28, 282–322.

Hendrie, J. (2004) A review of a multiple retailer's labour turnover, *International Journal of Retail and Distribution Management*, 32, 434–441.

Hentz, B. (2006) Enhancing presentation narratives through written and visual integration, *Business Communication Quarterly*, 69, 425–429.

Henwood, K. and Pidgeon, N. (1995) Grounded theory and psychological research, *The Psychologist*, 8, 115–118.

Herington, C., Scott, D. and Johnson, L. (2005) Focus group exploration of firm–employee relationship strength, *Qualitative Market Research*, 8, 256–276.

Herrmann, A.F. (2007) Stockholders in cyberspace: Weick's sensemaking online, *Journal of Business Communication*, 44, 13–35.

Higgins, J.M., McAllaster, C., Certo, S.C. and Gilbert, J.P. (2006) Using cultural artefacts to change and perpetuate strategy, *Journal of Change Management*, 6, 397–415.

Hinrichs, J. (1964) Communication activity of industrial research personnel, *Personnel Psychology*, 17, 193–204.

Hodge, B.J., Anthony, W. and Gales, L. (2003) *Organization Theory – A Strategic Approach* (6th edn), Englewood Cliffs, NJ: Prentice Hall.

Hofstede, G. (1998) Attitudes, values and organizational culture: Disentangling the concepts, *Organization Studies*, 19, 477–492.

Hogard, E. (2007) Using consultative methods to investigate professional–client interaction as an aspect of process evaluation, *American Journal of Evaluation*, 28, 304–317.

Hogard, E. and Ellis, R. (2006) Evaluation and communication: Using a communication audit to evaluate organizational communication, *Evaluation Review*, 30, 171–187.

Hogard, E., Ellis, R., Ellis, J. and Barker, C. (2005) Using a communication audit to improve communication on clinical placement in pre-registration nursing, *Nurse Education Today*, 25, 119–125.

Holbert, N. and Speece, M. (1993) *Practical Market Research: An Integrated Global Perspective*, London: Prentice Hall.

Houtkoop-Steenstra, H. (1996) Probing behaviour of interviewers in the standardized semi-open research interview, *Quality and Quantity*, 30, 205–230.

Huang, E.M., Russell, D.M. and Sue, A.E. (2004) IM here: Public instant messaging on large, shared displays for workgroup interactions, *Proceedings of the SIGCHI Conference on Human Factors in Computing Systems*, Vienna, 24–29 April, pp. 279–286.

Hudson (2007) *Cull or Cure: The Secret of an Efficient Company?*, London: Hudson Management Consultancy.

Hughes, R. (2004) Competencies for effective public health nutrition practice: A developing consensus, *Public Health Nutrition*, 7, 683–691.

Human, S.E. and Provan, K.G. (1997) An emergent theory of structure and outcomes in small-firm strategic manufacturing networks, *Academy of Management Journal*, 40, 368–403.

Hunt, O., Tourish, D. and Hargie, O. (2000) The communication experiences of education managers: Identifying strengths, weaknesses and critical incidents, *International Journal of Educational Management*, 14, 120–129.

Hurst, B. (1991) *The Handbook of Communication Skills*, London: Kogan Page.

Hutton, J. (1996) Making the connection between public relations and marketing, *Journal of Communication Management*, 1, 37–48.

Ibarra, H. and Andrews, S.B. (1993) Power, social influence, and sense making: Effects of network centrality and proximity on employee perceptions, *Administrative Science Quarterly*, 38, 277–303.

Ilgen, D. and Davis, C. (2000) Bearing bad news: Reactions to negative performance feedback, *Applied Psychology*, 49, 550–565.

Isabella, L.A. (1990) Evolving interpretations as a change unfolds: How managers construe key organizational events, *Academy of Management Journal*, 33, 7–42.

Ivory, M. and Megraw, R. (2005) Evolution of web site design patterns, *ACM Transactions on Information Systems*, 23, 463–497.

Jaccaud, S. and Quirke, B. (2006) Structuring global communication to improve efficiency, *Strategic Communication Management*, 10, 18–21.

Jackson, J., Dawson, R. and Wilson, D. (2003) Reducing the effect of email interruptions on employees, *International Journal of Information Management*, 23, 55–65.

Jacobs, G. (2006) Communication for commitment in remote technical workforces, *Journal of Communication Management*, 10, 353–370.

Jacobs, M., Jacobs, A., Feldman, G. and Cavior, N. (1973) The 'credibility gap': Delivery of positive and negative emotional and behavioural feedback in groups, *Journal of Consulting and Clinical Psychology*, 41, 215–223.

Jamtvedt, G., Young, J., Kristoffersen, D., O'Brien, M. and Oxman, A. (2008) *Audit and Feedback: Effects on Professional Practice and Health Care Outcomes (Review)*, New York: Wiley. Accessed 3 February 2008 from http://mrw.interscience.wiley.com/cochrane/clsysrev/articles/CD000259/pdf_fs.html

Jeffery, G., Hache, G. and Lehr, R. (1995) A group-based Delphi application: Defining rural career counselling needs, *Measurement and Evaluation in Counseling and Development*, 28, 45–60.

Jennings, C., McCarthy, W. and Undy, R. (1990) *Employee Relations Audits*, London: Routledge.

Jesson, J. (2004) Mystery shopping demystified: Is it a justifiable research method? *The Pharmaceutical Journal*, 272, 615–617.

Johnson, P., Fidler, C. and Rogerson, S. (1998) Management communication: A technological revolution?, *Management Decision*, 36, 160–170.

Johnston, R. (1995) The determinants of service quality: Satisfiers and dissatisfiers, *International Journal of Service Industry Management*, 6, 53–71.

Jones, D. (2002) The interpretive auditor: Reframing the communication audit, *Management Communication Quarterly*, 15, 466–471.

Jones, D. and Stubbe, M. (2004) Communication and the reflective practitioner: A shared perspective from sociolinguistics and organizational communication, *International Journal of Applied Linguistics*, 14, 185–211.

Jones, T. (1997) Create the write impression, Special Supplement: Communicating With Your Customer, *The Times*, 18 February, 8.

Kalla, H. (2005) Integrated internal communications: A multidisciplinary perspective, *Corporate Communications: An International Journal*, 10, 302–314.

Kammeyer-Mueller, J.D. (2002) *The Well-adjusted Newcomer: The Roles of Pre-entry Knowledge, Proactive Personality and Socialization*, PhD thesis, University of Minnesota.

Kanter, R. (1988) Three tiers for innovation research, *Communication Research*, 15, 509–523.

Kanter, R. (1991) Change-master skills: What it takes to be creative, in J. Henry and D. Walker (eds) *Managing Innovation*, London: Sage.

Karp, T. (2006) Transforming organizations for organic growth: The DNA of change leadership, *Journal of Change Management*, 6, 3–20.

Kassing, J. (2007) Going around the boss: Exploring the consequences of circumvention, *Management Communication Quarterly*, 21, 55–74.

Kaynak, E. and Cavlek, N. (2007) Measurement of tourism market potential of Croatia by use of Delphi qualitative research, *Journal of East–West Business*, 12, 105–123.

Kazoleas, D. and Wright, A. (2001) Improving corporate and organizational communications: A new look at developing and implementing the communication audit, in R. Heath (ed.) *Handbook of Public Relations*, Thousand Oaks, CA: Sage.

Keatinge, D. (2002) Versatility and flexibility: Attributes of the critical incident technique in nursing research, *Nursing and Health Sciences*, 4, 33–39.

Keeney, S., Hasson, F. and McKenna, H. (2006) Consulting the oracle: Ten lessons from using the Delphi technique in nursing research, *Journal of Advanced Nursing*, 53, 205–212.

Keers, C. (2007) Using appreciative inquiry to measure employee engagement, *Strategic HR Review*, 6, 10–12.

Kelle, U. (1998) *Computer-Aided Qualitative Data Analysis: Theory, Methods and Practice*, London: Sage.

Kelleher, T. and Miller, B.M. (2006) Organizational blogs and the human voice: Relational strategies and relation outcomes, *Journal of Computer-Mediated Communication*, 11, 395–414.

Kelley, K. (2006) Creating measurable leadership communication standards at Owens Corning, *The Business Communicator*, 7, 8–9.

Kennedy, H. (2004) Enhancing Delphi research: Methods and results, *Journal of Advanced Nursing*, 45, 504–511.

Kennedy, S. and McCarthy, T. (2008) Be in to win, in R. Burke and C. Cooper (eds) *Building More Effective Organizations: HR Management and Performance in Practice*, Cambridge: Cambridge University Press.

Kent, G., Wills, G., Faulkner, A., Parry, G. *et al.* (1996) Patient reactions to met and unmet psychological need: A critical incident analysis, *Patient Education and Counseling*, 28, 187–190.

Kent, K. (1996) Communication as a core management discipline, *Journal of Communication Management*, 1, 29–36.

Kesner, I.F. and Sebora, T.C. (1994) Executive succession: Past, present, and future. *Journal of Management*, 20, 327–372.

Keys, R. (2008) IFRS Blog: Prepare to explain the effects – new business combinations standards. Accessed 1 February 2008 from http://pwc.blogs.com/ifrs/

Kidd, P.S. and Parshall, M.B. (2000) Getting the focus and the group: Enhancing analytical rigour in focus group research, *Qualitative Health Research*, 10, 293–308.

Kiely, J. and Peek, G. (2002) The culture of the British police: Views of police officers, *The Service Industries Journal*, 22, 167–183.

Kim, W. and Mauborgne, R. (2003) Tipping point leadership, *Harvard Business Review*, April, 60–69.

King, N. (1994) The qualitative research interview, in C. Cassell and G. Symon (eds) *Qualitative Methods in Organizational Research. A Practical Guide*, London: Sage.

King, N., Bailey, J. and Newton, P. (1994) Analysing general practitioner' referral decisions. 1. Developing an analytical framework, *Family Practice*, 11, 3–8.

Kippendorf, K. (1980) *Content Analysis: An Introduction to its Methodology*, Beverly Hills, CA: Sage.

Kitzinger, J. (1994) The methodology of focus group interviews: The importance of interaction between research participants, *Sociology of Health and Illness*, 16, 103–121.

Klassen, R.D. and Jacobs, J. (2001) Experimental comparison of web, electronic and mail survey technologies in operations management, *Journal of Operations Management*, 19, 713–728.

Koiso-Kanttila, N. (2005) Time, attention, authenticity and consumer benefits of the web, *Business Horizons*, 48, 63–70.

Koo, M., Krass, I. and Aslani, P. (2003) Factors influencing consumer use of written drug information, *The Annals of Pharmacotherapy*, 37, 259–267.

Kopec, J. (1982) The communication audit, *Public Relations Journal*, 39, 24–27.

Kotter, J. (1982) *The General Managers*, New York: Free Press.

Kramlinger, T. (1998) How to deliver a change message, *Training and Development*, April, 44–47.

Kressel, K., Kennedy, C., Lev, E., Taylor, L. and Hyman, J. (2002) Managing conflict in an urban health care setting: What do 'experts' know?, *Journal of Health Care Law and Policy*, 5, 364–446.

Krueger, R. (1988) *Focus Groups: A Practical Guide for Applied Research*, Newbury Park, CA: Sage.

Krueger, R. (1998a) *Developing Questions for Focus Groups*, Thousand Oaks, CA: Sage.

Krueger, R. (1998b) *Moderating Focus Groups*, Thousand Oaks, CA: Sage.

Krueger, R. (1998c) *Analyzing and Reporting Focus Group Results*, Thousand Oaks, CA: Sage.

Krueger, R. and Casey, M. (2000) *Focus Groups: A Practical Guide for Applied Research* (3rd edn), Thousand Oaks, CA: Sage.

Ladner, D., Wingenbach, G. and Raven, M. (2002) Internet and paper-based data collection methods in agricultural education research, *Journal of Southern Agricultural Education Research*, 52, 40–51.

Laine, P.-M. and Vaara, E. (2007) Struggling over subjectivity: A discursive analysis of strategic development in an engineering group, *Human Relations*, 60, 29–58.

Lamb, S. (2006) How to write it: Business plans and reports, *Business and Economic Review*, October–December, 17–24.

Langley, A. and Royer, I. (2006) Perspectives on doing case study research in organizations, *M@n@gement*, 9, 73–86.

Lanigan, D. (1997) The focus group groupies, *Campaign*, 26 September, 36–37.

Larsen, J. (2008) De-exoticizing tourist travel: Everyday life and sociality on the move, *Leisure Studies*, 27, 21–34.

Latif, D. (2000) The link between moral reasoning scores, social desirability, and patient care performance scores: Empirical evidence from the retail pharmacy setting, *Journal of Business Ethics*, 25, 255–269.

Lauer, L. (1996) Are you using the power of assessments and audits?, *Nonprofit World*, 14, 43–47.

Leana, C. and Van Buren, H. (2000) Eroding organizational social capital among US firms: The price of job instability, in R. Burke and C. Cooper (eds) *The Organization in Crisis: Downsizing, Restructuring and Privatization*, Oxford: Blackwell.

Lee, T. (1999) *Using Qualitative Methods in Organizational Research*, London: Sage.

Lee, W., Tan, T. and Hameed, S. (2005) Polychronicity, the Internet, and the mass media: A Singapore study, *Journal of Computer-Mediated Communication*, 11(1), article 14. Accessed 8 February 2008 from http://jcmc.indiana.edu/vol11/issue1/wplee.html

Leeds, B. (1992) Mystery shopping offers clues to quality service, *Bank Marketing*, 24, 24–26.

Leeds, B. (1995) Mystery shopping: From novelty to necessity, *Bank Marketing*, 27, 17–21.

Leek, S., Turnbull, P. and Naude, P. (2003) How is information technology affecting business relationships? Results from a UK survey, *Industrial Marketing Management*, 32, 119–126.

Leipzig, J. and More, E. (1982) Organizational communication: A review and analysis of three current approaches to the field, *Journal of Business Communication*, 19, 78–89.

Levering, R. and Moskowitz, M. (2006) And the winners are, *Fortune (Europe Edition)*, 30 January, 63.

Levin, D. and Cross, R. (2004) The strength of weak ties you can trust: The mediating role of trust in effective knowledge transfer, *Management Science*, 50, 1477–1490.

Li, F. (2007) *What is e-business? How the Internet Transforms Organizations*, Oxford: Blackwell.

Lidén S. and Skålén, P. (2003) The effect of service guarantees on service recovery, *International Journal of Service Industry Management*, 14, 36–58.

Lightfoot W., Hefti, A. and Mariotti, A. (2005) Using a Delphi panel to survey criteria for successful periodontal therapy in posterior teeth, *Journal of Periodontology*, 76, 1502–1507.

Linstone, H. and Turoff, M. (1975) *The Delphi Method: Techniques and Applications*, Reading, MA: Addison-Wesley.

Linstone, H. and Turoff, M. (2002) *The Delphi Method: Techniques and Applications*,

Information Systems Department at the New Jersey Institute of Technology. Available from www.is.njit.edu/pubs/delphibook/

Litosseliti, L. (2003) *Using Focus Groups in Research*, London: Continuum.

Litterick, D. (2006) Somewhere, someone is watching you as British habit bites Big Apple, *Daily Telegraph*, 25 March, 35.

Lloyd, H. and Varey, R. (2003) Factors affecting internal communication in a strategic alliance project, *Corporate Communications: An International Journal*, 8, 197–207.

Lockshin, L. and McDougall, G. (1998) Service problems and recovery startegies: An examination of the critical incident technique in a business-to-business market, *International Journal of Retail and Distribution Management*, 26, 429–438.

Loeb, S., Penrod, J. and Hupcey, J. (2006) Focus groups: Tactics for success, *Journal of Gerontological Nursing*, 32, 32–38.

Loftus, E. (2004) Memories of things unseen, *Current Directions in Psychological Science*, 13, 145–147.

Lombard, M., Snyder-Duch, J. and Bracken, C.C. (2002) Content analysis in mass communication: Assessment and reporting of intercoder reliability, *Human Communication Research*, 28, 587–604.

Lorenzo, C. and Gómez, M. (2007) Website design and e-consumer: Effects and responses, *International Journal of Internet Marketing and Advertising*, 4, 114–141.

Louis, M.R. (1985) An investigator's guide to workplace culture, in P. Frost, L.F. Moore, M.R. Louis, C.C. Lundenberg and J. Martin (eds) *Organizational Culture*, Beverly Hills, CA: Sage.

Lount, M. (1997) *Interpersonal Communication Processes in the Pastoral Ministry of Catholic Clergy*, DPhil thesis, Northern Ireland: University of Ulster.

Lount, M. and Hargie, O. (1997) The priest as counsellor: An investigation of critical incidents in the pastoral work of Catholic priests, *Counselling Psychology Quarterly*, 10, 247–259.

Love, M. (2006) Cutting through the clutter at Microsoft, *Strategic Communication Management*, 10, 18–21.

Loyd, B. and Loyd, D. (1985) The reliability and validity of an instrument for the assessment of computer attitudes, *Educational and Psychological Measurement*, 45, 903–908.

Lucius, R.H. and Kuhnert, K.W. (1997) Using sociometry to predict team performance in the work place, *Journal of Psychology*, 131, 21–32.

Lui, S., Ngo, H. and Tsang, A. (2001) Interrole conflict as a predictor of job satisfaction and propensity to leave: A study of professional accountants, *Journal of Managerial Psychology*, 16, 469–484.

Lumb, R. and Breazeale, R. (2002) Police officer attitudes and community policing implementation: Developing strategies for durable organizational change, *Policing and Society*, 13, 91–106.

Lundberg, C.G. (1975) Patterns of acquaintanceship in society and complex organization: A comparative study of the small world problem, *Pacific Sociological Review*, 18, 206–221.

Lundberg, M. (2008) A word-of-mouth approach to informal information sharing among part-time and short-term employed front-line workers in tourism, *Journal of Vacation Marketing*, 14, 23–39.

Lunt, P. and Livingstone, S. (1996) Rethinking the focus group in media and communication research, *Journal of Communication*, 46, 79–98.

Luthans, F. and Larsen, J. (1986) How managers really communicate, *Human Relations*, 39, 161–178.

Mabrito, M. (1997) Writing on the front line: A study of workplace writing, *Business Communication Quarterly*, 60, 58–70.

Macht, J. (1998) The new market research, *Inc.*, 20(10), 86–93.

Mackellar, A., Ashcroft, D., Bell, D., James, D. and Marriott, J. (2007) Identifying criteria for the assessment of pharmacy students' communication skills with patients, *American Journal of Pharmaceutical Education*, 71(3). Accessed 17 February 2008 from www.ajpe.org/aj7103/aj710350/aj710350.pdf

MacPhail, A. (2001) Nominal group technique: A useful method for working with young people, *British Educational Research Journal*, 27, 161–170.

Madden, K. and Perry, C. (2003) How do customers of a financial services institution judge its communications?, *Journal of Marketing Communications*, 9, 113–127.

Madlock, P. (2008) The link between leadership style, communicator competence, and employee satisfaction, *Journal of Business Communication*, 45, 61–78.

Maitlis, S. and Lawrence, T.B. (2007) Triggers and enablers of sensegiving in organizations, *Academy of Management Journal*, 50, 57–84.

Malby, R. (1995) The whys and wherefores of audit, in R. Malby (ed.) *Clinical Audit for Nurses and Therapists*, London: Scutari Press.

Mallak, L., Lyth, D., Olson, S., Ulshafer, S. and Sardone, F. (2003) Diagnosing culture in health-care organizations using critical incidents, *International Journal of Health Care Quality Assurance*, 16, 180–190.

Management Decisions Systems (1993) *Employee Surveys: Current and Future Practices*, Darien, CT: MDS.

Manfreda, K., Bosnjak, M., Berzelak, J., Haas, I. and Vehovar, V. (2008) Web surveys versus other survey modes, *International Journal of Market Research*, 50, 79–104.

Manfredi, C., Lacey, L., Warnecke, R. and Balch, G. (1997) Method effects in survey and focus group findings: Understanding smoking cessation in low-SES African American women, *Health Education and Behaviour*, 24, 786–800.

Marcoulides, G. (1989) Measuring computer anxiety: The computer anxiety scale, *Educational and Psychological Measurement*, 49, 733–739.

Marinker, M. (1986) Performance review and professional values, in D. Pendleton, T. Schofield and M. Marinker (eds) *In Pursuit of Quality: Approaches to Performance Review in General Practice*, Exeter, Devon: Royal College of General Practitioners.

Markar, T. and Mahadeshwar, S. (1998) Audit on communication between general practitioners and psychiatrists following an initial outpatient assessment of patients with learning disabilities, *British Journal of Developmental Disabilities*, 44, 38–41.

Markey, R., Hodgkinson, A. and Kowalczyk, J. (2002) Gender, part-time employment and employee participation in Australian workplaces, *Employee Relations*, 24, 129–150.

Marks, P. (2007) Up to no good? It'll be in your emails, *The New Scientist*, 196 (2632), 30.

Marsden, J., Dolan, B. and Holt, L. (2003) Nurse practitioner practice and deployment: Electronic mail Delphi study, *Journal of Advanced Nursing*, 43, 595–605.

Martensson, J., Dracup, K. and Fridlund, B. (2001) Decisive situations influencing spouses' support of patients with heart failure: A critical incident technique analysis, *Heart and Lung*, 30, 341–350.

Martin, J. (2002) *Organizational Culture: Mapping the Terrain*, Thousand Oaks, CA: Sage.

Martínez-Iñigo, D., Totterdell, P., Alcover, C. and Holman, D. (2007) Emotional labour and emotional exhaustion: Interpersonal and intrapersonal mechanisms, *Work and Stress*, 21, 30–47.

Mason, S. (2005) Email and compliance, *Computer Fraud and Security*, December, 8–11.

Mavis, B. and Brocato, J. (1998) Postal surveys versus electronic mail surveys: The tortoise and the hare revisited, *Evaluation and The Health Professions*, 21, 395–408.

Mayfield, C., Wingenbach, G. and Chalmers, D. (2005) Assessing stakeholder needs: Delphi meets the internet, *Journal of Extension*, 43(3), Article Number 3IAW1. Available from www.joe.org/joe/2005june/iw1.shtml

Mayfield, J. and Mayfield, M. (2006) The benefits of leader communication on part-time worker outcomes: A comparison between part-time and full-time workers using motivating language, *Journal of Business Strategies*, 23, 131–154.

Mazzoni, G. and Memon, A. (2003) Imagination can create false autobiographical memories, *Psychological Science*, 14, 186–188.

McAleese, D. and Hargie, O. (2004) Five guiding principles of culture management: A synthesis of best practice, *Journal of Communication Management*, 9, 155–170.

McBride, A., Pates, R., Ramadan, R. and McGowan, C. (2003) Delphi survey of experts' opinions on strategies used by community pharmacists to reduce over-the-counter drug misuse, *Addiction*, 98, 487–497.

McComb, S.A., Bourne, K.A. and Barringer, M.W. (2003) Reconciling the paradox of part-time service work, *Organizational Dynamics*, 32, 342–356.

McCoy, M. and Hargie, O. (2001) Evaluating evaluation: Implications for assessing quality, *International Journal of Health Care Quality Assurance*, 14, 317–327.

McCoy, M. and Hargie, O. (2003) Implications of mass communication theory for asymmetric public relations evaluation, *Journal of Communication Management*, 7, 304–316.

McFadyen, M. and Cannella, A. (2004) Social capital and knowledge creation: Diminishing returns of the number and strength of exchange relationships, *Academy of Management Journal*, 47, 735–746.

McGrane, F., Wilson, J. and Cammock, T. (2005) Leading employees in one-to-one dispute resolution, *Leadership and Organization Development Journal*, 26, 263–279.

McKeans, P. (1990) GM division builds a classic system to share internal information, *Public Relations Journal*, 46, 24–41.

McKechnie, D., Grant, J. and Bagaria, V. (2007) Observation of listening behaviors in retail service encounters, *Managing Service Quality*, 17, 116–133.

McKenna, H. (1994) The Delphi technique: A worthwhile research approach for nursing?, *Journal of Advanced Nursing*, 19, 1221–1225.

McKenna, H., Hasson, F. and Smith, M. (2002) A Delphi survey of midwives and midwifery students to identify non-midwifery duties, *International Journal of Midwifery*, 18, 314–322.

McKenzie, T. (2007) Lessons learned about change at Sun Microsystems, *Strategic Communication Management*, 11, 14–17.

Mehan, H. (1979) *Learning Lessons: Social Organization in the Classroom*, Cambridge, MA: Harvard University Press.

Merton, R. (1987) The focussed interview and focus groups: Continuities and discontinuities, *Public Opinion Quarterly*, 51, 550–566.

Messe, L., Kerr, N. and Sattler, D. (1992) 'But some animals are more equal than others': The supervisor as a privileged status in group contexts, in S. Worchel, W. Wood and J. Simpson (eds) *Group Process and Productivity*, London: Sage.

Messmer, M. (2003) The write stuff: How to prepare effective reports, *Strategic Finance*, July, 15–16.

Meyer, H. (1997) Health care mata hari, *Hospitals and Health Networks*, 71, 46–48.

Meyer, J. (2002) Organizational communication assessment: Fuzzy methods and the accessibility of symbols, *Management Communication Quarterly*, 15, 472–479.

Miceli, M., de Rosis, F. and Poggi, I. (2006) Emotional and non-emotional persuasion, *Applied Artificial Intelligence*, 20, 849–879.

Michel, S. (2001) Analyzing service failures and recoveries: A process approach, *International Journal of Service Industry Management*, 12, 20–33.

Miles, L. (1993) Rise of the mystery shopper, *Marketing*, July, 19–20.

Miles, M.B. and Huberman, M.A. (1984) *Qualitative Data Analysis: A Sourcebook of New Methods*, Newbury Park, CA: Sage.

Milewa, T., Dowswell, G. and Harrison, S. (2002) Partnerships, power and the 'new' politics of community participation in British health care, *Social Policy and Administration*, 36, 796–809.

Milgram, S. (1967) The small world problem, *Psychology Today*, 1, 61–67.

Millar, R., Crute, V. and Hargie, O. (1992) *Professional Interviewing*, London: Routledge.

Millar, R. and Tracey, A. (2006) The employment interview, in O. Hargie (ed.) *The Handbook of Communication Skills* (3rd edn), London: Routledge.

Miller, C., Burgoon, M., Grandpre, J. and Alvaro, E. (2006) Identifying principal risk factors for the initiation of adolescent smoking behaviors: The significance of psychological reactance, *Health Communication*, 19, 241–252.

Miller, G. (2001) The development of indicators for sustainable tourism: Results of a Delphi survey of tourism researchers, *Tourism Management*, 22, 351–362.

Miller, K., Hartman-Ellis, B., Zook, E. and Lyles, J. (1990) An integrated model of communication, stress and burnout in the workplace, *Communication Research*, 17, 300–326.

Miller, R. (1998) Undercover shopping, *Marketing*, May, 27–29.

Milliken, F. and Morrison, E. (2003) Shades of silence: Emerging themes and future directions for research on silence in organizations, *Journal of Management Studies*, 40, 1563–1568.

Milliken, F., Morrison, E. and Hewlin, P. (2003) An exploratory study of employee silence: Issues that employees don't communicate upward and why, *Journal of Management Studies* (Special Edition), 40, 1453–1476.

Mills, C. (2000) The interfaces of communication, sensemaking and change, *Australian Journal of Communication*, 27, 95–110.

Mills, C. (2002) The hidden dimension of blue-collar sensemaking about workplace communication, *Journal of Business Communication*, 39, 288–313.

Mills, C.E. (2004) The subjectivities of change: Key factors in making sense of formal change communication, *Australian and New Zealand Communication Association Conference 2004 Electronic Journal*, University of Sydney, Australia: Australian and New Zealand Communication Association. Available from http://conferences. arts.usyd.edu.au/viewabstract.php?id=71&cf=3

Mills, C.E. (2005) Moving forward by looking back: A model for making sense of organizational communication, *Australian Journal of Communication*, 32, 19–43.

Mills, C.E. (2006) Modelling sensemaking about communication: How affect and intellect combine, *Southern Review*, 38, 9–23.

Millward, L. (2006) Focus groups, in G. Breakwell, S. Hammond, C. Fife-Schaw and J.A. Smith (eds) *Research Methods in Psychology*, London: Sage.

Milne, S. (1999) Call to regulate growth in workplace 'spying', *The Guardian*, 18 February, 9.

Miltiades, H. (2008) Interview as a social event: Cultural influences experienced while interviewing older adults in India, *International Journal of Social Research Methodology*, 11, 1–15.

Mintzberg, H. (1989) *Mintzberg on Management*, New York: The Free Press.

Mintzberg, H. (1996) Musings on management, *Harvard Business Review*, 74, 61–67.

Mintzberg, H. (2005) Developing theory about the development of theory, in K. Smith and M. Hitt (eds) *Great Minds in Management*, Oxford: Oxford University Press.

Mintzberg, H. (2007) *Tracking Strategies: Towards a General Theory of Strategy Formation*, Oxford: Oxford University Press.

Monge, P.R. and Contractor, N.S. (2001) Emergence of communication networks, in F. Jablin and L. Putnam (eds) *The New Handbook of Organizational Communication*, Thousand Oaks, CA: Sage.

Monge, P.R. and Contractor, N.S. (2003) *Theories of Communication Networks*, New York: Oxford University Press.

Montgomery, D., Wiesman, D. and DeCaro, P. (2001) Towards a code of ethics for organizational communication professional: A working proposal, *American Communication Journal*, 5(1), Fall Issue. Available from www.acjournal.org/holdings/index.htm

Moore, F. and Rees, C. (2008) Culture against cohesion global corporate strategy and employee diversity in the UK plant of a German MNC, *Employee Relations*, 30, 176–189.

Morgan, D. (1997) *Focus Groups and Qualitative Research* (2nd edn), Thousand Oaks, CA: Sage.

Morgan, D. (1998) *The Focus Group Guidebook*, Thousand Oaks, CA: Sage.

Morgan, D. and Scannell, A. (1998) *Planning Focus Groups*, Thousand Oaks, CA: Sage.

Morris, G. and LoVerde, M. (1993) Consortium surveys, in P. Rosenfeld, J. Edwards and M. Thomas (eds) *Improving Organizational Surveys: New Directions, Methods and Applications*, Newbury Park, CA: Sage.

Morris, J., Cascio, W. and Young, C. (1999) Downsizing after all these years: Questions and answers about who did it, how many did it, and who benefited from it, *Organizational Dynamics*, 27, 78–87.

Morrison, L., Colman, A. and Preston, C. (1997) Mystery customer research: Cognitive processes affecting accuracy, *Journal of the Market Research Society*, 39, 349–361.

Morwitz, V., Steckel, J. and Gupta, A. (1997) When do purchase intentions predict sales?, *Marketing Science Institute*, Working Paper Report No. 97–112, June, 1–38.

Moss, S. and Sanchez, J. (2004) Are your employees avoiding you? Managerial strategies for closing the feedback gap, *Academy of Management Executive*, 18, 32–44.

Mulder, M., Lans, T., Verstegen, J., Biemans, H. and Meijer, Y. (2007) Competence development of entrepreneurs in innovative horticulture, *Journal of Workplace Learning*, 19, 32–44.

Mumby, D. (2007) Organizational communication, in G. Ritzer (ed.) *The Encyclopedia of Sociology*, London: Blackwell, pp. 3290–3299.

Mumby, D. and Stohl, C. (1996) Disciplining organizational communication studies, *Communication Quarterly*, 10, 50–72.

Murgolo-Poore, M., Pitt, L., Berthon, P. and Prendegast, G. (2003) Corporate intelligence dissemination as a consequence of intranet effectiveness: An empirical study, *Public Relations Review*, 29, 171–184.

Murgolo-Poore, M., Pitt, L. and Ewing, M. (2002) Intranet effectiveness: A public relations paper-and-pencil checklist, *Public Relations Review*, 28, 113–123.

Murphy, C., Coover, D. and Owen, S. (1989) Development and validation of the computer self-efficacy scale, *Educational and Psychological Measurement*, 49, 893–899.

Murphy, M. (1997) Conducting survey research: A practical guide, in T. Brannick and W. Roche (eds) *Business Research Methods: Strategies, Techniques, and Sources*, Dublin: Oak Tree Press.

Murray, H. (1989) Training in giving and receiving criticism, *Training and Development*, January, 19–20.

Nah, F. (2004) A study on tolerable waiting time: How long are web users willing to wait?, *Behaviour and Information Technology*, 23, 153–163.

Narayanasamy, A. and Owens, J. (2001) A critical incident study of nurses' responses to the spiritual needs of their patients, *Journal of Advanced Nursing*, 33, 446–455.

Ng Kwet Shing, M. and Spence, L. (2002) Investigating the limits of competitive intelligence gathering: Is mystery shopping ethical?, *Business Ethics: A European Review*, 11, 343–353.

NHS Management Executive (1995) *Setting Standards for NHS Communications: Consultation Document*, London: NHS Management Executive.

Nickell, G.S. and Pinto, J.N. (1986) The computer attitude scale, *Computers in Human Behavior*, 2, 301–306.

Nixon, J.C. and Dawson, G.A. (2002) Reasons for cross-cultural communication training, *Corporate Communications: An International Journal*, 7, 184–191.

Norris, P. (2004) Reasons why mystery shopping is a useful and justifiable research method, *The Pharmaceutical Journal*, 272, 746–747.

Norton, R.W. (1980) Nonmetric multidimensional scaling in communication research: Smallest space analysis, in P. Monge and N. Cappella (eds) *Multivariate Techniques in Human Communication Research*, New York: Academic Press.

Oakley, A. (1981) Interviewing women: A contradiction in terms, in H. Roberts (ed.) *Doing Feminist Research*, Boston, MA: Routledge and Kegan Paul.

O'Connor, H. and Madge, C. (2003) 'Focus groups in cyberspace': Using the internet for qualitative research, *Qualitative Market Research*, 6, 133–143.

Odiorne, G. (1954) An application of the communications audit, *Personnel Psychology*, 7, 235–243.

Odom, M. (1993) Kissing up really works on boss, *San Diego Union-Tribune*, 12 August 1993, E12.

Office of Communications (Ofcom) (2005) *SME Tracking Study*, London: Ofcom.

Ogawa, R. (1991) Enchantment, disenchantment, and accommodation: How a faculty made sense of the succession of its principal, *Educational Administration Quarterly*, 27, 30–60.

O'Kane, P. (2004) *The Impact of Technology on Organizational Communication*, Unpublished PhD dissertation, University of Ulster.

O'Kane, P. and Hargie, O. (2004) We have the technology, but can we communicate with it? Investigating e-communications in a Norwegian company, in B. Dale, R. Karlsdottir and O. Strandhagen (eds) *Bedrifter I Nettverk*, Trondheim, Norway: Tapir Akademisk Forlag.

O'Kane, P. and Hargie, O. (2007) Intentional and unintentional consequences of substituting face-to-face interaction with e-mail: An employee-based perspective, *Interacting with Computers*, 19, 20–31.

O'Kane, P., Hargie, O. and Tourish, D. (2004) Communication without frontiers, in D. Tourish and O. Hargie (eds) *Key Issues in Organizational Communication*, London: Routledge.

O'Kane, P., Palmer, M. and Hargie, O. (2007) Workplace interactions and the polymorphic role of e-mail, *Leadership and Organization Development Journal*, 28, 308–324.

O'Keefe, D. (2006) Persuasion, in O. Hargie (ed.) *The Handbook of Communication Skills*, London: Routledge.

Olsson, E., Tuyet, L., Nguyen H. and Stålsby Lundborg, C. (2002) Health professionals' and consumers' views on the role of the pharmacy personnel and the pharmacy service in Hanoi, Vietnam – a qualitative study, *Journal of Clinical Pharmacy and Therapeutics*, 27, 273–280.

O'Muircheartaigh, C. and Campanelli, P. (1998) The relative impact of interviewer effects and sample design effects on survey precision, *Journal of the Royal Statistical Society*, 161, 63–77.

Onwuegbuzie, A. and Leech, N. (2007) Validity and qualitative research: An oxymoron?, *Quality and Quantity*, 41, 233–249.

O'Reilly, C. and Pfeffer, J. (2000) *Hidden Value: How Great Companies Achieve Extraordinary Results with Ordinary People*, Boston, MA: Harvard Business School Press.

Organ, D. (1988) *Organizational Citizenship Behavior: The Good Soldier Syndrome*, Lexington, MA: Lexington Books.

O'Shea, J., McAuliffe, E. and Wyness, L. (2007) Successful large system change: At what cost?, *Journal of Change Management*, 17, 107–120.

Othman, R. (2008) Organizational politics: The role of justice, trust and job ambiguity, *Singapore Management Review*, 30, 43–53.

Padfield, A. and Procter, I. (1996) The effect of interviewer's gender on the interviewing process: A comparative enquiry, *Sociology*, 30, 355–366.

Padgett, D. (2004) *The Qualitative Research Experience*, Belmont, CA: Wadsworth/ Thomson.

Patterson, M., Warr, P. and West, M. (2004) Organizational climate and company productivity: The role of employee affect and employee level, *Journal of Occupational and Organizational Psychology*, 77, 193–216.

Payne, J. (1996) Developing and implementing strategies for communicating bad news, *Journal of Communication Management*, 1, 80–88.

Payne, S. (1999) Interview in qualitative research, in A. Memon and R. Bull (eds) *Handbook of the Psychology of Interviewing*, Chichester: Wiley.

Pearson, A. (1991) Managing innovation: An uncertainty reduction process, in J. Henry and D. Walker, (eds) *Managing Innovation*, London: Sage.

Peltokorpi, V. (2008) Synthesising the paradox of organizational routine flexibility and stability: A processual view, *International Journal of Technology Management*, 41, 7–21.

Perlmutter, D. (2000) *Policing the Media: Street Cops and Public Perceptions of Law Enforcement*, Thousand Oaks, CA: Sage.

Perloff, R. (2007) *The Dynamics of Persuasion: Communication and Attitudes in the 21st Century* (3rd edn), Mahwah, NJ: Lawrence Erlbaum Associates, Inc.

Perriss, R., Graham, R. and Scarsbrook, A. (2006) Understanding the Internet, website design and intranet development: A primer for radiologists, *Clinical Radiology*, 61, 377–389.

Peters, L.D. and Fletcher, K.P. (2004) Communication strategies and marketing performance: An application of the Mohr and Nevin Framework to intra-organizational cross-functional teams, *Journal of Marketing Management*, 20, 741–770.

Peterson, C., Maier, S. and Seligman, M. (1993) *Learned Helplessness: A Theory for the Age of Personal Control*, Oxford: Oxford University Press.

Petit, J., Goris, J. and Vaught, B. (1997) An examination of organizational communication as a moderator of the relationship between job performance and job satisfaction, *Journal of Business Communication*, 34, 81–98.

Pew Internet and American Life Project Surveys (2007) *Internet Adoption*. Accessed 5 February 2008 from www.pewinternet.org/trends/Internet_Adoption_12%2005%2007.pdf

Pfeffer, J. (2007) *What Were They Thinking? Unconventional Wisdom About Management*, Boston, MA: Harvard Business School Press.

Pfeffer, J. and Sutton, R. (2000) *The Knowing–Doing Gap: How Smart Companies Turn Knowledge Into Action*, Boston, MA: Harvard Business School Press.

Pfeffer, J. and Sutton, R. (2006) *Hard Facts, Dangerous Half-truths and Total Nonsense: Profiting From Evidence-based Management*, Boston, MA: Harvard Business School Press.

Pfeil, M., Setterberg, A. and O'Rourke, J. (2003) The art of downsizing: Communicating lay-offs to key stakeholders, *Journal of Communication Management*, 8, 130–141.

Pierce, E. (2007) The proposal project, *Business Communication Quarterly*, 70, 320–324.

Pikka-Maaria, L. and Vaara, E. (2007) Struggling over subjectivity: A discursive analysis of strategic development in an engineering group, *Human Relations*, 60, 29–58.

Pincus, J.D. (1986) Communication satisfaction, job satisfaction, and job performance, *Human Communication Research*, 12, 395–419.

Poggi, I. (2005) A goal and belief model of persuasion, *Pragmatics and Cognition*, 13, 297–336.

Pollner, M. (1998) The effects of interviewer gender in mental health interviews, *Journal of Nervous and Mental Disease*, 186, 369–373.

Porter, D.T. (1988) Diagnosing communication networks, in C. Downs (ed.) *Communication Audits*, New York: Harper Collins.

Porter, D.T. and Adrian, A.D. (2004) Diagnosing communication networks, in C.W. Downs and A.D. Adrian (eds) *Assessing Organizational Communication: Strategic Communication Audits*, New York: Guilford Press.

Potter, L. (2006) Strategic planning: Timeless wisdom still shapes successful communication programs, in T. Gillis (ed.) *The IABC Handbook of Organizational Communication*, San Francisco, CA: Jossey-Bass.

Potter, W.J. and Levine-Donnerstein, D. (1999) Rethinking validity and reliability in content analysis, *Journal of Applied Communication Research*, 27, 258–284.

Poulin, B., Hackman, M. and Barbarasa-Mihai, C. (2007) Leadership and succession: The challenge to succeed and the vortex of failure, *Leadership*, 3, 301–324.

Powell, C. (2003) The Delphi technique: Myths and realities, *Journal of Advanced Nursing*, 41, 376–382.

Power, M. and Rienstra, B. (1999) Internal communication in new corporate conglomerates: Developing a corporate communication model for loosely coupled businesses in local government, *International Journal of Public Sector Management*, 12, 501–515.

Pratkanis, A. (2007) Social influence analysis: An index of tactics, in A. Pratkanis (ed.) *The Science of Social Influence: Advances and Future Progress*, New York: Psychology Press.

Pratto, F. and John, O. (1991) Automatic vigilance: The attention grabbing power of negative social information, *Journal of Personality and Social Psychology*, 51, 380–391.

Prein, G., Kelle, U. and Bird, K. (1998) An overview of software, in U. Kelle (ed.) *Computer-aided Qualitative Data Analysis: Theory, Methods and Practice*, London: Sage.

Proctor, T. and Doukakis, I. (2003) Change management: The role of internal communication and employee development, *Corporate Communications: An International Journal*, 8, 268–277.

Pryce-Jones, M. (1993) Critical incident technique as a method of assessing patient satisfaction, in R. Fitzpatrick and A. Hopkins (eds) *Measurement of Patients' Satisfaction with their Care*, London: Royal College of Physicians.

Puchta, C. and Potter, J. (2004) *Focus Group Practice*, London: Sage.

Putnam, L.L. (1983) Organizational communication: Toward a research agenda, in L.L. Putnam and M.E. Pacanowsky (eds) *Communication and Organizations: An Interpretive Approach*, Beverly Hills, CA: Sage, pp. 31–54.

Quible, Z. (1998) A focus on focus groups, *Business Communication Quarterly*, 61, 28–38.

Quinn, D. and Hargie, O. (2004) Internal communication audits: A case study, *Corporate Communications: An International Journal*, 9, 146–158.

Quirke, B. (1996) *Communicating Corporate Change*, London: McGraw-Hill.

Rackham, N. and Carlisle, J. (1978) The effective negotiator – Part 1, *Journal of European Industrial Training*, 2, 6–10.

Ramani, G. and Kumar, V. (2008) Interaction orientation and firm performance, *Journal of Marketing*, 72, 27–45.

Rauch, W. (1979) The decision Delphi, *Technological Forecasting and Social Change*, 15, 159–169.

Ravlin, E. (2005) Status and stratification processes in organizational life, *Journal of Management*, 31, 966–987.

Rawlins, W. (1998) Theorizing public and private domains and practices of communication, *Communication Theory*, 8, 369–380.

Redding, W. (1972) *Communication Within the Organization: An Interpretive Review of Theory and Research*, New York: Industrial Communication Council.

Redding, W. (1985) Stumbling toward identity: The emergence of organizational communication as a field of study, in R. McPhee and P. Tompkins (eds) *Organizational Communication: Traditional Themes and New Directions*, Beverly Hills, CA: Sage.

Redman, J. (2008) Creating and recreating the NHS: The importance of ensuring nurse involvement, *Journal of Nursing Management*, 16, 21–28.

Reichheld, F. (1996) *The Loyalty Effect*, Boston, MA: Harvard Business School Press.

Reichheld, F. (2003) *Loyalty Rules: How Leaders Build Lasting Relationships*, Boston, MA: Harvard Business School Press.

Reichheld, F. (2006) *The Ultimate Question: Driving Good Profits and True Growth*, Boston, MA: Harvard Business School Press.

Reid, D. and Reid, F. (2005) Online focus groups: An in-depth comparison of computer-mediated and conventional focus group discussions, *International Journal of Market Research*, 47, 131–162.

Reid, N. (1988) The Delphi technique: Its contribution to the evaluation of professional practice, in R. Ellis (ed.) *Professional Competence and Quality Assurance in the Caring Professions*, London: Croom Helm.

Reid, W., Pease, J. and Taylor, R. (1990) The Delphi technique as an aid to organization development activities, *Organization Development Journal*, 8, 37–42.

Remenyi, D., Williams, B., Money, A. and Swartz, E. (1998) *Doing Research in Business and Management: An Introduction to Process and Method*, London: Sage.

Renkema, J. and Hoeken, H. (1998) The influence of negative newspaper publicity on corporate image in the Netherlands, *Journal of Business Communication*, 35, 521–535.

Rentsch, D., Luthy, C., Perneger, T. and Allaz, A. (2003) Hospitalization process seen by patients and health care professionals, *Social Science and Medicine*, 57, 571–576.

Rice, R.E. and Aydin, C. (1991), Attitudes toward new organizational technology: Network proximity as a mechanism for social information processing, *Administrative Science Quarterly*, 36, 219–244.

Richards, L. (2005) *Handling Qualitative Data: A Practical Guide*, London: Sage.

Richards, L. (2006) *Teach Yourself Nvivo 7: The Introductory Tutorials*. Available from www.lynrichards.org

Riketta, M. and Van Dick, R. (2005) Foci of attachment in organizations: A meta-analytic comparison of the strength and correlates of workgroup versus organizational identification and commitment, *Journal of Vocational Behavior*, 67, 490–510.

Riley, D., Newby, C. and Leal-Almeraz, T. (2006) Incorporating ethnographic methods in multidisciplinary approaches to risk assessment and communication: Cultural and religious issues of mercury in Latino and Caribbean communities, *Risk Analysis*, 26, 1205–1221.

Roberts, K.H. and O'Reilly, C.A. (1973) Measuring organizational communication, *Journal of Applied Psychology*, 59, 321–326.

Robertson, E. (2003) How to use a communication climate model, *Strategic Communication Management*, 7, 28–32.

Robertson, E. (2005) Placing leaders at the heart of organizational communication, *Strategic Communication Management*, 9, 4–37.

Robinson, M. and Cottrell, D. (2005) Health professionals in multi-disciplinary and multi-agency teams: Changing professional practice, *Journal of Interprofessional Care*, 19, 547–560.

Robson, P. and Tourish, D. (2005) Managing internal communication: An organizational case study, *Corporate Communications: An International Journal*, 10, 213–222.

Rod, M., Ashill, N. and Carruthers, J. (2008) The relationship between job demand stressors, service recovery performance and job outcomes in a state-owned enterprise, *Journal of Retailing and Consumer Services*, 15, 22–31.

Roethlisberger, F.J. and Dickson, W.J. (1939) *Management and the Worker*, Cambridge, MA: Harvard University Press.

Rogers, E.M. and Argawala-Rogers, R. (1995) Communication networks in organizations, in S.R. Corman, S.P. Banks, C.R. Bantz and M.E. Mayer (eds) *Foundations of Organizational Communication: A Reader*, New York: Longman.

Rogers, L. (2006) Britons the most spied-on people in the Western world, *The Sunday Times*, 29 October, 13.

Romm, C., Pliskin, N. and Rifkin, W. (1996) Diffusion of e-mail: An organizational learning perspective, *Information and Management*, 31, 37–46.

Roos, I. (1999) Switching processes in customer relationships, *Journal of Service Research*, 2, 68–85.

Roos, I. (2002) Methods of investigating critical incidents, *Journal of Service Research*, 4, 193–204.

Rosenfeld, P., Giacalone, R. and Riordan, C. (1995) *Impression Management in Organizations*, London: Routledge.

Rosenhan, D. (1973) On being sane in insane places, *Science*, 179, 250–258.

Rouleau, L. (2005) Micro-practices of strategic sensemaking and sensegiving: How middle managers interpret and sell change every day, *Journal of Management Studies*, 42, 1413–1441.

Rousseau, D.M. (1990) Normative beliefs in fund-raising organizations: Linking culture to organizational performance and individual responses, *Group and Organization Studies*, 15, 448–460.

Rowley, J. (2006) *Information Marketing* (2nd edn), Aldershot: Ashgate.

Roy, J.L., White, A. and Greaney, M. (2006) Using face-to-face and online focus groups to study motivators and barriers to maintaining healthy weight in young adults, *The FASEB Journal*, 20, A1010.

Rubin, J. (1996) New corporate practice, new classroom pedagogy: Toward a redefinition of management communication, *Business Communication Quarterly*, 59, 7–19.

Rubin, R., Palmgreen, P. and Sypher, H. (eds) (1994) *Communication Research Measures: A Sourcebook*, New York: Guilford Press.

Rucci, A., Kirn, S. and Quinn, R. (1998) The employee–customer–profit chain at Sears, *Harvard Business Review*, 76, 82–98.

Rutten, L., Arora, N., Bakos, A., Aziz, N. and Rowland, J. (2005) Information needs and sources of information among cancer patients: A systematic review of research (1980–2003), *Patient Education and Counseling*, 57, 250–261.

Ryder, I. (1998) Moments of truth management, *Strategic Communication Management*, February–March, 16–21.

Saks, A.M. and Ashforth, B.E. (2000) The role of dispositions, entry stressors, and behavioural plasticity theory in predicting newcomers' adjustment to work, *Journal of Organizational Behavior*, 21, 43–62.

Salem, P. (2002) Assessment, change and complexity, *Management Communication Quarterly*, 15, 442–450.

Sallis, P. and Kassabova, D. (2000) Computer-mediated communication: Experiments with e-mail readability, *Information Sciences*, 123, 43–53.

Saludadez, J. and Taylor, J. (2006) The structuring of collaborative research networks in the stories researchers tell, in F. Cooren, J. Taylor and E. Van Every (eds) *Communication as Organizing: Empirical and Theoretical Explorations in the Dynamic of Text and Conversation*, Mahwah, NJ: Lawrence Erlbaum Associates, Inc.

Sanchez, P. and McCann, B. (2005) How to be effective in the major areas of CEO communication, *The Business Communicator*, 6, 10–11.

Sanson-Fisher, R., Girgis, A., Boyes, A., Bonevski, B., Burton, L. and Cook, P. (2000) The unmet supportive care needs of patients with cancer, *Cancer*, 88, 226–237.

Sarangi, S. (1994) Accounting for mismatches in intercultural selection interviews, *Multilingua*, 13, 163–194.

Saunders, C. (1986) Opening and closing, in O.Hargie (ed.), *A Handbook of Communication Skills*. London: Croom Helm.

Saunders, C. and Caves, R. (1986) An empirical approach to the identification of communication skills with reference to speech therapy, *Journal of Further and Higher Education*, 10, 29–44.

Saunders, C. and Saunders, E.D. (1993a) Expert teachers' perceptions of university teaching: The identification of teaching skills, in R. Ellis (ed.) *Quality Assurance for University Teaching*, Buckingham: Open University Press.

Saunders, C. and Saunders, E.D. (1993b) *Expert Teachers' Perceptions of University Teaching: The Identification of Teaching Skills*, Northern Ireland: University of Ulster.

Scammell, A. (2006) Business writing for strategic communications: The marketing and communications mix, *Business Information Review*, 23, 23–43.

Schaefer, D.R. and Dillman, D.A. (1999) Development of a standard e-mail methodology: Results of an experiment, *Public Opinion Quarterly*, 62, 378–397.

Schaeffer, N. and Presser, S. (2003) The science of asking questions, *Annual Review of Sociology*, 29, 65–88.

Schein, E.H. (2004) *Organizational Culture and Leadership* (3rd edn), San Francisco, CA: Jossey-Bass.

Schimmel, K., Clark, J., Irwin, R. and Lachowetz, T. (2007) What communication methods work for sports events? An analysis of the FedEx, *International Journal of Sport Management and Marketing*, 2, 301–315.

Schluter, J., Seaton, P. and Chaboyer, W. (2008) Critical incident technique: A user's guide for nurse researchers, *Journal of Advanced Nursing*, 61, 107–114.

Schwartz, D.F. and Jacobson, E. (1977) Organizational communication network analysis: The liaison communication role, *Organizational Behavior and Human Performance*, 18, 158–174.

Schwartzbaum, A. and Gruenfeld, L. (1969) Factors influencing subject–observer interaction in an organizational study, *Administrative Science Quarterly*, 14, 443–450.

Scott, C., Shaw, S., Timmerman, E., Frank, V. and Quinn, L. (1999) Using communication audits to teach organizational communication to students and employees, *Business Communication Quarterly*, 62, 53–70.

Scott, J. (2000) *Social Network Analysis: A Handbook* (2nd edn), London: Sage.

Scott, M. (1996) Can consumers change corporations?, *Executive Female*, 19, 42–46.

Seidman, I.E. (1998) *Interviewing as Qualitative Research. A Guide for Researchers in Education and the Social Sciences* (2nd edn), New York: Teachers College Press.

Sellnow, T., Seeger, M. and Ulmer, R. (2002) Chaos theory, informational needs and natural disasters, *Journal of Applied Communication Research*, 30, 269–292.

Selltiz, C., Wrightsman, L. and Cook, S. (1976) *Research Methods in Social Relations*, New York: Holt, Rinehart & Winston.

Semler, R. (1989) Managing without managers, *Harvard Business Review*, 67, 76–85.

Semler, R. (1993) *Maverick*, London: Century.

Sewell, G. and Barker, J. (2006) Coercion versus care: Using irony to make sense of organizational surveillance, *Academy of Management Review*, 31, 934–961.

Shapiro, J. (1999) Implementing change with audit: The role of management, in R. Baker, H. Hearnshaw and N. Robertson (eds) *Implementing Change With Clinical Audit*, Chichester: Wiley.

Shapiro, J., Quinones, M. and King, E. (2007) Expectations of obese trainee characteristics: Influence training effectiveness, *Journal of Applied Psychology*, 92, 239–249.

Sharbrough, W.C., Simmons, S.A. and Cantrill, D.A. (2006) Motivating language in industry: Its impact on job satisfaction and perceived supervisor effectiveness, *Journal of Business Communication*, 43, 322–343.

Shelby, A. and Reinsch, N. (1996) The communication audit: A framework for teaching management communication, *Business Communication Quarterly*, 59, 95–108.

Sherer, P.D. and Coakley, L.A. (1999) Questioning and developing your part-time employee practices, *Workforce*, October, 4–7.

Shih, T. and Fan, X. (2008) Comparing response rates from web amd mail surveys: A meta-analysis, *Field Methods*, 20, 249–271.

Sias, P.M. and Cahill, D.J. (1998) From coworkers to friends: The development of peer friendships in the workplace, *Western Journal of Communication*, 62, 273–299.

Sifry, D. (2004) *Sifry's Alert: October 2004 State of the Blogosphere*. Retrieved 30 March 2005 from www.sifry.com/alerts/archives/000390.html

Sillince, J., MacDonald, S., Lefang, B. and Frost, B. (1998) Email adoption, diffusion, use and impact within small firms: A survey of UK companies, *International Journal of Information Management*, 18, 231–242.

Silverman, D. (2005) *Doing Qualitative Research* (2nd edn), London: Sage.

Sim, J. (1998) Collecting and analysing qualitative data: Issues raised by the focus group, *Journal of Advanced Nursing*, 28, 345–352.

Sims, H. and Lorenzi, P. (1992) *The New Leadership Paradigm: Social Learning and Cognition in Organizations*, London: Sage.

Singh, J. (2004) Tackling measurement problems with item response theory: Principles, characteristics, and assessment, with an illustrative example, *Journal of Business Research*, 57, 184–208.

Singleton, T. and Singleton, A. (2007) Why don't we detect more fraud?, *Journal of Accounting and Finance*, 18, 7–10.

Sinickas, A. (1998) Communication measurement, *Strategic Communication Management*, 2, 8–9.

Sirota, D., Mischkind, L. and Meltzer, M. (2008) Enthusiastic employees, in R. Burke and C. Cooper (eds) *Building More Effective Organizations: HR Management and Performance in Practice*, Cambridge: Cambridge University Press.

Skinner, B.F. (1954) The science of learning and the art of teaching, *Harvard Educational Review*, 24, 86–97.

Skinner, D. (1999) The reality of equal opportunities: The expectations and experiences of part-time staff and their managers, *Personnel Review*, 28, 425–433.

Slack, F. and Rowley, J. (2001) Observation: Perspectives on research methodologies for leisure managers, *Management Research News*, 24, 35–42.

Sloan, J., Bodpati, M. and Ticker, T. (2004) Respondent misreporting of drug use in self-reports: Social desirability and other correlates, *Journal of Drug Issues*, 34, 269–292.

Smircich, L. (1985) Is the concept of culture a paradigm for understanding organizations and ourselves?, in P.J. Frost, L.F. Moore, M. Reis Louis, C.C. Lundberg and J. Martin (eds) *Organizational Culture*, Beverly Hills, CA: Sage.

Smircich, L. and Morgan, G. (1982). Leadership: The management of meaning, *Journal of Applied Behavioral Science*, 18, 257–273.

Smith, A. (1991) *Innovative Employee Communication: New Approaches to Improving Trust, Teamwork and Performance*, Englewood Cliffs, NJ: Prentice Hall.

Smith, F., Salkind M. and Jolly, B. (1990) Community pharmacy: A method of assessing quality of care, *Social Science and Medicine*, 31, 603–607.

Smith, J., Harre, R. and van Langenhove, L. (1995) Idiography and the case study, in J. Smith, R. Harre and L. van Langenhove (eds) *Rethinking Psychology*, London: Sage.

Smith, K. and Hitt, M. (eds) (2005) *Great Minds in Management: The Process of Theory Development*, Oxford: Oxford University Press.

Smith, M. and Robertson, I.T. (1993) *The Theory and Practice of Systematic Personnel Selection* (2nd edn), London: Macmillan.

Smith, R. (2007) Why employees are more trusted than the CEO, *Strategic Communication Management*, 11, 7.

Smythe, J. (2007) *The CEO: Chief Engagement Officer: Turning Hierarchy Upside Down to Drive Performance*, Aldershot: Gower.

Somers, K., Baker, G. and Isbell, C. (1984) How to use the Delphi technique to forecast training needs, *Performance and Instruction Journal*, 23, 26–28.

Sonenshein, S. (2007) The role of construction, intuition, and justification in responding to ethical issues at work: The sensemaking-intuition mode, *Academy of Management Review*, 32, 1022–1041.

Sorensen, R. and Iedema, R. (2008) Redefining accountability in health care: Managing the plurality of medical interests, *Health*, 12, 87–106.

Spitzberg, B. (2003) Methods of interpersonal skill assessment, in J. Greene and B. Burleson (eds) *Handbook of Communication and Social Interaction Skills*, Mahwah, NJ: Lawrence Erlbaum Associates, Inc.

Srivastav, A. (2006) Organizational climate as a dependent variable, *Journal of Management Research*, 6, 125–136.

Stablein, R. (2006) Data in organization studies, in S. Clegg, C. Hardy, T. Lawrence and W. Nord (eds) *The Sage Handbook of Organization Studies* (2nd edn), London: Sage.

Stake, R. (2000) Case studies, in N. Denzin and Y. Lincoln (eds) *Handbook of Qualitative Research*, London: Sage.

Stallworth, Y. and Roberts-Gray, C. (1987) The craft of evaluation: Reporting to the busy decision maker, *Evaluation Review*, 13, 91–103.

Stamper, C.L. and Van Dyne, L. (2003) Organizational citizenship: A comparison between part-time and full-time service employees, *Cornell Hotel and Restaurant Administration Quarterly*, February, 33–42.

Stanton, M. (1981) How to audit communications, *Management Today*, November, 69–73.

Staw, B., Sandelands, L. and Dutton, J. (1981) Threat-rigidity effects in organizational behavior: A multilevel analysis, *Administrative Science Quarterly*, 26, 501–524.

Stengel, R. (2000) *You're Too Kind*, London: Simon & Schuster.

Stensaker, I. and Falkenberg, J. (2007) Making sense of different responses to corporate change, *Human Relations*, 60, 137–177.

Stevenson, W.B., Davidson, B., Manev, I. and Walsh, K. (1997) The small world of the university: A classroom exercise in the study of networks, *Connections*, 20, 23–33.

Stevenson, W. and Gilly, M. (1991) Information processing and problem solving: The migration of problems through formal positions and networks of ties, *Academy of Management Journal*, 34, 918–928.

Stevenson, W.B. and Gilly, M.C. (1993) Problem-solving networks in organizations: Intentional design and emergent structure, *Social Science Research*, 22, 92–113.

Stewart, C.J. and Cash, W.B. (2000) *Interviewing. Principles and Practices* (9th edn), Boston, MA: McGraw-Hill.

Stewart, D., Shamdasani, P. and Rook, D. (2007) *Focus Groups: Theory and Practice*, Thousand Oaks, CA: Sage.

Stewart, T. (1999) The status of communication today, *Strategic Communication Management*, 3, 22–25.

Stinchcomb, J. (2004) Searching for stress in all the wrong places: Combating chronic organizational stressors in policing, *Policy Practice and Research*, 5, 259–277.

Stokes, D. and Bergin, R. (2006) Methodology or 'methodolatory'? An evaluation of focus groups and depth interviews, *Qualitative Market Research*, 9, 26–37.

Stone, B. (1995) Strategic marketing and communications audits, *Marketing Health Services*, 15, 54–56.

Strategic Direction (2006) Blogging4Business Report, *Strategic Direction*, 22, 18–21.

Strauss, A.L. and Corbin, J. (1990) *Basics of Qualitative Research: Grounded Theory Procedures and Techniques*, Newbury Park, CA: Sage.

Strauss, A.L. and Corbin, J. (1998) *Basics of Qualitative Research: Grounded Theory Procedures and Techniques* (2nd edn), Newbury Park, CA: Sage.

Strenski, J. (1984) The communications audit: Basic to business development, *Public Relations Quarterly*, Spring, 14–17.

Sudhakar, B. and Patil, S. (2006) Measuring up, *Communication World*, 23, 32–34.

Sunday Times (2006) The 100 best companies to work for, *Sunday Times*, Special Supplement, 5 March.

Sutherland, S. (1992) *Irrationality: The Enemy Within*, London: Constable.

Swallow, V., Newton, J. and Van Lottum, C. (2003) How to manage and display qualitative data using 'Framework' and Microsoft Excel, *Journal of Clinical Nursing*, 12, 610–612.

Sweet, C. (2001) Designing and conducting virtual focus groups, *Qualitative Market Research*, 4, 130–135.

Tallman, K., Janisse, T., Frankel, R., Sung, S., Krupat, E. and Hsu, J. (2007) Communication practices of physicians with high patient-satisfaction ratings, *The Permanente Journal*, 11, 19–29.

Tang, T. and Ibrahim, A. (1998) Antecedents of organizational citizenship behaviour revisited: Public personnel in the United States and in the Middle East, *Public Personnel Management*, 27, 529–549.

Tardy, C. and Dindia, K. (2006) Self-disclosure: Strategic revelation of information in personal and professional relationships, in O. Hargie (ed.) *The Handbook of Communication Skills* (3rd edn), London: Routledge.

Taylor, K. (2008) Hey boss, you're boring, *Associations Now*, January, 39–42.

Thach, E. and Murphy, K. (1995) Competencies for distance education professionals, *Educational Technology Research and Development*, 43, 57–79.

The Radicati Group (2006) *Market Numbers Summary Update, Q3 2006*, 11 October, Palo Alto, CA: The Radicati Group.

The Radicati Group (2007) *Market Numbers Summary Update, Q3 2007*, 15 October, Palo Alto, CA: The Radicati Group.

Thiele, C., Laireiter, A. and Baumann, U. (2002) Diaries in clinical psychology and psychotherapy: A selective review, *Clinical Psychology and Psychotherapy*, 9, 1–37.

Thornbory, G. and White, C. (2007) How to write reports effectively, *Occupational Health*, February, 20–21.

Tichy, N. and Charan, R. (1995) The CEO as coach: An interview with Allied Signal's Lawrence Bossidy, *Harvard Business Review*, March–April, 68–79.

Tittmar, H. (1978) Seasonal fluctuation in condom retrieval, *IRCS Medical Science*, 6, 135.

Toch, H. (2008) Police officers as change agents in police reform, *Policing and Society*, 18, 60–71.

Torkzadeh, G. and Van Dyke, T. (2002) Effects of training on internet self-efficacy and computer user attitudes, *Computers in Human Behavior*, 18, 479–494.

Tourangeau, R. (2000) *The Psychology of Survey Response*, New York: Cambridge University Press.

Tourangeau, R. (2004) Survey research and societal change, *Annual Review of Psychology*, 55, 775–801.

Tourangeau, R., Couper, M. and Conrad, F. (2004) Spacing, position and order – interpretive heuristics for visual features of survey questions, *Public Opinion Quarterly*, 68, 368–393.

Tourish, B. and Tourish, D. (1997) Auditing internal communications in local authority leisure facilities: A case study from a leisure complex, *Managing Leisure: An International Journal*, 2, 155–173.

Tourish, D. (1996) *Internal Communication and the NHS: The Results of a Fieldwork Analysis, and Implications for Corporate Practice*, Unpublished DPhil thesis, Northern Ireland: University of Ulster.

Tourish, D. (1997) Transforming internal corporate communications: The power of symbolic gestures, and barriers to change, *Corporate Communications: An International Journal*, 2, 109–116.

Tourish, D. (1998) 'The God that failed': Replacing visionary leadership with open communication, *Australian Journal of Communication*, 25, 99–114.

Tourish, D. (2005) Critical upward communication: Ten commandments for improving strategy and decision making, *Long Range Planning*, 38, 485–503.

Tourish, D. (2006) The appraisal interview reappraised, in O. Hargie (ed.) *A Handbook of Communication Skills* (3rd edn), London: Routledge.

Tourish, D. (2007a) Review article: Communication, discourse and leadership, *Human Relations*, 60, 1727–1740.

Tourish, D. and Hargie, O. (1996a) Communication audits and the management of change: A case study from an NHS Unit of Management, *Health Services Management Research*, 9, 125–135.

Tourish, D. and Hargie, O. (1996b) Communication in the NHS: Using qualitative approaches to analyse effectiveness, *Journal of Management in Medicine*, 10, 38–54.

Tourish, D. and Hargie, C. (1996c) Internal communication: Key steps in evaluating and improving performance, *Corporate Communications*, 1, 11–16.

Tourish, D. and Hargie, O. (1998) Communication between managers and staff in the NHS: Trends and prospects, *British Journal of Management*, 9, 53–71.

Tourish, D. and Hargie, O. (2004a) Communication audits: Building world class communication systems, in S. Oliver (ed.) *Handbook of Corporate Communication and Public Relations*, London: Routledge.

Tourish, D. and Hargie, O. (eds) (2004b) *Key Issues in Organizational Communication*, London: Routledge.

Tourish, D. and Hargie, O. (2004c) The communication consequences of downsizing trust, loyalty and commitment, in D. Tourish and O. Hargie (eds) *Key Issues in Organizational Communication*, London: Routledge.

Tourish, D. and Mulholland, J. (1997) Communication between nurses and nurse managers: A case study from an NHS Trust, *Journal of Nursing Management*, 5, 25–36.

Tourish, D., Paulsen, N., Hobman, E. and Bordia, P. (2004) The downsides of downsizing: Communication processes and information needs in the aftermath of a workforce reduction strategy, *Management Communication Quarterly*, 17, 485–516.

Tourish, D. and Robson, P. (2003) Critical upward feedback in organizations: Processes, problems and implications for communication management, *Journal of Communication Management*, 8, 150–167.

Tourish, D. and Robson, P. (2006) Sensemaking and the distortion of critical upward communication in organizations, *Journal of Management Studies*, 43, 711–730.

Tourish, D. and Tourish, B. (1996) Assessing staff–management relationships in local authority leisure facilities: The communication audit approach, *Managing Leisure: An International Journal*, 1, 91–104.

Tourish, N. (2007b) *The Dynamics of Upward Communication in Organizations*, PhD thesis, Aberdeen: Robert Gordon University.

Towers-Perrin (2006) *Ten Steps to Creating an Engaged Workforce*, Brussels: Towers-Perrin.

Tracey, A. (2006) '*Perpetual Loss and Pervasive Grief'. An Exploration of the Experiences of Daughters Bereaved of their Mother in Early Life*, DPhil thesis, Northern Ireland: University of Ulster.

Travers, J. and Milgram, S. (1969) An experimental study of the small world problem, *Sociometry*, 32, 425–443.

Travis, C. and Aronson, E. (2007) *Mistakes Were Made (But Not By Me): Why We Justify Foolish Beliefs, Bad Decisions, and Hurtful Acts*, London: Harcourt.

Trombetta, J.J. and Rogers, D.R. (1998) Communication climate, job satisfaction and organizational commitment: The effects of information adequacy, communication openness and decision participation, *Management Communication Quarterly*, 1, 494–514.

Tsang, E. (2002) Self-serving attributions in corporate annual reports: A replicated study, *Journal of Management Studies*, 39, 51–65.

Tsui, A., Ashford, S., St Clair, L. and Xin, K. (1995) Dealing with discrepant expectations: Response strategies and managerial effectiveness, *Academy of Management Journal*, 38, 1515–1543.

Tufte, E. (1983) *The Visual Display of Quantitative Information*, Cheshire, CT: Graphics Press.

Turnbull, P. and Wass, V. (1998) Marksist management: Sophisticated human relations in a high street retail store, *Industrial Relations Journal*, 29, 99–111.

Turner, J. and Reinsch, N. (2007) The business communicator as presence allocator: Multicommunicating, equivocality, and status at work, *Journal of Business Communication*, 44, 36–58.

Tuzovic, S. and Bruhn, M. (2005) Integrating customer orientation, employee compensation and performance management: A conceptual framework, *International Journal of Business Performance Management*, 7, 255–274.

Urbaczewski, A. and Jessup, L. (2003) Web browser, what's that secret you're keeping?, *Business Horizons*, 46, 25–32.

Urquhart, C., Light, A., Thomas, R., Barker, A., Yeoman, A. *et al.* (2003) Critical incident technique and explicitation interviewing in studies of information behavior, *Library and Information Science Research*, 25, 63–88.

van der Jagt, R. (2005) Senior business executives see communication and reputation as a crucial part of their leadership role, *Corporate Reputation Review*, 8, 179–186.

Van der Wiele, T., Hesselink, M. and Iwaarden, J. (2005) Mystery shopping: A tool to develop insight into customer service provision, *Total Quality Management and Business Excellence*, 16, 529–541.

van Ruler, B. (2004) The communication grid: An introduction of a model of four communication strategies, *Public Relations Review*, 30, 123–143.

van Schaik, P. and Ling, J. (2005) Five psychometric scales for online measurement of the quality of human–computer interaction in web sites, *International Journal of Human–Computer Interaction*, 18, 309–322.

van Tilburg, T. (1998) Interviewer effects in the measurement of personal network size: A nonexperimental study, *Sociological Methods and Research*, 26, 300–328.

Van Vuuren, M., de Jong, M. and Seydel, E. (2007) Direct and indirect effects of supervisor communication on organizational commitment, *Corporate Communications: An International Journal*, 12, 116–128.

van Zolingen, S. and Klaassen, C. (2003) Selection processes in a Delphi study about key qualifications in senior secondary vocational education, *Technological Forecasting and Social Change*, 70, 317–340.

Varey, R. (2006) Accounts in interactions: Implications of accounting practices for managing, in F. Cooren, J. Taylor and E. Van Every (eds) *Communication as Organizing: Empirical and Theoretical Explorations in the Dynamics of Text and Conversation*, London: Lawrence Erlbaum Associates Ltd.

Varney, G. (1990) A study of the core literature in organization development, *Organization Development Journal*, 8, 59–66.

Vaughn, S., Schumm, J. and Sinagub, J. (1996) *Focus Group Interviews in Education and Psychology*, Thousand Oaks, CA: Sage.

Vázquez-Ramos, R., Leahy, M. and Estrada Hernández, N. (2007) The Delphi method in rehabilitation counseling research, *Rehabilitation Counseling Bulletin*, 50, 111–118.

Vinten, G. (1994) Participant observation: A model for organizational observation?, *Journal of Managerial Psychology*, 9, 30–38.

von Eye, A. (1990) *Introduction to Configural Frequency Analysis*, Cambridge: Cambridge University Press.

Wadman, L. (2006) Show leaders the impact of comms, *Strategic Communication Management*, 10, 6–7.

Walker, A. and Smither, J. (2004) Are the characteristics of narrative comments related to improvement in multirater feedback ratings over time?, *Journal of Applied Psychology*, 89, 575–581.

Walton, D. and Reed, C. (2002) Argumentation schemes and defeasible inferences, in *Working Notes of the ECAI 2002 Workshop on Computational Models of Natural Argument*, Lyon, France.

Wasserman, S. and Faust, K. (1994) *Social Network Analysis: Methods and Applications*, New York: Cambridge University Press.

Watson, T. (2008) Public relations research priorities: A Delphi study, *Journal of Communication Management*, 12, 104–123.

Webb, C. and Kevern, J. (2001) Focus groups as a research method: A critique of some aspects of their use in nursing research, *Journal of Advanced Nursing*, 33, 798–805.

Webb, M. and Palmer, G. (1998) Evading surveillance and making time: An ethnographic view of the Japanese factory floor in Britain, *British Journal of Industrial Relations*, 36, 611–627.

Weber, K. and Glynn, M.A. (2006) Making sense without institutions: Context, thought and action in Karl Weick's theory, *Organization Studies*, 27, 1639–1660.

Weber, P.S. and Manning, M.R. (2001) Cause maps, sensemaking, and planned organizational change, *Journal of Applied Behavioural Science*, 37, 227–252.

Weick, K. (1979) *The Social Psychology of Organizing* (2nd edn), Reading, MA: Addison-Wesley.

Weick, K.E. (1995) *Sensemaking in Organizations*, Thousand Oaks, CA: Sage.

Weick, K.E. (2001) *Making Sense of the Organization*, Oxford: Blackwell.

Weick, K.E. (2007) The generative properties of richness, *Academy of Management Journal*, 50, 14–19.

Weick, K.E., Sutcliffe, K.M. and Obstfeld, D. (2005) Organizing and the process of sensemaking, *Organizational Science*, 16, 409–421.

Weinshall, T. (1979) *Managerial Communication: Concepts Approaches and Techniques*, London: Academic Press.

Welch, M. and Jackson, P. (2007) Rethinking internal communication: A stakeholder approach, *Corporate Communications: An International Journal*, 12, 177–198.

Wells, B. and Spinks, N. (1996) The good, the bad, the persuasive strategies for business managers, *Corporate Communications: An International Journal*, 1, 22–31.

Wengraf, T. (2001) *Qualitative Research Interviewing*, London: Sage.

Westwood, R. and Linstead, S. (2001) Language/organization: Introduction, in

R. Westwood and S. Linstead (eds) *The Language of Organization*, London: Sage, pp. 1–19.

White, G. and Thomson, A. (1995) Anonymized focus groups as a research tool for health professionals, *Qualitative Health Research*, 5, 256–261.

White, J. and Mazur, L. (1995) *Strategic Communications Management: Making Public Relations Work*, Wokingham: Addison-Wesley.

Whitty, M. and Carr, A. (2006) New rules in the workplace: Applying object-relations theory to explain problem Internet and email behaviour in the workplace, *Computers in Human Behavior*, 22, 235–250.

Wiio, O.A. (1975) *Systems of Information, Communication, and Organization*, Helsinki: Helsinki Research Institute for Business Economics.

Wiio, O.A. (1977) *Organizational Communication and its Development*, Helsinki: Viestintainstituuti (Institute for Human Communication).

Wiley, S. (2006) Culture changes help retention, *CPA Practice Management Forum*, 2, 18–20.

Wilkins, A.L. and Ouchi, W.G. (1983) Efficient cultures: Exploring the relationship between culture and organizational performance, *Administration Science Quarterly*, 28, 468–482.

Wilkinson, S. (2003) Focus groups, in J.A. Smith (ed.) *Qualitative Psychology: A Practical Guide to Research Methods*, London: Sage.

Willig, C. (ed.) (1999) *Applied Discourse Analysis: Social and Psychological Interventions*, Buckingham: Open University Press.

Willmott, H. (1993) Strength is ignorance: Slavery is freedom: Managing culture in modern organizations, *Journal of Management Studies*, 30, 515–552.

Wilmot, R. and McClelland, V. (1990) How to run a reality check, *Training*, 66–72.

Wilson, A. (2001) Mystery shopping: Using deception to measure service performance, *Psychology and Marketing*, 18, 721–734.

Wilson, A. and Gutmann, J. (1998) Public transport: The role of mystery shopping in investment decisions, *Journal of the Market Research Society*, 40, 285–293.

Wilson, M., Robinson, E. and Ellis, A. (1989) Studying communication between community pharmacists and their customers, *Counselling Psychology Quarterly*, 2, 367–380.

Wolfe Morrison, E. (2002) Newcomers' relationships: The role of social networks during socialization, *Academy of Management Journal*, 45, 1149–1160.

Wong, A. and Sohal, A. (2003) A critical incident approach to the examination of customer relationship management in a retail chain: An exploratory study, *Qualitative Market Research: An International Journal*, 6, 248–262.

Wooffitt, R. (2001) Researching psychic practitioners: Conversation analysis, in M. Wetherell, S. Taylor and S.J. Yates (eds) *Discourse as Data: A Guide for Analysis*, London: Sage.

Worrall, L. and Cooper, C. (2006) *The Quality Of Working Life: Managers' Health And Well Being*, London: Chartered Management Institute.

Wren, J. and Dulewicz, V. (2005) Leader competencies, activities and successful change in the Royal Air Force, *Journal of Change Management*, 5, 295–309.

Yellowlees, P. and Marks, S. (2007) Problematic Internet use or Internet addiction?, *Computers in Human Behavior*, 23, 1447–1453.

Yinger, J. (1998) Evidence on discrimination in consumer markets, *Journal of Economic Perspectives*, 12, 23–40.

Zack, M.H. and McKenney, J.L. (1995) Social context and interaction in ongoing computer-supported management groups, *Organization Science*, 6, 394–422.

Zhu, Y., May, S. and Rosenfeld, L. (2004) Information adequacy and job satisfaction during merger and acquisition, *Management Communication Quarterly*, 18, 241–270.

Zimmerman, S., Sypher, B. and Haas, J. (1996) A communication metamyth in the workplace: The assumption that more is better, *Journal of Business Communication*, 33, 185–204.

Zorn, T. (1995) Bosses and buddies: Constructing and performing simultaneously hierarchical and close friendship relationships, in J. Wood and S. Duck (eds) *Under-Studied Relationships*, London: Sage.

Zorn, T. (2002) Forum introduction: Current uses, critical appraisals and future prospects, *Management Communication Quarterly*, 15, 439–441.

Zorn, T.E., Roper, J., Broadfoot, K. and Weaver, C.K. (2006) Focus groups as sites of influential interaction: Building communicative self-efficacy and effective attitudinal change in discussing controversial topics, *Journal of Applied Communication Research*, 34, 115–140.

Zwijze-Koning, K. and de Jong, M. (2005) Auditing information structures in organizations: A review of data collection techniques for network analysis, *Organizational Research Methods*, 8, 429–453.

Zwijze-Koning, K.H. and de Jong, M.D.T. (2007) Measurement of communication satisfaction. Evaluating the Communication Satisfaction Questionnaire as a communication audit tool, *Management Communication Quarterly*, 20, 261–282.

Author index

Subject index